Foundations
of
Psychosomatics

Edited by

Professor Margaret J. Christie

School of Studies in Psychology
University of Bradford

and

Dr Peter G. Mellett

Horton Hospital, Epsom

JOHN WILEY & SONS

Chichester · New York · Brisbane · Toronto

British Library Cataloguing in Publication Data:

Foundations of psychosomatics.
  1. Medicine, Psychosomatic
  I. Christie, Margaret J.
  II. Mellett, Peter G.
  616.08   RC49   80-42011

ISBN 0 471 27855 6

Photosetting by Thomson Press (India) Ltd., New Delhi and printed in the United States of America.

£19.35

This book is to be returned on or before
the last date stamped below.

30 APR 1992
-3 OCT 1995

CHRISTIE, M. J.
+ MELLETT P. G.
(eds)

Foundations
of
Psychosomatics

ERRATA

Peter Venables is at the Department of Psychology, University of York, England, and not the University of Reading. We very much regret this error.

John Wiley & Sons

CONTRIBUTORS

DR SUE BAKER

Department of Psychology, University of Southampton, Southampton SO9 5NH.

MR JOHN BARRETT

Department of Psychology, University of Bristol, 8–10 Berkley Square, Bristol, B5 1TH.

DR MICHAEL BOARDER

Department of Psychiatry, Stanford University Medical Centre, Stanford, California, USA.

PROFESSOR MICHAEL BOND

Department of Psychological Medicine, University of Glasgow, 6 Whittinghame Gardens, Great Western Rd., Glasgow G1 2 OAA.

DR MALCOLM CARRUTHERS

Director of Clinical Laboratory Services, The Maudsley Hospital, Denmark Hill, London SE5 8AZ.

PROFESSOR MARGARET J. CHRISTIE

School of Studies in Psychology, University of Bradford, Bradford, W. Yorkshire BD7 1DP.

DR EDWIN COOK

Department of Psychology, University of Wisconsin, Madison, WI 55795, USA.

DR NICOLA DAVIS

Department of Experimental Psychology, University of Oxford, South Parks Road, Oxford, OX1 3UD.

DR NORMAN DIXON

Department of Psychology, University College London, Gower Street, London WC1E 6BT.

DR BERNARD T. ENGEL

Chief, Laboratory of Behavioral Sciences, Gerontology Research Center, Baltimore City Hospitals, Baltimore, Maryland, 21224, USA.

DR JORAM FELDON

Department of Psychology, Tel-Aviv University, Tel-Aviv, Israel.

PROFESSOR ANTHONY GALE

Department of Psychology, University of Southampton, Southampton SO9 5NH.

DR SONI GARTSHORE	*Menninger Clinic, Topeka, Kansas, USA.*
DR ALISTAIR GORDON	*The Retreat, Heslington Road, York YO1 5BN.*
DR JEFFREY GRAY	*Department of Experimental Psychology, University of Oxford, South Parks Road, Oxford, OX1 3UD.*
DR JACK INGHAM	*MRC Unit for Epidemiological Studies in Psychiatry, University Department of Psychiatry, Royal Edinburgh Hospital, Morningside, Edinburgh EH10 5HF.*
PROFESSOR MALCOLM LADER	*Institute of Psychiatry, De Crespigny Park, Denmark Hill, London SE5 8AF.*
DR JULIAN LEFF	*MRC Social Psychiatry Unit, Institute of Psychiatry, De Crespigny Park, London SE5 8AF.*
DR ARCHIE LEVEY	*Institute of Psychiatry, De Crespigny Park, Denmark Hill, London SE5 8AF.*
DR JAMES H. MCCROSKERY	*Department of Psychology, State University of New York, Oswego, NY 13126, USA.*
DR MICHAEL MARMOT	*Department of Medical Statistics and Epidemiology, London School of Hygiene and Tropical Medicine, Keppel Street, London WC1E 7HT.*
DR IRENE MARTIN	*Institute of Psychiatry, De Crespigny Park, Demnark Hill, London SE5 8AF.*
DR PETER G. MELLETT	*Horton Hospital, Epsom, Surrey.*
MS MAGGIE MILLS	*Department of Psychology, University of Reading, Building 3, Earley Gate, Reading RG6 2AL.*
DR SUSAN OWEN	*Department of Experimental Psychology, University of Oxford, South Parks Road, Oxford OX1 3UD.*
DR GUDRUN SARTORY	*Institute of Psychiatry, De Crespigny Park, Denmark Hill, London SE5 8AF.*
DR DAVID SIDDLE	*Department of Psychology, University of Southampton, Southampton, Herts SO9 5NH.*

PROFESSOR ROBERT M. STERN

Department of Psychology, The Pennsylvania State University, 417 Bruce V Moore Building, University Park, Pennsylvania 16802, USA.

DR NICHOLAS TARRIER

Clinical Department of Pharmacology, Institute of Psychiatry, De Crespigny Park, London SE5 8AF.

PROFESSOR GORDON TRASLER

Department of Psychology, University of Southampton, Southampton SO9 5NH.

PROFESSOR PETER H. VENABLES

Department of Psychology, University of York, Heslington, York YO1 5DD.

DR MICHAEL WADSWORTH

MRC National Survey of Health and Development, University of Bristol, Department of Community Health, Canynge Hall, Whiteladies Road, Bristol, BS8 2PR.

DR HELEN WINEFIELD

Department of Psychiatry, The University of Adelaide, PO BOX 498, Adelaide, South Australia 5001.

CONTENTS

PREFACE

The book began life in London, after discussions with Wiley's Michael Coombs and with the invaluable secretarial help of Janette Yap. This was, however, at a point in time much further back from the present than we would have wished: we feel, therefore, that those contributors who presented their chapters promptly deserve our special thanks—and our apologies! This does not imply that all the rest were inefficient: events were such that the editorial process slowed markedly when one of us moved to the University of Bradford.

The deceleration was such that Michael had time to be replaced by Celia Bird, whose wise and generous response to our difficulties and delays did much to ensure that we did, eventually, come to publication. In the final phases of preparation we had the help of two Bradford graduates: Diane Foulds and Judith Heeley, to whom we owe grateful thanks. A debt of gratitude is owed also to Penny Walker, whose invaluable secretarial activity saw us through the last stages: the book owes much to her typing, her cheerfulness, and her coffee.

Finally, acknowledgement is due to the Social Science Research Council: the first editor was in receipt of their support during the book's preparation and their research grants do much to maintain investigation in the foundations of psychosomatics—in areas of early experience, emotion, individual differences and environmental influence.

Margaret J. Christie
Peter G. Mellett

SECTION 1

Aims and Origins

Foundations of Psychosomatics
Edited by M. J. Christie and P. G. Mellett
© 1981 John Wiley & Sons Ltd.

1

FOUNDATIONS OF PSYCHOSOMATICS

MARGARET J. CHRISTIE

School of Studies in Psychology, University of Bradford, England.

AIMS AND INTENTIONS

This first chapter attempts to be dual purpose: to provide something of an introduction, in which the origins, aims and intentions of the book are made explicit and the reader is led round the contents, with explanations about the contributions, their perceived relations to each other and to the volume's general theme. Additionally, however, the chapter attempts to provide a swift review of the development, through the present century, of the psychosomatic approach to medicine, and to focus attention on the relevance of the behavioural sciences for provision of foundations to psychosomatics.

First, though, the origins of the book, which lie in the Society for Psychosomatic Research and particularly in its annual London Conferences. These give an opportunity for cross-disciplinary interactions of epidemiologists, neurologists, psychologists, sociologists, etc. with representatives of psychiatry and general medicine. The aim and intention of these annual meetings has always been less concerned with the presentation of today's scientific data, hot from the computer, and more with the provision of a conference programme which facilitates creative multidisciplinary interaction. One is introduced to other concepts and other languages, and provided with opportunity for the '. . . attempt to transcend the confines of interdisciplinary boundaries' (Lipowski, 1976). This, then, is the background to the book: our publisher suggested, after our joint efforts in mounting the 1975 Conference on 'Behaviour, Affect and Illness', that the aims and intentions behind the Conference programme were equally relevant for the planning of two volumes of contributed chapters. Two were envisaged, with the slightly differing aims which underpinned the programmes for the two days of the Conference: the first day was devoted to more academic, *foundational* papers, while the second day's programme carried material which focused on *clinical* relevance. This first volume, then, as its title suggests, collects together a selection of *foundational* material while a subsequent, complementary successor will focus on *clinical* applications.

In selecting the material we have attempted to choose authors who have a proven ability to communicate across disciplinary boundaries. Attempts have also been made to write at a level which is acceptable to a reader having minimal previous acquaintance with any specific area, but who has sufficient scientific background to allow assimilation of the general theme, and the ability (and willingness!) to consult the sources suggested by the authors. There is no intention of presenting a comprehensive coverage of relevant material: the chapters are a selection of topics which have interested the editors, and which, it is hoped, may stimulate and interest their readers.

One class of reader whom we have had particularly in mind is the academic from medicine or from the behavioural and life sciences, who has in recent years become associated with the teaching of psychology and sociology within medical education; those involved, as Chapter 2 notes, in the ' . . . unprecedented attempts to provide formal training for medical students in the behavioural sciences'. Many of these 'attempts' take place in the pre-clinical years when the question of presenting the 'relevance' of behavioural science to medicine looms large. Increasing numbers of such scientists have come as delegates to the Psychosomatic Conferences and appeared to glean from them material suitable for incorporation into their teaching programmes. We trust, also, that the book proves equally interesting and useful to students such as those who, in successive years of the Conferences, were stewards, invaluable aides who shepherded delegates and kept activities on schedule. Such students, whether from medical school and intercalating a year of psychology between pre- and clinical years, or from undergraduate psychology degree courses in which they had developed an interest in psychophysiology and psychosomatics, will, we very much hope, be among our readership.

One conference delegate was Dr Helen Winefield who, while on sabbatical leave from Australia, examined behavioural science components of medical education both in European and North American centres. It is, therefore, particularly appropriate that her contribution forms an early chapter of this book: her scholarly and very comprehensive overview provides an excellent background against which to assess the themes of succeeding chapters as possible teaching topics.

That foundational psychosomatics is a particularly relevant component of pre-clinical teaching has recently been vigorously argued (Christie, 1978): indeed it can be claimed the contemporary medicine requires a 'psychosomatic' approach to *all* of its areas and that this is an essential component of the whole-person view. As Weiner (1977) notes ' . . . it may well be that psychological and social factors in combination with genetic, viral, immunological, physiological and biochemical factors predispose, in some degree, to all disease'. To develop this theme, however, we need to turn to our swift review of developments through the present century, before returning to the introduction of our contributors, and to our perception of their interrelations.

THE DEVELOPMENT OF PSYCHOSOMATICS

Founding fathers

Although the first issue of *Psychosomatic Medicine* did not appear until 1939 it could be said that the first foundations of psychosomatics were laid at the turn of the century. Three figures—Freud, Pavlov, and Cannon—are of particular relevance, and their influence endures, being reflected throughout subsequent pages of this book. Thus Dixon's work on perceptual defence can be seen as a contemporary development of sophisticated experimental approaches to defence mechanisms, and conditioning is, in addition to being the central theme of the Levey and Martin chapter, an aspect of McCroskery and Engel, Siddle and Trasler, Sartory and Lader. Cannon is clearly reflected in Carruthers' work and indeed in any aspect of the book which has as its topic the physiological correlates of emotional state.

Early aims

The first issue of *Psychosomatic Medicine* was launched in 1939, with the twin aims of *studying the interaction of psychological and physiological aspects of all normal and abnormal bodily functions,* and of attempting to integrate both *somatic and psycho therapies.*

As Lipowski (1977) notes there is at this stage of the development a balance of study and research with treatment. There is, in the journal's editorial, no suggestion of causality, of the psychogenesis of specific somatic disorder, no holy seven 'psychosomatic disorders', no hint of the existence of 'psychosomatic patients'. These themes were to dominate the scene during two decades following the journal's first issue. Freud's influence seemed to be paramount through the activities of the Chicago Psychoanalytic Institute, and psychosomatics was *apparently* less influenced by Cannon and Pavlov. It was not, of course, the case that these founding fathers *had* ceased to influence the field: there is, for example, a natural succession from Cannon through Selye (1950) to contemporary stress research, to Mason (1968), and Levi and his colleagues (1971).

The Chicago Institute

In the 1940s, however, we do see a predominance of psychoanalytic viewpoints and a focus of attention on the work of the Chicago Psychoanalytic Institute. The impetus for their activities seems, however, to have been European rather than North American, originating from a reaction in Germany and Austria during the 1920s against the prevailing, somewhat mechanistic, view of medicine then current. The nineteenth century had seen major developments in medicine's basic sciences: the successes in, for example, microbiology and chemistry, had led to a perception of disease as a reflection of malfunctioning mechanisms, with attention focused on the faulty organ system. In reaction to this mechanistic attitude there had developed a psychosomatic orientation in the continent of Europe and the rise of Nazi persecution led to its dissemination beyond Austria and Germany. Wittkower went to London, Franz Alexander to Chicago, and from that centre spread the 1940s message for psychosomatics that origins of disorder lie in childhood experience, that unconscious conflicts remain into adulthood as part of a predisposing state which can be reactivated by external circumstances, by life events which can precipitate a 'psychosomatic disorder'. There are individual differences in organ weakness, which have a contribution to make, but the particular disorder which develops is seen as a consequence of a specific predisposing conflict. Thus, as we see from Chapter 11, peptic ulcer was regarded as the consequence of a conflict of dependency and self-sufficiency: the former being manifested in a wish to be fed and cared for which resulted in an excessive stimulation of gastric secretion which could ultimately lead to the development of peptic ulcer. The 'psychosomatic disorders'—the holy seven of bronchial asthma, rheumatoid arthritis, ulcerative colitis, essential hypertension, neurodermatitis, thyrotoxicosis, in addition to peptic ulcer—had their own specific predisposing unconscious determinants and generated an explanation of causation. The 'specificity' model had, however, its critics, not least because the molar levels of explanation were inadequate. There was heavy emphasis on clinical observation, without adequate back-up from experimental study of the ' . . . interaction of psychological and physiological aspects of all normal and abnormal bodily functions'. Further there were sterile disputes relating to criteria for 'psychosomatic disorders' and 'psychosomatic patients' which almost, but not quite ' . . . swept the field into oblivion. . .' (Lipowski, 1977).

Mid-century reaction

Work did, however, continue within the field of psychosomatics: an outstanding example is that of Weiner, and his recent appraisal of the Chicago work (Weiner, 1977), while being justifiably critical of its sweeping statements, reminds us that there is validity in a model which focuses attention on interactions between physiological and psychological predispositions and the precipitating factor of life stress. So, the 1950s saw a phase of development in psychosomatics in which Cannon and Pavlov were re-integrated, and a broader eclectic viewpoint emerged, one which re-emphasizes the findings from experimental investigation and combines these in a more productive fashion with clinical observation. Typical of this mid-century development is Hamilton's 1955 volume, after which came O'Neill (1955), the earlier volumes in Hill's series (Hill, 1970, 1976), then the full flow of literature from 'psychosomatics in the seventies' (Lipowski, 1976).

PSYCHOSOMATICS IN THE SEVENTIES

The role of psychophysiology

The broader eclectic view which we saw emerging is described by Crisp (1975) in these terms:

> the notion that disease arises from the complex interplay of multiple factors over the years, existing and arising with the environment and the individual's make-up appeals mostly to those of a divergent turn

of mind and perhaps also to those most prepared to tolerate a degree of uncertainty ... such characteristics are probably not of a kind that incline a person to systematic research with its, often, reductionist ethos and necessary discipline.

As we will see from subsequent chapters, however, there is a wealth of systematic research, able to provide foundations for contemporary psychosomatics, much of this originating, as will be apparent, from *psychophysiological* sources, and all of it concerned with the major themes of psychosomatics—early life, emotion, environment and individual differences. Siddle and Trasler (Chapter 13) provide us with a useful introduction to specific aspects of psychophysiology, for those unfamiliar with the field: at this point, therefore, we need only point out a few broad features. Its original impetus was towards development of methods for measurement of physiological correlates of emotion, though the remit has broadened considerably in recent years, as Siddle and Trasler note. Readers wishing to dig more deeply in the field are directed toward volumes from the 1970s such as the major handbook (Greenfield and Sternbach, 1972) a collection of research papers (Venables and Christie, 1975) and a volume devoted to the enduring theme of emotion (Grings and Dawson, 1978). An aspect of contemporary psychophysiology having particular relevance for psychosomatics is the capacity for taking a holistic view of man, for looking simultaneously at measurement of subjective state and behaviour, as well as attending to the physiological correlates of these. In focusing on such physiological correlates, however, the methods of psychophysiology are of particular value for examination of the mediating mechanisms—neurophysiological or endocrine—by which psyche is translated into soma, by which events at a symbolic level of organization are translated into physiological function of organ or tissue. An obvious example, and one which reminds us of the foundations laid by Cannon, is examination of the mechanisms whereby the perception of threat is translated into neuroendocrine response. The complex nature of normal and endocrine interaction is presented diagrammatically by Christie and Woodman in the most recent volume of psychophysiology (Martin and Venables, 1980), and a simplified schematic version can be found in Christie Little, and Gordon (1980). By analysis of interactions such as these psychophysiology is in a central position for examining mediating mechanisms in ways largely ignored by the psychosomatics of the 1940s. This aspect of the field has been highlighted by Graham (1971) who, as a physician elected to presidency of the American Society for Psychophysiological Research, described psychosomatics as 'clinical psychophysiology'. He emphasizes the reversal from the molar approach of the Chicago School to the molecular approach of the recent decade, where, he suggests, there is greater concern with 'small samples', with examination of 'small physiological steps in the direction of full blown illness', and writes that ' ... close attention to one aspect of organ function may be more informative than a global approach to a disease state...'. This approach, this concern with the earliest stages of disease development, is reflected at a number of points in subsequent chapters: Venables' report of growing interest in longitudinal studies and screening methods for 'at risk' subjects, Wadsworth and Ingham's discussion of the transition from the state labelled 'health' to that designated as 'illness'. This growing concern is, of course, to some extent a consequence of the changing nature of disease, of the increase in slowly developing, chronic disorder in contrast to the acute conditions of earlier decades: Wadsworth and Ingham note this in their chapter, and fuller discussion is available in Wadsworth Butterfield, and Blaney (1971). Thus interest in the pre-consultation period, increasingly evident among psychologists and sociologists, extends backwards until one is asking about the earliest experiences of man— in utero, during birth and as a neonate. This theme will be returned to in our appraisal of relations between subsequent chapters, but at this point it may be useful to summarize the present state of psychosomatics, and an invaluable form of such a summary is provided by Lipowski. This particular writer has contributed enormously to the development of psychosomatics as a coherent approach to medicine: his prolific output is available in numerous journals, he has an overview of 'psychosomatics in the seventies' in Hill's most recent volume (Lipowski, 1976) and his comprehensive collection of contributions to an edited volume (Lipowski, Lipsett, and Whybrow 1977) accurately reflects the nature of the contemporary scene.

Three aspects of psychosomatic endeavour

Lipowski (1976) describes contemporary psychosomatics as having three interrelated aspects:

(1) a science of the relations between biological, psychological and social variables as they pertain to human health and disease;
(2) an approach to the practice of medicine that advocates the inclusion of psychosocial factors in the study, prevention, diagnosis and management of all disease;
(3) clinical activities at the interface of medicine and the behavioural sciences subsumed under the term 'consultation liaison psychiatry'.

We see reflected in Lipowski's description the move away from psychodynamic formulations and towards consideration of *social* events and situations and their effects on psychophysiological functioning. This is, perhaps, an area of psychosomatic activity which was less evident in the first issue of *Psychosomatic Medicine*: we saw there the twin aims of studying psychological and physiological interaction in relation to all normal and abnormal bodily function and of attempting to integrate somatic and psychotherapies. Indeed, Kimball (1970), summarizing his comprehensive review of conceptual developments in psychosomatic medicine, writes that 'Its preoccupation has shifted from concern with intrapsychic events and disease to emphasis on the environments in which illness occurs'. We can note that alongside the growth of psychosomatic interest in the psychosocial environment there was a parallel development in psychophysiology: 1970 saw the first review of an area designated as 'social psychophysiology' (Shapiro and Schwarz, 1970), followed by Schwarz and Shapiro (1973) and Christie and Todd (1975). This topic will be returned to when we survey the chapters from our 'environment' section, in the next section's overview of the book and its relation to current themes and endeavours in contemporary psychosomatics.

SOME CONTEMPORARY FOUNDATIONS

We have noted, in earlier sections, the foundational nature of the behavioural and life sciences, and in particular the role of psychophysiology. We commented also on the inheritance from Freud, Cannon, and Pavlov, and suggested that the influence of these founding fathers was still much in evidence when one examined contemporary foundations of psychosomatics. In this concluding section, therefore, it becomes appropriate to introduce our contributors, and in so doing to attempt the editorial role of providing links between both them and the earlier influences on psychosomatics.

Freud

Chapter 6 reflects more clearly than any other the influence of Freud and the psychoanalytic input to psychosomatics. Dixon, however, represents a fascinating example of the experimental psychologist, using physiological monitoring to examine phenomena which are 'not conscious' and without doubt could be viewed as reflections of 'unconscious' motivation.

Chapters 3, 4, and 5 are, of course, in some ways reflecting this inheritance in that all are concerned with the earliest aspects of life. Further, Chapters 3 and 4 provide foundations from which to appraise *contemporary* interest in the birth experience and its immediate aftermath: psychosomatics may welcome enthusiastically the Janov and the Leboyer, but a cool appraisal of the nature of foetal and neonatal abilities is essential for an objective assessment of contemporary enthusiasms.

Venables provides a chapter which aids our understanding of the high-risk screening and longitudinal studies; these are of growing importance for medicine in an age when slowly developing, chronic conditions are more evident than acute states with swift onset. His chapter also introduces the topic of early *intervention*, with exploration of the effects on childhood behaviour of the nursery school experience in Mauritius: further information is available in Venables (1978).

Pavlov

Two influences are evident throughout the book: conditioning is relevant to Chapters 5, 7, 8, 9, 12, and 13, while the orienting response (OR)—Pavlov's 'what-is-it?' reflex—and the complementary phenomenon of habituation, form aspects of Chapters 5, 8, and 13. This capacity to respond with optimal use of sensory function to stimuli of importance has great survival value: the Russian tradition sees the OR as a response to *change*, and Mackworth (1969) has described this as a reflection, up the phylogenetic scale, of the evolutionary principle that 'change is dangerous'. In man we see that abnormalities such as pathological anxiety, schizorphrenia, or psychopathy are frequently accompanied by abnormalities of the fundamental responses of orienting and habituation.

The general area of Pavlovian conditioning is, of course, central to the chapter provided by Levey and Martin: these authors have for many years been associated with an institute where Pavlov's influence on Eysenck, and the latter's influence on contemporary research, are very evident. We see, for example, the latter reflected at the various points where the EPI and its dimensions of extraversion and neuroticism are described: in relation to individual differences in pain, in conditionability, in anti-social behaviour. Gray represents a third stage of development in that his interpretation of introverted behaviour as a reflection of sensitivity to situations of frustrative non-reward is a modification of the Eysenckian model. This aspect of his work is less evident in his chapter, but interested readers could find some account of it in Gray (1972).

McCroskery and Engel's chapter represents a wider perspective of conditioning in that operant and Pavlovian aspects are both relevant. Again we have a cool appraisal of foundational material, against which to assess a current clinical enthusiasm, for biofeedback treatment of organic dysfunction.

Cannon

There is a sense in which Cannon is reflected at almost any point where the physiological correlates of emotion are at the centre of interest; as emotion is one of the most fundamental and enduring themes of psychosomatics, we have Cannon in evidence throughout the book. He is probably most evident, however, in Chapters 10 and 8: Carruthers demonstrates the developments, from earlier work on adrenaline, of the notion that fear and anger are associated with specific output ratios of adrenaline and noradrenaline. That the latter could be associated with the angry aggressive state is of relevance for the current work on Type A behaviour and its significance as a possible risk factor for cardiovascular disease. It is interesting to note the absence of this from the holy seven, and the very obvious presence of interest in such disorder manifested in contemporary psychosomatics. Associations of noradrenaline or its metabolites with aggressive state have been reported in other contexts (see Christie and Woodman, 1980, for some relevant references), and it may well be that this particular example stimulus–response–specificity (SRS—see Sternbach, 1966) will have a considerable influence on future psychosomatic research. Another future development may well be that of ambulant monitoring of physiological state, as described by Carruthers. This technique offers the possibility of moving out from the laboratory environment, with its potential for generating anxiety and consequent questions about the ecological validity of data collected 'at the bench', while Gale and Baker offer guidance for those opting for the potential it offers for *controlled* investigation. Chapter 19 represents another approach to 'real life', that of schizophrenic patients at home and their psychophysiological responses to the emotional environment. We will, however, look again at the general topic of environments in a later section, and continue at this point with aspects of emotion.

One obvious development over the past decade has been the increasing use of psychoactive drugs. This topic forms part of Chapter 8, but we see interest in the theme reflected also in Chapters 7, 10, and 19. Gray's notion that our 'moral fibre' may be sapped by their use has a splendidly Victorian ring about it, while Leff and Tarrier's report of interactions between the effect of phenothiazines and the emotional quality of the family environment is intriguing. Carruthers' mention of the effects on *subjective* state of β-blockade leads us into consideration of contemporary interest in the James–Lange–Schachter–Valins saga, into the question of whether our emotional feeling reflects our physiological state: there are suggestions in Carruthers' and in McCroskery and Engel's chapters that this may be so.

Another fascinating 'update' relates to 'perception without awareness': this, and Dixon's chapter, were noted at an earlier point in this overview, but it could also be incorporated into the much broader and more comprehensive contemporary interest in cortical/subcortical integration. As Levey and Martin observe '. . . we deal which an organism equipped with a number of subcortical mechanisms designed to ensure survival in the jungle and a highly differentiated cortex which is nevertheless unable to inform the subcortex that we no longer live there'. Dixon deals with input to the central processing machinery, while other writers are concerned with output from it. All, however, contribute to development of ideas about hierarchical control of aspects of man's behaviour, lack of awareness of some of this, and the relevance of cortical/subcortical components. Paul MacLean is particularly appropriate to this theme (MacLean 1976) and, in view of his 1930s association with Papez, he really should have been introduced as something of a founding father. Given his continuing creativity and industry, however, he might well prefer this introduction, albeit belated, within the context of *contemporary* foundations!

Lastly, in this appraisal of emotion, we can note, somewhat regretfully, the emphasis on *dysphoric* aspects and dearth of material related to *euphoric* emotion. In the 1960s Wenger (1966) observed that we know considerably more about the psychophysiology of anxiety than about the nature of tranquillity, while Stern, Farr, and Ray (1975) reported the problems associated with giving an account of the psychophysiology of pleasure. There is, to be sure, a hint of the positive state in Chapter 9's reference to relaxation, but all in all we do have an absence of euphoria. The nearest approach is Marmot's description of the positive, supportive qualities of Japanese life, which we will encounter in the next section. But this absence is unfortunate, given the contemporary interest in phenomena such as transcendental meditation reflecting, as it does, psychosomatic concern with the search for tranquillity as well as the headlong rush into stimulation which Carruthers describes.

Environments

As we observed at an earlier point, the theme of environment is a late arrival on the psychosomatic scene, but we have in Chapters 15–19 a selection of diverse topics, as well as reference to relevant aspects in Chapters 3, 5, and 10.

Marmot focuses on the culture, Wadsworth and Ingham on subcultural influences, and Leff and Tarrier on the home. Gale and Baker alert us, as we noted previously, to the need for appraisal of the potential threat inherent in the laboratory environment, and a similar message comes from Gordon in his discussion of treatment environments. Given the widespread physiological response to threat which was described by Cannon it does indeed become relevant for psychosomatics to consider *environmental* sources of threat in situations of both psychophysiological research and therapy.

But, inevitably, there will be *individual differences* in response to environmental sources of threat, and our consideration of Roessler's work on ego-strength, with the emphasis on *perception and interpretation* noted in Chapter 11, directs our attention to this. We noted also, at an earlier point, the book's concern, in various ways, with the Eysenckian model of personality: these two approaches, of Eysenck and Roessler, reflect concern with *physiological* underpinnings and physiological *consequences* of 'personality'. Obviously there are those, within psychosomatics, who would take issue with *this* view of personality. But as Crisp (1975) notes, the field attracts '... those most prepared to tolerate a degree of uncertainty ...' so we trust his mature judgement in this matter, and look for this tolerance! Tolerance also of the attempt, in this concluding section, to make explicit the links which we perceived between our contributors' material, and between them and their predecessors. This particular section could have been continued indefinitely: there is, as a colleague (Martin, 1967) once noted, nothing quite as pleasant as being creative on somebody else's sidelines. But while Crisp (1975) *also* assures us that psychosomatics '... appeals mostly to those of a divergent turn of mind ...' we feel that our readers would regard indefinite continuation as creativity unacceptably rampant. We hope, therefore, that sufficient has been said to give the book coherence, but not enough to bore readers into premature closure.

REFERENCES

Christie, M. J. (1978). Bodies and minds revisited. *Bulletin of the British Psychological Society*, **31**, 355–357.
Christie, M. J., Little, B. C., and Gordon, A. M. (1980). Peripheral indices of depressive states. In van Praag, H. M., Lader M. H., Rafaelsen, O. J., and Sachar, J. (Eds.),

Handbook of Biological Psychiatry, Vol. III: *Brain Mechanisms and Abnormal Behaviour*. New York: Dekker.

Christie, M. J. and Todd, J. L. (1975). Experimenter–subject–situational interactions. In Venables, P. H., and Christie, M. J. (Eds.), *Research in Psychophysiology*. London: John Wiley & Sons.

Christie, M. H., and Woodman, D. D. (1980). Biochemical methods. In Martin, I., and Venables, P. H. (Eds.), *Techniques in Psychophysiology*. Chichester: John Wiley & Sons.

Crisp, A. M. (1975). Psychosomatic research today: a clinician's overview. *International Journal of Psychiatry in Medicine*, **6**, 159–166.

Graham, D. T. (1971). Psychophysiology and medicine. *Psychophysiology*, **8**, 121–131.

Gray, J. A. (1972). The psychophysiological nature of introversion–extraversion: A modification of Eysenck's theory. In Nebylitsyn, V. D., and Gray, J.A. (Eds.), *Biological Bases of Individual Behaviour*. New York: Academic Press.

Greenfield, N. S. and Sternbach, R. A. (1972). *Handbook of Psychophysiology*. New York: Holt, Rinehart & Winston, Inc.

Grings, W. W., and Dawson, M. E. (1978). *Emotions and Bodily Responses: A Psychophysiological Approach*. New York: Academic Press.

Hamilton, M. (1955). *Psychosomatics*. London: Chapman & Hall.

Hill, O. W. (1970). *Modern Trends in Psychosomatic Medicine—2*. London: Butterworths.

Hill, O. W. (1976). *Modern Trends in Psychosomatic Medicine—3*. London: Butterworths.

Kimball, C. P. (1970). Conceptual developments in psychosomatic medicine: 1939–1969. *Annals of Internal Medicine*, **73**, 307–316.

Levi, L. (1971). *Society, Stress and Disease*, Vol. 1: *The Psychosocial Environment and Psychosomatic Diseases*. London: Oxford University Press.

Lipowski, Z. J. (1976). Psychosomatic medicine: an overview. In Hill, O. W. (Ed.), *Modern Trends in Psychosomatic Medicine—3*. London: Butterworths.

Lipowski, Z. J. (1977). Psychosomatic medicine: current trends and clinical applications. In Lipowski, Z. J., Lipsett, D. R. and Whybrow, P. C. (Eds.), *Psychosomatic Medicine: Current Trends and Clinical Applications*. New York: Oxford University Press.

Lipowski, Z. J., Lipsett, D. R., and Whybrow, P. C. (1977). *Psychosomatic Medicine: Current Trends and Clinical Applications*. New York: Oxford University Press.

Mackworth, J. F. (1969). *Vigilance and Habituation*. Harmondsworth: Penguin.

MacLean, P. D. (1976). 'The triune brain in conflict'. Paper presented to the 11th European Conference on Psychosomatic Research, Heidelberg.

Martin, I., and Venables, P. H. (1980). *Techniques in Psychophysiology*. Chichester: John Wiley & Sons.

Martin, J. (1967). Personal communication.

Mason, J. W. (1968). Organization of psychoendocrine mechanisms. *Psychosomatic Medicine*, **30**, (5), part 11.

O'Neill, D. (1955). *Modern Trends in Psychosomatic Medicine—1*. London: Butterworths.

Selye, H. (1950). *The Physiology and Pathology of Exposure to Stress*. Montreal: Acta, Inc.

Schwartz, G. E. and Shapiro, D. (1973). Social psychophysiology. In Prokasy, W. F., and Raskin, D. C. (Eds.), *Electrodermal Activity in Psychological Research*. New York: Academic Press.

Shapiro, D., and Schwartz, G. E. (1970). Psychophysiological contributions to social psychology. *Annual Review of Psychology*, **21**, 87–112.

Stern, R. M., Farr, J. H., and Ray, W. J. (1975). Pleasure. In Venables, P. H., and Christie, M. J. (Eds.), *Research in Psychophysiology*. London, John Wiley & Sons.

Sternbach, R. A. (1966). *Principles of Psychophysiology*. New York: Academic Press.

Venables, P. H. (1978). Psychophysiology and psychometrics, *Psychophysiology*, **15**, 302–315.

Venables, P. H., and Christie, M. J. (1975). *Research in Psychophysiology*. London: John Wiley & Sons.

Wadsworth, M., Butterfield, W. J. H., and Blaney, R. (1971). *Health and Sickness: The Choice of Treatment*. London: Tavistock.
Weiner, H. (1977). *Psychobiology and Human Disease*. New York: Elsevier.
Wenger, M. A. (1966). Studies of autonomic balance: a summary. *Psychophysiology*, **2**, 173–186.

Foundations of Psychosomatics
Edited by M. J. Christie and P. G. Mellett
© 1981 John Wiley & Sons Ltd.

2

BEHAVIOURAL SCIENCE IN THE MEDICAL CURRICULUM: WHY AND HOW

HELEN R. WINEFIELD
Department of Psychiatry, University of Adelaide, South Australia.

Although doctors have always acted as applied social scientists, observing and reflecting upon human nature, and trying to induce their patients to behave in certain health-relevant ways, at present we are witnessing unprecedented efforts to provide formal training for medical students in the behavioural sciences. The first section of this chapter explores in some detail five different aspects of human behaviour which are of special interest to doctors. Compliance with medical instructions with regard to both treatment and prevention of illness are the first and second, and the third is the appropriate utilization of the available health-care facilities. Also included are the doctor's own professional functioning and personal adjustment in a very demanding role, and lastly his or her influence upon non-patient decision-makers in the community. In reviewing these areas I hope to show why a detailed and sophisticated study of human behaviour is a vital part of medical education, and also to indicate some of the most exciting areas of current research at the confluence of the medical and behavioural sciences.

Useful preliminary reading in the application of the principles and concepts of psychology and sociology to medical concerns is available in recent interdisciplinary publications such as the report of the American Psychological Association Task Force on Health Research (1976), Freeman, Levine, and and Reeder (1972), Millon (1975), Rachman and Philips (1975), and Winefield and Peay (1980).

In the second section of the chapter I shall discuss the Behavioural Science courses which are now a standard part of medical curricula in many parts of the world. Special consideration will be given to the content which is appropriate, and the determinants of student response. Throughout, I have necessarily been selective in the references provided, and hope that those chosen may be helpful as starting points for the interested reader.

BEHAVIOURS OF SPECIAL INTEREST TO DOCTORS

Compliance with treatment instructions

It has now been clearly recognized that many patients, sometimes the majority, do not carry out the treatment measures prescribed by their medical advisers.

Drugs are not taken, diet is not changed, and advice is not followed, by an alarming number of health-care 'users' (Ley and Spelman, 1967). Doctors may well feel that unless patients are prepared to follow their expert advice about how to overcome a particular episode of illness, the whole basis of medicine is threatened.

Whether or not instructions will be followed seems to be associated with both cognitive and motivational factors in the patient: these will be evaluated in turn. Messages which are difficult to understand or remember are unlikely to be acted upon adequately. The elderly, and those who are upset or anxious, whether about their illness, their home situation, or their toddler devastating the doctor's office, are particularly likely to forget at least some salient points in the doctor's instructions, even if they heard and understood them in the first place. At the same time, many people simply fail to comprehend what they are being told, due to an overestimation on the doctor's part of their understanding of anatomical or technical terms. Boyle (1970) for example found that 58 per cent of patients did not know where their heart was; 80 per cent were wrong about the location of the stomach, and 49 per cent about the lungs.

An understanding of the principles of perception, information-processing, and memory enables the doctor to transmit information clearly and devise checks and prompts to help patients with this cognitive aspect of the compliance problem. Ley (1979) has concluded that giving instructions first, and thus increasing their perceived importance, helps to reduce forgetting of the doctor's advice, as does using concrete and specific, rather than vague or abstract, terminology. In ensuring that information is adequately grasped by patients, the doctor will raise their satisfaction with the consultation, and thus the likelihood of compliance (Korsch and Negrete, 1972).

If the doctor understands the principles of human learning, he or she may strengthen medication-taking behaviour by arranging for specific cues and reinforcers of appropriate habits on the patient's part (Kegeles, Lund, and Weisenberg, 1978; Zifferblatt, 1975). This suggestion implies that the patient is an active partner in the treatment regimen, a point stressed by Stimson (1974), who reviewed factors such as the patient's beliefs and attitudes towards medicines, his assessment of the doctor's competence and concern, and the extent to which his expectations had been fulfilled. These emotional and motivational determinants of compliance necessitate consideration of the crucial but elusive 'doctor–patient relationship'. This rather nebulous concept can be operationally defined in terms of the behaviours through which the doctor communicates an impression of competence, hopefulness, concern, and respect for the patient as an individual person, and fosters the patient's trust, confidence, and active co-operation.

With the disappearance of epidemics of infectious diseases—thanks to improved public health measures, vaccinations, and antibiotics—many patients suffer relatively chronic health problems, which are not life-threatening, and which require the patient's active co-operation in treatment. The successful management of many health problems including diabetes, heart disease, psychiatric disorders, and ageing, all depend on mutual participation in treatment by doctor and patient. This and other variations of the doctor–patient relationship were first described by Szasz and Hollender (1956). Seeing the doctor as a persuader (Frank, 1973) and behaviour modifier makes clear the need for communication and counselling skills in his repertoire of healing activities (Bernstein, Bernstein, and Dana, 1974; Bowden and Burstein, 1974; Edinburg, Zinberg, and Kelman, 1975; Enelow and Swisher, 1972). The use of open-ended rather than leading questions, encouraging the patient to express doubts and worries, knowing how and when to confront people with inconsistencies in their story (or between their story and their expression), and communicating genuine empathy and concern for the person are all important. Such skills can be systematically taught to medical students, and behavioural science is an appropriate context for an introductory analysis.

Much of what has been discussed so far is equally relevant to the doctor's role as an agent of preventive medicine. Before this is examined in more detail, however, it may be a suitable moment to comment upon the fact that in many cases the most effective treatment for bodily dysfunction may be a behavioural one. Treatments based on the principles of behaviour modification are being developed for insomnia, obesity, sexual difficulties, anxiety, depression, and pain (including headaches) (Annon, 1974; Davidson, 1976; Fordyce, 1976; Kingsley and Wilson, 1977; Lazarus, 1972; Lick and Heffler, 1977). Problems such as bedwetting, nervous habits and compulsions, phobias, and childish misbehaviour are by now fairly widely accepted as suitable targets for the application of techniques derived from the psychology of learning (Bandura, 1969; Yates, 1970). It is not suggested that doctors should all feel obliged to develop expertise in methods of behaviour modification, although some may wish to do that; rather I believe that an awareness of the existence and rationale of such methods is required by every medical practitioner to increase his or her own therapeutic scope, as well as to keep abreast of developments in knowledge which bear directly upon the problems of sickness and health. Talk of influencing and modifying the behaviour of others need not call up images of a 1984 society. As one who keeps pain and death at bay, and as an educated and prestigious member of the community, the doctor is a powerful reinforcement agent and model, and would no doubt prefer to use that potential knowingly and systematically.

Compliance with preventive advice

Mortality statistics, as in Tables 2.1 and 2.2 (extracted from the WHO report, 1974), dramatize the contribution to premature death and presumably also to morbidity in industrialized cultures, of behaviours which are in principle modifiable. Some of the accidents which are the leading cause of premature death are certainly just that—unavoidable 'acts of God'—but many may be related to child abuse, suicide efforts, and the effects of excessive alcohol. 'Accident-proneness' is not randomly distributed in the population but tends to co-vary

TABLE 2.1. Leading causes of death at different ages in 27 North American, European, and Oceanic countries, 1971

Age group (years)	Most frequent cause of death	Second most frequent cause of death	Third most frequent cause of death
1–4	Accidents (25)	Congenital anomalies (14); influenza and pneumonia (6)	Malignant-neoplasms (19); congenital anomalies (7)
5–14	Accidents (27)	Malignant neoplasms (26)	Congenital anomalies (22)
15–44	Accidents (26)	Malignant neoplasms (24)	Heart diseases (18); suicide (7)
45–64	Malignant neoplasms (14); heart diseases (13)	Heart diseases (14); malignant neoplasms (13)	Cerebrovascular disease (21); accidents (3)
65+	Heart diseases (27)	Cerebrovascular disease (14); malignant neoplasms (13)	Cerebrovascular disease (14); malignant neoplasms (13)

Numbers in parentheses indicate in how many of the countries surveyed the cited cause of death has the rank given. Data source: WHO, 1974.

TABLE 2.2. Causes of death between 15 and 44 years in USA, England, and Australia

Cause of death	USA (1970)		England and Wales (1971)		Australia (1971)	
Accidents	30.8	(1)	21.7	(2)	37.2	(1)
Malignant neoplasms	13.2	(2)	23.8	(1)	14.4	(2)
Heart diseases	12.7	(3)	17.0	(3)	13.0	(3)
All other external causes (e.g. assault)	9.1	(4)	2.7	(7)	2.2	(6)
Suicide and self-inflicted injuries	6.7	(5)	6.1	(4)	10.2	(4)
Cirrhosis of the liver	3.7	(6)			1.4	(9)
Cerebrovascular disease	3.4	(7)	4.8	(5)	4.3	(5)
Influenza and pneumonia	2.4	(8)	2.8	(6)	1.5	(8)
Diabetes mellitus	1.3	(9)				
Congenital anomalies	1.0	(10)	1.7	(9)		
Bronchitis, emphysema and asthma			2.1	(8)	1.8	(7)
Nephritis and nephrosis			1.2	(10)	1.0	(10)
All other causes	15.7		16.1		13.0	

Numbers are percentages of deaths in the age-group attributed to the given cause; numbers in parentheses show the rank of each cause of death in each country. Data source: WHO, 1974.

with certain social and personality variables (e.g. Waller and Whorton, 1973). At least some of the congenital anomalies responsible for death in childhood could be averted through genetic counselling. A combination of drug abuse (alcohol, nicotine, and analgesics as well as narcotics) and incorrect lifestyle (diet, lack of exercise, and tension) is clearly implicated in many ills of early and middle age (Duggin, 1977; Gil, 1970; Jenkins, 1976). Cancer due to contact with environmental carcinogens is preventable, and in any case would be much more readily treated if people did not delay seeking help for as long as they do (Cullen, Fox, and Isom, 1976).

The WHO conclusion (1974, p. 568) is that '. . . it would be worth-while to re-examine the preventive approach. Health education of the public should be undertaken by all levels of health workers.' An understanding of the principles of behavioural influence and attitude change appears to be at least as valuable in this endeavour as knowledge of physiology and microbiology. In less-developed countries diarrhoeal and other infectious diseases such as measles, for which effective preventive and treatment measures exist, predominate as causes of death, especially in children. The applications of behavioural theories to preventive medicine in general have been reviewed by Berkanovic (1976) and by Pomerleau, Bass, and Crown (1975) who also comment on some problems of choosing the most suitable research designs.

It is appropriate for doctors to be concerned not only with behaviours which contribute to needless deaths and illnesses, but also those relevant to health and recovery. For example, mother's presence can reduce maladaptive responses to hospitalization in preschool children (Bowlby, 1975; Robertson, 1970). Providing information about the aftermath of surgery helps to speed recovery and reduce the need for postoperative narcotics (Egbert et al., 1964; Janis, 1958). The psychological state of the patient often determines the effectiveness of pharmacological methods of pain control (Weisenberg, 1977), and antenatal education measures can reduce childbirth pain (Cogan, Henneborn, and Klopfer, 1976). Rahe, Ward, and Hayes (1979) report that postmyocardial infarction patients who received group therapy showed less coronary morbidity and mortality, and more returned to work, compared with controls over a 3–4-year follow-up.

Enduring characteristics of the patient which may affect health include personality and coping resources in the face of life stresses. The Coronary Prone Behaviour Pattern (Type A) characterized by time urgency, aggressiveness, and competitiveness, has been associated with the prevalence of coronary disease in different populations and the risk of its development in healthy persons, or its recurrence (Jenkins, 1976; Rosenman et al., 1964). The 'cancer-prone' personality has also been described, as one characterized by despair and hopelessness in response to loss (LeShan, 1966; Schmale and Iker, 1966), use of denial and somatic regression (Bahnson, 1969), and restricted emotional expressiveness, particularly with regard to hostile feelings (Greer and Morris, 1975, Kissen, Brown, and Kissen, 1969). There are many hazards associated with relating particular personality patterns to specific diseases (Freyhan, 1976;

Surawicz, et al., 1976). It is difficult to disentangle cause-and-effect relationships between being ill and giving certain sorts of answers to personality tests and assessments. Long-term prospective studies such as that carried out by Thomas and Duszynski (1974) on over a thousand medical students are all too rare. The problems of research design are also great, especially in the area of choosing exactly who might best serve as appropriate control or comparison subjects (Greer and Morris, 1978; Fox, 1978).

These difficulties of retrospectivity and inadequacy of controls have also troubled another vigorous area of research into the role of psychological factors in illness, namely the work on significant life changes and readjustments as antecedents of illness (e.g. Rahe et al., 1971). The onset of major fatal diseases has been related to important stressful events in the victim's life, for example in the work of Ulf (1975) on heart disease in twins, and Greene and Miller (1958) and Townes, Wold, and Holmes (1974) on childhood leukemia. Many other somatic and psychiatric illnesses have also been shown to be associated with preceding stressful events.

However, while purely physical/genetic/constitutional variables may lack the predictive power implied by a dualistic Cartesian viewpoint, life events can explain relatively little of the remainder of the variability in individual illness rates. Hinkle (1974) summarized several long-term studies of groups of 'healthy' people sharing a similar environment with the conclusion that risk of illness is not evenly distributed throughout the population. For people who have an established pattern of physiological susceptibility to illness, episodes of illness are likely to follow significant social or interpersonal changes in their lives. Many people, however, have few, and some have no, illnesses, despite facing the same levels of life change. Dohrenwend and Dohrenwend (1978) called for better definition of the events to be studied, and estimations of their magnitude, as well as for more precise research designs. All of these issues have been the subject of lively argument, for example Tennant and Andrews (1978) concluded that it is the distressfulness of life events, rather than the magnitude of change they cause, which is associated with impairment.

It is in trying to account for individual differences in vulnerability to illness that much fascinating although challenging work is being carried out at present. We have realized that many, if not most, diseases, and not just the 'holy seven' of hypertension, ulcerative colitis, asthma, peptic ulcer, neurodermatitis, thyrotoxicosis, and rheumatoid arthritis (Greene, 1975), are or can be causally associated with stresses such as psychological losses or threats of loss (including self-esteem and familiar secure habits). From the stance of a practising physician, such information alone has some direct implications for prevention and treatment of illness, mainly in alerting him or her to keep a close watch on definably 'at risk' patients: those who are undergoing re-adjustment in their lives such as parenthood, bereavement, divorce, changes of residence and of employment, and so on. Additional factors, however, are being discovered to influence susceptibility to illness independently of life stress.

So far, understanding of the physiological concomitants of individual differences in illness-proneness are at a frustratingly primitive stage of development. There is some evidence, for example, that immunological system function may be affected by experiential factors (Amkraut and Solomon, 1974), and hormonal influences are another possible pathway (Greer, 1979). While the study of innate genetic or constitutional differences is important, these are likely to remain unmodifiable in the near future. Non-physiological, potentially modifiable factors have been suggested to predict, and possibly eventually allow medical control of, individual illness-risk. One is the social support available to the stressed person, and the other is whether that individual responds to stress with helplessness or not.

Before going on to discuss these developments, it is worth emphasizing that usually we are restricted to basing our observations and theories on reported illnesses, not illness *per se*. Many aches and pains, colds, infections, diseases, and the like are never reported to doctors. Illness behaviour, to be discussed more fully later, determines which are reported, when the majority are not, and what causes a person to consult a doctor over a condition which does not cause that response in another person, and to which he himself may have made a different response on another occasion.

In 1976 Cobb reviewed a considerable body of evidence for the buffering role of feelings of being loved and esteemed, and of belonging to a network of communication and mutual obligation, when stressful life events occur. Cassel (1976) reached similar conclusions, and suggested that concentration of preventive efforts on strengthening social supports for isolated and stressed individuals would do more to prevent a wide range of diseases than do current expensive screening programmes. Brown, Bhrolchain, and Harris (1975), and Miller and Ingham (1976), have shown how having friends, both intimate and casual, acts to break the stress–illness spiral. Lynch (1977) has reviewed evidence for an association between loneliness or social disorganization and premature death, and Brown and Harris (1978) found that women without a close confiding relationship were more vulnerable to develop depression when provoking events occurred.

That visitors should be encouraged rather than tolerated in hospitals is a minor deduction from this evidence. Cobb's conclusion (p. 312) is that doctors should start now to teach all their patients, both well and sick, how to give and receive social support. This may seem to imply considerable changes in the doctor's role. Techniques for teaching social skills are available (Trower, Bryaant and Argyle, 1978): psychologists and social workers might find themselves actively involved in treatment and prevention. Pilisuk and Froland (1978) analyse what social support is, and how it might be delivered in the context of health care.

The second factor which has been claimed to mediate the health response of a stressed individual is his psychological state, particularly with regard to feelings of helplessness. Helplessness and hopelessness and consequent 'giving-up' have been found by Schmale (1972, p. 23) to precede

> diseases of all categories, from infectious and metabolic to those of
> degenerative and neoplastic origin in the medical group and from acute

organic brain syndromes and schizophrenic reactions to psychoneurotic disorders and the clinical syndromes of depression in the psychiatric
group.

Seligman (1975) described learned helplessness as the result of an organism's
experience of lack of control over undesirable events, and linked it to depression,
illness, and sudden death. Normal people made to feel helpless by repeated
experiences of failure to control events, like depressives, perform tasks more
poorly, lower their expectancies of success, and suffer a dysphoric mood.
Although the usefulness of learned helplessness as an analogue of depression
has been questionned, the theory has given fresh impetus to the application of
experimental psychology to clinical disorders, and also suggested new approaches to treatment. In revised form (Abramson, Seligman, and Teasdale, 1978;
Wortman and Dintzer, 1978), the theory focuses more on how people interpret
their failures and frustrations, for example as due to temporary or permanent
inadequacies.

   Feelings of helplessness have also been investigated through the concept
of internal versus external locus of control (Rotter, 1966). Strickland (1978)
concluded, from a review of research into locus of control and health-related
behaviours, that internals are generally more likely to engage in preventive
health practices, and to follow remedial instructions than are externally oriented
individuals. However (p. 1205):

> change agents such as health personnel will be most effective when
> techniques are tailored to individual expectancies. External indivi-
> duals evidently respond more easily to conditions in which structure is

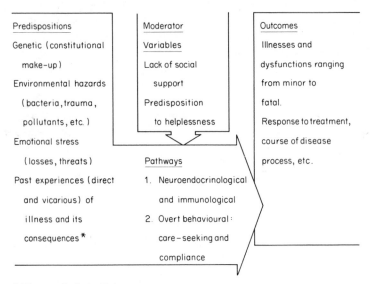

* Discussed in the text below.

FIGURE 2.1. Determinants of individual health and illness

imposed from outside. Internals prefer situations in which they can assume responsibility and work independently.

Although much more has been and could yet be written about prediction and prevention of illness in individuals, the above gives some indication of the main lines of current research. Figure 2.1 attempts to summarize some of the factors discussed. It is apparent that the medical practitioner who wishes to understand and apply the concepts involved will do so more readily with a background of knowledge in the following areas of behavioural science: behavioural modification, pursuasion and attitude change, communication skills, group dynamics, the assessment of personality and of its various measuring instruments, research design, and statistical analysis.

Use of health-care facilities

The third kind of behaviour of special interest to doctors concerns the process whereby an individual decides that given experiences of discomfort warrant medical attention. In presenting themselves and their 'symptoms' to a doctor, people seek to adopt the sick role, a well-defined set of obligations and privileges (Parsons, 1951; Mechanic, 1968). The person who has been designated by an authority on the subject (i.e. the doctor) as sick, has the right of exemption from normal duties, is not regarded as responsible for his plight, and is required to seek to regain good health, by obtaining competent treatment. If the impairment of function is seen as a result of conscious behaviour, such as in venereal disease or drug addictions, or where the motivation of the patient to recover and take up his normal duties again is suspect, as in hypochondriasis, sick role status may be withheld. Exemption from the demands of life may be highly valued by people who prefer to be seen as sick rather than as incompetent in one way or another (Shuval, Antonovsky, and Davies, 1973).

On the other side of the coin are those who would readily be accepted by doctors as sick, but who avoid medical attention. Financial difficulties, a dislike of the dependence implied by sickness, or an anxious wish not to have to admit to oneself the possibility of physical disease or illness may be some of the determinants of this inappropriate avoidance of the sick role. Mechanic (1966) referred to all these non-biological determinants of the use of medical services as 'illness behaviour'. Pilowsky (1969, 1978) has discussed abnormal illness behaviour as that where there is a conflict between the doctor's diagnosis and the patient's illness behaviour. This therefore covers both those who seek admission to the sick role when the doctor can find no pathology, and those who deny illness when it is objectively present. Behaviour may be abnormal with respect to either somatic or psychological illness. The Illness Behaviour Questionnaire (Pilowsky and Spence, 1975) has been developed to help describe the constituents of abnormal illness behaviour. The major dimensions, derived by factor analysis, are phobic concern about one's health, conviction of disease, perception of somatic *vs* psychological illness, affective inhibition, affective disturbance, denial of other problems, and irritability.

Cultural background affects illness behaviour in both the meaning attributed to pain (Zborowski, 1952) and in the kinds of symptoms likely to be regarded as serious, and the extent of complaining (Zola, 1966). Sex-role stereotypes within a culture have also been implicated as determinants of illness behaviour: masculine 'toughness' about health may be one reason, along with masculine competitiveness, aggression, smoking and drinking patterns, for the higher male mortality rate in all developed countries (Nathanson, 1977; Waldron, 1976).

Illness behaviour training within the family can be expected to reflect not only cultural and subcultural health values and attitudes, but also those unique to the particular family. Both through identification with parents and through direct training by them, children presumably learn how much significance is to be attached to different bodily sensations, and what response is appropriate. Although genetic and constitutional characteristics may determine in which physiological system stress is expressed (Grossman and Greenberg, 1957), socialization within the family may determine the illness behaviour response, as we know it determines other patterns of response such as the expression of aggression and dependency, sex-typing, and need for achievement (Mussen, Conger, and Kagan, 1974). Unfortunately very little solid information is available about illness behaviour training (Mechanic, 1964), although several authors have provided speculations and suggestions concerning past parent – child relations where illness has already been established (e.g. Ader, 1974, Jonas and Jonas 1975; Livsey, 1972; Meissner, 1974). The sort of detailed facts currently required concern the relation between illness behaviour patterns in children of different ages and in their relatives, peers, teachers, doctors, and other models of 'normal' illness behaviour for the society. It may be noted in passing that doctors train parents in what sort of illness behaviour is medically appropriate, for example what is an appropriate and what is an 'over-protective' response to a child's fever or vomiting, but this training proceeds by trial and error on the parent's part rather than by guidance in advance.

Illness behaviour is a central issue in the whole question of when and how people make use of the health care facilities provided. Much has been written on the latter from a more sociological perspective (e.g. Anderson and Anderson, 1972; Rainwater, 1975). It seems evident that comprehension of this important aspect of patient behaviour depends on a very broad social science training ranging from developmental psychology to sociology. Hopefully the behavioural science-trained general practitioners, paediatricians and child psychiatrists of tomorrow will fill in some of the serious gaps in the fabric of present understanding.

Professional function and personal adjustment of doctors

Medicine as a profession is, or can be, a very demanding one, with mushrooming amounts of new information to be digested and applied, increasing support by public money and consequent public accountability, and with serious potential consequences for any mistake. 'Although the relief of suffering is a noble vocation, it has always been a desperately competitive profession, with the ways of advancement carefully guarded and narrowly routed' (Poynter, 1973, p. 5). With all these sources of stress, health problems in the members of the medical profession are predictable. In fact doctors' rates of alcoholism, drug abuse, and suicide are high (Bowden, 1974). Taught as students to regard themselves as an intellectual élite, in most Western societies accorded high prestige and a certain mystique, and trained for constant battle against disease, doctors understandably feel threatened by unco-operative or dying patients and by signs of illness in themselves.

In terms of Figure 2.1 it is possible to make suggestions for the better health of doctors, but as usual the active participation of the 'patient' (in this case doctor) in the recommended preventive régime is vital. Thus doctors need to understand their own needs and habits as clearly as those of their designated patients. Firstly, some of the stress of medical practice can be relieved by equipping doctors with competence in coping with the behavioural aspects of their patient's health. Special instruction is needed about sex (Lief, 1973) and death (Bloch, 1976) to remove embarrassment and anxiety related to these sensitive topics. Interviewing and counselling skills need to be acquired, together with acceptance of personal limits and fallibility. Helplessness can be avoided by setting realistic goals, practising 'detached concern' (Lief and Fox, 1963), and getting feedback about the successes as well as the failures of treatment. Social support will probably come from the doctor's own family, close friends, and professional colleagues, and these personal resources deserve cultivation rather than neglect by the doctor. Relationships with colleagues may be smoother if communication lines are open and role conflicts solved, so that team morale is high. Such recommendations, if followed (see also Bowden, 1974) could hopefully reduce the risk of illness, as well as making appropriate acceptance of the sick role easier for doctors.

Health-relevant behaviours of non-patients

Just as the patient-behaviours of greatest medical concern described in the first three parts of this section are as applicable to the doctor as to the patient, we may also consider them in relation to non-patients whom the doctor may be in a position to influence. In a sense it is wasteful for the expensively produced doctor to insist upon, or to expect, a solely face-to-face practice. The possibilities of the public media, and the increased acceptance of social responsibilities by educational and to a lesser extent by entertainment organizations, mean that the doctor's expertise may benefit many more people than those who directly request treatment. Robertson (1975) after analysing the costs and chances of implementation of a variety of preventive measures such as advice to stop smoking, to wear safety belts, or to get children immunized, concluded that the behaviour of a few key decision-makers is a more effective

target than that of every individual in a large population. Lung cancer prevention in uranium miners was similarly found to result from coercion of one
organization by another (Fox and Goldsmith, 1976). 'Health education'
courses in schools, which now commonly include discussions of sexuality,
death, and personal adjustment as well as admonitions about washing hands
before eating, is an obvious area where community- rather than individual-
oriented medicine can be practised. Local government, and local pressure

TABLE 2.3. Contributions of behavioural sciences to medical practice

---

Level I: Behaviours relevant to medical practice
  NB: Each of the following is shown by (a) patients, (b) non-patients (including opinion
  leaders and decision-makers within the community), and (c) doctors.
1. Response to treatment: (i) compliance with instructions regarding pharmacological
   agents, diet, exercise and habits of life as below; (ii) speedy recovery from surgery and
   hospitalization without untoward physical or psychological side-effects; and (iii) coping
   with sensory defects, physical disabilities and chronic diseases, with minimal impairment
   of human potential.
2. Everyday habits of diet, lifestyle, response to stress, usage of alcohol, nicotine,
   analgesics, and other drugs, all of which are causally related to incidence and prevalence
   of fatal and crippling accidents (in cars, falls, drownings, etc.), violence (suicide,
   homicide, rape, child-battering), and illness (heart disease, cancer, liver and kidney
   disease, and many others, perhaps almost all).
3. Symptoms of sleeplessness, over-eating, depression, chronic pain including headaches,
   sexual difficulties, anxiety states, childhood behaviour disorders, etc.
4. Usage and delivery of health-care services: (i) on the patient's part appropriateness of
   demands for medical attention; (ii) on the doctor's part the arrangements for delivery
   of health care efficiently and justly; (iii) on society's part suitable allocation of resources
   to health care; responsiveness to medical advice.

Level II: Resultant questions which arise about behaviour
1. Why do people behave as they do, and how can their behaviour be influenced so as to
   reduce illness and disability and promote health?
2. How do people solve problems, arrive at decisions, learn, and communicate, alone and
   in groups, usually and under stress, and at different stages in the lifecycle?
3. What is the extent and source of individual variability?
4. How do beliefs, values, and attitudes about health, illness, medicine, doctors, hospitals,
   drugs, etc. arise, and how may they be modified?

Level III: Related areas of behavioural sciences
1. Individual psychological processes: perception, learning, thinking, emotion, personality, and their disorders. Also methods of assessment of each and how to evaluate same.
2. Psychosocial development through the lifespan, as influenced by biological (genetic,
   constitutional, and species-specific) factors and by learning (within the family, the
   social class, the ethnic group, the culture, etc.).
3. Behaviour change and interpersonal influence: behaviour therapy and modification,
   social skills training, counselling, communication (verbal and non-verbal), conformity,
   attitude change.
4. Social psychology: person-perception, role theory, group dynamics and leadership,
   co-operation and competition, helping behaviour, etc. Social systems and sociology.
5. Research design and methodology, and statistical analysis.

---

groups concerned with improving the quality of life, provide other possibilities. Without going into great detail, and without presuming to define the doctor's role exactly, it seems clear that the doctor may be conceived as a logical pivot and catalyst for a broadly based community initiative for health. For this he or she will require not only wide professional competence, but also persuasive and political skills, possibly enhanced by scientific study of decision-making and social influence processes.

The foregoing survey of types of human behaviour of particular interest to doctors has aimed to demonstrate the potential contribution to medical education of the behavioural sciences. These relationships are summarized in Table 2.3. Research on the more molecular aspects of human behaviour such as the psychophysiology of motivation, sleep, drug actions, memory, etc. constitutes a necessary underpinning to advances in understanding of the body, but has been omitted from the present discussion. Collaboration between behavioural and other scientists seems likely to be fruitful in these areas. From the point of view of the practice rather than the science of medicine— and it is in practice that the majority of medical graduates are going to spend their time—the contributions of a psychosocial behavioural viewpoint are immediately applicable and valuable. We can now proceed to review how behavioural science content is being incorporated into medical curricula, and what future directions seem desirable.

CURRENT AND FUTURE BEHAVIOURAL SCIENCE COURSES

Having, as I hope, established in the preceding section the value for medical practitioners of an understanding of human behaviour, I shall now discuss how this might best be achieved.

The addition of behavioural science courses to medical curricula already acknowledged as overloaded, has proceeded quite rapidly during the last 15 years or so. Such courses are now the rule in medical schools throughout the world, as described for example by Badgley and Bloom (1973), Coe (1975), Cohen and Kelner (1976), Dacey and Wintrob (1973), Davis (1970), Gadd (1973), Fletcher (1974), Sheldrake (1974), and Winefield (1977). The reasons for this change, and the corresponding hopes for what behavioural science courses would achieve, seem to have been several. Disillusionment with the potential benefits to health of more and more technology, and a parallel renewal of interest in preventive medicine, can be discerned as one. Another would be the realization derived from a study of medical history (Risse, 1975), and of anthropology (Swift, 1969; Maretzki, 1976), of the therapeutic power of the 'doctor–patient relationship', and a wish to give students maximal skill in the use of this tool. A third impetus may derive in fact from the medical profession's response to the non-biological analyses of illness and medicine provided by Illich (1975), Fabrega (1976), and Fabrega and Van Egeren (1976), the ideas of the first-named having had considerable popular impact. To the extent then that the physician is working directly with patients, and has a holistic, long-term prevention and containment orientation towards their health care, he is likely to value behavioural science education (Van Egeren and Fabrega, 1976).

It is probably worth noting here, in order to avoid any possible confusion, that such an understanding of the dynamics and principles of human behaviour in both 'normality' and 'abnormality' and in health and disease, is quite distinct from the traditional instruction in clinical psychiatry. Although behavioural science may form a useful foundation for the latter, at both undergraduate and postgraduate levels, that is too narrow a justification for its inclusion in the curriculum (Bloch, 1973). Van Egeren and Fabrega (1976) also exclude as components of behavioural science specific training in interview techniques, and the detailed consideration of how to arrange delivery of health care. These are important parts of a student's education, but more appropriately located in a later clinical behavioural science course, as discussed below. Preclinical students need to master the principles which will allow them to evaluate new evidence, carry out their own researches in a competent scientific way, and continue their own education life-long; a course which consisted solely of technical training would not achieve this (Volpe, 1975).

Many authors have described the basic assumptions upon which a successful behavioural science course should be founded, and the ways in which it should be taught (e.g. Herman, 1975; McKinlay, 1971; Olmsted and Kennedy, 1972; Pattishall, 1972, 1973; Richards, 1975; Tait, 1973, 1974). The initial honeymoon period of unrealistic expectations and unrealizable promises for the results of introducing behavioural science courses is over. There are even some signs of disillusionment with social science input, for example in the call of some American medical schools for the inclusion of humanities subjects to make the students sensitive and person-oriented (Banks, 1974), and in the reduction of behavioural science contact hours at some places (Wintrob, 1977, personal communication). On the other hand the recent development of centres and units of Behavioural Medicine in America suggests a most desirable integration of behavioural and biomedical knowledge and techniques, being applied to a wide range of health-care problems (Schwartz and Weiss, 1978).

Based on the accumulated experiences of preclinical behavioural science teachers, realistic and valid appreciations of what can be achieved, and how, are emerging. Several issues can be expediently separated out and will be discussed below. These are course content, student response, and projections towards the future.

Course content

Although diversity of subject-matter within behavioural science courses is still widespread, a consensus is becoming apparent that even at the preclinical level more than lip service should be given to the goal of clinical relevance. Recent writers (Cohen and Kelner, 1976; Griffiths, 1976; Wexler, 1976) are agreed that in order to maximize the usefulness and therefore memorability of behavioural science for students, the teachers concerned need to know in detail what medical practice involves. This knowledge is not part of the standard training in psychology or sociology. Therefore specialist behavioural science teachers need to be created (or to create themselves), probably by undertaking a special study of the doctor's job. Certainly physical and emotional incorporation within a medical setting seems desirable; service courses run from within pure academic departments have on the whole met with indifference and even hostility from students, and in terms of retention and application of the facts presented, seem likely to be a waste of everybody's time. The poor response to 'irrelevant'-perceived courses is unsurprising in view of the acknowledged cognitive overload imposed on medical students, and of the socialization process they are undergoing concurrently, of which I shall say more below.

Novice behavioural science teachers may feel some disquiet about the replacement of their formative environment by a medical school, and about their obligation to stress 'clinical applications', particularly as, to date, there are few adequate role models for them. Psychological and sociological research on health-relevant topics, which can frequently be carried out only by those affiliated with medical institutions, has a great deal to offer the parent disciplines as well as to medicine. Table 2.3 indicates the relationship between specifically medical concerns and traditional social science issues. Medical acceptance of social scientists as academic and professional colleagues makes possible explorations of how social science may be applied to solve human problems, in a way which is of great value to interested social scientists.

As far as successful teaching is concerned, an important factor is likely to be the explicit links drawn between levels 1, 2, and 3 of Table 2.2 by the teacher. To give a couple of simple examples: in order to understand pain, medical students need a grounding in the principles of perception, and how perception is related to attention, needs, and habits; for illness behaviour they need to know what kinds of learning experiences affect human habits; yet if perception and learning are taught as from an introductory psychology text, only a tiny fraction of the most able students will independently see the connections to medical practice, and perhaps not even those at the stage in their training where clinical experience is absent.

Older (1977) has written entertainingly about teaching techniques, giving a prescription for a 'benign' behavioural science course. Needless to say, similar questions about the methodology of instruction are germane to every subject in the medical curriculum, not least the other 'basic sciences' whose contributions are at present also undergoing some scrutiny (e.g. Tomlinson et al., 1977).

Training in interviewing, communication skills, and the like can be provided after, or in parallel with, the preclinical behavioural science course. Selected references include Engel (1972), Magarey, Whaite, and Pigott (1976), Pollack and Manning (1967), Shaw and Gath (1975), Soule and Gulledge (1977), Topham and Smith (1973), and Ward and Stein (1975). Many reported programmes emphasize immediate feedback on progress (via videotape recorders, etc.), direction of attention to both verbal and non-verbal information, and skill rehearsal in a non-threatening educational setting.

A major problem of all innovatory educational efforts in the medical curriculum, and one perhaps especially keenly felt by teachers trained in the scientific study of behaviour is the difficulty in specifying objectively the goals of behavioural science courses, and of devising means to evaluate progress towards them. The teacher wants to inculcate not only knowledge, as reflected by examination performances, but attitudes and conceptual tools which will influence problem-solving capabilities for the duration of the professional career. The difficulties of expressing this aim in measurable terms are enormous, given the absence of any adequate measuring device for quality of medical practice, even in one defined field such as family medicine.

At present some correlation of behavioural science performance with other measures of undergraduate and postgraduate examination performance seems an easy, although rather unsatisfactory, way to evaluate the impact of the behavioural science course; for example Brownstein et al. (1976) found that a class which had had a 50-week rather than a 15-week behavioural science course did about 10 per cent better in their later clinical rotations. The unsatisfactoriness of such efforts lies partly in the almost inevitable presence of simultaneous changes in the rest of the curriculum, for example (i) the introduction of community or social and preventive, or family medicine courses; (ii) changes in emphasis upon subjects; or (iii) changes in the teachers themselves. A further problem is the suspect validity of written examinations as measures or predictors of medical skill (Becker et al., 1972). In practice the content of the behavioural science course is likely to depend upon the immediate feedback to teachers in the form of student response. This would be more acceptable if preclinical students were informed judges of what is relevant to medical practice.

Student response

As has been intimated, student demands for 'relevance' legitimately influence what forms part of a behavioural science course, although there are some frustrations in assessing the long-term outcomes. A major influence upon the students themselves at this stage of their lives (and hence upon what they see as educationally relevant) derives from the role models available to them in the form of physician-relatives, older students, and, as they enter the clinical years of their education, the clinical consultants and teachers. Many aspects of medical training are stressful, such as learning to perform dissections, to probe people manually and verbally, and to maintain an appropriate but not excessive degree of idealism and emotional involvement. The anxieties aroused by these threatening experiences and tasks are allayed by identifying with the prestigious practising doctors who act as teachers. Here lies a possibly subversive influence upon the student response to behavioural science courses. The medicine of the teaching hospital, dealing as it does with a procession of patients who tend to be transitory and relatively disadvantaged due to old age, poverty, and/or major trauma, is a very different proposition from the medicine most graduates will practise, where patients are younger, permanent residents of the area, more comparable to the doctor in terms of income and education, and suffering from relatively minor and chronic health problems. At least until a cadre of clinical teachers who themselves know the benefits of behavioural science understanding is available, which should occur in most parts of the world within the next few years, 'Clinical Behavioural Science' needs to be deliberately provided for students. The concepts and techniques learned beforehand should be reinforced and extended in the context of clinical problems, probably by a multidisciplinary teaching team. Opposition to this expansion of behavioural science on account of its demands on student time and staff energy can safely be predicted. Harper (1971) suggested that behavioural scientists should be teaching their clinical-physician colleagues rather than undergraduates, while Hunt (1974) and Burgess and Willis (1970) have analysed some of the conflicts in roles and in orientation which make that unlikely.

In general the directions of change at the moment appear to include both the downward extension of clinical material and clinical co-teaching into the behavioural science course (Weiner, 1972), and the upward extension (Cohen and Kelner, 1976; Griffiths, 1976) of behavioural science into the clinical years. Entire relocation of behavioural science into the clinical years was suggested by O'Farrell (1974), but the restrictions on time, and the students' lack of receptivity to new theoretical material at that stage, appear to reduce the desirability of this alternative. Active student participation through assessable practical project involvement has many advantages (Fransella, 1978; Weinman, 1978).

The future

If, as Wexler (1976) and others have advocated, preclinical behavioural science teaching comes to focus clearly upon the practice of primary care medicine (as for example Winefield and Peay, 1980), with reinforcement during clinical years, provision is still needed for students with a particularly keen interest to be able to take advanced elective courses. This arrangement would of course also be beneficial for the morale and enthusiasm of the teachers. Behavioural science components of the intercalated science or medical science honours degree frequently offered in Britain, or the M.D.–Ph.D. offered at the Johns Hopkins and other American universities (Rubin et al., 1975) are steps in the right direction.

Bergen (1974) has analysed the sources of the resistance felt by many doctors towards taking psychosocial aspects of illness and recovery seriously. Such considerations run counter to the doctor's traditional belief that illness can be known and understood by attention to the visible world of the patient's body. Re-evaluation of this belief is now called for, in the light of accumulating evidence partly summarized in the first section of this chapter. As Jefferys (1974) pointed out, medicine at present stands somewhat at a crossroads, the alternative future pathways being the roles either of super-technologist or of applied behavioural scientist. It is hard to imagine all of the intelligent, ambitious, and often idealistic youth who enter medical schools being content with ending up as the highly trained body-plumbers implied by the first alternative. The behavioural sciences furnish medicine with the opportunity to embrace the widest possible conception of health care.

REFERENCES

Abramson, L. Y., Seligman, M. E. P., and Teasdale, J. D. (1978). Learned helplessness in humans: critique and reformulation. *Journal of Abnormal Psychology*, **87**, 49–74.

Ader, R. (1974). The role of developmental factors in susceptibility to disease. *International Journal of Psychiatry in Medicine*, **5**, 367–376.

American Psychological Association Task Force on Health Research (1976). Contributions of psychology to health research. *American Psychologist*, **31**, 263–274.

Amkraut, A., and Solomon, G. F. (1974). From the symbolic stimulus to the pathophysiologic response: immune mechanisms. *International Journal of Psychiatry in Medicine*, **5**, 541–563.

Anderson, O. W., and Anderson, R. M. (1972). Patterns of use of health services. In Freeman, H. E., Levine, S., and Reeder, L. G. (Eds.), *Handbook of Medical Sociology* (2nd edn), pp. 386–406. New Jersey: Prentice-Hall.

Annon, J. S. (1974). *The Behavioral Treatment of Sexual Problems*. Hawaii: Enabling Systems Inc.

Badgley, R. F., and Bloom, S. W. (1973). Behavioral sciences and medical education: the case of sociology. *Social Science and Medicine*, **7**, 927–941.

Bahnson, C. B. (1969). Psychophysiological complementarity in malignancies: past work and future vistas. *Annals of the New York Academy of Sciences*, **164**, 319–334.

Bandura, A. (1969). *Principles of Behavior Modification*. New York: Holt, Rinehart & Winston.

Banks, S. A. (1974). The newcomers: humanities and social sciences in medical education. *Texas Reports on Biology and Medicine*, **32**, 19–30.

Becker, H. S., Geer, B., and Miller, S. A. (1972). Medical education. In Freeman, H. E., Levine, S., and Reeder, L. G. (Eds.), *Handbook of Medical Sociology* (2nd edn), pp. 191–205. New Jersey: Prentice-Hall.

Bergen, B. J. (1974). Psychosomatic knowledge and the role of the physician: a sociological view. *International Journal of Psychiatry in Medicine*, **5**, 431–442.

Berkanovic, E. (1976). Behavioral science and prevention. *Preventive Medicine*, **5**, 92–105.

Bernstein, L., Bernstein R. S., and Dana, R. H. (1974). *Interviewing: A Guide for Health Professionals* (2nd edn). New York: Appleton-Century-Crofts.

Bloch, S. (1973). Goals in the teaching of behavioural sciences to medical students. *British Journal of Medical Education*, **7**, 239–243.

Bloch, S. (1976). Instruction on death and dying for the medical student. *Medical Education*, **10**, 269–273.

Bowden, C. L. (1974). The physician's adaptation to his role. In Bowden, C. L., and Burstein, A. G. *Psychosocial Basis of Medical Practice: An Introduction to Human Behavior*, pp. 217–223. Baltimore: Williams & Wilkins Co.

Bowden, C. L., and Burstein, A. G. (1974). *Psychosocial Basis of Medical Practice: An Introduction to Human Behavior*. Baltimore: Williams & Wilkins Co.

Bowlby, J. (1975). *Separation: Anxiety and Anger*. Harmondsworth: Penguin Books.

Boyle, C. M. (1970). Difference between patients' and doctors' interpretations of some common medical terms. *British Medical Journal*, **2**, 286–289.

Brown, G. W., Bhrolchain, M., and Harris, T. (1975). Social class and psychiatric disturbance among women in an urban population. *Sociology*, **9**, 225–254.

Brown, G. W., and Harris, T., (1978). *Social Origins of Depression: A Study of Psychiatric disorder in Women*. London: Tavistock.

Brownstein, E. J., Singer, O., Dornbush, R., Lilienfield, D. M., Shaker, R., and Freedman, A. M. (1976). Teaching behavioral science in the preclinical curriculum. *Journal of Medical Education*, **51**, 59–62.

Burgess, M. M., and Willis, F. N. (1970). In a medical school psychology is black. *International Journal of Social Psychiatry*, **16**, 201–204.

Cassel, J. (1976). The contribution of the social environment to host resistance. *American Journal of Epidemiology*, **104**, 107–123.

Cobb, S. (1976). Social support as a moderator of life stress. *Psychosomatic Medicine*, **38**, 300–314.

Coe, R. M. (1975). Teaching behavioral sciences in schools of medicine: some observations on some Latin-American schools. *Social Science and Medicine*, **9**, 221–225.

Cogan, R., Henneborn, W., and Klopfer, F. (1976). Predictors of pain during prepared childbirth. *Journal of Psychosomatic Research*, **20**, 523–533.

Cohen, R., and Kelner, M. (1976). Teaching behavioural science in Canadian medical schools. *Social Science and Medicine*, **10**, 23–27.

Cullen, J. W., Fox, B. H., and Isom, R. N. (eds.) (1976). *Cancer: The Behavioral Dimensions*. New York: Raven Press.

Dacey, M. L., and Wintrob, R. M. (1973). Human behavior: the teaching of social and behavioral sciences in medical schools. *Social Science and Medicine*, **7**, 943–957.

Davidson, P. O. (1976). *The Behavioral Management of Anxiety, Depression and Pain*. New York: Brunner-Mazel.

Davis, D. R. (1970). Behavioural science in the preclinical curriculum. *British Journal of Medical Education*, **4**, 194–197.

Dohrenwend, B. S., and Dohrenwend, B. P. (1978). Some issues in research on stressful life events. *Journal of Nervous and Mental Disease*, **166**, 7–15.

Duggin, G. (1977). The Australian disease: Analgesia abuse. *New Doctor*, No. 4, 22–25.

Edinburg, G. M., Zinberg, N. E., and Kelman, W. (1975). *Clinical Interviewing and Counselling: Principles and Techniques*. New York: Appleton-Century-Crofts.

Egbert, L. D., Battit, G. E., Welch, C. E., and Bartlett, M. K. (1964). Reduction of postoperative pain by encouragement and instruction of patients. *New England Journal of Medicine*, **270**, 825–827.

Enelow, A. J., and Swisher, S. N. (1972). *Interviewing and Patient Care*. New York: Oxford University Press.

Engel, G. L. (1972). The education of the physician for clinical observation. *Journal of Nervous and Mental Disease*, **154**, 159–164.

Fabrega, H. (1976). Toward a theory of human disease. *Journal of Nervous and Mental Disease*, **162**, 299–312.

Fabrega, H., and Van Egeren, L. (1976). A behavioral framework for the study of human disease. *Annals of Internal Medicine*, **84**, 200–208.

Fletcher, C. R. (1974). Study of behavioral science teaching in schools of medicine. *Journal of Medical Education*, **49**, 188–189.

Fordyce, W. E. (1976). *Behavioral Methods for Chronic Pain and Illness*. Saint Louis: Mosby.

Fox, B. H. (1978). Premorbid psychological factors related to cancer incidence. *Journal of Behavioral Medicine*, **1**, 45–133.

Fox, B. H., and Goldsmith, J. R. (1976). Behavioral issues in prevention of cancer. *Preventive Medicine*, **5**, 106–121.

Frank, J. D. (1973). *Persuasion and Healing* (rev. edn). Baltimore and London: Johns Hopkins University Press.

Fransella, F. (1978). Content or practice? *Bulletin of the British Psychological Society*, **32**, 345–348.

Freeman, H. E., Levine, S., and Reeder, L. G. (Eds.) (1972). *Handbook of Medical Sociology* (2nd edn). New Jersey: Prentice-Hall.

Freyhan, F. A. (1976). Is psychosomatic obsolete? A psychiatric reappraisal. *Comprehensive Psychiatry*, **17**, 381–386.

Gadd, A. (1973). Educational aspects of integrating social sciences in the medical curriculum. *Social Science and Medicine*, **7**, 975–984.

Gil, D. R. (1970). *Violence against Children*. Cambridge, Massachusetts: Harvard University Press.

Greene, W. A. (1975). Hematology and the derivation of psychosomatic concepts. *Archives of Internal Medicine*, **135**, 1338–1343.

Greene, W. A., and Miller, G. (1958). Psychological factors and reticuloendothelial disease, IV. Observations on a group of children and adolescents with leukemia: an interpretation of disease development in terms of the mother–child unit. *Psychosomatic Medicine*, **20**, 124–144.

Greer, S. (1979). Psychological enquiry: a contribution to cancer research. *Psychological Medicine*, **9**, 81–89.

Greer, S., and Morris, T. (1975). Psychological attributes of women who develop breast cancer: a controlled study. *Journal of Psychosomatic Research*, **19**, 147–153.

Greer, S., and Morris, T. (1978). The study of psychological factors in breast cancer: problems of method. *Social Science and Medicine*, **12**, 129–134.

Griffiths, R. D. P. (1976). The teaching of psychology in medical schools: a pat on the back or a kick in the pants? *Bulletin of the British Psychological Society*, **29**, 269–273.

Grossman, H. J., and Greenberg, N. H. (1957). Psychosomatic differentiation in infancy. I. Autonomic activity in the newborn. *Psychosomatic Medicine*, **19**, 293–306.

Harper, A. C. (1971). The social scientist in medical education: the specialist's safeguard. *Social Science and Medicine*, **5**, 663–665.

Herman, M. W. (1975). Developing objectives for a core program on social aspects of medicine. *Journal of Medical Education*, **50**, 389–391.

Hinkle, L. E. (1974). The effect of exposure to culture change, social change and changes in interpersonal relationships on health. In Dohrenwend B. S., and Dohrenwend, B. P. (eds.), *Stressful Life Events: Their Nature and Effects*, pp. 9–44. New York: Wiley.

Hunt, S. (1974). The relationship between psychology and medicine. *Social Science and Medicine*, **8**, 105–109.

Illich, I. (1975). *Medical Nemesis: The Expropriation of Health*. London: Lothian.

Janis, O. L. (1958). *Psychological Stress: Psychoanalytic and Behavioral Studies of Surgical Patients*. New York: Wiley.

Jefferys, M. (1974). Social science and medical education in Britain: a sociologic analysis of their relationship. *International Journal of Health Services*, **4**, 549–563.

Jenkins, C. D. (1976). Recent evidence supporting psychologic and social risk factors for coronary disease. *New England Journal of Medicine*, **294**, 987–994, 1033–1038.

Jonas, A. D., and Jonas, D. F. (1975). The influences of early training on the varieties of stress response–an ethological approach. *Journal of Psychosomatic Research*, **19**, 325–335.

Kegeles, S. S., Lund, A. K., and Weisenberg, M. (1978). Acceptance by children of a daily home mouthrinse program. *Social Science and Medicine*, **12**, 199–210.

Kingsley, R. G., and Wilson, G. T. (1977). Behavior therapy for obesity: a comparative investigation of long-term efficacy. *Journal of Consulting and Clinical Psychology*, **45**, 288–298.

Kissen, D. M., Brown, R. I. F., and Kissen, M. (1969). A further report on personality and psychosocial factors in lung cancer. *Annals of the New York Academy of Sciences*, **164**, 535.

Korsch, B. M., and Negrete, V. F. (1972). Doctor–patient communication. *Scientific American*, August, 66–74.

Lazarus, A. A. (Ed.) (1972). *Clinical Behavior Therapy*. New York: Brunner-Mazel.

LeShan, L. (1966). An emotional life history pattern associated with neoplastic disease. *Annals of the New York Academy of Sciences*, **125**, 780–793.

Ley, P. (1979). Memory for medical information. *British Journal of Social and Clinical Psychology*, **18**, 245–255.

Ley, P., and Spelman, M. S. (1967). *Communicating with the Patient*. London: Staples Press.

Lick, J. R. and Heffler, D. (1977). Relaxation training and attention placebo in the treatment of severe insomnia. *Journal of Consulting and Clinical Psychology*, **45**, 153–161.

Lief, H. I. (1973). Obstacles to the ideal and complete sex education of the medical student and physician. In Zubin, J., and Money, J. (eds.), *Contemporary Sexual Behavior: Critical Issues in the 1970s*, pp. 441–453. Baltimore and London: Johns Hopkins University Press.

Lief, H. I., and Fox, R. C. (1963). Training for 'detached concern' in medical students. In Lief, H. I. Lief, V. F., and Lief, N. R. (eds.), *The Psychological Basis of Medical Practice*, pp. 12–35. New York: Harper and Row.

Livsey, C. G. (1972). Physical illness and family dynamics. *Advances in Psychosomatic Medicine*, **8**, 237–251.

Lynch, J. J. (1977). *The Broken Heart*. New York: Basic Books.

Magarey, C. J., Whaite, A., and Pigott, B. (1976). An academic course in human communication for first year medical students. *Australian Family Physician*, **5**, 976–978.

Maretzki, T. W. (1976). What difference does anthropological knowledge make to mental health. *Australian and New Zealand Journal of Psychiatry*, **10**, 83–88.

McKinlay, J. B. (1971). The concept 'patient career' as a heuristic device for making medical sociology relevant to medical students. *Social Science and Medicine*, **5**, 441–460.

Mechanic, D. (1964). The influence of mothers on their children's health attitudes and behavior. *Pediatrics*, **33**, 444–453.

Mechanic, D. (1966). Response factors in illness: the study of illness behavior. *Social Psychiatry*, **1**, 11–20.

Mechanic, D. (1968). *Medical Sociology*. New York: Free Press.

Meissner, W. W. (1974). Family process and psychosomatic disease. *International Journal of Psychiatry in Medicine*, **5**, 411–430.

Miller, P. McC. and Ingham, J. A. (1976). Friends, confidants, and symptoms. *Social Psychiatry*, **11**, 51–58.

Millon, T. (ed.) (1975). *Medical Behavioral Science*. Philadelphia: W. B. Saunders.

Mussen, P. H., Conger, J. J., and Kagan, J. (1974). *Child Development and Personality* (4th edn.). New York: Harper & Row.

Nathanson, C. A. (1977). Sex, illness and medical care: a review of data, theory, and method. *Social Science and Medicine*, **11**, 13–25.

O'Farrell, V. (1974). Effect of context on teaching of psychology to medical students. *British Journal of Medical Education*, **8**, 251–254.

Older, J. (1977). Building a benign behavioral-science course. *New England Journal of Medicine*, **296**, 627–628.

Olmsted, R. W., and Kennedy, D. A. (eds.) (1972). *Behavioral Science and Medical Education: A Report of Four Conferences*. US Department of Health Education and Welfare Publication No. (NIH) 72–41.

Parsons, T. (1951). *The Social System*. Illinois: Free Press.

Pattishall, E. C. (1972). Integration of the behavioral sciences in the medical curriculum.

Alabama Journal of Medical Sciences, **9**, 158–163.

Pattishall, E. C. (1973). Basic assumptions for the teaching of behavioral science in medical schools. *Social Science and Medicine*, **7**, 923–926.

Pilisuk, M., and Froland, C. (1978). Kinship, social networks, social support and health. *Social Science and Medicine*, **12B**, 273–280.

Pilowsky, I. (1969). Abnormal illness behaviour. *British Journal of Medical Psychology*, **42**, 347–351.

Pilowsky, I. (1978). A general classification of abnormal illness behaviours. *British Journal of Medical Psychology*, **51**, 131–137.

Pilowsky, I., and Spence, N. D. (1975). Patterns of illness behaviour in patients with intractable pain. *Journal of Psychosomatic Research*, **19**, 279–287.

Pollack, S., and Manning, P. R. (1967). An experience in teaching the doctor–patient relationship to first-year medical students. *Journal of Medical Education*, **42**, 770–774.

Pomerleau, P., Base, F., and Crown, V. (1975). Role of behavior modification in preventive medicine. *New England Journal of Medicine*, **292**, 1277–1282.

Poynter, N. (1973). *Medicine and Man*. Harmondsworth: Penguin.

Rachman, S. J., and Philips, C. (1975). *Psychology and Medicine*. London: Temple Smith.

Rahe, R. H., Meyer, M., Smith, M., Kjaer, G., and Holmes, T. H. (1971). Social stress and illness onset. *Journal of Psychosomatic Research*, **15**, 19–24.

Rahe, R. H., Ward, H. W., and Hayes, V. (1979). Brief group therapy in myocardial infarction rehabilitation: three- to four-year follow-up of a controlled trial. *Psychosomatic Medicine*, **41**, 229–242.

Rainwater, L. (1975). The lower class: health, illness and medical institutions. In T. Millon, (ed.), *Medical Behavioral Science*, pp. 514–522. Philadelphia: W. B. Saunders.

Richards, N. D. (1975). Methods and effectiveness of health education: the past, present and future of social scientific involvement. *Social Science and Medicine*, **9**, 141–156.

Risse, G. B. (1975). The role of medical history in the education of the 'humanist' physician: A re-evaluation. *Journal of Medical Education*, **50**, 458–465.

Robertson, J. (1970). *Young Children in Hospital* (2nd edn.). London: Tavistock Publications.

Robertson, L. S. (1975). Behavioral research and strategies in public health: a demur. *Social Science and Medicine*, **9**, 165–170.

Rosenman, R. H., Friedman, M., Straus, R., Wurm, M., Kositchek, R., Hahn, W., and Werthessen, N. T. (1964). A predictive study of coronary heart disease. *Journal of the American Medical Association*, **189**, 15–22.

Rotter, J. B. (1966). Generalized expectancies for internal versus external control of reinforcement. *Psychological Monographs*, **80**, (1) Whole No. 609.

Rubin, R. R., Elkes, J., Maris, R. W., and Dietz, P. E. (1975). Medicine and the behavioral sciences: the Johns Hopkins M. D.–Ph.D. program. *The Johns Hopkins Medical Journal*, **136**, 268–270.

Schmale, A. H. (1972). Giving up as a final common pathway to changes in health. *Advances in Psychosomatic Medicine*, **8**, 20–40.

Schmale, A., and Iker, H. (1966). The psychological setting of uterine cervical cancer. *Annals of the New York Academy of Sciences*, **125**, 807–813.

Schwartz, G. E., and Weiss, S. M. (1978). Behavioral medicine revisited: an amended definition. *Journal of Behavioral Medicine*, **1**, 249–251.

Seligman, M. E. P. (1975). *Helplessness: On Depression, Development, and Death*. San Francisco: W. H. Freeman & Co.

Shaw, P. M., and Gath, D. H. (1975). Teaching the doctor–patient relation to medical students. *British Journal of Medical Education*, **9**, 176–181.

Sheldrake, P. (1974). Behavioural science: medical students' expectations and reactions. *British Journal of Medical Education*, **8**, 31–48.

Shuval, J. T., Antonovsky, A., and Davies, A. M. (1973). Illness: a mechanism for coping with failure. *Social Science and Medicine*, **7**, 259–265.

Soule, D. J., and Gulledge, A. D. (1977). Facilitating the learning of communications and interviewing skills. *Psychosomatics*, **18**, 37–43.

Stimson, G. V. (1974). Obeying doctor's orders: a view from the other side. *Social Science and Medicine*, **8**, 97–104.

Strickland, B. (1978). Internal–external expectancies and health-related behaviors. *Journal of Consulting and Clinical Psychology*, **46**, 1192–1211.

Surawicz, F. G., Brightwell, D. R. Weitzel, W. D., and Othmer, E. (1976). Cancer, emotions, and mental illness: the present state of understanding. *American Journal of Psychiatry*, **133**, 1306–1309.

Swift, M. G. (1969). The role of the behavioural sciences in medicine: anthropology and medicine. *Medical Journal of Australia*, **2**, 35–38.

Szasz, T. S., and Hollender, M. H. (1956). A contribution to the philosophy of medicine: the basic models of the doctor–patient relationship. *Archives of Internal Medicine*, **97**, 585–592.

Tait, I. (1973). Behavioural science in medical education and clinical practice. *Social Science and Medicine*, **7**, 1003–1011.

Tait, I. (1974). Person-centred perspectives in medicine. *Journal of the Royal College of General Practitioners*, **24**, 151–160.

Tennant, C., and Andrews, G. (1978). The pathogenic quality of life event stress in neurotic impairment. *Archives of General Psychiatry*, **35**, 859–863.

Thomas, C. B., and Duszynski, K. R. (1974). Closeness to parents and the family constellation in a prospective study of five disease states: suicide, mental illness, malignant tumour, hypertension and coronary heart disease. *The Johns Hopkins Medical Journal*, **134**, 251–270.

Tomlinson, R. W. S., Clack, G. B., Pettingale, K. W., Anderson, J., and Ryan, K. C. (1977). The relative role of 'A' level chemistry, physics and biology in the medical course. *Medical Education*, **11**, 103–108.

Topham, M., and Smith, J. S. (1973). The use of experiential learning in undergraduate medical training. *Medical Journal of Australia*, **1**, 1155–1158.

Townes, B. D., Wold, D. A., and Holmes, T. H. (1974). Parental adjustment to childhood leukemia. *Journal of Psychosomatic Research*, **18**, 9–14.

Trower, P., Bryant, B., and Argyle, M. (1978). *Social Skills and Mental Health*. London: Methuen.

Ulf, De F. (1975). Life change patterns prior to death in ischaemic heart disease: a study on death-discordant twins. *Journal of Psychosomatic Research*, **19**, 273–278.

Van Egeren, L., and Fabrega, H. (1976). Behavioral science and medical education: a biobehavioral perspective. *Social Science and Medicine*, **10**, 535–539.

Volpe, R. (1975). Behavioral science theory in medical education. *Social Science and Medicine*, **9**, 493–499.

Waldron, I. (1976). Why do women live longer than men? *Social Science and Medicine*, **10**, 349–362.

Waller, J. A., and Whorton, E. B. (1973). Unintentional shootings, highway crashes and acts of violence–a behavior paradigm. *Accident Analysis and Prevention*, **5**, 351–356.

Ward, N. G., and Stein, L. (1975). Reducing emotional distance: a new method to teach interviewing skills. *Journal of Medical Education*, **50**, 605–614.

Weiner, H. (1972). Experiences in the development of a preclinical curriculum in the sciences related to behavior. *Journal of Nervous and Mental Disease*, **154**, 165–172.

Weinman, J. (1978). Integrating psychology with general medicine. *Bulletin of the British Psychological Society*, **32**, 352–355.

Weisenberg, M. (1977). Pain and pain control. *Psychological Bulletin*, **84**, 1008–1044.

Wexler, M. (1976). The behavioral sciences in medical education: a view from psychology. *American Psychologist*, **31**, 275–283.

Winefield, H. R. (1977). The teaching of psychology to medical students in Australia and New Zealand. *Australian Psychologist*, **12**, 199–203.

Winefield, H. R., and Peay, M. Y. (1980). *Behavioural Science in Medicine*. London: George Allen & Unwin, and Beaconsfield: Beaconsfield Publishers.

World Health Organization (WHO) (1974). The ten leading causes of death for selected countries in North America, Europe and Oceania, 1969, 1970 and 1971. *World Health Statistics Report*, **27**, 563–652.

Wortman, C. B., and Dintzer, L. (1978). Is an attributional analysis of the learned helplessness phenomenon viable? A critique of the Abramson–Seligman–Teasdale reformulation. *Journal of Abnormal Psychology*, **87**, 75–90.

Yates, A. J. (1970). *Behavior Therapy*. New York: Wiley.

Zborowski, M. (1952). Cultural components in response to pain. *Journal of Social Issues*, **8**, 16–30.

Zifferblatt, S. M. (1975). Increasing patient compliance through the applied analysis of behavior. *Preventive Medicine*, **4**, 173–182.

Zola, I. K. (1966). Culture and symptoms—an analysis of patients' presenting complaints. *American Sociological Review*, **31**, 615–630.

SECTION 2

Earliest Aspects

Foundations of Psychosomatics
Edited by M. J. Christie and P. G. Mellett
© 1981 John Wiley & Sons Ltd.

3

INTRA-UTERINE EXPERIENCE AND ITS LONG-TERM OUTCOME

JOHN H. W. BARRETT
Department of Psychology, University of Bristol, England.

OVERVIEW

'Look what baby can do!' Recent research on the abilities of infants has confirmed a level of competence in the newborn child far greater than was suspected in the textbooks of paediatrics and psychology of a decade ago. But what about the child before birth? Do we also need to revise our ideas about foetal competence? Although birth initiates profound changes in some physiological systems, for the brain birth does not in itself appear to be a significant event. Opportunity for experience is clearly radically altered, but studies in animals and humans of sensory and motor systems, brain metabolism and electrophysiology, indicate that surprising levels of competence are present long before the normal time for birth.

Do the competence and reactivity of the foetal brain have long-term implications for cognitive and emotional development? Attempts to answer this question are caught in a minefield of methodological problems, but large numbers of studies have been inspired by the potential clinical, social, and scientific importance of the area. For example, what are the effects on her child's achievement of such influences on the pregnant mother as nutrition, especially deficiencies and additives; environmental pollutants; infections; and addictions, including narcotics, alcohol, and smoking? Does the prenatal environment contribute to the aetiology of the many cases of mental retardation (70 per cent according to Turnbull and Woodford, 1976) where there is no identifiable anatomic, metabolic, or other cause? Do maternal schizophrenia or emotional stress during pregnancy influence personality development, or contribute to maladjustment in the child? Can some adult sexual problems be attributed to hormonal tuning of the foetal hypothalamus? Do any of the recent rapid changes in the management of pregnancy have an influence on postnatal behavioural development? Are chemical contraceptives or induced abortion likely to have effects on the behaviour of subsequent children? To what extent do uterine influences on the child interact with the mother's earlier medical history, particularly her health during childhood and adolescence? What about transgenerational or 'granny' influences? In addition to its relevance to clinical and social problems, the study of prenatal influences on behaviour has potential theoretical and methodological implications for many areas of research, including behaviour genetics, developmental psychology, psychopathology, and psychosomatic medicine.

The behavioural problems associated with easily detectable physical defects brought about by prenatal environmental influences have been discussed frequently and comprehensively elsewhere. This review will be mainly concerned with those influences which appear to have an effect on behaviour in the absence of any obvious effect on morphology. After a brief overview of the empirical findings to date, and of some of the difficulties of interpreting them, it will concentrate on the problem of the long term outcome of intra-uterine experience.

Foetal competence

First, how competent is the foetus? There are obvious difficulties in investigating this, and the ages at which behaviours have been first noted tend to be revised downwards as research continues. The earliest human behaviour appears to be the bending of the head and trunk when the skin around the mouth is lightly touched. This is sometimes known as the perioral withdrawal reflex, and occurs in the 7th week after conception (Humphrey, 1969). At about the same age the earliest intrinsic electroencephalogram activity has been recorded. It is presumably subcortical, but by 12 weeks cortical activity is likely to be involved (Timiras et al., 1968). The first reflexes are 'total', with the whole body tending to respond to any stimulus, but responses rapidly become more specific. Ultrasound studies have picked up foetal breathing movements at 11 weeks, and studies of breathing movements later in pregnancy have shown them to react sensitively to maternal blood sugar and adrenalin levels (Body and Dawes, 1975). Sucking and swallowing movements also appear about this time, as do components of the grasp and Babinski reflexes, and the 'foetal position' is assumed: arms in front of the face and knees bent in to the abdomen. By about 13 weeks sensitivity to touch has spread downwards to most parts of the body, and the foetus has become much more active. Its repertoire of movements increases rapidly, and soon includes most of the tactile reflexes found in the normal neonate. Much self-stimulation appears to occur, including thumb-sucking. By 16 weeks the mother is often aware of the movements. At 21 weeks rest–activity cycles have been recorded, but their relation to sleep–waking remains problematic. However, from 28 weeks there are clear sleep–waking cycles, and REM and non-REM phases of sleep can be distinguished (Schulte, 1974).

Given very intensive care, a few foetuses are viable by about 24 weeks. The structures of eye and ear have long been well developed, and premature infants of this age already show evoked responses in the brain to visual and auditory as well as tactile stimuli. These responses are most prominent over the corresponding cortical projection areas (Weitzman and Graziani, 1968; Hrbek, Karlberg, and Olsson, 1970). However, 'to know that the various sensory systems are capable of functioning prenatally and to know that they actually *do* function prenatally are two different things' (Gottlieb, 1976).

There is strong evidence that hearing actually does function prenatally. Many mothers have reported that startle responses and other changes in foetal movement are evoked by sounds such as loud music, the clunk of a typewriter carriage, or the vibrations of a washing machine. Here maternal mediation cannot be ruled out, since delayed indirect foetal responses have been recorded after auditory stimulation of the mother. However, a number of controlled studies (Grimwade, Walker, and Wood, 1971) carried out during the last 3 months of pregnancy have shown direct foetal responses, in the form of changes in heart-rate and body-movement, within 5 seconds of sudden loud low-frequency sounds in the mother's environment. Walker, Grimwade, and Wood, (1971) placed small microphones close to the heads of foetuses and found that the womb is a surprisingly noisy place. The rhythm of the maternal circulation combines with the less regular peristaltic activity to produce mean sound pressure levels of 95 dB, roughly equivalent to the noise of heavy traffic on a busy street corner. Consequently, only very loud external sounds are likely to reach the level to which the foetus is continuously exposed. (One possible implication of this is that to keep the noise levels after birth deliberately low may well increase rather than decrease the contrast between the prenatal and postnatal environments. In any case for the first few days after birth sound will be dampened to some extent by fluid in the middle ear.) Although low external frequencies (up to 200 Hz or so) are relatively little attenuated by the womb, attenuation increases with frequency, and frequencies above 1000 Hz are greatly reduced. Foetal responses have also been evoked by frequencies below the audible range, and this suggests that non-cochlear routes, such as cutaneous and vestibular organs, are involved. These, no doubt, also mediate the foetal movements triggered by changes in maternal posture or activity.

Very little is known about foetal visual function. Visual evoked responses, as already noted, are present in the youngest prems, and bright lights cause them to blink and turn their heads away. The pupillary light reflex develops at about 30 weeks, and from 33 weeks the head turns towards 'soft' light (Harcourt, 1974).

Although the taste buds are anatomically mature by 12 weeks from conception, and the basic tastes of sweet, salt, sour, and bitter can already be differentiated by the youngest prems, studies of taste *in utero* are lacking until 34 weeks. At this age injection of an unpleasant-tasting substance into the amniotic fluid is quickly followed by reduced swallowing of the fluid. Similarly, injection of a sweet flavour appears to increase swallowing (Mistretta and Bradley, 1975). By this time, too, the prem displays clear smiling movements.

Can the foetus feel pain? What about foetal awareness? The controlled research throws no light on these fascinating, but particularly intractable, 'other minds' problems, and discussion of them is thus outside the scope of the present review.

There is mounting evidence that foetal functioning, including behaviour, influences not only neural but also anatomical development (Hamberger,

1975; Gottlieb, 1976). For example, normal behaviour may be necessary for the normal development of joints and musculature, and when it is inhibited such disorders as cleft palate, dislocated hip, and club foot may result. Much of the brain is made while its functioning is already in progress, and stimulation of foetal sense receptors may influence the pattern of synaptic connectivity and the enzyme composition of the brain (McIlwain, 1970). The foetus actively sucks in and swallows amniotic fluid, which contributes significantly to its nutrition, and actively makes use of its behavioural repertoire to achieve the vertex presentation. Changes in the foetal pituitary–adrenal system may be responsible for the initiation of birth (Challis and Thorburn, 1975).

Studies of prenatal influences

The sensitivity of the foetus to experience is clear. Indeed, Joffe (1969) concluded that the extreme sensitivity of the foetus largely offsets the protection from external stimuli provided by the womb. But do prenatal experiences have long-term significance? Do they influence postnatal development? On account of methodological and practical difficulties, and of the many significant gaps in the existing research, the answers to these questions are much less clear. It is important to bear in mind that most of the studies are of an epidemiological nature and were set up to do no more than detect associations between prenatal and post-natal variables. Such associations as are found may be causally spurious, and failure to find associations may be just as spurious. The interpretation of the associations requires the evaluation of a large number of methodological and theoretical considerations, and even then can be no more than provisional. Some of the problems of interpretation will be discussed at greater length in the second part of this chapter. Let us here try to gain an overview and look at some representative findings. (For more comprehensive treatments, together with methodological evaluation, the reader is referred to Joffe (1969) and Barrett (1971)).

The groups of pregnancy influences which have been most frequently studied in man are nutrition, infection, oxygen deprivation, hormones, emotions, sound, complications, smoking, alcohol, and psychotropic drugs. The range of behaviours which have been reported to be affected includes intelligence and ability, school achievement, motor coordination, attention, temperament, activity level, irritability and 'behaviour disturbance'.

By far the commonest outcome measure which has been used to monitor the effects of prenatal experience is IQ. Most of the influences investigated are associated with reductions in IQ, especially when it is assessed in the first 5–7 years of life. Most of them are likely to affect the availability to the foetus of nutrition or oxygen. Such influences include maternal malnutrition, anaemia, proteinuria, alcoholism, and urinary and cytomegalovirus infections, along with twin pregnancy, postmaturity and very short interbirth interval. Foetal undernutrition is also reflected by some categories of low birthweight. There is a large literature on the relation of low birthweight not only to IQ, but also to perceptual-motor abilities, reading, and school achievement. Adverse effects have been reported until at least 15 years, but their interpretation is particularly complex and will be further discussed in the section on Enduring Effects.

The effects of complications of pregnancy are also difficult to unravel. This is no doubt partly due to the problem of the concept of 'complications', a non-unitary miscellany of conditions of widely varying type and severity. In some studies complications are associated with reduced IQ and school achievement, and with increased reading difficulties and behaviour disturbance, but in others such associations have not been discovered. (Detailed discussions can be found in Sameroff and Chandler (1975) and Hunt (1976).) Some workers (e.g. Mura, 1974) have reported a higher incidence of complications in mothers with psychiatric conditions such as schizophrenia. However, in most studies there is a possibility of confounding with the effects of medication for the condition, and most of the more recent research (e.g. McNeil, Persson-Blennow, and Kaji, 1974, Mirdal et al., 1977) has resulted in negative findings.

A few prenatal influences have been associated with enhanced ability and achievement. The claims for antenatal abdominal decompression in normal pregnancies (Heyns et al., 1962) have not been supported by a series of better controlled studies (Liddicoat, 1968; Murdoch, 1968; Murdoch et al., 1976). Another apparent enhancement followed the treatment with progesterone of mothers suffering from toxaemia of pregnancy. Toxaemia is associated in some studies with diminished school achievement, but Dalton (1968) found that compared with both toxaemia and normal controls, children of progesterone-treated pregnancies walked earlier and showed higher attainment in a variety of school subjects at 9–10 years. A further follow-up at 18 years (Dalton, 1976) suggested that the effect had persisted: the progesterone children performed better in examinations (at both O and A levels) and obtained many more university admissions. The enhancement was especially strong in arithmetic, verbal reasoning, and science subjects. But the study suffers from problems of design and control. Lynch and Mychalkiw (1978) re-examined the data and found that many of the differences were not statistically significant, and their own two studies also found no significant differences. Taken together, the studies of the effect of progesterone on ability present a mixture of suggestive trends and negative or contradictory results. This is not surprising given the variety of agents, some with androgenic components; the differing doses and timing; and the many other methodological problems. However, there is greater support for an effect on aspects of personality, some of which might be expected to influence cognitive function. Further, rat studies have found increases in DNA and MAO activity and in cortical thickness.

The maternal emotions during pregnancy which have been reported to be associated with offspring behaviour are mainly of the unpleasant sort, ranging from mild tenseness to severe anxiety, grief, and fear. Death or illness in the family, marital discord, absent or disinterested husband, bad relations with neighbours, housing problems, and distress at interruption of career are the life events which most commonly appear to precipitate these emotions. They also encompass more chronic anxiety states, including those reflected in unusually strong fears regarding childbirth and competence in child-rearing. It has been observed in a few subjects that severe anxiety in the mother is followed shortly afterwards by dramatic increases in foetal heart-rate and body movements (Sontag, 1966). These stressful emotions are sometimes associated postnatally with irritability, restlessness, excessive crying, sleep problems and 'behaviour disturbance' in the child. However, few studies followed the children beyond the first weeks, and most have assessment problems and fail to control for the possible postnatal transmission of the effects. Further, mothers with high levels of anxiety or stress tend to have more pregnancy complications and more physical problems in their offspring. They also tend to have more delivery problems, longer labours and more medication in labour. (Useful reviews of the effects of maternal emotions during pregnancy have recently been provided by Copans (1974) and Sameroff and Chandler (1975).)

Can animal studies help? In view of the difficulties of carrying out and interpreting studies in man, it will be useful to take a brief look at the implications of some of the more controlled studies of prenatal influences on animals. That some effects appear to be not only species-specific but also strain-specific underlines the need for great caution in extrapolating findings from animals: in general, extrapolation is unwarranted unless there is independent evidence of similar associations in man. The large number of animal studies has been comprehensively reviewed by Joffe (1969). Most have used the rat as subject. The pregnancy variables reported to have significant postnatal effects include nutrition; oxygen; hormones; drugs; pollutants such as herbicides, pesticides, and lead; radiation; magnetic fields; sound; and various types of stress, including anxiety, overcrowding, heat, and illumination. The offspring behaviours affected also cover a wide range, and include activity level, exploration, emotionality (as measured in the open-field test), aggression, motor performance, mating behaviour, and various forms of learning. The rat studies are, or course, not without their own problems of methodology and interpretation (see, for example, Cravens, 1974, and Masterpasqua, Chapman, and Lore, 1976). However, Barrett's (1971) summary of the general conclusions of the animal findings still appears to hold:

(1) In some mammals environmental events during pregnancy can alter the intrauterine environment and, without obvious morphological effects, influence offspring behaviour.

(2) The range of maternal experiences and treatments during pregnancy which can influence offspring behaviour is wide, and includes emotional disturbances and events of a relatively subtle nature.

(3) The occurrence and quality of an effect on offspring behaviour

depend on the interaction of a prenatal influence with other variables, amongst which foetal genotype, stage of pregnancy, and postnatal experience are often particularly important.

(4) Offspring behaviour can be influenced during pregnancy by experiences undergone by the mother before mating or during infancy, and also by experiences undergone by the maternal grandmother.

Pre-conception and 'granny' influences

Pre-conception and 'granny' influences are also suggested by the human data. For example, a variety of maternal infections acquired before conception, including some sexually transmitted diseases, can lead to placental anomalies and hence to foetal growth retardation and its consequences, including physical and mental disadvantage. A high incidence of such infections, and of other problems, is associated with some forms of previous induced abortion, particularly where early and specialized antenatal management is absent in subsequent pregnancies (Wynn and Wynn, 1977). Even after allowing for parental social class and education, the National Child Development survey found a relationship between a child's reading attainment and the social class of his maternal grandfather (Davie, Butler, and Goldstein, 1972). In this study, uterine transmission of the effect is only one of a number of possible routes. However, Drillien (1957) found that the incidence of low birthweight was more strongly associated with the social class of the maternal grandfather than with that of the father, and suggested that the mother's childhood nutrition and health affected placental adequacy. Thus, non-genetic transgenerational processes may influence the foetus in the womb, and may contribute to the perpetuation of cycles of disadvantage (Rutter and Madge, 1976). It follows that medical and social measures and policies, particularly those affecting women, should be evaluated from the point of view of possible effects on the next generation, and that to be more effective preventive medicine and psychiatry may need to develop a much stronger transgenerational perspective.

Underlying processes and foetal learning

So far, we have talked in terms of correlations and associations: what about the underlying processes? The foetus can be directly reached by components of the environment in which its mother lives, for example radiation and sound. It can be indirectly influenced by the sensory stimulation of its mother, for example when this leads to emotional stress and hormonal change, as well as by the effect on the mother's internal environment of nutrition, infections, drugs, and pollutants. The indirect influences can be communicated by diffusion through the amniotic fluid, or mechanically through changes in uterine pressure and movement, as well as through the placenta. Although it provides a barrier for blood cells and large bacteria, the placenta is, in general, an efficient transmitter. However, it does not play a merely passive role: it makes its own very active contribution, and interacts in a complex manner with both mother and foetus. For example, in addition to ferrying hormones in both directions, it actively and independently manufactures them. The autonomous role of the placenta has led some workers to talk in terms of the mother–placenta–foetus triad, and it significantly complicates the interpretation of prenatal influences. In principle at least, maternal stimulation can reach the foetus by several routes simultaneously. For example, in addition to influencing the hormones of mother and foetus, maternal anxiety affects the absorption, metabolism, and availability of nutrients, together with resistance to infection, and can also provoke increased uterine motility.

Can the foetus learn? Although this question has attracted much interest and speculation, it has not surprisingly been little studied either in the foetus, or in the prem. The answer depends in part on what is meant by learning: there are many kinds and many problems of definition. Despite the great amount of valuable research that has been carried out, notions of learning and memory in general are still far from mature, particularly so with regard to the preverbal infant. In the light of current views on the development of such aspects as attention, cognitive representation, information capacity, and contingency analysis, and on the role of experience in their development, it is unlikely that learning of much cognitive complexity could occur in the foetus. The classical (!) study remains that of Spelt (1948). Working with foetuses during their last 3 months in the womb, he used Pavlovian procedures to try to set up a conditioned foetal body movement response to a signal in the form of a mild vibration of the mother's abdomen. He claimed success; but although it was a careful investigation, full control of various sources of possible artifact was inevitably not possible, and criticism and scepticism have been frequent. Attempts at replication do not appear to have been published. Further, it is unlikely that the foetus could be more easily conditioned than the neonate. The demonstration of unequivocal classical conditioning in the neonate has proved particularly difficult and controversial. Many well-controlled attempts to produce it have failed. This suggests that 'Pavlovian tactics may be inappropriate and that in order to demonstrate early learning, investigators should resort to instrumental or operant techniques' (Millar, 1974). However, the success of some attempts, including a number of recent studies using heart-rate as a conditioned response, suggests that when the neonate is in an appropriate state classical conditioning does occur at least in some modalities (Crowell, et al., 1976). Perhaps on account of the formidable problems involved, there are no reports of attempts to use operant conditioning with the human foetus. On the other hand, operant conditioning has frequently been demonstrated in the neonate and can therefore be regarded as a possibility, at least in late foetal life.

However, learning embraces much more than classical and operant conditioning, which now appear to be rather special cases. 'From a cognitive point of view, habituation is considered to indicate the retention of information about stimulation. In this respect it may represent the simplest and possibly earliest form of learning' (Millar, 1974). Habituation has been demonstrated in the newborn (Friedman, Nagy, and Carpenter, 1971), and has been put forward as a speculative interpretation of the temporary waning of the perioral withdrawal reflex upon repeated stimulation which occurs only 7 weeks from conception (Lipsitt, 1969). The relationship between intra-uterine position and neonatal posture may involve learning, and the sensory preferences shown by neonates may indicate that sensory expectations or adaptation levels can be acquired in the womb (Bronson, 1969). Some studies have found decreased crying and activity, and increased weight gain in neonates subjected to rhythmic light, sound, or movement at a frequency close to that of the maternal heart-beat, and it has been suggested that this may be related to uterine adaptation levels (Salk, 1973; Palmqvist, 1975). However, a recent more controlled study (Smith and Steinschneider, 1975) found that although the relation between prenatal maternal heart-rate and neonatal quieting was in the expected direction, it failed to reach statistical significance. More research is needed. Although there have been retrospective introspective reports of long-term retention of uterine and perinatal learning, controlled studies are predictably lacking.

Whatever the extent of foetal learning in the narrow sense, the reported correlations between prenatal influences and postnatal behaviour *can* be accounted for without invoking it. Traditional concepts of learning have not proved very useful in explaining the role of experience in the *development* of behaviour, and Gottlieb (1976) advocates thinking instead in terms of induction, facilitation, and maintenance. As Haith and Campos (1977) put it: 'Experience must be seen as involved not only in the reinforcement and acquisition of responses, but also in initiating and maintaining developmental changes.' Futher, explanations in terms of intrinsic physiological processes and largely extrinsic transactional processes must be seriously considered. The physiological possibilities include nutritional and hormonal processes; enzyme induction; the effect of sensory input on the chemical and cellular composition of the developing brain; and hormonal and autonomic tuning. (For fuller discussion, see Barrett (1971).) However, these processes may form part of the physiological substrate of learning; and some of them are examples of physiological adaptation, and as such might be held to fall within some of the wider definitions of learning. The transactional processes include the postnatal influence on the child of maternal behaviours which have been affected by prenatal events. They will be discussed at greater length in the second part of this chapter.

Conclusions

The correlational and non-manipulative nature of most of the human data makes it unlikely that any one study will permit confident separation of prenatal from genetic, pre-conception and postnatal factors. However, if studies using different methods and controls, and performed in different contexts, converge to implicate the same influences, and if there are animal findings and physiological mechanisms consistent with these, then we can be more confident in our conclusions.

At the end of his examination of the methodological status of the human research, Joffe (1969) concluded:

> The human studies provide sufficient evidence to enable preventive prenatal action to be initiated with regard to a variety of pregnancy and childhood disorders without waiting for the methodological issues to be unravelled precisely—though the action may be more effective when they are.

The research of the last decade leaves Joffe's conclusion as valid now as it was then. Does it permit us to conclude that psychosomatic relationships start before birth?

THE LONG-TERM OUTCOME

Nutrition and personality

'The authors have been able to test—and reject—the hypothesis that prenatal nutrition impairs subsequent mental performance' (Stone, 1976). This is a conclusion which has often been inspired by the elegant study of 20,000 18-year-old males born during the Dutch Hunger Winter of 1944–45 (Stein et al., 1975). However, Stein et al. restricted their conclusions to 'surviving adults in industrial societies', and themselves pointed out that prenatal nutrition, in combination with poor postnatal nutrition, could not be excluded as a possible determinant of adult mental competence. To poor postnatal nutrition might be added poor nutrition and health of the mother before conception, and a host of other factors. . . .

It is usually inappropriate to draw general conclusions from single studies, however comprehensive. Endemic undernutrition typically co-varies with other adverse social factors in an almost inextricable manner. Nevertheless, taken as a whole, the massive and controversy-laden literature on the effects of nutrition on behaviour provides much support for the conclusion that prenatal nutrition plays an important role in the team of environmental factors which *together* often have a major influence on intellectual development.

We shall not attempt here to review the evidence (see Cravioto, Hambraeus, and Valquist, 1973; Winick, 1974; Barrett, in press). Instead, it is intended to use the area of nutrition to illustrate some principles that are likely to have general relevance to the evaluation of the long-term effects of prenatal influences, and in particular to look at interactions between what are usually described as physical and psychological factors.

Intensity

Biological systems are resilient. Unless an insult to the foetus is sufficiently intense, or prolonged enough to stress its self-regulating processes beyond their limits of self-correction, it is unlikely in itself to have much effect. Some insults, however, including deficits in nutrition, infection, and stress, appear to damage the self-regulating systems themselves, and consequently increase general vulnerability, sometimes permanently. In view of their relatively high birth-weight it is questionable whether the Dutch famine children actually were malnourished at birth (Tizard, 1974). It is vital to distinguish between maternal undernutrition and foetal undernutrition.

Timing

Vulnerability is usually greatest when a system is developing fastest. The various parts of the brain develop at different times and different rates. Taken as a whole, the brain has two major growth spurts: from 10 to 18 weeks after conception, and from 20 weeks after conception to 2 years or so after birth. Foetal undernutrition can affect brain growth at any time, but maternal undernutrition is only likely to do so during the second half of pregnancy (Dobbing, 1974).

Duration

To bring about permanent deficits, a significant proportion of the brain growth spurt must be growth-restricted. Prolonged mild undernutrition is likely to have more severe effects than shorter periods of acute starvation. Within limits, 'catch-up' is possible: adequate nutrition after birth can overcome deficits produced by prenatal undernutrition. Nutrition has its most severe impact when inadequate both before and after birth (Dobbing, 1974).

Interaction with other prenatal influences

Undernutrition, infection, and emotional stress interact powerfully with each other both prenatally and postnatally, and also over time (Mata, 1974). Often these interactions are synergistic (that is, the action of two factors together will have a much greater effect than would be produced by merely adding their separate effects). Risks are cumulative and 'beyond a certain "concentration" there will be a sharp rise in defect attributable to any further trauma' (Stratton, 1977). Thus a degree of undernutrition, which might in itself be of little significance, can be decisive if suffered in the context of existing poor health. In areas of endemic food shortage a pregnant mother weakened by undernutrition and infection may undergo great emotional stress and fatigue in the battle to find food for herself and her family. Which factor is causal?

Interaction with pre-conception and transgenerational factors

Even when well-nourished during pregnancy, a mother may be unable to support a normal growth-rate in her foetus because her own growth was stunted during or before adolescence by undernutrition or infection (Ounstead and Ounstead, 1973). Where there is a history of problems of this kind, even mild maternal undernutrition in later pregnancy is likely to have significant effects. The availability to the foetus of some important nutrients can be affected by the previous use of some chemical contraceptives (Wynn and Wynn, 1977). Animal studies suggest that both undernutrition and anxiety in the maternal grandmother can have significant and enduring effects on the foetus (Denenberg and Rosenberg, 1967; Bresler, Ellison, and Zamenhof, 1975). And Brazelton *et al.* (1977) conclude that their data on undernourished Guatemalan infants point to 'non-genetic variables which can affect intra-uterine conditions unfavourably and perpetuate the depleting effects of poverty from one generation to another.' (Other examples of pre-conception and 'granny' effects were discussed in the Overview.)

Interaction with delivery factors

Prenatal disadvantages make complications of delivery more likely, and they in their turn can exacerbate the effects of earlier problems.

Interaction with postnatal factors and the role of effects on personality

Discussion of the complexities of interactions with postnatal factors will occupy most of the rest of this review. At this point we will confine ourselves to two aspects that provide examples of the complex relationships between psychological and physical processes. Perhaps we should say 'the unity of ...'? First, there is evidence from both animal and human studies (Fraňková, 1974; Richardson, 1976) that a rearing environment which is cognitively and socially stimulating can compensate to a marked degree for early undernutrition. Home stimulation and nutrition appear to act synergistically.

Secondly, when associations between foetal undernutrition and later intellectual development were first reported it was usually assumed that the causal chain involved effects on the brain which influenced learning capacity. Much research, both in humans and animals, indicates this can indeed be the case, especially where the trauma is severe and persisting. However, there is also much data to suggest that other processes may account for the associations, either in part, or sometimes even exclusively.

For example, nutritional variables may influence personality characteristics, and the intellectual deficits may be secondary to these. Prenatal undernutrition is associated with a variety of effects on motivation and emotional behaviour in rats. They can be hyperactive, more aggressive, less able to adapt to stress, less exploratory and less demanding (Halas, Hanlon, and Sandstead, 1975; Massaro, Levitsky, and Barnes, 1977). And they elicit less effective maternal behaviour (Wiener *et al.*, 1977).

Passiveness, docility, lack of curiosity, and lack of popularity have been observed at school age in children previously rehabilitated from severe early undernutrition (Birch and Gussow, 1970). Full-term low-birth-weight babies are often lethargic, unresponsive, and less rewarding as neonates (Brazelton *et al.*, 1977) and later show a higher incidence of the irritating characteristics dubbed 'mother-killers' by Thomas, Chess, and Birch, (1968). The consequences of the effect of undernutrition on personality characteristics are made explicit in a study by Chavez, Martinez, and Yaschine, (1974). A group of pregnant women from an undernourished Mexican village were given food supplements for 3 years, starting in the 6th week of pregnancy. From 3 months after birth their children received food supplements too. Compared with non-supplemented controls, these children walked earlier, talked more, slept less, cried less, and left the house more often. They actively manipulated their environment, and generated more, and more varied, contacts with their parents and other adults. They acted as agents of change and created conditions which facilitated their own mental development. In other words, the nutritional supplements appeared to have changed a whole sequence of transactions.

Transactions

'What is not justified on present evidence is any belief in the possibility of long-term prediction with existing measures.' After discussing the criteria for assessing the possible long-term consequences of obstetric circumstances, Stratton (1977) reached that apparently pessimistic conclusion. Why are long-term outcomes so unpredictable? Quite apart from the complexity of the area and our current ignorance of many of the factors involved, it is likely that a more fundamental aspect of the answer lies in the appropriateness of the assumptions made about the nature of development; in other words the explicit or implicit developmental theory employed.

Part of the background to the problem was summarized, after a review of the findings and methodology, in Barrett's (1971) conclusions:

The child is born with an individuality which is a product of the interaction of genotype and pre-natal environment. The future development of the child then depends on the match between rearing practices and his particular characteristics. The same practices have different consequences depending on the characteristics of the particular infant .... This process is cumulative, and the long-term prognosis depends on the continual adjustment of the rearing of the child to match the existing mix. Provided damage to the brain is not too severe, the influence of an effective upbringing of this sort can often swamp even serious obstetric problems. Where the postnatal environ-

ment is not so favourable, problems developed in utero may be exacerbated.

From this it is clear that one-to one relationships between pregnancy influences and long-term development are hardly to be expected. Interactions
with the postnatal environment are particularly powerful and complex.
As Chavez, Martinez, and Yaschine, (1974) found, the child will have
an effect on his environment, particularly on his care-givers and their behaviour, including their behaviour towards him. During the development of
child and family, there will be reciprocal reactions: change in one member
will lead to change in the others which in turn will lead to change in the original,
and so on in a continuing transactional manner. The long-term outcome
depends on the whole of the intervening transactions. Help!

This daunting conclusion is of course not specific to evaluating the effects
of pregnancy influences. It is an example of the problem shared by all attempts
at tracing the influence of earlier experiences on later development, and is
therefore basic to developmental theory as a whole. The general problem
has been discussed at length by Sameroff and Chandler (1975) and Sameroff
(1975), and both papers also include specific discussions of obstetric influences.
They distinguish three models of development:

(1) The main-effect model, characterized by the one-to-one relationships
    already referred to, where influences, whether constitutional or environ-
    mental, have independent additive effects on development.
(2) The interactional model, where the effect of a given factor is *statically*
    dependent on the contribution of other factors. An example is provided
    by the usual interpretation of the frequent finding that perinatal disadvant-
    ages tend to 'wash out' in favourable rearing situations but to persist in
    less favourable ones. 'The major reason behind the inadequacy of this
    model is that neither constitution nor environment are necessarily constant
    over time' (Sameroff, 1975).
(3) The transactional model, where in a continually developing interplay
    the child *dynamically* alters his environment and is in turn influenced by
    the changed world he himself has brought about. This model views 'children
    and their environments as undergoing regular restructuring in ways that
    relegate past events and characteristics to the status of ancient history....
    Early factors that have enduring consequences are assumed to do so
    because of persistent influences acting throughout the life span, rather
    than at discrete points in development.... Transactions between the
    child and his caretaking environment serve to break or maintain the linkage
    between earlier trauma and later disorder and must... be taken into
    account if successful predictions are to be made' (Sameroff and Chandler,
    1975).

As we have seen, the postnatal environment can reduce or exacerbate the
long-term effects of obstetric problems. How does this happen? Sameroff

and Chandler (1975) put forward the concept of a 'continuum of caretaking causalty' to incorporate the environmental risk factors which lead toward unfavourable developmental outcomes. Persistent inappropriate caretaking by deprived, stressed or poorly educated parents often appears to play a decisive role. The New York Longitudinal Study (Thomas, Chess, and Birch, 1968) provides good examples of this. Few significant correlations were found between temperamental characteristics in the 1st and 5th years, and where an initially 'difficult' temperament did persist there was evidence that the parents had been unable to adjust to the greater demands made on them. Where the parents were able to respond more positively, the problems tended to 'wash out'.

The caretaking skills of parents can be stressed and disrupted over many years by infant behaviours, such as disturbances in alertness, vigour, stability, or sleep–waking cycles, which may be the aftermath of obstetric disadvantages. In turn, the disrupted caretaking may serve to perpetuate problem behaviour in the child. This transactional sequence highlights the role of the effect of an infant on its caregiver, somewhat neglected in child studies until about a decade ago, but recently the subject of intensive research (see Lewis and Rosenblum, 1974). The study by Chavez et al. (1974) already discussed provides examples of the ways in which the child appears to construct his own environment. As Schneirla (1957) pointed out, an organism does not wait passively for the environment to stimulate it to respond: it is always active and the circular feedback effects of its own activity, or transactions with itself, create an important 'third source' of its own development. A child is an agent of change, an active participant in his own development, and in this sense development is in part a self-generated phenomenon. Schneirla's approach to development has been labelled the constructivist or ipsative approach (see Lerner, 1976). It provides a link between developmental theory and some 'self' theories of personality. The constructivist approach has not yet been developed very far, but it is currently generating great interest, and has implications which add to the difficulties of long-term prediction.

How adaptable are we? Many of the studies of prenatal influences are underpinned, either explicitly or implicitly, by the main-effect or interactional models, and these often make the assumption that associations between early experience and outcome are determined by persisting internal processes. However, the transactional model allows for the possibility that such associations may be determined by transactional or even largely external processes, and that given different environmental transactions the internal processes would fade or 'wash out'. In other words, the earlier models may have underestimated the adaptability and plasticity of the individual as well as the extent to which apparent developmental continuities may be maintained by the rigidity of some environments. There is abundant statistical evidence that disadvantages tend to hunt in packs, and that environments which are associated with higher incidences of obstetric problems are often those which are also likely through transactional processes to exacerbate the effects postnatally.

The reversibility of early influences has recently been stressed by many, especially Clarke and Clarke (1976). However, as Stratton (1977) has noted:

> While Clarke and Clarke make an important point in emphasising the resilience of the child, this only shows that early trauma *can* be remedied. There remains the question, in any specific case, of whether it *will* be remedied, and the evidence clearly shows that in some cases the answer is 'no'.

It follows from the transactional model that where there are predictable continuities in environmental disadvantages long-term predictions are likely to be more accurate, and that by disturbing the transactional sequence even relatively mild influences on the foetus may make a significant contribution to the risks to the child.

From its inception, psychiatry has been powerfully influenced by assumptions about the effects of early experience. However although dynamic and transactional in some respects, many schools of thought within psychiatry and personality have conceived of development, and particularly of interactions with the environment, in somewhat static terms. In his recent Mapother lecture at the Institute of Psychiatry, Eisenberg (1977) made a plea for a more dynamically developmental approach to clinical problems. To the various important ideas he discussed may be added the transactional and constructivist models of development. As well as throwing much light on the long-term prediction problem, they would appear to have valuable wider implications for psychiatry, developmental medicine, and psychosomatic medicine.

Discontinuity and 'wash-out'

Development is often thought of as a set of smooth, continuous, incremental processes where characteristics are gained, and once gained rarely lost. Although this may hold for some characteristics, many show discontinuity, instability, and reversal, sometimes multiple reversal (Bower, 1976).

Temperamental characteristics are frequently unstable. For example, in the New York Longitudinal Study only 1 of 9 characteristics showed significant correlations between assessments in the first and fifth years (Thomas *et al.*, 1968). Significant negative correlations have been observed between newborn and 3-year measurements of aspects of arousal and reactivity (Bell, Weller, and Waldrop, 1971; Yang and Halverson, 1976).

IQ, now generally thought of as an indicator of current performance in a limited group of mainly intellectual skills, is often considered to be one of the most stable characteristics. It is also the outcome measure most frequently used in the published studies of prenatal influences. Yet longitudinal surveys of the development of IQ from infancy to adulthood have found large changes. Even during the school years, when its stability is relatively high, over a third of individual scores change by more than 20 points, and occasionally variations of more than 50 points are recorded. What is more, the amount and direction of change reflect ecological variables including rearing practices and life events (McCall, Hogarty, and Hurlbut, 1972).

Research findings are contingent on the methodology used. Much of the data on prenatal influences are based on assessments of outcome at a single point in time, usually shortly after birth or during the first 5 years. Such studies, particularly when retrospective, often point to adverse outcomes. However, where prospective methods are employed, the prognosis usually appears much more favourable, and in the few prospective surveys already published which report repeated assessments over time, change and 'wash-out' have often been found, particularly in advantaged families. For instance, their detailed review of the evidence leads Sameroff and Chandler (1975) to conclude that the effects of pregnancy complications and perinatal hypoxia frequently wash out. Of special relevance here is their further conclusion that psychosomatic factors, particularly maternal emotional stress and anxiety during pregnancy, do appear to increase sharply the risk of complications and the risk of developmental problems in the child.

An illuminating example of 'wash-out' is provided by a longitudinal study of perinatal hypoxia (Corah et al., 1965). Specific impairments were found during the first few days of life, and again at 3 years, but by 7 years there were no IQ differences between the hypoxic group and the controls. However some mild effects were still evident at 7 years and these included problems with conceptualizing and motor co-ordination as well as attention difficulties and distractibility. The results point to the need to employ repeated multiple measures of outcome. In this study effects on aspects of temperament appeared to outlive effects on IQ, and this emphasizes the danger that studies using IQ or any other single outcome measure may lead to an underestimation of the significance of prenatal influences.

Taking the pregnancy research as a whole, the most consistent and robust conclusion to emerge is that psychosocial factors have a much stronger influence on development than specific obstetric problems. Except where severe, persistent, or cumulative disadvantages have damaged the self-correcting mechanisms themselves, intrinsic development is characterized by plasticity and discontinuity: apparent continuities often derive largely from the environmental contribution to the transaction.

Enduring effects

Do all prenatal influences on behaviour wash out during the early years? A survey of the literature reveals many reports of effects up to the age of 4 years, fewer up to the age of 7 years, and very few after 7 years. It is tempting to draw the conclusion that wash-out is general. Tempting, but invalid! Such a conclusion might well prove to be an artifact of the current state of the research. Most of the literature reports assessments either at a single early age, or at a small number of early ages. Even though there are long-term longitudinal studies under way, few have yet reported the relevant analyses for ages beyond 7 years.

From 7 years onwards, associations with behaviour have been reported for low birthweight, for smoking (after allowance for low birthweight), and for excess androgen and progesterone exposure. In most cases the measures were of IQ, ability, or aspects of school achievement. Impairments have been reported up to 11 years for smoking (Goldstein, 1977), and up to 15 years for low birthweight (Malhotra, 1972). Enhancements, and also effects on personality, have been reported up to 16 years for androgen and 18 years for progesterone. The interpretation of most of these reports is not straightforward. Space precludes systematic evaluation here, but let us indicate just a few of the difficulties since many of them illustrate the tight interdependence between the 'psyche' and the 'soma'.

Does the deficit in the child's reading age associated with smoking reflect personality differences between smoking and non-smoking mothers? (The incidence of low birthweight associated with smoking in pregnancy is a separate and serious problem.) The low-birthweight issue is particularly complex. Birthweight is not a unitary category and reflects many very different conditions. In the low-birthweight range, there is a higher incidence of physically and mentally handicapped children, but they are often excluded from the studies. And many of these handicaps can be attributed to foetal undernutrition (Sabel, Olegard, and Victorin, 1976; Wynn and Wynn, 1977). In most studies the effects associated with low birthweight tend to wash out in higher occupational classes, and the results reflect their persistence in lower occupational classes. Does maternal separation or distress while the neonate is in intensive care play a part? Is there an iatrogenic component? Are parents over-anxious or over-protective in their later behaviour toward low-birthweight children? Recent studies (Blake, Stewart, and Turcan, 1977) suggest that improvement in the intensive care of very low-birthweight babies is greatly reducing the incidence of major long-term problems. Are the outcome measures too crude to detect lesser problems?

The data on exposure of the foetal brain to high androgen levels come from girls born with the adrenogenital syndrome (AGS). In some samples 60 per cent had IQs above 110 points (25 per cent would be expected) and a few 'tomboyish' behaviours were reported, although gender role was clearly female and there were no homosexual trends. However, Baker and Ehrhardt (1974) found there was no IQ difference between the 27 patients and their parents and sibs—they all had elevated IQs. Van de Wiele (1974) pointed out that despite large doses of cortisone androgen suppression was often not adequate, and so the tomboy effects might be due to current, not foetal, androgen levels. And one of the AGS girls had a non-AGS sister who was also a tomboy! As for the aetiology of sex differences in behaviour and emotion in 'normal' humans, some reviews (Reinisch, 1974; Maccoby and Jacklin, 1974) have concluded that the effect of foetal hormones is to produce a mild but culturally reversible predisposition or greater 'readiness to learn' one gender role rather than the other. But Archer (1976) in a detailed review of the biological evidence finds even this too strong and stresses the role of cultural transactions.

We are left with progesterone. The status of Dalton's (1976) findings was discussed on page 45. Another study (Reinisch and Karow, 1977) assessed 71 children whose mothers had received different combinations of synthetic progestins and oestrogens for the maintenance of at-risk pregnancies. After scores had been adjusted for prenatal and perinatal complications, there was no relationship between the different combinations and IQ; but there was a relationship with personality. High progestin: oestrogen ratios were associated with sensitivity, independence, self-confidence, and self-sufficiency, characteristics found by Cattell to be predictive of school success...

Much of the research which promises to throw most light on the question of the longevity of intra-uterine experiences is still in progress. It might well be that intra-uterine experiences have powerful and enduring effects on aspects of development not reflected by the extremely limited range of outcome measures employed in the published work—at present that is a matter for speculation. However, it is already clear that in some circumstances some intra-uterine experiences do contribute significantly to a package whose long-term consequences are all too predictable. The success of both research and intervention is highly dependent on the assumptions or model, whether explicit or implicit, on which they are based. The transactional model has its problems, one of which is its complexity, but the reality it is attempting to mirror is also complex, and it may prove to be more fruitful than simple models which, while having the advantage of simplicity, have the disadvantage of matching the real world less well. Much depends on the extent to which the transactional approach can be made operational and practicable within the context of current research.

Signs of its utility and potential are already forthcoming. An example is provided by a prospective longitudinal study of the relationship between a mother's perception of her first-born child and his subsequent emotional development (Broussard, 1976). A questionnaire was administered to mothers in the first days after the birth and again a month later, and their children were psychiatrically assessed at $4\frac{1}{2}$ and 11 years. There was no association between the first maternal questionnaire and either child assessment. There was, however, a significant association between the second maternal questionnaire and the children's need for psychiatric intervention at both ages. Broussard postulated that by 1 month a mother's attitude towards her child may have an important effect on the development of emotional disorder. The finding that there were no relationships with maternal perception measured in the first few days suggests that the child's early behaviour shaped his mother's attitude which in turn influenced his development. As we have seen, many associations have been found between *early* behaviour and prenatal influences. In the subgroup of infants viewed negatively by their mothers at the time of both questionnaires, only 7.7 per cent had no mental disorder at 11 years. It seems that if it were based on a transactional model involving assessments of both child and parents at a few carefully chosen times, long-term predictivity might be significantly improved.

Conclusions

The behaviour of the foetus affects its anatomical development. Maternal anxiety in pregnancy is associated with a higher incidence of complications. Psychosocial factors often seem to 'wash out' the effects of prenatal under-nutrition or low birthweight. These are just three of the many examples of psychosomatic relationships which we have met while reviewing the complexities of intra-uterine influences. Intra-uterine influences can perhaps best be thought of as contributing to long-term outcome by distorting the socio-psychosomatic transaction. Where problems have already arisen, information about the conditions which facilitate wash-out might help to make medical, educational, or social intervention more effective. Consideration of the possible effects on long-term transactions might be added to the criteria used in making decisions and shaping policy with regard to antenatal and perinatal care. Evidence of the potential value of such an approach comes from the evaluation of the management of intensive care for children of very low birthweight. Blake *et al.* (1977) suggested that part of the improvement in outcome over the past decade might be attributed to the effect on the long-term transaction of involving the mother and family as much as possible in the care of the infant while in the baby unit. Such involvement reduces anxiety, reduces separation, facilitates the development of infant–family communication, and above all encourages the mother to become an active agent in the developmental transaction rather than its depressed and passive victim.

REFERENCES

Archer, J. (1976). Biological Explanations of psychological sex differences. In Lloyd, B., and Archer, J. (eds.), *Exploring Sex Differences*. London and New York: Academic Press.

Baker, S. W., and Ehrhardt, A. A. (1974). Prenatal androgen, intelligence, and cognitive sex differences. In R. C. Friedman, R. M. Richart, R. L. Van de Wiele, and L. O. Stern (eds.), *Sex Differences in Behavior*. New York: John Wiley.

Barrett, J. H. W. (1971). Pre-natal environmental influences on behaviour. In G. F. Batstone, A. W. Blair, and J. M. Slater (eds.), *A Handbook of Pre-Natal Paediatrics*. Aylesbury: MTP Press.

Barrett, J. H. W. (In press). Prenatal influences on adaptation in the newborn. In P. M. Stratton (ed.), *The Psychobiology of the Human Newborn*. London: Wiley.

Bell, R. Q., Weller, G. M., and Waldrop, M. F. (1971). Newborn and preschooler: organisation of behaviour and relations between periods. *Monog. Soc. Res. Child Develop.*, **36**, 2 (whole no. 142).

Birch, H. G., and Gussow, J. D. (1970). *Disadvantaged Children: Health, Nutrition and School Failure*. New York: Grune & Stratton.

Blake, A., Stewart, A., and Turcan, D. (1977). Perinatal intensive care. *J. Psychosom. Res.*, **21** (4), 261–272.

Boddy, K., and Dawes, G. S. (1975). Fetal breathing. *Br. Med. Bull.*, **31** (1), 3–7.

Bower, T. G. R. (1976). Repetitive processes in child development. *Sci. Amer.*, **235** (5), 38–47.

Brazelton, T. B., Tronick, G., Lechtig, A., Lasky, R. E., and Klein, R. E. (1977). The behavior of nutritionally deprived Guatemalan infants. *Devel. Med. Child Neurol.*, **19**, 364–372.

Bresler, D. E., Ellison, G., and Zamenhof, S. (1975). Learning deficits in rats with malnourished grandmothers. *Devel. Psychobiol.*, **8** (4), 315–323.

Bronson, G. (1969). Discussion of T. Humphrey, Postnatal repetition of human prenatal activity sequences. In R. J. Robinson, (ed.), *Brain and early Behaviour*, pp. 73–74. London: Academic Press.

Broussard, E. R. (1976). Neonatal prediction and outcome at 10/11 years. *Child Psychiatry and Human Development*, **7** (2), 85–93.

Challis, J. R. G., and Thorburn, G. D. (1975). Prenatal endocrine function. *Br. Med. Bull.*, **31** (1), 32–36.

Chavez, A., Martinez, C., and Yaschine, T. (1974). The importance of nutrition and stimuli on child mental and social development. In J. Cravioto, L. Hambraeus, and B. Vahlquist (eds.), *Early Malnutrition and Mental Development*. Uppsala: Almqvist & Wiksell.

Clarke, A. M., and Clarke, A. D. B. (1976). *Early Experience: Myth and Evidence*. London: Open Books.

Copans, S. A. (1974). Human prenatal effects: methodological problems and some suggested solutions. *Merrill-Palmer Quart.*, **20** (1), 43–52.

Corah, N. L., Anthony, E. J., Painter, P., Stern, J. A., and Thurston, D. (1965). Effects of perinatal anoxia after 7 years. *Psychol. Monogr.*, **79**, 1–34.

Cravens, R. W. (1974). Effects of maternal undernutrition on offspring behavior: incentive value of a food reward and ability to escape from water. *Devel. Psychobiol.*, **7** (1), 61–69.

Cravioto, J., Hambraeus, L., and Valquist, B. (eds.), (1974). *Early Malnutrition and Mental Development*. Uppsala; Almqvist & Wiksell.

Crowell, D. H., Blurton, L. B., Kobayashi, L. R., McFarland, J. L., and Yang, R. K. (1976). Studies in early infant learning: classical conditioning of the neonatal heart rate. *Psychol. Monogr.*, **12** (4), 373–397.

Dalton, K. (1968). Antenatal progesterone and intelligence. *Br. J. Psychiat.*, **114**, 1377–83.

Dalton, K. (1976). Prenatal progesterone and educational attainment. *Br. J. Psychiat.*, **129**, 438–442.

Davie, R., Butler, N., and Goldstein, H. (1972). *From Birth to Seven*. London. Longman.

Denenberg, V. H., and Rosenberg, K. M. (1967). Nongenetic transmission of information. *Nature*, **216**, 549.

Dobbing, J. (1974). Prenatal nutrition and neurological development. In J. Cravioto *et al.* (eds.), *Early Malnutrition and Mental Development*. Uppsala: Almqvist & Wiksell.

Drillien, C. M. (1957). Social and economic factors affecting the incidence of premature birth. *J. Obst. Gynec. Br. Commonw.*, **64**, 161.

Eisenberg, L. (1977). Development as a unifying concept in psychiatry. *Br. J. Psychiat.*, **131**, 225–237.

Fraňková, A. (1974). Interaction between early malnutrition and stimulation in animals. In J. Cravioto *et al.* (eds.) *Early Malnutrition and Mental Development*. Uppsala: Almqvist & Wiksell.

Friedman, S., Nagy, A. N., and Carpenter, G. C. (1971). Newborn attention: differential decrement to visual stimuli: *J. Exp. Child Psychol.*, **10**, 44–51.

Goldstein, H. (1977). Smoking in pregnancy: some notes on the statistical controversy. *Br. J. Prev. Soc. Med.*, **31**, 13–17.

Gottlieb, G. (1976). Conceptions of prenatal development: behavioral embryology. *Psychol. Rev.*, **83** (3), 215–234.

Grimwade, J. C., Walker, D., and Wood, C. (1971). Human foetal heartrate change and movement in response to sound and vibration. *Am. J. Obstet. Gynec.*, **109**, 86–90.

Haith, M. H. and Campos, J. J. (1977). Human infancy. *Ann. Rev. Psychol.*, **28**, 251–293.

Halas, E. S., Hanlon, M. J., and Sandstead, H. H. (1975). Intrauterine nutrition and aggression. *Nature*, **257** (5523), 221–222.

Hamberger, V. (1975). Fetal behavior. In E. S. E. Hafez (ed.), *The Mammalian Fetus*. Springfield, Illinois: Charles Thomas.

Harcourt, B. (1974). The visual system. In J. A. Davis, and J. Dobbing (eds.), *Scientific Foundations of Paediatrics*. London: Heinemann.

Heyns, O. S., Samson, J. M., and Roberts, W. A. B. (1962). An analysis of infants whose mothers had decompression during pregnancy. *Med. Proc.*, **8**, 307–311.

Hrbek, A., Karlberg, P., and Olsson, T. (1970). 'Assessment of maturity of premature children by variations in evoked responses.' Paper presented at Second European Congress of Perinatal Medicine, London, April 1970.

Humphrey, T. (1969). Postnatal repetition of human pre-natal activity sequences. In R. J. Robinson (ed.), *Brain and Early Behaviour*. London and New York: Academic Press.

Hunt, J. V. (1976). Environmental risk in fetal and neonatal life and measured infant intelligence. In M. Lewis (ed.), *Origins of Intelligence*. London: Wiley.

Joffe, J. M. (1969). *Prenatal Determinants of Behaviour*. Oxford: Pergamon Press.

Lerner, R. M. (1976). *Concepts and Theories of Human Development*. Reading, Massachusetts: Addison-Wesley.

Lewis, M., and Rosenblum, L. A. (eds.) (1974). *The Effect of the Infant on its Caregiver*. New York: Wiley.

Liddicoat, R. (1968). Effects of maternal antenatal decompression treatment on infant mental development. *S. Afr. Med. J.*, **42**, 203–211.

Lipsitt, L. P. (1969). Learning capacities of the human infant. In R. J. Robinson (ed.), *Brain and Early Behaviour*. London and New York: Academic Press.

Lynch, A., and Mychalkiw, W. (1978): Prenatal progesterone II. Its role in the treatment of pre-eclamptic toxaemia and its effect on the offspring's intelligence: a re-appraisal. *Early Hum, Dev.*, **2**, 323–339.

McCall, R. B., Hogarty, P. S., and Hurlbut, N. (1972). Transitions in infant sensori-motor development and the prediction of childhood IQ. *Am. Psychol.*, **27**, 728–748.

McIlwain, H. (1970). Metabolic adaptation in the brain. *Nature*, **226**, 803.

McNeil, T. F., Persson-Blennow, I., and Kaji, L. (1974). Reproduction in female psychiatric patients: severity of mental disturbance near reproduction and rates of obstetric complications. *Acta Psychiat. Scand.*, **50** (1), 23–32.

Maccoby, E. E., and Jacklin, C. N. (1974). *The Psychology of Sex Differences*. London: Oxford University Press.

Malhotra, M. K. (1972). Geburtsgewicht, neurologischer Status and geistige Entwicklung. *Praxis der Kinderpsychologie und Kinderpsychiatrie*, **21**, 1, 22–30.

Massaro, T. F., Levitsky, D. A., and Barnes, R. H. (1977). Protein malnutrition induced during gestation: Its effects on pup development and mating behaviour. *Devel. Psychobiol.* **10** (4), 339–345.

Masterpasqua, F., Chapman, R. H., and Lore, R. K. (1976). The effects of prenatal psychological stress on the sexual behaviour and reactivity of male rats. *Devel. Psychobiol.*, **9** (5), 403–411.

Mata, L. J. (1974). The relationship of maternal infection to fetal growth and development. In J. Cravioto *et al.* (eds.), *Early Malnutrition and Mental Development*. Uppsala: Almqvist & Wiksell.

Millar, W. S. (1974). Conditioning and learning in early infancy. In B. Foss (ed.), *New Perspectives on Child Development*. Harmondsworth: Penguin.

Mirdal, G. M., Rosenthal, D., Wender, P. M., and Schulsinger, F. (1977). Perinatal complications in offspring of psychotic parents. *Br. J. Psychiat.*, **130**, 495–505.

Mistretta, C. M., and Bradley, R. M. (1975). Taste and swallowing in utero. *Br. Med. Bull.*, **31**, (1), 80–84.

Mura, E. L. (1974). Perinatal differences. A comparison of child psychiatric patients and their siblings. *Psychiat. Quart.*, **48** (2), 239–255.

Murdoch, B. D. (1968). Effects of pre-natal maternal decompression on EEG development of 3-year old children. *S. Afr. Med. J.*, **42**, 1067–1071.

Murdoch, B. D., Griesel, R. D., Burnett, L. S., and Bartel, P. R. (1976). Antenatal maternal decompression and CNS function in the child: cognitive, neurological and electrocortical investigation. *Psychologia Africana*, **16** (2), 117–123.

Ounstead, M., and Ounstead, C. (1973). *On Foetal Growth Rate*. London: Heinemann.

Palmqvist, H. (1975). The effect of heartbeat sound stimulation on the weight development of newborn infants. *Child Develop.*, **46** (1), 292–295.

Reinisch, J. M. (1974). Fetal hormones, the brain, and human sex differences: a heuristic, integrative review of the recent research. *Arch. Sexual Behav.*, **3** (1), 51–90.

Reinisch, J. M., and Karow, W. G. (1977). Prenatal exposure to synthetic progestins and estrogens: effects on human development. *Arch. Sexual Behav.*, **6** (4), 257–288.

Richardson, S. A. (1976). The relation of severe malnutrition in infancy to the intelligence of school children with differing life histories. *Pediat. Res.*, **10**, 57–61.

Rutter, M., and Madge, N. (1976). *Cycles of Disadvantage*. London: Heinemann.

Sabel, K. G., Olegard, R., and Victorin, L. (1976). Remaining sequelae with modern perinatal care. *Pediatrics*, **57**, 625–658.

Salk, L., (1973). The role of the heartbeat in the relations between mother and infant. *Sci. Amer.*, **228**, 5, 24–29.

Sameroff, A. J. (1975). Early influences on development: fact or fancy? *Merrill-Palmer Quart.*, **21** (4), 267–294.

Sameroff, A. J., and Chandler, M. J. (1975). Reproductive risk and the continuum of caretaking casualty. In F. D. Horowitz, (ed.), *Review of Child Development Research*, Vol. 4. Chicago: University of Chicago Press.

Schneirla, T. C. (1957). The concept of development in comparative psychology. In D. B. Harris, (ed.), *The Concept of Development*. Minneapolis: University of Minnesota Press.

Schulte, F. J. (1974). The neurological development of the neonate. In J. A., Davis, and J. Dobbing (eds.), *Scientific Foundations of Paediatrics*. London: Heinemann.

Smith, C. R., and Steinschneider, A. (1975). Differential effects of prenatal rhythmic stimulation on neonatal arousal states. *Child Develop.*, **46** (2), 574–578.

Sontag, L. W. (1966). Implications of fetal behavior and environment for adult personalities. *Ann. NY Acad. Sci.*, **134**, 782–786.

Spelt, D. K. (1948). The conditioning of the human fetus in utero. *J. Exp. Psychol.*, **38**, 338–346.

Stein, Z., Susser, M., Saenger, G., and Marolla, F. (1975). *Famine and Human Development: The Dutch Hunger Winter of 1944–1945*. New York: Oxford University Press.

Stone, D. H. (1976). Review of Z. Stein *et al.*, Famine and human development. *Devel. Med. Child Neurol.*, **18**, 825.

Stratton, P. M. (1977). Criteria for assessing the influence of obstetric circumstances on later development. In T. Chard, and M. Richards (eds.), *Benefits and Hazards of the New Obstetrics*. London: Heinemann.

Thomas, A., Chess, S., and Birch, H. (1968). *Temperament and Behavior Disorders in Children*. New York: New York University Press.

Timiras, P. S., Vernadakis, A., and Sherwood, N. M. (1968). Development and plasticity of the nervous system. In N. S. Assali (ed.), *The Biology of Gestation*, Vol. II: *The Fetus and Neonate*. London and New York: Academic Press.

Tizard, J. (1974). Early malnutrition, growth and mental development in man. *Br. Med. Bull.*, **30** (2), 169–174.

Turnbull, A. C., and Woodford, F. P. (eds.) (1976). *Prevention of Handicap Through Antenatal Care*. Amsterdam: Elsevier.

Walker, D., Grimwade, J., and Wood, C. (1971). Intrauterine noise: a component of the fetal environment. *Am. J. Obst. Gynec.*, **109**, 91–95.

Weitzman, E. D., and Graziani, L. J. (1968). Maturation and topography of auditory evoked response of the prematurely born infant. *Devel. Psychobiol.*, **1** (2), 79.

Wiele, R. L. van de, (1974). (Discussion). The effect of hormones on the development of behaviour. In R. C. Friedman, R. M. Richart, R. L. van de Wiele, and L. O. Stern (eds.), *Sex Differences in Behaviour*, p. 77. New York: Wiley.

Wiener, S. G., Fitzpatrick, K. M., Levin, R., Smotherman, W. P., and Levine, S. (1977). Alterations in the maternal behavior of rats rearing malnourished offspring. *Devel. Psychobiol.*, **10** (3), 243–254.

Winick, M. (ed.) (1974). Nutrition and metal development. *Current Concepts in Nutrition*, Vol. 2. New York: Wiley.

Wynn, M., and Wynn, A. (1977). *Prevention of Preterm Birth.* London: Foundation for Education and Research in Child-Bearing.

Yang, R. K., and Halverson, C. F. (1976). A study of the 'inversion of intensity' between newborn and pre-school-age behavior. *Child Develop.*, **47**, 350–359.

Foundations of Psychosomatics
Edited by M. J. Christie and P. G. Mellett
© 1981 John Wiley & Sons Ltd.

4

INDIVIDUAL DIFFERENCES IN THE FIRST WEEK OF LIFE

MAGGIE MILLS
Department of Psychology, University of Reading, England.

NEWBORN CAPABILITIES

From birth, babies display organized, replicable patterns of behaviour, and from the beginning hold a reciprocal relationship with their environment. As part of a large study on the interrelationship of certain pre- peri- and postnatal variables* we were able to observe 116 infants for the first hour after delivery, beginning time-sampled observations of behaviour as they delivered. (Rosenblatt and Packer, 1978). In the first 20 minutes, three-quarters of the subjects spontaneously scanned their world (mean scan time 3.7 minutes) and when, after 20 minutes, we tested the visual and auditory responses of those infants who were alert (88 per cent), using part of the Brazelton Neonatal Assessment Scale (1973), we found that most infants changed their behaviour on auditory stimulation and were capable of some focused following. There was much individual variation (see Figure 4.1) but some babies were performing extremely well on the visual measures.

Visual perception

Despite evidence of ocular motor immaturity, experimental studies with newborns confirm the naturalistic observations we were able to make in the first hour of life. The neonate, 1 or 2 days old, can direct his gaze to part of the environment. Using a corneal reflection technique, Mendelson and Haith (1976) demonstrated better eye control, smaller eye movements and smoother scanning in darkness (using infrared film) than in light. In view of these findings, the argument that only reflexive visual activity is present in newborns makes little sense. Salapatek (1975) has shown different scanning patterns depending on whether the infant is viewing a homogeneous visual field or the presence of black–white figures. With the latter, foveal fixations cluster on regions of contour with frequent edge crossings and are adapted to the size of the figure. Haith also found a prevalence of horizontal eye movements at birth which is conducive to vertical contour scanning. Further, Miranda (1970), using a visual

* Joint Bedford College/St Mary's Hospital Medical School project on the effects of obstetrical medication on the human neonate, funded by the MRC.

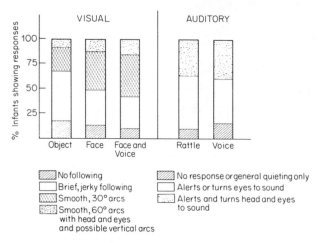

FIGURE 4.1. Visual and auditory responses to inanimate and
animate stimuli in the first hour after birth

preference technique, found longer fixations for patterns with more or larger
details and for curved contours. There seems little doubt, then, that newborns
can modify their pattern of visual scanning according to target features, and
are capable of contour discrimination. This is likely to be more important than
the content of early perceptual experience.

If we examine other motor systems, 2-day-old babies have conjugate fixations and eye movements (Hershenson, 1964) and show convergence (Slater,
1975). The earliest, systematic study of co-ordinated head and eye movements,
under strictly controlled conditions, was carried out by Tronick and Clanton
(1971) when infants were 1 month of age. The four search patterns that they
described as typical of adult functioning, were observed by the author while
administering visual attention measures to babies in the first week of life.
(Our sample comprised 145 infants, each of whom was tested three times in the
first week.)

The newborn eye movement system also codes target direction. Radial
location of moving objects in the first week of life is suggested by the fact that
infants' avoidance responses can be elicited by a moving object on a hit path
but not by a similar object whose trajectory would not result in a collision
(Ball and Tronick, 1971; Bower, 1977). Butterworth (1978) suggests an innate
link between optical flow patterns and the child's relation to external space
which would allow an infant to make allowances for changes of posture independently of motor activity.

Studies on the perception of the location of stationary objects in space which
use pre-reaching (Trevarthen, Hubley, and Shevren, 1975) or adjusted hand-
swiping (Bower, Broughton, and Moore, 1970) as the dependent variable would
be strong evidence of spatial perception at birth since they take account of
the distal properties of stimulation. Unfortunately, they are flawed by difficul-

ties of interpretation, and Dodwell, Muir and Difranco (1976) failed to replicate Bower's findings. There is, however, convincing evidence (Harris and Macfarlane, 1974) on the location of peripheral targets.

Neonates can locate a peripheral target within 25 degrees of visual angle although this is reduced to 15 degrees of visual angle if there is also a central target (Macfarlane, Harris, and Barnes, 1976). Interestingly, the extent of the first saccadic eye movement taken to locate the target depends on target distance (Aslim and Salapatek, 1975) and the latency to initiate the saccade is greater at 1 than at 7 weeks of age. So while there is clearly development in the early weeks, the neonatal perceptual system can code object position accurately, and probably use feedback to monitor position changes (see Harris, 1977 for discussion).

Further work by Bower, Broughton, and Moore, (1971) with respect to external space, shows that neonates can perceive stereoscopic depth in Julesz random dot patterns. As for object constancy and the constancy of an object's identity as the object's position in space or time varies, empirical investigation does not seem to begin on subjects younger than 6 weeks of age at the earliest (Day and MacKenzie, 1971) and is therefore beyond the scope of this review.

Auditory perception

Several studies now (Hutt et al., 1968; Bench, 1973; Hecox, 1975, and Weir, 1976 and 1978) indicate high-frequency loss for the newborn. When compared to an adult evoked potential, the neonate has a 20 dB loss and this loss is greater for the higher frequencies—that is those above 1 kHz (Hecox, 1975). When tested asleep in an auditory response cradle, using reflex movement and respiration change as indications of acoustic sensitivity, Bennett (1978) found that 50 per cent of newborns would respond to an intensity of 74 dB sound pressure level (SPL) for 250 Hz and 85 dB SPL for 1 kHz. Weir (1978) found comparable values, but was forced to conclude that variability in responding is the main feature of the neonatal auditory system in the first week, since none of her 18 babies responded to all five sine wave tones, and on average only 50 per cent of subjects responded to each stimulus. In a later experiment, with louder stimuli an increase of 5 dB on the threshold of the first experiment) 75 per cent of a larger sample of infants responded to each frequency.

Using stimuli that resemble the human voice in differing degrees, we have seen the same variability in neonatal responding in our laboratory. In one experiment (Mc Bride, 1978) 12 infants between 3 and 7 days old heard, contingent on their sucking activity, either a natural female voice, the fundamental frequency of that natural voice, or recorded from the larynx a simulated fundamental frequency recording which had certain characteristics altered. A natural laryngograph recording is composed of vocal fold vibration which determines the fundamental frequency of voiced sounds, and is the primary physical correlate of their pitch. Thus, babies were hearing intonation patterns with characteristics changed, or intonation patterns without any vocal tract contribution to the sound. It was found that subjects either suppressed sucking when hearing the voice stimuli, or increased their rate, but which response occurred varied between infants and sometimes even within an infant.

A second experiment videotaped responses to changes between periods of natural voice and laryngograph, which were delivered not contingent on the infant sucking, although a pacifier was available to them. Again, large individual differences in responding were observed in sucking, in state changes, in startling to sound, and in other motor activity. Although the behaviour was not very law-abiding, an analysis of the videotapes clearly showed that voice-like sounds are discriminated by infants in the first week of life.

Interestingly, normal auditory stimuli result in delayed responsiveness for this age-group, which suggests some higher nervous system immaturity. Anatomically, the auditory system is advanced at birth: the inner ear reaches adult maturation at 30 weeks gestation and the external auditory meatus is complete at birth (Northern and Downs, 1974). Middle-ear resistance also occurs in the first week of life (Bennett, 1975). Weir (1976) has suggested that the greater hearing loss which neonates exhibit for 2 and 4 Hz, rather than for 125 and 250 Hz tones, when compared to adults, could be a result of the neonate possessing bone conduction hearing only.

Fourcin (1978) suggests that low-frequency, square-wave forms are effective stimulation to neonates because of the preferential masking of high-frequency energy by low, in hearing. He suggests that incomplete myelinization at birth impedes high-frequency transmission rates rather than low-frequency rates. He further suggests that the nature of the voiced speech sounds, which the newborn hears most often, is such that their greatest energy is at the fundamental frequency which will have the greatest pulling power for the young baby's auditory attention. For diagnostic purposes in identifying neonates with hearing loss, a methodological advance has been achieved with the auditory response cradle (Bennett, 1975), in providing a more adequate control of state and a reliable sound-delivery system. But the high rate of response failure that Weir reports makes it difficult to provide a normative account of the neonate's early acoustic sensitivity and data on the developmental course of their response variability are still needed.

Intersensory co-ordination

The newborn exhibits a certain measure of intersensory co-ordination. Motor quietening certainly occurs to auditory stimulation (see Figure 4.1). The orienting reflex can be elicited by sound, as can the direction of the oculogyric reflex, so that when presented with a sound the newborn will turn his eyes to look at the place the sound came from (Butterworth and Castillo, 1976). Turkewitz et al. (1966), after an experimental investigation of this phenomenon in newborns using electro-oculography, concluded that reflexive organization was indicated since the stimuli they used were brief and the ocular-motor response was found to be state-dependent. Loud sounds produced eye movements away from the source and soft sounds produced the opposite. It has also been shown that babies, if supported, will orient their bodies towards a visual target in a co-ordinated way (Bullinger, 1976).

Using the corneal reflection technique, judges blind to the experimental condition, and normal 1-to 4-day-old infants, Haith (1979) investigated the types of relations between vision and audition. Sound presented at midline in a blank visual field caused the newborn to increase eye-opening, centralize fixations and constrain them, and generally manifest more eye control. Sound presented at midline of a stimulus again centralized fixations, but did not increase other activity. Sound presented laterally caused an initial fixation towards the source and then fixations away from it, and concentrated figure scanning. The type of sound, whether it was a voice or tone, made no difference. Thus auditory spatial information influenced visual activity.

It may well be that a newborn lacks differentiation between the senses— he may not know whether he is hearing or seeing something but these data suggest that he may be predisposed to learn about spatially related events and is an integrated organism from the outset. Sound, as Haith says, initiates the scanning routine which enables him to find a visual change which is perhaps associated with an auditory change. This investigation complements Piaget's contention that the most important task of the early months of life is to coordinate the processing activities of different modalities.

Inter-modal equivalence

Maratos (1973) played tapes to infants, under a month old, reproducing their own cry and other vocalizations. From analysis of her tapes she suggested tentatively that infants this age were capable of matching their previous auditory output. Meltzoff and Moore (1977) suggest that imitation of visually and proprioceptively perceived models is indeed an innate ability of newborn infants. In an admirably controlled study they presented 18 infants ranging in age from between 12 and 21 days with a live human face to look at. Mouth-openings, tongue-protrusion, lip-protrusion and sequential finger movements were shown to the infants for a 15 second stimulus period after which the newborn's responses were videotaped for a further 20 seconds. To prevent the model's movements being influenced by the baby's attempts to copy, a dummy was put into the babies' mouths for the second experiment.

Taped segments of the responses were judged by people who did not know what condition the babies were looking at. They were asked to decide whether behaviour described by the categories they were given—mouth-opening, tongue-protrusion etc.—occurred or not. A better control might have been for them to describe the behaviour they saw, rather than it being suggested to them that they look for the specific behaviours the baby saw the model perform. It was found that significantly more tongue-protrusion responses occurred after that gesture had been presented by the model than during either the baseline period or the mouth-opening session. The same occurred for mouth-opening, so that neonates, albeit a small sample, were shown to imitate tongue-protrusion and mouth-opening reliably. It seems unlikely that such a complicated task, requiring an active matching process mediated by some abstract representational system, could already have been acquired in the first days of life, especially since this procedure has now been successfully used with several newborns. It is hard to think of a more useful device for successful interaction with a caretaker than the ability Meltzoff recently demonstrated.

Autonomic reactivity

Autonomic indices such as heart-rate, electrodermal activity, and respiration, when taken in conjunction with behavioural measures, can be used to reflect the infant's interest in parts of his early environment (Clifton and Nelson, 1976). They may help to identify aversive responses (Lipsitt, 1976) and they may also help in the interpretation of the meaning of infant responses. They may also be important as one component of emotional responsivity which is just beginning to attract the researcher's attention again (Sroufe, 1979; Zelazo, 1972; Campos, 1976; Watson, 1970). Venables (1980), however, points out that heart-rate measures, which are extremely well documented in the first weeks, boast hardly any longitudinal studies, while normative electrodermal data on infants are sparse, and little is known of autonomic activity that accompanies newborn motor behaviour.

Cardiac responding

The infant heart-rate literature (Lewis, 1974; Clifton, 1974) suggests that most stimuli produce acceleration in the newborn, a response that has been linked to high-intensity stimuli and a defensive reaction. Cardiac responding is, however, maximally influenced by state, and since neonates spend a goodly part of their day asleep this artifact may have promoted the belief that neonates were only capable of accelerated heart-rate responses until around 4 months of age (Berg, Berg, and Graham, 1971). Heart-rate, of course, can either increase or decrease to a stimulus and, following work with adult humans (Lacey, 1967), a decelerative response is considered a component of the orienting reflex. It appears that decelerative responses can in fact be elicited in newborns with stimuli of moderate intensity, either visual or auditory, and with auditory stimuli having a slow rise time (Samaroff, Cashmore, and Dykes, 1973, Kearsley, 1973).

The nature of the response is, however, extremely delicate; Pomeleau-Malcuit and Clifton (1973) for instance, found that sleeping neonates presented with the tactile stimulus of a pinch on the earlobe had accelerated heart-rates regardless of whether the tactile stimulus elicited a motor response, but when they were presented with a stroke on the chin (a function stimulus which promotes the rooting reflex), their heart-rate decelerated. There was heart-rate acceleration in the latter situation only if the infant produced a motor response to the tactile stimulus. As was mentioned earlier, by far the most important determinant of heart-rate responding is state. Heart-rate responding to the same stimuli may differ in two groups of infants, depending on how soon the newborn passes into a drowsy condition preparatory to going to sleep. Even when, behaviourally, they qualify for testing as being in an alert state, Clifton and Nelson (1976), with 2-day-old subjects, and Lewis, Day and Harnitz (1969) with 2-week-old subjects, found that awake subjects gave heart-rate decelerations to initial tone presentations, as if habituating, but showed accelerations as they actually fell asleep. Thus, habituation or state change can be evidenced by decelerative or accelerative responding; a change from wakefulness to sleep appears to negate habituation.

It seems clear that developmental changes in heart-rate are occurring. The third-trimester foetus has a primarily accelerative response (Sontag, Steel, and Lewis, 1969; Tanaka and Arayama, 1969). Heart-rate in premature infants (Berkson, Wasserman, and Behrman, 1974) shows the same pattern. Clifton's neonatal data make it clear that the adult decelerative pattern can be demonstrated in neonates but Adkinson and Berg (1976) were able to show better heart-rate habituation even in 3-day-old babies compared with 1-day-old subjects. It may well be that as the time infants spend in a spontaneously alert state increases, so does the adult pattern of heart-rate response become definitely established (Berg, Berg, and Graham, 1971).

Electrodermal Activity

Skin conductance and skin potential measures, while apparently recordable from birth (for general review see Venables, 1978) have scarcely been exploited in infant research as part of the responses of a total system. Newborns in the first 2 days of life, when stimulated by light, tones, and odours amongst other stimuli, gave electrodermal responses to only 18 per cent of the stimuli, of which an 80 dB tone was the most effective (Crowell et al., 1965). SCR latencies were short (0.7–1.4 seconds), recovery times were similar to adult values (2.4–3.8 seconds), but the rise times were quite different from adult values. Skin conductance levels in newborns have also been sampled (Kaye, 1964). Testing on palmar and plantar sites was done over 4 days and, after an initial fall in the first few hours, a rising developmental trend was reported.

Responding is again influenced by state (Weller and Bell, 1965) so that the higher the state attained in Prechtl terms, the higher the levels of conductance that were obtained. Developmentally, it is of interest that Appel et al. (1971) found skin potential, but not skin conductance responses, from 1-month-old subjects when they were presented with auditory stimulation. The present interest in children's autonomic responding comes from studies which seek to predict later psychiatric breakdown from these measures, or to use them in treating hyperkinetic childhood behaviour, and described in the next chapter. Given the relative difficulty of eliciting electrodermal activity in neonatal subjects, together with the early lack of heart-rate stability, it is perhaps unlikely that these measures can ever be used in the early weeks for their predictive force.

Olfactory perception

MacFarlane (1975) carried out an ingenious experiment in which he used the newborn's head-turning response as an indication of its ability to discriminate the smell of its mother's breast milk from that of another lactating mother. Forty-seven term infants, when they were 2 days of age, did not make significantly more head-turns to their mother's breast pad when lying inert on their cot, but by 10 days a significantly greater number of infants was making more head-turns to the assumedly familiar smell. In a further experiment, it appeared that at birth discrimination may be possible, but that only later in the first week can the infant use smell to locate the preferred stimulus. Laboratory work supports MacFarlane's findings for Lipsitt, Engen, and Kaye, (1963) in an admirably controlled study found that habituation of respiration responses occurred in neonates in a constant sleep state within 10 trials, when the odorants presented were such combinations as anise with asafoetida, and amyl acetate with heptanal. Response recovery was demonstrated when one of these smells, presented at original intensity, was presented alone.

Taste perception

Johnson and Salisbury (1975) demonstrated that newborns in the first week of life exhibited different patterns of sucking and breathing, depending on whether they were drinking human or artificial milk. They observed 44 normal infants sucking on a specially designed bottle with an electromagnetic flow transducer, which measured milk volume swallowed (mean volume per suck was found to be 0.6 ml), and which also had a valve system which allowed a smooth flow of milk without negative pressure building up during sucking. It was demonstrated that infants in the first 48 hours swallow water and do not inhale it, but prolonged apnoea was easily induced by feeding saline.

Human infants typically suck in bursts interspersed with pauses. When cow's milk is delivered, the same total number of sucks as for human milk was recorded over each 1-minute test period, but the inter-suck interval was much greater for cow's milk — 1.5 as opposed to 0.5 per second. The total number of breaths is also reduced during cow's milk feeding, and there are longer intervals between breaths. Breast milk feeding produced far greater variation in sucking pattern. The authors conclude that there may be one or more chemosensory afferent pathways in the upper airway of the human neonate, and its stimulation during feeding modifies the sucking rhythm and the breathing pattern, so that discrimination for different types of fluid—perhaps in terms of viscosity—can be seen.

This study raises the question of whether artificial milk feeding as opposed to breast milk has a different effect on the neuroegulation of breathing. There may be implications for cases of sudden infant death. It is suggested that the interrelationship between sucking, swallowing, and breathing, which is one of the most sophisticated feats the newborn must achieve, may be of value in providing an assessment measure of 'the effects of a natural challenge to respiration'.

Crook and Lipsitt (1976) who have demonstrated that the quantitative properties of fluid delivered during nutritive feeding also affect sucking rhythm and autonomic activity, have commented that observations from the Brown University Child Study Centre suggest newborns often have difficulty with fast fluid flow when taken from a normal bottle if the solution is of low viscosity. They also conclude that 'failure to adjust the rhythm of sucking and swallowing may result in temporary respiration occlusion and bradycardia'. Lipsitt (1976) supposes that practice in these congenital patterns of behaviour such as sucking, breathing, and swallowing may be essential.

Thoman, Miane, and Freesem, (1977) screened respiration and apnoeic attacks in 22 term infants, by monitoring their behaviour asleep at home over a 2-week period. Infants showing little apnoea differed from the rest of the group in having variable respirations in sleep and marked instability. Although periods of apnoea during sucking and in sleep may be different, it is argued that those infants with little experience of coping with apnoea may be in difficulty if additionally stressed. Soule (1974) reports heart-rate variability in a subject who had sudden infant death syndrome (SIDS). Hoppenbrouwers (1977) gathered information on the respiration rates of siblings of SIDS infants and found higher rates of respiration at 3 and 6 weeks of age than amongst a control group. The evidence is fairly tenuous, but the suggestion is that respiration patterns exhibiting low amounts of apnoea in early sleep may be genetically determined, and perhaps predispose certain infants to SIDS.

Taste discrimination in the newborn was also found by Crook and Lipsitt (1976) in a series of experiments, one of which changed the fluid to be sucked from less sweet to sweeter fluids. They found that the mean heart-rate for the subjects became progressively higher, although a slower sucking rate was seen, due to longer inter-suck intervals. This paradoxical phenomenon is interpreted as the engagement of a hedonistic or savouring response, which Lipsitt suggests occurs in naturalistic conditions where the infant is offered the opportunity to self-regulate. The argument goes that if elevated heart-rate were just to mean increased energy expenditure then it is odd that slower sucking is not accompanied by lower rather than higher heart-rate, which is, in fact, found to be the case. Incidentally, this series of findings on sucking patterns and taste may render obsolete the received view that non-nutritive and nutritive sucking rhythms are qualitatively different and probably organized by different brain mechanisms.

SLEEP CYCLES AND STATE OF AROUSAL

It has been shown that the human newborn experiences a period of prolonged alertness immediately after delivery (Rosenblatt and Packer, 1978) and spends several hours awake on day one (Theorell et al., 1973; Trevarthen, 1975). As the first week progresses, less frequent periods of quiet alertness are seen with a corresponding increase in sleeping time (Thoman, 1975). Such findings are confirmed by studies of neonatal electroencephalogram (EEG) at this time. It has been shown (Kleitman, 1963) that the basic activity and rest cycle (BRAC) is approximately 50 minutes in the newborn infant; half that of the human adult.

In the first week of life, we found bouts of sleep lasted 40 minutes or less, although, due to hospital routine, not all awakenings were spontaneous. Wolff (1973) reports that the mean duration of quiet sleep after birth is 20 minutes, and no developmental trend is seen up to 3 months of age. Active sleep lasts for about the same period. Organization of sleep patterns, however, changes fast. At first, 60 per cent of deep sleep is preceded or followed by active sleep (Prechtl, 1974). Korner (1972) found that approximately one quarter of active sleep periods were preceded by quiet sleep after birth. In general, however, the infant does move through intervening states when progressing from wakefulness to quiet sleep, and vice-versa. Wolff (1973) found that direct transitions from quiet sleep to wakefulness occurred only in about 1 per cent of newborns and he never saw changes in the opposite direction.

Clifton and Nelson (1976) point out that the concept of an underlying periodicity to behaviour implies quantitative changes in arousal along a continuum, yet the neonatal data base does not support such an underlying arousal continuum. Bell and Haaf (1971) tried to treat state measures as if they belonged on a continuum from low (sleep) to high (crying). They found no correlation between changes in the sucking response or the prone-head reflex, and state. In the face of so much evidence to the contrary (see Clifton and Nelson's review in 1976) it may be inappropriate to order state measures in a continuous linear fashion. Most infant researchers, therefore, have specified qualitative state categories which range from deep sleep with regular respiration and no startles, to light sleep characterized by irregular respiration and the presence of REM, through to drowsy behaviour, alert wakefulness, fretting with high motor activity and some vocalization, and finally, full-blown, rhythmic crying that occurs for more than a certain period of time. It is certainly the case that qualitatively different states of organization can be seen in the human newborn, similar to those described above, and the response characteristics that can be elicited, experimentally or socially, from newborns will vary, depending on which state the infant is in (Prechtl, 1974; Korner, 1972; Thoman, 1975). Both the intensity of an individual response in any response system and the organizational patterns across various response systems change as a function of state. Reactivity must be viewed as a function of state together with response system, stimulus modality and intensity and prandial condition (Ashton, 1973).

Nevertheless, if discreet categories are used, transitional states, perhaps best exemplified by drowsy behaviour, then become a problem; for instance heart-rate responding (Clifton and Nelson, 1976), pattern of sucking rhythm on a non-nutritive teat (McBride, 1978) and sleep patterns (Wolff, 1973; Parmelee and Stern, 1972) show marked changes as the infant becomes drowsy. Also, as Clifton points out, as response orientation changes from state to state, 'so does the nature of potentially confounding influences of state change'. State changes, for instance, can mimic habituation phenomena or even look like disinhabituation.

Bennett (1978) doubts that even time-sampled observations of behavioural state are subtle enough to indicate a transitional period of state change, which can be done by recording heart-rate, respiration, and EEG (Prechtl, Akiyamaya, and Grant, 1968). While, for experimental purposes, electrodes can be put in place during the infant's sleep, naturalistic observation, particularly of social behaviour, precludes simultaneous recording of autonomic phenomena. Clifton suggests that state changes should not be allowed to occur for experimental purposes; in which case, procedures must be brief and discards are likely. Perturbed by most neonatal researchers' inattention to the limitations of state, Clifton and Nelson (1976) calculated, from data available, the state changes and state duration criteria that would be expected for unstimulated infants who entered their specified initial state spontaneously. Adjustments would be needed for intensity of stimulation, and it is important to mark the difference between manipulated and spontaneous state. A whole range of experimental treatments available in the literature was then evaluated and it was found that in over 90 per cent of infants the procedures were of such a length that it would be reasonable to expect state changes to occur, yet these were mostly either ignored, or not reported.

Another solution is to monitor changes of state concomitantly, and correlate them with experimental conditions (Moffit, 1971) such that state change becomes a dependent variable. Almost any environmental change is likely to produce a state change, while state can also be determined by temperature, continuous auditory stimulation, and swaddling, whether the baby is propped vertically, and if testing occurs pre- or post-prandially. Visual and auditory responsiveness depends on feeding, as do periods of quiet sleep. Even the type of feeding can produce differences since breast-fed babies often have periods of alertness prior to feeding, and bottle-fed infants are found to be alert afterwards (Wolff, 1973).

Ninety per cent of alert periods in the newborn last less than 10 minutes (Berg, Berg, and Graham, 1971) unless they occur during feeding. Brown et al. (1975) reported that during feeding sessions, newborns kept their eyes open for nearly half of the 30 minutes' observation period, and were most likely to have their eyes open when the mother presented the bottle. Time alert shows a rapidly accelerating developmental trend (Wolff, 1973), but we have frequently noted that interesting stimuli, such as the live human face, can maintain orientation and alertness for much longer periods in the first week of life. At delivery, the infant typically shifted into a new state about every 90 seconds, and 75 per cent of infants never went into state I or II (Rosenblatt and Packer, 1978). From day 1 onwards three-quarters of the infants were in a predominantly alert state during administration of the Brazelton neonatal assessment. By day 3, three-quarters of the sample were attentive to human face and voice. It may well be that in a social context, the duration of unstimulated periods of alertness is less relevant as a condition of infant learning than is the ability to come to, and maintain, an appropriate state for the type of stimulation on offer.

Substantial individual differences between newborns have already been discussed, such as the predominance of a particular state and state lability, but individual differences and consistencies in state cycling have been reported for neonates. Thoman (1975) took behavioural measures of state on 24 infants for an hour in the morning and another hour in the afternoon of the same day. She found significant correlations for quiet sleep and active sleep when this was later divided into three different types—no REM, with REM, and dense REM. Taking all states together, both waking and sleeping, in 41 infants, there was no intercorrelation on time spent in each, but when all state categories were clustered empirically so that, for instance, active sleep went with waking activity and crying, then the newborn's organizational system was found to be reliable. Thoman suggests that individual profiles of sleep and state cycling of this kind might be of use clinically in identifying SIDS in infancy, or, as Dreyfuss-Brisac (1974) showed, in assessing the mother–infant relationship.

In contrast, Dittrichova et al. (1976) took physiological recordings through the first 5 months of life, and provided EEG, respiration, REM, and body-movement records. Early individual differences in the duration of quiet sleep faded out and no striking differences in paradoxical sleep were seen. EEG patterns and frequency of respiration during quiet sleep showed stable individual differences, as did the frequency of rapid-eye movements and body movements during paradoxical sleep. Sleep-bout duration did not reflect individual differences, perhaps because it forms part of a complicated homeostatic mechanism which is still maturing at birth. Both these studies were carried out in specific controlled conditions and may not generalize beyond them.

An infant's behavioural state is perhaps the most salient characteristic he presents to his environment and can be easily manipulated. Developmental trends are shown for almost all aspects that have been discussed here. Adequate documentation of these trends, together with an understanding of the individual differences that occur and their possible significance, are essential for both clinical and experimental evaluation of the newborn. Concomitant with these trends is, of course, neurological development, while behavioural states in infancy are often correlated with patterning of physiological responses. Some associations between state and neurological defects are also known to occur. Infants with a birthweight which is low in comparison to their gestational age have an immature EEG (Schulte et al., 1972) and deviations in sleep patterns can be shown for children with mongolism or phyenylketonuria and for those suffering from high bilirubinaemia levels (Prechtl, Theorell, and Blair, 1973). Ornitz and co-workers (1969) have also shown a delay in the development of sleep patterns for autistic children. The relationship between individual differences in state and subsequent behaviour is discussed later on in this chapter.

INFANT TESTING

It is now time to ask how this increased cognizance of the neonate's perceptual abilities and response repertoire is used in current assessment. With some exceptions (Brazelton, 1973; Miranda *et al.*, 1977) descriptive infant psychometrics has not explored with much imagination the range of abilities we now know infants possess. Successful infancy assessment measures are themselves in their infancy.

Traditionally, the medical profession has relied on the 1- and 5-minute Apgar (1953) score, taken immediately after birth as a check on the status of the newborn. Such a procedure does not pick up delayed stress signals common even in normal babies (Brazelton, 1970). In our obstetrical analgesia study the Apgar score failed to correlate with other, more sophisticated, behavioural measures taken after delivery. Other work on obstetrical medication (Thalme, Belfrage, and Raabe, 1974, Wingate, 1974) indicates that the Apgar measure does not differentiate experimental from control groups.

Routine neurological examinations of the human newborn—for instance, those of Prechtl and Beintema (1964), Dargassies (1952), and Touwen (1977) have no predictive value except in cases of gross motor damage (Miranda *et al.*, 1977). These tests tap none of the basic intellectual skills of infants which this chapter has elaborated on, and even where abnormal signs are reported in the first weeks, these fail to correlate with later performance (Kalverboer, 1975). Dargassies (1977) claims that diagnosis of quite gross damage can often not be confirmed with any accuracy until 8 months of age. Touwen (1977) recently devised a quickly administered test (a duration of 10 minutes) based on the fuller Prechtl scales, but its validity is in question since, of the 48 babies tested, half proved to be false-positives when their performance was correlated with that obtained from a full Prechtl examination.

Also, the Prechtl examination, like other later development tests, such as the Griffiths (1964) or the Bayley (1969), relentlessly tests motor activity, but we have little evidence, either intuitively or experimentally, that testing motor activity can tell us anything in a direct way about cognitive development (see Zelazo (1977) for an account of babies with cerebral palsy and infants damaged by thalidomide poisoning). Even where, as with the Brazelton Neonatal Assessment Scale, neuromotor behaviours have been discarded in favour of a multi-dimensional approach, reflex indices are still included. Rosenblith (1974) in an enormous sample of over 1000 newborns looked in an enlightened way at various different indices of functioning at birth, but still correlated these with the Bayley scale at 8 months of age. Not surprisingly, continuities were most soundly demonstrated on motor variables such as muscle tone, tactile adaptation, and motor activity.

The practice of sampling a large range of different baby behaviours has now popularly displaced the single variable investigation. (The latter, for instance, might be like the Bell sucking test (Bell, 1975) which measures rate and latency to cry on removal of the teat and tries somewhat unsuccessfully to relate these measures to later temperamental difficulties in children.) A multivariable—or pot-pourri approach, as it has been called—has the advantage of observing those behaviours—alert-looking, and listening, habituation to relevant stimuli and adaptation to new stimuli that could be regarded as socially useful in early interaction with a caretaker. (For an itemized account of the Brazelton Neonatal Assessment Scale see Table 4.1). Such an approach also takes account of integrated behaviour such as that described earlier, i.e. sucking and looking, or listening and turning to sound. It also explores the interactive nature of infant behaviour—drowsy babies do not suck or even show good motor tone, while alert attention to stimuli is difficult to elicit in the fretful, crying or hungry baby (Thoman, 1975).

Relevant as auditory and visual processing and systematic state changes are to interaction, tests like those of Brazelton and Rosenblith are open to the criticism that they do not describe what the infant does for most of the first week of life—viz. sleeping, sucking and crying. Yang, Federman, and Duithiet, (1976) has devised a dimensional analysis of baby behaviour that seeks to describe each individual baby by deriving factors of behaviour from 26 variables, measured during periods of spontaneous activity and sleep. Some induced behaviour is included, and observations are taken over a 6-hour period. The factors they obtain are reactivity/irritability which would be similar to responses obtained from the Brazelton measures of fretting and crying and aversive stimulation (Bakow, 1973) and may correspond to the 15 per cent of consistently irritable babies seen in our own sample. A second factor was a description of maturity that included body size, gestational age, high respiration rate and low autonomic variability during sleep, and a third factor featured high-frequency sucking and infants who were sensitive to differences in sucking stimuli. Clifton and Nelson (1976) put average alert periods for babies in the first week of life at a few minutes only, but according to diary data, our sample showed that they had average sleep periods of only 40 minutes at a time. While these times may be attributable to the exigencies of hospital routine, the potential for displaying the behaviour studied in the Brazelton assessments may be greater for infants than had previously been supposed.

More recently still (Miranda et al., 1977; Hack, Mastow, and Miranda 1976; Soule, 1978) have used a technique which confined sampling to a fairly small number of theoretically determined responses, usually of the information-processing kind. This kind of approach, particularly with babies at risk, may prove more fruitful than simply collecting clusters of global characteristics.

Having collected normative visual fixation responses to pattern stimuli for low-risk term newborns, premature infants, and Down-syndrome subjects (Miranda and Fantz, 1973), Miranda et al. (1977) took 33 premature infants (average gestation age 34 weeks with a mean birthweight of 1.9 kg) who were considered to be at risk because of perinatal, antenatal, or neonatal difficulties, and tested their latency to fixate and the duration of their fixation when they were at 39 weeks' gestational age. They also received a paediatric neurological examination. An observer, using a criterion of target and pupil overlap in judging the corneal reflection in the baby's eye, rated each infant's visual performance as normal (strong preference for stimuli in two-choice task with prominent patterning, evidenced by accurate, open-eyed fixation of short latency and some scanning and motor quieting) or abnormal, if the infant failed to fixate despite open eyes, or had consistently deviant fixations as judged by the behaviour of the several hundred other low-risk, term infants that the experimenters had already tested. Follow-ups were based on autopsies, and on infant psychological tests administered at 18 months, or between the ages of 3 and 5 years. Of the 23 infants rated normal on the visual test soon after birth, only one had a developmental quotient (DQ) below 70, and 3 had an IQ below 84, on later testing. Of the 8 babies rated abnormal at birth, none was found to be functioning normally on follow-up. Over all, the predictions made on fixation tests were correct in 27 out of the 33 infants, while the neurological examination only made correct predictions in 21 cases.

It is likely that this kind of responsivity to the environment is among the highest forms of neurological functioning of which the neonatal brain is capable, but the authors view their results as preliminary, because their tests failed to discriminate differentially 5 infants whose IQ was below 84 points on follow-up. Further, while this technique clearly has potential and is relatively easy to administer, we still lack data on its efficacy with clinically normal populations. Developmentally, a visual rating scale (Hack et al., 1976) derived from these measures and including binocular viewing, scanning, eye brightening and interruption of sucking behaviour on presentation of the stimuli has proved of value. Hack et al. (1976) took 25 pre-term infants not suffering from respiration problems or jaundice and tested them at 31 weeks and then again at 35 weeks. Their rating improved two whole points during that period with fixation behaviour increasing in frequency. It would be useful to regard this measure as one of degree of alertness but unfortunately no state observations were taken. Visual focusing, orientation, and habituation measures were also taken by Soule (1978) on 19 babies aged 2–3 days (birthweight on average 2.6 kg) whose mothers were on methadone. Visual processing was found to be extremely poor while auditory processing was not affected. Using Brazelton-type measures, sick infants were described as labile in state, difficult to console, hypertonic, and tremulous. It is not clear, however, whether the observers knew these babies were likely to suffer withdrawal symptoms.

Methodological problems in infant assessment

None of the new procedures that have been described escapes the methodological difficulties peculiar to infant research. First, there is the supreme difficulty of attributing meaning to infant responses, which will be discussed in more detail later. Second, while the choice of variables depends on the researcher's interest, the type of medication being studied, or the kind of 'at-risk' population being evaluated, they are usually only sampled cross-sectionally, so that no measures of their stability can be established. For early infant auditory responses, variability across an hour's session is apparently the norm (Weir, 1976). It can be shown (Lipsitt *et al.*, 1976) that newborn heart-rate pattern is predictable between testing sessions, but few researchers have documented the consistency of a particular response when it is measured repeatedly in the same day. Yang *et al.* (1976) in the study previously mentioned, observed 137 3-day-old babies for two 3-hourly periods which were separated only by 30 minutes. Heart-rate measures, respiration, eye movements, and continuous observation of state assessments were made. For the last half-hour's sucking, prone-head responses and induced aversive reactions were all studied. Of the initial set of 26 variables, only eight had test–retest reliabilities greater than 0.50. The authors conclude that, such poor retest reliabilities are not perhaps unexpected given only the very gross descriptions of frequent state transitions of which they were capable.

Not surprisingly, administration of the Brazelton assessment to our sample on days one, three and seven in the first week of life, showed marked visual improvement and some increase in auditory alertness across babies (see Table 4.2). There were, however, consistent individual patterns of responding for state-regulated behaviour (Rosenblatt and Packer, 1978). Most babies became quiet when held and rocked after being disturbed by stimulation, but a group of between 12 and 15 per cent of the sample consistently failed to quiet themselves and were extremely difficult to soothe.

Third, comparability of abilities across subjects can yield equivocal information. There is no precise set of criteria designating the 'normal' baby. Most subjects, when so described, tell us only that we have a population of 40 weeks' gestational age. Important variables are often not reported or controlled, such as the minimum drug dose the mother had in labour, the mother's parity, the degree of jaundice developed by the baby (it has been reliably reported that jaundice impairs neonatal functioning (Rosenblatt, 1977)). Even the class and race of the parents can affect findings, since cross-cultural studies yield different values on the Brazelton scale (Wooson and Wooson, 1977).

Comparable subject samples also depend on the discard rate which, in neonatal studies, can be high (Lewis and Johnson, 1971). In one study of visual habituation (Friedman, 1972) as much subject data was discarded as was analysed. It is quite likely that subjects whose data are discarded are either less fully recovered from their birth experience or are simply less mature. There is considerable variability in subjects showing a gestation age of 40 weeks (Dubowitz, Dubowitz, and Goldberg, 1970) and one study (Day, 1974) retested on visual discrimination measures the subjects whose data had been discarded, and found that they performed effectively on a second testing. They concluded that these subjects had been less mature at first testing.

In summary, the Brazelton investigation and variants of it which other researchers have adopted for their own purposes, tap information-processing

differential elicitation of stage changes. There is also the difficulty of finding an accurate statistical description of state variables. Further, we still await prospective studies to show us whether a test such as the Brazelton assessment which, in a broad sense, investigates individual differences and might be considered as a test of temperament in the first week of life, shows any continuity with behaviour later on. One study (Hall, 1978) suggests that the drowsy, unalert baby during Brazelton testing in the first week of life, may become the difficult, demanding 2-year-old when followed up at home.

INDIVIDUAL DIFFERENCES: AT BIRTH

The data reviewed so far clearly demonstrate that there are individual differences in newborns at birth. We have seen differences in responding to auditory events, in meeting the challenge of the Brazelton examination (see Table 4.2) in visual alertness (Barten et al., 1971), in irritability, in amounts of activity, and in the organization of sucking patterns (Rutter, 1977).

It is perhaps relevant to mention here data taken early in infancy from a now famous study (Thomas et al., 1963) which identified, from mothers' descriptions, nine dimensions of temperament on which infants differed. They were able to distinguish these infants on how regular their sleep, eating, and toilet habits were; how physically active they were and how easily distracted they

TABLE 4.2. The development of orienting skills over the first six weeks (percentage of infants)

	Birth	Day 1	Day 3	Day 7	Day 21	Day 42
Visual following: object						
(a) Brief, jerky	83	95	92	95	98	100
(b) Smooth, $\geq 30°$ area	50	57	67	75	79	95
Visual: Face						
(b) Brief, jerky	86	97	97	98	100	100
(b) Smooth, $\geq 30°$ area	50	71	74	81	74	97
Visual and auditory: face + voice						
(a) Brief, jerky	89	95	95	98	99	100
(b) Smooth, $\geq 30°$	58	74	80	85	87	97
Auditory: rattle						
(a) Alert to, or eyes turn	89	90	98	97	98	100
(b) Turn head and eyes	36	61	70	63	60	70
Auditory: voice						
(a) Alert to, or eyes turn	84	90	95	94	94	98
(b) Turn head and eyes	38	54	59	61	54	69
Average n	89	120	125	121	131	126

were; on how they reacted to change and whether they sought new experiences or avoided them; on how receptive to stimulation they were, and on how they differed in mood. Clearly, these categories are far from independent and are in fact very global descriptions of the mothers' judgements. A more recent methodological study compared items from the Brazelton scale with Thomas's temperamental constructs using the same population of babies (Sostek and Anders, 1977). It was found that state control and social perception measured on the Brazelton scales predicted 'distractable' infants on the Carey temperament scale (1970) which was adapted for infancy. (The Carey scale measures temperamental dimensions similar to those of Thomas *et al.*, 1963.) Motor items, on the other hand, related to 'intense' babies. These two Carey items predicted better DQ scores when a Bailey test was administered at 10 weeks of age.

How are these individual differences determined? Theoretically, genetic factors may be responsible (Rutter *et al.*, 1964). (Twin studies have shown as heritable, social behaviour (Scarr-Salapatek, 1976) and temperamental traits (Torgeson and Kringler, 1980) at least for the first year of life.) The newborn's intra-uterine environment may play a part, or a variety of perinatal influences, particularly medical intervention during labour and delivery, may effect at least early outcome. Further, a differential recovery from birth trauma and adjustment in the first days after birth, which may be influenced by prenatal circumstances, may be implicated.

In practice these sources of variation, whether they come from the environment or are experienced intrapersonally, are seldom independent, which makes the task of isolating a particular prenatal or perinatal effect from other influences particularly hazardous (see Barrett, Chapter 3 in this volume). In our study, which investigated the association between maternal obstetric medication and newborn outcome, parity, length of first stage of labour, mother's drug dose and type of delivery, were all factors that covaried. When this occurs there has been speculation on the possibility of synergistic effects on the neonate if several adverse physical factors occur in combination (Tronick *et al.*, 1976). Hall (1977) reports that in a sample of 50 firstborns tested at 6 days of age, 33 per cent of the variance on the Brazelton test item, alertness, was accounted for by a combination of the following factors—toxaemia in the mother, high drug dosage (pethidine), her height and age and class, together with the newborn's birthweight.

The link between an alert baby, the mother's characteristics, and the maternal medication, could have been formed in any number of ways. The differences in maternal well-being might directly affect the mother's intra-uterine transmission of oxygen to the foetus, which in turn could lead to low levels of cortical activity in the neonate early on. Perhaps the perinatal factors of maternal height indirectly affect the newborn as short women tend to have more prolonged and difficult labours (Drillien, 1962) or the experience of pethidine during labour could have made the babies drowsy. It is even possible that differences in the foetuses could independently have contributed either to the mother manifesting toxaemia or to her difficulties in labour, which are likely to lead to more drug being administered to her. The inclusion of birthweight as a factor contributing to the variance would support this speculation if low-weight foetuses are likely to be more traumatized by the effects of toxaemia, long labour, or high drug dosage. Finally, perhaps alertness reflects a handling effect, if women of different social class, and possibly age, stimulate their babies and interact with them in different ways. Dunn (1979) for instance, reports that babies who cried a lot and had difficulty in feeding in the first days of life also had experienced high doses of medication and long labours. Unravelling the complexity of these factors, whose interrelation is as yet imperfectly understood, is clearly a necessary step to discovering the origins of individual differences.

In practice, few studies are uncontaminated by postnatal handling, which introduces additional variables such as poor feeding (Dunn, 1975) or even maternal anxiety (McDonnald, 1968). We were lucky to observe infant behaviour immediately after birth (although observations taken immediately after delivery turned out to be largely uncorrelated with scores on later days in the first week). However, most experimental investigations of newborn characteristics are confounded by the fact that, simultaneously, the baby is engaged in a much more important dialogue of learning to adapt and modify his behaviour to that of his mother, just as his mother is doing to him. Not even naturalistic studies of interaction are free of this difficulty. First, most so-called 'interaction' studies measure frequencies separately for the two participants: or use correlations of infant and maternal behaviour; few have developed a methodology for detailed dependent, sequential analysis of the behaviour of each member of the dyad. And, as Dunn (1975) states, 'there is no measure of behaviour of either mothers or infants that can be assumed to be independent of the course of previous interaction between the two since birth'. It cannot even be assumed that hospital routine will ensure a negligible amount of contact between mother and child in the early postnatal days (Copans, 1974), given the increased use of Laboyer-type deliveries, the relaxation of strict feed-schedules in hospitals, and the fact that on Day 1, newborns possibly spend more time awake than on any day in the first week (Lieberman et al., 1979, Theorell et al., 1973).

INDIVIDUAL DIFFERENCES: MATERNAL MEDICATION AND NEONATAL BEHAVIOUR

Studies of the effects on the neonate of the pain-relieving drugs given to the mother in labour have been methodologically crude. Firstly, there is the basic pharmacology of the perinatal period with complex relationships obtaining between the mother's physiology, the placental unit, the foetus, and the neonate. Little is known about the uptake of drugs in the foetus, their distribution, the drug metabolism in the neonate after birth, or how labour may have influenced the placental passage of drugs. Secondly, there is the difficulty of identifying one influence amongst a host of covarying perinatal factors, particularly if, as seems likely, there are synergistic effects. Thirdly, the human newborn is a rapidly changing organism where day-to-day differences can be the result of maturation, recovery from birth trauma, social interaction, or sleep and feed problems. It is also difficult to know how physiological changes at birth interact with drug distribution and what neonatal behaviours can be expected to vary as a result of circulating drug levels or metabolic transformations.

Lastly, even if differences in neonatal behaviour due to drugs are established through methodologically sound procedures, what is the significance of these differences? It subtle differences in state, sleep responsivity, or alertness are demonstrated in the newborn such as might influence a developing social relationship with the caretaker, we still need a detailed account of the dynamics of early interaction against which to evaluate the importance of these drug-related changes. Though relatively long-term effects are found (for instance, a month to 6 weeks after delivery), perhaps the mother simply adapts to the baby's induced behaviour. If such effects, on the other hand, are transient, there may still be an altered equilibrium in the neonate's nervous system and cortical organization, which can determine his ability to function.

The purpose of the St Mary's Hospital study, which investigated the effects of maternal medication on the behaviour of 145 newborns five times in the first 6 weeks, was to produce a research design that controlled for the following methodological flaws that had been noted in earlier studies. A large sample was studied, so that statistical techniques such as multiple regression analysis could be used to interpret the variance in behaviour which was due to the independent factors which were the subject of interest. No mother received a combination of drugs in labour and all subjects had normal pregnancies. The drugs under study were bupivacaine ($n = 59$), a marcaine derivative administered by epidural anaesthesia (doses of 10–14 ml volume were given in concentrations of 0.375 per cent); pethidine ($n = 51$), plus an anti-emetic, given in doses of 100mg, or 150 mg,—the former being the most common dosage and usually administered once only. A control group ($n = 35$) of mothers had no drug at all.

No infants of low birthweight, or with neonatal complications, or who were small for dates, were included. Observers testing the babies did not know which drug group the mothers were in. Babies were tested by different psychologists on different days to avoid bias in testing. The behavioural tests were compared with performance on a neurological assessment performed independently at 6 days of age by a paediatrician. Infants were not found to differ significantly on these two assessments.

Psychosomatic data on the course of the mother's pregnancy in the form of self-administered questionnaires on her physical and mental state, together with information about her anxieties, and her plans for the baby's birth, was taken by the Obstetric Study midwife in the third trimester of pregnancy. After birth, ratings were made on the mother's adjustment to the demands made by her baby, and the hospital routine. Since women self-selected to each drug group, the study could be considered quasi-experimental. Analysis of the antenatal information has only just begun, but neither maternal expectations nor mood at 36 weeks' gestation related to choice of drug group.

Alper et al. (1975) point out that there is an assumption in maternal drug studies that the magnitude of the foetus' exposure does not reflect individual differences so long as the same dose is received by the mother. We were able to investigate the relationship between actual drug levels in the neonate, amounts given to the mother, and excretion and metabolic rates in the infant, with subsequent behaviour. More sophisticated and more widely sampled aspects of neonatal behaviour were recorded, and included sleep data taken from mother's diary during the first week of life, nutritive feedings recorded during the first week, and non-nutritive sucking measures taken at the same time as the Brazelton neonatal assessment scale was administered.

Briefly, the main findings of previous studies have been that maternal doses of meperidine (pethidine) impaired a neonate's ability to shut out repeated, meaningless, auditory stimulation in the first week of life (Brackbill et al., 1974). Aleksandrowicz et al. (1974) also found drug effects which related to decreased habituation to auditory stimuli. Maternal epidural anaesthesia (lidocaine, mepivacaine) has shown associations with muscular hypotonia, lowered Moro-reflex, and decreased rooting behaviour in the first 8 hours of life (Scanlon, 1974). Various drug types such as tranquillizers, local and general anaesthetics, analgesic narcotics, and barbiturates, amongst others—when given in various combinations, are associated with decreased visual and auditory responsiveness to the human face and voice. This was found on the first day of life, but some associations persisted even when subjects were 1 month old and showed their greatest effect then; other drug-related changes peaced in intensity earlier on in life (Aleksandrowicz et al., 1974).

In contrast, Tronick et al. (1976) report only minimal drug effects. Using the Brazelton Assessment Scale, they tested a homogeneous sample of 54 normal infants, coming from eight drug groups, for the first 5 days of life, and then again on days 7 and 10. Cord-blood levels, showing drug concentration in the newborn, were also taken. Medication doses were low and not more than two were administered in the 4 hours before delivery. Babies whose mother had had analgesics showed motor behaviour and orientation that improved over the first week, while babies whose mothers had lidocaine administered by epidural anaesthesia showed worse motor tone at 12 hours, but showed no difference in responsivity, state, motor behaviour, or reaction to stress thereafter.

Results of the St Mary's study (Rosenblatt, et al., 1978) show that between-group analysis of epidural, pethidine, and no-drug groups yields few significant differences in infant behaviour, as measured by the Brazelton Assessment Scale, given over the first 6 weeks of life. A multiple-regression analysis was performed. Drug is only seen to affect behaviour consistently and significantly when the pharmacological effects are examined. The amount of drug in the baby's cord at delivery, and his ability to metabolize and/or excrete the drug (as measured by half-life taken from heel-pricks on infants during the first 48 hours of life) are strongly related to subsequent behaviour. Further, although there were differences between the three groups on certain labour variables, such as how likely they were to have long labours, induced labours, or instrumental delivery (more likely with epidural anaesthesia), no labour variable accounted for the variation in infant behaviour.

Returning to the differences within each drug group, and taking first those babies who had high delivery levels of bupivacaine—in the first week, these newborns were likely to be very irritable, to show great liability of state, to cry early on in the test administered on day 3 and to tremor on day 7. High delivery levels of bupivacaine consistently predicted poor orienting behaviour both in the visual and auditory mode, and poor alertness throughout the first week. These subjects also scored less well on defensive movements. On testing, at 3 and 6 weeks, the effects of high cord levels of drug, amount given to the mother, and drug half-life were still to be seen. Orientation was still poor, and these babies smiled less and demonstrated greater physiological reaction to stress. Thus, bupivacaine exerts a strong effect on social behaviour for 6 weeks

TABLE 4.3 Epidural group: Brazelton items on which infants performed well in relation to dose-related drug measures (regression analysis; obstetric variables held constant)

		Days
Attention and social responsiveness (7 items)	Inanimate visual (object)	1, 7, 21, 42
	Inanimate auditory (rattle)	3
	Animate visual (face)	1, 21, 42
	Animate auditory (voice)	7
	Animate visual and auditory (face and voice)	7, 21, 42
	Alertness	1, 42
	Consolability	1
Motor organization (5 items)	Tone	1, 7
	Activity	7, 42
	Hand-to-mouth	1
	Defensive movements (to an occluding cloth)	1, 3, 7
Control of state of consciousness (8 items)	Response decrement to:	
	light	7
	rattle	42
	Tolerance of handling before crying	3
	Irritability	3
	Lability of state	3
Physiological response to stress (2 items)	Startles	3, 42
	Tremor	7, 21

after delivery and results in depressive behaviour throughout the first week (see Table 4.3).

Pethidine is also seen to have a depressive effect. At delivery, pethidine administration was more likely to result in respiratory depression, but this did not necessarily lead to decreased performance on Brazelton items. Longer half-life of the drug in the baby in the first week did, however, lead to decreased alertness and lower orienting behaviour. Half-life, delivery cord level of drug, and the amount the mother received, all together accounted for decreased habituation, orientation, alertness and defensive skill. At 3 weeks, infants who had high delivery levels of pethidine were much more irritable, labile in their state changes, difficult to console and also smiled less (see Table 4.4).

Interestingly, newborn behaviour immediately after delivery showed no drug effects. It seems likely that the changes brought about by the trauma of the birth are great enough to swamp any drug-induced effects, so that all babies could produce adequate elicited and spontaneous behaviour. It might be of interest to researchers in this field to know that half-life is more likely to predict behaviour in the pethidine group, while delivery cord levels are a better discriminator for bupivacaine. Further, drug effects are greatest on the first and third day of life, so that the clinician might perhaps be less concerned by depressive behaviour early in the first week, but might look for causes other than drugs, should labile states or depressed motor behaviour persevere beyond that time.

TABLE 4.4. Pethidine group: Brazelton items on which infants performed well in relation to dose-related drug measures (regression analysis; obstetric variables held constant)

		Days
Attention and social responsiveness (7 items)	Inanimate visual (object)	1, 3, 7
	Inanimate auditory (rattle)	7
	Animate visual (face)	1
	Animate visual and auditory (face and voice)	1
	Alertness	1, 7
	Consolability	1, 21
Motor organization (5 items)	Hand-to-mouth	3, 42
	Defensive movements (to an occluding cloth)	1
Control of state of consciousness (8 items)	Response Decrement to: rattle	3
	bell	3
	Peak of excitement	21
	Self-quieting	21
	Lability of state	21
Physiological response to stress (2 items)	Tremor	3, 7

While it is clear from our study that high drug levels in the baby at delivery, and the persisting presence of drug over the first 2 days of life in the newborn, can effect behaviour both in the first week and indeed for longer, it looks as if careful control of drug dosage and timing reduces these drug effects to a minimum. Mothers who receive analgesics or anaesthetic for pain relief in labour often have babies who, as assessed by the Brazelton scale, are performing as well, or better, when obstetric variables are held constant, than those whose mothers had no drugs. It is suggested that careful management of labour with successful relief, may lead to a reduction in hypertension and maternal anxiety that can, in turn, reduce foetal heart-rate changes and consequent serious respiratory distress. Alper *et al.* (1975) comment that natural childbirth and psychoprophylaxis can result in prolonged second stage and a significant degree of asphyxia, and he calls for neurobehavioural studies to evaluate the relative benefits of this type of delivery, as opposed to optimally administered anaesthetics or analgesics.

There is some impairment of what is termed the newborn's social repertoire, particularly where drug dose affects the onset of smiling behaviour around 3 weeks of age. Pain relief is clearly beneficial to the mother who receives a successful epidural, but mothers who received large amounts of pethidine interacted less with their babies immediately after delivery. While individual differences in neonatal behaviour that are related to drugs have practical implications for the organization of paediatric and obstetric care, the meaning of drug-induced changes depends on the model of early infant bonding which is being put forward (Hales *et al.*, 1977; Dunn, 1977; Stern, 1977, Trevarthen, 1975; Kaye, 1978).

Studies on the way in which the mother and child relate to each other in the early days show that the human neonate's social world is peculiarly adapted to his needs and the kind of personal organization he is able to display. During feed times, mothers hold their infants about 8 inches away from their own face, and this is about the distance of the newborn's fixed accommodation focusing (Haynes, White, and Held 1965). Thus, the newborn gets a unblurred picture of his caretaker. Mothers echo the intonation patterns of their babies' spontaneous vocalizations in such a way as to maximize the baby's possibility of acquiring the sounds of the language he hears around him (Fourcin, 1978). In the first days of life, infants can imitate human facial gestures (Meltzoff and Moore, 1977). When a mother starts to talk to her infant, the infant immediately looks at her eyes (Haith, Bergman, and Moore, 1977). Eye gaze is important to a mother (Klaus and Kennell, 1970; Robson and Moss, 1970), perhaps because when a baby opens his eyes the mother has a mirror into his consciousness.

Mothers do not distract their infants when they are actually sucking on the teat; auditory stimulation interrupts sucking (Crook, and Lipsitt, 1976) so they talk affectionately to their newborns when the babies are taking rest pauses (Dunn, 1977) or they talk, but do not look at the infant, to stimulate attention at the same time (Stern, 1977). Mothers fit in with their infant's social behaviour;

they chat to the baby in temporally predictable sequences and repeat intonations which are easy for the baby to process cognitively (Jaffe, Stern and Perry, 1973, Trevarthen, 1975; Sylvester-Bradley and Trevarthen, 1978). They slow down the speed of their speech (Stern, 1977) and they take aspects of the infant's behaviour as turns in their conversation: a baby's hiccup, for example, might be interpreted by the mother as a reply to her question, if its timing was appropriate (Snow, 1977). Packer (1978) has described a maternal plan according to which the organization of early feeds takes place, and Kaye (1978) has illustrated how the mother exerts control during the feeding situation. As has been mentioned before, the human infant sucks in a rhythmic pattern, in which a burst of sucks is interspersed with pauses. In the first week mothers attempt to stimulate the baby to suck again as soon as he pauses; in fact this behaviour on her part simply prolongs the pause so that the baby waits until the end of the mother's jiggling of the bottle or breast and then resumes sucking. The mother has perceived the regularity of her infant's behaviour, but is responding inappropriately for efficient feeding. After about 2 weeks, however, the mothers change their response to a faster jiggling and then stop, so that the infant's natural response is no longer being impeded. From these observations, taken on 30 mother and newborn pairs, Kaye (1978) suggests that the mother builds a pattern of interaction on the regularity and predictability of her own infant's responses, and to do this she must rely upon mutual monitoring of the baby's behaviour. All these phenomena are the basis of a mutual reciprocal relationship between mother and child.

THE PERSISTENCE OF EARLY INDIVIDUAL DIFFERENCES

It is clearly important that the caring professions should be able to identify at an early stage those infants likely to encounter problems, and so be able to monitor their developmental progress. Prospective psychological studies are obviously of most use if they can predict which variables should be recorded, while subjects are still a captive sample for testing, during their mandatory stay in hospital after delivery. Unfortunately, there are factors influenceing the continuity of individual differences that work against any such ideal, clear-cut predictions of later vulnerability (Sameroff and Chandler, 1975).

For reasons already given, infant assessment scales have little intellectual predictive value (Lewis, 1976) except at the extreme end of the range (Kagan, 1971; McCall, 1976). Plasticity in behavioural development is perhaps only to be expected when 80 per cent of the growth of the brain occurs postnatally (Dobbing and Smart, 1974). Measurements made during the lying-in period can reflect the transient effects of perinatal treatment, such as medication (Tronick et al., 1976), which may yet be strong enough to mask other characteristics. Even with drug-free deliveries, Brazelton, Robey, and Collier, (1969) found different recovery rates from birth between Mexican and American newborns. The latter showed continuities in performance over the first week, while the Indian babies got progressively better at coping with their environment even though, cross-culturally, the American babies manifest more crying and sleeping while the Mexican infants spent longer awake. Lower birth-weight, perhaps indicating less satisfactory levels of nutrition, might account for the Indian babies taking longer to recover from birth stress, although, of course, genetic differences cannot be ruled out.

The ordinary processes of rapid maturation and development may also render transitory a particular individual difference. Is heart-rate recorded at 1 month, for instance, registering the same cognitive mechanisms of attention as it does at 4 months? Is the baby who happily accepts a stranger at 7 months, yet protests vehemently at a year, primarily a person who, in the terminology of Thomas and his colleagues (1963) approaches new situations or avoids them, or is he simply manifesting a normal (and well-documented) develop-mental discontinuity? And what of behaviours, like smiling, that simply do not appear at birth at all? Zelazo (1976) recounts how reflex smiling occasioned by particular stimulus configurations (Ahrens, 1954; Allyn, 1971) becomes a smile of success (Watson, 1970) after effortful assimilation of some mental task. Surely the latter has quite a different meaning for infant cognition?

Myrtle McGraw, who was filming the course of early motor development in the 1930s, asked what it meant if 'one perfectly normal infant should walk alone at nine months and another not until he is 18 or 20 months'. And does it follow that the former would display mental superiority? Only empirical evidence can tell us just which behaviour measures may be related at different ages and whether they are important for development.

We have already encountered the view that congenital patterns of behaviour which are discernible at birth may need practice (Lipsitt et al., 1976; Thoman et al., 1978). It is also the case that certain motor reflexes, such as stepping and walking, which are elicited by infant neurological examinations, can be ex-perimentally maintained (Zelazo, 1977) after they would normally have died out. It may be that certain child-rearing practices may also maintain them. If early experience can so modify newborn motor reflexes, how much more may the mutual modification that goes on between mother and child affect behaviour that may be the result of temperament or characteristics usually described as 'constitutional'?

The mutual modification of behaviour that goes on between mother and child certainly complicates any search for continuity. Pratt (1978) asked mothers to interpret the meaning of their babies' crying, by playing them videotaped recordings taken at home during the first year. At first a high proportion of their descriptions were related to physiological discomfort, such as hunger and pain, but later on, towards the fifth month, mothers' interpretations shifted dramatically to psychological explanations such as boredom or frust-ration. Even attributing meaning to such a basic, and ostensibly easily identi-fiable, response as infant crying, can thus be problematic.

In a now well-known longitudinal study tracing the behaviour of mother and child together over the first 5 years of life, Dunn (1975) was unable to trace individual continuity in either mother or child alone beyond the first year. Mothers seen as warm, affectionate, and stimulating in newborn feeding sessions stayed that way with their children through much of the first year of life, although stable baby characteristics were acknowledged as contributing to this maternal continuity. Hall (1977), however, with both normal women and mothers with psychiatric problems, found no differences in the baby measures taken at 3 months, but only mothering differences. Dunn identified mothers who differed in their accepting attitude towards their children's attempts at communication in the second year of life (mother's high on this variable had children with higher Stanford–Binet IQ scores at $4\frac{1}{2}$ years). Yet these compliant mothers were not necessarily the affectionate ones during the first year. At this point in the study new patterns of maternal differences appeared. These environmental discontinuities are thus the result of developmental changes in the child affecting the mother, who may herself derive differential enjoyment from the different stages of childhood. These findings also illustrate the importance of looking for individual differences between mother and child pairs, since certain child characteristics (higher sucking rates as newborns and frequency of vocal approaches at 14 months) were also correlated with the mothers' behaviour.

The influence of environment is nowhere seen more clearly than in the study of newborn characteristics attributable to perinatal events (Davie, Butler and Goldstein, 1972). Ucko (1975) traced, from their birth records, children who had suffered from asphyxia at birth. They showed various neonatal characteristics, such as lack of adaptability, hypersensitivity to stimuli, and unpredictability in sleep habits, which could be supposed to lead to them being difficult to handle. On school entry, these same children were seen as anxious and difficult to control, which suggests that their style of behaving had not changed much over the years. Nevertheless, Neligman, Prudhen, and Steiner, (1974) in an epidemiological study relating perinatal trauma to children's physical and mental outcome at 5 and 10 years, found that the effects of even 20 minutes' asphyxia after birth were totally swamped by the kind of family that the child was subsequently brought up in. No neonatal characteristics are known for this study, but while height and weight did not vary between socioeconomic groups on follow-up, intelligence did—slightly at 5 years and very appreciably at 10 years. Interestingly, Dunn (1978) also reports that continuities between neonatal differences and behaviour at 5 in a medically low-risk sample only persisted for the children of low socioeconomic status families.

A number of studies link aspects of early childhood behaviour to later psychiatric disorder, behaviour problems and reading difficulties. Few, however, have taken detailed measures during the first week of life. Two studies that have now reported (Bernal, 1973; Blurton-Jones et al., 1978) demonstrate individual differences in neonatal behaviour which are associated with sleep problems that are relatively long-lasting. Children who experienced these difficulties also show other behavioural and temperamental differences.

During the first 10 days of life the mothers of Dunn's (1977), Cambridge study (who all were delivered at home) kept a diary of their babies' daily cycle which included information on sleep patterns. Those newborns, who slept for shorter periods in the first 10 days of life, took longer to cry and breathe regularly at birth, were more likely to cry on removal of a non-nutritive teat after sucking, and were more irritable. On follow-up at 14 months, these infants were night-wakers who consistently slept 2 hours less per night than the rest of the cohort. (A sleep problem is judged to be present when maternal questionnaires revealed the infant to wake as many as four or five times a night.) At 3 years their sleep problems persisted; and their mothers expressed difficulty in coping with them because they were stubborn, awkward in strange social situations, and did not go to strangers easily (Dunn, 1978). At 5 these children were significantly more likely to score above the medium on behaviour-problem ratings (Dunn, 1978b). There were, however, children in the study who had behaviour problems but no sleep difficulties.

Graham, Rutter, and George, (1973) also found a relationship between irregularity of habits like sleeping, and later behaviour problems which require psychiatric guidance. Dunn (1978) notes that strong emotional reactions to the birth of a new sibling result in sleeping difficulties. It was further noted that the siblings who already had sleep difficulties themselves showed a 'distinctive' pattern of reaction to the new birth, and in this connection it is interesting to note that Carey (1974) found infants with sleep difficulties in the first year had low sensory thresholds. A clear picture thus emerges of an individual difference in temperament, identifiable in the neonatal period and persisting as sleep disturbance and unpredictable behaviour through the early years of childhood, which sometimes manifests itself through behavioural disorder later, and is likely to appear in circumstances of stress.

EFFECTS OF EARLY SEPARATION

Early separation, either immediately after delivery or during the first weeks of life, is an inescapable fact of institutionalized birth. It has been estimated that one in six of all live births in this country are followed by a referral, albeit sometimes brief, to a special care unit (DHSS, 1974; Richards and Chard, 1978). Since separations in the first week of life, apart from those routinely occurring in the post-delivery period, are usually occasioned by medical care being deemed necessary for either mother or baby (Garrow and Smith, 1976), and most usually the latter, it is useful in this context to assess the psychological consequences of contact and separation as they affect both mother and child.

There is little convincing evidence for the existence of a 'sensitive period' during which the establishing of mothering behaviour must occur if bonding is to be successful. Such a notion derives from animal studies where imprinting may be biologically necessary for survival and, more importantly, there are no antenatal maternal expectancies, plans and attitudes to offset early setbacks in the relationships that may be occasioned by prematurity, low birthweight or neonatal illness.

It may be profitable to examine how normal, unseparated women see the process of adjustment to their child. Over the 3-month period after birth, Robson and Moss (1970) interviewed 50 mothers. At delivery they were concerned with their babies' appearance and their own post-delivery well-being, and many could remember no feelings about the baby at all. Rosenblatt and Packer (1978) also observed that first contact was not long or satisfying, even though mothers were given the baby within the first 5 minutes of birth. After 1 month's contact Robson's mothers were preoccupied by the baby, recognizing it and feeling that smiling, visual contact and cessation of crying on their babies' part was evidence that their infants recognized them. By 3 months, they reported total involvement with their child and felt 'attached'.

These accounts suggest that one outcome of contact is emotional involvement. Another has to do with gaining confidence in coping with their baby, particularly coping with feeding, since most mothers feel their primary target is getting nutriment into their infants. Both outcomes, of course, stem from the mother having had the opportunity of getting to know her infant through frequent handling and being able to understand his individual capabilities and requirements.

Evidence on how lack of early contact may change the adjustment process Robson describes, comes either from experimental, random allocation of mothers to groups who are given more or less time with their infants, at different times after birth, and the more fortuitous incubator separations resulting from admittance to a special-care unit.

Of the former, the type of family unit to which the baby returns is the determining factor in the persistence of difficulties after lack of contact. Where separation has occurred for term babies due to minor illness requiring admittance to special care units (Whiten, 1977), for term babies whose mothers (randomly allocated) were given more time with their infants than normal hospital routine allowed (Klaus and Kennell, 1970) for premature infants (Seashore et al., 1973), and for low-birthweight infants randomly allocated to a programme of contact or no contact (Leifer et al., 1972) their mothers, in comparison with unseparated mothers, all show differences in maternal attitude and feel less confident and competent with their infants. When the mothers' behaviour with their babies is observed at various stages in the first 2 years of life (no follow-up on separation has gone beyond that age), various differences are reported: Leifer et al. (1972) found no caretaking differences between their low-birthweight groups. Whiten (1977), Seashore et al. (1973), and Klaus and Kennell (1970) all report that separated mothers hold their babies less, smile and talk affectionately less often, and engage in less eye-to-eye contact in the early weeks. Klaus and Kennell (1970) also report differences in touching and stroking behaviour soon after birth.

These differences must be viewed in perspective, however. After 2 months there was no difference in social interchange for white, middle-class mothers who had term babies. By 1 year, in the study by Seashore et al. (1973), middle-class mothers who had had premature infants were performing like their control group, but the separated mothers did have a greater divorce rate. Klaus and Kennell's sample, which comprised black, low-income mothers, was reported as seeming detached when the infants were being examined at 1 year of age, and they had reported more marital difficulties. At 2 and 5 years, when a random sub-sample of these mother–infant pairs was followed up, the extended-contact mothers were less controlling, and talked more to their children. At 5, these children had significantly higher IQ scores.

Dunn (1975) has suggested an early buffering period for mother and child in the first week of life. The relatively short-lived separation effects that are reported are thus likely to be overcome, unless the family is severely stressed by other social, personal, or economic factors.

Families under stress

Stressed families who have come to the attention of the medical or social services because of the possibility of child abuse, are often found to have low birthweight or admission to an intensive care unit in the history of the child at risk (Beswick, Lynch, and Roberts, 1976; Lynch, 1975; Lynch and Roberts, 1978; Helfer and Kempe, 1972). Often, these infants are born into existing vulnerable circumstances. It should be stressed, however, that two studies (although not planned prospective investigations of child abuse) on very low birthweight infants, do not report an association between non-accidental injury and prematurity. For instance, Blake et al. (1975) report an incidence of 3 per cent of cases of abuse, but the mothers were thought to have been at risk psychiatrically and for personality problems even before conception. Nevertheless, in this study continuous high-quality nursing and psychological support was available to parents throughout a long follow-up period, and this may well have provided a model of infant care as well as advice on management problems.

Lynch and Roberts (1978) compared 50 families referred to a special hospital unit for actual or threatened child abuse and 50 control families whose infants had been born in the same maternity unit. All findings were checked against medical records. Forty-two per cent of the at-risk group had spent time in an intensive-care unit as a result of prematurity, but only 10 per cent of the controls had. Hanson (1978), in the Birmingham child abuse study, also found low birthweight to be associated with later abuse. Interestingly, maternity staff attending the mothers studied by Lynch and Roberts (1978) had already recorded that 44 per cent of the at-risk group mothers were experiencing mothering difficulties, even before discharge. Reasons given for these judgements were infrequent visiting, and mothers being unable to cope with feeding or crying.

Abused children were then compared with their siblings and, within families, it was much more likely for the abused group to have had abnormal labours (60 per cent as opposed to 40 per cent) and perinatal complications (40 per cent as opposed to 20 per cent). Forty per cent of the at-risk group were admitted to an intensive care unit for more than 48 hours, against only 6 per cent of their siblings. On follow-up, the siblings had robust physical histories, while the abused children were frequently ill. In fact, looking at mothers and children together in the at-risk group, 84 per cent had physical illnesses immediately prior to admittance.

While admittance of a baby to an intensive care unit presents many additional problems for parents, such as anxieties to do with abnormality, eventual outcome, and the risks of treatment; and feelings relating to a lack of autonomy over the child who is left behind in hospital to be cared for by experts, it seems that separation, which precludes familiarity with the baby, does frequently occur (as does continued illness) in the sequence of medical factors that altogether lead to an increase in the probability of child abuse.

THE EFFECTS OF LOW BIRTHWEIGHT

Assessing outcome in cases of low birthweight is complicated for the following reasons. It was mentioned earlier (Neligman, Prudhen, and Steiner, 1974) that family socioeconomic status (SES) interacts with perinatal complications to determine infant outcome. Independent variables such as maternal history of pregnancy, gestation, intra-uterine growth, birthweight of the infant, sex of the infant, and year of birth, all have to be taken into account. Yet it may be impossible to assess the individual influence of any one factor where several covary (here separation effects should not be forgotten), and where cohort size is small, and complete follow-ups are unattainable. Even if different study samples are compared, they may not be strictly comparable in terms of SES, type of birthweight evaluated, methods of data collection and the type of specialized care the subjects have received in hospital (Dawkins, 1975). All these variables are also differentially affected by the continuing technological changes occurring in neonatal intensive-care units (Schlesinger, 1973) as a result of improved knowledge of the biology and functioning of the low-birthweight newborn. This progress has led to increased chances of survival, particularly amongst the smallest babies: 17 per cent of infants under 1300 g at birth, survived in 1948; 30 per cent 10 years later (Drillien, 1962), and 66 per cent in 1975 (Stewart et al., 1977).

What measures, however, of the quality of survival are acceptable? Severe handicap or abnormality presented Dargassies (1977) with diagnostic problems in over half her sample of premature infants who had later severe neurological sequelae. Indeed 17 per cent of this sample were assessed, on the Dargassies neurological assessment, as normal up to 8 months of age. Handicap is usually evident by 3 years of age. Stewart (1977) and Stewart et al. (1978) were able to identify, at $3\frac{1}{2}$ years of age, children who had low birthweights and would be abnormal at 8 years, using psychological testing and DQ screening. Ability to cope with normal school is tested at 5 years of age in this country, but Stewart was able to identify (although not clearly define) the 18 per cent of her sample who were in normal schools but requiring some extra help, $1\frac{1}{2}$ years before they actually went to school.

Nevertheless emotional, learning, or social difficulties are often not apparent until later, while we know nothing, of course, of the adult potential of infants who were inmates of intensive-care units. Strain on the family both in the early weeks (Blake, Stewart, and Turcan, 1975) and in the long-term, where handicapped or learning problems exist, needs also to be assessed (Boyle, Giffen, and Fitzharding 1977). Medical staff reporting effects often concentrate too narrowly on neurological sequelae. It is important also to take into account the influence of family life on development, which is reflected globally in numerous SES findings and in the areas of cognitive support (Tizard 1978; Dunn and Wooding, 1976) opportunities for learning (Newson and Newson, 1976) and peer and sibling stimulation.

Dargassies (1977), who is following 286 premature infants at least to school age, comments in summary that

> consequences of prematurity constitute a problem with multiple components: the neurological sequelae are only a negative aspect . . . and alone cannot give a general prognosis for the future of premature infants. To be of value studies must be placed in a realistic life context.

Even though family help and attitudes can make considerable difference to DQ and possibly IQ (which is based on a different set of measures) it will not obscure the existence of cerebral palsy, for instance.

Francis-Williams and Davies (1974) found no association between IQ score (mean full scale score was 97 using the Wechseer Intelligence Scale for Children (WISC) and Wechsler Preschool and Primary Scale of Intelligence (WPPSI) and birthweight or gestational age, in 105 children tested between 4 and 12 years of age who were born in the 1960s and weighed less than 1500 g. This is contrary to earlier studies and shows definite improvement in the prognosis for very low weight babies. Interestingly, social class more closely predicted IQ. Singificant differences in IQ were found between social classes 1, 2, and non-manual 3 when they were compared with manual 3, 4, and 5 (scores of 107 and 90 respectively). While there were no controls, a mean of 97 is still probably lower than normative population data. Where survivors of the same birthweight were tested between the ages of $3\frac{1}{2}$ and 5 over a 6-year period (Turcan et al., 1977) IQ increased markedly in the last 2 years of testing (96 compared with 112). Outcome may well be less favourable when we consider the present school population. In 1967, Drillien tested infants below 2,000 g birthweight and found severe behaviour problems in 22 per cent. Stewart reports 18 per cent of her sample had minor handicaps, but only 6 per cent were attending special schools.

Davies (1976) took the view that children with an IQ between 70 and 85 were likely still to be at a considerable disadvantage at school, particularly if their SES background was poor. Estimates were made from three studies of children born in the 1960s, all below 1500 g in birthweight (2 per cent of the live births in this country are less than 1500 g birthweight). The first study done in Montreal examined 32 infants, 18 per cent of whom had an IQ below 85 (Fitzehardinge and Ramsay, 1973). The second study carried out at University College Hospital, London, was of a predominantly middle-class sample with 95 infants, 21 per cent of which were small-for-dates (SFD). Of 65 infants tested, 21 per cent had an IQ lower than 85 (Stewart and Reynolds, 1974). The third study was conducted at the Hammersmith Hospital, London, on 120 infants, 33 per cent of whom were SFD. Of 105 infants tested, 25 per cent had an IQ below 85, and the sample was predominantly working-class. (Complete follow-up details of drop-out rates are given in Davies, 1976.) Twenty-five per cent of the infants in the Montreal study had learning problems, and perceptual-motor difficulties were noted even where IQ was normal. In the Hammersmith study performance and verbal IQ showed discrepancies of 15 points in 20 per cent of children with normal IQ. The University College Hospital (UCH) sample was then too young for learning difficulties to be part of Davies' assessment.

Thus, if handicap is broadly defined as an IQ below 85 and specific learning difficulties, then 59 per cent of the Montreal sample, and 47 per cent of the Hammersmith study, were affected (babies born at home were slightly worse off). Turcan, Rawlings, and Stewart, (1977) report that of the 50 oldest UCH children examined at 8 years of age, 16 had learning difficulties, but were all receiving special help within normal schools. Including the numbers launched from neonatal intensive-care units within this broadly defined handicap problem in the period from 1961 to 1968, Davies (1976) estimates there may be 8000 children implicated. In fact, additional behavioural disorders may stem from these learning difficulties. Birch and Gussow (1970) report an association between behaviour and personality disorders and low birthweight, which is exacerbated, yet again, by low SES.

Blake, Stewart, and Turcan, (1977), following up 50 very low birthweight infants, report maladjusted behaviour problems for some 8-year-olds who were shy and over-dependent. This behaviour is further substantiated by Douglas and Gear (1976) who found that children at 13 and 15 who had a birthweight below 2000 g were rated by teachers as significantly more likely to be nervous. Those born at home had the tendency to be even shyer. It was hypothesized that lack of early contact made parents over-protective. Blake et al. (1975) reported that some parents of very low birthweight infants were seen as over-protective and unable to allow their children the peer contact they needed for development. Since 1970, when early visiting and contact inside the special-care unit has been encouraged for mothers, over-protective attitudes are seen less frequently, although Blake still describes parents of very low birthweight infants as over-anxious.

Parents interviewed about their preoccupations with their 3-year-old children who had been below 1500 g at birth (Boyle et al., 1977) reported significantly more anxiety over the children's vulnerability to accidents than did a control group whose infants were over 2500 g at birth. This study by Boyle is one of the few to look at the experience of having a low birthweight child within the family. An index representing parental evaluations of the child in the areas of health, feeding, sleeping, discipline, play, and general development was drawn up from questionnaire material administered to the parents, and comparison was made with medical assessments of the children. The majority of developmental anxieties expressed by parents were found to have major neurological or intellectual deficits as their basis when assessed clinically. 70 per cent of the low birthweight children had IQs over 80 and were free of neurological defects, but it is of course too early to assess possible learning difficulties. Indices of strain in these families, who were mostly intact, of average SES and capable of some self-help, suggest that the existence of a low birthweight infant is not a disruptive family factor where the handicap rate is low. 69 of the 75 couples who were together at the birth of the child, were still together on follow-up when the child was between $3\frac{1}{2}$ and 5 years of age. The divorce and separation rate was 13 per cent of cases, and psychiatric services were used by the parents in 5 per cent of cases. There were *no* cases of failure to thrive in these children and hospital records revealed *no* documented or suspect cases of child abuse.

Most of these parents sustained a 5-week separation after birth, during which they could not care for and handle their infant, although there were no visiting restrictions on the nursery after that. Such deprivation, nowadays, would be unthinkable as a low-contact, experimental manipulation. While these parents may have minimized the difficulties experienced after birth when reporting on adjustment several years later, and indeed may still be minimizing their current problems when they report, this study should be viewed as evidence that early adverse circumstances are certainly not irreversible. It is clear that, together with the increased use of Caesarian section to deliver mothers, specialized centres have resulted in a decrease in mortality for low birthweight infants and a greatly increased chance of survival for very low birthweight infants. IQ has risen and the incidence of major handicap does not seem to have changed. Findings on intensive care also suggest that the newborn's experience in and around birth affect its outcome perhaps more than prenatal or genetically determined disease (Davies and Stewart, 1975). Hypoxia in the perinatal period is clearly implicated in the aetiology of handicap and may come about from a variety of neonatal illnesses and complications and be potentiated by jaundice. Survivors of Mechanical ventilation, particularly where there is a history of fits, seem especially at risk for major handicap if they are of low birthweight (Stewart, 1977; Marriage and Davies, 1977). The authors, however, stressed the small sample sizes of the studies that led to these conclusions. Stewart (1977) states that of the indications for ventilation, hyaline membrane disease without other complication resulted in no major handicaps, whereas 25 per cent of the children below 1500 g had handicaps if they were ventilated for apnoeic spells or where there was respiratory failure associated with abnormal

CNS signs. Stewart further reports significant correlations between DQ and perinatal complications or treatment variables. After a multiple-regression analysis was carried out, two neonatal factors were found to contribute significantly to the variance: illnesses associated with convulsions accounted for 5.6 per cent, and infant arterial pH measured within 2 hours of birth was responsible for 2.4 per cent of the variance. Twenty-two other perinatal complication factors accounted altogether for 16.7 per cent of the variance of DQ.

In the days before intensive remedial care was available, Dargassies (1977) reporting on a sample born before 1962, and Douglas and Gear (1976) reporting on a study born before 1948, found that the handicap rate for infants between 28 and 38 weeks' gestational age was 21 per cent; 31 per cent of the infants showed neurological impairment at 28 weeks compared to 9 per cent at 37 weeks. For those infants with a birthweight under 2000 g, Douglas found the handicap rate was 17 per cent on follow-up. These studies followed 163 and 286 infants respectively with matched controls, at least until school age, and a sub-sample of subjects to 18 years of age. It has been noted here that the handicap rate is not greatly different for birthweight and gestational age from that of the intensive care survivors nowadays.

Events in and around birth that lead to later handicap were shown in the Dargassies study to cluster in an interesting way. Compared with the 226 control infants, who had no or only minor impairments, the handicapped group had no more single obstetric complications, gestational anomalies, anomalies at delivery, or neonatal disorders. One single factor occurred significantly more often in the handicap group and that was apnoea (23/60 as against 28/226). Indeed, jaundice and respiratory conditions at birth occurred more frequently in the control group. When all these antecedent factors were combined, however, multiple neonatal disorders such as initial respiratory problems, repeated apnoea, convulsions, idiopathic coma, intracranial haemorrage, severe jaundice, and neonatal anaemia, were more frequently seen together in the handicap group (70 per cent against 46 per cent) and the combination of neonatal and obstetric complications was twice as great in the handicap group.

Since malformations are found no more often in premature than in full-term infants, and metabolic diseases do not interfere with the progression of pregnancy to term, and neither do genetic anomalies produce premature birth— although they may cause intra-uterine growth retardation—and since prematurity is twice as high in the lower socioeconomic groups (Dargassies, 1977), it would seem that later social circumstances, together with the events in and around birth that have been identified as contributing to later handicap, are likely to be most important in the long-term status of the low birthweight infant.

CONCLUSION

The study of early development seeks to explain normative, ontogenetic changes in behaviour and skill that appear to be universal, and to describe the mechanisms by which the interaction between maturational and environmental factors brings about these changes. It also seeks to explain variations in behaviour among infants at birth and to account for the origin of some of the influences pre-, peri- and immediately postnatal, that determine outcome. It further seeks to predict early behaviours that may be associated with later deviance or developmental retardation. Lastly, there is the task of explaining intra-individual variation in behaviour during the neonatal period and specifying how particular contexts and events influence the different aspects—cognitive, emotional, and social—of development.

While human infants show marked individual differences at birth, they are all equipped with the capacity to attend, in all modalities, to changes in physical stimulation, contour, movement etc., and to use this attention selectively. Despite his limited motor abilities the neonate is competent at exercising activities like sucking and the regulation of breathing and swallowing, or the coordination of head and eye movements which are essential to survival. Thus his physically dependent state does not prevent him in engaging the world around him with a lively interest. Indeed, this physically dependent state is compensated for in a certain pre-adaptation to socially relevant stimuli. What is also certain is that human infants show great plasticity in their ability to shape dissimilar social and learning environments in order to achieve, by a variety of different routes, the same developmental ends.

Acknowledgement

My grateful thanks to Brian Foss for his many helpful comments during the preparation of this manuscript.

REFERENCES

Adkinson, C., and Berg, W. K. (1976). Cardiac deceleration in newborns: habituation, dishabituation and offset responses. *J. Exp. Child Psychol.* **21**, 46–60.

Ahrens, R. (1954). Beitrag zur Entwicklung des Psysiognomie- und Mimikerkennes. *Z. Exp. Angew. Psychol.*, **2**, Part I, 412–454.

Aleksandrowicz, M., Kaye, L., and Aleksandrowicz, D. (1974). Obstetrical pain-relieving drugs as predictors of neonatal behavioural variability. *Child Dev.* **45**, 935–945.

Allyn, G. (1971). Infant social perception. Unpublished doctoral dissertation. University of London.

Alper, M., Brown, W., Ostheiner, G., and Scanlon, J. (1975). Effects of maternal analgesia and anaesthesia on newborns. *Clin. Obstet. Gynecol.*, **2**. (3), 661–671.

Apgar, V. (1953). A proposal for a new method of evaluation of the Newborn Infant. *Curr. Res. Anesth.*, **32**, 260–267.

Appel, M. A., Campos, J. J., Silverman, S., and Conway, E. (1971). Electrodermal responding of the human infant. Paper mentioned in Venables (1978), p. 1978.

Ashton, R. (1973). The influence of state and prandial condition upon the reactivity of the newborn to auditory stimulation. *J. Exp. Child Psychol.*, **15**, 315.

Aslim, I. N., and Salapatek, P. (1975). Saccadic localisation of visual attention in human infants. *Percept. Psychophys.* **17**, 293–302.

Bakow, H. (1973). The relation between newborn behaviour and mother–child interaction. Paper presented at SSRCD, March.

Ball, W., and Tronick, E. (1971). Infant responses impending collision optical and real. *Science*, **171**, 818–820.

Barnes, F. (1975). Accidents in the first three years of life. *Child Care, Health Dev.* **1**, 421–433.

Barten, S., Birns, B., and Rouch, J. (1971). Individual differences in the visual pursuit behaviour of neonates. *Child Dev.* **42**, 313–319.

Bayley, N. (1969). *Bayley Scales of Infant Development*. New York: Psychological Corporation.

Bell, R., and Haaf, R. (1971). Irrelevance of newborn waking states to some motor and appetitional responses. *Child Dev.* **42**, 66–72.

Bell, R. Q. (1975). *The Congenital Contribution of Emotional Responses* in *Early Infancy* (CIBA Foundation Symposium No. 33). Hague Mouton.

Bench, J. (1973). 'Square-wave stimuli' and neonatal auditory behaviour. *J. Exp. Child Psychol.* **16**, 521–527

Bennett, M. J. (1975). The auditory response cradle. A device for the objective assessment of auditory states in the neonate. In R. Birch., A. Pie, and J. Pie, (eds), *Sound Reception in Mammals*. London: Academic Press.

Bennett, M. J. (1978). Trials with the auditory response cradle: neonatal responses to auditory stimuli (Submitted for publication).

Berg, K.M., Berg, W.K., and Graham, S.K. (1971). Infant heart response as a function of stimulus and state. *Psychophysiology*, **8**, 30–44.

Berg, W., Adkinson, C., and Strock, B. (1973). Duration and frequency of periods of alertness in neonates. *Dev. Psychol.*, **9**, 434.

Berkson, B., Wasserman, G. A., and Behrman, R. E. (1974). Heart-rate response to auditory stimuli in immature infants. *Psychophysiology*, **11**, 244–246.

Bernal, J. F. (1973). Night waking in the first 14 months. *Dev. Med. Child Neurol.*, **15**, 760–769.

Beswick, K., Lynch, M. A., and Roberts, J. (1976). Child abuse and general practice. *Br. Med. J.*, **2**, 800–802.

Birch, A. D., and Gussow, J. D. (1970). *Disadvantaged Children. Health Factors and School Failure*. New York: Grune & Stratton.

Blake, A., Stewart, A and Turcan, D. Perinatal intensive care (1977). *J. Psychosom. Res.*, **21**, 261–272.

Blake, A., Stewart, A., and Turcan, D. (1975). Parents of babies of very low birth weight: a long-term follow-up. In R. Porter, and M. O'Connor (eds), *Parent–Infant Interaction*, (CIBA Symposium 33) Amsterdam: Associated Scientific Publishers.

Blurton-Jones, N., Fereira, M., Farquhar-Brown, M., and MacDonald, L. (1978). Does parental behaviour explain the association between perinatal factors and night waking? *Dev. Med. Child Neurol.*, **20**, 427–434.

Bower, T. G. R. (1977). Comment on Yonas *et al.*, 'Development of sensitivity to information for impending collision', *Percept. Psychophys.*, **21** (3), 281–282.

Bower, T. G. R., Broughton, J., and Moore, M. (1970). The demonstration of intention in the reaching of neonate humans. *Nature*, **288**, 679–683.

Bower, T. G. R., Broughton, J., and Moore, M. (1971). Infants' responses to approaching objects. *Percept. Psychophys.*, **9**, 193–196.

Boyle, M., Giffen, A., and Fitzeharding, P. (1977). The very low birth weight infant: impact on parents in the pre-school years. *Early Human Dev.*, **1/2**, 191–201.

Brackbill, Y., Kane, J., Maniel, O. P., and Abramson, D. (1974). Obstetric meperidine usage and assessment of neonatal behaviour. *Anaesthiology*, **40**, 116–120.

Brazelton, T. B. (1970). Effects of prenatal drugs on the behaviour of the neonate. *Am. J. Psychiatry*, **126**, 1261–1266.

Brazelton, T. B. (1973). *Neonatal Assessment scale. London Clinics in Developmental Medicine*. London: Heinemann Medical.

Brazelton, T. B., Robey, M. D., and Collier, D. A. (1969). Infant development in the Zinacanteco Indians of Southern Mexico. *Pediatrics*, **44** (2), 274–289.

Brown, J., Bakeman, R., Shyder, P., Frederickson, W., Morgan, P., and Hepler, R. (1975). Interaction of black inner city mothers with their newborn infants. *Child Dev.* **46**, 677–686.

Bullinger, A. (1976). Orientation de la tete du nouveau né en presence d'un stimulus visuel. Paper from the International Congress of Psychology, Paris.

Butterworth, G. E. (1978). Thoughts and things: Piaget's theory. In J. Radford, and L. Burton (eds.), *Thinking in Perspective*. London: Methuen.

Butterworth, G. E., and Castillo, M. (1976). Co-ordination of auditory and visual space in newborn human infants. *Perception*, **5**, 155–160.

Campos, J. (1976). Heart rate: a sensitive tool for the study of emotional development. In (Ed.) L. Lipsitt (ed.), *Developmental Psychobiology: the Significance of Infancy.* Hillsdale, N. J.: Lawrence Erlbaum Associates.

Carey, W. B. (1970). A simplified method for measuring infant temperament. *Pediatrics*, **77** (2), 188–194.

Carey, W. B. (1974). Night waking and temperament in infancy. *Behav. Paediat.*, **84** (5), 756–758.

Clifton, R. W. (1974). Cardiac conditioning and orienting in the infant. In Obrist, Black, A. H., Brener, J., and Du Cane, L. V. (eds.), *Cardiovascular Psychophysiology.* Chicago: Aldine.

Clifton, R., and Nelson, M. (1976). Habituation in infants: the improvement of paradigm response system and state. In Tighe, H. R. and Leaton L. T. (eds.), *Habituation.* Hillsdale, N. J.: Lawrence Erlbaum Associates.

Copans, S. (1974). Human prenatal effects: methodological problems and some suggested solutions. *Merill Palmer Quart.*, **20**, 43–52.

Crook, C. K., and Lipsitt, L. P. (1976). Neonatal sucking and effects of quantity of the response-contingent fluid effects of rhythm and heart rate. *J. Exp. Child Psychol.*, **21**, 539–548.

Crowell, D. H., Dowes, C. M., Chun, B. J., and Spellacy, F. J. (1965). Galvanic skin reflex in human newborns. *Science*, **148**, 1108–1111.

Dargassies, S. (1952). *Etude Neurologique Sur Le Nouveau-Né.* Paris: Masson.

Dargassies, S. (1977). Long term neurological follow-up study of 286 truly premature infants. I. Neurological sequelae. *Dev. Med. Child Neurol.*, **19**, 462–478.

Davie, R., Butler, N., and Goldstein, H. (1972). *From Birth to Seven. A Report of the National Child Development Study.* London: Longman.

Davies, P.A. (1976). Outlook for low birth-weight infants. *Arch. Dis. Childh.*, **51**, 817–819.

Davies, P. A., and Stewart, A. L. (1975). A study of low birth-weight infants. *Br. Med. Bull.*, **31** (1), 85–91.

Dawkins, N. (1975). Gestational age, size and maturity. In W.G. MacGregor (ed.), *Clinics in Developmental Medicine*, No. 19 London: Spartics Society Heinemann.

Day, R. H. and MacKenzie, B. (1971). Perceptual shape constancy in early infancey. *Perception*, **2**, 315–320.

Day, R. H. (1974). Perceptual processes in early infancy. *Austr., Psychol.* **9**, 15–34.

Dean, M. (1978). Home sweet hospital. *World Medicine*, April, 21–24.

DHSS (1974). *On the state of public health.* (Annual report of the Medical Advisor to the DHSS for the year 1973). London: HMSO.

Dittrichova, J., Paul, K., and Vondrac, E. K. J. (1976). Individual differences in infant sleep. *Dev. Med. Child Neurol.*, **18**, 182–188.

Dobbing, J., and Smart, J. B. (1974). Vulnerability of the developing brain and behaviour. *Br. Med. Bull.*, **30**, 164–168.

Dodwell, P. C., Muir, D., and Di Franco, D. (1976). Responses of infants to visually presented objects. *Science*, **194**, 209–211.

Douglas, J. W. B., and Gear, R. (1976). *Arch. Dis. Childh.*, **51**, 820–827

Dreyfuss-Brisac, C. (1974). Organisation and sleep in prematures: implications for care-giving. In M. Lewis and A. Roseblum, (eds.), *The Effect of the Infant on its*

Caregiver. New York: Wiley.

Drillien, C. M. (1962). Abnormal neurologic signs in the first year of life in low birth-weight infants. *Dev. Med. Child Neurol.*, **14**, 575–584.

Drillien, C. M. (1967). The long term prospects for babies of low birth-weight, *Hosp. Med.*, **1**, 937–944

Dubowitz, L. M. S., Dubowitz, V., and Goldberg, L. (1970). Clinical assessment of gestational age in new born infants. *Pediatrics*, **77**, 1.

Dunn, J. F. (1975). Continuities in early mother–infant interaction. In *Parent–Infant Interaction*. (CIBA Foundation Symposium No. 33). Amsterdam: Scientific Publishers.

Dunn, J. F. (1977). Patterns of early interaction: continuities and consequences. In Schaffer, H. R., (ed.). Studies of mother–infant interaction. London: Academic Press.

Dunn, J. F. (1979). Individual differences in temperament. In M. Rutter, (ed.), The Scientific Foundations of Developmental Psychiatry.

Dunn, J. F. (1978). In D. Schaffer, and J. Dunn, (eds.), *The First Year of Life*. London: Wiley.

Dunn, J. and Wooding, C. (1976). Play in the home: its implications for learning. In Tizard, B. and Harvey, D. (eds.), *The Biology of Play*. London: Lavenham Press.

Fitzhardinge, P., and Ramsay, M. (1973). The improving outlook for the small, prematurely-born infant. *Dev. Med. Child Neurol.*, **15**, 447–459.

Fourcin, A. (1978). Acoustic patterns and speech acquisition. In N. Waterson, and C. Snow, (eds.), *The Development of Communication*. London: Wiley.

Francis-Williams, J., and Davies, P. (1974). Very low birthweight and later intelligence. *Dev. Med. Child Neurol.*, **16**, 709–728.

Friedman, S. (1972). Habituation and recovery of visual response in the alert human newborn. *J. Exp. Child Psychol.*, **13**, 339–349.

Garrow, D. H., and Smith, D. (1976). The modern practice of separating a newborn baby from its mother. *Proc. R. Soc. Med.*, **69**, 22–25.

Graham, P., Rutter, M., and George, S. (1973). Temperamental characteristics as predictors of behavioural disorders in children. *Am. J. Psychiat.*, **43** (2), 329–339.

Griffiths, R. (1964). *The Abilities of Babies*. London: University Press.

Hack, N., Mastow, T., and Miranda, S. B. (1976). Pattern vision in low birth-weight infants. *J. Paediatr.*, **88**, 669–674.

Haith, M .M. (1979). Visual competence in early infancy. In R. H. Held, H. Leibowitz, and H. L. Teuber (eds.), *Handbook of Sensory Physiology*, VIII. Berlin: Springer-Verlag.

Haith, M. M., Bergman, T., and Moore, M. (1977). Eye contact and face scanning in early infancy. *Science*, **198**, 853.

Hales, D. H., Lozoff, B., Sousa, R., and Kennel, I. H. (1977). Defining the limits of the maternal sensitive period. *Dev. Med. Child Neurol.* **19**, 454–461.

Hall, F. (1977). Prenatal events and later infant behaviour. *J. Psychosom. Res.*, **21**, 253–257.

Hall, F. (1978). Personal communication.

Hanson, R. (1978). Key characteristics and child abuse. In H. Kempe, (ed.), *Child Abuse and Neglect: Family and Community*. Cambridge, Massachusetts: Ballinger.

Harris, P. (1977). The child's representation of space. In G. Butterworth, (ed.), *The Child's Representation of the World*. New York: Plenum Press.

Harris, P. L., and MacFarlane, A. (1974). The growth of the effective visual field from birth to seven weeks. *J. Exp. Child Psychol.*, **18**, 340–348.

Haynes, H., White, B., and Held, R. (1965). Visual accommodation in infants. *Science*, **148**, 528–530.

Hecox, M. (1975). Research on evoked potentials in infancy. In L. B. Cohen and P. Salapatek (eds.), *infant Perception*, Vol. I. New York: Academic Press.

Helfer, R. F., and Kempe, C. H. (1972). The child's need for early recognition immediate care and protection. In C. H. Kempe, and H. F. Helfer (eds.), *Helping the Battered*

Child and his Family. Philadelphia: J. B. Lippincott.

Hershenson, M. (1964). Visual discrimination in the human newborn. *J. Comp. Physiol. Psychol.*, **58**, 270–276.

Hoppenbrouwers, T. (1977). Respiration rates and apnoea in infants at risk for SIDS. *Clin. Res.*, **25**, 189a.

Hutt, S. J., Hutt, C., Lenard, H. G., Bernuth, H., and Muntjewerff, W. J. (1968). Auditory responsivity in the human neonate. *Nature*, **218**, 888–890.

Jaffe, J., Stern, D., and Perry, J. C. (1973). Conversational coupling of gaze behaviours in prelinguistic human development. *J. Psycholinguist. Res.*, **2**, 321–330.

Johnson, P., and Salisbury, D. M. (1975). *Breathing and Sucking During Feeding in the Newborn* (CIBA Foundation Symposium No. 33). The Hague: Mouton.

Kagan, J. (1971). *Change and Continuity in Infancy*. New York: Wiley.

Kalverboer, U. (1975). Neurobehavioural studies of pre-school children. In *Clinics in Developmental Medicine*, No. 54. *Spastics Society*. London: Heinemann.

Kaye, K. (1964). Skin conduction in the human neonate. *Child Dev.* **35**, 1297–1305.

Kaye, K. (1980). The micropsychology of feeding in the first two weeks of life. SRCD Monographs (in press)

Kearsley, R. (1973). Neonatal response to auditory stimulation. A demonstration of orienting behaviour. *Child Dev.* **44**, 582–590.

Klaus, M., and Kennell, J. H. (1970). Mothers separated from their infants. *Pediatr. Clin. North Am.*, **186**, 1013–1037.

Kleitman, N. (1963). *Sleep and Wakefulness*. Chicago: University of Chicago Press.

Korner, A. F. (1972). State variables as obstacle and as mediator of stimulation in infant research. *Merrill Palmer Quart.*, **18**, 77–94.

Lacey, J. I. (1967). Somatic response patterning and stress. Some revisions of activation theory. In M. A. Appleby, and R. Trumbull (eds.), *Psychological Stress*. New York: Appleton-Century-Crofts.

Leifer, A. D., Liederman, P. H., Barnett, C. R., and Williams, J. A. (1972). Effects of infant separation on maternal attachment behaviour. *Child Dev.*, **43**, 1203–1218.

Lewis, M. (1974). The cardiac response in infancy. In Thompson, R. F., and M. Patterson (eds.), *Bioelectric Recording Techniques*. New York: Academic Press.

Lewis, M. (1976). *Origins of Intelligence in Infancy*. New York: Plenum Press.

Lewis, M., Day, C., and Harnitz, M. (1969). Cardiac responsivity to tactile stimulation in waking and sleeping infants. *Percept. Mot. Skills*, **29**, 259–269.

Lewis, M., and Johnson, N. (1971). What's thrown out with the bath water? A baby? *Child Dev.*, **42**, 1053–1055.

Lieberman, B. A., Rosenblatt, D. B., Belsey, E., Mills, M., Packer, M., Redshaw, M., Caldwell, J., Natariarri, L., Smith, R. L., Williams, M., and Beard, R. W. (1979). The effects of maternally administered pethidine or epidural bupivacaine on the foetus and newborn. *Br. J. Obst. Gynaecol.*, **86**, 598–607.

Lipsitt, L. (1976). *Developmental Psychobiology: the Significance of Infancy*. New York: Plenum Press.

Lipsitt, L. P., Engen, T., and Kaye, E. H. (1963). Developmental changes in the olfactory threshold of the neonate. *Child Dev.*, **34**, 371–376.

Lipsitt, L., Reilly, B., Butcher, M., and Greenwood, B. (1976). Stability and interrelationship of newborn sucking and heart rate. *Dev. Psychobiol.*, **9**, 305–311.

Lynch, M. A. (1975). Child health and child abuse. *Lancet*, **2**, 317–319.

Lynch, M. A., and Roberts, J. (1978). Early alerting signs. In A. Franklin, (ed.), *Child Abuse*. London: Open Books.

MacFarlane, J. A. (1975). *Olfaction in the Development of Social Preference in the Human Neonate. Parent–Infant Interaction* (CIBA Foundation Symposium. No. 33) Amsterdam: Associated Scientific Publishers.

MacFarlane, J. L., Harris, P., and Barnes, I. (1976). Central and peripheral vision in the neonate. *J. Exp. Child Psychol.*, **21**, 532–538.

Maratos, O. (1973). The origin and development of imitation in the first six months of life. Unpublished Ph.D. Thesis, University of Geneva.

Marriage, K., and Davies, P A. (1977). Neurological sequelae in children surviving mechanical ventilation in the neonatal period. *Arch. Dis. Childh.* **52**, 176–182.

McBride, A. (1978). The ability of the human neonate to discriminate between speech and non-speech vocalisation. Unpublished M.Sc. Thesis, University of London.

McCall, R. B. (1976). Towards an epigenetic conception of mental development. In M. Lewis, (ed.), *Origins of Intelligence in Infancy.* New York: Plenum Press.

McDonnald, R. L. (1968). The role of emotional factors in obstetric complications. *J. Psychosom. Med.*, **30**, 222–234.

Mackenzie, B., and Day, R. H. (1971). Operant learning of visual pattern discrimination. *J. Exp. Child Psychol.*, **11**, 45–53.

Meltzoff, A., and Moore, K. (1977). Imitation of physical and manual gestures by human neonates. *Science*, **198**, 75–78.

Mendelson, M., and Haith, K. (1976). The relation between vision and audition in the human newborn. *Monogr. Soc. Res. Child Deve.*, No. **167**.

Miranda, S. B. (1970). Visual abilities and pattern preferences of premature infants and full-term neonates. *J. Exp. Child Psychol.*, **10**, 189–205.

Miranda, S. B., and Fantz, R. L. (1973). Visual preferences of Down's syndrome and normal infants. *Child Dev.*, **44**, 555–561.

Miranda, S. B., Hack, M. B., Robert, C., Fantz, L., Fanaroff, A., and Klaus, M. (1977). Neonatal pattern vision: a predictor of future mental abilities. *J. Pediatr.*, **91** (4), 642–647.

Moffit, A. (1971). Consonant perception by twenty to twenty-four-week old infants. *Child Dev.*, **42**, 717–731.

Neligman, G., Prudhen, D., and Steiner, H. (1974). The formative years: birth, family and development in Newcastle-upon-Tyne. Oxford: O. U. P.

Newson, E. and Newson, J. (1976). *Seven Years Old in the Home Environment.* London: George Allen & Unwin.

Northern, J. L., and Downs, M. P. (1974). *Hearing in Children.* Baltimore, Maryland: Williams & Wilkins.

Ornitz, E. M., Ritvo, E. R., Lee, Y. H., Panman, L. M., Walter, R. O., and Mason, A. (1969). The auditory evoked response in babies during Remsleep. *Electroencephal Ogr. Clin. Neurophysiol.*, **27**, 195–198.

Packer, M. (1978). Mother–infant interaction in the first week of life. Unpublished report, Nuffield Foundation. (Research carried out at Bedford College and funded by the Nuffield Foundation on mother–infant interaction in the first week of life).

Parmelee, H. A. H., and Stern, F. (1972). Development of states in infancy. In C. D. C., Clemente, P. P., Purpura, and F. Mayer (eds.), *Sleep and the Maturing Nervous System.* New York: Academic Press.

Pomeleau-Malcuit, A., and Clifton, K. (1973). Neonatal heart rate response of tactile auditory and vestibular stimulation in different states. *Child Dev.*, **44**, 485–496.

Pratt, C. (1978). A study of infant crying behaviour in the home environment during the first year of life. Unpublished Ph.D. dissertation, University of Oxford.

Prechtl, H. F. R. (1974). The behavioural state of the newborn infant. *Brain Res.*, **76**, 188–210.

Prechtl. H. F. R. (1977). Neurological examination of the full-term newborn infant. *Clinics in Developmental Medicine*, No. 63. London: Spastics Society/Heinemann.

Prechtl, H. F. R., and Beintema, D. (1964). Neurological examination of the full-term newborn infant. *Clinics in Developmental Medicine*, No. 12, Spastics Society, London:

Prechtl, H., Akiyamaya, Z., and Grant, D. K. (1968). Polygraphic studies of the full-term newborn. (Eds.) R., Keith, and M. Baxs (eds.), *Studies in Infancy.* London: Heinemann Medical.

Prechtl, H. F. R., Theorell, K., and Blair, A. (1973). Behavioural state cycles in abnormal infants. *Devl. Med. Child Neurol.*, **15** (5), 606–615.

Richards, M. P. M. (1979). Possible effects of early separation on later development of children: a review. In F., Brimblecombe, and M. P. M. Richards (eds.), *Early Separation and Special Care Nurseries. Clinics in Developmental Medicine.* London: Heinemann.

Richards, M. P. M. and Chard, T. (1978). Benefits and hazards of the new obstetrics. *Clinics in Developmental Medicine*, No. 64. London: Spastics Society/Heinemann.

Robson, K. and Moss, H. A. (1970). Patterns and determinants of maternal attachment. *Pediatrics*, **77**, 976–985.

Rosenblith, J. P. (1974). Relations between neonatal behaviours and those at 8 months. *Dev. Psychol.*, **10**, 779–92.

Rosenblatt, D. (1977). Personal communication.

Rosenblatt, D. and Packer, M. (1978). Issues in the study of social behaviour in the first week of life. In D. Schaffer and J. Dunn (eds.), *The First Year of Life.* London: Wiley.

Rutter, M. (1977). Individual differences. In M. Rutter and L. A. Hersov, (eds.), *Recent Approaches to Child Psychiatry.* Oxford: Blackwell. Scientific Publications.

Rutter, M., Birch, H., Thomas, H., and Chess, S. (1964). Temperamental characteristics in infancy in the later development of behavioural disorders. *Br. J. Psychiatry*, **110**, 651–661.

Salapatek, P. (1975). In L. B. Cohen, and P. Salapatek, (eds.), *Infant Perception: From Sensation to Perception.*, Vol. 1: *Basic Visual Processes.* New York: Academic Press.

Samaroff, A., Cashmore, T. F., and Dykes, A. (1973). Heart rate deceleration during visual fixation in human newborns. Dev. *Psychol.*, **8**, 117–119.

Samaroff, A., and Chandler, M. J. (1975). Reproductive risk and the continuum of caretaking causality. In F. D. Horowitz, M. Hetherington, S., Scarr-Salapatek and G. Siegel (eds.), *Review of Child Development Research*, Vol. **4**, Chicago: University of Chicago Press.

Scanlon, J. W. (1974). Obstetric anaesthesia as a neonatal risk factor in normal labour and delivery. *Clin. Perinatol.*, **1** (2), 465–482.

Scarr-Salapatek, S. (1976). Genetic determinants of infant development: an overstated case. In L. Lipsitt, (ed.), *Developmental Psychobiology: The Significance of Infancy.* Hillsdale, N. J.: Laurence Erlbaum Associates.

Schlesinger, E. R. (1973). Neonatal intensive-care planning for services and outcomes following care. *J. Pediat.*, **82**, 916–920.

Schulte, F., Hinzeg, L. and Schremph, G. (1972). Maternal toxaemia, foetal malnutrition and bioelectric brain activity of the newborn. In C. D., Clemente, D., Purpura, and F. Mayer (eds.), *Sleep and the Maturing Nervous System.* New York: Academic Press.

Seashore, M. J., Leifer, A. O., Barnett, C. R., and Liederman, P. H. (1973). The effects of denial of early mother–infant interaction on maternal self-confidence. *J. Person. Soc. Psychol.*, **26** (3), 369–378.

Slater, A. M. (1975). Personal communication.

Snow, C. (1977). The development of conversations between mothers and babies. *J. Child Lang.*, 4, 129–152.

Sontag, L. W., Steel, W. G. and Lewis, M. (1969). The foetal and maternal cardiac response to environmental stress. *Human Dev.*, **12**, 1–9.

Sostek, A. M., and Anders, P. F. (1977). Relationships among the Brazelton neonatal scale, Bailey infant scales and early temperament. *Child Dev.*, **48**, 320–323.

Soule, A. B. (1974). Clinical uses of the Brazelton Neonatal Assessment Scale. *Pediatrics*, **54**, 583–586.

Soule, A. B. (1978). Personal communication.

Sroufe, L. A. (1979). Emotional development in infancy. In J. Osofsky (ed.), *Handbook of Infancy.* New York: Wiley.

Stern, D. (1977). *The First Relationship: Infant and Mother.* London: Fontana Open Books.

Stewart, A. (1977). The survival of low weight infants. *Br. J. Hosp. Med.*, September, 182–188.

Stewart, A. L., and Reynolds E. (1974). Improved prognosis for infants of very low birth weight. *Pediatrics*, **54**, 724–735.

Stewart, A., Turcan, D., Rawlings, G., and Reynolds, E. (1977). Prognosis for infants weighing 1000 g. or less at birth. *Ārch. Dis. Childh.*, **52** (2), 97–104.

Stewart, A., Turcan, D., Rawlings, G., Hart, S., and Gregory, S. (1978). Outcome of infants at high risk of major handicap. CIBA Symposium. *Mother–Infant Interaction* London: CIBA Foundation.

Sylvester-Bradley, B. and Trevarthen, C. (1978). Baby talk as an adaptation to the infant's communication. In M. Waterson, and C. Snow, (eds.), *The Development of Communication.* London: Wiley.

Tanaka, Y., and Arayama, T. (1969). Foetal response to acoustic stimuli. *Prac. Otorhinolaryngol.*, **31**, 269–273.

Thalme, B., Belfrage, P., and Raabe, R. (1974). Lumbar epidural analgesia in labour. *Acta Obstet. Gynecol. Scand.*, **53**, 27–35.

Theorell, K., Prechtl, H. F. R., Blaim, A. W., and Lind, J. (1973). Behavioural state cycles of normal newborn infants. *Dev. Med. Child Neurol.*, **15**, 597–605.

Thoman, E. (1975). Sleep and wake behaviours in neonates: consistencies and consequences. *Merrill Palmer Quart.*, **21** (4), 295–314.

Thoman, E., Miane, V., and Freesem, M. P. (1977). The role of respiratory instability in the S. I. D. syndrome. *Dev. Med. and Child. Neurol.*, **19**, 729–738.

Thomas, A., Chess, S., Birch, H. D., Hertzog, M. E., and Korn, S. (1963). *Behavioural Individuality in Early Childhood.* New York: Behavioural Press.

Tizard, B. (1978). *Adoption.* London: Open Books.

Torgeson, A., and Kringler, E. (1980). Temperamental differences in infants: a study of newborn twins. *Child Psychol. Psychiat.* (Submitted for publication).

Touwen, B. (1977). Neurological development in infancy. *Clinics in Developmental Medicine*, No. 58 London: Spastics Society/Heinemann.

Trevarthen, C. (1975). Basic patterns of psychogenetic change in fancy. In *Proceedings of the P. E. C. D. Conference on Dips in Learning.* St. Paul De Vence. March 1975.

Trevarthen, C., Hubley, P., and Shevren, L. (1975). Les activitiés innees du nourrison. *La Recherche*, **6** (56), 447–458.

Tronick, E., and Clanton, C. (1971). Infant looking patterns. *Vision Res.*, **11**, 1479–1486.

Tronick, E., Wise, S., Als, H., Adamson, L., Scanlon, J. B., and Brazelton, T. B. (1976). Regional obstetric anaesthetic and newborn behaviour: effect over the first ten days of life. *J. Pediat.*, **58**, 94–100.

Turcan, D. M., Rawlings, G., and Stewart, A. L. (1977). School abilities at 8 years of infants who weighed less than 1500 g. at birth. *Paediat. Res.*, **9**, 1025 (Abstract).

Turkewitz, G., Moreau, T., Birch, H. G., Levy, L., and Cornwell, A. C. (1966). Effect of intensity of auditory stimulation on directional eye movements in the human neonate. *Anim. Behav.*, **14**, 93–101.

Ucko, E. (1975). Comparative study of asphyxiated and non-asphyxiated babies from birth to 5 years. *Dev. Med. Child Neurol.*, **7**, 643–657.

Venables, P. (1980). Autonomic reactivity. In M. Rutter (ed.) *The Scientific Foundations of Developmental Psychiatry.* London: Heinemann Medical Books.

Watson, J. S. (1970). Cognitive perceptual development in infancy. Paper presented at Merrill Palmer Conference on Research and Teaching of Infant Development, Detroit.

Weir, C. (1976). Auditory frequency sensitivity in the neonate: a signal detection analysis. *J. Exp. Child Psychol.*, **21**, 219–225.

Weller, G. M. and Bell, R. J. (1965). Basal skin conductance and neonatal state. *Child Dev.*, **36**, 647–657.

Whiten, A. (1977). Separation of term infants. In Schaffer, H. (ed.), *Studies of Interaction of Infancy* (Loch-Lomond Symposium). London: Academic Press.

Wingate, P. (1974). The effect of epidural analgesic upon foetal and neonatal status. *Am. J. Obst. Gynecol.*, 1102–1106.

Wolff, P. H. (1972). The interaction of state and non-nutritive sucking. In J. F. Bosma (ed.), *Third Symposium on Oral Sensation and Perception*. Springfield, Illinois: Charles Thomas.

Wolff, P. H. (1973). Organisation of behaviour in the first three months of life. In J. I. Nurnberger, (ed.), *Biological and Environmental Determinants of Early Development.*, Vol. 51. (Association for Research in Nervous and Mental Disease). Baltimore: Williams and Wilkins.

Wooson, R. and Wooson, E. (1977). Personal Communication.

Yang, R. K., Federman, E. J., and Duithilt, T. C. (1976). The characterisation of neonatal behaviour: a dimensional analysis. *Dev. Psychol.*, **12**, 204.

Zelazo, P. R. (1972). Smiling and vocalising: a cognitive emphasis. *Merrill Palmer Quart.*, **18**, 349–365.

Zelazo, P. R. (1976). From reflexive to instrumental behaviour. In L. P. Lipsett (ed.), *Developmental Psychobiology: the Significance of Infancy*. New York: Plenum Press.

Zelazo, P. R. (1977). Reactivity to perceptual cognitive events: application for infant assessment. In (eds.), R. Kearsley and I. Siegal. *Infants at Risk: the Assessment of Cognitive Functioning*. N. Y. L. Erlbaum Associates.

Zelazo, P. R., Zelazo, N. A., and Colb, S. (1972). Walking in the newborn. *Science*, **176**, 314–315.

Foundations of Psychosomatics
Edited by M. J. Christie and P. G. Mellett
© 1981 John Wiley & Sons Ltd.

5

STUDIES OF CHILDREN AT HIGH RISK FOR SCHIZOPHRENIA: SOME METHODOLOGICAL CONSIDERATIONS

PETER H. VENABLES

Department of Psychology, University of Reading, England.

INTRODUCTION

Research which attempts to examine the mechanisms which might be responsible for schizophrenic breakdown by studying adult schizophrenics exhibiting the disease is made difficult by a number of factors. As Mednick and McNeil outlined in 1968 the behaviour of identified schizophrenics

> may be markedly altered in response to correlates of the illness such as educational, economic, and social failure; pre-hospital, hospital and post-hospital drug regimens; bachelorhood, long-term institutionalization, chronic illness and sheer misery.

Because of these factors the schizophrenic as investigated in hospital may present a picture which is an inseparable amalgam of primary disease processes and secondary factors which result from the patient's own reaction to the onset of his symptoms, the public's reaction to the unusual behaviour he begins to exhibit, and the results of his contacts with health services.

These considerations strongly suggest that it is worth while attempting to study the primary aspects of the disease as it develops by examination of subjects in the pre-morbid state. However, this is not a simple undertaking, necessitating as it does the longitudinal investigation of numbers of subjects of whom only a few may eventually break down.

In 1957 Pearson and Kley published a paper which laid the foundations for what in 1974(a) Rosenthal called the 'bandwagon rush to high-risk studies'. In their paper, which has not perhaps received the credit it deserves, they suggested that different 'base-rates' for the incidence of illness in different populations should be used to engender economies of design in longitudinal studies. They proposed that the potential usefulness of the long-acknowledged fact that abnormality of behaviour 'runs in families', whether the cause is social or biological, might lie

> in the fact that individuals with a known and relatively high incidence rate for a particular disorder may be submitted to longitudinal investi-

gation of a kind which would not be economical in samples drawn from the general population.

Thus, if 1000 children drawn at random from the general population were examined at age 10 and then followed up until age 55 only eight or nine schizophrenics would be expected to be found on the basis of a standard figure of lifetime risk for the disease of 0.85 per cent. On the the other hand, if the 1000 children all had one schizophrenic parent, then over the same time some 100 schiozophrenics would be expected to be diagnosed and the outcome of the study would be reasonably viable.

The importance of Pearson and Kley's paper was that they laid the foundation for prospective studies with the emphasis on reliable data collection at the start of a developmental period, in contrast to the often biased and inaccurate data available to retrospective studies from memory or past records.

Jones (1973) has reviewed the current methods used for studying the development of schizophrenia. In general all retrospective methods are shown to be in some way less than appropriate for the task.

Studies have shown that when anamnestic interview data are compared with factual records collected at the remembered time the two sets of data correlated only about $+0.2$ and $+0.3$ (Burton, 1970; Yarrow, Campbell, and Burton, 1970). Even over a period as short as 3 years Robbins (1963) has shown that mothers are very inaccurate in remembering the details of the way in which they brought up their children. If distortions occur over short periods with normal mothers of normal children, then long-period recall of the developmental features of children's lives in a possibly pathogenic environment is clearly open to even greater disturbance. Consequently, research on the aetiology of schizophrenia which places major reliance on recalled developmental data must be treated with extreme caution.

A more acceptable form of retrospective research is that which has been called the 'follow-back' design. In this, the earlier life data are in the form of records of past observations. These may, for instance, be from school records or case notes from clinics. While these data are much more reliable than anamnestic data they nevertheless may be either relatively scanty if drawn from school records or contain a population bias if derived from the case notes of those children who attended a clinic. Furthermore, the type of data available may not be wholly appropriate for the investigation in hand.

In the case of 'follow-up' or prospective designs, some of the major disadvantages of the retrospective paradigm can be eliminated. However, the prospective design has its own disadvantages which need to be recognized if the obvious enthusiasm for the prospective mode is not to be adopted in a blinkered fashion. The first difficulty arises from the common use of the familial high-risk method, derived from the principles advocated by Pearson and Kley (1957). If, to obtain the obvious economies inherent in the high-risk design, the subjects in the study are those at familial risk then clearly there is a bias in that those developing disorders but who do not have a sick parent are thus not studied. Rosenthal

(1970), for instance, cites data that indicate that only about 5 per cent of schizophrenics have a schizophrenic parent.

A second bias arises from the fact that the choice of measures taken at the initial stage is dependent on the then-current climate in which the investigation is carried out, and unless these are soundly and broadly based they may be superseded as time passes. More narrowly, although the concepts underlying the measurement may be appropriate, the techniques and apparatus available in the initial stages may suggest that the earlier measurements are inadequate or even not fully exploited.

Mednick (1978) points out a further difficulty in the use of the high-risk prospective method which needs to be recognized. This is the intrusion of error in design according to what has become known as Berkson's fallacy. The error arises, according to Berkson (1955), if the experimental high-risk group and the control low-risk group are not representative on a particular characteristic of the distribution of this characteristic in the general population. The major difficulty is that it is not possible to say, *a priori*, what particular characteristics ought to be selected and matched for in experimental and control populations. This type of error is not, of course, confined to prospective types of study but is perhaps more evident when the detailed characteristics of control and experimental populations develop as the study proceeds.

A further major difficulty in high-risk studies, as, of course, in any longitudinal work, is that of obtaining continued support for the study. This is particularly the case in a study of a population at high risk for schizophrenia where there are reasons (e.g. Mednick, 1970) to suggest that one aetiological factor lies in complications at or around the time of birth, and yet the disease is one which only has its first major manifestations in early adulthood and indeed the period of risk of onset may extend to age 55. Thus, even a study which starts as late as possible in the premorbid period, for instance at age 15, has to extend for some 20 years to cover the major time at risk, and the optimal study probably needs to cover a 56-year period. In addition to the difficulty of obtaining continuing support for a study which has little intermediate 'yield' from a large data collection exercise, it is inevitable that most studies will outlive the working life of a single major investigator with consequent difficulties in maintenance of enthusiastic commitment.

Nevertheless, the review by Garmezy (1974) shows that a large number of high-risk studies have been undertaken and the enthusiasm for the design which Rosenthal (1974a) notes is probably warranted. Most studies which have been undertaken are founded on expectations of a higher than normal base rate because of *genetic* risk, although the design used in selecting children with one schizophrenic parent is more strictly that of *familial* risk, insofar as it is not usual to take only those offspring of a schizophrenic parent who are separated from the parent as subjects for the study. The most often cited study in support of genetic risk is that of Heston (1966) who showed that in 47 children who were separated from their schizophrenic mothers at age 3 days, five developed schizophrenia by age 36, which gives an age-corrected rate over a risk period of 15–45 years of 16.6 per cent. Another study where children were raised apart from the schizophrenic parent, the well-known adoptee investigation of Rosenthal et al. (1971), produces a risk figure of 11.6 per cent for children with one schizophrenic parent. Hanson, Gottesman, and Meehl (1977) summarize the presently available data which suggest a mean risk for children with one schizophrenic parent of 9.2 per cent, the range over several studies being from 2.2 to 16.9 per cent. As Hanson *et al.* point out, part of this variation may be due to the inconsistencies in selection of cases for the studies due to vagaries of diagnosis of the parent, and also due to variation in cut-off points of classification as schizophrenic in the diagnosis of the offspring. Also arising, for instance, from the Heston (1966) study is the notion that children of a schizophrenic parent may suffer from disorders other than that of schizophrenia, a topic reviewed by Rosenthal (1974b), which leads to the expectation of a larger 'yield' from high-risk investigations than about 10 per cent of the population studied, if psychiatric diagnoses other than schizophrenia are considered. In this instance, the possibilities of finding offspring with a range or spectrum of abnormalities may be as high as 50 per cent.

Although elevated risk due to familial factors has been most commonly the characteristic employed in studies which have been undertaken, other methods may be employed. Jones (1973), for instance, identifies deviant childhood behaviour, pathological family interaction systems, social disadvantage, prenatal and perinatal influences, and cognitive style variables as criteria for identifying high-risk populations. To this list might be added deviant physiological function in so far as the study of children at risk in Mauritius, which will be discussed later, is based on this principle. Since Jones' review a further development in research technique appears to be gaining momentum; this is the investigation of schizotypy (Meehl, 1962) in the socially 'normal' population. This is proposed firstly in its own right as possibly providing a non-contaminated model for studying schizophrenia, and secondly because of the assumption of a higher risk for the development of schizophrenia among those who might be labelled as schizotypic.

The term schizotypy, although brought into usage by Rado (1956) was given particular emphasis by Meehl (1962). He suggested that the term *schizotaxia* be used for a neural integrative defect which was inherited and that 'the imposition of a social learning history upon schizotaxic individuals' results in a personality organization which he called, following Rado (1956), the *schizotype*.

Chapman *et al.* (1978) have developed some of Meehl's ideas and have constructed scales for 'anhedonia' and 'perceptual aberration' which embody factors said by Meehl to characterize schizotypy. Chapman *et al.* suggest that a reasonable case may be made out that persons exhibiting schizotypy may be considered to form a high-risk sample. In support of this view they cite the findings of Hoch and Cattell (1959) and Hoch *et al.* (1962) who showed that 20 per cent of subjects diagnosed as showing pseudoneurotic schizophrenia, which closely resembles Meehl's descriptions of schizotypy, were found to develop overt schizophrenia in a 5–20-year follow-up. Nielsen and Petersen (1976), in a study somewhat akin to that of Chapman *et al.* (1978), developed a scale of '*schizophrenism*' on the basis of phenomenological reports of experience of schizophrenic patients given by Chapman (1966). While the 'schizophrenism' scale is significantly correlated with EPI Neuroticism (Eysenck and Eysenck, 1967), what is of considerable interest is that schizophrenism was correlated ($r = 0.62$) to skin conductance response (SCR) recovery rate, while neuroticism did not significantly correlate with this electrodermal variable. In this context it should be noted that schizophrenic subjects are reported to show faster than normal SCR recovery (Ax and Bamford, 1970; Gruzelier and Venables, 1972; Zahn, Carpenter, & McGlashan, 1975a). The association of schizophrenism with neuroticism is perhaps in accord with suggestions above that schizotypy is akin to *pseudoneurotic* schizophrenia.

One potential advantage of the use of a design based on elevated risk due to the presence of schizotypy is that the population studied is probably adult and the developmental factors which have to be taken into account in the other high-risk studies do not intrude. Furthermore, when starting from a sample which is already adult the length of time of follow-up is thus reduced. However, as a means of studying the full development of schizophrenia due to the onset of a primary disease process, a study of the adult schizotype does not offer the potential advantages of the fully prospective longitudinal study starting from childhood. A very full coverage of the studies of this kind that were under way in 1974 is given by Garmezy (1974).

THE 1962 HIGH-RISK STUDY IN COPENHAGEN AND STUDIES WHICH HAVE DEVELOPED FROM IT

In 1960 Mednick (Mednick and Higgins, 1960) proposed the start of a research project in the Detroit area, the aim of which was the interviewing, and psychological and psychophysiological testing, of children who might become schizophrenic. These children would be considered to be at high risk because either or both of their parents were schizophrenic. The attempt to start this study in 1961 showed, however, that the necessary records were inadequate and the possibility of carring out a longitudinal study in a country with a high level of geographical mobility promised to present major difficulties and to result in an unacceptable loss of subjects. How far this decision was correct when seen in the light of those projects since started in the United States remains to be seen. However, the abandonment led Mednick to transfer his proposed work to Denmark where the existence of population registers makes the possibility of successfully carrying out a longitudinal study, lasting upwards of 20 years, much higher. In support of this belief Mednick (Mednick and Schulsinger, 1968) was able to cite the experience of Fremming (1951) who reported a success rate of 92 per cent in locating 5500 Danish subjects in a follow-up after 60 years.

The design adopted by Mednick and Schulsinger involved the testing of twice as many children at risk as controls at low risk. It was expected that for every vulnerable subject who succumbed with psychiatric disorder there would be the possibility of matching with another vulnerable subject who did not so succumb and also with a low-risk non-vulnerable subject. As pointed out by Rosenthal (1974a) this well-conceived strategy did not succeed, largely because the original matching did not include the subjects' psychiatric status at the time of the first examination. Mednick and Schulsinger (1968) state that many otherwise matched pairs were discrepant on the psychiatric rating of 'level of adjustment'. They therefore rematched subjects who broke down (the sick group) with one high-risk but 'well' subject and one low-risk subject, the matching variables being age, sex, social class, and level of adjustment at the time of the initial assessment. Rosenthal (1974a) points out that acceptance of this revised strategy might suggest that some of the measures carried out on the sick group during the initial examination in 1962 might not be reflecting aetiological factors but might be measuring the extent to which the disorder had already developed. It should be noted that Mednick and Schulsinger decided to carry out this study on subjects of mean age 15 years, largely in order that the length of eventual follow-up before breakdown would not be too extended. However, it may be that the study of subjects so close to the beginning of the period of risk presents difficulties in that increasing maladjustment in those who are going to break down already modifies some of the variables measured in the 'premorbid' period, thus to some extent annulling some of the value of the high-risk method. Nevertheless, no subjects in the study were overtly abnormal and thus the aims of studying a high-risk population premorbidly seem to have been maintained.

The choice of measures used in this study was to a very large extent determined by the theory of the development of schizophrenia which Mednick had presented in 1958. This model, derived from the then currently topical aspects of learning theory, suggested that 'schizophrenics to be' were more conditionable, generalized more readily, and showed higher levels of 'arousal' which dissipated more slowly than comparable normals. Thus a major aspect of the testing of the subjects was in essence a 'GSR' conditioning paradigm with measures of heart rate and electromyogram (EMG) being collected at the same time. All stimuli were presented by the use of a standard auditory tape, both conditioned stimulus (CS) and unconditioned stimulus (UCS) being auditory, the latter being an unpleasant noise of 96 dB.

One aspect of the procedure which reflects the 1960 'state of the art' was the short CS–UCS interval of $\frac{1}{2}$ second, thus allowing no possibility of obtaining the full characteristics of the response to the CS on reinforced trials.

Other measures which were obtained were the Wechsler Intelligence Scale for Children (WISC), the Minnesota Multiphasic Personality Inventory (MMPI) and a version of the Kent–Rosenoff word-association test. A self-administered adjective checklist was also employed and the same adjectives were also used by the investigators to describe the subject. Many descriptions of this study and the association of the measures taken in 1962 with subsequent breakdown have been provided. Perhaps the most important of these are the following Mednick (1967); Mednick and Schulsinger (1968, 1973); Mednick, Schulsinger, and Garfinkel (1975); Mednick (1978); and Mednick *et al.* (1978). The latest description of this material in Mednick *et al.* (1978) suggests that electrodermal data collected in 1962 is capable of predicting schizophrenic breakdown in 1972, and that this psychophysiological indication of the status of the subject in 1962 was itself related to perinatal conditions 15 years earlier.

The most informative statistical method used in Mednick *et al.* (1978) to demonstrate the implications of the data was path analysis, using the LISREL computer program (Jöreskog and van Thello, 1972). This provides a system for using multiple indicators of each construct used and indications of the extent of the linkage between each construct. Consequently the variables—perinatal birth complications, electrodermal data, and schizophrenic breakdown—are statistically defined constructs derived from several variables. The measure of perinatal birth complications is derived from a scale described by Mirdal *et al.* (1974). This scale weighted severity of items on a five-point basis: e.g. severe eclampsia, 5; forceps or vacuum extraction, 3; birthweight 2500–3000 g, 1; birthweight less than 1000 g, 5. The construct uses as metrics: the number of complications, a weighting for the most severe complication, and the total weighted score for all complications. The electrodermal data comprise the product of percentage of electrodermal responses (responsivity) and mean recovery rate of the skin conductance response during three sections of the GSR paradigm—conditioning, test for conditioning, and generalization. The measure of schizophrenic breakdown is derived from the combination of 18 symptom clusters from data collected in 1972 (H. Schulsinger, 1976) under four heads: hallucinations and delusions, 'hebephrenic' features, thought disorder, and autistic features.

Path analysis reveals that perinatal birth complications predict the 1962 electrodermal data ($p = 0.004$ males; $p = 0.003$ females) and that for males the 1972 schizophrenia construct is predicted ($p = 0.001$) for males. However, for females no such association is found. Mednick *et al.* (1978) discuss this sex discrepancy but any suggestions to account for it can only be considered to be tentative.

Although this last report of the findings of the 1962 Copenhagen study has been taken here as an example, the results have been outlined in earlier reports. Two aspects are of particular importance. The first of these is the reported role of obstetric and perinatal complications as possible precursors of schizophrenia. The second is the reliance of the findings on one particular aspect of the electrodermal response, namely the recovery limb. The suggestion that faster skin conductance (SC) recovery might be important was first indicated by Mednick (1967) in a report which showed that the high-risk and low-risk samples were differentiated on this variable with the high-risk group showing faster recovery than the low risk. The suggestion that fast SCR recovery might be associated with schizophrenia was subsequently supported, as stated earlier, by Ax and Bamford (1970), Gruzelier and Venables (1972), and Zahn, Carpenter, and McGlashan (1975) who showed that recovery of the SCR was faster in adult schizophrenics than in normals.

These two aspects have influenced the design of two further studies, one in Copenhagen and one in Mauritius. The finding of the apparent importance of perinatal variables suggested that a further study should be undertaken in which this variable was examined with better data. Consequently a study was carried out in which the selection of subjects was based on a sample of 9006 consecutive births fully recorded in Copenhagen between 1959 and 1961. From this sample, sub-groups of children of schizophrenic, 'character disorder', and matched normal parents were chosen. The sample and its selection are described by Mednick, *et al.*, (1971). This new study, begun in 1972 when the children were aged between 9 and 11 years, will thus permit confirmation of the findings of the earlier study which relate perinatal to subsequent data but with a much stronger set of perinatal data than in the earlier 1962 study, where these data were taken from available records not collected in a standard fashion. Besides a considerable amount of other data, psychophysiological data were again collected. Electrodermal and cardiovascular responses to standard taped stimuli were recorded. The tape format on this occasion was modified to provide an initial orientation section and a subsequent conditioning paradigm but on this occasion with a longer CS–UCS interval to enable first, second, and third interval responses to be measured (Prokasy and Kumpfer, 1973). Electroencephalogram (EEG) data collected at this time by Itil and his colleagues (Itil, *et al.*, 1974) have been published from a sub-sample of the material, and analysis of the resting EEG indicates that the high-risk (for schizophrenia) children show more slow delta, more fast beta, and less alpha activity than the control children. These findings are strongest for data recorded from the right temporal parietal leads. In the case of auditory evoked potential measures the high-risk children showed shorter latency of P_2, P_3, and N_3 components. No differences were shown in the amplitude of these components.

Before turning to the study in Mauritius, it is worth while describing two other studies in which the psychophysiological aspects of the 1962 Copenhagen study have received 'constructive replication' (Lykken, 1968). One of these is by Erlenmeyer-Kimling and her associates in New York, preliminary results of which are reported in Erlenmeyer-Kimling (1975). In this study, again of familial risk design, the children were between 7 and 12 years old and were tested between 1971 and 1973. In this study, as with the Copenhagen replication, the children are not yet at an age when breakdown can have occurred and where any form of proper validation can therefore take place. However, while in the 1962 Copenhagen study electrodermal differences between high- and low-risk groups were evident pre-breakdown (Mednick, 1967), no such differences have yet become evident in the Erlenmeyer-Kimling study. The disparity between this study and the original Mednick and Schulsinger project is suggested possibly to lie (*inter alia*) in the age differences between the two samples (Erlenmeyer-Kimling, 1975), or because of the factor of family intactness

(Mednick, 1978), the level of intactness being lower in the Copenhagen than in the New York sample. Data presented by Schulsinger and Mednick (1975) showed that family intactness was a variable influencing autonomic activity of the children some years after the break-up had occurred.

The second example of a study, in which part of the data collected replicates the Copenhagen example, is the work at the University of Rochester where the psychophysiological data have been collected by Salzman and his colleagues and a report of the analysis of some of the elctrodermal data is given in Salzman and Klein (1978).

These data provide a partial confirmation of the Mednick and Schulsinger material in so far as the children of schizophrenic parents (as a group) are shown to tend towards hyper-responsivity although the difference between high- and low-risk groups is only significant in the case of responses to the more intense (UCS) stimuli. The data on skin conductance recovery do not show an overall faster recovery for the high-risk subjects although there is an indication of faster recovery of the response to the first stimulus of the series. Salzman and Klein's data are from children aged 10 and as this is in the same age range as the Erlenmeyer-Kimling material it suggests that age does not appear to be a factor in the non-replication of the Mednick and Schulsinger material in this instance. It is probably important to emphasize that the selection of subjects in the 1962 Copenhagen study was on the basis of the *severe* nature of the schizophrenia suffered by their mothers. Hanson *et al.* (1977) have suggested that the risk factor is only high when the parental illness is severe, and in populations where risk does not have this feature the probability of breakdown may not exceed that of the base rate of the general population.

THE MAURITIAN STUDY

The majority of studies which have involved the use of psychophysiological measurements as part of the early assessment of the subjects have been based on the familial risk model. The exception is the study in Mauritius in which the assessment of risk has been based on the determination of aspects of electrodermal activity thought to be indicators of predisposition to schizophrenic breakdown, or possibly in Meehl's (1962) terminology schizotaxia. The bases for this study are thus in part the findings of the earlier work in Copenhagen. The dangers in adopting this approach are obviously those of relying on a single major area of measurement as an indicator of risk at the commencement of a longitudinal study. Consequently, intermediate assessment of development of the risk groups so determined is important if the criticism of Garmezy (1974) is not to be taken as too damning. In discussing the project Garmezy states 'the critical question that remains, however, is the appropriateness of using deviant psychophysiological functioning in children as a criterion of risk'.

The work commenced with screening of the total population of 3-year-olds —some 1800 children—in two towns in Mauritius chosen to have a racial mix which was characteristic of the total island population. Approximately two-thirds of the sample are of Indian origin, while the remainder are mainly of African descent.

During 1972 and 1973 the 1800 children underwent a psychophysiological investigation and in addition were extensively studied using developmental psychological and paediatric techniques. Data were collected on the social background of the subjects and in about 65 per cent of cases perinatal data were available.

The psychophysiological data were electrodermal and heart-rate responses elicited by a standard stimulus tape which was a shortened version of that employed in the second Copenhagen study. Six orienting stimuli were followed by 12 stimuli in a conditioning paradigm and 6 further stimuli to examine extinction.

The aspects of skin conductance which were measured were the level (SCL) at the start of each response and the latency, amplitude, and recovery of the response. Specific responses were carefully defined using latency window critieria. Sixty responses were potentially available for measurement, six to each of the orienting stimuli and 18×3 to the stimuli in the conditioning paradigm. The three responses in this instance were the response to the CS, and to the UCS, and the 'second interval' or 'pre-UCS' response possibly occurring as a conditioned response before the presentation of the UCS. From these 60 possible responses, 12 were chosen as being those of most potential usefulness in providing indications of 'schizotaxic' tendencies. Using these responses, four types of subject were selected. The first group were non-responders who show no electrodermal activity whatsoever, and who consequently might be thought to have characteristics similar to those of some adult schizophrenics. Venables (1977) reviewed the phenomenon of non-responsivity in schizophrenics and both the data examined at this time and that subsequently reported suggest that about half an adult schizophrenic population might be expected to display this phenomenon, or at least minimal responsivity, by giving only one or two responses. The second class of subject comprised those who exhibited SCR characteristics similar to the vulnerable subjects in the Copenhagen studies. They were selected to have SC responses with amplitudes greater than 1μmho/cm^2 and half recovery times shorter than 2.5 seconds. The third group of subjects were selected to have SC responses within a normal range, having amplitudes between 0.4 and 0.9 μmho/cm^2 and half-recovery times between 2.5 and 9.0 seconds. A fourth class of subjects was introduced because of the inability to achieve perfect matching of sex and race characteristics across groups. These were children whose SC responses were potentially those of children at high risk for psychopathy or delinquency by the virtue of exhibiting half recovery times longer than 9.0 seconds. Data reported by Mednick (1977) have shown that children of criminal fathers show a longer SCR half recovery time than children of non-criminal fathers, and the work in this area reviewed by Siddle (1977) supports this finding. It should, of course, be noted that hyperactive/minimal brain dysfunction children exhibit this characteristic

(Zahn *et al.*, 1975b) and it is possible that in this instance this class of children has been selected. However, in so far as it has been suggested (e.g. Cantwell, 1972) that an association exists between hyperactivity and sociopathy, alcoholism, and hysteria, the selection of these children as possibly at risk for characteristics associated with criminality may not be misplaced.

From the 1800 children originally tested, 200 were selected in 1973 in the manner briefly described above and fully detailed in Venables (1978). One hundred of this selected group were placed in two specially created nursery schools and the other 100 children matched with them on race, sex, and electrodermal characteristics, remained in the community to follow the typical development pattern of the 3-year-old Mauritian child. This included, for some, the attendance at informal nursery schools (*p'tits écoles*), but formal primary schooling for all did not commence until 6 years of age was reached. The numbers in the four electrodermally selected risk groups were: non-responders, 37; children with short recovery SCRs, 99; children with long recovery SCRs, 11; controls, 53. These were, as nearly as possible, evenly distributed among the 'nursery school' and 'community' groups. These children have been followed up and data collected both before and after they entered primary school, and analyses of these data are being carried out.

In a longitudinal study designed to last for more than 20 years, it is clear that preliminary intermediate results are important as means of showing that the original measurement procedures have some validity in relation to the general aims of the study. Attempts to examine the procedure and reliability of the selection procedure have been presented by Venables (1978). In summary, the exercise suggests that the original choice of responses on which selection was based could have been carried out in a somewhat better fashion. Factor analysis of amplitudes of responses indicated the appearance of three orthogonal factors. These could be labelled as: (1) responses to the first set of orientation stimuli, (2) responses to the second set of orientation stimuli, and (3) responses to unconditioned stimuli in the conditioning paradigm. The difference between stimuli (1) and (2) is that of auditory frequency and between (1) or (2) and (3) is intensity. Perhaps the most interesting aspect of these analyses is that the response to the first UCS loads with the orientation stimuli and not at all with the rest of the UCRs despite the similarity of intensity of all UCSs. This suggests that the element of novelty is a characteristic of the first factor described above. The opportunity to obtain a figure for the retest reliability of the electrodermal data was presented by a second testing of the 200 selected children approximately 18 months after the original testing at age 3. Test–retest correlations were significant for factors 1 ($p < 0.01$) and 3 ($p < 0.02$) but not for factor 2 ($p = 0.49$).

The difficulty in all this work is the choice of the most efficient means of summarizing the welter of data obtained. As mentioned earlier in discussing the most recent analysis of the 1962 Copenhagen data, use of path analysis had shown the usefulness of an index of electrodermal activity which was a product of percentage responsivity and mean recovery *rate* of SCRs. Application of this measure to the Mauritian data showed as expected that it differentiated the risk groups but more importantly had an encouragingly high test–retest reliability ($p < 0.001$). The analyses, overall, provide a feeling of cautious optimism that the procedures used had a degree of consistency over time, but it is quite clear that there is a marked degree of change due to age developmental factors and that these influence the measurement of apparent test–retest reliability. Notably, a cross-sectional study carried out in Mauritius using the same procedures as those employed in the main longitudinal investigation showed that the number of subjects who are non-responders is about 55 per cent at age 3 and this falls to about 5 per cent at age 15. Thus the selection of subjects as non-responders at age 3, with the idea that they might be displaying a pathological characteristic, is clearly erroneous. A very extensive retest of the majority of the original sample of 1800, which it is proposed to carry out at age 11, will enable an accurate assessment of the extent of continued non-responding which might be regarded as pathological as against the early non-responding which disappears with development.

While one concern is with the internal consistency of the measures used in the selection procedure and their reliability over time, these should be validly related to the measurement of the presumed variable, 'schizophrenic tendency' or 'schizotaxia', otherwise the exercise is clearly not of particular relevance.

An attempt was made to eastablish this 'interim validity' by assessing how far the members of the different 'risk' groups behaved differently in a standard play situation at age 6, just before entering nursery school. The study is described by Venables, et al.

The children in this study were the 200 who were selected from the original 1800 for intensive investigation. It is convenient to consider them as being in four groups, one from each of the two nursery schools and one from each of the two 'groups' matched with them but not attending nursery school. Thus for the purpose of this study one child could be drawn from each group and a sample of four children used as subjects in the play assessment procedure. Several steps were taken to eliminate, as far as possible, any bias in the rating of the children which might arise due to the identification of their group origin. The children were tested in the project's research centre which they had not visited since their original screening nearly 3 years before. To avoid identification they were provided with fresh identical uniforms which they wore to visit the centre.

Two workers who did not know the children were trained in the rating and observation technique which was modified from that outlined by Bell, Weller, and Wardrop (1971). The children were observed indoors playing with equipment and toys which as far as possible were not similar to those which the nursery school children had previously experienced.

Before entering the observation playroom the children played outside in a playground with swings, see-saw, and a sandpit, and thus were not entirely unfamiliar with each other when in the observation room.

Each child's behaviour was rated over an 8-minute period. During this time, counts of types of behaviour were made and some aspects of behaviour were timed. These aspects were: (a) 'constructive play alone', recorded when the child plays constructively with a toy or toys by himself; (b) 'positive inter-action', in which was included talking, helping, and co-operative play; and (c) 'watching' in which the child watched a peer or adult while not otherwise interacting or playing.

The results indicated that, as expected, the electrodermally selected control children who had attended nursery school spent significantly more time in constructive play than those who had not. In the case of the short recovery 'high-risk' children there was no difference in the amount of constructive play shown by the children who had attended nursery school and those who had not, but both groups showed more play than the 'normal' children who had not attended nursery school. It is interesting to note that since this study was carried out Kimmel and Deboskey (1978) have reported that gifted children appear to have some of the same electrodermal characteristics as the 'high-risk' children in this study, and we may be led to draw the parallel in the pre-morbid state between schizotypic and gifted children as that drawn between schizophrenic and creative adults by Dykes and McGhie (1976).

Although, as explained earlier, some doubts were felt about the extent to which those children who showed no electrodermal responses were a distinct 'pathological group, their behaviour on the variable 'watching' showed them to behave differently from the other children. While each of the members of the other 'risk' groups who attended nursery school showed the benefit of that experience by evidencing less 'watching', this was not the case with the non-responding children. It is possible, therefore, that by selecting children for this electrodermal characteristic one selects either those who may continue to show non-responsivity in a pathological fashion or those who in this instance were slow developers and who showed behavioural as well as electrodermal retardation.

The number of children who were selected because of long recovery time of their skin conductance response was small, but their behaviour distinguish-ed them from the other groups. Those children from this electrodermal cate-gory who had attended nursery school spent about three times longer in 'positive interaction' than any of the other groups of children and are thus, as suggested earlier, possibly akin to hyperactive children. However, it is important to note that children who had the same electrodermal characteristics but who had not attended nursery school did not show this excess of interactive be-haviour.

In summary, while it would undoubtedly be premature to suggest that the electrodermal selection procedure had been validated, nevertheless, it was shown that children who could be differentiated electrodermally at age 3 showed different types of behaviour at age 6, thus providing encouragement for a procedure that had not previously been undertaken.

CONCLUSION

The main emphasis of this review has been on the procedures adopted in high-risk studies and some indications of their promise. With the notable exception of the 1962 Copenhagen study, no full validation of the undoubtedly attractive logitudinal paradigm has been possible, and thus at this time the results from the area can only be eagerly awaited.

Particular attention has been paid to studies employing psychophysiological techniques. While the results from the measurement of electrodermal activity have undoubtedly been given greatest prominence, possibly because of the relative apparent simplicity of analytical procedures, the reliance on this measure is dangerous and more attention should be paid to other measures— electroencephalographic, cardiovascular, and electro-oculographic—in order to broaden the base of study in this area.

Acknowledgement

This paper was prepared while the author was in receipt of a grant from the Wellcome Trust which supports the work at present under way in Mauritius, and a grant from the US Public Health Service for work on the analysis of data collected in Copenhagen.

REFERENCES

Ax, A. F., and Bamford, J. L. (1970). The GSR recovery limb in chronic schizophrenia. *Psychophysiology*, 7, 145–147.

Bell, R. Q., Weller, G. M., and Waldrop, M. F. (1971). Newborn and preschooler: organization and behavior and relations between periods. *Monographs of the Society for Research in Child Development*, 36, 1–145.

Berkson, J. (1955). The statistical study of association between smoking and lung cancer. *Proceedings of Staff Meetings Mayo Clinic*, 319–348.

Burton, R. V. (1970). Validity of retrospective reports assessed by the multi-track multi-method analysis. *Developmental Psychology Monographs*, 3, 1–15.

Cantwell, D. P. (1972). Psychiatric illness in the families of hyperactive children. *Archives of General Psychiatry*, 27, 414–417.

Chapman, J. (1966). The early symptoms of schizophrenia. *British Journal of Psychiatry*, 112, 225–251.

Chapman, L. J., Chapman, J. P., Raulin, M. L., and Edell, W. S. (1978). Schizotypy and thought disorder as a high-risk approach to schizophrenia. In G. Serban (ed.), *Cognitive Defects in the Development of Mental Illness*. New York: Brunner/Mazel.

Dykes, M., and McGhie, A. (1976). A comparative study of attentional strategies in schizophrenic and highly creative normal subjects. *British Journal of Psychiatry*, 128, 50–56.

Erlenmeyer-Kimling, L. (1975). A prospective study of children at risk for schizophrenia: methodological considerations and some preliminary findings. In R. D. Wirt, G. Winokur, and M. Roff (eds.), *Life History Research in Psychopathology*, Vol. 4. Minneapolis: University of Minnesota Press.

Eysenck, H. J., and Eysenck, S. B. G. (1967). On the unitary nature of extraversion. *Acta Psychologica*, 26, 283–390.

Fremming, K. H. (1951). *The expectation of mental infirmity in a sample of the Danish population. Papers on Eugenics, No. 7.* London: The Eugenics Society.

Garmezy, N. (with Streitman, S.) (1974). Children at risk: the search for the antecedents of schizophrenia. Part I: Conceptual models and research methods. Part II: Ongoing research programs, issues and intervention. *Schizophrenia Bulletin*, **8**, 14–90; **9**, 55–125.

Gruzelier, J. H., and Venables, P. H. (1972). Skin conductance orienting activity in a heterogeneous sample of schizophrenics. *Journal of Nervous and Mental Disease*, **155**, 277–287.

Hanson, D. R., Gottesman, I. I., and Meehl, P. E. (1977). Genetic theories and the validation of psychiatric diagnoses: implications for the study of children of schizophrenics. *Journal of Abnormal Psychology*, **86**, 575–588.

Heston, L. L. (1966). Psychiatric disorders in foster-home reared children of schizophrenic mothers. *British Journal of Psychiatry*, **112**, 819–825.

Hoch, P. H., and Cattell, J. P. (1959). The diagnosis of pseudoneurotic schizophrenia. *Psychiatric Quarterly*, **33**, 17–43.

Hoch, P. H., Cattell, J. P., Strahl, M. O. and Pennes, H. H. (1962). The course and outcome of pseudoneurotic schizophrenia. *American Journal of Psychiatry*, **11**, 106–115.

Itil, T. M., Hsu, W., Saletu, B., and Mednick, S. A. (1974). Computer EEG and auditory evoked potential investigations in children at high risk for schizophrenia. *American Journal of Psychiatry*, **131**, 892–900.

Jones, F. H. (1973). Current methodologies for studying the development of schizophrenia: a critical review. *Journal of Nervous and Mental Disease*, **157**, 154–178.

Jöreskog, K. G., and van Thello, M. (1972). LISREL: a general computer program for estimating a linear standard equation system involving multiple indicators of unmeasured variables. *Research Bulletin*, 72–86. Princeton, New Jersey: Educational Testing Service.

Kimmel, H. D., and Deboskey, D. (1978). Habituation and conditioning of the orienting reflex in intellectually gifted and average children. *Physiological Psychology*, **6**, 377–380.

Lykken, D. T. (1968). Statistical significance in psychological research. *Psychological Bulletin*, **70**, 151–159.

Mednick, S. A. (1958). A learning theory approach to research in schizophrenia. *Psychological Bulletin*, **55**, 316–327.

Mednick, S. A. (1967). The children of schizophrenics: serious difficulties in current research methodologies which suggest the use of the 'High-risk-group' methods. In Romano, J. (ed.), *Origins of Schizophrenia*. Amsterdam: Excerpta Medica.

Mednick, S. A. (1970). Breakdown in individuals at high risk for schizophrenia: possible pre-dispositional perinatal factors. *Mental Hygiene*, **54**, 50–63.

Mednick, S. A. (1977). A bio-social theory of the learning of law-abiding behaviour. In S. A. Mednick and K. O. Christiansen (eds.), *Bio-social Bases of Criminal Behaviour*. New York: Gardner Press.

Mednick, S. A. (1978). Berkson's fallacy and high-risk research. In L. C. Wynne, R. L. Cromwell, and S. Matthysse, (eds.), *The Nature of Schizophrenia*. New York: Wiley.

Mednick, S. A., and Higgins, J. (eds.). (1960). *Current Research in Schizophrenia*. Ann Arbor: Edwards.

Mednick, S. A., and McNeil, T. F. (1968). Current methodology in research on the etiology of schizophrenia: serious difficulties which suggest the use of the high-risk-group method. *Psychological Bulletin*, **70**, 681–693.

Mednick, S. A., Mura, E., Schulsinger, F., and Mednick, B. (1971). Perinatal conditions and infant development in children with schizophrenic parents. *Social Biology*, **18**, 103–113.

Mednick, S. A., and Schulsinger, F. (1968). Some pre-morbid characteristics related to breakdown in children with schizophrenic mothers. In D. Rosenthal, and S. S. Kety, (eds.), *The Transmission of Schizophrenia.* New York: Pergamon Press.

Mednick, S. A., and Schulsinger, F. (1973). A learning theory of schizophrenia thirteen years later. In M. Hammer, K. Salzinger, and S. Sutton (eds.), *Psychopathology.* New York: Wiley.

Mednick, S. A., Schulsinger, F., and Garfinkel, R. (1975). Children at high risk for schizophrenia: Predisposing factors and intervention. In M. K. Kietzman, S. Sutton, and J. Zubin (eds.), *Experimental Approaches to Psychopathology.* New York: Academic Press.

Mednick, S. A., Schulsinger, F., Teasdale, T. W., Schulsinger, H., Venables, P. H., and Rock, D. R. (1978). Schizophrenia in high-risk children: sex differences in predisposing factors. In G. Serban (ed.), *Cognitive Defects in the Development of Mental Illness.* New York: Brunner/Mazel.

Meehl, P. E. (1962). Schizotaxia, schizotypy and schizophrenia. *American Psychologist,* 17, 827–838.

Mirdal, S., Mednick, S. A., Schulsinger, F., and Fuchs, F. (1974). Perinatal complications in children of schizophrenic mothers. *Acta Psychiatrica Scandinavica,* 50, 553–568.

Nielsen, T. C., and Petersen, K. E. (1976). Electrodermal correlates of extraversion, trait anxiety and schizophrenism. *Scandinavian Journal of Psychology,* 17, 73–80.

Pearson, J. S., and Kley, I. B. (1957). On the application of genetic expectancies as age-specific base rates in the study of human behavior disorders. *Psychological Bulletin,* 54, 406–420.

Prokasy, W. F., and Kumpfer, K. L. (1973). Classical conditioning. In W. F. Prokasy and D. C. Raskin (eds.), *Electrodermal Activity in Psychological Research.* New York: Academic Press.

Rado, S. (1956). *Psychonalysis of Behavior.* New York: Grune and Stratton.

Robbins, L. C. (1963). The accuracy of parental recall of aspects of child development and of child-rearing practices. *Journal of Abnormal and Social Psychology,* 66, 261–270.

Rosenthal, D. (1970). *Genetic Theory and Abnormal Behavior.* New York: McGraw.

Rosenthal, D. (1974a). Issues in high-risk studies of schizophrenia. In D. F. Ricks, A. Thomas and M. Roff (eds.), *Life History Research in Psychopathology,* Vol. 3. Minneapolis: University of Minnesota Press.

Rosenthal, D. (1974b). The concept of subschizophrenic disorders. In S. A. Mednick, F., Schulsinger, J., Higgins, and B. Bell, (eds.), *Genetics, Environment and Psychopathology.* Amsterdam: North Holland.

Rosenthal, D., Wender, P., Kety, S., Welner, J., and Schulsinger, F. (1971). The adopted away offspring of schizophrenics. *American Journal of Psychiatry,* 128, 307–311.

Salzman, L. F., and Klein, R. H. (1978). Habituation and conditioning of electrodermal responses in high-risk children. *Schizophrenia Bulletin,* 4, 210–222.

Siddle, D. A. T. (1977). Electrodermal activity and psychopathy. In S. A. Mednick and K. O. Christiansen (eds.), *Biosocial Bases of Criminal Behavior.* New York: Gardner Press.

Schulsinger, F., and Mednick, S. A. (1975). Nature–nurture aspects of schizophrenia: early detection and prevention. In M. H. Lader, (ed.), *Studies of Schizophrenia.* Ashford: Headley.

Schulsinger, H. (1976). A ten-year follow-up of children of schizophrenic mothers: clinical assessment. *Acta Psychiatrica Scandinavica,* 53, 371–386.

Venables, P. H. (1977). The electrodermal psychophysiology of schizophrenics and children at risk for schizophrenia: controversies and development. *Schizophrenia Bulletin,* 3, 28–48.

Venables, P. H. (1978). Psychophysiology and psychometrics. *Psychophysiology,* 15, 302–315.

Venables, P. H., Mednick, S. A., Schulsinger, F., Raman, A. C., Bell, B., Dalais, J. C., and

Fletcher, R. P. (1978). Screening for risk of mental illness. In G. Serban (Ed.), *Cognitive Defects in Development of Mental Illness*. New York: Brunner/Mazel.

Yarrow, M. R., Campbell, J. D., and Burton, R. V. (1970). Recollections of childhood: a study of the retrospective method. *Monograph of the Society for Research in Child Development*, **35** (No. 5, Serial No. 138), 1–83.

Zahn, T. P., Abate, F., Little, B. C., and Wender, P. H. (1975b). Minimal brain dysfunction, stimulant drugs and autonomic nervous system activity. *Archives of General Psychiatry*, **32**, 381–387.

Zahn, T. P., Carpenter, W. T., and McGlashan, T. H. (1975a). Autonomic variables related to short-term outcome in acute schizophrenic patients. Paper presented to the Society of Psychophysiological Research, Toronto.

SECTION 3

Emotion

Foundations of Psychosomatics
Edited by M. J. Christie and P. G. Mellett
© 1981 John Wiley & Sons Ltd.

6

PSYCHOSOMATIC DISORDER: A SPECIAL CASE OF SUBLIMINAL PERCEPTION

NORMAN F. DIXON
Department of Psychology, University College London.

In an earlier paper (Dixon, 1964) it was suggested that phenomena associated with subliminal perception may have considerable relevance for our understanding of the processes underlying psychosomatic illness. Over the years, a great deal of further evidence (see Dixon, 1971; Erdelyi, 1974; Silverman, 1976; Shevrin, 1975) relating to perception without awareness and perceptual defence has added weight to the suggestion. Not only are there some remarkable similarities between the data from laboratory investigations of these phenomena in normal subjects and those from studies of people suffering various sorts of psychosomatic illness, but it also seems likely, in the light of this most recent research, that they may make a significant contribution to our understanding and treatment of all those disorders which have, as their common denominator, the fact that psychic material can, quite unconsciously and involuntarily, eventuate in somatic symptoms.

The case for this thesis rests on five frequently occurring features of psychosomatic disorders.

Firstly a variety of psychic stresses may eventuate in a limited range of somatic symptoms. Secondly, the nature of these symptoms suggest that they may be mediated in several ways—by the direct action of the autonomic and adrenocortical systems on target organs, by maladaptive overt behaviour (for example, in the case of obesity), and by translation of the psychic stress into an appropriately symbolic form, so called hysterical conversion symptoms.

A third feature of at least some psychosomatic illnesses is that they appear to involve a learning component, and imply that unconscious complexes of emotionally loaded memories play a significant role in the genesis of somatic dysfunction. Yet a fourth aspect of some psychosomatic disorders is that even if intellectually cognisant of the fact that a relationship exists between particular psychological stressors and his somatic symptoms, the patient remains totally unaware of the sequence of events between the exacerbating stimulus and its somatic outlet. He is without real insight into his condition and, unless given psychotherapeutic assistance, quite unable to rid himself of his symptom.

Finally, and related to this latter point, some psychosomatic patients (Nemiah and Sifneos, 1970) show a remarkable absence of feeling about their illness. In a very real sense they seem to have traded the threat of negative affect for a physical disorder.

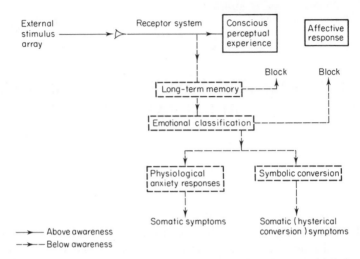

FIGURE 6.1. According to this hypothetical flow diagram critical external events, which may or may not be consciously perceived, also activate unconscious long-term memory complexes of emotionally charged ideas. Despite emotional classification of this impact between the present stimulus and past experience, affective responses are blocked. Emotional outlet occurs through ANS activity and/or symbolic conversion leading to somatic symptoms

Taken together these features of many psychosomatic disorders, as depicted in Figure 6.1, suggest a remarkable similarity between the processes underlying psychogenic causation in physical illness and those underlying laboratory demonstrations of subliminal perception by normal subjects. In this figure, information received via the special senses in conjunction with unconscious memory schemata triggers an emotional response which, because of being associated with unpleasant feelings, is immediately rerouted via the central nervous system or autonomic nervous system to a somatic outlet.

The diagram distinguishes between information flow and events of which the individual is conscious (solid lines) and those of which he remains unaware (dashed lines). It is suggested that, in psychosomatic disorders, aspects of incoming information may activate existing complexes and thus initiate an emotional response. With affective experience being blocked the resulting ANS activity finds an outlet in bodily symptoms. The site and nature of such symptoms may themselves be determined by the effects of ANS discharge upon unconscious memory systems. According to this account of what would appear to be going on in some psychosomatic patients, a therapeutic interpretation which results in alleviating symptoms follows a similar pattern to that taken by the aforementioned precipitating stimulus. In this case, however, by making contact with the underlying complex and exposing the symbolism of the symptom, the interpretation evidently undoes the block on affective experience, thus bringing about a re-routing of the emotional discharge.

This analysis in itself is little more than a description, in information-processing terms, of phenomena observed by many clinicians. It leaves unanswered such questions as to why some individuals show these effects while others do not, and how it is that interpretation of a symbolic conversion can alter the effects of psychic stress.

Perhaps further light might be thrown on these problems by considering what happens when a normal subject is artificially denied awareness of incoming sensory stimuli—the situation which is entailed by laboratory studies of subliminal perception.

Subliminal perception may be said to occur when a stimulus which, though so brief or of such low intensity as to elude conscious detection, can nevertheless evoke some measurable response from the subject. He does not consciously see it or hear it but it affects him. Subliminal perception is mediated by stimuli which are above the physiological threshold but below the thresholds of recognition and awareness (Dixon, 1971).

An information-processing flow diagram of what is entailed in subliminal perception is shown in Figure 6.2. Denied phenomenal representation by reason of its low signal/noise ratio the stimulus nevertheless undergoes structural and semantic analysis, makes contact with long-term memory, and receives emotional categorization. As a consequence of its meaning and emotional classification the stimulus may result in one or more of the following effects:

(1) change in the perception of a concurrent supraliminal stimulus array;
(2) symbolic conversion in free association;
(3) intrusions in the recall of learned material;

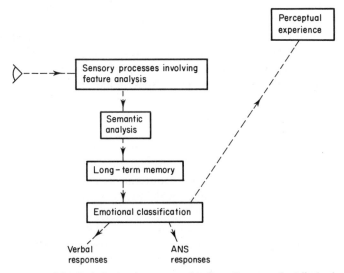

FIGURE 6.2. An information-processing flow diagram of subliminal perception

(4) dreams experienced during or following stimulation;
(5) changes in sensory and recognition thresholds;
(6) changes in autonomic activity—e.g. as reflected in electrodermal activity;
(7) changes in evoked cortical responses and the tonic EEG.

These areas of research are particularly pertinent—neurophysiological studies of the relationship between external stimulation, cerebral responses and conscious experience, work on sleep and dreams, and laboratory studies of subliminal perception, perceptual defence, attention, and masking.

For the first, neurophysiological studies by Libet *et al.* (1967) are important for showing that the brain can register the effects of external stimuli so slight that they fail to achieve conscious representation. The paradigm involved recording cortical evoked potentials (CEPs) from subdural electrodes placed directly on the somatosensory cortex of patients who were in the course of receiving stereotaxic therapy for intractable pain. Evoking stimuli were applied to an area of the skin whose central afferent projection involved that region of the somatic cortex, the post-central gyrus, from which the CEPs were taken.

The crucial finding from this research was that stimulation sufficient to produce the primary components of an evoked potential did so without eliciting any sensation in the fully conscious subjects. Since prolonged repetition of the same stimuli did produce sensation, *pari passu* with the later components of the compound evoked potential, it may be assumed that the same fibres were involved in the two cases.

While the research by Libet *et al.* confirms the physiological possibility of subliminal perception, other investigations (reviewed elsewhere (Dixon, 1971)), which also relied upon recording cortical evoked responses, leave little doubt that in addition to detecting the presence of a subliminal stimulus the brain may analyse and respond to its meaning. Thus, research by Shevrin and Fritzler (1968) has shown that the meanings of pictures flashed for only 0.001 seconds were nevertheless encoded in a visual evoked response and, moreover, exerted an influence upon subsequent free association. (See also Shevrin and Dickman (1980); and discussion of other studies by Shevrin and his colleagues in Dixon (1971).)

All in all there is nothing very surprising about these data. They accord with the discovery (Magoun 1954; see also Samuels, 1959) that whereas the transmission of information from sensory receptors to cortex is carried by the fast conducting lemniscal system of the brain, consciousness of this information depends upon sufficient contribution from the ascending reticular system. Whereas the first appears responsible for the primary components of the compound evoked potential, the second, that underlying consciousness of the input, is associated with the later components. Either system may operate independently of the other. Just as it is possible to experience dreams and hallucinations without any external initiating stimulus, so is it possible for information to enter the brain and produce an effect without the consciousness and knowledge of the recipient.

SLEEP AND DREAMS

Of particular relevance to the validity of subliminal perception and the latter's implication for psychosomatic processes is the effect of external stimuli on sleep and dreams (Dixon, 1971). Thus, there are two studies (Oswald, Taylor and Treisman, 1960; Berger, 1963) which have shown that even in the deepest sleep the presentation of an emotionally important stimulus (e.g. the subject's own name or the name of someone with whom he is emotionally involved) will evoke respectively a large amplitude deflection in the sleeping EEG and stimulus related dreams. Since auditorily presented words, which have no particular emotional significance, do *not* affect the EEG we may conclude that incoming auditory stimuli are subjected to at least three stages of processing—structural, semantic, and emotive.

This cycle of events depends upon a happening of some significance for psychosomatic disorders—stimulus access to long-term memory. Without such access, neither the initial discrimination of critical words, nor the selective emotional response to particular stimuli, nor the elaborating of a content relevant dream, would be possible. This conclusion, and the implications for the relationship between subliminal perception and psychosomatics, receives strong support from studies of the Poetzl effect—the assimilation and storage of information which at the time of its arrival, appears to bypass conscious registration. (For a detailed history of the research into this phenomenon see

Figure 6.3. The picture 'Three Kings' used by Fisher (1954)

Dixon, 1971.) Of the many investigations of this effect, first noted by Poetzl (1917), those carried out by Fisher (1954) are of particular relevance in the present context. In a typical study a young female patient, hospitalized for a severe psychosomatic ileitis, was asked to draw and describe the picture shown in Figure 6.3. However, since this stimulus picture was only presented for one-hundredth of a second the amount of information which she consciously obtained from it was severely limited (see Figure 6.4). The following day, however, the patient was recalled to the laboratory and asked to draw and describe any dreams she might have had the preceding night. Her 'dream' picture is shown in Figure 6.5. She was then asked for associations to her dream.

When we consider the results from this study three features emerge which are of interest for the student of psychosomatic disease. First, when, at the end of the experiment, the subject was shown the original stimulus picture she expressed great surprise at its resemblance of her dream picture and readily confirmed the identity between the three figures in her dream and the three Kings. Evidently she had, up to that moment, been unaware of those parts of the stimulus pictures which featured in her dream. Secondly, her associations to the elements in her dream suggested that its latent content represented a complex of highly emotional ideas and attitudes. In her dream she had, so to speak, combined attitudes towards her doctor and fellow patients (the human figures in the dream drawing) with feelings about her psychosomatic disorders and also with her underlying fear of cancer. The building blocks for the expression of psychopathology were those very features of the original picture which had escaped her conscious scrutiny.

Whether or not she had unconsciously selected these items at the original exposure, or whether the dream just made use of material that had, for other reasons, remained inaccessible, is of course debatable. Suffice it to say that this example of the Poetzl effect, like many other subsequent studies, not only shows

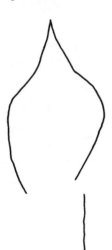

FIGURE 6.4. Subject's drawing of what she saw after tachistoscopic exposure of Figure 6.3. It shows a dome with a spire. The open rectangle below represents the window which the subject experienced as if it were in the dome, although she saw it below (Fisher, 1954)

FIGURE 6.5. Subject's drawing of her dream. The three figures and then location on 'piles' closely resemble the general outline of the 'Three Kings' in Figure 6.3. A girl known to the subject, who appeared in her dream is represented by the king on the right, the two men in the dream by the two kings on the left. The four vertical lines probably represent the two men in the picture. The pathway was taken from rather obscure outlines in the foreground of Figure 6.3. The mound on which the torsos of the two men rest was the pile of coal in the dream (from Fisher, 1954)

that the brain may register and store events that failed to enter consciousness, but also provides for a better understanding of those unconscious processes which in this instance gave rise to a severe psychosomatic illness.

While the role of specific memories may be disputed as a factor in the aetiology of *all* psychosomatic disorders there is ample evidence, not the least from cases of 'massive psychic trauma' (Krystal, 1968) to suggest that such physical responses to psychological stress as duodenal ulcer, asthma, ulcerative colitis, and hypertension, occurring in the survivors of major disasters, owe much to pre-existing psychopathology. It is as if the present crisis activates hitherto repressed memories of much earlier traumatic events. The vivid reactivation of early memories in cases of near drowning, noted by Janis (1969), is a case in point. Components of the processes underlying these clinical phenomena have also been demonstrated in laboratory experiments. Thus, an experiment by Spence and Gordon (1967) has shown this effect, most strikingly, for those people who habitually rely upon oral indulgence to alleviate feelings of depression and anxiety. When they are exposed to the traumatic experience of being socially rejected by their peers, retrieval from long-term memory suffers a curious distortion. Asked to learn a list of words, including associates to the word 'milk', and then flashed 'milk' below the threshold of consciousness their subsequent recall of the list was found to contain words like 'suck' and 'nipple' which had never featured in the list as learned, but which *did* relate to a much earlier feeding situation!

Subjects who were *not* oral types or who were *not* made to feel rejected, or who did *not* have the subliminal stimulus 'milk', showed no such effect.

Involving, as it does, the activation of an early complex by the influence on memory of an external stimulus below the conscious threshold, this experiment would seem to have considerable implications for psychosomatic medicine—and all the more so since the findings were specific to a particular sort of personality—one long associated with a special predisposition towards psychosomatic disorders!

As implied by these data, there is a sense in which some, if not all, psychosomatic disorders result from the capacity to store information. The existence of a complex—that system of emotionally charged ideas from which symptoms spring—necessitates the notion of unconscious memory. However, while neurosis and psychosomatic disorders may be regarded as part of the price paid for our capacity to retain at least the ghostly vestiges of past events, the translation of stored information into a neurotic or somatic symptom is frequently obscured by the symbolic conversion of the material concerned.

Here again laboratory studies of subliminal perception may cast some light on the processes involved. In addition to the symbolic conversions found in demonstrations of the Poetzl effect, and in dreams elicited by auditory stimuli presented during sleep (Berger, 1963), there have been those revealed by studies (Dixon, 1956, 1958(a); Bach, 1959; Arey, 1960; Pine, 1960, 1964) of subliminal perception in the waking state. These latter investigations have shown that response to words or pictures of which the recipient is unaware tend to bear a symbolic relationship to the stimuli. Thus, when asked to say the first word that comes to mind, during subliminal stimulation with the words 'penis' or 'vagina', subjects not only gave significantly large electrodermal responses but also responded with such suggestive words as 'cheroot', 'brush', 'screw', 'poppycock', 'tunnel', 'ring', and 'mouth'—responses which they were subsequently able to match with the appropriate stimulus items significantly more often than could be explained by chance.

Unadmitted to conscious scrutiny, by reason of their low signal-to-noise ratio, such meaningful subliminal stimuli were evidently not subjected to what Spence and Holland (1962) have called 'the restricting effects of awareness', and so gave rise to primary process responses.

This conclusion gains support from more recent researches. In the first (Marcel and Patterson, 1979) it has been shown not only that pattern-masked verbal stimuli give rise to symbolic-like responses, but also that in this type of perception without awareness the preconscious lexical access of polysemous words (e.g. 'palm') tends to evoke not one but all its meanings.

Comparable effects have been reported from studies of amnesic patients (Weiskrantz, 1977), aphasics (Werner, 1956), and schizophrenics (Maher, 1966) Whether a low signal-to-noise ratio is achieved by using a weak stimulus, by masking, by organic disease, or by psychosis, the end result seems to be a lifting of the inhibitory control upon associative activity which normally attends entry into consciousness. One consequence of this disinhibition is the possibility of symbolic conversion, a type of transformation which appears to characterize a proportion of somatic symptoms.

The second piece of research of relevance to symbolic conversion implicates the role of laterality in this phenomenon. In a study of normal subjects Fonagy (1977) has shown that whereas subliminal words presented in the right visual field tend to evoke normal semantic associates those displayed in the *left* visual field evoked verbal responses of objects having a similar visual appearance. For example the stimulus 'grass' evoked such responses as 'hair, needles, and bed of nails', while 'arrow' evoked such visually similar objects as 'hook, screwdriver, and staple'. This finding makes good sense in the light of those properties which have been ascribed (Ornstein, 1977) to right hemisphere function, that is to say a proclivity for visuo-spatial, parallel, primary, non-logical, processing—a type of processing which would appear to be involved in symbol formation. When set alongside the finding by Sackeim, Packer, and Gur (1977) that people showing right hemisphericity are the most susceptible to influence by subliminal stimuli, these data suggest the interesting possibility that patients who tend to convert psychic stress into symbolic somatic symptomatology may have a general tendency towards right hemisphericity.

PERCEPTUAL DEFENCE

In drawing parallels between subliminal perception and psychosomatic phenomena it is reasonable to consider the two in the context of psychological defences.

More specifically, since some, if not all, psychosomatic disorders may be viewed as manifestations of a fairly primitive defence mechanism, whose aim and object is to keep conscious experience free from emotionally disturbing information, they may be likened, at least in this respect, to the laboratory-produced phenomena of perceptual defence.

The term 'perceptual defence' was originally coined to describe the fact that a person's recognition threshold for a threatening stimulus tends to be higher than for a neutral stimulus. Thus, a longer tachistoscopic exposure is needed for perception of words like 'cancer' or 'death' than for words of equal length and familiarity but lacking any particular emotional significance.

So surprising (to some psychologists) was this finding that it gave rise to one of the most heated controversies in the whole history of psychology. The apparently anthropomorphic implications of a situation in which 'recognition' by 'brains' could evidently delay recognition by minds, initiated some hundreds of experiments to try and nail the phenomenon down as due to nothing more exciting than biases in verbal response behaviour; e.g. that people hesitate more about reporting rude words than non-rude words.

However, despite many attempts to disprove something which appeared to border on the supernatural, four lines of research have emerged which seem to have established the reality of perceptual defence as a genuine sensory perceptual phenomena.

Firstly, it has been shown (Dixon 1958(b), 1960; Dixon and Haider, 1961) that a threatening stimulus word, presented below the awareness threshold to one eye, may change visual sensitivity for a spot of light presented to the other eye. Since the subject in this paradigm was totally unaware of the subliminal stimulus to one eye and did not have to do anything more dangerous or embarrassing than adjust the brightness of a spot of light seen by his other eye, explanations of significant effects in terms of response biases are scarcely relevant.

The same may be said of a related research (Hardy and Legge, 1968) in which threatening stimuli, below the auditory threshold, raised the visual threshold for a neutral stimulus, and vice-versa. Moreover, by using a method of data analysis (based on the tenets of signal detection theory) which distinguishes between pure sensory effects (d') and response effects (β) this latter study, like subsequent investigations by Broadbent and Gregory (1967) and by Dorfman (1967), showed that manifestations of perceptual defence were purely sensory in origin.

A clue as to the physiological mechanism underlying these phenomena has been provided by a number of researches (Dixon and Lear, 1963, 1964; Emrich and Heinemann, 1966) which involved measuring pre-awareness changes in the EEG during the subliminal presentation of meaningful visual stimuli.

Results from this approach not only suggest that cortical discrimination of sensory inflow may occur for stimuli at intensities far below the awareness threshold, but that one consequence of such preconscious processing may be to depress or enhance output from the ascending reticular activating system (ARAS). Since a sufficient contribution from the ARAS is believed to be a necessary condition for consciousness of a stimulus, this chain of events would account for the perceptual defence effect. That there is time for the brain to adjust its threshold for consciousness of a discriminated stimulus, follows from the fact that those fibres conveying specific information from eye to cortex are faster-conducting than those responsible for non-specific activation of the reticular system.

The possible significance of perceptual defence for psychosomatic disorders is twofold. Firstly, the mechanisms involved could well be implicated in such gross hysterical symptoms as psychogenic blindness, deafness, and anaesthesia. Secondly, the fact that in perceptual defence the involuntary blocking of conscious awareness for a threatening stimulus may be preceded by such autonomic responses as changes in heart-rate and skin conductance, sounds uncommonly like the trade-off between experienced anxiety and such bodily symptoms (often mediated by the autonomic nervous system) as characterize psychosomatic illness. Indeed, the latter may well be regarded as a chronic state of perceptual defence. By the same token the so-called subception effect, wherein subjects give electrodermal responses to threatening stimuli before they consciously recognize such stimuli, might be said to have *its* counterpart in the psychosomatic patient's lack of insight regarding the contingency between particular psychic events and their somatic consequences.

ATTENTIONAL SPAN AND THE CAPACITY TO DO TWO THINGS AT ONCE

There is a sense in which some neurotic and psychosomatic disorders may be said to caricature, albeit in a gross and distressing way, the normal human capacity for doing two things at once.

Let us enlarge on this theme. Whatever else they may be, people are complex devices for receiving, analysing, storing, rearranging, and passing on information. Where they differ from most other devices that carry out these functions is in their capacity for examining and reporting back upon some part of the information which flows through their damp and complex circuitry. Whether dignified as consciousness, awareness, perceptual experience, phenomenal representation or, most 'scientific' of all, 'central channel capacity' this inner window on what they are about is both a hindrance and a help. The advantages of conscious experience would appear to be its intense concentration on essentials, its penchant for what is novel, hyper-relevant, threatening or pleasurable, and the possibility it provides for modification, and so-called cognitive reappraisal, of its content. Its disadvantages are the limitations on its capacity, the fact that its content may be highly susceptible to bias and distraction by the intrusive pressures of emotion and motivation and, most serious of all, that the possessor of a capacity for conscious experience may be incapable of distinguishing between those ingredients of his experience which are veridical—coming from the outside—and those which, coming solely from the inside, are illusory or delusional.

It is surely no exaggeration to aver that it is just this anomalous position, which the conscious experience system occupies in relationship to the total organism, that contributes to, if not causes, so many forms of psychiatric ill health. On the one hand there are the affective disorders—various forms of schizophrenia, phobias, and obsessions, which are characterized by the fact that conscious experience is taken up by mental content that is alien, unjustified, incomprehensible, ruminative, or just plain frightening; and on the other hand there are such malaises as conversion hysteria and some psychosomatic disorders wherein information which should achieve conscious representation becomes shunted straight through to some unwanted somatic outlet. Well may it be said that the schizophrenias are disorders of attention (see McGhie and Chapman, 1961; Frith, 1979). Indeed there is a sense in which all disorders which include a psychic factor reflect some dysfunction of the proper relationship between the ability to process information and the capacity to be conscious of this ability.

In considering the likely evolutionary origins of this susceptibility to so many sorts of breakdown in total functioning, is to arrive again at the starting point of this discussion—the evolution of a secondary system for phenomenal representation of some small part of all those informational events which, from inside or outside the living organism, determine his behaviour. There are several implications of all this for the genesis of some psychosomatic disorders. Firstly, since the channel capacity of the secondary system is very limited, whilst that of the special senses is very large—the possibility of overloading central channel capacity is extremely high. Secondly, since channel capacity is limited and may become more so under stress—e.g. as in so-called 'tunnel vision'—large amounts of information may be monitored by the special senses and enter the system without ever achieving phenomenal representation. Some proportion of this information may be of a kind to exacerbate existing complexes and initiate those autonomic effects which eventuate in stress disorders. There is evidence for both these contributions to psychosomatic disorder. Firstly, as Lipowski (1974) has suggested, information overload may lead to such disabilities as coronary disease and hypertension.

Secondly, as demonstrated in experiments by Corteen and Wood (1972) and Corteen and Dunn (1974), when conscious channel capacity is taken up with processing one stream of information, a secondary input may be monitored, analysed, and eventuate in a somatic output without, it seems, causing so much as a ripple in consciousness.

In these studies people had to 'shadow' (repeat back) prose presented to one ear, while words, some of which had been previously associated with electric shock, were presented, at low intensities, to the other ear. The results were of considerable significance for psychosomatic disorders. Though never entering awareness, those words on the unattended channel which had previously been associated with electric shock produced significant electrodermal responses (EDRs) from the subject's hand. From the fact that while unrelated non-shock words had no such effect but EDRs *were* produced by non-shock words which bore a semantic relation to the shock words, we must assume that all the subliminal inputs were being unconsciously analysed for meaning, a conclusion recently confirmed by Forster and Govier (1978). No less interesting was the finding that nothing on the unattended channel seemed to affect the primary, conscious task of shadowing prose on the other ear.

It seems the brain, at least under the conditions of these experiments, is quite capable of performing a semantic analysis of two simultaneous streams of information and of responding to each without any interaction between them. We have to ask whether the apparent autonomy and intractable nature of some psychosomatic and conversion symptoms is perhaps a consequence of this particular cerebral accomplishment; and, perhaps of even greater importance from the standpoint of possible therapeutic measures, whether, and under what conditions, interaction between two simultaneous inputs can be achieved. Three lines of research are of some relevance to this issue. In dichotic listening Lewis (1970) and Mackay (1973) have shown that when material on an unattended channel *is* of relevance to a primary processing task, then interaction between two pieces of information arriving simultaneously over different channels will occur. Thus, in the Mackay experiment subliminal words as, for example, 'money' or 'river' on one ear, determined the recipient's response to such ambiguous sentences as 'she sat by the bank' arriving on his other ear.

In the Lewis study, reaction times to single words on one ear were affected differentially by synonyms, antonyms, or unrelated words presented to the other ear.

While the emotional significance of information on a secondary 'subliminal' channel may evoke a somatic response without achieving conscious representation, as in the experiment by Corteen and Wood, it may also, if sufficiently important, gain momentary precedence over, and interrupt, another stream of information which was being consciously analysed. Thus, subjects who had been oblivious of material arriving on an unattended channel were immediately conscious of hearing their own name if this was embedded in the otherwise meaningless succession of unheard words (Moray, 1959).

For meaningful material from an unattended source to have an effect upon ongoing perceptual experience it is not, however, necessary that it should gain access to consciousness. In a study by Henley and Dixon (1974) which has been successfully replicated by Mykel and Daves (1979), subjects were required to report imagery evoked by music presented to the left ear. As predicted, the imagery they experienced was significantly influenced by cue words which entered the other ear at subliminal intensities. The subjects in this experiment were totally unaware of the cue words or of the fact that their imagery was in any way being shaped by other than the music. An interesting feature of this research was that no effects were observed if the music went to the right ear and the words to the left. It seems the routing of material to that part of the brain which is specialized for its reception (i.e. musical stimuli to the right hemisphere and verbal items to the left), may be an important condition for the sort of interaction effects observed.

Taken together, these various experiments illustrate two general features of information-processing which may be of some significance for psychosomatic disorders. They are:

(1) Though the conscious span of apprehension may be very limited, actual amounts of information received and processed by the organism could be very large.
(2) Incoming information which does not achieve phenomenal representation may nevertheless initiate a range of different responses, some of which could result in somatic symptomatology.

Experiments by Walker (1975) are particularly relevant to this issue. When a patch of red light is exposed to one eye, and green light to the other, this produces a state of binocular rivalry. Since the recipient of these two 'messages' alternates between seeing red and seeing green the question arises as to whether, during these alternations, the non-dominant eye is in fact transmitting anything throughout its period of non-dominance. Walker tested this possibility by adding a subliminal stimulus to the green patch whenever the subject reported seeing 'red'. The results were unequivocal. Introduction of the subliminal stimulus evoked immediate perception of 'green' and blindness for red. In other words, during binocular rivalry (as in dichotic listening) both receptors are evidently feeding information into the central nervous system but only one of these simultaneous inputs achieves conscious representation at any one time. However, according to the principle (one of obvious biological advantage) that the novelty of a stimulus increases its chances of conscious representation, any change in the 'unseen' input 'switches' it into awareness.

As Walker points out, this phenomenon in normal subjects probably has its pathological counterpart in the clinical phenomenon of cortical blindness described by Poppel, Held, and Frost (1973) and amblyopia as investigated by Ikeda and Wright (1974). In both these conditions 'blind' eyes have been found to follow moving stimuli even though their owners deny any awareness of that which is triggering their eye movements. Neurophysiological evidence suggests that this so-called 'blind sight' (also reported by Weiskrantz et al., 1974) is mediated by a retina–midbrain circuit which, via the pulvinar and association cortex, exercises control over opto-motor centres. It is just because such a monitoring system underlies the orienting response that it could quite possibly play a significant role in some psychosomatic disorders. Having evolved as a sort of psychological early warning system, operating totally outside of awareness, it provides a convenient route, from receptor input to somatic output, for just such threatening stimuli as are best kept out of awareness.

IMPLICATIONS OF WORK ON SUBLIMINAL PERCEPTION FOR DIAGNOSIS AND THERAPY

Whatever else it may have achieved I hope this brief outline of research on subliminal perception has shown some remarkable parallels between the laboratory findings on normal people and phenomena associated with at least some psychosomatic disorders.

The effect on brain processes, memory, autonomic responses, dreams, and defence mechanisms, of stimuli below the conscious threshold, suggest that:

(1) People with a predisposition towards psychosomatic disorder may have an inbuilt or learned capacity for short-circuiting incoming information which is itself brought about by an inability to analyse complex perceptual displays. The finding by Witkin (1965) that the cognitive style of field dependency (global non-articulated response to visual stimuli) is related to a predisposition towards hysterical and psychosomatic disorder would seem to bear out this contention, as does also the work of Sackeim et al. (1977) on the relationship between hemisphericity and susceptibility to stimuli below the conscious threshold.
(2) If psychosomatic disorder reflects a hiving-off of the conscious experience system from that which mediates the flow of information through an organism, this would explain the virtual impossibility of effecting cures by

conscious deliberation or exhortation. In order to break into the vicious chain of events between psychic content and somatic outlet some method must be used which bypasses the censoring functions of conscious scrutiny. One way is by the elliptical interpretation. Another, and more certain way, may be by using stimuli which are themselves below the conscious threshold. In effect the therapist would be using the psychosomatic route itself to effect suppression of the symptom.

Let us then look at some applications of subliminal stimulation to the problems of diagnosis and therapy.

DIAGNOSTIC POTENTIAL

Despite many attempts to find links between specific psychic contents and particular psychosomatic symptoms (see Alexander, 1952; Kline, 1972) little in the way of invariant relationships between psychic states and somatic consequences has been discovered. The discovery of such specific relationships as that found between the mother–child relationship and subsequent appendicitis appears to be the exception rather than the rule (Eylon, 1967).

There is a case therefore for attempting to use subliminal stimuli in a diagnostic or exploratory role. Three examples from existing research should suggest what might be achieved. The first is a study of anorexia nervosa (Beech, 1959) in which it was hypothesized that the disorder in question results from an unconscious confusion between food and sexual objects. Twenty-five girls with anorexia nervosa, and three normal controls, gave pre-recognition guesses as to the nature of subliminally presented words. Seven of the patients and none of the controls produced food-related responses to those stimulus words with sexual connotations.

A second, very different, study involving the Defence Mechanism Test (Kragh, 1962) centred around the problem of identifying those applicants to the Swedish Airforce who, during or after training, would be prone to flying accidents and psychosomatic disorder. The tachistoscopic test, which consists of measuring the effects on perception of the central 'hero' figure of a peripheral 'ugly male face', was validated over a 15-year period by the Swedish Airforce. So successful was the test in sorting 'safe sheep' from 'unsafe goats' that it has now been adopted as a standard part of selection procedure in Sweden and is being considered for adoption by the airforces of other countries which have suffered high levels of pilot wastage. As to why the test works, two non-mutually exclusive theories may be invoked.

A psychoanalytic explanation would be that the subject identifies with the 'hero' figure. Consequent upon this identification the peripheral 'threat' is unconsciously registered and activates early castration anxieties which, in turn, give rise to such unconscious defences as denial and isolation. It is the operation of these defensive measures which is revealed in the subject's drawing.

A simpler explanation would be merely that, in some individuals, anxiety engendered by a subliminal threatening stimulus disrupts those perceptual and other cognitive processes underlying a central task. It does so presumably by taking up conscious channel capacity!

Whichever sort of explanation is preferred, the plain fact remains that here is a technique which not only distinguishes those liable to psychosomatic breakdown under stress but also provides information about two aspects of psychopathology—the nature of an underlying complex and the sorts of defence mechanisms which it elicits. Other applications of subliminal stimulation to clinical phenomena have been initiated by Silverman (1976), Henley and Dixon (1976), Smith, Sjoholm and Nielzen (1974), Anderson, Fries and Smith (1970), and Shevrin (1975). Their various approaches have in common the recording of effects on different responses of content-specific subliminal stimuli. From studying a wide range of such dependent variables as changes in responses to projective tests, changes in the visual threshold, alterations in form and duration of after-images and movement after-effects, and variations in the visual evoked response—these several investigations go a long way towards helping to unravel the psychogenic causes of mental breakdowns. They do so by providing clues as to the otherwise hidden relationships between particular external events and those psychopathological complexes with which these same events collide. The most extensive work in this direction has been carried out by Silverman (1972, 1975). Known as the method of 'subliminal dynamic activation', Silverman's approach involves the use of projective and other tests to examine the effect on psychopathology of presenting subliminal words and pictures specifically designed to activate unconscious wishes and fantasies.

Working within the general framework of psychoanalytic theory Silverman has used this paradigm to obtain data consistent with Freudian hypotheses regarding the unconscious origins of a variety of disorders. Thus, a dozen or so experiments have shown the exacerbating effect upon schizophrenic pathology of stimuli symbolizing oral aggression, upon homosexuals of stimuli designed to stir up conflict over *incestuous* wishes (Silverman *et al.*, 1973), and upon the psychopathology of stutterers of stmuli to do with conflict over anal wishes (Silverman *et al.*, 1972). Using the same paradigm other researchers (Rutstein and Goldberger, 1973; Varga, 1973; Miller, 1973) have produced strong support for the psychoanalytic theory of depression—namely that the malaise results from the turning of unconscious aggressive wishes against the self.

It would be surprising, to say the least, if the feelings about, and attitudes towards, their bodies which people have, did not play a significant role in the genesis of some psychosomatic disorder. Judging from the work of Fisher and Cleveland (1968) this is indeed the case. Thus, even such serious disorders as cancer and arthritis have become associated with particular constellations of the body image. But here again the use of subliminal stimulation has proved rewarding. In a typical study, for example, Fisher (1976) has shown that Rorschach barrier scores (a measure of the extent to which the individual needs to feel his body is protected from the outside) may be significantly changed by the administration of subliminal auditory stimuli. Since a person's barrier scores are evidently related to the sort of psychosomatic disease he might contract, the possibility of manipulating symptoms by altering the body image seems worthy of further investigation.

Before leaving the question of diagnosis mention should be made of a recent research (Spence, Scarborough, and Ginsberg, 1978; Spence, 1980) which, though not employing external subliminal stimuli, is of considerable relevance to the relationship between bodily disease and unconscious perception. The subjects in this study were 62 women who, on the basis of abnormal smear tests, were considered to be at risk for cervical cancer. Prior to cone biopsy, which would confirm whether or not they in fact had the disease, each woman had an open-ended interview with the hospital physician. After each interview the physician made a 'guess' as to whether the patient in question would or would not be subsequently diagnosed as cancerous. To his surprise he was correct in 74 per cent of cases. On the hunch that the doctor had unconsciously responded to actual words used by the interviewees Spence *et al.* submitted the interview protocols to a computer analysis. The results yielded two findings of considerable interest. First, those 27 patients who were ultimately found to have cancer had in fact used significantly more words connoting feelings of hopelessness and fewer words of a hopeful nature than had the women with negative biopsies. Secondly, the lexical decisions of the cancer group seemed designed to conceal from themselves, and from the physician, the diagnostic information which they were communicating. For example, the word 'death' used significantly more often by the women who were subsequently found to have positive biopsies was invariably employed in a metaphorical context— 'I was tickled to death' or 'He'll be the death of me' rather than in its direct literal sense. There are, of course, at least two quite different interpretations of these data. On the one hand it is possible that the lexical decisions of these patients were in some way biased by unconscious perception of internal bodily change. On the other hand it is possible, perhaps indeed more likely, that these data reflect a relationship between personality factors and proneness to cancer which has been suggested by several researches (see Totman, 1979). According to this hypothesis, pessimistic lexical decisions in a stress situation and a predisposition towards cancer would both be outcomes of the same underlying personality structure. Either way this research would seem to have important implications for the use of diagnostic procedures in which the patient remains unaware of what he or she is communicating.

Given that probing with subliminal stimuli can be used in a diagnostic capacity one naturally asks whether similar treatments might not be used in a therapeutic role. A start in this direction has also been initiated by Silverman. In two studies (Silverman *et al.*, 1978) he has shown how a group of obese women may be helped to reduce weight by giving them repeated subliminal presentations of words which, as previous research has shown, tend to diminish the underlying anxiety that gave rise to over-eating.

In both studies behaviour modification programmes, extending over a period of weeks, were accompanied by subliminal stimulation, with half the subjects receiving the verbal message 'Mommy and I are one, (intended to stimulate symbiotic gratification fantasies) and the other half, a neutral control message. The dependent value, weight-loss, was measured at the end of the programme and at follow-up times of 4 and 12 weeks later.

In both studies treatment with the symbiotic message resulted in significant weight-loss for the experimental group.

To most normal adults the idea of oneness with the maternal parent may not seem terribly important, which is perhaps why Silverman's rather startling results with this symbiotic gratification stimulus have occasioned some surprise. However that may be, the words 'Mommy and I are one' have proved to be such an effective unconscious 'comforter' that they have also been of value in the treatment of schizophrenics (Silverman, 1971; Silverman and Candell, 1970; Lieter, 1973; and Kaye, 1975) and women suffering from insect phobias (Silverman, Frank, and Dachinger, 1974).

The symbiotic gratification stimulus is not, however, unique as a therapeutic stimulus. Following a very recent study (Tyrer, Lewis, and Lee 1978), in which it was shown that self-ratings of anxiety could be increased by showing normals a subliminal cine film depicting frightening events, Tyrer and his co-workers (Tyrer, Lee, and Horn, 1978) have utilized the same technique for the successful reduction of agoraphobic anxiety.

How successful these sorts of treatments may be for psychosomatic disorders other than obesity remains to be seen.

SUMMARY

The thesis has been advanced that processes involved in the genesis and maintenance of some psychosomatic disorders are akin to, if not identical with, those underlying manifestations of subliminal perception. In both cases external events make contact with, and activate, preconscious levels of memory, thereby giving rise to a somatic outlet—and all this below conscious awareness.

It has also been suggested that the symbolic conversion of subliminal external stimuli, and the effects of such stimuli upon drive schemata and autonomic responses produced by subliminal stimulation, may well involve the same processes as underlie certain somatic conversion symptoms.

By the same token perceptual defence, the Poetzl effect, and phenomena associated with binocular rivalry and dichotic listening, suggest what is in effect a *sine qua non* for at least some psychosomatic disorders—namely a capacity for preconscious monitoring of the external scene followed by a somatic response to particular features of that scene.

Finally the start that has already been made in using subliminal techniques for diagnosis and therapy holds considerable promise for future applications of stimulation below awareness.

REFERENCES

Alexander, F. (1952). *Psychosomatic Medicine. Its Principles and Applications.* London: Allen & Unwin.

Anderson, A., Fries, I., and Smith, G. L. W. (1970). Change in after-image and spiral after-effect serials due to anxiety caused by subliminal threat. *Scandinavian Journal of psychology.* 11, 7–16.

Arey, L. B. (1960). The indirect representation of sexual stimuli by schizophrenic and normal subjects. *Journal of Abnormal and Social Psychology,* 61, 424–441.

Bach, S. (1959). The symbolic effects of words in subliminal, supraliminal, and incidental presentation. Unpublished doctoral dissertation, New York University.

Beech, H. R. (1959). An experimental investigation of sexual symbolism in anorexia nervosa employing a subliminal stimulation technique: preliminary report. *Psychosomatic Medicine,* 21, 277–280.

Berger, R. J. (1963). Experimental modification of dream content by meaningful verbal stimuli. *British Journal of Psychiatry,* 109, 722–740.

Broadbent, D. E., and Gregory, M. (1967). Perception of emotionally toned words. *Nature,* 215, (5101), 581–584.

Corteen, R. S., and Dunn, D. (1974). Shock-associated words in a nonattended message: a test for momentary awareness. *Journal of Experimental Psychology,* 102, 1143–1144.

Corteen, R. S., and Wood, B. (1972). Autonomic responses to shock-associated words. *Journal of Experimental Psychology,* 94, 308–313.

Dixon, N. F. (1956). Symbolic associations following subliminal stimulation. *International Journal of Psycho-Analysis,* 37, 159–170.

Dixon, N. F. (1958a). The effect of subliminal stimulation upon autonomic and verbal behaviour. *Journal of Abnormal and Social Psychology,* 57, 29–36.

Dixon, N. F. (1958b). Apparent changes in the visual threshold as a function of subliminal stimulation. A preliminary report. *Quarterly Journal of Experimental Psychology,* 10, 211–219.

Dixon, N. F. (1960). Apparent changes in the visual threshold: central or peripheral? *British Journal of Psychology,* 51, 297–309.

Dixon, N. F. (1964). Communication without awareness: the implications of subliminal perception. *Journal of Psychosomatic Research,* 8, 337–341.

Dixon, N. F. (1971). *Subliminal Perception: The Nature of a Controversy.* London: McGraw Hill.

Dixon, N. F., and Haider, M. (1961). Changes in the visual threshold as a function of subception. *Quarterly Journal of Experimental Psychology,* 13, 229–235.

Dixon, N. F., and Lear, T. E. (1963). Electroencephalograph correlates of threshold regulation. *Nature* (London), 198, 870–872.

Dixon, N. F., and Lear, T. E. (1964). Incidence of theta rhythm prior to awareness of a visual stimulus. *Nature* (London), 203, 167–170.

Dorfman, D. D. (1967). Recognition of taboo words as a function of a priori probability. *Journal of Personality and Social Psychology,* 7, 1–10.

Emrich, H., and Heinemann, L. G. (1966). EEG bei unterschwelliger wahrenhmung emotional bedeutsamer wörter. *Psychologische Forschung,* 29, 285–296.

Erdelyi, M. (1974). A new look at the New Look: perceptual defence and vigilance. *Psychological Review,* 81, 1–25.

Eylon, Y. (1967). Birth events, appendicitis, and appendectomy. *British Journal of Medical Psychology,* 40, 317.

Fisher, C. (1954). Dreams and perception. The role of preconscious and primary modes of perception in dream formation. *Journal of the American Psychoanalytic Association,* 2, 389–445.

Fisher, S. (1976). Conditions affecting boundary response to messages out of awareness. *Journal of Nervous and Mental Diseases,* 162, 313–322.

Fisher, S., and Cleveland, S. (1968). *Body Image and Personality*. New York: Holt, Rinehart & Winston.

Fonagy, P. (1977). The use of subliminal stimuli in highlighting function differences between the two hemispheres. Paper given to December meeting of the Experimental Psychology Society at Birkbeck College, London.

Forster, P. M., and Govier, E. (1978). Discrimination without awareness? *Quarterly Journal of Experimental Psychology*, **30**, 282–295.

Frith, C. D. (1979). Consciousness, information processing and schizophrenia. *British Journal of Psychiatry*, **134**, 225–235.

Hardy, G. R., and Legge, D. (1968). Cross-model induction of changes in sensory thresholds. *Quarterly Journal of Experimental Psychology*, **20**, 20–29.

Henley, S. H. A., and Dixon, N. F. (1974). Laterality differences in the effects of incidental stimuli upon evoked imagery. *British Journal of Psychology*, **65**, 529–536.

Henley, S. H. A., and Dixon, N. F. (1976). Preconscious processing in schizophrenics: an exploratory investigation. *British Journal of Medical Psychology*, **49**, 161–166.

Ikeda, H., and Wright, M. J. (1974). Is amblyopia due to inappropriate stimulation of the 'sustained' pathway during development? *British Journal of Ophthamology*, **58**, 165–175.

Janis, I. L. (1969). *Stress and Frustration*. New York: Harcourt Brace Inc.

Kaye, M. (1975). The therapeutic value of three merging stimuli for male schizophrenics. Unpublished doctoral dissertation, Yeshiva University.

Kline, P. (1972). *Fact and Fantasy in Freudian Theory*. London: Methuen.

Kragh, U. (1962). Precognitive defensive organization with threatening and non-threatening peripheral stimuli. *Scandinavian Journal of Psychology*, **3**, 65–68.

Krystal, H. (1968). *Massive Psychic Trauma*. New York: International University Press Inc.

Lewis, J. L. (1970). Semantic processing of unattended messages using dichotic listening. *Journal of Experimental Psychology*, **85**, 225–228.

Libet, B., Alberts, W. W., Wright, E. W., and Feinstein, B. (1967). Responses of human somato-sensory cortex to stimuli below the threshold for conscious sensation. *Science*, **158** (3808), 1597–1600.

Lieter, E. (1973). A study of the effects of subliminal activation of merging fantasies in differentiated and non-differentiated schizophrenics. Unpublished doctoral dissertation, New York University.

Lipowski, Z. J. (1974). Sensory overloads, information overloads and behaviour. *Psychotherapy and Psychosomatics*, **23**, 264–271.

McGhie, A., and Chapman, J. (1961). Disorders of attention and perception in early schizophrenia. *British Journal of Medical Psychology*, **34**, 103–116.

Mackay, D. G. (1973). Aspects of the theory of comprehension, memory and attention. *Quaterly Journal of Experimental Psychology*, **25**, 22–40.

Magoun, H. W. (1954). The ascending reticular system and wakefulness. In E. D. Adrian and H. Jasper (eds.), *Brain Mechanisms and Consciousness*, pp. 1–27. Springfield, Illinois: Thomas.

Maher, B. A. (1966). *Principles of Psychopathology: An Experimental Approach*. New York: McGraw-Hill.

Marcel, A., and Patterson, K. (1978). Word recognition and production: reciprocity in clinical and normal studies. In J. Requin (ed.), *Attention and Performance VII*. New Jersey, Lawrence Erlbaum Associates.

Miller, J. (1973). The effects of aggressive stimulation upon adults who have experienced the death of a parent during childhood and adolescence. Unpublished doctoral dissertation, New York University.

Moray, W. (1959). Attention in dichotic listening, affective cues and the influence of instructions. *Quaterly Journal of Experimental Psychology*, **11**, 56–60.

Mykel, N., and Daves, W. (1979). Emergence of unreported stimuli into imagery as a function of laterality of presentation: replication and extension of work by Henley and Dixon. *British Journal of Psychology*, **70**, 253–258.

Nemiah, J. C., and Sifneos, P. E. (1970). Affect and fantasy in patients with psychosomatic disorders. In O. W. Hill (ed.), *Modern Trends in Psychosomatic Medicine*, Vol. 11, pp. 26–34. London: Butterworth.

Ornstein, R. E. (1977). *The Psychology of Consciousness*. Harmondsworth: Penguin Books.

Oswald, I., Taylor, A. M., and Treisman, M. (1960). Discriminative responses to stimulation during human sleep. *Brain*, **83**, 440–453.

Pine, F. (1960). Incidental stimulation: a study of preconscious transformations. *Journal of Abnormal and Social Psychology*, **60**, 68–75.

Pine, F. (1964). The bearing of psychoanalytic theory on selected issues in research on marginal stimuli. *Journal of Nervous and Mental Disease*, **138**, 205–222.

Poetzl, O. (1917, 1960). The relationship between experimentally induced dream images and indirect vision. Monogr. No. 7, *Psychological Issues*, **2**, 41–120.

Poppel, E., Held, R., and Frost, D. (1973). Residual visual function after brain wounds involving the central visual pathways in man. *Nature* (London), **243**, 295–296.

Rutstein, E. H., and Goldberger, L. (1973). The effects of aggressive stimulation on suicidal patients: an experimental study of the psychoanalytic theory of suicide. In B. Rubinstein (ed.), *Psychoanalysis and Contemporary Science*, Vol. 2. New York: Macmillan.

Sackeim, H. A., Packer, I. K., and Gur R. C. (1977). Hemisphericity, cognitive set and susceptibility to subliminal perception. *Journal of Abnormal Psychology*, **86**, 624–630.

Samuels, L. (1959). Reticular mechanisms and behaviour. *Psychological Bulletin*, **56**, 1–25.

Shevrin, H. (1975). Does the averaged evoked response encode subliminal perception? Yes: A reply to Schwartz and Rem. *Psychophysiology*, **12**, 395–398.

Shevrin, H., and Dickman, S. (1980). The psychological unconscious: a necessary assumption for all psychological theory.' *American Psychologist*. (In press.)

Shevrin, H., and Fritzler, D. E. (1968). Brain response correlates of repressiveness. *Psychological Reports*, **23**, 887–892.

Silverman, L. H. (1971). An experimental technique for the study of unconscious conflict. *British Journal of Medical Psychology*, **44**, 17–25.

Silverman, L. H. (1972). Drive stimulation and psychopathology: on the conditions under which drive-related external events evoke pathological reactions. In R. R. Holt (ed.), *Psychoanalysis and Contemporary Science*, Vol. 1. New York: Macmillan.

Silverman, L. H. (1975). On the role of data from laboratory experiments in the development of the clinical theory of psychoanalysis. *International Review of Psycho-Analysis*, **2**, 1–22.

Silverman, L. H. (1976). Psychoanalytic theory: 'the reports of my death are greatly exaggerated. *American Psychologist*, **31**, 621–637.

Silverman, L. H., Bronstein, A., and Mendelsohn, E. (1976). The further use of the subliminal psychodynamic activation method for the experimental study of the clinical theory of psychoanalysis: on the specificity of relationships between manifest psychopathology and unconscious conflict. *Psychotherapy: Theory Research and Practice*, **13**, 2–16.

Silverman, L. H., and Candell, P. (1970). On the relationship between aggressive activation, symbiotic merging, intactness of body boundaries and manifest pathology in schizophrenics. *Journal of Nervous and Mental Disease*, **150**, 387–339.

Silverman, L. H., Frank, S. C., and Dachinger, P. (1974). A psychoanalytic reinterpretation of the effectiveness of systematic desensitization: experimental data bearing on the role of merging fantasies. *Journal of Abnormal Psychology*, **83**, 313–318.

Silverman, L. H., Klinger, H., Lustbader, L., Farrell, J., and Martin A. (1972). The effects of subliminal drive stimulation on the speech of stutterers. *Journal of Nervous and Mental Disease*, **155**, 14–21.

Silverman, L. H., Kwawer, J. S., Wolitzky, C., and Coron, M. (1973). An experimental study of aspects of the psychoanalytic theory of male homosexuality. *Journal of Abnormal Psychology*, **82**, 178–188.

Silverman, L. H., Martin, A., Ungaro, R., and Mendelsohn, E. (1978). The effect of subliminal stimulation of symbiotic fantasies on behaviour modification treatment of obesity. *Journal of Consulting and Clinical Psychology*, **46**, 432–441.

Smith, G. J. W., Sjoholm, L., and Nielzen, S. (1974). Sensitive reactions and afterimage variegation. *Journal of Personality Assessment*, **38**, 41–47.

Spence, D. P. (1980). Lawfulness in lexical choice. *Journal of the American Psychoanalytic Association*, **28**, 115–132.

Spence, D. P., and Gordon, C. M. (1967). Activation and measurement of an early oral fantasy: an exploratory study. *Journal of the American Psychoanalytic Association*, **15**, 99–129.

Spence, D. P., and Holland, B. (1962). The restricting effects of awareness: a paradox and an explanation. *Journal of Abnormal and Social Psychology*, **64**, 163–174.

Spence, D. P., Scarborough, H. S., and Ginsberg, E. H. (1978). Lexical correlates of cervical cancer. *Social Science and Medicine*, **12**, 141–145.

Totman, R. (1979). *Social Causes of Illness*. London: Souvenir Press/Cordon Books.

Tyrer, P., Lee, I., and Horn, P. (1978). Treatment of agoraphobia by subliminal and supraliminal exposure to phobic cine film. *Lancet*, **1**, 358–360.

Tyrer, P., Lewis, P., and Lee, I. (1978). Effects of subliminal and supraliminal stress on symptoms of anxiety. *Journal of Nervous and Mental Disease*, **166**, 88–95.

Varga, M. (1973). An experimental study of aspects of the psychoanalytic study of elation. Unpublished doctoral dissertation, New York University.

Walker, P. (1975). The subliminal perception of movement and the 'suppression' in binocular rivalry. *British Journal of Psychology*, **66**, 347–356.

Weiskrantz, L. (1977). Trying to bridge some neurophysiological gaps between monkey and man. *British Journal of Psychology*, **68**, 431–445.

Weiskrantz, L., Warrington, E. K., Sanders, M. D., and Marshall, J. (1974). Visual capacity in the hemianopic field following a restricted occipital ablation. *Brain*, **97**, 709–728.

Werner, H. (1956). Microgenesis and aphasia. *Journal of Abnormal and Social Psychology*, **52**, 347–353.

Witkin, H. A. (1965). Psychological differentiation and forms of pathology. *Journal of Abnormal Psychology*, **70**, 317–336.

Foundations of Psychosomatics
Edited by M. J. Christie and P. G. Mellett
© 1981 John Wiley & Sons Ltd.

7

STRESS TOLERANCE: POSSIBLE NEURAL MECHANISMS

JEFFREY A. GRAY, NICOLA DAVIS AND SUSAN OWEN
Department of Experimental Psychology, University of Oxford, England.

JORAM FELDON
Department of Psychology, Tel-Aviv University Israel

and

MICHAEL BOARDER
*Department of Psychiatry, Stanford University Medical Center, California,
U.S.A.*

Consider the following four experiments.

1. Two groups of rats are trained to run in an alley for a food reward.
One of them (which we shall term the 'partial punishment' or PP group),
together with the food in the goalbox, is given an electric shock initially of low
intensity but gradually increasing in intensity on successive trials. The other
group is simply given, during this first 'training' phase of the experiment, a
reward on every trial; this is known as 'continuous reinforcement' (CRF). In
the second 'test' phase of the experiment both groups are given reward together
with a high-intensity shock on every trial. It is normally found in such an experiment that, during the test phase, the CRF group shows a much greater reluctance
(which one can measure as the time taken to reach the goalbox) to go to food-
plus-shock than does the PP group (e.g. Brown and Wagner, 1964). The PP
group, in other words, has developed tolerance for the shock. We shall call
this phenomenon the 'partial punishment effect' or PPE.

2. Two groups of rats are again trained to run in an alley for a food reward.
One is a simple CRF group as in the first experiment. The second is trained with
a 'partial reinforcement' (PRF) schedule, i.e. each rat is given a reward on a
proportion of trials only, the rewarded trials being selected in a random fashion
so that, on any given trial, the animal cannot tell whether it will be rewarded
for running or not. In the test phase of this experiment no further rewards
are given to the animals in either group (a procedure known as 'extinction').
It is found that the PRF group continues to run to the now-empty goalbox
much more persistently than the CRF group. The PRF group, in other words,
has developed tolerance for 'frustrative non-reward' (i.e. the omission of the
reward which both groups have come to expect for running in the alley). This
phenomenon is known as the 'partial reinforcement extinction effect' (PREE)
(Lewis, 1960).

3. A group of rats is given a single session in which it is exposed to inescapable electric shocks (a procedure which is sometimes said to produce
'learned helplessness': Seligman, Maier, and Solomon, 1971). Each animal is

then trained in a task in which it is again shocked, but in which it is possible to escape from or avoid the shock by jumping from side to side of a two-compartment apparatus known as a 'shuttlebox'. A control group is also tested in the shuttlebox, but without exposure to the initial inescapable shocks. The group that had the learned helplessness experience is worse at escaping from shock in the shuttlebox than the control group. We now repeat the experiment, but give the learned helplessness group 15 daily sessions of inescapable shock before the shuttlebox test. It is found that such animals are just as good at learning to escape shock as the controls which have never had inescapable shock. Thus repeated exposure to inescapable shocks allows the animal to overcome the deleterious effects of a single session of inescapable shock (Weiss and Glazer, 1975; Weiss et al., 1975). Miller (1976) has termed this effect 'toughening up'.

4. The fourth experiment is identical to the third except that, in place of the inescapable shock sessions, the rats are made to swim in cold water (2°C) for 3–4 minutes before the shuttlebox test session. This treatment impairs shuttlebox performance in the same way as does inescapable shock; and, also like inescapable shock, 15 consecutive daily sessions of 'cold swim' overcome the initial deficit, so that shuttlebox performance tested after the final swim is normal (Weiss and Glazer, 1975; Weiss et al., 1975).

In each of these four experiments the animal is exposed repeatedly to a stressor (shock, non-reward, cold swim) and comes, in consequence, to show reduced behavioural responses to the stressor. (In case the reader is in any doubt about the status of non-reward as a 'stressor', it should be said that there is much behavioural evidence that animals find it aversive—see Gray, 1975. It has also been shown that non-reward elicits a rise in plasma corticosterone, which is widely used as a physiological measure of stress: Goldman, Coover, and Levine, 1973; Valero, Gray, and Mellanby, unpublished results.) In these cases, then, the animal develops tolerance for the stressor to which it is exposed.

Besides these 'direct tolerance' effects, there are also clear demonstrations of 'cross-tolerance'. Thus, exposure to a PPE schedule (as in example 1 above) gives rise to increased resistance to extinction (as in example 2); and conversely exposure to a PRF schedule gives rise to increased resistance to punishment (Brown and Wagner, 1964). Exposure to repeated inescapable shock (as in example 3) has also recently been shown to lead to increased resistance to extinction (Chen and Amsel, 1977). In addition, Weiss et al. (1975) showed that repeated exposure to shock prevents cold swim from impairing shuttlebox performance, and repeated exposure to cold swim prevents inescapable shock from having this effect. Thus cross-tolerance has been demonstrated in both directions for the pairs, shock and non-reward, shock and cold swim; the pair, non-reward and cold swim, does not appear to have been investigated as yet.

Our own interest in these phenomena arose in the first instance from our research into the psychological and physiological effects of the anti-anxiety drugs, i.e. the benzodiazepines, the barbiturates, and alcohol (Gray, 1977).

There is much evidence that these drugs attenuate the behavioural effects of anticipated shock and of anticipated non-reward (see Gray, 1977 for review) For example, if we train rats to run in an alley for a reward on a CRF schedule and then shock them in the goalbox (as in example 1) or extinguish them (as in example 2), running speed declines in both cases. But if we inject these animals with chlordiazepoxide (librium) or sodium amylobarbitone (sodium amytal) during the test phase of the experiment, running speeds decline much less: the drugged animal is apparently less worried about the prospect of shock or non-reward.

These effects are, of course, what one would expect of substances which are used to control anxiety in Man, and they have been used (Gray, 1976, 1978) as the basis for a general theory of the psychology of anxiety. According to this theory 'anxiety' is a central state which is elicited by exposure to one of three classes of stimuli: stimuli associated with punishment (e.g. with electric shock); stimuli associated with frustrative non-reward; and novel stimuli. (The behavioural effects of the latter kind of stimulus are also attenuated by the anti-anxiety drugs; but we shall ignore them in this chapter.) The behavioural outputs of the state of anxiety (which have been deduced both from the effects of the anti-anxiety drugs and from results in the experimental study of learning—see Gray, 1975) include: inhibition of ongoing behaviour; an increased level of arousal (Gray, 1964); and increased attention to novel features of the environment. The function of anxiety considered in this way is, then, to 'stop, look, and listen': that is to say, in the face of stimuli which warn of danger, frustration, or the unknown, it is necessary for the animal to interrupt its current activities and scan its environment for cues as to better alternatives.

Now, there are conditions in which there is no better alternative than to continue with the initial behavioural strategy, even though this strategy has adverse consequences. Such are the conditions which have been used in the experiments on the development of tolerance to stress which we have described above. On a partial punishment or partial reinforcement schedule there is no alternative behaviour which will obtain the reward but to persevere with running to the goalbox; the only alternative to continued swimming in the Weiss et al. (1975) experiment is to drown; and no alternative at all is allowed in the inescapable shock procedure—the animal must 'grin and bear it'. Under these circumstances the response which many of us would find natural is to reach for a bottle of whisky or at any rate for a valium tablet. An older and more Puritan generation would have regarded both courses of action as 'sapping the moral fibre'. Experiments on rats make it clear that this suspicion would have been well-founded. *For the anti-anxiety drugs rather clearly prevent the development of behavioural tolerance to stress.*

This was first demonstrated in experiments on the partial reinforcement extinction effect using sodium amylobarbitone (Ison and Pennes, 1969; Gray, 1969). In these early experiments rats were run in the straight alley for several trials a day (6–8) at an inter-trial interval (ITI) of 3–5 minutes. Recently we have modified the experiment by running the animals for only one trial a day.

The principal reason for this change was a theoretical one. As indicated above the anti-anxiety drugs block the behavioural effects of *anticipated* non-reward; but they do not appear to affect responses directly controlled by non-reward itself (nor, for that matter, responses directly elicited by electric shock) (Gray, 1977; Feldon *et al.*, 1979). Now there is good evidence that the PREE is produced in two separate but complementary ways (Mackintosh, 1974). In the first way, the animal comes to associate the immediate after-effect of non-reward on a particular trial with the probability of reward on the next (Capaldi, 1967). Sodium amylobarbitone leaves the PREE produced in this way intact (Ziff and Capaldi, 1971). In the second way the animal develops an emotional response in anticipation of non-reward, called by Amsel (1962) 'anticipatory frustration'. The immediate effect of this emotional state is to cause the animal to inhibit the non-rewarded response; but, on a PRF schedule, the animal develops tolerance for the disruptive effects of anticipatory frustration and the PREE ensues (Amsel, 1962). It is this second, emotional, process which we would expect to be sensitive to the action of anti-anxiety agents.

The reason for shifting to the one-trial-a-day PREE in our drug studies can now be made clear. At one trial a day there is no opportunity for the im-

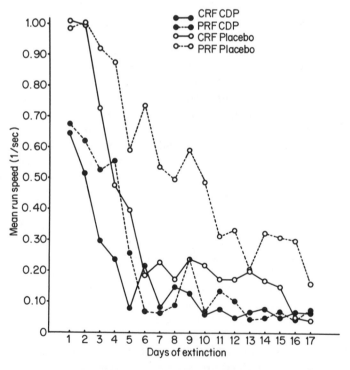

FIGURE 7.1. Effect of 5mg/kg chlordiazepoxide HCl (CDP), injected daily throughout acquisition of a running response, on subsequent resistance to extinction as a function of continuous (CRF) or partial (PRF) reinforcement

mediate after-effect of non-reward to become associated with events on the next trial—the 24-hour ITI is simply too long. Thus one can investigate the effects of the drugs of interest on a PREE which is under the control purely of anticipatory frustration. And indeed it turns out that the effects of both sodium amylobarbitone (Feldon et al., 1979) and chlordiazepoxide (Feldon and Gray, in press, a) are very clear-cut when we use the one-trial-a-day PREE.

In describing these effects we have to distinguish between those the drug produces in virtue of its presence during acquisition of the running response and those it produces in virtue of its presence during extinction. Figures 7.1–7.3 show the data collected in our laboratory by Joram Feldon using chlordiazepoxide (CDP) (Feldon and Gray, in press a); his results with sodium amylobarbitone were very similar (Feldon et al., 1979). The rats were injected with CDP (5 mg/kg) before the daily trial either throughout acquisition only, or throughout extinction only, or both, or neither. It can be seen that, injected during acquisition only, the drug virtually abolished the PREE by reducing resistance to extinction in the PRF group, CRF-trained animals remaining essentially unaffected in their extinction performance (Figure 7.1). Injected during extinction only, CDP increased resistance to extinction in both CRF and PRF groups, and the PREE remained intact (Figure 7.2). When the drug was injected throughout the entire experiment the acquisition and extinction effects combined together: in the CRF condition there was an increase in resistance to extinction (due to the effect of the drug during extinction); in the PRF condition the acquisition effect of the drug (reducing resistance to extinction)

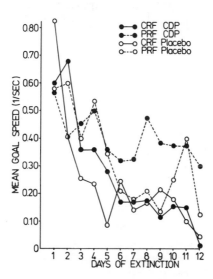

FIGURE 7.2. Effect of 5mg/kg chlordiazepoxide HCl (CDP), injected daily throughout extinction, on resistance to extionction as a function of continuous (CRF) or partial (PRF) reinforcement

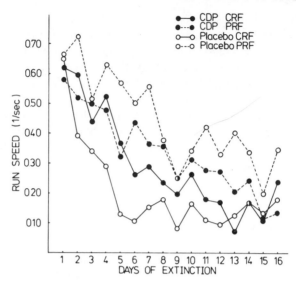

FIGURE 7.3. Effect of 5mg/kg chlordiazepoxide HCl
(CDP), injected daily throughout both acquisition and
extinction, on resistance to extinction as a function of
continuous (CRF) or partial (PRF) reinforcement

and the extinction effect (increasing resistance to extinction) cancelled each
other out, so that there was very little change from the placebo-injected controls;
and the PREE was again virtually abolished (Figure 7.3).

Thus, when exposed to occasional non-reward mixed with reward, animals
maintained on a minor tranquillizer fail to learn persistence (the PREE).
All the effects of the drug, both those due to its presence during acquisition
and those due to its presence during extinction, can be understood in the light
of the hypothesis (Gray, 1967, 1977) that it attenuates the behavioural significance of stimuli associated with frustrative non-reward. If these stimuli
are rendered psychologically nugatory, it is not possible for the animal to
learn to tolerate them.

Recently we have extended our research in this direction to the partial
punishment effect at one trial a day. Nicola Davis used an experimental design
very closely modelled on that employed by Feldon. During acquisition, instead
of non-rewarded trials as received by the PRF group in Feldon's experiment,
her partial punishment group received shocks in the goalbox on the same
schedule (every trial being rewarded with food). The shocks started out at
a very low intensity, but by the end of training they had reached 0.3 mA. This
value of shock was sufficient to cause the control group to give up running to
the goalbox quite smartly when they first encountered it in the test phase of
the experiment, but the PP group continued to run to the goalbox (the PPE:
Figure 7.4). The effects of CDP were strikingly similar to those seen in the
PREE experiment. Given in acquisition, the drug blocked the PPE, principally
by decreasing resistance to punishment in the PP group; given during conti-

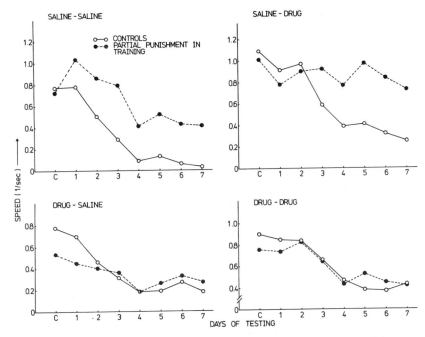

FIGURE 7.4. Effect of 5mg/kg chlordiazepoxide HCl on resistance to punishment as a function of presence or absence of partial punishment in training. Saline–saline: saline in both training and testing. Saline–drug: drug in testing only. Drug–saline: drug in training only. Drug–drug: drug in both training and testing. The point 'C' on the abscissa is the final day of training (without shock). Ordinate: running speed in the goal section of the alloy. From: N. H. Davis, S. Brookes, J. A. Gray and J. N. P. Rawlins (in press), chlordiazepoxide and resistance to punishment, *Quart. J. Exp. Phychol*

nuous punishment testing, it increased resistance to punishment in both the PP and the CRF groups, preserving the PPE; given during both acquisition and extinction, it abolished the PPE by increasing resistance to punishment in the CRF group (Figure 7.4). Working along similar lines Dyck, Lussier and Ossenkopp (1975) have also shown that cross-tolerance from punishment during acquisition to punished extinction during testing is blocked by injection of sodium amylobarbitone during acquisition. Their results and ours provide welcome confirmation of the hypothesis that there are important psychological and physiological communalities between the effects produced by (a) stimuli associated with non-reward and (b) stimuli associated with punishment (Gray, 1967, 1975; Wagner, 1966), at least as far as their susceptibility to blockade by the anti-anxiety drugs is concerned.

These results raise a number of interesting questions about physiological mechanisms. What changes in the brain underlie the development of tolerance to punishment or to non-reward? What changes underlie the development of cross-tolerance between each of these (and other) stresses? And how do the anti-anxiety drugs prevent these changes from taking place? In the remainder of this paper we will describe some of our speculations and research bearing on these questions.

Our first incursion into the neurology of persistence was aimed at the septal area, the hippocampus and their interconnections (Gray, 1970). This is not the place to tell that story in detail (see Gray et al., 1978). Suffice it is to say that the septohippocampal system (Whelan, 1978) undoubtedly does play a part in the development of persistence as measured by the PREE: roughly speaking, destruction of the medial septal area (which contains the pacemaker cells which control the hippocampal theta rhythm: Stumpf, 1965; Gray and Ball, 1970; Rawlins et al., 1979) produces a syndrome rather like that caused by CDP or sodium amylobarbitone injected during extinction only; while destruction of the lateral septal area (to which the hippocampus makes its major subcortical projection: Swanson and Cowan, 1976) produces a syndrome like that caused by one of these drugs injected during acquisition only (Feldon and Gray 1979a, b). Destruction of the entire septal area (Henke, 1974, 1977), produces a syndrome like that seen when CDP or sodium amylobarbitone is injected throughout acquisition and extinction, thus making possible the hypothesis that these drugs act sequentially on the lateral septal area (during acquisition) and the medial septal area (during extinction (Feldon and Gray, in press b).

There is, however, a lack of parsimony about this hypothesis which renders it unattractive. In any case, we have other reasons for preferring an alternative hypothesis: one which incorporates the role of the septohippocampal system, but also draws attention to the possible role played by the major monoaminergic afferents this receives from the brain stem.

We were led in this direction by the results of some neuropharmacological experiments in which we investigated the effects of anti-anxiety drugs on the threshold for septal driving of the hippocampal theta rhythm as a function of stimulation frequency. In these experiments stimulation is applied (in the free-moving rat) to the pacemaker cells for theta located in the medial septal area by way of electrodes permanently implanted in that region (Gray and Ball, 1970). If the frequency of the applied stimulation lies within the naturally occurring theta range (about 6–12 Hz in the rat), it is possible to drive the theta rhythm in this way. In the undrugged male rat it is found when this is done that there is a minimum current for driving theta at a frequency of 7.7 Hz (Gray and Ball, 1970; James et al., 1977). Now this happens to be the frequency of theta which is elicited by non-reward in the alley (Gray and Ball, 1970; Kimsey, Dyer, and Petri, 1974). When reward is delivered, a lower frequency (about 6–7 Hz) occurs; and when the animal is running towards the reward, a higher frequency (about 8.5–10 Hz).

We therefore predicted that, since the anti-anxiety drugs block the behavioural effects of non-reward but not those of reward (Gray, 1977), these agents ought to impair septal control of hippocampal theta selectively at frequencies close to 7.7 Hz. It was a striking confirmation of this prediction to discover that several benzodiazepines, sodium amylobarbitone, and alcohol all abolish the 7.7 Hz minimum in what we have come to call the 'theta-driving curve', doing so by selectively raising the threshold at this frequency (Gray and Ball, 1970; McNaughton *et al.*, 1977; Nettleton, personal communication, 1976).

At this point we determined to discover something about the way in which the anti-anxiety drugs perform this strange trick. Our researches have built up a strong case for the hypothesis that they do it by impairing (in some as yet unknown way) conduction in the dorsal ascending noradrenergic bundle, which brings noradrenergic fibres from the locus coeruleus to both the septal area and the hippocampus (Ungerstedt, 1971; Moore, 1978). For pharmacological blockade of noradrenaline (McNaughton *et al.*, 1977) and destruction of the dorsal bundle using 6-hydroxydopamine (6-OHDA) (Gray *et al.*, 1975) both lead to the same changes in the theta-driving curve as do the anti-anxiety drugs.

Confirmation that this is not simply an isolated neuropharmacological phenomenon of doubtful significance, but is related to the behavioural effects of the anti-anxiety drugs, has come from experiments conducted in our laboratory by Susan Owen and Michael Boarder. In these experiments the dorsal noradrenergic bundle has been destroyed by local injection of 6-OHDA. At the end of the experiment regional assay of the brain for levels of noradrenaline and dopamine is used to confirm that the intended lesion has been successfully produced; and levels of noradrenaline in the hippocampus are typically reduced to well below 10 per cent of control values.

Owen and Boarder have investigated the behaviour of such animals in a number of tasks involving non-reward or novelty; and the overall pattern of their results is very similar to the pattern seen after injection of sodium amylobarbitone or CDP. In particular they find (Figure 7.5) that the PREE is

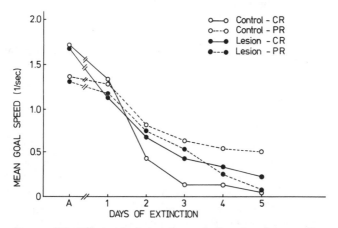

FIGURE 7.5. Effect of destruction of the dorsal ascending noradrenergic bundle ('lesion') on resistance to extinction as a function of continuous (CR) or partial (PR) reinforcement. The point 'A' on the abscissa is the last day of acquisition

abolished by destruction of the dorsal bundle, and that the behaviour observed closely resembles that seen in intact animals injected with one of the anti-anxiety drugs during both acquisition and extinction: resistance to extinction is increased after CRF but decreased after PRF (compare Figure 7.5 with Figure 7.3).

Owen and Boarder also have evidence that the role of the dorsal bundle in promoting the PREE involves the septohippocampal system. It was reported by Henke (1974) that destruction of the entire septal area abolishes the PREE when short ITIs are used and 48 acquisition trials are run, but leaves it intact if acquisition is extended to 96 trials. We have confirmed this finding using lesions restricted to the lateral septal area (Feldon and Gray, 1979b). Owen and Boarder have similarly shown that the dorsal bundle lesion abolishes the PREE at 50 acquisition trials but leaves it intact at 100 trials. This similar dependence of the two lesion effects on number of training trials strongly suggests that the dorsal bundle affects persistence by way of its input to the septohippocampal system.

At present, then, we believe that the development of tolerance for non-reward depends, at least in part, upon events occurring in the dorsal ascending noradrenergic bundle, and affecting in particular the input from this fibre bundle to the septohippocampal system. There is also evidence that stressors other than non-reward give rise to activity in the dorsal bundle. Thus it has been shown that immobilization stress causes an increase in the turn-over of noradrenaline in the forebrain and that this increase is counteracted by benzodiazepines, barbiturates, and alcohol (Corrodi et al., 1971; Lidbrink et al., 1972). Weiss et al. (1975) and Glazer et al. (1975) have shown that when acute exposure to inescapable electric shock or to swim stress leads to helplessness in the shuttlebox, this is accompanied by a fall in the level of noradrenaline in the brain, indicating that the requirement for activity in central noradrenergic neurone set up by the conditions of the experiment has been too great for synthesis of new transmitter to keep up with it. These workers also report a particularly striking phenomenon in the animals 'toughened up' by repeated exposure to inescapable shock: pari passu with the disappearance of helplessness in these animals, the levels of central noradrenaline returned to normal. Thus the development of tolerance for shock in Weiss's experiments was accompanied by—and may have been mediated by—long-term changes in the function of noradrenergic neurons in the brain.

There is some indication from physiological experiments of the mechanism by which such long-term changes might take place (Fillenz, 1977).

Like other substances released by neurons, noradrenaline is stored in special organelles—the synaptic vesicles—from which it is released by exocytosis on arrival of a nerve impulse. Synaptic vesicles in noradrenergic neurons differ, however, from those in all other neurons described to date in that they are responsible not only for the storage and release of the neurotransmitter, but also for its synthesis. For this purpose they contain the enzyme dopamine-β-hydroxylase, which catalyses the last step in the synthesis of noradrenaline.

The synaptic vesicles are themselves synthesized in the cell body of the neuron and transported to the nerve terminal by an axoplasmic transport mechanism with a velocity of around 10 mm/hour. The vesicles have only a limited life-span in the terminal, since they cannot refill with noradrenaline after they have undergone exocytosis (Fillenz and West, 1976; West and Fillenz, in preparation). Thus, in order to maintain the stores of releasable noradrenaline in the terminals there has to be a constant supply of new vesicles by axoplasmic transport.

Another requirement for maintaining the stores of noradrenaline in the nerve terminal is the replacement of released noradrenaline by new synthesis of the neurotransmitter itself. This is controlled by the enzyme, tyrosine hydroxylase, which catalyses the rate-limiting step in noradrenaline synthesis. It is known that acute stress leads to an increased release of noradrenaline from peripheral neurons. This increased release can be maintained for a limited period of time, since there is a rapid acceleration of noradrenaline synthesis to replace the lost transmitter. When the store of functional vesicles becomes depleted, however, noradrenaline release begins to fail (Benedict, Fillenz, and Stanford, 1977). It is possible that a similar failure in noradrenaline release, but in the *central* nervous system, is one of the mechanisms underlying the behavioural helplessness described by Weiss *et al.* (1975) after acute exposure to electric shock or swim stress.

In the periphery, it has been shown that the stimulus which causes neurons to release noradrenaline also sets in train an increase in the rate of synthesis of the two key enzymes controlling the levels of this transmitter: tyrosine hydroxylase, the rate-limiting enzyme, and dopamine-β-hydroxylase, the marker enzyme for vesicles. This is the phenomenon of 'trans-neuronal enzyme induction' (Thoenen, 1975; Fillenz, 1977). Increased levels of enzyme begin to appear in the cell body 16–18 hours after the original stimulus and remain elevated for a number of days (Thoenen, 1975). In order to exert an effect on releasable transmitter the enzymes have to reach the nerve terminal. This introduces a further delay, different for the two enzymes, since they are trans-ported at different rates: 10 mm/hour for dopamine-β-hydroxylase, which is particle-bound, and 5–10 mm/day for tyrosine hydroxylase, which is extra-vesicular and largely in solution in the cytoplasm. Thus the elevated enzyme levels appear in the nerve *terminals* long after the cessation of the original stimulus. Furthermore, the delay in the rise in enzyme level will vary with the distance of the nerve terminal from the cell body (Black, 1975). In the case of the noradrenergic input from the locus coeruleus to the hippocampus (as an example which is particularly relevant to the concerns of this chapter), there is likely to be a delay of 6–7 days between the exposure of an animal to a stimulus which might give rise to enzyme induction and the appearance of higher levels of tyrosine hydroxylase in the hippocampal nerve terminals.

Induction of tyrosine hydroxylase has been shown to occur in the central nervous system in response to the injection of reserpine (Reis *et al.*, 1974), which depletes catecholamine stores, and cold stress (Zigmond, Schon, and

Iversen, 1974); furthermore, these changes have been observed in the terminal areas served by the dorsal noradrenergic bundle, including the hippocampus (Boarder and Fillenz, 1979). What is not known is whether the observed increase in the activity of tyrosine hydroxylase gives rise to the possibility of increased release of neurotransmitter. On the assumption that this does indeed occur as a result of the induction of tyrosine hydroxylase, we have here a mechanism which might account for the kind of behavioural tolerance for stress with which this chapter has been concerned. That is to say, initial exposure to a stressor would cause an increased level of activity in noradrenergic neurons in the forebrain, as described by Lidbrink et al. (1972: see above). If the demands imposed on noradrenergic impulse traffic by the stressor are excessively severe, there will be a fall in the availability of noradrenaline for release and the kind of behavioural incapacity described by Weiss et al. (1975) in their experiments on helplessness. But the increased noradrenergic impulse traffic (or the conditions which give rise to it) will also set in motion a chain of events which results in increased synthesis of noradrenaline and thus an increased availability of this neurotransmitter for release at nerve terminals. When this occurs we shall see—according to the hypothesis developed here—the kind of behavioural tolerance to stress which has been described above.

This hypothesis has, in fact, been proposed before by Weiss et al. (1975) and Miller (1976) in connection with their 'toughening-up' experiments. They report one key observation which offers support for the hypothesis. In the animals which came to show normal avoidance behaviour in the shuttlebox in consequence of repeated exposure to shock, along with the return of noradrenaline levels to normal values there was also a rise in the activity of tyrosine hydroxylase measured in whole-brain homogenates. (This may have reflected an increase in the actual amount of this enzyme in the brain—which would constitute enzyme induction sensu stricto—or some other change which could increase the activity of a given amount of enzyme (Kuczenski, 1975). For the purpose of the present argument this distinction is unimportant.) Rather surprisingly (given that there is other evidence that cold stress can result in induction of tyrosine hydroxylase in the central nervous system: Thoenen, 1975; Zigmond, Schon, and Iversen, 1974), Weiss et al. did not find increased activity of tyrosine hydroxylase in the animals which were 'toughened up' by repeated exposure to a cold swim, though the levels of noradrenaline returned to normal in these animals, as did performance in the shuttlebox. Conceivably, different detailed mechanisms mediate the two kinds of phenomena which we distinguished above as 'direct tolerance' and 'cross-tolerance'; though both mechanisms appear to involve long-term adaptive changes in central noradrenergic neurons, judging from the experiments reported by Weiss's group.

In our own experiments we are investigating the possibility that there are long-term changes in the function of the noradrenergic neurons of the dorsal bundle as a result of exposure to different schedules of reward, non-reward and punishment in the straight alley. These experiments are not yet sufficiently advanced, however, to warrant description. Thus we offer the hypothesis developed above, in the approved Popperian manner, as a hostage to fortune.

Acknowledgements

Our own research described in this chapter is supported by the UK Medical Research Council. We are grateful to our colleague, Dr M. Fillenz, for her considerable help both in the writing of this paper and the thinking that has gone into it. We are also grateful to those of our colleagues who have allowed us to describe their as yet unpublished results.

REFERENCES

Amsel, A. (1962). Frustrative nonreward in partial reinforcement and discrimination learning: some recent history and a theoretical extension. *Psychol. Rev.*, **69**, 306–328.

Benedict, C. R., Fillenz, M., and Stanford, S. C. (1977). Plasma noradrenaline levels during exposure to cold. *J. Physiol.*, **269**, 47–48.

Black, I. B. (1975). Increased tyrosine hydroxylase activity in frontal cortex and cerebellum after reserpine. *Brain Res.*, **95**, 170–175.

Boarder, M. R., and Fillenz, M. (1979. Absence of increased tyrosine hydroxylation after induction of tyrosine hydroxylase following reserpine administration. *Biochem. Pharmacol.*, **28**, 1675–1677.

Brown, R. T., and Wagner, A. R. (1964). Resistance to punishment and extinction following training with shock or nonreinforcement. *J. Exp. Psychol.*, **68**, 503–507.

Capaldi, E. J. (1967). A sequential hypothesis of instrumental learning. In K. W., Spence and J. T. Spence (eds.), *The Psychology of Learning and Motivation*, Vol. 1, pp. 67–156. New York and London: Academic Press.

Chen, J. S., and Amsel, A. (1977). Prolonged, unsignaled, inescapable shocks increase persistence in subsequent appetitive instrumental learning. *Anim. Learn. Behav.*, **5**, 377–385.

Corrodi, H., Fuxe, K., Lidbrink, P., and Olson, L. (1971). Minor tranquilizers, stress and central catecholamine neurons. *Brain Res.*, **29**, 1–16.

Dyck, D. G., Lussier, D., and Ossenkopp, K.-P. (1975). Partial punishment effect following minimal acquisition training: sodium amobarbital and the stimulus properties of early punished trials. *Learn. Motiv.*, **6**, 412–420.

Feldon, J., and Gray, J. A. (1979a). Effects of medial and lateral septal lesions on the partial reinforcement extinction effect at one trial a day. *Quart. J. Exp. Psychol.*, **31**, 693–674.

Feldon, J., and Gray, J. A. (1979b). Medial and lateral septal lesions on the partial reinforcement extinction effect at short inter-trial intervals. *Quart. J. Exp. Psychol.*, **31**, 675–690.

Feldon, J., and Gray, J. A. (1981a). Partial reinforcement extinction effect after treatment with chlordiozepoxide. *Psychopharmacology*, in press.

Feldon, J., and Gray, J. A. (1981b). The partial reinforcement extinction effect: influence of chlordiazepoxide in septallesioned rats. *Psychopharmacology*, in press.

Feldon, J., Guillamon, A., Gray, J. A., De Wit, H., and McNaughton, N. (1979). Sodium amylobarbitone and responses to non reward. *Quart. J. Exp. Psychol.*, **31**, 19–50.

Fillenz, M. (1977). The factors which provide short-term and long-term control of transmitter release. *Progr. Neurobiol.*, **8**, 251–278.

Fillenz, M., and West, D. P. (1976). Fate of noradrenaline storage vesicles after release. *Neurosci. Lett.*, **2**, 285–287.

Glazer, H. J., Weiss, J. M., Pohorecky, L. A., and Miller, N. E. (1975). Monoamines as mediators of avoidance-escape behaviour. *Psychosom. Med.*, **37**, 535–543.

Goldman, L., Coover, G. D., and Levine, S. (1973). Bidirectional effects of reinforcement shifts on pituitary adrenal activity. *Physiol. Behav.*, **10**, 209–214.

Gray, J. A. (1964). Strength of the nervous system and levels of arousal: a reinterpretation. In J. A. Gray (ed.), *Pavlov's Typology*, pp. 289–366. Oxford: Pergamon Press.

Gray, J. A. (1967). Disappointment and drugs in the rat. *Adv. Sci.*, **23**, 595–605.

Gray, J. A. (1969). Sodium amobarbital and effects of frustrative non-reward. *J. Comp. Physiol. Psychol.*, **69**, 55–64.

Gray, J. A. (1970). Sodium amobarbital, the hippocampal theta rhythm and the partial reinforcement extinction effect. *Psychol. Rev.*, **77**, 465–480.

Gray, J. A. (1975). *Elements of a Two-Process Theory of Learning*. London: Academic Press.

Gray, J. A. (1976). The behavioural inhibition system: a possible substrate for anxiety. In M. P. Feldman, and A. Broadhurst (eds.), *Theoretical and Experimental Bases of the Behaviour Therapies*, pp. 3–41. London: Wiley.

Gray, J. A. (1977). Drug effects on fear and frustration: possible limbic site of action of minor tranquilizers. In L. L. Iversen, S. D., Iversen, and S. H. Snyder (eds.), *Handbook of Psychopharmacology*, Vol. 8, pp. 433–529. New York: Plenum Press.

Gray, J. A. (1978). The Myers Lecture: the neuropsychology of anxiety. *Br. J. Psychol.*, **69**, 417–434.

Gray, J. A., and Ball, G. G. (1970). Frequency-specific relation between hippocampal theta rhythm, behavior, and amobarbital action. *Science*, **168**, 1246–1248.

Gray, J. A., Feldon, J., Rawlins, J. N. P., Owen, S., and McNaughton, N. (1978). The role of the septo-hippocampal system and its noradrenergic afferents in behavioural responses to nonreward. In J. Whelan (ed.), *Functions of the Septo-Hippocampal System*, pp. 275–307. Ciba Foundation Symposium No. 58 (new series).

Gray, J. A., McNaughton, N., James, D. T. D., and Kelly, P. H. (1975). Effects of minor tranquillisers on hippocampal theta rhythm mimicked by depletion of forebrain noradrenaline. *Nature (London)*, **258**, 424–425.

Henke, P. G. (1974). Persistence of runway performance after septal lesions in rats. *J. Comp. Physiol. Psychol.*, **86**, 760–767.

Henke, P. G. (1977). Dissociation of the frustration effect and the partial reinforcement extinction effect after limbic lesions in rats. *J. Comp. Physiol. Psychol.*, **91**, 1032–1038.

Ison, J. R., and Pennes, E. S. (1969). Interaction of amobarbital sodium and reinforcement schedule in determining resistance to extinction of an instrumental running response. *J. Comp. Physiol. Psychol.*, **68**, 215–219.

James, D. T. D., McNaughton, N., Rawlins, J. N. P., Feldon, J., and Gray, J. A. (1977). Septal driving of the hippocampal theta rhythm as a function of frequency in the free-moving male rat. *Neuroscience*, **2**, 1007–1017.

Kimsey, R. A., Dyer, R. S., and Petri, H. L. (1974). Relationship between hippocampal EEG, novelty and frustration in the rat. *Behav. Biol.*, **11**, 561–568.

Kuczenski, R. (1975). Conformational adaptability of tyrosine hydroxylase in the regulation of striatal dopamine biosynthesis. In A. J. Mandell (ed.), *Neurobiological Mechanisms of Adaptation and Behavior*, pp. 109–125. New York: Raven Press.

Lewis, D. J. (1960). Partial reinforcement: a selective review of the literature since 1950. *Psychol. Bull.*, **57**, 1–28.

Lidbrink, P., Corrodi, H., Fuxe, K., and Olson, L. (1972). Barbiturates and meprobamate: decreases in catecholamine turnover of central dopamine and noradrenaline neuronal systems and the influence of immobilization stress. *Brain Res.*, **45**, 507–524.

Mackintosh, N. J. (1974). *The Psychology of Animal Learning*. London: Academic Press.

McNaughton, N., James, D. T. D., Stewart, J., Gray, J. A., Valero, I., and Drewnowski, A. (1977). Septal driving of the hippocampal theta rhythm as a function of frequency in the male rat: effects of drugs. *Neuroscience*, **2**, 1019–1027.

Miller, N. E. (1976). Learning, stress and psychosomatic symptoms. *Acta Neurobiol. Exp.*, **36**, 141–156.

Moore, R. Y. (1978). Catecholamine innervation of the basal forebrain. I. The septal area. *J. Comp. Neurol.*, **177**, 665–683.

Rawlins, J. N. P., Feldon, J., and Gray, J. A. (1979). Septo-hippocampal connections and the hippocampal theta rhythm. *Exp. Brain Res.*, **37**, 49–63.

Reis, D. J., Joh, T. H., Ross, R. A., and Pickel, V. M. (1974). Reserpine selectively increases tyrosine hydroxylase and dopamine-β-hydroxylasenzyme protein in central noradrenergic neurones. *Brain Res.*, **81**, 380–386.

Seligman, M. E. P., Maier, S. F., and Solomon, R. L. (1971). Unpredictable and uncontrollable aversive events. In F. R. Brush (ed.), *Aversive Conditioning and Learning*, pp. 347–400. New York: Academic Press.

Stumpf, C. (1965). Drug action on the electrical activity of the hippocampus. *Int. Rev. Neurobiol.*, **8**, 77–138.

Swanson, L. W., and Cowan, W. M. (1976). Autoradiographic studies of the development and connections of the septal area in the rat. In J. F. DeFrance (ed.), *The Septal Nuclei*, pp. 37–64. New York: Plenum Press.

Thoenen, H. (1975). Transsynaptic regulation of neuronal enzyme synthesis. In L. L. Iversen, S. D. Iversen and S. H. Snyder (eds.), *Handbook of Psychopharmacology*, Vol. 3, pp. 443–475. New York: Plenum Press.

Ungerstedt, U. (1971). Stereotaxic mapping of monoamine pathways in the rat brain. *Acta Physiol. Scand.*, **82** (Suppl. 367), 1–48.

Wagner, A. R. (1966). Frustration and punishment. In R. M. Haber (ed.), *Current Research on Motivation*, pp. 229–239. New York: Holt, Rinehart & Winston.

Weiss, J. M., and Glazer, H. I. (1975). Effects of acute exposure to stressors on subsequent avoidance–escape behavior. *Psychosom. Med.*, **37**, 499–521.

Weiss, J. M., Glazer, H. I., Pohorecky, L. A., Brick, J., and Miller, N. E. (1975). Effects of chronic exposure to stressors on avoidance escape behavior and on brain norepinephrine. *Psychosom. Med.*, **37**, 522–534.

Whelan, J. (ed.) (1978). *Functions of the Septo-Hippocampal System*. Ciba Foundation Symposium No. 58 (new series). Amsterdam: Associated Scientific Publishers.

Ziff, D. R., and Capaldi, E. J. (1971). Amytal and the small trial partial reinforcement effect: stimulus properties of early trial nonrewards. *J. Exp. Psychol.*, **87**, 263–269.

Zigmond, R. E., Schon, F., and Iversen, L. L. (1974). Increased tryosine hydroxylase activity in the locus coeruleus of rat brain stem after reserpine treatment and cold stress. *Brain Res.*, **70**, 547–552.

Foundations of Psychosomatics
Edited by M. J. Christie and P. G. Mellett
© 1981 John Wiley & Sons Ltd.

8

PSYCHOPHYSIOLOGY AND DRUGS IN ANXIETY AND PHOBIAS

GUDRUN SARTORY AND MALCOLM LADER
Institute of Psychiatry, University of London.

The principal feature which distinguishes emotions from other mental pheno-mena is the extent to which autonomic arousal is generated as an integral part of emotional states. The sympathetic and parasympathetic nervous system activity which characterizes these states gives psychophysiological measures a unique role in recording emotional states and their changes.

Even a quick review of the literature reveals that the relationships of phy-siology and pharmacology are complex. The affect of anxiety provides the best opportunity to unravel some of these relationships and therefore we have limited our discussion to anxiety. In particular, we are concerned with three aspects: (i) to discuss the psychophysiology of anxiety as in both normal subjects and anxious patients; (ii) to review physiological changes accompanying alterations in anxiety, both increases as in the development of phobic states and decreases as in fear reduction; (iii) to outline the ways in which drugs can modify the relationships between physiology and affect.

PSYCHOPHYSIOLOGY OF ANXIETY AND FEAR

Considerable effort has been devoted to studying the psychophysiological characteristics of pathological states, with the aim of establishing reliable response patterns which may eventually serve as a diagnostic tool. This is generally done by comparing the patient sample of interest with another patient group or with a sample of non-pathological subjects. The experi-mental procedures in this type of study comprise the recording of: (1) resting levels of various psychophysiological indices; (2) responses to emotionally neutral stimulation such as tones and white noise; (3) responses to physical discomfort, for example, as induced by the cold pressor test in which subjects immerse an arm in a bucket of ice; and, (4) well-established paradigms such as that used to evaluate habituation. In these studies emotions are regarded as traits which manifest themselves in all types of reactions without being elicited by appropriate stimuli.

In addition, increasing attention is being given to emotional states, or more specifically, the state of anxiety evoked by phobic stimulation. The broad aim of these studies is to validate assumptions about response patterns in fearful states. Subject samples of volunteers and patients with specific phobias of animals are usually compared with non-phobic volunteers. Both groups are presented with the appropriate phobic stimuli, and changes in response patterns in the phobic group contrasted with those in the non-phobic group; alternatively, within-subject comparisons using responses to neutral and phobic stimuli are made. Patients with specific phobias differ from other phobic patients such as social phobics and agoraphobics in their response to neutral stimulation (Lader, 1967). Specific phobics showed the same rate of electrodermal response (EDR) habituation to tones as normal volunteers, whereas other groups of phobic patients habituated at a significantly slower rate. However, when presented with the appropriate phobic stimulus, specific phobics exhibit response patterns similar to those of other phobics with respect to direction, magnitude, and frequency of responses.

Finally, painful stimulation such as an electric shock or the threat thereof has been frequently used to evoke response patterns resembling phobic reactions. Intuitively, the fear of painful stimuli seems rationally justified whereas fear of harmless animals is not, and the two responses seem to differ at least as far as their cognitive component and respective acquisition are concerned. However, given the appropriate experimental paradigm, psychophysiological response patterns look similar in both cases with respect to direction if not magnitude.

Relatively few studies have been carried out on changes in anxiety states. Ethical considerations preclude extensive testing of assumptions about the genesis of phobic reactions. Systematic psychophysiological monitoring during fear-reduction procedures, on the other hand, has been facilitated by the standardization of treatment procedures during the past few decades. Its heuristic value has, however, only recently been acknowledged. The aim of these studies is to elucidate the mechanisms underlying therapeutic interventions and to relate changes in autonomic responses to behavioural and cognitive changes.

(1) Response patterns of psychophysiological indices during anxiety states

(a) Cardiovascular measures

Heart-rate Heart-rate, or pulse-rate, is largely controlled by the balance between sympathetic nervous activity and parasympathetic nervous activity. As a result, it is a prime contender for the measurement of anxiety states. In the past the evidence of elevated heart-rate in anxious patients compared with normal control subjects has not always been conclusive (Altschule, 1953). Recently, improved diagnostic procedures with the selection of a more homogeneous patient sample and exclusion of anxiety-prone controls have uncovered highly significant differences.

Bond, James and Lader (1974) reported a higher pulse-rate during rest in patients suffering from chronic anxiety when compared with controls. Wing (1964) demonstrated significantly higher heart-rates in patients suffering from anxiety states than in normal controls during a resting condition and during a short colour-naming stress task. After the colour-naming both groups returned to their original resting level. Change in heart-rate due to experimental conditions was parallel in the two groups with the patient group maintaining a consistently higher level. A similar result was found by Lader and Wing (1966) when testing anxious patients and normal controls during rest and the administration of a series of tones. Both groups showed the same degree of habituation over time yet patients did so at a level approximately 15 beats per minute higher than controls. In a similar study there were differences in accelerative and decelerative response components between anxious patients and normal controls (Hart, 1974). Pairs of tones of varying intensity were administered to subjects with an interstimulus interval of 4 seconds. During initial trials phasic changes in heart-rate between the first tone, or signal, and the second tone contained a decelerative component characteristic of orienting reactions in normal controls which was, however, absent in anxious patients. After repeated trials the decelerative component habituated and the two groups' heart-rate changes were similar. The author concluded that anxiety was characterized by a deficit in orienting behaviour. In this study the general level of heart-rate during rest, as well as during administration of single tones, failed to distinguish between anxious and non-anxious subjects; but as the author pointed out, some of the anxious patients suffered from specific phobias which were not manifest in the testing situation.

Increased heart-rate correlates not only with trait anxiety, a factor derived from a number of tests designed to measure anxiety, but also with state anxiety (Cattell, 1963). Lang (1968) substantiated this finding by showing that change in heart-rate reliably discriminated between presence and absence of anxiety-eliciting stimuli. The close link between heart-rate acceleration and fearful states was further supported by demonstrations that the same stimulus material prompted acceleration responses in subjects fearful of that material, and heart-rate deceleration in unafraid subjects. This deceleration is generally accepted as part of the normal orienting response (Graham and Clifton, 1966). Hare (1973) selected spider phobic subjects and a non-phobic group on the basis of the questionnaire and showed both groups a number of landscape slides considered emotionally neutral, and several slides of spiders. Spider phobics showed a sharp accelerative response when confronted with slides of spiders. Subjects of the non-phobic group, on the other hand, responded with significant heart-rate deceleration to slides of spiders. Neither of the two groups showed any significant shifts in response to landscape slides. Thus phobic and non-phobic subjects differed in their respective response direction to relevant stimuli in addition to which phobic subjects also showed a differential response depending on whether stimuli were relevant to their phobic condition or irrelevant. The same response patterns, namely HR acceleration in spider phobics, could be elicited by tones after pairing them repeatedly with slides of spiders (Hare and Blevings, 1975a). A replication of this study (Hare and Blevings, 1975b) yielded similar results with respect to phobic stimuli. Neutral stimuli, however, elicited heart-rate deceleration in phobic subjects but not in non-phobic subjects. When spider phobic and non-phobic subjects were exposed not only to seascape slides and spider slides but also to unpleasant surgical pictures (Prigatano and Johnson, 1974), responses to the latter were indistinguishable in both groups from responses to the neutral seascape slides. In fact, non-phobic subjects exhibited the same mean heart-rate and variance to all three types of stimulus material. Phobic subjects, on the other hand, had a higher mean heart-rate and a more variable heart-rate in response to spider pictures compared with the other slides.

In a similarly designed study (Klorman et al., 1977) subjects who indicated a fear of mutilation scenes were compared with subjects who were not afraid of such material. Independent groups were shown either neutral slides, incongruous slides, or else mutilation scenes. There were similar decelerative responses to neutral and incongruous slides in both mutilation-fearful and non-fearful groups. Mutilation slides, however, elicited distinct decelerative responses in the non-fearful group only. The mutilation-fearful group responded with heart-rate acceleration during the first few slides. The accelerative component decreased over the course of the twelve slides and a decelerative response emerged in the mutilation-fearful group towards the end of the procedure. This shift in direction of responses may well be indicative of mechanisms relevant during fear reduction. Unfortunately, subjective fear ratings were not analysed in detail.

A number of studies have shown that the extent of heart-rate acceleration is related to the amount of fear experienced in response to fear-eliciting stimulation in fantasy (Lang, Melamed, and Hart, 1970; Marks, Marset, and Boulougouris, 1971) and to in vivo objects (Sartory, Rachman, and Grey, 1977). In the latter study patients and volunteers suffering from specific phobias were exposed to the phobic object at distances which elicited fear ratings of four different magnitudes between 0 (relaxed state) and 100 (maximum fear tolerated).

The resulting changes in heart-rate (Figure 8.1) differentiated reliably between fear states on the upper part of the scale but less so between mild and non-fear states, perhaps accounting in part for the generally low correlations between the two variables. The correlations reported range from 0.2 to 0.5 (Kelly and Walter, 1968; Lang, Melamed, and Hart, 1970; Cattell, 1963).

In summary, heart-rate is increased in anxiety states and fear, and in heightened fear states relates to the magnitude of experienced fear. So far no consistent pattern has emerged relating to conditions where the presence of anxiety alters orienting reactions to neutral stimulation.

Blood flow Anxiety-eliciting stimulation is assumed to cause vasoconstriction in the periphery but to increase muscular circulation, presumably to render the organism better able to cope with a stressful situation. Peripheral blood flow is measured by finger pulse volume or cephalic vasomotor responses and changes in muscular circulation are recorded in the forearm. Cephalic vasomotor responses have been recorded using photoplethysmographic techniques.

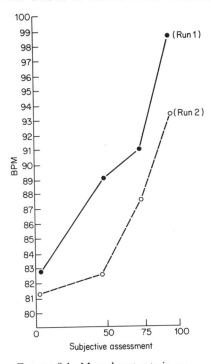

FIGURE 8.1. Mean heart-rate in response to phobic stimuli which were presented at various distances to elicit subjective fear ratings of 0 (relaxed) to 100 (maximum fear tolerated). The initial presentations (Run 1) were repeated (Run 2) with adjusted distances

Ackner (1956) reviewed the literature on finger pulse volume in anxious patients and control subjects and concluded that the former tended to have a smaller pulse volume, but with much overlap between the groups. A recent study (Bloom, Houston, and Burish, 1976) demonstrated that finger pulse volume is sensitive to threat of painful stimuli in volunteers. Two groups of subjects were given a mild shock initially and subjects in the threat condition were then told that they would receive increasingly stronger shocks. Control subjects were informed that the experimenter was merely interested in the after-effects of the shock; neither of the two groups received any further shocks. Subjects in the threat condition had significantly lower finger pulse volumes, indicating more peripheral vasoconstriction. They also reported more anxiety than non-threatened subjects. In a second study (Bloom and Trautt, 1977), the sensitivity of the finger pulse volume to manipulations of anxiety level was confirmed.

In a study of spider phobics, cephalic vasomotor responses differentiated between phobic and non-phobic volunteers when exposed to slides of spiders

(Hare, 1973; Hare and Blevings, 1975a, b). Fearful volunteers reacted to phobic material with vasoconstriction whereas non-fearful ones responded with vasodilatation. The latter response is assumed to form part of an orienting reaction (Sokolov, 1963). Neither group exhibited appreciable changes in response to neutral landscape slides.

Forearm blood flow is significantly higher in patients suffering from anxiety states than in normal controls during rest (Kelly, 1966; Kelly, Brown, and Shaffer, 1970), but both groups attained similar levels of blood flow during mental arithmetic.

(b) Electrodermal activity (EDA)

EDA has been a popular measure in this area. A sample of patients with chronic anxiety states had significantly more spontaneous fluctuations than a control sample throughout 10 minutes of a rest period and the administration of 20 tones (Lader and Wing, 1966). Skin conductance level (SCL) in the patient sample was also significantly higher towards the end of both the rest period and stimulation phase due to a differential habituation rate: controls habituated rapidly within both periods whereas the patient group maintained the same high level of skin conductance. Skin conductance responses (SCRs), on the other hand, were larger in controls than in patients at the beginning of the experiment, and over time decreased in controls to an amplitude smaller than that in patients. This measure is assumed to represent part of the orienting response. In another study the SCR was also smaller in response to neutral stimulation in anxious subjects than non-anxious ones (Neary and Zuckerman, 1976). However, both groups of subjects habituated. Habituation rate of SCR itself seems a good indicator of the severity of anxiety states (Lader, 1967). Specific phobics showed the most rapid habituation, followed by social phobics, agoraphobics, and finally patients with free-floating anxiety and with depression-anxiety. The last four groups of patients were, in fact, indistinguishable in their habituation rate and their frequency of spontaneous fluctuation, but they differed significantly from specific phobics who, in turn, resembled normal controls (Lader, Gelder, and Marks, 1967). Level of skin conductance was not indicative of anxiety in this study. Katkin and McCubbin (1969) also found a negative relation between frequency of spontaneous fluctuations and habituation rate of SCR amplitude in volunteers. That habituation of the SCR is impaired in anxious patients has been confirmed in two further studies (Raskin, 1975; Horvath and Meares, 1979).

Studies investigating electrodermal phenomena in response to fear-eliciting stimulation yielded varied results regarding the type of measurements which are sensitive to differences in emotional states. Spontaneous fluctuations are numerous during threat of shock in volunteers (Katkin, 1965; Orne and Paskewitz, 1974) and in phobics when imagining anxiety-eliciting scenes (Marks et al., 1971). Spider phobics produce more spontaneous fluctuations than non-phobic subjects when viewing slides of spiders (Prigatano and Johnson,

1974). SCR amplitude, on the other hand, failed to differentiate between phobic and non-phobic subjects in the later study because, as the authors pointed out, this measure showed marked habituation during the course of the experiment. Subjects had been presented with each slide for 10 seconds. When exposed to three slides of spiders for 2 seconds each, spider phobics showed greater SCR amplitudes than unafraid subjects (Geer, 1966). In another study, spider phobic and non-phobic subjects were exposed to 12 spider slides each for 5 seconds (Hare and Blevings, 1975b). Again, spider phobics showed a greater increase in SCR amplitude from neutral to phobic material than unafraid subjects, but habituation of response magnitude over trials was not apparent at this short duration of presentation. Tonic activity, i.e. SCL, was the same in the two groups, as might have been expected when comparing specific phobics with controls (Lader and Wing, 1966). SCL also failed to distinguish between mutilation-fearful and unafraid persons, as defined by questionnaire, when viewing gruesome slides of mutilated bodies (Klorman et al., 1977). Interestingly enough, SCRs increased equally in both groups of subjects during these aversive slides compared to neutral ones, whilst concomitant phasic heart-rate changes showed acceleration in the fearful group and deceleration in the unafraid subjects; the latter is indicative of orienting responses.

When summarizing the evidence to date on measures of electrodermal activity in anxiety states, it appears that SCL is a fairly crude measure which will only separate extreme groups, i.e. severe phobics and controls. Spontaneous fluctuations, on the other hand, have so far yielded the most consistent results when investigating anxiety states in severely phobic patients and monosymptomatic volunteers alike. This measure, however, seems unsuited to short-term recording. Recommended durations of recording to obtain reliable counts range between 30 seconds (Lacey and Lacey, 1958) and 40 seconds. (Lader and Wing, 1966) which far exceeds the stimulation period typical of studies in which anxiety is elicited.

SCR is the most complicated measure of the three: there are strong indications that it represents an orienting reaction which is increased in volunteers in response to phobic stimulation yet decreased in severe phobics to neutral stimulation. The possible inverse relationship between orienting reaction and anxiety states as measured by SCR amplitude needs further study before conclusions from the above results can be drawn. The lack or delay in habituation of SCR amplitude in phobics (Lader and Wing, 1966) and emotionally labile subjects (Katkin, 1975) compared to emotionally stable subjects may provide a valuable manoeuvre for distinguishing defensive reactions (Sokolov, 1963) characteristic of anxiety states, from orienting ones.

(c) Electroencephalogram measures

Research on electroencephalogram (EEG) measures in anxiety has focused mainly on the presence or suppression of phasic cortical activity ranging from 8 to 13 Hz, commonly identified as alpha rhythm. Its presence was deemed to indicate a state of low arousal with low perceptual input. The high arousal state characteristic of anxiety could therefore be expected to engender reduction of alpha activity which has, in fact, been demonstrated by several studies. Recordings of resting EEG in psychoneurotics showed less alpha activity than that of normal control subjects (Strauss, 1945; Lindsley, 1950; Bond, James, and Lader, 1974) and the alpha activity present in anxious patients consists of higher frequency components than those of control subjects (Brazier, Finesinger, and Cobb, 1945). Furthermore, anxiety-arousing stimuli suppress alpha activity (Berger, 1929). These findings support the notion of a unitary tonic level of arousal in autonomic and cortical response systems (Duffy, 1962). Recently, however, this view of a unidimensional arousal system has been challenged, first on the strength of data collected in volunteers under mildly stressful conditions (e.g. Lacey, 1967), and, more directly, by studies demonstrating stimulus-bound alpha activity. Orne and Paskewitz (1974) trained subjects to enhance their alpha activity with the aid of auditory feedback. In two further sessions the subjects were warned they might be given shocks, but only when alpha was absent. The shock instructions failed to diminish alpha density in both sessions although the anxiety-provoking properties of the situation were apparent in verbal reports, significantly raised heart-rate and increased spontaneous fluctuations of dermal activity. In a similar study, the popular assumption of the anxiety-reducing effects of alpha-abundance was being tested (Chisholm, DeGood, and Hartz, 1977). Tones and shocks were administered to subjects who were subsequently allocated to one of three groups: one underwent feedback training contingent upon the production of alpha activity; another acted as yoked controls receiving non-contingent feedback; and the third group simply listened to music. After the 'treatment' all subjects were again exposed to pairs of tones and shocks, part of the time with alpha feedback and for the remainder without. There were no significant differences in decrease of subjective anxiety between groups but heart-rate was significantly higher in the contingent feedback group during phases of increased alpha density. The only significant reduction in heart-rate resulting from treatment occurred in the group which had listened to music. The results thus failed to substantiate the assumption of a relationship between suppression of alpha rhythm and anxiety.

Consideration of the mechanisms underlying alpha blocking might elucidate the inconsistent results in alpha activity during anxiety states. Mulholland (1972) demonstrated in a series of experiments that alpha blocking is a function of oculomotor activity rather than of visual input, as had been assumed so far (Chapman, Shelbourne, and Bragdon, 1970). Future research should explore whether anxiety states are associated with increased oculomotor activity which might be associated with decreased alpha activity.

While the mechanisms controlling the contingent negative variation (CNV) remain obscure, it is difficult to interpret the smaller CNV amplitude in anxious patients as compared to normal subjects (Bond, James, and Lader, 1974; McCallum and Walter, 1968). As the anxious patients' CNV appeared to be similar to that of normal controls when given a distracting noise, McCallum and Walter concluded that anxiety induced a state of constant distraction.

In summary, the diagnostic value of EEG measures in anxiety states is limited; this applies to alpha blocking as it appears to be mediated by reactions other than autonomic arousal; little is known of the factors affecting CNV amplitude, which makes it impossible to evaluate its functional relationship with anxiety.

(d) Pupil size

Costly electronic equipment may be necessary for reliable measurement of changes in pupil size, which is probably the reason for the paucity of research with this sensitive index of sympathetic arousal (see review: Janisse, 1976). Fear states are commonly found to be associated with pupil dilatation. Rubin (1964) compared pupil sizes in patients suffering from anxiety states with those of a control sample during rest, a cold pressor test, and recovery from the latter. No differences were apparent between the two groups during the first two conditions. During recovery from the cold pressor test, however, the patients showed a considerable delay in pupil constriction compared to the control sample. Pupillary dilatations during the presentation of anxiety-arousing words were associated with high scores on the Eysenck Personality Inventory (EPI) (1967) neuroticism scale (Francis, 1969). In a more recent study audience-anxious subjects had significantly larger pupils when performing digit transformation and short-term memory tasks compared to calm subjects (Simpson and Molloy, 1971) even though the 'audience' consisted of the experimenter alone.

(e) Electromyogram

Muscle tension during anxiety states has been recorded from a large number of different striated muscle sites without providing consistent results. There seem to be as many studies with findings of higher muscle tension in anxious subjects as there are with negative results (see review Lader and Wing, 1966). The sites most frequently used for recording are the frontalis muscle (e.g. Malmstrom, 1968) and the forearm extensors (e.g. Kelly *et al.*, 1970). Studies with multiple site measurement (Balshan, 1962; Goldstein, 1964) have an obvious advantage over single site measurement and have usually provided positive results. Differences in muscle activity between anxious and calm subjects seem to involve more groups of muscles during stimulation than during resting levels. Goldstein (1964) found higher levels of muscle activity with respect to masseter and forearm extensors in anxious patients compared to controls during rest. During white noise, however, sternomastoid, frontalis, forearm extensor, and gastrocnemius muscle activity was higher in patients than in controls.

Electromyogram (EMG) recordings have yielded differential results when taken from sites which formed part of muscle groups involved in a specific complaint about muscle tension. Sainsbury and Gibson (1954) assessed bodily complaints due to muscular overactivity in anxious patients. Patients who complained of headache at the time of recording exhibited higher EMG levels in the frontalis muscle than other patients; by contrast, patients with complaints of stiffness and aching in the arms had higher forearm muscle potentials than the remainder.

Summarizing the evidence so far, it seems that if anxiety states produce high muscle tension they involve different muscle groups in different individuals, which may explain the inconsistent results in studies employing single site measurements.

(2) Studies on the acquisition of anxiety reactions

Few studies have examined the induction in man of the strong autonomic reactions characteristic of fear and anxiety because of ethical considerations. Data collected so far have been derived from a classical conditioning paradigm whereby a neutral stimulus, the conditioned stimulus, is presented with an unconditioned stimulus such as pain which is capable of eliciting autonomic reactions. The same autonomic reactions may then be elicited by the previously neutral stimulus on its own, a process explained a long associationistic principles. It is thus hypothesized that one way in which specific phobias arise is by associating situations or objects generally considered harmless with a painful or traumatic experience.

Campbell, Sanderson, and Laverty (1964) recorded heart-rate, respiration, EMG and EDA while subjecting a small number of alcoholic patients to an extremely unpleasant conditioning procedure. The neutral or conditioned stimulus consisted of a tone which was initially presented several times until habituation ensued. Following that, subjects were given a paralysing drug, succinylcholine ('scoline') which left them conscious yet suspended respiratory activity for about 100 seconds. The tone was presented throughout respiratory paralysis. Two control groups were given either the drug or the tone on its own. After the single conditioning trial subjects were allowed to recover for 5 minutes and asked to describe their experiences. Most experimental subjects believed they were dying and all considered the experience extremely harrowing. Subsequently all subjects were administered 30 extinction trials during which the tone was presented alone. A further series of 30 extinction trials was given a week later. The rate of spontaneous fluctuation of the subjects' SCRs showed a significant shift between the periods of the experiments. The rate increased very sharply in the experimental group following the conditioning trial, and in the two subsequent extinction series it rose even further. Subjects in the experimental group responded consistently throughout the extinction procedure without response decrement. Control subjects, by contrast, showed no significant increase in responses over the procedure.

Marked shifts in cardiac responses occurred during 85 per cent of extinction trials, in respiratory responses during 80 per cent of trials, and in muscle tension changes during 55 per cent of trials in the experimental group. None

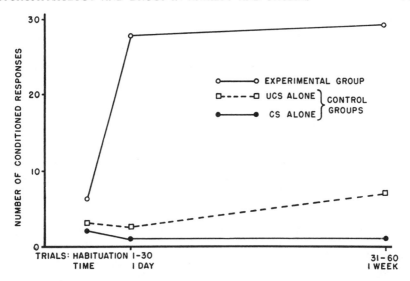

FIGURE 8.2. Mean number of conditioned SCRs for experimental and control subjects during extinction trials. Responses during the initial habituation trials represent the unconditioned responses prior to the conditioning procedure

of these responses occurred in more than 5 per cent of extinction trials in the two control groups. The experiment demonstrated that a single conditioning trial suffices to engender intense autonomic responses to a previously neutral stimulus if the unconditioned stimulus is perceived as life-threatening.

Studies employing electric shocks as the unconditioned stimulus were, on the whole, less successful in producing strong fear reactions. Mild feelings of unpleasantness could be induced in response to words after they had been paired with electric shock (Staats, Staats, and Crawford, 1962) and EDA or SCR amplitude was also raised compared to other words. Nevertheless, the responses failed to reach the intensity characteristic of phobic reactions. Similarly, electrical aversion therapy in alcoholics and sexual deviants seemingly never produced fear reactions even in successfully treated cases (Hallam and Rachman, 1972). Hallam and Rachman (1976) found that heart-rate and SCR amplitude were reduced during extinction trials when no more shocks were expected, and furthermore, if many conditioning trials were administered (up to 200) habituation to the unconditioned stimulus developed. It may be argued, however, that the conditioned stimuli, i.e. drinking cues or sexual fantasies, were by no means emotionally neutral prior to the conditioning procedure, and that therefore only a slight shift towards unpleasantness in their emotional evaluation could be expected.

Electric shocks proved to be successful unconditioned stimuli when paired with material frequently forming the content of phobic reactions (Öhman et al., 1975a, b, 1976). The authors compared the effectiveness of spider and snake slides with that of neutral material such as houses, plants, faces, and geometric forms in bringing about conditioned SCRs. During acquisition trials response amplitudes were generally the same for the different materials or only slightly raised in response to the phobic material. Groups in which slide presentations were paired with shocks exhibited higher SCR amplitudes than controls, shown the slides alone, for all stimulus materials. Following the conditioning trials, however, groups previously exposed to phobic material in conjunction with shocks showed greater resistance to extinction than any of the other groups. Although small, the effect is consistent with replications of the study (Fredrikson, Hugdahl, and Öhman, 1976; Öhman et al., 1978b). It would have been interesting to know whether there were any concomitant changes in the subjective assessment of the stimuli. However, these have not been recorded.

The results indicate that mild electric shocks can induce conditioned dermal responses which persist throughout extinction, provided appropriate conditioned stimuli are chosen (Öhman, Fredrikson, and Hugdahl, 1978a). The reason why some stimuli are more appropriate than others remains subject to further research and theoretical debate. Nor is it clear which SCRs and finger pulse volume responses show this effect while heart-rate does not (Fredrikson and Öhman, 1979).

(3) Studies on fear reduction

Most studies in which psychophysiological indices were monitored during anxiety-reducing treatment procedures have centred on whether fear reduction is a process of counter-conditioning or of habituation of autonomic reactions. Wolpe (1958) maintained that fear could be effectively combated only by conditioning a physiologically incompatible response such as relaxation to the phobic stimulus. Counter-conditioning was supposed to take place only if stimuli were mildly fear-provoking; otherwise fear responses would prove too strong to be inhibited. Wolpe's theorizing led to development of systematic desensitization during which a hierarchy of fear stimuli is formed and exposure to the stimuli administered in stepwise fashion starting with the item rated lowest. This notion of counter-conditioning derived some support from a study by Van Egeren, Feather, and Hein, (1971) although this study did not altogether adhere to the systematic sensitization technique. The authors chose subjects with public speech phobias among college students and elaborated a hierarchy of five fear-provoking scenes for each individual. Half the subjects were taught relaxation prior to treatment and underwent the two treatment sessions while being relaxed. The others were merely exposed to the scenes. Respiration-rate, heart-rate, digital pulse amplitude and SC were recorded throughout the procedure. The hypothesis that relaxation leads to fewer autonomic responses was borne out only with respect to SC and only in response to mild fear-arousing scenes, as indeed Wolpe would have predicted. As to decreases in autonomic responses over presentations, only vasomotor responses declined more in relaxed subjects compared to non-relaxed ones.

Contrary to Wolpe's prediction, however, the decline was greater for high fear-provoking scenes than for mild fear-arousing ones. According to Wolpe's theory (1958) only mild fear states could be inhibited effectively by relaxation.

Lader and Mathews (1968) put forward an alternative model of fear reduction suggesting that during exposure to phobic stimuli fear reduction could be conceptualized more parsimoniously as habituation of autonomic responses. In order to accommodate data which indicate that relaxation is indeed beneficial to fear reduction, the authors postulated that the rate of habituation to fearful material was partly a function of the general level of arousal, i.e. habituation was considered to be more rapid with low 'background' arousal than under conditions of high autonomic arousal. Individual differences in autonomic responses support this notion. Lader, Gelder and Marhs (1967) divided phobic patients into 'habituators' and 'non-habituators' on the basis of their SCR diminution to a series of tones. Habituators had a better clinical outcome in desensitization treatment than non-habituators. The former, mostly comprising specific phobics, also exhibited less spontaneous fluctuations than the latter who consisted mainly of agoraphobics.

Given a similar level of 'background' arousal, however, some of the more recent studies have tended to confirm Van Egeren et al.'s (1971) result which suggested more rapid habituation of autonomic responses to strong fear-inducing stimuli than to mild ones. Boulougouris, Marks, and Marset (1971) subjected phobic patients to six sessions of flooding treatment with intense fear-inducing stimuli and to six sessions of systematic desensitization in a crossover design. Before and after each treatment condition heart-rate and EDR were recorded during neutral fantasies and phobic fantasies. Before treatment onset, heart-rate, spontaneous fluctuations and SCR amplitude increased sharply from neutral scenes to phobic scenes in both groups. However, only the flooding condition brought about significant treatment effects in all three measures alike. After treatment, level of heart-rate during phobic scenes was indistinguishable from that during neutral scenes. Spontaneous fluctuations and SCR amplitude were also lower than before treatment, although still higher during phobic scenes than during neutral ones. Systematic desensitization failed to change any of the three measures. Measures of subjective anxiety paralleled the two EDR indicators. Although still elevated during phobic scenes after treatment they were significantly lower in the flooding condition alone. In this study treatment was administered three times weekly in addition to which patients were instructed to practise between sessions. When treatment was administered at greater intervals (Grey, Sartory, and Rachman, 1979; Borkovec, 1972) no difference was found in heart-rate reduction between the flooding and desensitization groups although both showed a greater decrease during treatment than a control group. It appears therefore that processes occurring during the intervals between treatment sessions contribute to the final outcome. At follow-up measurements, groups treated by systematic desensitization tend to show a more stable fear reduction than those treated with flooding (De Moor, 1970; Gelder et al., 1973). Thus the controversy of how to conceptualize processes leading to fear reduction is far from being resolved.

SOME PHARMACOLOGICAL ASPECTS

As we have seen in the previous sections the relations between psychophysiological measures and emotional states are complex; indeed, with pathological emotional states like depressive illnesses the interactions are so complicated as to preclude any facile insights. The introduction of drugs into these systems piles Pelion upon Ossa but, nevertheless, useful information can be obtained although the interpretations must be guarded (Stroebel, 1972).

With drug experiments a basic dichotomy is between: (a) the use of drugs to investigate the mechanisms underlying psychophysiological measures and thus, indirectly, of emotional states; and (b) more commonly, the use of psychophysiological measures to indicate the presence and the magnitude of psychotropic drug action. A further subdivision of category (a) concerns the type of effect elicited: (1) peripheral physiological, (2) central physiological, (3) emotional state. Examples of each of these types of experimental approach will be presented to illustrate the uses and limitations of the data obtained.

(1) Use of drugs to evaluate psychophysiological mechanisms

(a) Peripheral

An example concerns the use of the beta-adrenoceptor blocking agent, propranolol, to evaluate the mechanisms governing the diurnal variation in finger tremor amplitude. As this rhythm was abolished by beta-blockade, it seemed likely that such fluctuations were related to the catecholamine fluxes in the body known to occur during the day (Tyrer and Bond, 1974).

This approach is of psychophysiological interest for elucidating mechanisms. As such it is essential for methodological reasons, e.g. to avoid artifacts, but it tells us nothing about emotion or psychosomatics.

(b) *Central physiological*

A commonly used test in this category is the Sedation Threshold Test (Shagass, 1954). In this technique a barbiturate is slowly injected intravenously until an end-point is reached: EEG (abrupt increase in fast wave activity), autonomic (abolition of SCRs), neurological (slurring of speech), or behavioural (inability to do mental arithmetic). The variable of interest is the dosage of drug in mg/kg required to reach this criterion. Shagass and Jones (1958) reported that the sedation threshold was low in psychotic depression and high in neurotic depression and anxiety states. Although, some studies supported these initial reports (Perez-Reyes, 1968; Perris, and Brattemo, 1963), others failed to confirm any clear distinction between psychotic and neurotic depression (Ackner and Pampliglione, 1959; Martin and Davies, 1962; Nymgaard, 1959). A further problem has been the difficulty in defining a reliable end-point.

Even more problematical is the interpretation of such findings. It could be supposed that the amount of barbiturate required to reach the end-point depends on the sensitivity of neuronal elements such as receptors, and that this sensitivity varies among patient groups and emotional states. However, peripheral mechanisms may still be paramount. Thus, high muscle blood flow facilitates the uptake of barbiturate from the circulation into fat tissues in the muscles (Balasubramanian, Mawer, and Simons 1970). Thus barbiturate plasma concentrations after intravenous injection will be inversely related to muscle blood flow. As this flow is raised in anxious and agitated patients, more barbiturate will be extracted from the circulation per unit time and consequently more must be injected before the CNS is affected. Estimations of plasma barbiturate levels during the injection or measures of muscle mass blood flow would help settle this question.

(c) Emotional state

Several studies have approached the tricky problem of the relation between physiological changes and emotions by examining the effects of adrenaline and noradrenaline given by injection (Breggin, 1964). For example, Basowitz and his associates (1956) interviewed 12 normal subjects (hospital interns) to ascertain any past history of stress and to list any specific reactions to it, such as tremor, perspiration, palpitations and apprehensiveness. Using double-blind procedures and a cross-over design, adrenaline was infused intravenously in a dosage of 5 µg/kg body weight per hour and its effects compared with those of saline. Measurements included blood pressure and pulse-rate, psychological tests such as hand steadiness and digit span, physical persistence in keeping a leg raised, and subjective reports. Adrenaline produced a distinct elevation in pulse pressure and a rise in heart-rate averaging 13 beats/minute. Hand steadiness and physical persistence were impaired. The commonest symptom was palpitations. Symptoms were reported on the saline occasions as well as on the adrenaline occasions, but only half as frequently and usually only when saline was the first treatment given. Adrenaline elicited symptoms which generally resembled those elicited at the initial interview as occurring in the subjects in response to stress. Most interestingly, in emotionally labile subjects many symptoms but minimal cardio-vascular changes were noted; in rigid personalities few symptoms but marked physiological changes occurred.

In a similar experiment with medical students, adrenaline infusions produced a tachycardia, rise in systolic, and drop in diastolic blood pressure. No systematic relation between the intensities of the physiological and the subjective reaction were seen. Subjective effects declined steadily as each infusion proceeded (Frankenhaueser and Järpe, 1963). When a mixture of adrenaline and noradrenaline was infused, the systolic blood pressure rose while the diastolic fell, but the pulse rate was not altered consistently (Frankenhaueser and Järpe, 1962), suggesting that the effects of adrenaline predominated. Most of the 11 subjects reported palpitations, tremor, and general discomfort; about a half had symptoms of restlessness, apprehensiveness, tenseness, and dyspnoea.

The classic experiments of Schachter and Singer (1962) showed that the experience of subjective emotion was greatly influenced by cognitive factors. They injected subjects either with small doses of adrenaline or saline, half the subjects being told what symptoms to expect, half remaining naïve. Some subjects were placed in a situation conducive to euphoria by being introduced to a stooge who joked and ridiculed the experiment. The others were placed with another stooge who carped and complained about the tasks set in the experiment and angrily criticized the experimenters. At the end of the session the subjects rated themselves and were objectively assessed for their emotional states. Those with the euphoric stooge rated themselves as happy, the second group as angry. The crucial finding was that subjects ignorant of the effects of adrenaline rated themselves, and were rated, as having higher intensities of emotion than subjects forewarned which symptoms to expect. Schachter and Singer conclude that 'given a state of physiological arousal for which an individual has no immediate explanation, he will label this state and describe his feelings in terms of the cognitions available to him'. Thus, awareness of physiological arousal seems to be the substrate on which cognitive clues induce a specific emotion. Although other interpretations exist, a reasonable hypothesis is that an emotion is induced by the interaction of at least two states: high physiological arousal and appropriate sensory input.

Schachter and Wheeler (1962) also carried out the reverse experiment using a pharmacological antagonist. Subjects who had been given either adrenaline, a placebo, or chlorpromazine, watched a comedy film. The adrenaline subjects showed more amusement than those given the sympathetic blocking agent chlorpromazine.

The corollary to the adrenaline experiments involves the administration of sympathetic blocking agents such as propranolol. In a series of studies, Tyrer (1976) examined the effects of such drugs on psychophysiological measures, somatic sensations, and feelings of anxiety. In general, marked effects of a predictable nature were noted on the physiological measures, e.g. bradycardia and reduction in tremor. Somatic feelings were also reduced, especially in anxious patients. However, by and large, central feelings of anxiety were unaffected except in certain patients with marked somatic symptoms such as palpitations or gastrointestinal disturbance. The most tenable conclusions were that peripheral responses are not essential to the experience of an emotion such as anxiety but that such changes may reinforce or perpetuate the emotion. Thus, there is no support for the James–Lange hypothesis which implies that the actual experience of emotion is secondary to the perception of bodily changes.

(2) Use of psychophysiological measures to evaluate drugs

This approach is perhaps of less interest to the researcher into psychophysiological and psychosomatic mechanisms. Again three broad divisions can be made.

(a) Peripheral effects

Many psychotropic drugs have anticholinergic and/or antiadrenergic properties and hence have many peripheral actions. For example, chlorpromazine lowers standing blood pressure producing a reflex tachycardia, it constricts the pupil, and lessens sweat-gland activity and salivation. Any of these measures can be used to monitor chlorpromazine therapy. Of course, it is impossible to derive any information regarding the central effects of chlorpromazine using any of these variables because the physiological measures themselves are distorted by the drug.

(b) Central effects

However, if the drug of interest is known to be devoid of peripheral effects useful information can be obtained regarding some aspect of central functioning. Unfortunately the central correlates of psychophysiological variables are either poorly understood or interpretable only in terms of some intervening construct such as 'arousal'. There can be little rational use of these measures in the sense of a logical coherent, conceptual analysis so that an empirical approach must suffice.

The main groups of drugs appropriate for such evaluations are the depressant anxiolytics like the barbiturates and the benzodiazepines, and the stimulants such as amphetamines. A variety of measures have been used as indicators including heart-rate, EDA, forearm blood flow and finger tremor.

(c) EEG effects

This has been made a separate, if somewhat artificial, category because of the special and ambiguous position of the EEG and its evoked responses. The physiological mechanisms underlying the EEG are not clear, so that it must be used in an entirely empirical way with cautious interpretation of data and avoidance of extrapolation or widespread deductions.

Because of these limitations, each drug's effects on the EEG have to be evaluated afresh, although particular types of drugs tend to produce similar effects, e.g. barbiturates producing fast-wave activity. A further limitation is that each method of analysis needs separate evaluation with respect to drug effects. Thus, broad band-pass filter analysis will not distinguish between increased beta activity due to alertness and barbiturate fast-wave activity. Nevertheless, knowing the effects of a drug or class of drugs on the EEG analysed in a particular way can provide a most sensitive way of detecting those drug effects. Thus, significant barbiturate effects can be noted up to 18 hours after a single dose, at a time when chemical methods of estimation would be insensitive.

(3) Drugs, physiological measures, and psychiatric patients

An example of a more complex relationship was found in a recent study

(Bond, James, and Lader, 1974). The effects of anxiolytic drug therapy—benzo-diazepines and a barbiturate, compared with placebo each given for 2–4 weeks to 20 anxious patients—were examined clinically and on a variety of measures including the auditory EEG averaged evoked response (AER). All components of the AER were significantly reduced by the benzodiazepines as compared with placebo, but not by the barbiturate. This corresponded to the clinical findings that the benzodiazepines were therapeutically effective, whereas neither the amylobarbitone nor the placebo produced any worth-while improvement.

When drugs with peripheral effects are involved, the problem of artifactual findings obtrudes. It is extremely difficult to find 'drug-free' schizophrenics for psychophysiological studies. Both central and peripheral measures are known to be affected by antipsychotic medication, for example, SC and saliva-tion in both decrease markedly when a patient is placed on chlorpromazine. Consequently, claims that schizophrenic patients are hypo- or non-responsive must be carefully considered in the light of any concurrent drug therapy. For example, in the study by Spohn, Thetford, and Cancro (1970), a group of 32 male schizophrenics were compared with normal subjects with respect to SC recorded during a tachistoscopic task. Mean levels were initially the same, but during the task those of the normal group rose and gradually adapted back to resting levels; in the patients the SC first dropped and then rose up to resting levels. However, the patients were receiving phenothiazines, and when these were withdrawn both resting and task SCLs were significantly higher than they had been in the patients before withdrawal, and than they were in the normal subjects when retested. Also it must be remembered that normal subjects and patients are self-administering many drugs, caffeine and theo-bromine from coffee and tea, alcohol, and nicotine.

Finally, another complication relates to the frequent finding that many groups of psychiatric patients differ from normal in psychophysiological values. Thus, in normal subjects single doses of imipramine produce a dose- and time-related reduction in sweating and salivation due to the anticholiner-gic actions of the drug. In patients treated with 50 mg three times daily for 4 weeks, a similar drop occurs in the first week followed by a steady recovery almost to pretreatment levels. The most immediate explanation is that the sweat and salivary glands have become 'tolerant' to the anticholinergic effects of imipramine. However, on average, depressives have abnormally low sweat and salivary activity, but as clinical improvement occurred the measures would rise towards normal values. Thus, the levels in the last week of treatment would be the net effect of imipramine lowering glandular activity and clinical improvement being associated with an increase.

CONCLUSIONS

One major research strategy has been to compare psychophysiological measures in individuals labelled as suffering from anxiety states with individuals not so labelled. The differences described are often not clear-cut. In these between-group comparisons it must be remembered that the effect of anxiety can vary greatly from moment to moment in patients. Futhermore, in abnormal laboratory situations anxiety may not be manifest in patients or, as is more likely, may be induced in calm subjects. Despite these difficulties the differences which have been obtained show consistently physiological overactivity in anxious patients.

The complementary approach is to use subjects as their own controls either as anxiety is increased by the induction of phobias or as anxiety is decreased by effective treatment. This allows a more direct manipulation of supposedly relevant parameters together with a more meaningful monitoring of subjective responses. Inevitably the results are more complex, but again the general principle of over-arousal in anxiety seems upheld. The main refinement is that the anxiety has to be perceived in order that physiological measures become elevated.

Another way of manipulating mood is by the means of drugs. This method has the disadvantage of usually introducing major complications, namely that drugs act on many structures with disparate physiological functions so that the behavioural and even physiological changes are the end-point of complex effects. In our present state of knowledge and with our relatively non-specific psychotropic drugs, great care is needed both in the use of drugs and in the interpretation of the effects.

REFERENCES

Ackner, B. (1956). Emotions and the peripheral vasomotor system. A review of previous work. *Journal of Psychosomtic Research*, 1, 3–20.

Ackner, B., and Pampiglione, G. (1959). An evaluation of the sedation threshold test. *Journal of Psychosomtic Research*, 3, 271–281.

Altschule, M. D. (1953). *Bodily Physiology in Mental and Emotional Disorder*. New York: Grune & Stratton.

Balasubramanian, K., Mawrer, G. E., and Simons, P. J. (1970). The influence of dose on the distribution and elimination of amylobarbitone in healthy subjects. *British Journal of Pharmacology*, 40, 578–579.

Balshan, I. D. (1962). Muscle tension and personality in women. *Archives of General Psychiatry*, 7, 436–448.

Basowitz, H., Korchin, S. J., Oken, D., Goldstein, M. S., and Gussack, H. (1956). Anxiety and performance changes with a minimal dose of epinephrine. *Archives of Neurology and Psychiatry*, 76, 98–108.

Berger, H. (1929). über das Elektroenkephalogram des Menschen. *Archiv für Psychiatrie und Nervenkrankheiten*, 87, 527–570.

Bloom, L. J., Houston, B. K., and Burish, T. G. (1976). An evaluation of finger pulse volume as a psychophysiological measure of anxiety. *Psychophysiology*, 13, 40–42.

Bloom, L. J., and Trautt, G. M. (1977). Finger pulse volume as a measure of anxiety: further evaluation. *Psychophysiology*, 14, 541–544.

Bond, A. J., James, D. C., and Lader, M. H. (1974). Physiological and psychological measures in anxious patients. *Psychological Medicine*, 4, 364–373.

Borkovec, T. D. (1972). Effects of expectancy on the outcome of systematic desensitisation and implosive treatments for analogue anxiety. *Behavior Therapy*, **3**, 29–40.

Boulougouris, J. C., Marks, I. M., and Marset, P. (1971). Superiority of flooding (implosion) to desensitisation for reducing pathological fear. *Behaviour Research and Therapy*, **9**, 7–16.

Brazier, M. A. B., Finesinger, J. E., and Cobb, S. A. (1945). A contrast between the electroencephalograms of 100 psychoneurotic patients and those of 500 normal adults. *American Journal of Psychiatry*, **101**, 433–448.

Breggin, P. R. (1964). The psychophysiology of anxiety with a review of the literature concerning adrenaline. *Journal of Nervous and Mental Disease*, **139**, 558–568.

Campbell, D., Sanderson, R. E., and Laverty, S. G. (1964). Characteristics of a conditioned response in human subjects during extinction trials following a single traumatic conditioning trial. *Journal of Abnormal and Social Psychology*, **68**, 627–639.

Cattell, R. B. (1963). The nature and measurement of anxiety. *Scientific American*, **208**, 96–104.

Chapman, R., Shelbourne, S., and Bragdon, H. (1970). EEG alpha activity influenced by visual input and not by eye position. *Electroencephalography and Clinical Neurophysiology*, **28**, 183–189.

Chisholm, R. C., DeGood, D. E., and Hartz, M. A. (1977). Effects of alpha feedback training on occipital EEG, heart rate and experiential reactivity to a laboratory stressor. *Psychophysiology*, **14**, 157–163.

De Moor, W. (1970). Systematic desensitisation versus prolonged high intensity stimulation (flooding). *Journal of Behaviour Therapy and Experimental Psychiatry*, **1**, 45–52.

Duffy, E. (1962). *Activation and Behaviour*. New York: Wiley.

Eysenck, H. J. (1967). *The Biological Basis of Personality*. Springfield, Ill.: Charles C. Thomas.

Francis, R. D. (1969). Neuroticism and optical pupil changes in response to auditory stimuli. *British Journal of Social and Clinical Psychology*, **8**, 344–349.

Frankenhaeuser, M., and Järpe, G. (1962). Psychophysiological reactions to infusions of a mixture of adrenaline and noradrenaline. *Scandinavian Journal of Psychology*, **3**, 21–29.

Frankenhaeuser, M., and Järpe, G. (1963). Psychophysiological changes during infusions of adrenaline in various doses. *Psychopharmacologia*, **4**, 424–432.

Fredrikson, M., Hugdahl, K., and Öhman, A. (1976). Electrodermal conditioning to potentially phobic stimuli in male and female subjects. *Biological Psychology*, **4**, 305–314.

Fredrikson, M. and Öhman, A. (1979). Cardiovascular and electrodermal responses conditioned to fear-relevant stimuli. *Psychophysiology*, **16**, 1–7.

Geer, J. H. (1966). Fear and autonomic arousal. *Journal of Abnormal Psychology*, **71**, 253–255.

Gelder, M. G., Bancroft, J. H. J., Gath, D. H., Johnston, D. W., Mathews, A. M. and Shaw, P. M. (1973). Specific and non-specific factors in behaviour therapy. *British Journal of Psychiatry*, **123**, 445–462.

Goldstein, I. B. (1964). Psysiological responses in anxious women patients. A study of autonomic activity and muscle tension. *Archives of General Psychiatry*, **10**, 382–388.

Graham, F. K., and Clifton, R. K. (1966). Heart rate change as a component of the orienting response. *Psychological Bulletin*, **65** (5), 305–320.

Grey, S., Sartory, G., and Rachman, S. (1979). Synchronous and desynchronous changes during fear reduction. *Behaviour Research and Therapy*, **17**, 137–147.

Hallam, R. S., and Rachman, S. (1972). Some effects of aversion therapy on patients with sexual disorders. *Behaviour Research and Therapy*, **10**, 171–180.

Hallam, R. S., and Rachman, S. (1976). Current status of aversion therapy. In M. Hersen, R. M. Eisler, and P. M. Miller (eds.), *Progress in Behaviour Modification*. New York/London: Academic Press.

Hare, R. D. (1973). Orienting and defensive responses to visual stimuli. *Psychophysiology*, **10**, 453–464.

Hare, R. D., and Blevings, G. (1975a). Conditioned orienting and defensive responses. *Psychophysiology*, **12**, 289–297.

Hare, R. D., and Blevings, G. (1975b). Defensive responses to visual stimuli. *Biological Psychology*, **3**, 1–13.

Hart, J. D. (1974). Physiological responses of anxious and normal subjects to simple signal and non-signal auditory stimuli. *Psychophysiology*, **11**, 443–451.

Horvath, T., and Meares, R. (1979). The sensory filter in schizophrenia: a study of habituation, arousal, and the dopamine hypothesis. *British Journal of Psychiatry*, **134**, 39–45.

Janisse, M. P. (1976). The relationship between pupil size and anxiety: a review. In Sarason, I. G., and Spielberger, C. D. (eds.), *Stress and Anxiety*, Vol. 3. New York: John Wiley & Sons.

Katkin, E. S. (1965). Relationship between manifest anxiety and two indices of autonomic response to stress. *Journal of Personality and Social Psychology*, **2**, 324–333.

Katkin, E. S. (1975). Electrodermal lability: a psychophysiological analysis of individual differences in response to stress. In I. G., Sarason and C. D. Spielberger (eds.), *Stress and Anxiety*, Vol. 2. New York: John Wiley & Sons.

Katkin, E. S., and McCubbin, R. J. (1969). Habituation of the orienting response as a function of individual differences in anxiety and autonomic lability. *Journal of Abnormal Psychology*, **74**, 54–60.

Kelly, D. H. W. (1966). Measurement of anxiety by forearm blood flow. *British Journal of Psychiatry*, **112**, 789–798.

Kelly, D., Brown, C. C., and Shaffer, J. W. (1970). A comparison of physiological measurements on anxious patients and normal controls. *Psychophysiology*, **6**, 429–441.

Kelly, D. H. W., and Walter, C. J. S. (1968). The relationship between clinical diagnosis and anxiety, assessed by forearm blood flow and other measurements. *British Journal of Psychiatry*, **114**, 611–626.

Klorman, R., Weissberg, R. D., and Wiesenfeld, A. R. (1977). Individual differences in fear and autonomic reactions to affective stimulation. *Psychophysiology*, **14**, 45–51.

Lacey, J. I. (1967). Somatic response patterning and stress: some revisions of activation theory. In M. H., Appley, R. Trumbull (eds.), *Psychological Stress: Issues in Research*, pp. 14–37. New York: Appleton-Century, Crofts.

Lacey, J. I., and Lacey, B. C. (1958). The relationship of resting autonomic activity to motor impulsivity. *Proceedings of the Association for Research into Mental Disease*, **36**, 144–209.

Lader, M. H. (1967). Palmar skin conductance measures in anxiety and phobic states. *Journal of Psychosomatic Research*, **11**, 271–281.

Lader, M. H., Gelder, M. G., and Marks, I. M. (1967). Palmar conductance measures as predictors of response to desensitization. *Journal of Psychosomatic Research*, **11**, 283–290.

Lader, M. H., and Mathews, A. M. (1968). A physiological model of phobic anxiety and desensitisation. *Behaviour Research and Therapy*, **6**, 411–421.

Lader, M. H., and Wing, L. (1966). *Physiological Measures, Sedative Drugs and Morbid Anxiety*. Maudsley Monograph No. 14. London: Oxford University Press.

Lang, P. J. (1968). Fear reduction and fear behavior: problems in treating a construct. In J. M. Schlien (ed.), *Research in Psychotherapy*, Vol. 3. Washington D. C.: A. P. A.

Lang, P. J., Melamed, B. G., and Hart, J. (1970). A psychophysiological analysis of fear modification using an automated desensitization procedure. *Journal of Abnormal Psychology*, **176**, 220–234.

Lindsley, D. B. (1950). Emotions and the electroencephalogram. In Reymert, M. L. (ed.), *Feelings and Emotions*, pp. 238–246. New York: McGraw-Hill.

McCallum, W., and Walter, W. G. (1968). The effects of attention and distraction on the contingent negative variation in normal and neurotic subjects. *Electroencephalography and Clinical Neurophysiology*, **25**, 319–329.

Malmstrom, E. J. (1968). The effect of prestimulus variability upon physiological reactivity scores. *Psychophysiology*, **5**, 149–165.

Marks, I., Marset, P., Boulougouris, J., and Huson, J. (1971). Physiological accompaniments of neutral and phobic imagery. *Psychological Medicine*, **1**, 299–307.

Martin, I., and Davies, B. M. (1962). Sleep threshold in depression. *Journal of Mental Science*, **108**, 466–473.

Mulholland, T. B. (1972). Occipital alpha revisited. *Psychological Bulletin*, **78**, 176–182.

Neary, R. S. and Zuckerman, M. (1976). Sensation seeking, trait and state anxiety, and the electrodermal orienting response. *Psychophysiology*, **13**, 205–211.

Nymgaard, K. (1959). Studies on the sedation threshold. *Archives of General Psychiatry*, **1**, 530–536.

Öhman, A., Eriksson, A., and Olofsson, C. (1975a). One-trial learning and superior resistance to extinction of autonomic responses conditioned to potentially phobic stimuli. *Journal of Comparative Physiology and Psychology*, **88**, 619–627.

Öhman, A., Eriksson, G., and Lofberg, I. (1975b). Phobias and preparedness: phobic versus neütral pictures as conditioned stimuli for human autonomic responses. *Journal of Abnormal Psychology*, **84**, 41–45.

Öhman, A., Fredrikson, M. and Hugdahl, K. (1978a). Towards an experimental model for simple phobic reactions. *Behavioural Analysis and Modification*, **2**, 97–114.

Öhman, A., Fredrikson, M., and Hugdahl, K. (1978b). Orienting and defensive responding in the electrodermal system: palmar–dorsal differences and recovery rate during conditioning to potentially phobic stimuli. *Psychophysiology*, **15**, 93–101.

Öhman, A., Frederikson, M., Hugdahl, K., and Rimmo, P. A. (1976). The premise of equipotentiality in human classical conditioning: conditioned electrodermal responses to potentially phobic stimuli. *Journal of Experimental Psychology*, **105**, 313–337.

Orne, M. T., and Paskewitz, D. (1974). Adversive situational effects of alpha feedback training. *Science*, **186**, 458–460.

Perez-Reyes, M. (1968). Differences in sedative susceptibility between types of depression, clinical and neurophysiological. *Archives of General Psychiatry*, **19**, 64–71.

Perris, C., and Brattemo, C. E. (1963). The sedation threshold as a method of evaluating antidepressive treatments. *Acta Psychiatrica Scandinavica*, **39** (suppl., 169), 111–119.

Prigatano, G. P., and Johnson, H. J. (1974). Autonomic nervous system changes associated with a spider phobic reaction. *Journal of Abnormal Psychology*, **83**, 169–177.

Raskin, M. (1975). Decreased skin conductance response habituation in chronically anxious patients. *Biological Psychology*, **2**, 309–319.

Rubin, L. S. (1964). Autonomic dysfunction as a concomitant of neurotic behavior. *Journal of Nervous and Mental Disease*, **138**, 558–574.

Sainsbury, P., and Gibson, J. G. (1954). Symptoms of anxiety and tension and the accompanying physiological changes in the muscular system. *Journal of Neurology, Neurosurgery and Psychiatry*, **17**, 216–224.

Sartory, G., Rachman, S., and Grey, S. (1977). An investigation of the relation between reported fear and heart rate. *Behaviour Research and Therapy*, **15**, 435–438.

Schachter, S., and Singer, J. E. (1962). Cognitive, social and physiological determinants of emotional state. *Psychological Review*, **69**, 379–399.

Schachter, S., and Wheeler, L. (1962). Epinephrine, chlorpromazine and amusement. *Journal of Abnormal and Social Psychology*, **65**, 121–128.

Shagass, C. (1954). The sedation threshold. A method for estimating tension in psychiatric patients. *Electroencephalography and Clinical Neurophysiology*, **6**, 221–233.

Shagass, C., and Jones, A. L. (1958). A neurophysiological test for psychiatric diagnosis: results in 750 patients. *American Journal Psychiatry*, **114**, 1002–1009.

Simpson, H. M., and Molloy, F. M. (1971). Effects of audience anxiety on pupil size. *Psychophysiology*, **8**, 491–496.

Sokolov, E. N. (1963). *Perception and the Conditioned Reflex.* New York: Macmillan.

Spohn, H. I., Thetford, P. E., and Cancro, R. (1970). Attention, psychophysiology, and scanning in the schizophrenic syndrome. In R. Cancro (ed.), *The Schizophrenic Reactions: a Critique of the Concept, Hospital Treatment, and Current Research*, pp. 259–269. New York: Brunner Mazel.

Staats, A. W., Staats, C. K., and Crawford, H. L. (1962). First-order conditioning of meaning and the parallel conditioning of a GSR. *Journal of General Psychology*, **67**, 159–167.

Strauss, H. (1945). Clinical and electroencephalographic studies: the electroencephalogram in psychoneurotics. *Journal of Nervous and Mental Disease*, **101**, 19–27.

Stroebel, C. F. (1972). Psychophysiological pharmacology. In N. S. Greenfield and R. A. Sternbach (eds.), *Handbook of Psychophysiology*, pp. 787–838. New York: Rinehart & Winston.

Tyrer, P. (1976). *The Role of Bodily Feelings in Anxiety.* London: Oxford University Press.

Tyrer, P. J., and Bond, A. (1974). Diurnal variation in physiological tremor. *Electroencephalography and Clinical Neurophysiology*, **37**, 35–40.

Van Egeren, L. F., Feather, B. W., and Hein, P. L. (1971). Desensitization of phobias: some psychophysiological propositions. *Psychophysiology*, **8**, 213–228.

Wing, L. (1964). Physiological effects of performing a difficult task in patients with anxiety states. *Journal of Psychosomatic Research*, **7**, 283–294.

Wolpe, J. (1958). *Psychotherapy by Reciprocal Inhibition.* Stanford: Stanford University Press.

Foundations of Psychosomatics
Edited by M. J. Christie and P. G. Mellett
© 1981 John Wiley & Sons Ltd.

9

BIOFEEDBACK AND EMOTIONAL BEHAVIOUR

JAMES H. MCCROSKERY, PH.D.
Department of Psychology, State University of New York, U.S.A.

and

BERNARD T. ENGEL, PH.D.
Laboratory of Behavioral Science, Baltimore City Hospitals, U.S.A.

INTRODUCTION

In this chapter we shall examine three classes of behaviours (i.e. verbal, physiological, and approach/avoidance) as they occur in situations which most investigators would agree are important in understanding emotional behaviour. We are especially interested in reviewing the data which are relevant to an issue raised by Lang, Rice, and Sternbach (1972) in their chapter on the psychophysiology of emotion. They speculated that: '... operant control of selected autonomic events should be a powerful tool for the investigation of relationships between the peripheral physiology and other systems of behaviour'. They asked:

> will subjects who were trained to control autonomic responses be able to maintain control when subjected to stress? ... [will] operant conditioning of autonomic responses ... also prove helpful in the treatment of those anxious or depressive states in which physiological responses are paramount in the symptom picture? (p. 639).

Operant conditioning of physiological responses has come to be referred to as biofeedback. In operant conditioning behaviour is changed by arranging consequences contingent upon the behaviour to be changed (see Reynolds, 1975). With biofeedback the consequence is usually an external signal such as tone or light, or an internal signal such as pain, or a visceral sensation that is made contingent upon the occurrence of a prescribed physiological response (see Beatty and Legewie, 1977). By means of such biofeedback procedures a number of physiological responses mediated by the autonomic nervous system have been shown to be capable of coming under operant control. Furthermore, it has been shown that such conditioning can significantly modify a number of clinical states such as aberrant heart rhythms, high blood pressure or vasospasm.

The most fruitful research designs usually have three phases. First, the verbal, physiological and approach/avoidance indices are characterized. These responses may be elicited by specific stimuli or they may be emitted in a prescribed situation. Second, biofeedback training is given to alter a physiological— i.e. autonomic or somatic—response in a direction which is opposite to the aberrant response. Finally, subjects are tested to determine whether the stimuli which elicited the responses still do so, or to determine whether the prevalence of emitted responses has changed. This paradigm raises a number of questions which we will consider:

(1) Will biofeedback training for a particular physiological response enable subjects to alter their usual response in a stressful situation?
(2) Do all three response classes change or can they be dissociated?
(3) Within each response class do all responses covary or can they be dissociated (e.g. will relaxation in one muscle group lead to relaxation in others)?
(4) Is the biofeedback training of a particular physiological response necessary or are a number of autonomic and somatic changes equally effective in altering emotional behaviours?

The answers to these questions will provide information about the possible limits of biofeedback training, about the interrelationships among the response classes of the emotional complex, about possible clinical applications of biofeedback training, and about the mechanisms of emotional responding. For example, if biofeedback training cannot change the physiological response to an aversive stimulus, then the clinical usefulness of such training is questionable. If the physiological response is altered, but the subjects continue to report fear and avoid the threatening situation, then the usefulness of the training alone is questionable in that altering the physiological response does not lead to alterations in other components. Should physiological training lead to changes in verbal and motor behaviour, then it suggests that such training might be a helpful therapy for individuals with specific phobias or as a counter to pain onset such as occurs during muscle contraction headaches.

In the following section, operant conditioning of heart-rate, muscle group activity levels, electrodermal activity, and alpha brain waves will be considered. These four target areas have been chosen because there is research with these physiological responses bearing on our questions. We have chosen to limit our review to acute fear- and pain-arousing situations which in the laboratory can be modelled by stimuli such as electric shock, and in the clinic studied by specific phobias or pain onset. More diffuse emotional states, such as chronic anxiety, generalized phobias, or depression, will not be discussed. Muscle contraction headaches regulated by biofeedback of muscle tension levels were selected as a clinical example of pain onset; the possible regulation of migraine headaches by thermal or vascular control has not been included. The possible use of false physiological information also will be considered.

REVIEW OF THE LITERATURE

(1) Heart-rate changes

(a) Experimental studies

The first published report on the control of human heart-rate in relation to an emotionally charged situation is by Sirota, Schwartz, and Shapiro (1974). They asked two questions: (1) can human subjects be trained to alter their heart-rates while anticipating noxious stimulation; and (2) would such training change judgements of the noxious stimulation? In their study, female subjects were given training in heart-rate control (half to increase and half to decrease). There were seventy-two 15-second trials, half of which were followed by signalled electric shock to the forearm. During training trials, feedback was provided by a light and tone which came on whenever the subject's heart rate met or exceeded criterion. Following each shock trial the subjects verbally rated the intensity of the shock on a 0–100 scale. In answer to the first question, they found that while there was a slight tendency for tonic heart-rate to be greater in both groups on shock trials, analysis of phasic heart-rate changes over the 15-second anticipatory period showed marked increases (shock *vs.* no shock) for those trained to increase, and slight decreases (shock *vs.* no shock) for those trained to decrease, showing that anticipation of shock did not disrupt heart-rate control. The second question was answered by the shock ratings. The subjects trained to increase heart-rate consistently rated the shock intensities higher than those trained to decrease heart-rate.

More recently, Sirota, Schwartz, and Shapiro (1976) attempted to replicate these findings with some changes in procedure and design. The major change was that half of the female subjects had 25 trials of increase training followed by 25 trials of decrease training, while the other half had the reverse order. Although the obtained differences were not as striking as in the initial study, the essential features were replicated. Subjects were able to change heart-rate while anticipating shock. The increase to decrease subjects showed appropriate increases and decreases with training. On the other hand, the decrease to increase subjects showed appropriate decreases but then could not effect increases over the increase trials. The shock ratings also differed as a function of the training condition: the combined group rating was greater when increasing than when decreasing.

The above two studies demonstrate that human subjects can learn heart-rate control in a situation of impending electric shock. Use of a different aversive stimulus would show the generality of this skill. Such a study has been done by Mainardi, Victor, and Shapiro (1977)—(see Shapiro, 1977, for details) in which a cold pressor test was used as a stressful stimulus. There were two experimental groups and two control groups. One experimental group was trained to increase heart-rate; the other experimental group was trained to decrease heart-rate. All four groups had a cold pressor test (30 seconds) before and after the training trials. In comparing the second cold pressor test with the first cold pressor test, the feedback increase subjects showed an increase of 11.5 beats per minute (bpm), the feedback decrease subjects showed a decrease of 3.4 bpm. These changes are consistent with the training trial results where the feedback increase group showed increases in heart-rate and the feedback decrease group showed decreases. The pain ratings also supported the previous studies. On the second test, the feedback increase group rated the pain highest, the feedback decrease rated the pain lowest, while the two control groups were intermediate in pain judgements. These studies show that normal, human subjects can be trained to modify heart-rate, and that such training will influence not only heart-rate responses, to a noxious stimulus, but also verbal responses about the severity of the discomfort elicited by the stimulus.

A study by Ainslie and Engel (1974) bears on the question of the generalization of cardiac conditioning to other physiological responses. Monkeys were given various sequences of classical and operant (heart-rate slowing or heart-rate speeding) conditioning sessions in order to determine if operant conditioning could alter the cardiac response to impending electric shock, and also to see whether cardiac operant conditioning generalized to other physiological responses which also were classically conditioned. In three of the four monkeys in which classical conditioning preceded operant conditioning, the response to the warning clicks was a significant increase in heart-rate in relation to the neutral clicks, and in all four monkeys there was an increase in blood pressure. All four monkeys initially trained to slow heart-rate and both monkeys initially trained to increase heart-rate learned successfully while blood pressure responses were variable. When the classical and operant procedures were combined it was found that: (1) the heart-rate response to the warning clicks was changed both in magnitude and direction; (2) the operant contingencies produced changes which persisted; and (3) changes following heart-rate slowing were different from changes following heart-rate speeding. These data demonstrate that the response to an impending aversive stimulus can be modified in monkeys by operant conditioning. However, the data also show that such training does not necessarily generalize to other physiological responses, in this case blood pressure.

The results of the Ainslie and Engel study raise another question. If cardiac conditioning does not necessarily generalize to other physiological responses, will training in control of other physiological responses generalize to cardiac responses? This question is relevant to that of the necessary role of cardiac conditioning in the Shapiro, *et al.* studies reviewed earlier. If conditioning of other physiological responses does not alter the cardiac responses but does alter verbal reports about the aversive stimulus, then cardiac change is not necessary to alter verbal responses. If this should be the case, then either training in control of any one of a number of autonomic or somatic responses will modify the emotional behaviour complex, or the characteristics of the experimental situation that generate 'demands' upon the subjects or raise their 'expectations' are influencing the emotional behaviour complex.

DeGood and Adams (1976) offer some data on the specific role that cardiac-rate conditioning plays in changing cardiac-rate to aversive stimuli. They studied normal woman subjects and compared cardiac responses to an aversive stimulus in subjects who had received cardiac biofeedback training, deep muscle relaxation training, and no-feedback/music training. Prior to training, heart-rate responses to a signalled painful shock to fingers on the right hand were re-corded. Before training there was an increase in heart-rate on the aversive trials. During training there were decreases in heart-rate in the biofeedback and no-feedback/music groups. On the post-training aversive trials all groups showed a reduction in heart-rate responses to the signalled shock trials, but the largest reductions were on the part of the biofeedback group. These results are further evidence that physiological changes tend to be specific to the response being trained. With respect to cardiac changes in general, one of us has reviewed this literature in greater detail elsewhere (Engel, 1977).

Results bearing on the question of the extent to which cardiac rate con-ditioning influences approach/avoidance behaviours come from a study by DiCara and Weiss (1969). Following the initial research on the modification of autonomic responses by Miller and his colleagues, DiCara and Weiss asked how the regulation of cardiac responses would affect avoidance responses. Rats were trained under curare to increase or decrease their heart-rates, tested for transfer to a free-moving situation, and then tested for gross motor behaviour in a one-way avoidance situation. Of interest is the avoidance learning test in which the slow-heart-rate rats learned to avoid shock by running to the safe side; the fast-heart-rate rats generally did not even learn to escape the shock. DiCara and Weiss reported that the fast-heart-rate rats were hyper-reactive, jumping and squealing to the shocks, whereas the slow-heart-rate rats had more inhibited reactions. Although these data give support to the hypothesis that altering a physiological aspect of an emotional response will alter subsequent approach/avoidance behaviours, they primarily show that fast-heart-rate learners are at a disadvantage rather than that slow-heart-rate learners are at an advantage.

(b) Clinical studies

The above studies have consistently shown that while anticipating or while experiencing a variety of stressful stimuli, human and animal subjects can control heart-rate, and that the direction of control leads to a change in be-haviour related to the stressful situation. These studies also have raised the possibility that control of heart-rate may be therapeutically effective in phasic pain and anxiety management. The following clinical studies are based on this premise.

One of the first clinical studies was reported by Prigatano and Johnson (1972) who used biofeedback in an attempt to control heart-rate variability in subjects with spider phobia such that they could decrease heart-rate variability while looking at slides of spiders. Twenty-six spider-phobic subjects were assigned to either visual feedback training of heart-rate variability or placebo conditions of viewing the same visual display. During the test trials in which spider, seascape, and surgical slides were presented, feedback was continuously provided. The procedures did not lead to differences in heart-rate variability between the two groups; both groups decreased variability during training. Both groups showed decreases after treatment, based on two fear survey reports and on a behavioural avoidance measure (approach to a caged tarantula). In another study, with animal-phobic patients, Nunes and Marks (1975) were successful in demonstrating greater heart-rate decreases during feedback than during non-feedback in the presence of the feared stimulus. Ten women received either two or four 2-hour treatment sessions. In $\frac{1}{2}$-hour segments of training, heart-rate visual feedback was either present or absent (the order was counterbalanced across patients), while every 10 minutes the patients gave self-ratings of anxiety, and skin conductance responses were measured. Over treatment there was a decline in heart rate and in anxiety ratings; skin conductance did not change. Although heart-rate was significantly lower during feedback segments than during non-feedback segments, changes in verbal reports of anxiety did not parallel the feedback manipulation.

Gatchel and Proctor (1976) also tried to determine whether learned control of heart-rate through biofeedback training would bring about fear reduction. Thirty-six speech-anxious, male and female college-aged subjects, selected on the basis of their responses on a fear survey schedule, were assigned to either biofeedback of heart-rate slowing or a control group. Prior to training, each subject was tested for public speaking anxiety before two female observers, who rated overt signs of anxiety while measures of heart-rate and skin conductance were taken. Following the second training session, the subjects were asked to give two speeches. As in the pre-test speech, two observers rated overt anxiety while heart-rate and skin conductance were monitored. As expected, the subjects given feedback for decreases in heart-rate slowed their heart-rate while those given the control task showed no change; this skill also transferred to the no-feedback periods. The pivotal data are heart-rate change before and during the post-test speeches and the anxiety measures. There was a greater decrease in both self-reported and observed anxiety in the biofeedback group as compared to the control group. Heart-rate and skin conductance measures taken before the speech and during the 3-minute speech showed that the biofeedback groups had less of a heart-rate increase than the tracking groups and had a lower skin conductance level. Contrary to the finding by Ainslie and Engel (1974), DeGood and Adams (1976), and Nunes and Marks (1975) on specificity, this latter finding of skin conductance shows change within the response class. These results suggest that the biofeedback subjects, by putting into effect the heart-rate slowing skills they had acquired, were able to reduce the levels of anxiety in an anxiety-evoking situation. However, these results still leave open the question of whether the therapeutic effect was specific to the cardiac training: i.e. is learning of heat-rate slowing a necessary factor in anxiety reduction?

Blanchard and Abel (1976) report on a woman who had been experiencing 'blackout spells' and episodes of sinus tachycardia subsequent to being raped at age 14. Following at least 10 years of detailed medical work-ups she became involved in group therapy which led to the biofeedback programme. A unique feature of this study is the use of prepared audio tapes in which rape and other sexual situations that she described were played. Prior to heart-rate training, her heart-rate increased an average of 10 bpm, with moments of absolute levels of 150 bpm. Following 33 feedback training sessions, she lowered heart-rate from 4 to 6 bpm without feedback in the presence of the training tape and was able to generalize to a new tape. Clinically, the patient reported reduced anxiety to the rape tape, and concomitant with feedback training in the presence of tape, the 'black out spells' began to disappear and were gone by the end of treatment. It would seem that heart-rate lowering training in the presence of aversive stimulation was a major factor in her treatment course. In view of the data reviewed earlier that cardiac conditioning can lower cardiac-rate to aversive stimuli, this finding seems quite reasonable. However, it should be remembered that this patient differed from the phobic or speech-anxious subjects in that her cardiac response was, in Lang, Rice, and Sternbach's (1972) terms, 'paramount in [her] symptom picture'.

(c) Comment

The data reviewed in this section show clearly that heart-rates can be operantly conditioned, and that subjects who are so trained will modify their cardiac responses to noxious stimuli. Furthermore, the data also indicate that such training will alter other response classes, for, in all but one study, those subjects trained to reduce heart-rate reported that noxious stimuli now seem less aversive, and they also showed increased approach behaviour in the aversive situation. The question of variation within a response class is less clear. One study showed that heart-rate changes to aversive stimulation did not alter blood pressure responses; another study showed that heart-rate biofeedback was more effective than deep muscle relaxation for lowering heart-rate, while a third study showed that decreases in heart-rate were accompanied by decreases in skin conductance. Although there is some evidence that cardiac conditioning may have a therapeutic effect in patients in whom cardiac activity is prominent part of the symptom picture (see also Engel and Bleecker, 1974), there is little evidence that cardiac conditioning is *specifically* therapeutic in patients in whom cardiac activity is functionally irrelevant. It would be helpful to compare cardiac to other forms of biofeedback in such patients.

(2) Muscle tension changes

(a) Experimental studies

In the late 1960s and early 1970s there were a number of articles describing various biofeedback apparatus and procedures for deep muscle relaxation (Budzynski and Stoyva, 1969; Green *et al.*, 1969; Leaf and Gaarder, 1971). In these initial papers it was suggested that electromyogram (EMG) biofeedback training might be of value for patients with chronic anxiety and insomnia, for patients with muscle contraction headaches, and as an adjunct to systematic desensitization. (For a review of the use of EMG biofeedback for chronic anxiety and insomnia see Stoyva, 1977.) Despite this extraordinary range of putative therapeutic applications, there have been surprisingly few experimental studies in which feedback-assisted muscle relaxation has been studied to see whether subjects so trained will react less and report a reduction in aversive properties of noxious stimulation.

There are probably two reasons for this dearth of basic research. First, with the exception of muscle contraction headaches which are phasic events, most of the proposed clinical applications are to state-related problems which do not lend themselves to simple experimental analogues. Second, whereas autonomic responses are organ-specific—e.g. cardiac, vasomotor—muscular responses have been conceptualized as general. Thus, while investigators have usually trained their subjects to control tension in the muscles of the forehead, there has been an implicit faith that such training is readily generalized to most muscles of the body. As a matter of fact, there is evidence that this is not true (see Alexander, 1975), and minimal experimental evidence that it is true. Thus, archival evidence suggests that for feedback training there is considerable specificity of learning within the muscular system just as there is in the cardiovascular system.

We found no studies in which concomitant autonomic responses were measured during muscular conditioning. Thus, while the rationale for the therapeutic benefit for biofeedback-assisted muscle relaxation derives in part from theories which relate neuromuscular to autonomic responses (Gellhorn, 1967; Germana, 1969), and in part from well-established studies which show cardiovascular changes during exercise, we know of no evidence that shows that biofeedback-produced reductions in muscle activity have any effects on autonomic function (however, see Stoyva and Budzynski, 1974, for possible cortical activity and theta wave correlates). There is evidence that meditative forms of relaxation are associated with reductions in blood pressure (Benson *et al.*, 1974) and with reductions in the prevalence of premature ventricular beats (Benson, Alexander, and Feldman, 1975). However, no such data exist for biofeedback-assisted muscle training. There is one finding from experimental research, however, which seems to be generally accepted: biofeedback-assisted muscle relaxation is more effective than verbal feedback in facilitating relaxation in specific muscle groups. Kinsman *et al.*, (1975) have shown that biofeedback-assisted frontalis muscle relaxation training was more effective than verbal feedback within sessions and between sessions. Furthermore, muscle feedback groups showed evidence of transfer to non-feedback trials whereas verbal feedback groups showed no transfer (see also Reinking and Kohl, 1975; Coursey, 1975).

(b) Clinical studies

Muscle contraction headaches: Although muscle contraction headaches are not always elicited by specific external or environmental stimuli, the internal prodromal signs of pain onset can be considered as a cue to impending aversive stimulation. If so, can patients be trained to reduce frontalis muscle levels to signalled pain, and will they report less headaches? The first report on the possible application of EMG feedback for patients with muscle contraction headaches is by Budzynski, Stoyva, and Adler (1970). Their procedures have been used by most subsequent researchers. Patients were asked to keep some form of a daily log or diary in which they reported frequency, intensity, and duration of headaches. Following baseline determination, the patients received biofeedback training for lowering the activity of the frontalis muscles. In the initial study it was found that as the mean level of frontalis EMG dropped, the mean level of 'headache activity' (from the self-reports) also dropped. Two- to three-month follow-ups showed that headache activities remained at low levels especially when the patients continued to practise relaxation at home. In their discussion of day-to-day changes, Budzynski, Stoyva, and Adler (1970) attributed the beneficial clinical results to both a learned situational tension-reduction skill *and* to a general lowering of arousal level. In a subsequent report, Budzynski et al., (1973) showed that EMG feedback was more effective than pseudofeedback or no treatment, in reducing frontalis level and in reducing self-reports of headaches. They hypothesized that the patient goes through three stages of control. At first the patient becomes more aware of preceding tension, then he refines his relaxation skills so as to abort some headaches, and finally he reaches a level of automatic relaxation without 'conscious effort'. Thus, although these authors initially suggest that the patient acquires and uses a situationally specific skill through EMG-feedback, they later emphasize the notion that the headache changes are due to general decreases in arousal (Budzynski and Stoyva, 1975).

Several other investigators (Wickramasekera, 1972a, and 1973; Cox, Freundlich, and Meyer, 1975; Hutchings and Reinking, 1976) also have found a correlation between a decrease in EMG levels and a reduction in self-reports of headache activity. In all of these studies, mean frontalis EMG levels rather than changes from daily baseline are reported, so that even from the training data the issue of a general lowering versus a learned ability to bring about immediate changes cannot be assessed. In some of these studies no-feedback sessions were interpolated throughout training but the data from these sessions are not reported. Philips (1977) recently measured groups of patients in biofeedback and pseudo-feedback conditions for 4 minutes prior to beginning each session. She called these pre-session periods voluntary control measures because the patients were asked to put into effect any skill they had learned to lower muscle tension. Over the 12 training sessions only the biofeedback subjects showed a decline; but again, resting levels were not reported. A study by Epstein and Abel (1977) looked specifically at self-control in the laboratory. Six patients received 16 sessions of feedback for lowering frontalis tension. Each session consisted of 10 minutes baseline, 20 minute, feedback, and 20 minutes no-feedback (but instruction to relax using acquired skills). Results of feedback were reported as change from baseline and results of no-feedback were reported as change from feedback. Although all but one patient showed slight decreases during feedback, no patient was able to maintain self-control when feedback was discontinued. Since only change scores were presented, the question of general lowering cannot be answered. However, by showing that their patients could not maintain self-control in the laboratory, they raise the question of whether patients are able to effect self-control in response to naturally occurring headache episodes. Thus, despite all of the speculations about the merits of biofeedback-assisted muscle relaxation as a 'coping skill', there still are no data to show that this skill either is learned or is used.

Systematic desensitization: In their first paper Budzynski and Stoyva (1969) suggested that behaviour therapy might be improved by including biofeedback-assisted muscle training to facilitate systematic desensitization, since there are several 'problems with the relaxation procedures usually used in such therapy:

(1) the therapist cannot be sure that the patient is relaxed since he never monitors tension or relaxation;
(2) there is no technique available to assist a patient who reports difficulty in relaxing.

Furthermore, Leaf and Gaarder (1971) have noted that many patients are unable to recognize their levels of tension; and Green et al., (1969) have noted that the time needed to train patients to relax seems inordinately long. Budzynski and Stoyva provided analogue feedback from the frontalis muscles which were chosen because they are reportedly difficult to relax. Fifteen subjects were randomly assigned to an experimental group which was to try to keep a tone frequency low, or to an irrelevant feedback group which heard a constant low tone, or to a group which was not given any tone. After only three 30-minute sessions the experimental group had a 50 per cent decline in muscle action potential levels, the low-tone group had an increase of 28 per cent, and the no-tone group a decrease of 25 per cent Green et al. provided visual feedback from dorsal forearm muscles groups and reported that seven out of 21 subjects were able to approximate 'zero' levels of muscle tension within 20 minutes of training. These initial results were hailed as suggesting that biofeedback procedures might facilitate deep muscle relaxation and thereby facilitate the course of systematic desensitization.

Subsequently, more details of application have been provided by Budzynski and Stoyva (1972) who suggest that biofeedback for EMG muscle relaxation could be employed both in the relaxation training and in the desensitization phases of behaviour therapy. After working with about 20 patients they suggested a number of advantages of EMG feedback-assisted desensitization:

(1) initial training assures greater relaxation for desensitization;
(2) the visualization can be terminated before the patients experience anxiety;
(3) the use of feedback between visualizations quickens return to the relaxed state; and
(4) the muscle quantification will assist research.

They report a case study of a woman who had been unable to learn muscle relaxation and so could not proceed with systematic desensitization of her social anxiety. They provided feedback training for her forearm muscles, then masseter muscles, and finally frontalis muscles. After she had learned to relax she returned to her therapist for successful treatment.

Of special interest is the use of EMG monitoring and feedback during the presentation of scenes from the hierarchy for patients with specific phobias. This would provide the opportunity to study the learned changes in a physiological response in the presence of anxiety-evoking stimuli. Could patients achieve muscle relaxation in the presence of such scenes? Would this change lead to a modification of other behaviour (judgements and avoidances) of the anxiety situation? Wickramasekera (1972b) reports a case study in which EMG biofeedback was successfully used during relaxation training and during hierarchy visualizations in a woman with examination phobias. Budzynski and Stoyva (1972) report that EMG levels rise during the visualizations and may be more sensitive indices of anxiety than the overt finger signal. However, just as the explanation for the headache results shifted from one of a specific skill to one of a general change, so the touted application of EMG feedback in desensitization therapy has shifted from specific phobias to generalized phobias. Budzynski (1973) contends that relaxation training may not be necessary with circumscribed phobias but becomes more helpful with generalized phobias. This point is subsequently expanded by Budzynski and Stoyva (1975) who argue that arousal level is lower in individuals with specific phobias than in individuals with generalized phobias (see also Lader and Mathews, 1968). In the latter case, such as with social phobias or agoraphobia, the fearful situations are so frequently encountered that long-term relaxation training may be needed to achieve low arousal. In the former case, desensitization may well proceed via habituation without any relaxation training.

(c) Comment

The clinical literature on biofeedback-assisted relaxation training is replete with hypotheses on how such training might facilitate desensitization therapy, or how such training might provide a technique that patients can use at the onset of muscle contraction headaches. But there are few experimental data or systematic observations of patients to support any of these hypotheses. Experiments are needed which show that muscle relaxation can be learned during acute stress, and that such learning will transfer both to other stressors and to no-feedback test trials. Experiments are needed to show that visualized scenes are accompanied by heightened muscle tension and that reductions in tension are accompanied by changes in autonomic activity and by changes in verbal reports of arousal. Experiments are needed to show whether there are differences in muscular and autonomic indices of arousal among various kinds of phobic patients, and whether reductions in these indices accurately predict reductions in verbal reports. As it stands, it would appear from the clinical literature that the application of feedback-assisted muscle group training as a specific skill or for specific situations is an idea whose time has gone.

(3) Electrodermal response changes

(a) Experimental studies

Kimmel et al. (1967) attempted to modify the electrodermal orienting response of children. They sought to answer two questions:

(1) will operant techniques modify elicited skin responses (as opposed to spontaneous skin responses)? and
(2) would such modification transfer to a more complex intelligence test situation?

The first question was one of feasibility of acquiring a physiological response. The second question was one of extension to overt behavioural components of the response. They compared normal children with retarded children. One month prior to training each child was tested individually on the Sequin form board, and the time required to replace all the pieces was recorded. A conditional stimulus was projected on a screen for 3.2 seconds. Half of the retarded and half of the normal children were reinforced ('good', and a piece of candy) each time a skin resistance response (SRR) occurred during the last 2 seconds of the stimulus presentation, while the other half in each group were reinforced each time a skin response had not occurred. At the conclusion of conditioning each child was again tested on the form board. The normal children who were reinforced for not responding showed the most change (albeit an increase in reponding) while the retarded children who were reinforced for responding showed the next largest change. The other two groups did not change appreciably in response magnitude. These findings demonstrated that elicited SRRs could be modified. Other data from this study suggested that modifying the orienting response transferred to another task. Ninety-two per cent of the retarded children who had been reinforced for making orienting responses improved on the form board test after conditioning while only 55 per cent of those reinforced for not making orienting responses improved. The authors concluded that the orienting responses were influenced by operant conditioning and that these changes mediated the differences obtained on the form board. Since 'improved' could mean as little as 1 second faster, it is unfortunate that the magnitude of improvement was not presented. Nevertheless, these are highly provocative findings which should be replicated.

Subsequent research has clearly demonstrated that elicited electrodermal responses (EDRs) can be modified by operant procedures. Shnidman has shown that skin potential responses (SPRs) can be modified both by negative reinforcement (1969) and by positive reinforcement (1970). One of her main questions was whether changes in skin potential were specific to the stimulation period or whether there was an overall change in response rate. She noted that the application of autonomic response modification to areas such as psychosomatic medicine require analysis of response to specific stimuli (i.e. 'stressors'). In the first study the experimental subjects received electric shock if they did not produce a criterion response to the stimulus while the subjects in the control group received a shock only on trials when the experimental subjects with whom they were matched received a shock. There were 40 acquisition trials, ten extinction trials, and a number of in-between 'blank trials'. In comparisons of frequency and of magnitude the experimental subjects responded more than the controls during extinction. Both groups responded more on stimulus trials than on blank trials, with the experimental subjects differentiating more between stimulus and blank trials. These findings show that elicited EDRs can be modified and that the change is not one of an overall increase in spontaneous activity. In the second paper (Shnidman, 1970), a related design was used to determine if the electrodermal response could be modified using positive reinforcement. The experimental subjects were reinforced if they produced a criterion SPR during the stimulus period. Control subjects received reinforcement on the same trials that their experimental counterparts did, independent of their skin responses. There were 40 acquisition trials and ten extinction trials and 'blank trial'. Those subjects receiving contingent reinforcement responded more during acquisition than the control subjects, and both groups responded more on stimulation trial than on blank trials. These data demonstrate increases in skin potential responding with positive reinforcement and also show that the increases are specific to stimulation and not an overall increase in spontaneous activity. As Shnidman pointed out, the procedures from these studies should be tested in those phobic patients in whom specific, elicited autonomic responses need to be counter-conditioned.

These studies have demonstrated that reinforcement procedures can increase the electrodermal component of the orienting response, but the question of decreasing the frequency or magnitude of the EDR is less clear. Earlier, Grings and Carlin (1966) had shown that the frequency of skin conductance responses (SCRs) could be increased or decreased depending on the contingency of electric shock stimulation.

Subsequently, Shnidman and Shapiro (1971) examined the effects of both positive reinforcement and punishment with differential conditioning. For the first two groups, contingencies were programmed for responding. In Group 1 the subjects received monetary reward if a response occurred; in Group 2 the subject lost money if a response occurred. For the other two groups contingencies were programmed for not responding. In Group 3 the subjects received money if they did not make a criterion response, and in Group 4 the subjects lost money if a response did not occur. They found a significant effect as a function of contingency, with Groups 1 and 2 showing a larger effect than Groups 3 and 4. There was no effect for type of reinforcer, nor was there an interaction. The response-contingent groups responded more than the non-response-contingent groups. The differences were not due to response sensitization or to an increase in general or spontaneous activity. Although their study again demonstrates that elicited SPRs can be modified, they did not show that such responses could be suppressed either by punishment (loss of money—Group 2) or by omission training (rewarding absence of a response—Group 3). The lack of decreases in these two groups compared to the findings of Carlin and Grings may be a function of shock punishment being more effective than loss of money.

A number of clinical investigators have used EDR feedback to facilitate muscle relaxation. It is noteworthy in this regard that Rice (1966) reported that he was able to dissociate operantly conditioned increases in unelicited EDRs from concomitant muscle responses in the fingers holding the EDR electrodes. It should be clear that this finding in no way negates the possibility that training to reduce EDR activity will facilitate reductions in muscle activity. However, it does indicate that experiments to test that hypothesis are needed.

(b) Clinical studies

There are few published clinical reports of the use of EDR in the control of elicited arousal. One abstract appears by Shapiro *et al.* (1972) in which they explored the modification of snake phobia. They studied 20 patients with 10 reinforced for increasing EDRs and 10 reinforced for decreasing EDRs. There were 10 baseline trials and then 60 conditioning trials. Each trial consisted of a 5-second presentation of a snake slide with about 30 seconds between trials. Reinforcement was a tone which indicated monetary reward. Half of the subjects were reinforced if the skin response was greater in amplitude than on the preceding trial, and half were reinforced if the skin response was smaller in amplitude. The last 10 trials (71–80) were extinction trials. Both groups showed decreases over trials but the decreases were greater in the 'decrease group' and this difference was significant over extinction. Before conditioning, and then after conditioning, a subjective fear questionnaire was administered. The 'decrease group' showed a greater reduction in fear of snakes (but not of spiders). Given that both groups showed a decrease it might have been that the decrease group received more reinforcements in the presence of snakes but it cannot be determined from the abstract. Patel (1977) has reported several studies in which she used EDR feedback to assist her hypertensive patients to relax and to lower their blood pressures. Although the clinical results with the patients were strong, it is not possible to assess the specific role that EDR conditioning might have played in the treatment since no EDR data or trial-specific blood pressure data are reported.

(c) Comment

In view of the many commercially available EDR trainers that exist, and in view of the number of clinical reports in which EDR feedback has been used to 'facilitate' relaxation, it is surprising how few systematic clinical results there are in the scientific literature. Does EDR conditioning facilitate reduction in recorded muscle tension? Does EDR conditioning facilitate reduction in blood pressure or other autonomic indices of arousal? Would EDR counter-conditioning of elicited responses in phobic patients (or any other patients for that matter) reduce subjective reports of fear? Serious investigators of biofeedback applications would do well to study these questions. This is an area where there are relatively few claims, temperate speculations, and virtually no data.

(4) EEG alpha changes

(a) Experimental studies

Modulation of EEG alpha density via biofeedback to counter situational stresses is based on two premises, each of which is now questioned. One premise derives from the reported decrease in EEG alpha density in situations of apprehension. The second premise is based on the reported elevations in mood which occur when EEG alpha densities are increased. These two observations have suggested to some investigators that if individuals could be trained to increase alpha activity, they might change other behaviours during a feared situation.

Orne and Paskewitz (1974) attempted to test the hypothesized relationship between apprehension and decreases in alpha activity and the attendant hypothesis that learned increases in alpha activity might prevent increases in physiological arousal and subjective reports of anxiety. Ten male college students who had shown acceptable levels of alpha density during a preliminary training session agreed to return and participate in an experiment involving 'harmless but quite painful electric shock'. For this second session conditions were arranged to augment apprehension. After training as in session one, they were told that at times when they were not producing alpha, a warning tone would sound during which they could be shocked. Orne and Paskewitz anticipated that baseline alpha would be decreased from the previous no-shock baseline session. However, they found no decreases in baseline alpha densities, and no increases in alpha density during feedback training. The difference between warning periods and non-warning periods was even more surprising; there was none. The shock instructions failed to lead to any decrease in alpha density, while at the same time there were increases in heart-rate (more than 10 bpm), in spontaneous skin conductance responses, and in subjective reports of discomfort and apprehension. The authors considered the possibility that the prior feedback training enabled the subject to maintain alpha densities in the situation of shock threat as 'unlikely'. They concluded that their findings questioned the validity of using biofeedback training of alpha activity to control acute anxiety.

Two reports are frequently cited as evidence that increased alpha density is associated with subjective reports of feelings of calm, pleasantness and relaxation (the 'alpha experience'). Brown (1970) asked subjects to attempt to identify feeling states which would keep a blue light turned on. After each session every subject filled out a questionnaire which asked what he experienced and what special techniques he used to control the light. Detailed results of subjective reports from the third session of those ten subjects who completed four sessions were given. Those subjects who reported drifting, floating, or loss of awareness (except of the light) were those with the highest levels of alpha activity. Half reported techniques of feeling relaxed or attempting to relax; however, the data do not show a clear relationship of such feelings to alpha abundance. Nevertheless, the results were interpreted as showing an association of feeling states with alpha activity. Nowlis and Kamiya (1970) conducted a study using auditory feedback to show that humans can learn to control alpha EEG, and to determine what subjective states are associated with controlling the tone. After a 2-minute baseline (with tone for alpha) the subjects were given time 'to try to figure out what made the tone' come on and off. After the session there was an open-ended interview to determine the subjects' methods of controlling the tone. There was a wide variety of reports by the subjects on how they controlled the tone, such as relaxation, floating, or not focusing, as ways to keep alpha on, and being alert and agitation as ways of keeping the tone off. Only among the eyes-open subjects there was agreement on 'visual attentiveness' as a way to keep the light off with nine of the ten reporting this method. After cautioning on the interpretation of the verbal reports, the authors concluded that the evidence is strongly towards associated differences in reports of mental activities for the various conditions.

Although the findings of Brown, and Nowles and Kamiya, suggested that biofeedback training to augment alpha activity might counter situational arousal, subsequent research has questioned the relationship between alpha feedback and 'alpha experience'. This research has generally taken two forms. Some authors argue that increases in alpha density do not directly lead to subjective reports but may be a function of demand characteristics or suggestion (see Plotkin, 1977). Another group of authors suggest that alpha experience may not be due to alpha feedback training per se, but rather may be related to other changes such as oculomotor processing (Plotkin and Cohen, 1976) or relaxation (Marshall and Bentler (1976)).

Orne and Paskewitz (1974) and Chisholm, DeGood, and Hartz (1977) are the only investigators we know who attempted to determine the effect of alpha biofeedback training in an aversive situation. They also looked at changes in heart-rate and in self-reports of anxiety and tension. Thirty-six volunteer subjects were randomly assigned to an EEG biofeedback group, a non-contingent control group, and a no-feedback music group. There were eight pre-training trials in which electric shock occurred 30 seconds after tone onset, 24 training trials, and then 12 post-training tone-shock test trials (eight with the feedback or music signal available and four without). On the training aversive trials alpha activity was suppressed during the tone-shock period, heart rate increased, and the subjects reported increased tension. During treatment the biofeedback group showed an increase in alpha activity as did the music control group, while the non-contingent control group showed a decrease. All groups reported a decrease in tension. In the post-training trials the biofeedback subjects had an increase in alpha activity (compared to pre-treatment) with the feedback signal present, but they could not maintain this increase when the signal was removed on the eyes-opened tests; however, on the eyes-closed tests they maintained the increased alpha. The two control groups did not show any reliable alpha changes. All groups reported decreases in tension from pre- to post-treatment with no group differences. Only the music group showed reliable tonic heart-rate decreases. So, despite evidence of an increase in alpha activity with biofeedback transferring to an aversive situation, there was no differential decrease in another physiological measure (heart-rate) nor in self-reports of anxiety or tension leading the authors to conclude that reduction in alpha suppression did not contribute to a general relaxation.

(b) Clinical studies

Biofeedback of alpha activity has been attempted for the remediation of pain onset in three studies. The first was based on the premise that a high alpha 'meditative state' would be incompatible with pain behaviour. In this case study Gannon and Sternbach (1971) provided over 50 training sessions to a man with intractable headaches. On the last four sessions there was no feedback, but the patient was given a report of his performance at the end of the session. There were three follow-up sessions over subsequent months. Over the course of treatment the patient showed increases in percentage of alpha activity with fairly equal amounts during eyes-closed and eyes-opened by the end of training. The pain findings were mixed. If the patient came to the laboratory with a headache, he could not achieve high alpha levels nor would his headache abate. However, he did report that he might be able to prevent a headache in a potentially provocative situation.

A second study (McKenzie *et al.*, 1974) used alpha training in the laboratory combined with home practice of relaxation. All patients showed an increase in alpha activity from the beginning to the end of training. By the end of training there was a 79 per cent decrease in reported headache activity, and 1 month after treatment there was a 77 per cent decrease. A control group given Silva relaxation training also showed symptom-alleviation. The authors assert that the patients learned more rapidly with alpha biofeedback. In a follow-up, Montgomery and Ehrisman (1976) sent questionnaires to those who had participated in their training programme. Those who returned the questionnaires indicated that symptom relief and an increased ability to relax had persisted over the 6-month to 3 year period after they finished the programme. A study that employed feedback and pseudofeedback groups (Lehman, Lang, and Debruyne, 1976) found that headache pain decreased systematically in both groups, and there was no difference in decrease between the two groups (suggesting expectation effects). There were increases in alpha density in both groups over sessions which, along with the finding of greater alpha during resting than during training, led the authors to conclude that alpha increases were a habituation effect.

In a different type of application, Budzynski and Stoyva (1972) initially attempted biofeedback control of alpha activity as a means to 'regain a state of calm after an anxiety episode'. They presented a brief case report of a man with phobias of death-related themes who after two sessions of training increased his alpha from 20 per cent to 80 per cent. However, when they attempted to maintain alpha relaxation and have him visualize hierarchy items, the alpha rhythm disappeared. This was true even with neutral scenes so they were unable to use alpha levels as indicators of anxiety. They did use alpha feedback between visualizations and reported successful treatment. They also noted that they often encountered individuals with very high initial alpha levels and individuals with very low initial alpha levels, and that both kinds of patients presented problems for desensitization. Consequently, they switched to muscle relaxation training.

(c) Comment

Most readers of this book probably are aware of the grandiose claims that proponents of alpha feedback have made about the clinical and prophylactic value of such training (see especially Brown, 1974). There is very little evidence for any such benefits. Most of the published claims are anecdotal and can be readily ascribed to various non-specific effects. Many researchers in this field have found that the popular claims about the 'alpha experience' have created a climate of scepticism about the merits of any research in this area. We suggest that this field would benefit most from a period of 'benign neglect' during which careful and systematic experimental studies might be pursued, but during which any further clinical investigations should be avoided.

(5) False physiological information

(a) Experimental studies

Valins (1970) argues that a major aspect of emotional behaviour is the perception and labelling of physiological change and the attribution of these to emotional stimuli. For example, if a person believes that his heart is pounding while in the presence of another person he may take this information into account and conclude a liking for this person. One implication of this approach is that a person's behaviour (judgements and approaches) may be influenced by false yet convincing physiological information. Valins (1966) demonstrated that male subjects who 'hear' their heart-rate change upon the presentation of certain slides of females, will then rate those slides as more attractive than slides for which no heart-rate change was 'heard'. More specifically, he argues that upon hearing that their heart-rates changed, they become selectively more attentive to features of those slides. Furthermore, he stated that the actual heart-rates did not seem to change as a function of the false feedback, and so contends that the effect is cognitive, not physiological.

Clearly this interpretation has implications for biofeedback and emotional behaviour. If individuals can be convinced that their heart-rate is decreasing in the presence of an anxiety-arousing stimulus, and they interpret or label this change as being due to decreased fear, they might behave differently towards the stimulus. This implication was tested in a provocative study by Valins and Ray (1967) in which they attempted to test whether systematic desensitization was effective for physiological or cognitive reasons. In the first experiment subjects were randomly assigned to an experimental group which received false heart rate information or a control group which heard the same sounds but were told that they were meaningless background noise. The subjects were presented with ten slides of the word 'SHOCK', 7 seconds after which they received a shock to their first and third fingers, and saw ten slides of snakes. When the snake slides were presented there were no changes in heart-rate sounds, whereas when the SHOCK slides were presented the sounds increased from 72 to 90 bpm. Presumably then, the experimental subjects heard that they were not affected by the snake slides but that they were affected by the shock slides. Following these presentations the subjects were given a snake-avoidance test in which they were asked to voluntarily approach a 30 inch boa constrictor. When all subjects in each group were included there was no difference in mean approach behaviour between the experimental and control subjects. However, when that subset of each group who had previously never touched a snake were compared, there was more approach behaviour on the part of those given the false feedback. This finding led Valins and Ray to conduct a second experiment like the first except that:

(1) subjects were selected on the basis of a questionnaire that indicated fear of harmless snakes;
(2) a second snake-shock session was conducted 1 week after the first during which the snake trials consisted of seeing a real snake in a cage; and
(3) for the approach/avoidance the subject was led into the room and pressured (with money incentives) to pick the snake up.

In the second experiment it was found that the experimental subjects required less pressure than the control subjects to touch the snake. However, the authors report that there were no differences in pressure required to pick up the snake between the two groups (but no data are presented). These findings led Valins and Ray to conclude that avoidance behaviour can be modified by information about physiological reactions, and that it is cognitions about internal changes that are the major determinants of the performance changes.

Although these papers appeared prior to the advent of clinical research in biofeedback and were meant to challenge assumptions regarding systematic desensitization, one major implication of the argument by Valins is that successful training in heart-rate (or other control may not be necessary, only 'apparent' success is needed. As a result, we will give some attention to attempted replications and alternative explanations of the false-information approach. This brief review will focus only on studies of false heart-rate information.

After a 'conceptual replication' by Sushinsky and Bootzin (1970) failed to confirm the findings of Valins and Ray, a more direct replication was attempted by Kent, Wilson, and Nelson (1972). Their only change in procedure was that of using a more conventional post-treatment behavioural avoidance test, arguing that the money inducement procedure thwarted comparison with other studies. Using the same snake slides used by Valins and Ray, they gave false information or no information to 26 undergraduate students who rated themselves as fearing snakes. After ten snake trials and ten SHOCK trials, the subjects were asked to approach a 3-foot boa constrictor in a glass cage. Following the behavioural test each subject filled out a number of scales and questionnaires regarding his anxiety and regarding his perceptions of the experiment. In spite of the finding that of the subjects who had received false information significantly more indicated that the heart-rate changes implied they were 'maybe less frightened' of snakes, none of the dependent measures significantly distinguished between feedback and control subjects. At the same time Gaupp, Stern, and Galbraith (1972) attempted to reinterpret the original findings in terms of an aversion relief model based on classical conditioning. Their results show that true heart-rate changes need to be monitored. Similar non-replication has been obtained by Rosen, Rosen, and Reid (1972) who included a no-treatment control and a group led to believe that the snake slide did affect them. Following the experimental manipulation there were no differences among the groups on a behavioural test of approaching a 3-foot boa constrictor or on fear rating scales.

Some experimental support for Valins and Ray comes from Borkovec, Wall, and Stone (1974) who have shown that false heart-rate increase information produced greater self-reported anxiety, overt anxiety, and speech difficulty with speech-anxious subjects than false decrease information and false no-change groups. Likewise, Holmes and Frost (1976) have reported that subjects given false heart-rate increase information between the first and second presentation of an electric shock reported increases in anxiety, and rated the second shock stronger than a group given false heart-rate decrease information. Neither of these studies has shown that false decrease information leads to a lessening of emotional behaviour.

In an attempt to clarify these reported differences, Conger, Conger, and Brehm (1976) compared high and low fearful subjects noting that some of the replication studies used more fearful subjects than did Valins and Ray. Based on a self-rating of snake fear, college females having low or high fear ratings were given the snake and SHOCK series and then tested for approach to a 30-inch garter snake. Although low-fear subjects showed greater approach behaviour if given false information than other low-fear subjects who were informed that the sounds were extraneous, the manipulation had no effect on the high-fear subjects. Conger, Conger, and Brehm point out that this finding minimizes the clinical usefulness of false physiological information.

An important study would be one comparing false changes in heart-rate with real changes in heart-rate via operant conditioning. An abstract of such a study has been reported by Sirota, Shapiro, and Schwartz (1977) as a follow-up to the work described earlier on heart-rate control and ratings of noxious stimuli. Although four groups were studied, only the first two are relevant to our concern. Group 1 was given true feedback for increasing and decreasing heart-rate, while Group 2 was given feedback for stabilizing heart-rate but were told that the feedback was for increasing and decreasing heart-rate. As in their replication study (Sirota, Schwartz, and Shapiro, 1976) trials consisted of a 15-second training period followed by electric shock on four of every five trials. There were 50 trials. The results were that these two groups showed 'analogous' heart-rate changes and shock ratings with a tendency for such changes to be greatest in Group 1. However, if, as it appears, the Group 2 subjects increased and decreased heart-rate, then it is not possible to separate the rating changes into 'belief' and 'physiological' changes (see Stern, Botto, and Herrick, 1972).

(b) Comment

Besides the replication problem, there are at least two other problems with these studies of false information. The Valins and Ray paradigm assumes explicitly that heart-rate variations are markers for variations in affect. If this is so, then regardless of whether it is the perception of the cardiac changes or the changes themselves which is the affect, the question immediately arises as to how this state of affairs ever came into being. If subjects (or for that matter, Valins and Ray believe that cardiac changes reflect changes in feeling, why do they believe this? Surely they must have an experiential basis for establishing this association. If physiological changes are reliable components of emotional behaviour, then it seems to us that the important question is how this came to be. Whether one chooses to define the changes as the emotion, or whether one prefers to call the perception of these changes the emotion, is trivial.

The second problem with the false information paradigm is that it focuses arbitrarily on one specific physiological response when there is considerable experimental and clinical evidence that different individuals tend to react in different organ systems (e.g. see Engel, 1972; Graham, 1972), and some subjects who report considerable anxiety report no or minimal physiological symptoms. It seems to us that if one wanted to test the validity of the false information hypothesis, one would have to select both subjects and physiological responses with these considerations in mind. An interesting experiment would be one which included three groups of subjects. Group one would be selected because they reported that they associated (say) cardiac activity with anxiety. Group two would be selected because they associated (say) electrodermal activity with anxiety. Group three would be selected because they denied that their anxiety had any physiological correlates. Each group would then be divided into four subgroups. One subgroup would receive veridical feedback in heart rate, the second would receive veridical feedback in electrodermal activity, the third would receive false cardiac information, and the fourth group would receive false electrodermal information. If all four groups responded alike—i.e. showed equivalent approach or avoidance behaviour—then that would be strong evidence that the physiological indices were epiphenomenal. If the feedback (false or veridical) was irrelevant, but the subject/physiological response match was important, that would be evidence for physiological specificity *and* for relevant (but not necessarily veridical) information, and it would reopen the question of the clinical usefulness of false (but relevant) information. Finally, if only veridical feedback was associated with approach/avoidance behaviour, it would be strong evidence for the clinical use of relevant biofeedback.

SUMMARY AND CONCLUSIONS

In this chapter we have looked at whether a physiological response elicited or emitted during acute emotional arousal can be modified by operant conditioning so that when a person is in the arousing situation the frequency and/or magnitude of that response will be attenuated; and we have looked at whether such a modification would be accompanied by changes in two other emotional indices: verbal and approach/avoidance responses. This review was prompted by speculation by Lang, Rice, and Sternbach (1972) that operant conditioning might be a 'powerful tool' for laboratory study and clinical treatment of emotional behaviour. Subsequently, Lang (1977) has concluded that continuous visceral feedback is not a 'uniquely powerful' treatment for anxiety and other general responses.

   To evaluate the effect of operant conditioning on the physiological component of emotional behaviour we proposed an experimental paradigm with three stages:

(1) a pre-treatment stage in which physiological, verbal, and approach/ avoidance responses are measured;
(2) a treatment stage during which a particular physiological (somatic or autonomic) response is modified through biofeedback training; and

(3) a post-treatment stage which essentially repeats the measurements of the first stage with the exception that the subject attempts to change the physiological response through whatever feedback (or control) skill he acquired in stage (2).

Given appropriate controls for treatment effects and for reactivity to post-test as a function of pre-test experience, variations of the above paradigm should provide evidence concerning four questions that we raised:

(1) Will biofeedback training for a particular physiological response enable subjects to alter that effector response in a stressful situation?
(2) Do all three response classes change or will they be dissociated?
(3) Within the physiological response class is change specific to the trained response or are there other correlated changes?
(4) Is the biofeedback of a particular physiological response necessary or are a number of autonomic and somatic changes equally effective in altering emotional behaviour?

The first two questions concern the feasibility of operant modification of a specific physiological response in an aversive situation and of the effects of such change on verbal and approach/avoidance responses. Studies with both animal and human subjects have shown that the usual increase in heart-rate to aversive stimulation can be modified. In laboratory studies the impending or present aversive stimulus was electric shock or ice-water. With clinical studies the aversive event was a speech presentation, a phobic stimulus, or audio tapes of an anxiety-arousing scene. In all but one study where tested, the successful decrease in heart-rate was accompanied by changes in judgement about the degree of aversiveness of the stimulus, or in self-reports of anxiety, or in overt approach responses. We believe that the effectiveness of true heart-rate decrease training as a counter to emotional arousal had been demonstrated such that future research should explore a wider range of aversive situations, collect data about beyond-the-laboratory changes, and follow up the patients in clinical studies. If false heart-rate information plays a larger role than presently appears to be the case, then we repeat our suggestion for more studies comparing true changes via operant conditioning with false information changes on subsequent verbal and approach responses.

With EEG alpha wave training there were two studies using aversive stimulation (electric shock): one study showed no change in alpha levels following brief training, while the second study showed that subjects could maintain an increase in alpha levels following biofeedback training. However, in this latter study the alpha change was not accompanied by changes in self-reports of anxiety. The clinical reports also are mixed: questions of the role of expectation effects and of home practice in relaxation need to be resolved. In our judgement, more laboratory research is needed to demonstrate modified alpha wave changes during aversive stimulation and concomitant changes in other emotional indices.

An early suggestive study on the electrodermal component of the orienting reflex should serve as a model for further research on the electrodermal component of emotional behaviour. Subsequent studies have shown that elicited skin potential responses can be altered by operant conditioning, although it is not clear whether they can be reduced, and whether they can be reduced in stressful situations. Laboratory research is needed to determine the effects of electrodermal training during aversive stimulation before clinical studies are attempted.

The muscle training data turned out to be far less conclusive than we expected. Probably because feedback-assisted muscle relaxation is conceptualized as a general treatment for cases of pervasive anxiety, EMG feedback is studied as a means of reducing general arousal rather than as a skill to apply for controlling specific phobias or 'tension' headaches at the time of early headache signals. We have urged that laboratory studies be conducted on altering muscle-group responses with biofeedback in the face of aversive stimulation.

Our third question focused on correlated changes within the physiological response class in an attempt to determine the specificity of training. Would decreases in heart-rate be accompanied by changes in blood pressure, or in electrodermal responses, or in muscle activity? Would changes in one muscle group be correlated with changes in other muscle groups, or in heart-rate, or in alpha wave activity? We strongly urge that in future research more physiological responses be measured along with the target response for operant conditioning. Such data could clarify mechanism by which physiological response modification may attenuate emotional reactivity. At this stage the evidence favours specificity, but there are scattered reports of correlated changes that need to be pursued. As matters now stand, it appears that biofeedback of a specific physiological response alters only that physiological response.

Our final question was directed at the relevance of training a particular response: might any number of physiological responses known to be involved in emotional or pain responses be equally trainable and equally effective in altering emotional behaviours? At this stage it is too early to tell; only heart-rate training has been shown effective with acute arousal. It is still not clear whether cardiac conditioning is the only response change therapeutic in patients showing a variety of physiological responses during arousal.

We will close by commenting on the use of controls for non-specific effects and by suggesting a symptom-matching hypothesis. Given that the verbal and approach/avoidance reponses being evaluated as measures of physiological feedback training effectiveness are vulnerable to response bias, we urge that more 'expectation' and 'demand characteristic' control groups be employed. Did subjects receiving heart-rate decrease training expect that the electric shocks would not feel as strong after training, or did they sense that they were expected to report that the shocks were less intense? Did those receiving heart-rate increase training expect that the iced water would be more intense after training or, at least, that they should report it as more intense? Further studies with physiological training might do well to include, for example, groups given training and then asked to anticipate how they would rate the post-training aversive stimulation and or approach/avoid in the presence of the aversive stimulus. Nonetheless, although expectation and demand controls were rarely used in the studies we reviewed, the reported successes with heart-rate, as compared to failures with alpha training, minimize the argument that these factors play a large part, unless one believes that the heart-rate investigators are better at raising expectations or generating demands.

It is our opinion that the clinical studies of arousal using biofeedback which have shown the strongest effect are those in which the physiological response chosen for feedback was 'paramount' in the symptom picture. A tachycardic response to sexual situations was reduced by heart-rate conditioning; frontalis muscle headaches (when due to such muscle contractions) seem to be reduced by frontalis muscle conditioning. These findings lead us to suggest that the most reactive physiological response should be determined and then made the target of the biofeedback training. In regard to this symptom-matching hypothesis, we urge that the experiment suggested at the end of our comments on false physiological information be conducted. We proposed that training be made either relevant or irrelevant to the patient's most salient response in order to assess the effectiveness of relevant training.

These speculations lead back to the recent conclusion by Lang (1977) that continuous visceral feedback is not a 'uniquely powerful treatment' for anxiety and other general responses. Lang contends that biofeedback training is too specific and no more effective than progressive relaxation or meditative relaxation, and argues against the routine use of biofeedback in treating anxiety. If he means pervasive or chronic anxiety then his conclusions are beyond the scope of this chapter. If he means those acute arousal reactions where the physiological response is arbitrarily selected for training, then we would say that more data are needed. However, in the treatment of acute anxiety or pain arousal associated with a specific paramount physiological responses, we believe that biofeedback training will prove an effective treatment for altering emotional behaviours.

REFERENCES

Ainslie, G. W., and Engel, B. T. (1974). Alternation of classically conditioned heart rate by operant reinforcement in monkeys. *Journal of Comparative and Physiological Psychology*, **87**, 373–382.

Alexander, A. B. (1975). An experimental test of assumptions relating to the use of electromyographic biofeedback as a general relaxation training technique. *Psychophysiology*, **12**, 656–662.

Beatty, J., and Legewie, H. (eds.) (1977). *Biofeedback and Behavior*. New York: Plenum Press.

Benson, H., Alexander, S., and Feldman, C. L. (1975). Decreased premature ventricular contractions through the use of the relaxation response in patients with stable ischemic heart disease. *Lancet*, 30 August, 380–382.

Benson, H., Rosner, B. A., Marzetta, B. R., and Klemchuk, H. P. (1974). Decreased blood pressure in borderline hypertensive subjects who practiced meditation, *Journal of Chronic Diseases*, **27**, 163–169.

Blanchard, E. B., and Abel, G. G. (1976). An experimental case study of the biofeedback treatment of a rape-induced psychophysiological cardiovascular disorder. *Behavior Therapy*, **7**, 113–119.

Borkovec, T. D., Wall, R. L., and Stone, N. M. (1974). False physiological feedback and the maintenance of speech anxiety. *Journal of Abnormal Psychology*, **83**, 164–168.

Brown, B. B. (1970). Recognition of aspects of consciousness through association with EEG alpha activity represented by a light signal. *Psychophysiology*, **6**, 442–452.

Brown, B. B. (1974). *New Mind, New Body: Bio-feedback: New Directions for the Mind.* New York: Harper & Row.

Budzynski, T. H. (1973). Biofeedback procedures in the clinic. *Seminars in Psychiatry*, **5**, 537–547.

Budzynski, T. H., and Stoyva, J. M. (1969). An instrument for producing deep muscle relaxation by means of analog information feedback. *Journal of Applied Behavior Analysis*, **2**, 231–237.

Budzynski, T. H., and Stoyva, J. (1972). Biofeedback techniques in behavior therapy. Reprinted in D. Shapiro, T. X. Barber, L. V. DiCara, J., Kamiya, N. W. Miller, and J. Stoyva (eds.), *Biofeedback and Self-control: 1972.* Chicago: Aldine.

Budzynski, T. H., and Stoyva, J. (1975). EMG biofeedback in generalized and specific anxiety disorders. In H. Legewie, and L. Nusselt (eds.), *Biofeedback-Therapie: Lernmethoden in der Psychosomatik, Neurologie und Rehabilitation (Fortschritte der Klinischen Psychologie*, Vol. 6). München–Berlin–Wien: Urban & Schwarzenberg.

Budzynski, T., Stoyva, J., and Adler, C. (1970). Feedback-induced muscle relaxation: application to tension headache. *Journal of Behavior Therapy and Experimental Psychiatry*, **1**, 205–211.

Budzynski, T. H., Stoyva, J. M., Adler, C. S., and Mullaney, D. J. (1973). EMG biofeedback and tension headache: a controlled outcome study. *Psychosomatic Medicine*, **35**, 484–496.

Chisolm, R. C., DeGood, D. E., and Hartz, M. A. (1977). Effects of alpha feedback training on occipital EEG, heart rate, and experential reactivity to a laboratory stressor. *Psychophysiology*, **14**, 157–163.

Conger, J. C., Conger, A. J., and Brehm, S. (1976). Fear level as a moderator of false feedback effects in snake phobias. *Journal of Consulting and Clinical Psychology*, **44**, 135–141.

Coursey, R. D. (1975). Electromyograph feedback as a relaxation technique. *Journal of Consulting and Clinical Psychology*, **43**, 825–834.

Cox, D. J., Freundlich, A., and Meyer, R. C. (1975). Differential effectiveness of electromyograph feedback, verbal relaxation instructions, and medication placebo with tension headaches. *Journal of Consulting and Clinical Psychology*, **43**, 892–898.

DeGood, D. E., and Adams, A. S. (1976). Control of cardiac response under aversive stimulation: superiority of a heart-rate feedback condition. *Biofeedback and Self-regulation*, **1**, 373–385.

DiCara, L. V., and Weiss, J. M. (1969). Effect of heart rate learning under curare on subsequent noncurarized avoidance learning. *Journal of Comparative and Physiological Psychology*, **69**, 368–374.

Engel, B. T. (1972). Response specificity. In N. S. Greenfield, and R. A. Sternbach (eds.), *Handbook of Psychophysiology.* New York: Holt, Rinehart and Winston, Inc.

Engel, B. T. (1977). Operant conditioning of cardiac function. In S. Rachman (ed.), *Contributions to Medical Psychology.* Oxford: Pergamon Press.

Engel, B. T., and Bleecker, E. R. (1974). Application of operant conditioning techniques to the control of cardiac arrhythmias. In P. A., Obrist, A. H., Black, J., Brener, and L. V. DiCara (eds.), *Cardiovascular Psychophysiology.* Chicago: Aldine.

Epstein, L. H., and Abel, G. G. (1977). An analysis of biofeedback training effects for tension headache patients. *Behavior Therapy*, **8**, 37–47.

Gannon, L., and Sternbach, R. A. (1971). Alpha enhancement as a treatment for pain: a case study. *Journal of Behavior Therapy and Experimental Psychiatry*, **2**, 209–213.

Gatchel, R. J., and Proctor, J. D. (1976). Effectiveness of voluntary heart rate control in reducing speech anxiety. *Journal of Consulting and Clinical Psychology*, **44**, 381–389.

Gaupp, L. A., Stern, R. M., and Galbraith, G. G. (1972). False heart-rate feedback and reciprocal inhibition by aversion relief in the treatment of snake avoidance behavior. *Behavior Therapy*, **3**, 7–20.

Gellhorn, E. (1967). *Principles of Autonomic–Somatic Integrations: Physiological Basis and Psychological and Clinical Implications*. Minneapolis: University of Minnesota Press.

Germana, J. (1969). Central efferent processes and autonomic–behavioral integration. *Psychophysiology*, **6**, 78–90.

Graham, D. T. (1972). Psychosomatic medicine. In N. S. Greenfield, R. A. Sternbach (eds.), *Handbook of Psychophysiology*. New York: Holt, Rinehart & Winston, Inc.

Green, E. E., Walters, E. D., Green, A. M., and Murphy, G. (1969). Feedback technique for deep relaxation. *Psychophysiology*, **6**, 371–377.

Grings, W. W., and Carlin, S. (1966). Instrumental modification of autonomic behavior. *The Psychological Record*, **16**, 153–159.

Holmes, D. S., and Frost, R. O. (1976). Effect of false autonomic feedback on self-reported anxiety, pain perception, and pulse rate. *Behavior Therapy*, **7**, 330–334.

Hutchings, D. F., and Reinking, R. H. (1976). Tension headaches: what form of therapy is most effective? *Biofeedback and Self-regulation*, **1**, 183–190.

Kent, R. N., Wilson, G. T., and Nelson, R. (1972). Effects of false heart-rate feedback on avoidance behavior: an investigation of cognitive desensitization. *Behavior Therapy*, **3**, 1–6.

Kimmel, H. D., Pendergrass, V. E., and Kimmel, E. B. (1967). Modifying children's orienting reactions instrumentally. *Conditional Reflex*, **2**, 227–235.

Kinsman, R. A., O'Banion, K., Robinson, S., and Staudenmayer, S. (1975). Continuous biofeedback and discrete post trial verbal feedback in frontalis muscle relaxation training. *Psychophysiology*, **12**, 30–35.

Lader, M. H., and Mathews, A. M. (1968). A physiological model of phobic anxiety and desensitization. *Behavior Research and Therapy*, **6**, 411–421.

Lang, P. J. (1977). Research on the specificity of feedback training: implications for the use of biofeedback in the treatment of anxiety and fear. In J. Beatty, and H. Legewie (eds.), *Biofeedback and Behavior*. New York: Plenum Press.

Lang, P. J., Rice, D. G., and Sternbach, R. A. (1972). The psychophysiology of emotion. In N. S. Greenfield, and R. A. Sternbach (eds.), *Handbook of Psychophysiology*. New York: Holt, Rinehart & Winston, Inc.

Leaf, W. B., and Gaarder, K. R. (1971). A simplified electromyograph feedback apparatus for relaxation training. *Journal of Behavior Therapy and Experimental Psychiatry*, **2**, 39–43.

Lehman, D., Lang, W., and Debruyne, P. (1976). Kontrolliertes EEG-Alpha-feedback-training bei Gesunden und Kopschmerzpatientinnen. *Archiv für Psychiatrie und Nervenkrankheiten*, **221**, 331–343.

Mainardi, J. A., Victor, R., and Shapiro, D. (1977). Voluntary control of heart rate: effects on heart rate and pain during the cold pressor test. *Psychophysiology*, **14**, 81 (abstract).

Marshall, M. S., and Bentler, P. M. (1976). The effects of deep physical relaxation and low-frequency-alpha brainwaves on alpha subjective reports. *Psychophysiology*, **13**, 505–516.

McKenzie, R. E., Ehrisman, W. J., Montgomery, P. S., and Barnes, R. H. (1974). The treatment of headache by means of electroencephalographic biofeedback. *Headache*, **14**, 164–172.

Montgomery, P. S., and Ehrisman, W. J. (1976). Biofeedback-alleviated headaches: a follow-up *Headache*, **16**, 64–65.

Nowlis, D. P., and Kamiya, J. (1970). The control of electroencephalographic alpha rhythms through auditory feedback and the associated mental activity. *Psychophysiology*, **6**, 476–484.

Nunes, J. S., and Marks, I. M. (1975). Feedback of true heart rate during exposure in vivo. *Archives of General Psychiatry*, **32**, 933–936.

Orne, M. T., and Paskewitz, D. A. (1974). Aversive situational effects on alpha feedback training. *Science*, **186**, 458–460.

Patel, C. H. (1977). Biofeedback-aided relaxation and meditation in the management of hypertension. *Biofeedback and Self-regulation*, **2**, 1–41.

Philips, C. (1977). The modification of tension headache pain using EMG biofeedback. *Behavior Research and Therapy*, **15**, 119–129.

Plotkin, W. B. (1977). On the social psychology of experiential states associated with EEG alpha biofeedback training. In J. Beatty, and H. Legewie (eds.), *Biofeedback and Behavior*. New York: Plenum Press.

Plotkin, W. B., and Cohen, R. (1976). Occipital alpha and the attributes of the 'alpha experience'. *Psychophysiology*, **13**, 16–21.

Prigatano, G. P., and Johnson, H. J. (1972). Biofeedback control of heart rate variability to phobic stimuli: a new approach to treating spider phobia. *Proceedings of the 80th Annual Convention of the American Psychological Association*, **7**, 403–404 (summary).

Reinking, R. H., and Kohl, M. L. (1975). Effects of various forms of relaxation training on physiological and self-report measures of relaxation. *Journal of Consulting and Clinical Psychology*, **43**, 595–600.

Reynolds, G. S. (1975). *A Primer of Operant Conditioning* (rev. edn). Glenview Ill.: Scott, Foresman & Co.

Rice, D. G. (1966). Operant conditioning and associated electromyogram responses. *Journal of Experimental Psychology*, **71**, 908–912.

Rosen, G. M., Rosen, E., and Reid, J. B. (1972). Cognitive desensitization and avoidance behavior. *Journal of Abnormal Psychology*, **80**, 176–182.

Shapiro, D. (1977). Biofeedback and the regulation of complex psychological processes. In J. Beatty, and H. Legewie (eds.), *Biofeedback and Behavior*. New York: Plenum Press.

Shapiro, D., Schwartz, G. E., Shnidman, S., Nelson, S., and Silverman, S. (1972). Operant control of fear-related electrodermal responses in snake-phobic subjects. *Psychophysiology*, **9**, 271 (abstract).

Shnidman, S. R. (1969). Avoidance conditioning of skin potential responses. *Psychophysiology*, **6**, 38–44.

Shnidman, S. R. (1970). Instrumental conditioning of orienting responses using positive reinforcement. *Journal of Experimental Psychology*, **83**, 491–494.

Shnidman, S. R., and Shapiro, D. (1971). Instrumental modification of elicited autonomic responses. *Psychophysiology*, **7**, 395–401.

Sirota, A. D., Schwartz, G. E., and Shapiro, D. (1974). Voluntary control of human heart rate: effect on reaction to aversive stimulation. *Journal of Abnormal Psychology*, **83**, 261–267.

Sirota, A. D., Schwartz, E. E., and Shapiro, D. (1976). Voluntary control of human heart rate: Effect on reaction to aversive stimulation: a replication and extension. *Journal of Abnormal Psychology*, **85**, 473–477.

Sirota, A. D., Shapiro, D., and Schwartz, G. E. (1977). Heart rate feedback and instructional effects on subjective reaction to aversive stimuli. *Psychophysiology*, **14**, (abstract).

Stern, R. M., Botto, R. W., and Herrick, C. D. (1972). Behavioral and physiological effects of false heart rate feedback: a replication and extension. *Psychophysiology*, **9**, 21–29.

Stoyva, J. (1977). Why should muscular relaxation be clinically useful? Some data and 2 1/2 models. In J. Beatty, and H. Legewie, (eds.), *Biofeedback and Behavior*. New York: Plenum Press.

Stoyva, J., and Budzynski, T. (1974). Cultivated low arousal—an antistress response?

In L. V. DiCara (ed.), *Limbic and Autonomic Nervous System Research*. New York: Plenum Press.

Sushinsky, L., and Bootzin, R. (1970). Cognitive desensitization as a model of systematic desensitization. *Behaviour Research and Therapy*, **8**, 29–34.

Valins, S. (1966). Cognitive effects of false heart-rate feedback. *Journal of Personality and Social Psychology*, **4**, 400–408.

Valins, S. (1970). The perception and labeling of bodily changes as determinants of emotional behavior. In A. H. Black (ed.), *Physiological Correlates of Emotion*. New York: Academic Press.

Valins, S., and Ray, A. A. (1967). Effects of cognitive desensitization on avoidance behavior. *Journal of Personality and Social Psychology*, **7**, 345–350..

Wickramasekera, I. (1972a). Electromyographic feedback training and tension headache: preliminary observations. *The American Journal of Clinical Hypnosis*, **15**, 83–85.

Wickramasekera, I. (1972b). Instructions and EMG feedback in systematic desensitization: a case report. *Behavior Therapy*, **3**, 460–465.

Wickramasekera, I. (1973). The application of verbal instructions and EMG feedback training to the management of tension headache—preliminary observations. *Headache*, **13**, 74–76.

Foundations of Psychosomatics
Edited by M. J. Christie and P. G. Mellett
© 1981 John Wiley & Sons Ltd.

10

'FIELD STUDIES': EMOTION AND β-BLOCKADE

MALCOLM CARRUTHERS

Clinical Laboratories, The Maudsley Hospital, London.

'Stress' is a very loose and unsatisfactory term to put forward as a cause of disease, because modern medicine has become very scientific, probably to the detriment of the art of medicine, and demands quantitive rather than qualitative data in support of any theory. However, the position is changing rapidly as it becomes possible to quantitate the physiological and biochemical effects of stress. Now that there are ways of putting a glamorous statistical wig on a few bald facts, stress-related theories are becoming more attractive and more acceptable.

As monitoring techniques get more portable, and field studies more practicable, it is easier to get away from the highly artificial laboratory situation and investigate the influence of factors in everyday life, under natural and realistic conditions. Nearly all laboratory experiments tend to be anxiety-provoking, and so the more positive responses of anger, enjoyment, or total absorption with the situation are rarely present. Yet these may be the very emotions that cause or prevent disease.

A further factor which is making stress-related theories of disease more acceptable is the increasing use of what could be regarded as 'stress-blocking' drugs, the beta-blockers. These compounds have chemical structures similar to the catecholamines, adrenaline and noradrenaline, and act by competitive inhibition of β-adrenergic nerve endings throughout the sympathetic division of the autonomic nervous system. This ability to produce a safe and easily reversible pharmacological sympathectomy makes them useful research tools for investigating the influence of emotion on the autonomic nervous system. They also have become the most commonly used drugs for the clinical treatment of a wide range of disorders such as coronary heart disease and 'essential' hypertension. This increases the acceptability of the idea that emotion may play an important part in initiating, or at least promoting, such disorders, and emphasizing their psychosomatic elements.

PHYSIOLOGICAL MEASURES

Procedures for measuring electrophysiological variables have been miniaturized and are now available in the form of compact, portable machines such as the 'Medilog' 4–24 recorder (Oxford Instruments). This portable physiological laboratory can record the electrocardiogram (ECG), blood pressure, body temperature, and electroencephalogram (EEG) for 24-hour periods in fully ambulant subjects, in their normal work situation (Carruthers et al., 1978). The recorder was initially used to study the ECG changes in pilots and passengers during the 20-hour flight from Buenos Aires to London (Carruthers, Argüelles, and Mosovich, 1976).

It must not be forgotten, however that the measurements themselves represent the end-result of many conflicting influences rather than absolute values. Pulse-rate, for example, is increased by adrenaline, reflexly decreased by noradrenaline, and further slowed by the parasympathetic nervous system.

Though most ECG studies concentrate on changes related to sympathetic activity, evidence of parasympathetic activity can also be obtained. One of the little-known effects of watching violence on films and television is its vagotonicity. This was seen in groups of people watching the film 'Clockwork Orange' (Carruthers and Taggart, 1973) where the more violent episodes caused a marked slowing of the heart despite the high level of sympathetic activity indicated by the increased catecholamine excretion. Also there was an increase in the sinus arrythmia effect or 'SA gap', which is the difference between the maximum heart-rate on inspiration and minimum heart-rate on expiration. This variability of heart-rate can now be analysed by computer (Mobbs, David and Thomas, 1971) from Medilog recordings, and adds another physiological measure to our ambulatory armamentarium.

Biochemical measures

Colorimetric chemical methods were used by Cannon (1929) to demonstrate glycosuria in medical students after they had watched an exciting football match, and also to measure rises in blood sugar in experimental animals stimulated with 'adrenin'. Newer methods are now available which enable glucose, cholesterol, and triglycerides to be measured in capillary samples of blood. It was the theory of the general adaptation syndrome, propounded by Selye (1936). however, which benefited most from investigation made possible by new methods of chemical analysis; these methods enabled investigators to detect increases in urinary oxogenic steroids during major illnesses or after operations. The corticosteroid response to emotional stress, on the other hand, was more variable, and people therefore began to wonder how general Selye's adaptation syndrome really was, and research into closer examination of the biochemical correlates of emotion was stimulated.

By distinguishing between the physiological and biochemical actions of adrenaline and those of noradrenaline, and by devising more sophisticated methods for their differential biochemical estimation, it becomes possible to develop more detailed theories capable of explaining responses to emotion. Funkenstein (1956) put forward an hypothesis that noradrenaline release would be specifically associated with an aggressive emotional state. Although originally largely conjectural, this hypothesis has since been backed by a considerable body of evidence of which the studies described are only a part.

Elmadjian, Hope, and Lanson (1957), who studied the behaviour of the urinary catecholamines in a wide variety of active and passive participants in sports, as well as in neuropsychiatric patients undergoing psychotherapy, concluded that active aggressive emotional displays were related to increased excretion of noradrenaline in association with normal excretion of adrenaline. Frankenhäuser's (1971) review of her own and related work emphasizes that the individual's psychoendocrine response to emotional stress is considerably modified by psychosocial and dispositional factors. Her researches in general confirmed that situations characterized by uncertainty and unpredictability produced an adrenaline response which diminished as uncertainty decreased. By contrast, noradrenaline release remained at an elevated level throughout the period during which the subject was engaged in attention-demanding activity.

Other workers in Sweden such as Carlson, Levi, and Orö (1972) and Levi (1975) have studied the effects of a wide variety of psychological stimuli on physiological and biochemical reactions in healthy human volunteers. The experimental settings included simulated industrial and office work, actual working situations in various occupations, public appearances, the viewing of films, simulated flight, action under simulated ground-combat conditions, prolonged confinement in experimental shelters, and control conditions of relaxation and rest.

These extensive studies were all based on urinary catecholamine excretion rates. Since, however, it is unlikely that unconjugated adrenaline and noradrenaline are excreted in the urine in amounts directly proportional to their rate of secretion by the sympathetic nervous system, and since it was desirable to relate transient lipid patterns and ECG changes to the catecholamime levels prevailing in the internal environment at a given moment in time, there were obvious advantages to be derived from measuring the plasma catecholamines. To carry out these measurements, fluorimetric methods up to a thousand times more sensitive than colorimetric procedures had to be used and difficulties in sample preservation had to be overcome.

EMOTION

Aggression

To illustrate the suggested chain of biochemical events which occur when aggression is the predominant emotion (Figure 10.1), the stress reactions of racing drivers, traffic drivers, and public speakers were studied. Modification of these responses by β-blockade was also investigated in these groups, both to provide additional evidence for this theory and to explore a potential remedy for some of its effects.

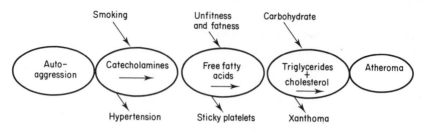

FIGURE 10.1. Suggested chain of events causing atheroma

Racing drivers

In 1967 Dr Peter Taggart, himself an international-class racing driver, reported the preliminary results of radio-electrocardiographic studies made on the drivers in competitive circuit races (Taggart and Gibbons, 1967). Three healthy, experienced racing drivers showed, during these events, an increase in the heart-rate to between 190 and 205 beats per minute (bpm). The rate was 150–180 bpm in the 15 minutes before the race, and at the signal indicating 2 minutes before the start a rate in excess of 180 was usual. This increased up to 200–205 at the start, and was usually maintained near this level throughout the event.

As well as suggesting an extremely high level of sympathetic activity, extension of these (Taggart, Gibbons, and Somerville, 1969) and other studies (Frost, Dryer, and Kohlstadt 1951; Walker, Collins, and McTaggart, 1969) indicated that racing driving might be the ideal test-bed for investigating acute aggressive emotion. Dr Taggart also observed, during these earlier studies, that the drivers' plasma samples, although clear before the race, often became markedly lipaemic after it. As the majority of drivers voluntarily fast for several hours, or even overnight, before racing, it appeared probable that the lipaemia resulted from increased synthesis of endogenous triglyceride induced by the emotional stress of racing driving. The catecholamine and lipid responses of a group of these drivers were therefore investigated to establish the biochemical mechanism giving rise to this secondary hyperlipidaemia.

One, two, or three plasma samples were taken from each of 16 drivers during the 3-hour period following a race. Two drivers were studied repeatedly throughout the season. The majority of events were of international status, taking place in England, Germany, Italy, Spain, and Belgium. The remainder were Club events and the drivers had the appropriate range of experience and ability. Their ages ranged from 22 to 39; all were apparently healthy and of average build.

Blood (20 ml) was drawn rapidly from an antecubital vein—with the driver still seated in his car for the immediately pre-race or post-race samples, or while he was seated in some convenient situation such as the first-aid post for the later samples.

All drivers had been fasting and abstained from alcohol. The biochemical methods of measuring plasma catecholamines (Carruthers *et al.*, 1970) and free fatty acids (Carruthers and Young, 1973) have been reported elsewhere, and the ECG methods were those of Taggart, Carruthers, and Somerville, 1973.

The results are shown in Figure 10.2. As would be expected from the stresses involved in these intensely competitive events, total catecholamine levels were greatly raised at the time of the race although, in the samples taken after 15 minutes, considerably lower values were obtained. The high levels were almost entirely due to noradrenaline, although there was also some elevation of adrenaline.

Free fatty acid (FFA) levels were high both before and immediately after the race. Samples taken after 1 hour or later showed lower values approaching normal resting levels. Triglyceride levels were slightly raised immediately after

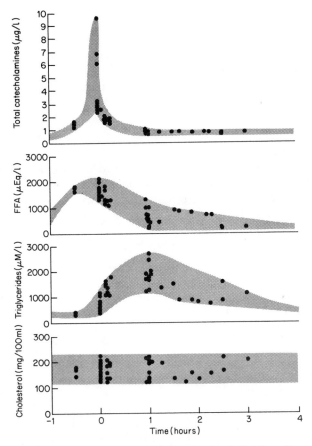

FIGURE 10.2. Racing drivers: plasma catecholamines, free fatty acid, triglyceride, and cholesterol levels before and at varying intervals after the end of races. They are plotted against a common time axis, demonstrating their temporal interrelationships. The ranges of each are represented by the shaded areas

the race, peak values being obtained after 1 hour. Cholesterol levels did not alter through the period studied.

Although a great deal of important work has already been done on stress-induced hyperlipidaemia (Carlson *et al.*, 1972), the emotional factor usually receives scantly attention when the types of hyper-lipidaemia thought to be associated with atherosclerosis are considered. The study indicated, however, that a maximal lipid response may be triggered by relatively low plasma catecholamine levels. It has been shown since (Taggart and Carruthers, 1972) that β-blockade can lessen the tachycardia, and prevent rises in lipids and glucose in this extremely stressful situation. Studies such as these may have relevance for town driving, and for the everyday experience of a more general population.

Traffic drivers

Eight drivers, six of whom were members of the Institute of Advanced Motorists, were studied on a total of twelve occasions. In view of the extensive ECG studies previously performed by Taggart and Gibbons (1968), Taggart *et al.* (1969), and by Bellet *et al.* (1968), it was decided not to include this method of investigation in these tests.

After fasting overnight, the subject was bled at home and the plasma samples separated. He then drove his own car through morning rush-hour traffic of approximately similar density for $\frac{1}{2}$ hour. Immediately after pulling up, while the subject was still in the driving seat, a further blood sample was taken for lipid and catecholamine analysis. These results are shown in Figure 10.3.

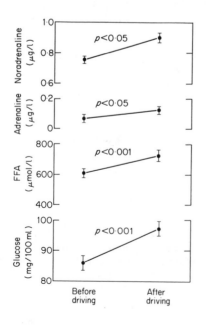

FIGURE 10.3. Traffic drivers: plasma catecholamines, free fatty acid, and glucose levels before and after a $\frac{1}{2}$-hour drive in traffic

From the limited number of drivers tested, it appears that the metabolic results of driving in traffic are similar in type, if not in scale, to those seen in racing drivers. The rise in noradrenaline previously reported in studed in studies carried out on urine by Bellet, Roman, and Kostis (1969) tends to confirm the impression frequently voiced by psychologists that motoring brings out the aggressive element in man's nature.

Public speakers

Many of our readers will have personal experience of the stress of public speaking. The most common sequence of sensations experienced by a speaker is a steady increase in anxiety for some minutes or even hours before speaking. In the more nervous it may be accompanied by palpitations and dryness of the lips and mouth, leading to hoarseness, and only partially relieved by the water traditionally provided for this purpose. Fear that the speaker, as well as his buccal secretions, will 'dry up' is the main dread of those unaccustomed to public speaking, and even of some of those that are.

Therefore, depending upon the personality of the speaker, his experience, the subject of the talk, and the likely or actual reaction of the audience, this situation represents a challenge of variable intensity. To stand up to speak requires a determined effort for the majority of people, although if the talk proceeds well a certain degree of elation may ensue, as he 'makes his points' at the expense of his mute, seated, captive audience. As in many other situations, a mood of anxiety and uncertainty is often succeeded by one of defiance and even anger if he is interrupted during the talk, or he feels his views are not being well received. It is the combination of aggression and anxiety, exprienced by many people in the groups most at risk from coronary heart disease, which suggested this topic for investigation as being more representative of the type of emotional stress present in modern urban life.

A wide range of speakers addressing audiences of greatly differing sizes was studied. These included medical students and housemen giving factual case histories to small groups of their colleagues, experienced lecturers talking to more critical audiences of up to several hundred people, and television performers appearing 'live' before an estimated ten million viewers.

Of the 30 subjects, seven had suffered myocardial infarcts 6 months to 10 years previously. To investigate the potential benefit of β-blockade under these conditions, 15 of the subjects, including all the post-infraction cases, were given a variable single oral dose of oxprenolol (Trasicor) $\frac{1}{2}-1$ before speaking. Continuous ECG recordings were obtained before, during, and after the speeches. In the majority of cases the C and M radio-electrocardiograph, linked to a UHER tape recorder, as in the racing-driver study, was used for this purpose. Later in the study the less fallible and cumbersome Vingmed 'Recard' system was used. Except for the subjects on television, who made it one of the features of their programme, the subjects were not allowed to reveal that they were being monitored lest the confession should alter their responses. Similarly, the pre- and post-speech blood samples were taken in another room without the knowledge of the audience.

The reactions of the individual subjects, regardless of experience, were found to be so varied that only those of the blocked and unblocked groups will be considered separately. The mean maximum heart-rate in the normal unblocked subjects was 151 bpm (range 125–180), usually reaching a peak within a few seconds of the start of the speech and being maintained at only a slightly lower level for most of its duration. The rapidity of this response was clearly seen in the television reporters, whose heart-rates were being recorded on cardiotachometers attached to the oscilloscopes displaying their electrocardiograms. Transient peaks were reached within 10–15 seconds of the television camera 'cutting' to them. Although considerable variation of heart-rate occurred due to sinus arrhythmia this initial marked acceleration often occurred during the rapid inspiration preceding an opening sentence, and was not repeated in the succeeding slow breaths accompanying speaking. Rates of up to 180 bpm were also reached by many of the 15 speakers when they were on placebo tablets, the mean maximum being 140 (standard error 4.29), and ectopic beats were observed in a few cases. However, in those subjects in whom they did occur they tended to be prolific and often multifocal. Additional evidence of high levels of circulating adrenaline was provided even in the healthy subjects by the characteristic sloping ST–depression referred to in the section on anxiety, as in the J–E wave (Taggart, Carruthers, and Somerville, 1973). In six out of seven post-coronary subjects ischaemic-like changes appeared on the ECG while they were speaking, and one of these experienced angina. Such changes were present in three of these before speaking, but in six subjects the ST configuration worsened during their talk.

After taking an average of 20 mg of the β-blocking drug, the mean maximum heart-rate was 82 (standard error 2.80) ($p < 0.001$) and no ectopic beats were seen. None of the post-coronary group showed any worsening in relation to their resting pre-speech ECG, or developed angina while speaking, after taking these small single doses of β-blockers. The biochemical results are shown in Figure 10.4

Public speaking appeared to be a moderately intense emotional stress for most people, although this was seldom evident from their calm exterior. Although anxiety was the predominant emotion leading up to the event, this merged with a more confident aggressive mood as the talk progressed. The biochemical changes accompanying this mood-swing were a slight decrease in adrenaline accompanied by an increase in noradrenaline. This was reflected in the electrocardiographic changes which were similar to those described by Lepeschkin *et al.* (1960) during infusions of both amines in healthy subjects. The thermogenic action of noradrenaline in promoting the release and oxidation of FFAs may explain the description of a heated argument (Carruthers, Taggart, and Somerville, 1973). This study confirms the marked techycardia reported by Ira, Whalen, and Bogdonoff (1963) as occurring even in experienced medical speakers.

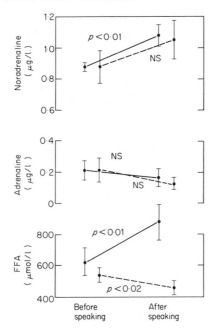

FIGURE 10.4. Public speakers: plasma catecholamines and free fatty acids in 15 subjects before and after speaking when taking placebo tablets (———) and oxprenolol (------)

The effectiveness of β-blocking drugs in preventing the electrocardiographic changes due to adrenaline (Suzman, 1971; Jackson, 1971), and the increases in FFAs and triglycerides brought about by noradrenaline, were just as marked as in what, for some people, is an everyday situation, as they had been in racing-drivers. Several of the speakers noticed a lessening of the apprehension they normally experienced before the event, when taking the drug. This may have been due to interruption of the self-perpetuating action of anxiety, postulated by Breggin (1964), as was demonstrated in stutterers taking diazepam (Leanderson and Levi, 1966). In no case was there any perceptible impairment of performance, and in some more anxious individuals it may even have been improved in that they felt and appeared less flustered and spoke more slowly and distinctly. It could be claimed that β-blockers can pace both the heart and the speech.

Anxiety

In many respects the effects of anxiety are both more distressing and more obvious than those of aggression. Anxiety and associated uncertainty often precede almost any form of emotional stress, and the symptomatology of 'panic in the breast', pallor, perspiration, pilo-erection, and pupillary and palpebral dilatation are more dramatic than the slight flush of anger. The extract of the adrenal medulla, known as 'adrenin' (Cannon, 1929), with which most of the early studies on the biochemistry of stress were carried out, is likely to have contained considerably more adrenaline than noradrenaline, both because of its greater stability and its higher concentration in the gland.

Thus the adrenaline : noradrenaline ratio in the peparation originally available was 4 : 1, about the same as in the human adrenal gland. Further, the tachycardia and glycosuria which adrenaline causes were more easily demonstrated than the increases in blood pressure and plasma lipids produced by noradrenaline, so that the former became the hallmarks of sympathetic action.

Only with the isolation of the two hormonal components of adrenin, and the development of methods for their separate estimation, did the biochemical differentiation of anxiety from aggression become possible. Even then the situation investigated tended to be of mixed emotional content rather than one of pure anxiety, and increases in the rate of secretion of both adrenaline and noradrenaline were reported. Also, the studies were mainly based on urinary catecholamine measurements over periods of an hour or more, during which time the subject could have undergone several changes of mood. It therefore appeared that the biochemical changes associated with anxiety could best be characterized from plasma samples taken during periods of acute anxiety, as occurred in parachute-jumping and rock-climbing, as well as in the previously reported studies on airline passengers (Carruthers, Taggart, and Somerville 1973) in subjects with dental phobia (Edmondson, Roscoe, and Vickers, 1972) and those reacting normally to dental procedures (Taggart, 1976).

Parachutists

Twenty-five young healthy parachutists were studied during a total of 30 jumps. Their degree of experience varied widely from the inexperienced doing their first jump (A) and moderately experienced 'free-fallers' (B) to the Parachute Regiment's 'Nomad' sky-diving team (C). All the subjects were fasting before dives, which was found to be no great hardship, particularly for the inexperienced group. Plasma samples were taken in eight cases immediately prior to the ascent. Using the 'Recard' system, ECG recordings were obtained with the subject in several different positions, including prone and while hanging upright in a training harness, to allow for postural variations during the descent. The subject then switched the ECG recorder on approximately 5 minutes before jumping and left it on during the descent, landing, and for several minutes afterwards to obtain a full record and 'recovery' tracing.

A further blood sample was taken as soon as the subject could be reached, which was usually within a minute for the more accurate experienced parachutists, but was sometimes up to 2 or 3 minutes if the less experienced fell wide of the mark. Samples were separated immediately using a centrifuge powered by a portable generator and placed in vacuum jars containing solid carbon dioxide or water–ice as appropriate.

The major interest of this study lay in the ECG rather than the biochemical changes. The most marked feature of the tracings was the extremely high heart-rate, commonly in the region of between 180 and 200 bpm. This usually returned to normal within 2 minutes of landing, demonstrating the rapidity of decay of adrenaline and the difficulties of obtaining a truly representative plasma sample. The most rapid deceleration of heart-rate, from 200 to 50 bpm within a minute, was seen in one subject who fractured his ankle on landing.

In addition, in the majority of subjects the recordings taken before and after the descents showed the characteristic ST–T depression which, together with the transitional stages of the J–E waves, is suggestive of the action of high circulating adrenaline levels on the heart (Taggart et al., 1973). These changes were not present when the same subjects exercised to a similar heart-rate, and were therefore unlikely to be produced by the tachycardia alone. They can be prevented by giving ß-blocking drugs (Jackson, 1971), aiding the important differentiation to be made between anxiety and cardiac ischaemia. The biochemical results showed large rises in adrenaline and glucose (Figure 10.5) with no change in lipid levels.

One of the major practical and ethical problems in the investigation of anxiety in healthy volunteers is the means of inducing a sufficiently intense response to produce clearly-defined changes in the variables being measured within a safe

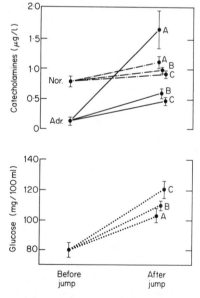

FIGURE 10.5. Parachutists: plasma catecholamines and glucose levels before and after jumping in nine inexperienced (A), twelve moderately experienced (B), and five experienced (C) parachutists

and acceptable experimental design. At the same time, as far as possible, other emotions such as anger and aversion, together with physical exertion, have to be excluded. For these reasons the extreme situation of parachute-jumping provides an ideal setting for the study of intense anxiety in a fairly pure form associated with little physical exertion.

In previous studies, von Euler and Lundberg (1954) demonstrated increased urinary adrenaline, and Basowitz et al. (1955) showed impaired performance of psychological tests in men undergoing parachute training. Increases in heart-rate up to 180 bpm during parachute descents were reported by Shane and Slinde (1968), but the radio-electrocardiographic tracings were not suitable for demonstrating the marked ST depression and other changes seen in this study. As would be expected, the transitory rise in plasma adrenaline, even when measured after a few minutes' delay, is proportionally greater than that measured in urine, which represents the average secretion rate over an extended period of time. As suggested by Frankenhäuser's (1971) work, the adrenaline response decreased with increased parachuting experience. The poor correlations between adrenaline levels and rises in blood sugar and heart-rate again emphasized the individuality of sympathetic responses.

Climbers

Eleven male climbers whose mean age was 31 years (range 22–48) were studied while scaling the limestone escarpment known as Bowles Rocks near Tunbridge Wells. Although not of great height the ascents were reasonably anxiety-provoking, even for these experienced climbers using ropes, because of the steepness of the rock face which had been recently moistened and made slippery by rain. On a single-blind basis, the fasting subjects were given placebo tablets an hour before their first climb, and 40 mg of oxprenolol an hour before the second. Blood samples were taken before the climb and within a minute of finishing. The ECG was continuously recorded throughout the climb by means of the 'Recard' tape-recorder system. Each climb lasted about 15 minutes and consisted of several ascents, descents, and traverses.

With oxprenolol the maximum heart-rate during the climb decreased from a mean of 166 bpm to a mean level of 120 bpm. Alterations in the configuration of the ST segment, similar to those observed in the parachutists, were abolished by this β-blocking compound. The drug also halved the rise in plasma adrenaline. No change was found in plasma noradrenaline, suggesting that the physical exertion involved was one of mild intensity and that most of the increase in heart-rate was due to the anxiety induced by the climb.

No change in FFAs, triglycerides, or glucose was observed in either group, although a slight increase in cholesterol occurred in the unblocked climbers, as in other exercising groups described elsewhere (Carruthers and Murray, 1976). No change of mood or agility was noticed in those taking oxprenolol.

The reduction in pulse-rate produced by β-blockade in this situation was not as marked as that occurring under conditions of intense emotion associated with little exertion, like racing-drivers (mean decrease 169 to 102 bpm) and public speakers (140 to 82 bpm). This supports previous claims that tachycardia due to emotional stress is predominantly mediated by β-receptors and hence is suppressed by β-blocking compounds, while that due to physical exertion mainly results from other physiological effects and is consequently less affected (Imhof and Brunner, 1970). Using the same oral dose of oxprenolol, Imhof and Brunner obtained closely similar results in ski-jumpers. The tachycardia associated with the ascent to the starting platform was reduced from 130 to 115 bpm, while the maximum heart-rate, which occurred 15 seconds after landing, was reduced from 150 to 100 bpm.

In the biochemical characterization of anxiety, three main approaches have previously been used (Breggin, 1964). First, comparisons were made between both the physiological and psychological responses to injected adrenaline and noradrenaline in healthy subjects and patients with a variety of mental disorders. In 1919 Tompkins, Sturgis, and Weam showed that the impure adrenal extract could cause anxiety in previously conditioned or 'neurotic' subjects. Since then a large number of studies, using the pure hormones, has demonstrated that the ability of physiological doses of adrenaline to provoke the signs and symptoms of anxiety is heavily dependent on environmental cues and the previous conditioning of the subject. It was also found that while small intermittent dose of adrenaline produced the sympathetic effects of 'arousal' in healthy subjects, large sustained dosage produced parasympathomimetic effects of 'fatigue', especially in neurotic subjects, possibly through a feedback action of adrenaline on the hypothalamic trophotropic functions (Rothballer, 1959). Thus even more than most drugs, adrenaline actions appear to be dependent on the dosage, on the subject, and on conditions of administration.

A second group of experiments involves the measurement of urinary catecholamine excretion, together with other physiological parameters in normal subjects, and patients with neuroses, anxiety states, or paranoia. In general the findings in these studies agree with those reported by Funkenstein (1956) of increased adrenaline excretion in anxious, depressed patients, and increased noradrenaline excretion in angry, paranoid patients.

The third group of experiments involves the investigation of subjects experiencing anxiety-provoking situations. The wide variety of situations studied is indicated by the reviews of Martin (1961) and Levi (1969). In general they support the early work done by Ax (1953). Within a contrived laboratory situation, he demonstrated that the physiological response to anxiety was similar to that of injected adrenaline, while with anger the response more closely resembled that produced by noradrenaline and adrenaline together, with the former hormone predominating. There were higher intercorrelations in the physiological variables studied in anger, indicating greater physiological integration. Conversely, between-subject variance was greater than within-subject variance, especially in anxiety, suggesting 'uniqueness in physiological expression of emotion'. Although the majority of studies of urinary catecholamines in these two types of emotional stress support this physiological evidence

(Levi, 1969), they also reflect a similar high degree of individuality in biochemical responses in different people.

The studies reported here reinforce the association between the emotion of anxiety, the secretion of adrenaline, and the consequent rise in pulse-rate and plasma glucose. They also suggest that the increase in plasma adrenaline, up to 10 times greater than that of the tranquil person, may form a chemical basis for the suggestion made by James in 1890 that anxiety symptoms can reinforce anxiety.

Thus the acute anxiety reaction could be self-perpetuating, a spiralling sequence of anxiety, adrenaline secretion, and learned sympathomimetic symptoms perpetuating the anxiety. An important action of β-blocking compounds in relieving anxiety might be to interrupt the cycle. Such a mechanism would explain the beneficial effects obtained with a low dosage of β-blocking drugs in anxiety states (Turner et al., 1965; Granville-Grossman and Turner, 1966) and in cardiac disorders related to anxiety (Besterman and Friedlander, 1965). This is consistent with the lesser increase and smaller rises in adrenaline secretion seen in the blocked airline passengers and climbers. It contrasts with the failure of sedatives such as diazepam to reduce adrenaline levels or heart-rate in phobic dental patients (Edmondson et al., 1972) or of amytal to decrease the sinus tachycardia of patients with anxiety states (Turner et al., 1965). For these reasons, as well as their lack of side-effects such as depression and impairment of concentration, β-blocking drugs may be more beneficial than sedatives in the treatment of anxiety.

The absence of effects on plasma noradrenaline or lipid levels in situations evoking only anxiety, shown in these and previous studies of dentistry (Edmondson and Roscoe, 1972) and of airline passengers (Carruthers, Taggart, and Somerville, 1973). suggests that anxiety is unlikely to be the form of emotional stress implicated in the long-term causation of atheromatous arterial disease. This coincides with the clinical finding (Friedman and Rosenman, 1959) that it is usually not the anxious 'always-ill' people who suffer most from coronary thrombosis, but the aggressive, tough, driving, high-denial, never-ill ones.

Lastly this chapter speculates on possible abnormalities of autonomic state and their relevance for development of organic dysfunction.

EFFECTS OF AUTONOMIC IMBALANCE

Disturbances of autonomic balance in response to stress play a part in all psychosomatic disorders. Their influence is most clearly seen in relation to what has been called the 'Western Way of Death' (Carruthers, 1974)—cardiovascular disease. According to this view the acceleration of the normal deterioration with age of many cardiovascular functions is caused by excessive or unbalanced sympathetic activity, giving rise to a range of what could be termed 'hypercatabolic diseases'. Patients with cardiovascular disease show evidence of increased sympathetic activity and decreased parasympathetic activity. There is often evidence of a hyperkinetic circulation with raised pulse-rate and blood pressure. This is usually associated with increased production, which is often stress-related, of hormones having a predominantly catabolic action such as catecholamines and corticosteroids. These have wide-ranging effects on lipid and carbohydrate metabolism, with repercussions throughout the cardio-vascular system.

These patients also show signs of a decrease in parasympathetic activity and corresponding reduction in hormones having mainly anabolic effects, particularly testosterone and insulin. Male patients with early atherosclerosis have shown reduced testosterone production, as have subjects with overt coronary disease. The latter also have high oestradiol levels. Patients with undescended testicles, whether operated on or not, are at risk from decreased testosterone production and those with operations for inguinal hernia may suffer damage to hormone production by both testes even though only one side is subject to surgical assault. By far the greater number of male patients with advanced cardiovas-cular disease have reduced penile erection or are impotent. This often follows psychogenic trauma, and a variety of different forms of stress—including even aircraft noise—have been shown to reduce testosterone production (Argüelles et al., 1978).

Contrary to what was expected from the low incidence of coronary disease in pre-menopausal women, administration of oestrogens to either sex can predispose to venous or arterial thrombosis. Oestradiol itself can cause ST-depression on the ECG.

What can be regarded as replacement therapy, by giving anabolic steroids to patients with advanced circulatory disease, can have a 'parasympathomimetic' action which reverses many of the associated physiological and biochemical changes. The patients show reduced pulse-rates and blood pressure, though this

TABLE 10.1. Autonomic factors in cardiovascular disease

	Sympathetic dominance	Parasympathetic dominance
Promoting factors	Stress (emotional, physical, thermal) Surgery Smoking	Physical training Mental training (autogenic training and yoga) Sleep Anabolic
Metabolic effects	Catabolic	Increased
Testosterone and Insulin	Decreased	Increased
Fibrinolytic activity	Decreased	
Catecholamines and Corticosteroids	Increased	Decreased Decreased
Lipids, glucose + uric acid	Increased	Decreased
Heart-rate + blood pressure	Increased	
Signs and symptoms of tissue hypoxia (e.g. angina, limb pain, ST–T depression)	Increased	Decreased

may also be contributed to by the increased physical activity which is encouraged. As well as the decrease in symptoms and signs of tissue hypoxia, fibrinolytic activity and carbohydrate tolerance are increased. Insulin requirements in diabetes fall, and non-diabetics may also experience hypoglycaemic episodes. Sympathetic predominance is seen in its most severe and acute form following major surgery (Carruthers *et al.*, 1974). There is intense catabolic activity with a negative nitrogen balance and increased ACTH, catecholamines, and corticosteroids, which often continues for 1–2 weeks after surgery. During this period there is also evidence of decreased parasympathetic activity, with reduction in testosterone and insulin levels, and impaired glucose tolerance and fibrinolytic activity. These changes are remarkably similar to those seen in cardiovascular disease, so it is not surprising that arterial and venous thromboses are some of the most common complications in the postoperative period.

What makes us stress-seekers

Hans Selye has described mankind's lemming-like search for stimulating situations, which can often be emotionally or physically damaging, as earning us the title of 'stress-seekers'. The field studies described in this chapter suggest a chemical reason for this. There are several reasons for considering noradrenaline to be the final common pathway to pleasure in many situations, including smoking. Neurophysiological experiments have shown noradrenaline release at pleasure centres' in the brain, particularly the hypothalamic region, in response to both electrical 'self-stimulation' (Wise and Stein, 1969) and to nicotine (Hall and Turner, 1972). As noradrenaline cross the blood–brain barrier, and adrenaline to a very limited extent, it is suggested that the peripheral release of noradrenaline from sympathetic post-ganglionic fibres and the adrenal medullae is associated with noradrenaline release in the brain. The extent to which this correlation holds is likely to vary from species to species, and further modification of the hypothesis derived from Stein's work on rats may be needed. Increased noradrenaline levels in plasma or urine have been described here and elsewhere in such physically inactive, but stimulating, events as racing driving, public speaking, exposure to cold (Carruthers *et al.*, 1974), watching exciting films (Fröberg, *et al.*, 1971) and drinking coffee (Levi, 1967). It is perhaps not entirely coincidental that cigarette advertising and sponsorship often tend to associate the pleasure of smoking with such events.

This viewpoint thus underlines the many ways in which men's Stone Age physiological and biochemical responses to emotion have become inappropriate in his Space Age setting, and can pave the way to psychosomatic diseases.

REFERENCES

Argüelles, A. E., Volmer, M. C., Hidalgo, H. E., and Cassini, J. H. (1978). *Plasmatic testosterone and cortisol levels in male workers chronically exposed to airplane turbine noise*. Proceedings of 16th International Congress of Aerospace Medicine, London.

Ax, A. F. (1953) The physiological differentiation between fear and anger in humans. *Psychosomatic Medicine*, 15, 433.

Basowitz, H., Persky, H., Korchine, S. J., and Grinker, R. (1955). *Anxiety and Stress*. New York: McGraw-Hill.

Bellet, S., Roman, L., Kostis, J., and Slater A. (1968) Continuous electrocardiographic monitoring during automobile driving: studies in normal subjects and patients with coronary disease. *American Journal of Cardiology*, 22, 856–862.

Bellet, S., Roman, L., and Kostis, J. (1969). The effects of automobile driving on catecholamine and adreno-cortical excretion. *American Journal of Cardiology*, 24, 365–358.

Besterman, E. M. M., and Friedlander, D. H. (1965). Clinical experiences with propranolol. *Postgraduate Medical Journal*, 41, 526.

Breggin, P. R. (1964). The psychophysiology of anxiety: with a review of the literature concerning adrenaline. *Journal of Nervous and Mental Disease*, 139, 558–568.

Cannon, W. B. (1929) *Bodily Changes in Pain, Hunger, Fear and Rage*, 2nd edn. New York: Appleton-Century-Crofts.

Carlson, L. A., Levi, L., and Oraö, L. (1972). Stressor induced changes in plasma lipids and urinary excretion of catecholamines and their modification by nicotinic acid. *Acta Medica Scandinavica*, 191, (Supplement 528), 91.

Carruthers, M. E. (1974). *The Western Way of Death*. London: Davis Poynter

Carruthers, M., Argüelles, A., and Mosovich, A. (1976). Man in transit: biochemical and physiological changes during intercontinental flights. *Lancet*, 1, 977–981.

Carruthers, M., Cooke, E., and Frewin, P. (1978). Ambulatory monitoring of aircrew. *ISAM 1977: Proceedings of the Second International Symposium on Ambulatory Monitoring*. London: Academic Press.

Carruthers, M., and Murray A. (1976). *F/40: Fitness on 40 Minutes a Week*. London: Futura Books.

Carruthers, M., and Taggart, P. (1973). Vagotonicity of violence: biochemical and cardiac responses to violent films and television programmes. *British Medical Journal*, 3, 384–389.

Carruthers, M., Taggart, P., Conway, N., Bates, D., and Somerville W. (1970). Validity of plasma catecholamine estimations. *Lancet*, 2, 62–67.

Carruthers, N., Taggart, P., Salpekar, P. D., and Gatt, J. A. (1974). Some metabolic effects of beta-blockade on temperature regulation and in the presence of trauma. In W. Schweizer (ed.), *Beta Blockers—Present Status and Future Prospects*. Berne: Hans Huber.

Carruthers, M., Taggart, P., and Somerville, W. (1973). Some effects of beta blockade on the lipid response to certain acute emotions. In D. M. Burley, J. H. Frier, R. K. and Rondel, S. H. Taylor (eds.), *New Perspectives in Beta Blockade*. Horsham: CIBA Laboratories.

Carruthers, M., and Young, D. A. B. (1973). Free fatty acid estimation by a semi-automated fluorimetric method. *Clinica Chimica Acta*, 49, 341–348.

Edmondson, H. D., Roscoe, B., and Vickers, M. D. (1972). Biochemical evidence for anxiety in dental patients. *British Medical Journal*, 4, 7–9.

Elmadjian F. H., Hope, J., and Lamson, E. T. (1957). Excretion of epinephrine and norepinephrine in various emotional states. *Journal of Clinical Endocrinology*, 17, 608.

Euler, U. S. von, and Lundberg, U. (1954). Effect of flying on the epinephrine excretion in Air Force personnel. *Journal of Applied Physiology*, 6, 551–555.

Frankenhäuser, M. (1971). Experimental approaches to the study of human behaviour as related to neuroendocrine functions. In L. Levi (ed.), *Society, Stress and Disease* vol. 1: *The Psychosocial Environment and Psychosomatic Diseases*, pp. 22–35. (Proceedings of International Interdisciplinary Symposium, Stockholm, 1970). Oxford University Press.

Friedman, M., and Rosenman, R. H. (1959). Association of specific overt behaviour pattern with blood and cardiovascular findings. *Journal of the American Medical Association*, **169**, 1286.

Fröberg, J., Karlsson, C. G., Levi, L., and Lidberg, L. (1971). Physiological and biochemical stress reactions induced by psycho-social stimuli. In L. Levi (ed.), *Society, Stress and Disease* vol. 1: *The Psychosocial Environment and Psychosomatic Diseases*, pp. 280–295. (Proceedings of International Interdisciplinary Symposium, Stockholm, 1970). Oxford University Press.

Frost, J. W., Dryer, R. L., and Kohlstadt, K. G. (1951). Stress studies on auto race drivers. *Journal of Laboratory and Clinical Medicine*, **38**, 523–525.

Funkenstein, D. H. (1956). Norepinephrine-like and epinephrine-like substances in relation to human behaviour. *Journal of Nervous and Mental Diseases*, **124**, 58–65.

Granville-Grossman, K. L., and Turner, P. (1966). The effect of propranolol on anxiety. *Lancet*, **2**, 788.

Hall, G. H., and Turner, D. M. (1972). Effects of nicotine on the release of 3H-noradrenaline from the hypothalamus. *Biochemical Pharmacology*, **21**, 1829–1838.

Imhof, P., and Brunner, H. (1970). The treatment of functional heart disorders with beta-adrenergic blocking agents. *Postgraduate Medical Journal*, **46**, (Supplement 22), 96–99.

Ira, G. H. Jr., Whalen, R. E., and Bogdonoff, M. D. (1963). Heart rate changes in physicians during daily 'stressful' tasks. *Journal Psychosomatic Research*, **7**, 147–150.

Jackson, W. B. (1971). The use of propranolol in ECG diagnosis. *New Zealand Medical Journal*, **73**, 65–68.

James, W. (1890). *Principles of Psychology*. New York: Holt.

Leanderson, R., and Levi, L. (1966). A new approach to the experimental study of stuttering and stress. *Acta-Otolaryngologica Suppl.*, **224**, 311.

Lepeschkin, E., Marchet, H., Schroder, G., Wagner R. P., De Paul, S., and Raab, W. (1960). Effects of epinephrine and norepinephrine on the ECG of 100 normal subjects. *American Journal of Cardiology*, **5**, 594–603.

Levi, L. (1967). The effect of coffee on the function of the sympathomedullary system in man. *Acta Medica Scandinavica*, **181**, Fasc. 4.

Levi, L. (1969). Neuro-endocrinology of anxiety. *British Journal of Psychiatry*, Special Publication No. 3.

Levi, L. (1975). Parameters of emotion. In Levi (ed.), *Emotions, their Parameters and Measurement*, pp. 705–711. New York: Raven Press.

Martin, B. (1961). The assessment of anxiety by physiological behaviour measures. *Psychological Bulletin*, **53**, 234.

Mobbs, R. F., David, G. C., and Thomas, J. M. (1971). An evaluation of the use of heart rate irregularity as a measure of mental workload in the steel industry. *BISRA Open Report* OR/HF/25/71.

Rothballer, A. B. (1959). The effect of catecholamines on the central nervous system. *Pharmacological Reviews*, **11**, 494–547.

Selye, Hans (1936). A syndrome produced by diverse nocuous agents. *Nature (London)*, **138**, 32.

Shane, W. P., and Slinde, K. E. (1968). Continuous ECG recording during free-fall parachuting. *Aerospace Medicine*, **39**, 597–603.

Suzman, M. (1971). Effect of beta blockade on the anxiety of electrocardiogram. *Postgraduate Medical Journal*, **47** (Supplement 104).

Taggart, P., and Carruthers, M. (1972). Suppression by oxprenolol of adrenergic response to stress. *Lancet*, **2**, 256–258.

Taggart, P., Carruthers, M., and Somerville, W. (1973). Electrocardiogram, plasma catecholamines and lipids, and their modification by oxprenolol when speaking before an audience, *Lancet*, **2**, 341–346.

Taggart, P., and Gibbons, D. (1967). Motor car driving and the heart rate. *British Medical Journal*, **1**, 411–412.

Taggart, P., and Gibbons, D. (1968). Some cardiovascular responses to driving. *British Medical Journal*, **2**, 1043–1044.

Taggart, P., Gibbons, D., and Somerville, W. (1969). Some effects of motor car driving on the normal and abnormal heart. *British Medical Journal*, **4**, 130.

Taggart, P., Hedworth-Whitty, R., Carruthers, M., and Gordon, P. (1976). Observations on electrocardiogram and plasma catecholamines during dental procedures: the forgotten vagus. *British Medical Journal*, **2**, 787–789.

Tompkins, E. H., Sturgis, C. C., and Weam, J. T. (1919). Studies in epinephrine. II. *American Medical Association, Archives of Internal Medicine*, **24**, 247–253.

Turner, P., Granville-Grossman, K. L., and Smart, J. V. (1965). Effect of adrenergic receptor blockade on the tachycardia of thyrotoxicosis and anxiety state. *Lancet*, **2**, 1316.

Walker, J. L., Collins, V. P., and McTaggart, W. G. (1969). Measurement of sympathetic neuro-hormones in the plasma of racing-car drivers. *Aerospace Medicine*, **40**, 140–141.

Wise, C. D., and Stein, L. (1969). Facilitation of brain self-stimulation by central administration of norepinephrine, *Science*, **163**, 299–301.

SECTION 4

Individual Differences

Foundations of Psychosomatics
Edited by M. J. Christie and P. G. Mellett
© 1981 John Wiley & Sons Ltd.

11

AFTER THE EXECUTIVE MONKEY

EDWIN COOK
Department of Psychology, University of Wisconsin, U.S.A.

MARGARET J. CHRISTIE
School of Studies in Psychology, University of Bradford, England.

SONI GARTSHORE
Menninger Clinic, Topeka, U.S.A.

ROBERT M. STERN
The Pennsylvania State University, U.S.A.

and

PETER H. VENABLES
Department of Psychology, University of York, England.

As Weiss (1977) notes in his chapter on gastrointestinal lesions, one can now conclude, with a certainty founded on experimental evidence, that '. . .psychological factors play a major role in regulating gastric pathology'. The evidence gathered by Weiss comes from studies of laboratory animals exposed to such stressors as immobilization, unpredictable trauma, and conflicting motivations. Such manipulations may, however, seem remote from the psychological factors thought by Alexander and the Chicago Psychanalytic Institute (1950) to be relevant for the production of *human* ulcer. Only the common ground of conflicting motivation would appear to link the rat experiencing electric shock at the food box and the human subject with an unconscious desire to assert independence and self-sufficiency while simultaneously having dependency wishes to be loved and cared for like a helpless infant. Weiner (1977) has detailed the various problems associated with Alexander's model, which predicts that a predisposing independence/dependence conflict, when associated with a specific precipitating life event, results in increased gastric secretion and subsequent pathology. Weiner, himself associated with one of the few predictive studies of human subjects (Weiner *et al.*, 1957), notes that in recent years, investigation of gastrointestinal pathology has turned to examination of the mechanisms through which psychological states are translated into gastrointestinal response. One such investigation, which generated widespread interest when first reported, was that of Brady *et al.* (1958), working with rhesus monkeys. This study will provide the starting point for the chapter which, however, does *not* attempt comprehensively to review psychological aspects of gastric pathology; for those hoping for such a review we suggest Weiner (1977), a briefer treatment by

Ackerman and Weiner (1976), or Weiss (1977). The chapter has, as its more modest aim, the attempt to trace lines of research which had their origins in some aspect of the 'executive monkey' work by Brady and his colleagues. In tracing the two decades of investigation since their report we hope to demonstrate one of the fascinating aspects of research, namely the way in which a study, which may itself have apparent weaknesses and even resist replication, has *heuristic* value, serving to stimulate a range of subsequent studies through a number of years. We trace the progress of psychophysiological work with humans, noting first the development of a non-invasive method for monitoring gastrointestinal (g.i.) activity, then the broadening of interest beyond the area of g.i. activity, to more general aspects of autonomic response to the challenge of being the 'executive', or to the possible stressor of being the 'control'—who has no control. We look at individual differences in response to these roles, and look also at autonomic state after the end of the testing period, when a stressed system may, perhaps, exhibit its weakness in delayed homeostatic recovery, or by some apparently maladaptive change in state.

We return, then, to animal studies, to Weiss's work with rodents, one aspect of which has particular relevance for this chapter, namely his theoretical model which has value for explaining the original 'executive monkey' findings. First, however, we need to look briefly at those findings, before undertaking our ramble through two decades of subsequent investigations.

AVOIDANCE BEHAVIOUR AND THE DEVELOPMENT OF GASTRODUODENAL ULCERS IN THE 'EXECUTIVE MONKEY'

The work of Brady and his colleagues is by now probably familiar to all our readers, but needs summarizing in order to set the scene. An early paper (Brady *et al.*, 1958) reported that their interest in psychological factors and g.i. function had been stimulated by observations of g.i. lesions in some 15 experimental monkeys, exposed to conditioning procedures which had involved noxious stimuli: 5 control monkeys had, in contrast, shown no g.i. complications. Brady *et al.* (1958) reported a study in which 4 pairs of rhesus monkeys were kept in restraining chairs for periods of up to 7 weeks. During these weeks the 4 pairs of animals were exposed to a Sidman avoidance schedule: that is, to a procedure in which shocks were presented, without warning, at regular intervals, but these could be postponed by a lever-press response from an experimental animal. Through each 24 hours the monkeys experienced alternate 6-hour periods of 'avoidance' and rest. The animals had been trained by exposure to an electric shock repeated at 20-second intervals: a lever could be pressed by either monkey of the pair, and when this was appropriately manipulated both animals avoided the next shock. The more efficient of the two was selected as the experimental 'executive' monkey, the less efficient being the 'control' animal who subsequently had no ability to manipulate a lever effective for avoidance, but was exposed to any shocks which, because of the 'executive's' inefficiency, were delivered to both animals. When these yoked pairs were in one of the 6-hour 'avoidance' periods this was signalled by a red light, which was extinguished during rest. Within a few hours the 'executives' developed stable avoidance response rates of 15–20 lever presses per minute, and received not more than two shocks per hour. In rest periods avoidance response rates dropped. Brady *et al.* (1958) reported the deaths of three of their 'executives' after 9, 23, and 25 days, the fourth being sacrificed in a moribund state after 7 weeks. All 'executives' had extensive g.i. lesions and ulcers, while the 'controls' remained unaffected. The authors suggested that further study should be directed towards examination of the original selection criteria whereby the more efficient monkey became the 'executive', towards the social aspects of the interaction between executive and control animals, and towards constitutional factors operating in the avoidance response and its consequences.

Subsequent publications reported that examination of gastric secretion, monitored by means of a fistula preparation, revealed *reductions* of activity during avoidance activity, but *increases* during the rest periods: there were, however, individual differences in this aspect of response to testing. The 6 hours on/off schedule seemed particularly relevant for the production of gastric pathology, and suggestions that post-stressor rebound interacted with rhythmic variation in function were offered as explanation of 'executive' morbidity.

DEVELOPMENTS FROM THE EXECUTIVE MONKEY—HUMANS

We trace now the two lines of development from the executive monkey studies: one leading into work with humans, one to experiments with rodents.

The human studies began with methodological developments: the Sidman avoidance paradigm being modified to substitute noise for shock stimuli, and a non-invasive technique being used for monitoring g.i. activity. Subsequently this noise-avoidance paradigm was retained, but interest broadened in the way we have noted. In passing we should also observe that Mason (1968) has reviewed extensively subsequent work with the monkey, in which the shock-avoidance paradigm has been retained, but interest broadened from the g.i. tract to the integration of neuroendocrine response in stress.

The possibility of recording electrical activity from the abdomen, at the skin surface in the region over the stomach, was first reported by Alvarez (1922): regular waveforms with a frequency of 3/minute could be obtained and the records were called electrogastrograms (EGG). Little use was made of the procedure until the 1950s and its rediscovery by R.C. Davis. Davis, Garafolo, and Gault (1957), introducing the report of an exploratory study with the EGG, drew attention to the clinical need for a method for surface recording of gastric function, similar to surface recording of cardiac activity by means of the electrocardiogram. They reported their recording, at the skin surface over the abdomen, of potential changes which they regarded as reflecting electrical and probably secretory behaviour of the underlying viscera. A second report (Davis

Garafolo, and K veim, 1959) examined 'hunger contractions': these, however, appeared in the EGG when an experimental balloon was present—the EGG from an empty stomach was relatively quiet and apparently free of Cannon's 'hunger contractions' (Cannon and Washburn, 1912).

What made the EGG particularly exciting for Davis and his associates was the fact that it appeared to offer a means of measuring gastric activity without disturbance of normal function: methods dependent on introduction of a foreign body into the g.i. system increase the possibility that local stimulation generates artifact. Methods used by Davis and his co-workers in validating the EGG, together with details of his recording techniques, were published in the 1960s by Russell and Stern (1967).

After the report of Brady *et al.* (1958) attention was turned to the possibility that the human EGG might be used in examination of g.i. motility during Sidman avoidance sessions. Davis and Berry (1963) examined the EGGs of 12 pairs of male and 12 of female students before, during, and after a 10-minute session of noise-avoidance. 'Executive' and 'control' subjects were randomly assigned to their respective roles, and the latter group was reported to be un-aware of the task being undertaken by the former. Amplitude of the waves of g.i. activity was measured, these being regarded as reflections of gastric motility, and the executive subjects showed a larger g.i. response than the controls in the avoidance and post-avoidance rest sessions. This result was somewhat sur-prising in view of Cannon's (1929) description of *reduced* g.i. activity in fear, and the monkey evidence of *suppressed* secretory activity during test sessions; Brady (1963), however, observed that, contrary to assumptions of covariance between secretion and molity, there may be questions raised about selective effects on secretion and motility. As Brady also observed, there were critical differences between the monkey and the human studies: obvious ones are the marked reduction in testing time from days to minutes of involvement, and the very strong possibility that no *conditioning* process operates in the human situation, but a positive coping strategy is planned by the executive. However, the theme of secretory/motility variation is pursued through a number of subsequent publications from the early 1960s.

Secretion and motility

White (1964) reviews briefly some pharmacological influences on g.i. motility noting that Sternbach (1962) had demonstrated that the effects of adrenaline were seen in a reduction in peristaltic *force* of contraction as evidenced by reduc-ed amplitude of waves, accompanied by increased *rate* of contraction. With atropine, however, amplitude was reduced while rate was unchanged. White (1964) notes that there seems to be independence of rate and force of contrac-tion. Further, she reports that Goodman and colleagues recorded a 3-cycle/ minute 'basic a.c. rhythm' which they believed reflected gastric contractions, and also a 'd.c. potential' thought to reflect the status of the gastric mucosa. Further, the amplitude of the a.c. record increased '. . . in pain and emotion'.

White notes, however, that the time-scale of Goodman's changes was relatively long, then reports her own investigation of amplitude changes in the 3-cycles/ minute waveform, recorded during passive reception of 'mild stimulation' as well as during avoidance behaviour. It is interesting to see that, again, marked variations of technique have crept in, and yet Brady's monkeys are still viewed as a departure point. White reported a reduction of amplitude in avoidance sessions, and the possibility of decreased secretory activity as evidenced by a shifting baseline record. Evidence of reduced secretory function, recorded by an intragastric radio transmitter, was reported by Norman (1969) from a study of avoidance responding: he also notes Brady's (1963) comment that there *may* be autonomic control of gastric acid production which is not related to gastric motility. Norman (1969) reminds us of the need to examine individual differences in the subjects' interpretation of a stressor situation: a theme which we will return to at a later point, when we describe Roessler's model relating ego strength to autonomic response and post-stimulus recovery.

Meanwhile, however, we take up a point made by White (1964) which stimulated Stern (1966) into a re-examination of the effects on g.i. motility, recorded with the EGG during the noise-avoidance procedure devised by Davis and his colleagues. Around this period of EGG development Fedor and Russell (1965) had found greater amplitude of 3/minute waveforms when human subjects had been unsuccessful in avoidance of the aversive noise, and the area had, as we have already noted, been reviewed by Russell and Stern (1967) for a manual of psychophysiological methods (Venables and Martin, 1967). Stern (1966) introduced into the design the situation of each subject being his own control, being successively 'executive' and 'control' when exposed to alternating periods of noise-avoidance (or 'response-contingent stimulation') and to similar amounts of auditory stress randomly presented. Amplitude was examined in periods of response-contingent and random scheduling and during the successful or unsuccessful avoidance of noise. Again there was greater amplitude of g.i. waveforms during unsuccessful responses (as in Fedor and Russell, 1965) and again there was greater amplitude during the response-contingent than during the random stimulation. So, the second half of the 1960s saw no resolution of this problem of apparent discrepancy between motility data, and while some subsequent work with humans moved into examination of *individual differences* in autonomic activation, further developments in g.i. electrophysiology threw light on the findings from the Davis tradition of work with the EGG, as described below.

The EGG revisited

A recent discussion of abdominal potentials, their origins, and their recording from surface sites, is available in Davis Stern, and Cook (1980), who cite Sarna (1975) and the description of two distinct potentials generated by the stomach: electrical control activity (ECA) and electrical response activity (ERA). ECA is the previously described rhythmic variation of electrical potential which, in man, has a frequency of 3/minute, and covaries with any contractions which occur. The ECA is always present: it facilitates the occurrence and controls the timing of contractions by making the gastric mucosa temporarily susceptible to the generation of a second potential (Daniel and Irwin, 1968), ERA, which consists of one or more spikes superimposed on the ECA, and coincides with contractions.

Given the nature of electrical changes in the g.i. tract, as briefly reviewed above, it seems likely that these could be adequately recorded from surface electrodes attached to appropriate areas over the abdomen: the situation is, as we noted earlier, similar to that of ECG recording, and in both cases potentials are being transmitted through a volume conductor. There have, however, been some changes in the method originally advocated by Davis, and described by Russell and Stern (1967). Stern and his co-workers have now abandoned their earlier quadrant system, and place a single electrode at the intersection of the midline and epigastric line (an imaginary line connecting the lower ribs of left and right sides): this point, in most subjects, is over the antrum of the stomach. Details of the revised technique are available in Stern, Ray, and Davis (1980), which also describes improvements in quantification of EGG records. A recent publication (Stern, *et al.*, 1978) provides information relating to EGG usage, both in basic research and medical applications: abnormalities of gastric motility have, for example, been diagnosed by Krapivin and Chernin (1967) and Martin and Thillier (1971).

Noise-avoidance studies have now been revisited, with the improved technique for EGG recording (Davis, Cook, and Stern, 1977): a pilot study of gastric activity in response-contingent stress was undertaken. Power spectral analysis showed that the 3 cycles/minute activity tended to increase during a $\frac{1}{2}$ hour rest following a standard meal, while such activity was reduced when a noise-avoidance task was undertaken in the post-prandial period. A study in which yoked controls receive noise stimuli but do not undertake avoidance activity is now needed before one can adequately answer the question, originally posed by the Davis studies, of the direction of change in g.i. motility which accompanies 'executive' function in a Sidman avoidance situation. Ongoing work in the psychophysiological laboratory, with normal human subjects having no g.i. abnormality, has, however, led to the 'tool-sharpening' exercise of EGG development, increasing its potential value for the *clinical* situation, increasing the scope of its application in ways originally envisaged by Davis *et al.* (1957).

Individual differences: autonomic response and recovery

The observation of individual differences in psychophysiological response to the Sidman avoidance situation has been noted earlier in the chapter: we turn now to examination of human subjects, participating in noise-avoidance studies, with recording of cardiac and electrodermal function replacing the

EGG, and attention directed to post-test *recovery* as well as to the *response* during this laboratory challenge.

The background to these studies, undertaken in London and York (in contrast to the American ones reported in the rest of this chapter) is a sabbatical visit by Stern to London at a time when some psychophysiological interest there was centred on stress response and recovery in human subjects. Explorations had been undertaken along the time-scale of a working week, with interest in the 'easements' (Handlon, 1962) of working life such as weekends (Christie and Venables, 1973; Venables and Christie, 1974) and the mid-day meal break (Christie, Cort, and Venables, 1976; Christie and McBrearty, 1979a). Post-challenge *recovery* has had little attention, in contrast to wide interest in the stress *response* (Freeman, 1939; Johansson and Frankenhäuser, 1973; Bull and Nethercott, 1972) and the presence of Stern in the London laboratories served as a reminder of the EGG studies, and of the original 'executive monkey' work which had noted the 'rebound' phenomena after stress-offset. The noise-avoidance task used by Stern (1966) seemed to offer a means whereby human subjects could be exposed to a mild stressor having both psychological and physical aspects. Further, responses to the roles of 'executive' and 'control' subjects could be examined in relation to personality differences, and post-challenge recovery to pre-stimulus resting values could be investigated.

Preliminary studies in London provided evidence from measurement of an electrodermal index, skin potential level (SPL), that the speed of relaxation to a criterion point (Christie and Venables, 1971) was significantly slower after 10 minutes' exposure to the noise-avoidance stressor (Christie and Venables, 1974). Examination of heart-rate response to the rest–test–rest paradigm showed that subjects with low neuroticism (N) scores, assessed by the Eysenck Personality Inventory (EPI) showed, as one might expect, lower heart-rates in rest, and higher rates during autonomic response to the challenge of the noise-avoidance period. In contrast, however, subjects with high N scores showed their fastest heart rate at the beginning of the post-test *rest*, and the biggest 'rebound', was seen in the least stable subjects. Findings such as these had stimulated interest in Roessler's (1973) account of a decade's American research in which the ego strength (E_s) dimension of the Minnesota Multiphasic Personality Inventory (MMPI) had been examined in the context of laboratory investigation of sympathetic nervous system (SNS) response to the challenge of mild stressors. Roessler had argued that high E_s is associated with *appropriate* SNS response, that is with greater activation when there is challenge, but greater relaxation in 'easement': this appropriate pattern of response and recovery he relates to the appropriateness of these subjects' perception and interpretation of situations and stimuli—their 'coping'. In contrast, low E_s subjects show an invariant response to challenge and easement. Roessler reported a significant inverse correlation between E_s and N scores, and it became of interest to replicate this American finding with a British population.

Expansion of the scope of this set of studies became possible when Gartshore joined Venables, who was by this time established in York. Investigation of the influence of the social stressor aspects of the executive or control 'role' was undertaken, in conjunction with assessment of EPI and E_s scores. Again there was a rest–test–rest design, and autonomic activity reflected in the ECG and electrodermal activity (EDA) was monitored during the rests and the yoked-pair Sidman avoidance task period. The initial rest provided baseline data from which the extent of change could be measured: after this roles were allocated and the test period required the 'executive' to attempt the task of avoiding successive presentation of a 100 dB, 1000 Hz, noise by pressing a button during an unknown critical interval between stimuli. Both subjects were exposed to the aversive noise, but the 'controls' were passive recipients of the stressor. The post-stimulus rest period (R2) provided an opportunity to examine *recovery* to the baseline values of pre-stimulus rest (R1).

Results from the 58 subjects of this study were examined to investigate the effects of role and personality on autonomic responses (ANS) to both task and post-stimulus recovery. Looking first at the tonic state, at mean values for heart-rate and skin conductance level (SCL): there were no significant differences between executive (EX) and control (CON) groups in he first rest period, R1, Bearing in mind that roles (EX or CON) were not allocated until the *end* of R1, it is therefore possible to attribute any subsequent differences—recorded during the noise-avoidance period (T) or post-stimulus rest, R2—as being due to other than differences in initial state of the ANS. Examining heart-rate there was evidence that this was faster in EX than in CON groups: the T value was significantly higher than that for R 1 ($p < 0.001$) in the EX group, and the T (EX) value was 10 beats per minutes (bpm) faster than the T value of the CON group ($p < 0.005$). In the R2 period the heart-rate of both groups was decreased to a level similar to that of R1. In contrast to the heart-rate values, the range corrected (Lykken and Venables, 1971) SCL of both groups decreased significantly within each of the periods R1, T, and R2. Looking at the transition points between R1, T, and R2, heart-rate *change* was examined, when the following responses to stimulus and rest were noted. The EX group showed a significant increase of 12.7 bpm ($p < 0.001$) at the transition of R1/T, while the CON group exhibited a non-significant increase of 3.6 bpm. At the T/R2 transition the heart-rate response of the EX group was minimal, while the CON group exhibited a significant *increase* of some 13 bpm ($p < 0.001$). The SCL data were similar at the T/R2 transition: the CON group showed a significant *increase* while the EX data remained relatively unchanged. At this point we inevitably recall the 'rebound' in Brady's monkeys, but this was found in his *'executives'*; and also note Roessler's model of potentially maladaptive ANS response associated with low ego-strength in human subjects, suggesting the next stage of data analysis in the Venables and Gartshore study. These workers replicated Roessler's finding of a significant inverse correlation between N scores (EPI) and E_s (MMPI) rating, and were able to show some support, from their data, for the model of low N or high E_s being associated with greater *adaptiveness* of autonomic response to challenge and easement. Thus their SCL data indicated that the test period values of high E_s executives were significantly greater than those of the low E_s group, while at the same time the SCL of the high E_s *control* group was *lower* than that of the low E_s subjects. The post-challenge *recovery* of the high E_s controls was also more efficient, as evidenced by the lower SCL value.

Looking briefly at the extraversion/introversion dimension, lower extraversion was, in executives, associated with faster heart-rate during T, but the main effects of role and task factors are seen in relation to those aspects of personality associated with the ego-strength or neuroticism dimension— effects which do suggest that Roessler's model has value for examination of 'coping' and its autonomic correlates. It is, of course, within a psychosomatic context, tempting to make the great leap from apparent maladaptiveness of psychophysiological response in the laboratory to invidual differences in the morbidity and mortality of 'real life'. Such speculative activity, however, needs answers which come from epidemiological and related sources, like those of Marmot in Chapter 15 of the present volume. What psychophysiologists *could* do, however, is begin to answer questions about individual differences in response and homeostatic recovery, endeavouring to define more precisely those somatic characteristics of a *stressed* system which *may* be the precursor of subsequent dysfunction or disease (Christie and McBrearty, 1979b). Roessler's (1973) model appears to have heuristic value, and the Sidman avoidance paradigm, as developed by Davis and subsequent workers such as Stern, offers a laboratory method for examining response to both psychological and physical stressors, to 'executive' activity and 'control' passivity, to coping, and to the consequences of inadequancy in these areas.

Other psychophysiologists have examined in a more comprehensive way the effects of having control: these studies are out of the mainstream of our review, but some are mentioned at this point for completeness. Geer, Davison, and Gatchel (1970) reported skin conductance (SC) and heart-rate data from a reaction time (RT) study in which electric shock was administered to human subjects. When subjects believed that they had control over the length of the stressor stimulus period, the shock duration being thought to be reduced by a fast RT, there appeared to be significantly less SC activity, though heart-rate data threw up no significant findings. Hokanson *et al.* (1971) used systolic blood pressure (SBP) as their dependent variable in a study which manipulated controllability: there was a reduction in SBP associated with human subjects having control over aversive stimulation. There are, however, problems in interpreting such studies when controllability is confounded with predictability. Ball and Vogler (1971), following Haggard (1943) and Pervin (1963), reported that 21 of 25 subjects in their study preferred self-administered shock stimuli because this reduced uncertainty and increased predictability. Geer and Maisel (1972) attempted, with somewhat equivocal results, to disentangle the prediction-control confound. Some reasons for the problems of this area are discussed by Seligman, Maier, and Soloman (1971), but into this more complex aspect of the area we will venture no further, returning instead to the mainstream of the chapter, and looking at further developments in research, after the executive monkey, specifically that of Weiss with rodents. It will eventually bring us back to Seligman in the context of 'learned helplessness' and the response of the yoked control in a Sidman avoidance paradigm, but our major interest is in the theoretical model generated by Weiss to interpret the original findings of Brady and his co-workers.

DEVELOPMENTS FROM THE EXECUTIVE MONKEY—RATS

The 'control' subject in the Sidman avoidance situation is helpless, is exposed to an unavoidable stimulus. Work by Seligman and his colleagues in Philadelphia has highlighted the consequences of such exposure to unavoidable trauma, and from the results of animal investigation has been developed the model of 'learned helplessness' which currently stimulates interpretation of human depressive states (Miller, Rosellini, and Seligman, 1977). At the level of *animal* work, however, Weiss has conducted a series of elegant studies which, while relevant for analysis of Seligman's experimental findings, have also contributions to make to the 'executive monkey' saga. Weiss argues that a psychological factor of importance in determining the somatic consequences of such traumatic stimulation is the amount of *control* experienced. In 1968 Weiss demonstrated that 'executive' rats having some control over the presentation of shock stimulation exhibited significantly less gastric erosion than yoked animals exposed to shock stimulation identical to that of the 'executives'. Restrained rats were tested in matched groups of three: the third of the triplet, being merely restrained and not exposed to shock, exhibited minimal gastric erosion, thus 'control' rather than shock was regarded as the factor relevant for protection of the 'executive'. This is, of course, in marked contrast to the 'executive' monkey finding, and in 1971 Weiss more closely followed the original paradigm of Brady and his colleagues by using an unsignalled Sidman avoidance schedule. In a range of studies Weiss has repeatedly demonstrated that 'executive' rats show less gastric erosion, and so has necessitated a reappraisal of the original monkey findings. Seligman (1977) for example, suggests that selection for the 'executive' role of those monkeys who more rapidly learnt to avoid shock stimuli resulted in more *emotional* animals being '*executives*', and thus animals more susceptible to the development of g.i. pathology. Weiss, however, argues that g.i. lesion development can be precisely predicted from assessment of two factors: firstly the number of *responses* made in the testing situation and secondly the amount of *revelant feedback* received after a coping attempt. Thus, lesions increase with increased responding and decreased informational feedback. In a Sidman avoidance situation there are low amounts of such feedback: there are no external signals which are terminated by a correct response. Thus, Weiss argues, the 'executive' monkeys of Brady *et al.* (1958) were selected because they had high response rates and were in a Sidman avoidance situation, both factors being ulcerogenic. When Weiss selected rats who had high response rates and exposed them to the low-feed-back condition of Sidman avoidance, they too developed the 'executive' ulcers. So, Weiss argues, the 'executive' role is not necessarily associated with increased risk of g.i. pathology, only in the somewhat exceptional situation of combining high rates of response with low information about efficacy. And the general message for humans from his rat studies is, perhaps, the one that the experience of control has prophylactic value, that the executive isn't neces-sarily the candidate for psychosomatic disorder *if* he feels he is at least the master of his fate!

AFTER THE 'EXECUTIVE' MONKEY—STOCKTAKING

In tracing lines of research which all owe something to the stimulus of the 'executive monkey' we have ranged through various areas. At the outset we avoided any suggestion that we would review the field of gastric pathology, but we did claim the heuristic value of the 'executive monkey' and it is, therefore, incumbent on us to take stock of the research we have described, assessing its value as foundational for psychosomatics.

Taking our first statement, from Weiss (1977), that 'psychological factors play a major role in gastric pathology' and Weiner's (1976) observation that current interest is focused on mechanisms whereby psychological states are translated in g.i. response, we can begin our stocktaking with examination of the work with *humans*. Here we find that research has been concerned with the g.i. response of *normal* subjects, exposed to *laboratory* situations of chal-lenge. This highlights the role which Graham (1971) saw for psychophysiology, in which normal states are examined, in order to detect the earliest stages in development of pathology: psychosomatics is, he said, clinical psychophy-siology, but within the laboratory context there has been development of record-ing methods, refinement of the EGG, which has potential value for clinical use. Further, we have seen a stimulation of interest in examination of g.i. physiology, in relation to the electrical activity associated with secretion and motility, and to the extent of independence of the mechanisms controlling these two aspects of g.i. function. A little more light has been thrown on the topic of g.i. response to foreign bodies introduced into the stomach, and the artifacts introduced into the data; and while the EGG represents a distinct advance of methodology, in terms of its non-invasive nature, contemporary psychophy-siology is now beginning to look for methods which can move from the arti-ficiality of the laboratory into real life. Perhaps the next stage of methods development will be concerned with ambulant monitoring. Carruthers' chapter makes us aware of possibilities for 'field' studies, if only the equipment is available.

Turning now from these aspects of their translation into g.i. response to the nature of the *psychological states* generated by the Sidman avoidance situation, and to information about other aspects of ANS function. We have seen that a challenge may not necessarily be a stressor, and that the latter may perhaps be defined in terms of *maladaptiveness* of response and recovery. The Roessler view of ego-strength is a far cry from Alexander's specificity hypothesis, but still reflects and enduring theme of psychosomatics—individual differences in perception of events, in response to them, in coping. Looking then at data from the London and York studies, we might argue that *reduction* of ANS response in challenge and *increase* in easement is evidence of a stressed organism: thus the links between lack of control, low ego-strength and apparently maladaptive response/recovery deserve further exploration within psychosomatics, and particularly within the context of so-called 'stress-induced disorder".

Lastly, the *animal* work has contributed to psychosomatics by refinement of methodology, by theoretical reformulation of the 'executive monkey' findings, and, of course, by contributing to analysis of the nature of depression and its precursors.

In conclusion, then, we would argue that the original studies of Brady and his 1950s colleagues *have* had a stimulating effect on psychosomatic research, with a broadening of interests to encompass a number of its major themes.

REFERENCES

Ackerman, S. H., and Weiner, H. (1976). Peptic ulcer disease: some considerations for psychosomatic research. In O. W. Hill (ed.), *Modern Trends in Psychosomatic Medicine*, Vol. 3. London: Butterworths.

Alexander, F. (1950). *Psychosomatic Medicine: Its Principles and Applications*. New York: W. W. Norton and Co. Inc.

Alvarez, W. C. (1922). The electrogastrogram and what it shows. *Journal of the American Medical Association*, **79**, 1281–1284.

Ball, T. S., and Vogler, R. E. (1971). Uncertain pain and the pain of uncertainty. *Perceptual and Motor Skills*, **33**, 1196–1203.

Brady, J. V. (1963). Further comments on the gastrointestinal system and avoidance behaviour. *Psychological Reports*, **12**, 742.

Brady, J. V., Porter, R. W., Conrad, O., and Mason, J. W. (1958). Avoidance behaviour and the development of gastroduodenal ulcers, *Journal of the Experimental Analysis of Behaviour*, **1**, 69–72.

Bull, R. H. C., and Nethercott, R. E. (1972). Physiological recovery and personality, *British Journal of Clinical Psychology*, **11**, 297.

Cannon, W. B. (1929). *Bodily Changes in Pain, Hunger, Fear and Rage*. New York: Appleton-Century-Crofts.

Cannon, W.B., and Washburn, A. L. (1912). An explanation of hunger. *American Journal of Physiology*, **29**, 441–454.

Christie, M. J., and McBrearty. M. T. (1979a). Psychophysiological investigations of post lunch state in male and female subjects. *Ergonomics*, **22**, 307–323.

Christie, M. J., and McBrearty, E. M. T. (1979b). Stress—response and recovery. In C. Mackay and T. Cox, (eds.), *Response to Stress: Occupational Aspects*. Surrey: IPC Science and Technology Press.

Christie, M. J., Cort, J., and Venables, P. H. (1976). Individual differences in post-prandial state: explorations with palmar skin potentials, *Journal of Psychosomatic Research*, **20**, 501–508.

Christie, M. J., and Venables, P. H. (1971). Characteristics of palmar skin potential and conductance in relaxed human subjects. *Psychophysiology*, **8**, 523–532.

Christie, M. J., and Venables, P. H. (1973). Mood changes in relation to age, EPI scores, time and day. *British Journal of Social and Clinical Psychology*, **12**, 61–72.

Christie, M. J., and Venables, P. H. (1974). Change in palmar skin potential level during relaxation after stress. *Journal of Psychosomatic Research*, **18**, 301–306.

Daniel, E. E., and Irwin, J. (1968). Electrical activity of gastric musculature, in C. F. Code, (ed.), *Handbook of Physiology, Section 6, Alimentary Canal*, Vol. IV: *Motility*. Washington, D. C. : American Physiological Society.

Davis, C. M., Cook, E. W., and Stern, R. M. (1977). Effects of a reaction time task on digestive motility of the human stomach. Paper presented to the Annual Meeting of the Society for Psychophysiological Research, Philadelphia.

Davis, C. M., Stern, R. M., and Cook, E. W. (1980). Abdominal potentials: their origins and the current status of surface recording. *Psychophysiology* (submitted).

Davis, R. C., and Berry, F. (1963). Gastrointestinal reactions during a noise avoidance task. *Psychological Reports*, **12**, 135–137.

Davis, R. C., Garafolo, L., and Gault, F. P. (1957). An exploration of abdominal potentials. *Journal of Comparative and Physiological Psychology*, **50**, 519–523.

Davis, R. C., Garafolo, L., and Kveim, K. (1959). Conditions associated with gastrointestinal activity. *Journal of Comparative and Physiological Psychology*, **52**, 466–474.

Fedor, J., and Russell, R. W. (1965). Gastrointestinal reactions to response-contingent stimulation. *Psychological Reports*, **16**, 95–113.

Freeman, G. L. (1939). Toward a psychiatric plimsoll mark : physiological recovery quotients in experimentally induced frustration. *Journal of Psychology*, **8**, 247–252.

Geer, J. H., Davison, G. C., and Gatchel, R. I. (1970). Reduction of stress in humans through nonveridical perceived control of aversive stimulation. *Journal of Personality and Social Psychology*, **16**, 731–738.

Geer, J. H., and Maisel, E. (1972). Evaluating the effects of the prediction-control confound. *Journal of Personality and Social Psychology*, **23**, 314–319.

Graham, D. T. (1971). Psychophysiology and medicine. *Psychophysiology*, **8**, 121–131.

Haggard, E. A. (1943). Experimental studies in affective processes. I: Some effects of cognitive structure and active participation on certain autonomic reactions during and following experimentally induced stress. *Journal of Experimental Psychology*, **33**, 257–284.

Handlon, J. H. (1962). Hormonal activity and individual responses to stresses and easements in everyday living. In R. Roessler and N. S. Greenfield (eds.), *Physiological Correlates of Psychological Disorder*. Madison: University of Wisconsin Press.

Hokanson, J. E., DeGood, D. E., Forrest, M. S., and Brittain, T. M. (1971). Availability of avoidance behaviours in modulating vascular-stress responses. *Journal of Personality and Social Behaviour*, **19**, 60–68.

Johansson, G. and Frankenhäuser, M. (1973). Temporal factors in sympathoadrenomedullary activity following acute behavioural activation. *Biological Psychology*, **1**, 53–73.

Krapivin, B. V., and Chernin, V. V. (1967). Study of the motor function of the stomach by the electrogastrographic method in patients with peptic ulcer. *Soviet Medicine*, **30**, 57–60.

Lykken, D. T., and Venables, P. H. (1971). Direct measurement of skin conductance: a proposal for standardization. *Psychophysiology*, **8**, 656–672.

Martin, A., and Thillier, J. L. (1971). Spatiotemporal organization and regulation of digestive motor activities in man: electro-gastroenterography (E.G.E.G.) method of physiological analysis. *Journal of Physiology* (Paris), **63**, 253A.

Mason, J. W. (1968). Organization of psychoendocrine mechanisms. *Psychosomatic Medicine*, **30** (5), part 11.

Miller, W. R., Rosellini, T. A., and Seligman, M. E. P. (1977). Learned helplessness and depression. In J. D. Maser and M. E. P. Seligman (eds.), *Psychopathology: Experimental Models*. San Francisco, W. H. Freeman & Co.

Norman, A. (1969). Response contingency and human gastric acidity. *Psychophysiology*, **5**, 673–682.

Pervin, L. A. (1963). The need to predict and control under conditions of threat. *Journal of Personality*, **31**, 570–587.

Roessler, R. (1973). Personality, physiology and performance. *Psychophysiology*, **10**, 315–327.

Russell, R. W., and Stern, R. M. (1967). Gastric motility: the electro-gastrogram. In P. H. Venables and I. Martin (eds.), *Manual of Psychophysiological Methods*. Amsterdam: North Holland Publishing Co.

Sarna, S. K. (1975). Gastrointestinal electrical activity: terminology. *Gastroenterology*, **68**, 1631–1635.

Seligman, M. E. P., Maier, S. F., and Soloman, R. L. (1971). Unpredictable and unavoidable aversive events. In F. R. Brush (ed.), *Aversive Conditioning and Learning*. New York: Academic Press.

Stern, R. M. (1966). A re-examination of the effects of response-contingent aversive tones on gastrointestinal activity. *Psychophysiology*, **2**, 217–223.

Stern, R. M., Denari, N., Macciochi, S., Davis, C. M., and Pessy (1978). Stomach Motility: A Selectively Annotated Bibliography. Unpublished manuscript, Dept. of Psychology, Pennsylvania State University.

Stern, R. M., Ray, W. J., and Davis, C. M. (1980). *An Introduction to Psychophysiological Recording*. New York: Oxford University Press.

Sternbach, R. A. (1962). Studies of chronic gastric motility in unanesthetized cats: technique and evidence for dissociation. *Psychophysiology Newsletter*, **8**, 37–44.

Venables, P. H., and Christie, M. J. (1974). Neuroticism, physiological state and mood: an exploratory study of Friday/Monday changes. *Biological Psychology*, **1**, 201–211.

Venables, P. H., and Martin, I. (1967). *A Manual of Psychophysiological Methods*. Amsterdam, North-Holland Publishing Co.

Weiner, H. (1977). *Psychobiology and Human Disease* New York: Elsevier.

Weiner, H., Thaler, M., Reiser, M. F., and Mirsky, I. A. (1957). Etiology of duodenal ulcer. I. Relation of specific psychological characteristics to rate of gastric secretion (serum pepsinogen). *Psychosomatic Medicine*, **19**, 1.

Weiss, J. M. (1968). Effects of coping responses on stress. *Journal of Comparative and Physiological Psychology*, **65**, 251–260.

Weiss, J. M. (1971). Effects of coping behaviour with and without a feedback signal on stress pathology in rats. *Journal of Comparative and Physiological Psychology*, **77**, 22–30.

Weiss, J. M. (1977). Ulcers. In J. D. Maser and M. E. P. Seligman (eds.), *Psychopathology: Experiment Models*. San Francisco: W. H. Freeman & Co.

White, E. H. (1964). Additional notes on gastrointestinal activity during avoidance behaviour. *Psychological Reports*, **14**, 343–347.

Foundations of Psychosomatics
Edited by M. J. Christie and P. G. Mellett
© 1981 John Wiley & Sons Ltd.

12

THE RELEVANCE OF CLASSICAL CONDITIONING TO PSYCHOSOMATIC DISORDER

A. B. LEVEY

and

IRENE MARTIN,

Department of Psychology, Institute of Psychiatry, London.

CLASSICAL CONDITIONING

The textbook vignette of classical conditioning is thoroughly familiar. A dog, held in a restraining harness, hears a buzzer and a moment later receives meat powder. After repeated pairings of these two events the buzzer comes to produce salivation as the meat powder did initially. Pavlov termed the meat powder an unconditioned stimulus (UCS), the initial salivation an unconditioned response (UCR), the buzzer a conditioned stimulus (CS), and the salivation to the buzzer a conditioned response (CR).

This simple experiment is the foundation on which more complex conditioning structures have been built, and the present purpose is to examine what contemporary classical conditioning has to offer for a psychosomatic view of medicine. It requires that the basic Pavlovian 'buzzer–meat powder–salivating dog' image be updated to accommodate recent findings such as:

(1) The increased range of physiological responses which it has been shown can be conditioned. These include autonomic, visceral and sytemic reactions.
(2) The range of stimuli to which physiological responses can be conditioned. These include simple and also complex stimuli like people, places, and social situations.
(3) The complexity of the conditioning schedules employed which can lead to intricate patterns of responses and to the maintenance of responding over long periods of time.
(4) The contribution of individual differences to the outcome of conditioning.

In the conditioning process we have a mechanism by which bodily reactions can become associated with many stimuli and events in the environment. These reactions may be specific to individuals, they may involve different kinds of stimuli from the original conditioned stimulus, and they may persist for many years. These are well-established observations, and the terminology which has been in use since Pavlov's early work is, very briefly, as follows:

If the UCS is omitted over a series of trials the CR eventually ceases to be given; this is the phenomenon of *experimental extinction*. After some hours or days away from the experimental situation, re-exposure to the CS will elicit the CR, an effect described as *spontaneous recovery*. Stimuli which are similar to the CS will effectively elicit the CR in the early stages of conditioning, which is thus said to *generalize* to the similar stimuli. However, if only the CS is paired with the UCS while similar stimuli are consistently presented without the UCS, the CR is eventually given to the CS only, a procedure known as *differential conditioning*.

A basic theoretical interest of conditioning lies in what is achieved by this attaching of complex physiological responses to such a variety of stimuli. Pavlov regarded the process of conditioning as a fundamental mechanism of adaptation, inasmuch as the CR anticipates the UCS and thus enables the organism to prepare its activity. This process can extend to complex response patterning of widespread body systems, and the nature of the response pattern can change over time. Sometimes, however, the endpoint of the conditioning process is maladaptive; the conditioned response may be too strong, persist too long, and—in the case of some conditioned reactions—may be judged by the individual as unpleasant and unwanted. Research is required into how the pattern of responding can be defined as maladaptive, and the circumstances under which such learning takes place, often without any conscious awareness by the individual.

It is in this context that conditioning as a causal mechanism in the aetiology and symptomatology of psychosomatic illness merits serious examination, and it is the purpose of this chapter to examine critically the candidacy of classical conditioning, and particularly of individual differences in classical conditioning, for this important role.

In the following pages the criteria for an adequate explanation of psychosomatic conditions are first examined; next, the overlap of classical conditioning with the phenomena of psychosomatic illness. New developments are then reviewed, together with a description of recent work on conditioning in specific response systems. Finally, the argument for classical conditioning as a causal mechanism in psychosomatic illness is considered.

It is important to stress that this chapter is not intended as a defence of classical conditioning in this field; its purpose is to examine the evidence with scepticism and to attempt to assess the possible role or roles of classical conditioning mechanisms in the production of psychosomatic illness.

PSYCHOSOMATIC ILLNESS AND CLASSICAL CONDITIONING

The early work on psychosomatic illness gave rise to several theoretical models of which four were particularly influential.

The view of Alexander (1952) that illness represents unconscious conflict, particularly relating to infantile experience, derived from psychoanalytic theory and enjoyed a considerable vogue. In later writings, Alexander and his colleagues endorsed a concept of disease specificity, moving away from a more general model (Alexander, French, and Pollock, 1968). The relationship of disease types to personality was explored by Dumbar (1943) who proposed what was probably the first theory to discuss explicitly the contribution of individual differences to psychophysiological disorder.

The stress theory proposed and elaborated by Selye (1956) was influential in pointing to the deleterious effects of prolonged stress and was significant in the development of the theory of psychosomatic illness. More recently Levi (1971) has extended the concept of stress to psychosocial stress, and has offered refinements of the stress concept which bring it more clearly in line with human illness factors.

Finally, the role of empirical epidemiology has been to demonstrate convincingly the importance of life events such as retirement, bereavement, onset of puberty, etc. in the genesis of illness. These four major theoretical models serve to underline the main components of psychosomatic illness, though they now stand in need of refinement.

There is today a fairly general agreement that the mechanisms underlying psychosomatic illness are complex and multidimensional, and that earlier models of a global psychogenic illness are inadequate for explanatory purposes. Weiner (1976) has argued eloquently for the abandonment of simplistic models and unitary causal mechanisms. He suggests the need to identify subforms of illness categories in place of globally defined concepts. Explicit causal mechanisms for these discrete illness patterns may then be specifiable. In similar vein, Mason (1968, 1970) has argued for the inclusion of neurophysiological and neuroendocrine mechanisms in any account of psychosomatic illness and has suggested that they should be considered in relation both to external life events and to the internal events of emotional experience.

There is probably also general agreement that the functional disturbance of a vegetative organ or system can be caused by emotional disturbance including conflict, stress, and life events, and that chronic functional disturbance gradually leads to tissue changes and to organic disease. Cannon's well known concept of an organism prepared for fight or flight has survived well as a general notion but to the sympathoadrenomedullary system with which he was concerned must be added other neuroendocrine systems and consideration of the interrelationships of somatic and visceral components of behaviour. In a general sense we deal with an organism equipped with a number of primitive subcortical mechanisms designed to ensure survival in the jungle, and a highly differentiated cortex which is nevertheless unable to inform the subcortex that we no longer live there.

What are the criteria that will determine the adequacy of psychosomatic models in accounting for the phenomena of psychosomatic illness?

In the first instance a causal model necessarily implies a process, and will be more powerful if it is possible to specify that process. The early psychoanalytic models, for example, offered plausible accounts of symbolism and organ language but failed to specify the process by which these would operate. Similarly, the descriptive epidemiological model offers convincing evidence but does not specify the underlying mechanisms. Merely to say that life events precipitate illness does nothing to account for symptom characteristics. Obviously a good theory should account for the role of precipitative factors since the evidence for such factors is undeniable. But the problem remains: how do extermal 'life' stimuli become linked with internal response mechanisms, and how can this lead to maladaptive symptoms? The role of internal factors themselves should also be considered by an adequate theory. How for example do over-arousal or underarousal translate into symptoms for some individuals and not for others?

Finally, there are three major characteristics of psychosomatic illness which a model should account for:

(1) the usual chronicity of the disease process, which may include periods of remission;
(2) the continuity of symptoms, including their characteristic patterns of recurrence;
(3) the specificity of symptoms within individuals.

One of the most striking features of psychosomatic illness is that it shows marked individual differences in susceptibility to illness, in modes of precipitation, and in the patterning of symptoms. Why one patient should develop gastric ulcer while another develops hypertension is a question that has often been asked and not yet satisfactorily answered.

It would be premature to suggest that a conditioning theory can fulfil all or any of these criteria. Nevertheless, it is an interesting exercise to 'map' the phenomena of classical conditioning to those of psychosomatic illness. When this is done the degree of fit is impressive and probably accounts for the largely untested conviction of some authors that classical conditioning is implicated.

A list of the visceral systems involved in interoceptive conditioning (Adam, 1967) is virtually a compendium of the organic systems involved in illness. Adam cites the following: gastrointestinal system, cardiovascular system, lymphatic system, urogenital system, respiratory system, the endocrine systems, red bone marrow, serous membranes, and the reticuloendothelial system. Each of these systems has been conditioned using the classical paradigm. The receptor mechanisms available to this form of conditioning include mechanoreceptors, chemoreceptors, baroreceptors, thermoreceptors, osmoreceptors, and volume receptors. It seems highly probable that each of these receptor types plays some part in the genesis of psychosomatic symptoms. Equally noteworthy is the fact that the changes induced in these organ systems by classical conditioning resemble the changes induced in psychosomatic illness. The experimental literature shows that among other changes increases in heart-rate and blood pressure, increased irritability and activity of mucosa increase and decrease in a number of blood constituents are readily conditionable. Thus autonomic/emotional, visceral, and systemic components are all involved.

Both classical conditioning and psychosomatic illness are remarkably susceptible to individual differences in response patterning. To some authors this fact is one of the most eloquent in considering a possible role for conditioning mechanisms in illness. If classical conditioning is involved in the genesis or maintenance of illness it must be on the basis of highly specific patterns of responding which are initially learned and which either fail to extinguish, or recover spontaneously. The continuity, chronicity, and specificity of symptoms refer to the recurrence of this pattern through time, and are highly consistent with the phenomena of conditioning.

Finally, and in a somewhat abstract sense, both psychosomatic illness and classical conditioning conform to the so-called stress/diathesis model; that is, to the interaction of individual susceptibility and appropriate external events. In other words, both are concerned with the transaction between the internal and external environment. Thus a comparison of the phenomena of classical conditioning with the characteristics of psychosomatic illness yields rather striking similarities.

Varieties of classical conditioning

The usual textbook descriptions of classical conditioning are given at a very simple level, and it is doubtful whether any material of relevance to psychosomatic medicine will be found in these early formulations. Modern techniques of classical conditioning extend to a wide variety of responses and to complex paradigms which are more likely to match the complexity of real-life situations.

This section therefore will review recent developments in the conditioning literature which refer to two kinds of variants. The first is the extension from a single response (e.g. salivation) to a range of responses which include autonomic, visceral, and systemic. The second is the extension from simple classical conditioning schedules (repeated trials of CS and UCS) to more elaborate procedures which have been studied in the laboratory in recent years.

Generalized autonomic responding

Pavlov's work was concerned with the salivary response and involved the accurate measurement of salivary flow by means of implanted cannulae, a technique which enabled investigators to quantify results with accuracy. Extension of the principles of classical conditioning was later made to skeletal-motor responses, usually withdrawal of the dog's forepaw from noxious stimulation. More important, however, was the extension to emotional reactions, usually fear, and to the measurement of visceral responses. This form of conditioning is robust and has been widely used in the laboratory with animal subjects. Indeed, the induction of increased sympathetic activity by classical aversive conditioning is now a standard laboratory technique (e.g. Ainslee and Engel, 1974; Obrist, 1976).

In the typical experiment an animal is exposed to shock preceded by a neutral stimulus such as click or tone, and after relatively few pairings the neutral stimulus comes to elicit a complex of autonomic events which is reasonably interpreted as the psychophysiological concomitant of the animal's fear of impending shock. Cardiovascular recordings have been particularly popular, partly because it is a measure which is easy to record and also because an increased heart-rate is a reliable response to unpleasant stimuli across many species.

This experimental prototype has been used as a model for the development of fears and phobias in human subjects, and might well be applicable to those psychosomatic conditions in which sustained autonomic arousal or precipitation by explicit environmental stimuli are prominent.

Visceral responding

Of more interest in the present context is the development of interoceptive conditioning, originated by Bykov in the 1930s. This form of conditioning involves the stimulation of interoceptors as either CS or UCS or both. Internal

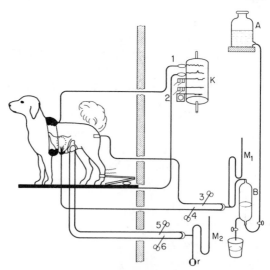

FIGURE 12.1. Apparatus used for interoceptive conditioning in the dog. A, B, delivery of water to implanted balloons; M_1, M_2, manometers monitoring intragastric and ileocaecal water pressure; 1, 6, tubes connecting the fistula to recording apparatus and water source. (Reproduced from Razran, 1961). Copyright (1980) by the American Psychological Association.

stimuli are typically those of pressure, warmth, or visceral distension produced by air or water. The simplest form of interoceptive conditioned reflex involves an internal CS and an external UCS. Figure 12.1 shows a dog in a conditioning situation and indicates that the procedure is nevertheless far from simple. As compared with his Pavlovian predecessor, the dog in the figure is equipped not only with one fistula for salivation but also with four others: one gastric, one rectal, and two ileocaecal (one to the ileum and one on the caecal side of the ileocaecal valve). Moreover provision is made for recording the dog's respiration and paw movements in response to electric shock and to the conditioned stimuli. Indeed, some Russian investigators also register the electroencephalograph (EEG), electrocardiograph (ECG), electrodermal activity (EDA), oculomotor, and pupillographic changes during conditioning.

In a simple prototype experiment the caecum is inflated with 30 cm^3 of air (CS) followed by a single electric shock (UCS) administered to the animal's left hindpaw. Within a few trials conditioned withdrawal of the paw occurs in response to the inflation, and this demonstrates the expected result of contingent pairing of CS and UCS. Using this type of preparation the laws of conditioning found for external receptors have been shown to apply to interoceptive conditioned reflexes.

An example of an experiment in which both stimuli are interoceptive in origin is the following. The CS, wetting of the gastric mucosa through a fistula, is followed by the introduction of water into the stomach, a UCS which produces a hyposmotic state. After the CS and UCS have been paired 20–25 times, wetting of the gastric mucosa alone elicits diuresis even though the water has been completely removed from the stomach through the fistula. Thus afferent impulses originating from gastric receptors evoke a response similar to the one resulting from hyposmosis.

The techniques of interoceptive conditioning have been well developed by Russian investigators and have been reviewed by Razran (1961). They have shown that interoceptive conditioning experiments follow the same general laws as conventional procedures. Sherrington's original division of receptors into exteroceptors, proprioceptors, and interoceptors has stood the test of time, and each of these receptor systems and their combinations can be conditioned. However, while the physiology of the receptor systems is well known, and in the case of the exteroceptors their inter-connection with CNS events is generally well documented, the interaction of interoceptive and CNS events is little understood (Adam, 1967).

Pavlov noted in 1912 that the cortex must contain some system analysers which monitor or keep track of all the internal events occurring within the organism. This view has a surprisingly modern ring in the light of the formulations to be discussed later in connection with taste aversion. Not only is the nervous system capable of responding to and integrating interoceptive messages, but it is apparently capable of predicting their consequences. This is the empirical basis on which interoceptive conditioning rests.

Systemic reactions

As well as being interested in specific visceral responses, conditioning theorists have studied more general systemic reactions. The Corsons and their co-workers (1962, 1963) studied conditioning of antidiuretic responses as part of a long-term programme designed to elucidate the role of the CNS in the regulation of renal function. In experiments concerned with electrolyte balance they observed that some of the response effects arose from emotional factors. This observation was followed up in conditioning experiments in which cannulae were implanted in the urinary bladders of dogs and a classical conditioning schedule applied using tones followed by shocks to the leg. Dogs were hydrated prior to the experiment, and the consequence of a number of pairings was to produce a decrease in urine output accompanied by increased urine osmolarity. It was also noted that the entire complex of the conditioning chamber was transformed into a CS so that the dog gave the antidiuretic response (CR) as soon as it was placed on the conditioning stand (see Figure 12.2). In other words the response had become conditioned to the environment as well as to the specific stimulus. These conditioned antidiuretic and electrolyte retention responses may be considered as examples of physiologically inappropriate responses when they become chronic, exaggerated, and generalized to diverse stimuli.

Experiments with renal function in human subjects by De Maria *et al.* (1963) employed an unusual paradigm in which acute anxiety or fear associated with anticipation of pain produced the visceral UCR, a constriction of the renal arteries at the point of their bifurcation, visible on the radiorenogram. The authors had observed that patients who are acutely anxious show changes in the radiorenogram, interpreted as a decrease in renal blood flow, comparable to that shown by adults with chronic hypertension. Using a group of 10 normal subjects, a series of 10 trials was given, in which a tone was paired with shock, and then an eleventh, tone-alone trial, following which a renogram was immediately recorded. Seven of the subjects demonstrated a renogram response to the CS on this test trial. In most of these reactive subjects a decrease in the vascular and concentration components was more pronounced in the right kidney than in the left, and the authors tentatively note that unilateral renal disease as a basis for hypertension tends to occur predominantly on the right side.

More recent work has suggested that blood glucose level can be classically conditioned (Woods and Kulkosky, 1976). In a typical experiment the administration of insulin or glucose (UCS) is repeatedly associated with CS (usually an auditory or olfactory stimulus). After a number of pairings of CS and insulin or glucose, the CS alone elicits a change in blood glucose. Using this technique it was possible to condition either hypoglycaemia or hyperglycaemia, depending on the UCS used in the experiment, the magnitude of the CR being of the order of from 10 to 35 mg glucose/100 ml blood.

The authors review a large number of factors relevant to this type of condi-

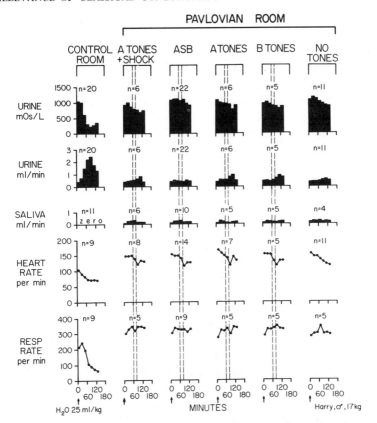

FIGURE 12.2. Conditioned respiratory, salivary, cardiac and anti-diuretic responses to psychologic stress in a dog; n = number of experiments in a given design. Broken vertical lines indicate the 20-minute period during which reinforced, unreinforced or inhibitory tones were presented. 'A tones and shock' indicate that 20 reinforced tones were administered, 'ASB' indicates that 10 reinforced tones were interspersed at random with 10 inhibitory B tones: 'A tones' signifies extinction sessions of 20 unreinforced A tones. 'B tones' signifies presentation of 20 inhibitory tones. 'No tones' signifies that the animal was placed in the conditioning chamber but that no stimuli were presented. Note that the conditioning chamber complex acted as a conditional stimulus, the dog exhibiting conditioned antidiuretic, cardiac and salivary responses while it was in the conditioning chamber. (Reproduced from Corson *et al.*, 1970)

tioning, e.g. the injection procedure itself as a CS, dose of insulin, etc. The CR exhibits all the properties of a classically conditioned response, and the underlying mechanism appears to be a CNS-mediated response of pancreatic insulin to the CS. One question which arises is whether this phenomenon, produced under the artificial conditions of the laboratory, can occur in normal life, and

Woods and Kulkosky review a considerable amount of evidence that stimuli which reliably predict the presence of food can elicit insulin secretion and hypoglycaemia.

Classical conditioning of the immunosuppressive response has also been demonstrated (Ader and Cohen, 1975; Rogers *et al.*, 1976), and this raises interesting possibilities in the present context. It has often been demonstrated that rats given a distinctively flavoured drinking solution such as saccharin (CS) followed by a toxic agent (UCS) capable of eliciting a temporary gastro-intestinal upset (UCR) will acquire a conditioned aversion to the saccharin solution.

Using a saccharin CS and a single intraperitoneal injection of 50 mg/kg cyclophosphamide as UCS, Ader and Cohen noted that their rats acquired the predicted aversion to saccharin, but more important they also observed that some of the cyclophosphamide-treated animals died, and that the mortality rate tended to vary directly with the volume of saccharin originally consumed. In order to account for this observation it was hypothesized that the pairing of a neutral CS with the chemical agent resulted in the conditioning of immuno-suppression. Investigation of antibody titres supported the hypothesis that the conditioned animals had become more vulnerable to superimposition of latent pathogens which may have existed in the environment.

Similar procedures were used in a second experiment in which lithium chloride, a non-immunosuppressive agent, was used as the UCS. While lithium chloride was effective in inducing a taste aversion, conditioned animals showed no reduction in antibody titres. These results suggest that conditioned immuno-suppression is not mediated directly by non-specific elevations in adrenocortical steroids that may accompany an illness-induced taste aversion. The authors suggest that there may be an intimate and virtually unexplored relationship between the CNS and immunological processes, and that behavioural condition-ing techniques provide a means for studying this relationship.

Organ systems relevant to psychosomatic illness

There has been a recent interest in examining eating behaviour as a form of conditioning, and this work has been extended to human subjects and to the treatment of obesity. Stunkard (1975) has suggested that, by the end of the meal, absorption is not great enough to explain the cessation of feeding and he postulates that satiety of a familiar food might be a conditioned response to the food. He argues that adjustment of meal size to varying caloric densities may represent a learned Pavlovian response. Stimulation of the oropharyngeal area, and particularly filling of the stomach, serve as CSs for ending a meal. Later, perhaps as much as 2 hours later, nutrients absorbed from the gastro-intestinal tract, or their metabolic products, are conveyed through the blood stream to satiety areas in the brain where they serve as unconditioned stimuli. Conditioning is therefore seen to arise from delayed after-effects of eating that food on earlier occasions.

Booth (1977) describes a series of experiments in support of the view that much of the control of feeding is not innately reflexive but learned. He suggests that satiety conditioning would be a relative aversion confined to the late stages of the meal, and that appetite and satiety are largely conditioned preferences and aversions which are state-dependent, the internal stimulus states being energy and amino acid metabolism or close correlates thereof. Obese human patients may be less sensitive to the internal signs of their caloric state and more than normally stimulated by the palatability of external feeding cues. A shift in the internal state could be produced by conditioning, and such a shift could become a chronic state. Thus conditioning may be implicated in the establishment of a precondition for subsequent illness.

In spite of speculative interest in the possibility that conditioning influences psychosomatic illness, very little work has been done in the conditioning of actual disease states. An exception is the investigation of bronchial asthma. Dekker and Groen (1956) observed reactions in patients which they attributed to conditioning and this possibility was tested experimentally by Dekker, Pelser, and Groen, (1957) who succeeded in eliciting asthmatic attacks to neutral stimuli in two patients. It should be noted that the procedure was attempted on 100 patients, of which only these two showed convincing evidence of conditioning (Purcell and Weiss, 1970). The method involved oral inhalation of an allergen aerosol to which the patients were sensitive. After establishing that the aerosol was an effective stimulus for asthmatic attack, it was associated with presentation of a neutral aerosol, previously shown to be ineffective in precipitating attacks. The investigators were careful to exclude contamination of the inhalation tube and mouthpiece by the active allergens. Each of the patients rapidly developed conditioned asthmatic attacks to the neutral solution, which generalized to the contact with the mouthpiece in the absence of the solution. The authors report that the conditioned asthmatic attacks were exceedingly difficult to extinguish, and note that an effective deconditioning procedure would be required to reverse the result of conditioning.

Conditioning of asthmatic attacks in guinea pigs was demonstrated by Ottenberg et al. (1958) but the criterion of the attack was limited to visual observation and the adequacy of this evidence has been questioned (Purcell and Weiss, 1970). The description by Gantt (1944) of a dog who developed apparent asthmatic attacks during the conditioning of an experimental neurosis has been widely quoted. One of the interesting features of this report is that the animal manifested increasing respiratory distress as it approached the conditioning chamber, which subsided as it was led away. In other words the conditioned behaviour had generalized to a complex situational CS. Purcell and Weiss (1970), reviewing this literature, sceptically report that 'with either animals or human beings, the successful conditioning of asthma remains to be demonstrated' (p. 607). It might be noted, however, that with the exception of the report by Gantt this work was done using very primitive conditioning paradigms, and more sophisticated techniques are required in this type of study.

Extensions of the basic paradigm

The essential events in the development of conditioned responses are complex, and the criteria which define classical conditioning have been greatly refined in recent years. The essential characteristic of classical conditioning is that the unconditioned stimulus (UCS) is presented regardless of the behaviour of the animal. In other words, the contingency between CS and UCS is determined by the experimenter (or the environment) and is not dependent on the nature of the subject's response. This differs from the operant conditioning paradigm (see Chapter 9) in which the subject 'learns' to increase those behaviours which are rewarded and decrease those which are punished.

An important development of the last decade has been the experimental manoeuvre of combining classical and operant schedules. The earliest experiments of this type were those in which CS–UCS pairings were first carried out in the usual way, the UCS typically being electric shock. The CS was then presented to the animal while it was performing a learned instrumental response, e.g. pressing a bar for food. The fear-inducing effect of the CS (and thus the effect of the prior classical conditioning) was measured as a decrement in the rate of the instrumental response, (Kamin, Brimen, and Black, 1963).

There are several variants on what has been termed 'two process' models of behaviour, that is, a model which supposes that observed behaviour is an outcome of the interaction between two underlying processes, one a classical conditioning component which accounts for the response becoming attached to the CS, and the other, an instrumental component, which is responsible for the guidance of behaviour in such a way as to maximize positive and minimize negative outcomes. These techniques offer a promising avenue to the understanding of autonomic and somatic relationships.

Two or three prototypes are of interest and appear potentially relevant to the problems of psychosomatic illness and its treatment. Furedy and Poulos (1976) have succeeded in classically conditioning a deceleration of heart-rate using postural tilt as the UCS, combined with operant training to maintain the lowered heart-rate. Ainslee and Engel (1974), using monkeys as subjects, have induced elevation of blood pressure and heart-rate by classical aversive conditioning, and subsequently used operant training to lower the cardiovascular response.

An interesting experiment on monkeys by Adam (1967) illustrates the potential complexity of the classical-operant interaction. An operantly conditioned lever-press was first established, followed by classical interoceptive conditioning using rhythmic distension of the small intestine, renal pelvis, or carotid artery as the UCS. Finally the animals were trained on a discrimination schedule by manipulating the interoceptive stimulus as a discriminative stimulus to initiate or terminate the lever-press response. The interest of this type of experiment lies in the fact that the interoceptive discriminative stimulus is below the level of awareness as monitored by orienting and EEG desynchronization, and yet is capable of controlling complicated behavioural interactions with the external environment.

Another development in the general two-process model of behaviour has been provided by Kimmel, McLeod, and Burns (1978) who have succeeded in producing classically conditioned changes in tonic arousal. The point to emphasize here is that a chronic state is by its nature a more persistent and long-lasting condition than a phasic or punctate response, and Kimmel *et al.* have demonstrated that this chronic state can be maintained by appropriate conditioned stimuli. Such a chronic state—e.g. of arousal or anxiety—can be brought under the experimenter's or environment's direct manipulation and control, and can be viewed as determining further operant learning.

Conditioning outside the laboratory

In a certain sense it is true to say that conditioning in the laboratory, is a delicate operation in which strict rules have to be observed if it is to take place. These include the fixed repetition of CS–UCS pairings, a constant and brief CS–UCS interval, and so on. As a result, a frequently expressed doubt is how far the results of laboratory investigations can be applied to real-life problems. In the laboratory an external stimulus schedule is applied by the experimenter and is under his control. In natural environments the critical relations of laboratory stimuli are unlikely to occur systematically. In particular, it is argued that the frequent occurrence of CS alone would result in extinction of the hypothetical conditioned response.

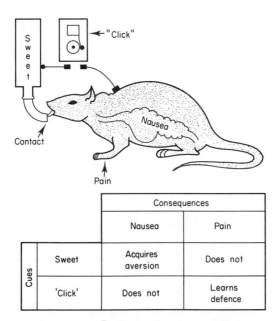

		Consequences	
		Nausea	Pain
Cues	Sweet	Acquires aversion	Does not
	'Click'	Does not	Learns defence

FIGURE 12.3. The effects of pairing a gustatory cue or an auditory cue with external pain or induced illness. (Reproduced from Garcia *et al.*, 1974)

Several lines of investigation bear on these problems. One of these concerns the fact that repeated exposure of the CS without the occurrence of the UCS does not necessarily lead to extinction of the CR, as Pavlov originally believed. Eysenck (1976) has drawn attention to the work of Napalkov (1963) which shows that, under some conditions, repeated unreinforced presentation of the CS may paradoxically result in an *increase* in the CR over a period of time; indeed, the strength of the CR may eventually exceed that of the original UCS (see Figure 12.3). Eysenck refers to this phenomenon as enhancement, pointing out that some CRs, such as those of anxiety, with associated physiological changes, are highly unpleasant for the subject to experience, and that their occurrence acts like a strong and unpleasant UCR, therefore resulting in an increase in CR strength. If this work is confirmed by future investigations it could demonstrate one of the ways in which classical conditioning can become maladaptive, for the subject continues to respond to a CS which is no longer appropriate. Eysenck has applied this concept to the explanation of neurotic behaviour, but it may equally well have significance for the explanation of psychosomatic illness.

Another line of investigation concerns the belief that the interstimulus interval between CS and UCS must be of limited duration, optimally 500 msec for skeletal responses, and of the order of seconds for autonomic responses. Recent work with the conditioning of taste aversions shows that rats can acquire an aversion to food or water of a specific flavour or odour even if the toxic reaction follows its ingestion after several hours. It was demonstrated some years ago that this kind of aversion to poison bait is frequently encountered in rats in the natural environment: tastes are paired with poisoning and the effects of poison do not usually begin immediately. Such learning gives a selective advantage in the process of survival.

A number of experimental studies have confirmed this observation, and a conditioning model has been proposed to account for the toxiphobia which develops. Ingestion of the food (CS) is followed by a UCS which produces delayed illness. Agents employed have included hypodermic injection of a hypertonic glucose solution, fairly large doses of insulin or amphetamine, and toxic irradiation.

This form of long-delayed conditioning appears to be a form of Pavlovian conditioning with the following distinctive features:

(1) the CS must be either taste or smell;
(2) the UCS must be a general dysphoric bodily state such as radiation sickness, fever, or nausea;
(3) the learning occurs with unusual rapidity, after as few as one CS–UCS pairing;
(4) the CS–UCS interval can be as long as 10 hours;
(5) the CR is unusually resistant to extinction;
(6) these delayed CRs are not easily modified by information or cognition.

It is not an uncommon experience in everyday life to eat a meal which is followed by nausea due to another cause such as gastric flu. Characteristically the meal is remembered as aversive, and the knowledge that 'flu and not the meal caused vomiting does not inhibit the aversion to the meal (Seligman and Hager, 1972).

It is significant that in the experiments just mentioned the animals learn to associate taste and odours rather than external cues such as lights with subsequent nausea. Figure 12.4, from Garcia, Harkins, and Rusiniak (1974) illustrates the design and results of a number of experiments which show the phenomenon of conditioned taste aversion. Rats punished by nausea acquire an aversion for the sweet taste of saccharin and refuse to drink. However, the animals will not acquire an aversion for a click, even if the click is repeatedly followed by delayed illness. On the other hand, if punished by electric shock the animals will quickly learn to defend against the shock by backing away from the source of the taste, i.e. the drinking spout, yet this will not be followed by an aversion for the sweet taste.

Seligman and Hager (1972) have applied the term 'preparedness' to the finding that certain stimuli become more easily conditioned to certain responses than others (in the example given, click with shock, taste with nausea). Another example comes from the literature on phobic states, which seem limited to fears of specific animals, heights, darkness, etc. Such fears, while not innate, are 'ready' to be elicited. Only rarely is there an electricity phobia or a hammer phobia, though these are likely to be associated with trauma in our world.

The belief proposed by the naïve behaviourism of the 1930s, that any stimulus can be conditioned with equal readiness to any response, has been long since discredited. However, the misunderstanding on which it was based has probably served to discredit conditioning theory, particularly as an explanation of

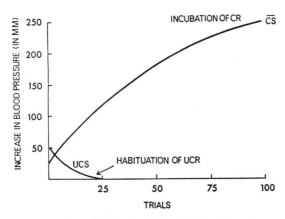

FIGURE 12.4. Increase in blood pressure as a function of repeated exposure of the dog to CS only (incubation) and decrease in blood pressure to UCS (habituation). (Reproduced from Eysenck, 1976)

real-life events. In this section we have attempted to show that some of the arguments against the use of classical conditioning as an explanatory model of behaviour are not justified in modern conditioning theory and observation.

Some important aspects of these conditioning techniques and their extension to visceral and systemic responses should be emphasized. The first concerns the nature of the responses that are actually conditioned in any experiment. The tendency of investigators in the West to concentrate attention on a single response component has probably led in the past to misunderstandings concerning the nature of classical conditioning. It is important to remember that when an unconditioned stimulus is applied, all the behaviour that accompanies it is potentially conditionable, though at different rates. Obrist (1976) discusses the view that single parameters of visceral functioning such as heart-rate can be trained independently of other cardiovascular processes such as blood pressure. He points out that in fact the heart-rate response which is apparently conditioned is the final product of a complex of changes in blood pressure and vagal tone mediated by baroreceptors and reflecting the preparation of the organism for somatic activity.

The second concerns the problem of subjective consciousness of the stimuli used in the conditioning process. The fact that impulses from the visceral field do not lead to subjective sensation, and hence fail to reach consciousness, is of particular importance in considering interoceptive conditioning. Distension of a hollow viscus is accompanied by pain, as is stretching of the visceral mesentery, and these occur as surgical symptoms. However, in the usual interoceptive conditioning experiment investigators are careful to avoid painful stimulation. Sherrington declared categorically that interoceptive stimuli never reach subjective awareness, while Sechenov referred to vague organ sensations which may reach consciousness but which are difficult to localize and interpret. A growing number of facts indicate that a surprisingly rich and extensive visceral receptor system sends a continuous stream of information about the state of the internal environment to the higher centres. Such information not only exerts a feedback control on other organ systems but explicitly influences behaviour, without entering consciousness. A part of the significance of conditioning without awareness is that it avoids the criticism sometimes levelled at the classical conditioning experiment that it can be explained in terms of cognitive expectation.

Finally, an interesting phenomenon discussed in several of the experiments reported above is the degree to which the conditioned response patterns generalize to stimuli other than the specific CS of the experiment. They may occur to various CS-related cues, such as the room, the experimenter, or the building in which the conditioning took place. In an extremely frightening experiment in which scoline was used to produce respiratory paralysis, one subject subsequently reported that he experienced profound anxiety whenever he entered the part of the building where he had been conditioned (Campbell, Sanderson and Laverty, 1964). Pavlov reported that after 5 or 6 injections of morphine the mere preliminaries of injection, including first sight of the experimenter, were in themselves sufficient to produce all the symptoms of nausea, secretion of saliva, vomiting, and sleep.

In summary, many experiments have been performed using humans, dogs, and monkeys as subjects. The conclusions from this work emphasize the ubiquity, the largely unconscious character, and all-round conditionability of interoceptive stimulation. Though the investigator's attention is fixed on a particular effector, what is being conditioned is a wide range of changes, particularly when visceral responses are elicited as part of the overall defensive reaction. These conditioned visceral responses have been shown to persist over long periods of time, long after the somatic components have dropped out, and they often result from prolonged exposure to the conditioning situation. It is important to re-emphasize that the classical conditioning situation invariably represents unavoidable and uncontrollable forms of stimulation.

The potential relevance of this work to psychosomatic illness is clear; feelings of anxiety or its unconscious viscero-motor accompaniments are capable of becoming conditioned stimuli for altered function in a variety of organ systems. The fact that this process can occur without awareness suggests that the individual might become conditioned to respond to inappropriate internal or external stimuli over long periods of time during which he would have no knowledge of the progressive disturbance of function.

Classical conditioning and individual differences

It has already been mentioned that the fact of marked individual differences in conditioning behaviour, and in the patterning of conditioned responses, is for some authors one of the most persuasive arguments for considering classical conditioning in relation to psychosomatic illness. It must be appreciated, however, that this aspect of conditioning has not been extensively studied.

In the 1920s Pavlov was led to investigate the role of individual differences in temperament in the conditioning performance of his dogs. He identified four temperamental types which he equated with the classical temperaments, sanguine, melancholic, choleric, and phlegmatic. He attributed these differences in temperament to the strength of the nervous system, by which he meant its resistance to inhibition, the equilibirum of inhibitory and excitatory processes within the nervous system, and the mobility or excitability of the nervous system.

In these terms the melancholic type was regarded as weak, while the choleric type was regarded as strong. The phlegmatic and sanguine types were regarded as 'normal' in strength but were differentiated by the factor of excitability. These differences were established by a series of objective 'tests' of the animal's performance across a range of conditioning procedures. Teplov (1964) extended these concepts to human subjects, working chiefly with the dimension of strength of the nervous system.

The work of Eysenck on the two major personality dimensions of neuroticism and introversion–extraversion is well known. He postulates that these two personality dimensions, defined by factor analysis, are orthogonal and thus form the four quadrants corresponding again to the four basic temperaments of classical theory. Eysenck (1967) has suggested that the temperamental dimension of introversion–extraversion has its physiological basis in the arousal system mediated by the reticular formation. He suggests that cortical arousal is more active in the introvert than the extravert. The dimension of neuroticism is referred to the autonomic nervous system, such that individuals high in neuroticism are characterized by labile autonomic responding.

On the basis of these postulates it was predicted that introverts would condition more readily than extraverts under normal circumstances, since the latter tend to summate inhibition more rapidly and excitation more slowly than the former. This prediction has been tested a number of times under differing experimental conditions which have led to its refinement. Introverts condition better, that is give more conditioned responses, under conditions which favour the development of inhibition. Under conditions in which inhibition is relatively lacking, extraverts may show superior levels of responding (Eysenck and Levey, 1972). Eysenck has attributed this to the Pavlovian phenomenon of paradoxical inhibition, in which stimulus conditions of high excitation can lead to inhibition of responding. The phenomenon was first observed by Pavlov in those dogs which exhibited a 'weak' nervous system, comparable to the introverted human subject.

Among the earliest systematic attempts to identify individual differences in conditioning was the work of Spence and Taylor (1951) who postulated that anxiety as measured by the Taylor Manifest Anxiety Scale would facilitate conditioning in normal subjects. A good deal of experimental work has shown that anxiety can facilitate conditioning provided the situation is such that anxiety is actively induced, and that the level of anxiety is not sufficiently strong that conditioning is interfered with. In short, anxiety effects show the inverted-U phenomenon, i.e. high and low anxiety levels impair performance, while moderate levels of anxiety are associated with optimum performance, and these can be demonstrated as a function of individual differences in human subjects. That anxiety is implicated in the development of psychosomatic illness is agreed by most authors, and the concept of heightened conditionability in specific organ systems in anxious subjects merits further investigation.

Gray (1975) has produced a theory of individual differences which incorporates the dimensions both of anxiety and of arousal. Rather than adopt a simple unitary concept of learning he has proposed nine distinct sub-categories of behaviour relevant to learning, which are differentially susceptible to the effects of arousal and anxiety. These include the phenomena of behavioural inhibition, habituation, excitatory conditioning, and so on. The experimental programme on which this work is based serves to identify the behaviours characteristic of each of these categories and the neural substrates underlying them. This theory structure, too complex to be described in detail in the present context, offers considerable promise for the eventual understanding of individual differences in conditioning.

The systematic investigation of individual differences in personality requires very large numbers of subjects, partly because the variance in frequency of conditioned responding is usually very high. This fact of itself points to the importance of individual variations in the classical conditioning process, whether they can be specified or not. Most of the work on personality and conditioning has been done with very simple skeletal-motor responses such as the eyeblink, or with simple autonomic responses such as the skin resistance response. These responses are of limited interest in the present context and it remains for the future to investigate the influence of individual differences on more elaborate forms of conditioning. For better or worse, most of the investigations of the conditioning phenomena of interest have been undertaken by Russian investigators, who traditionally work with very small samples, and indeed with individual animals. In this context individual differences, though reported frequently, are not studied systematically since the interoceptive conditioning experiments require lengthy preparation of subjects which makes large-scale studies unfeasible. Where studies of interoceptive conditioning have been reported in the West, individual differences in responding are again frequently reported. Corson and Corson (1976), for example, identify two distinct types of dogs, labelled low-adaptive and high-adaptive, which exhibit diametrically opposed response patterns in the antidiuretic conditioning experiment described earlier.

Among Western investigators individual differences have generally been considered under the rubric of personality, and a number of models of personality and individual differences are available. These have recently been reviewed by Claridge (1973) who concludes that most personality typologies are not readily accessible to experimental confirmation. The personality typology of Eysenck, mentioned earlier, is an exception and a large body of experimental work on these concepts is well known. During the past decade objective behavioural science has offered an alternative approach to the description of personality notably in the work of Mischel (1973) and Staats (1975). Both of these authors, from differing theoretical vantages, offer personality models which depend on the unique experiences of individuals to explain the continuity and patterning of personality. These are essentially learning models of personality and have the descriptive and theoretical advantage of appearing at least to account for some of the fine-grained qualitative differences which typological theories are forced to ignore. However, they are not in themselves able to account for individual differences in conditioning, though they rely on conditioning mechanisms to account for individual differences.

Apart from models of personality the work on individual differences in conditioning has tended to focus on specific traits such as anxiety, mentioned earlier in the work of Spence, which make no assumptions about personality as such. The past decade has seen the emergence of several unidimensional traits which may hold promise for the investigation of conditioning. The identification by Spielberger (1972) of separate components of trait and state anxiety, that is of tonic anxiety levels as opposed to situational anxiety, offers the possibility of identifying further those anxiety components in conditioning which are dependent on situational variables. Similarly Zuckerman's development of the sensation-seeking scale (Zuckerman, 1971) has been shown to reflect differences in an interesting variety of behaviours and might well be applied to systematic studies in conditioning. Finally the measurement of 'locus of control' (Rotter, 1966) recommends itself on intuitive grounds to the study of conditioning viewed as a transaction between the internal and external environment.

The chapters of this section, including the present one, are concerned with individual differences in relation to psychosomatic concepts. To summarize what has been said with regard to conditioning, those systematic studies of individual differences which have been undertaken with large numbers of subjects have shown marked effects of individual differences but have been limited to fairly trivial forms of the conditioning experiment. There is little doubt on the basis of anecdotal evidence and observation that individual differences in the patterning of responding are important in conditioning.

Further, it has been demonstrated that, within individuals, a reflex system which is 'lively' or readily aroused is more easily conditioned than relatively unreactive systems. Laboratory studies have mainly used autonomic variables but it seems reasonable that this principle could be extended to the case of organ system excitability. Thus an individual with an intrinsically hyperactive gastrointestinal tract, for example, might be more prone to develop colonic spasm or cardiospasm. These are speculative considerations, which serve to emphasize the importance of differential conditionability in any model of illness based on conditioning principles. Nevertheless, those who argue in favour of a classical conditioning model in the explanation of psychosomatic illness are obliged to rely heavily on the response specificity which conditioning demonstrates and which is observed in psychosomatic illness.

Classical conditioning and psychosomatic illness

The preceding sections have outlined some of the issues and developments in conditioning which may be judged to be relevant to the implication of classical conditioning in psychosomatic illness. It remains to re-examine the candidacy of classical conditioning for a role in the genesis of psychosomatic illness.

Three roles may be discerned for a conditioning process:

(1) causation of illness *de novo*;
(2) precipitation of attacks or episodes of an existing illness;
(3) initiation or maintenance of the psychological substrate underlying illness.

The first of these, direct causation of illness, represents a radical point of view which should be examined very critically. It implies that the visceral consequences of an illness, its signs and symptoms, be elicited first by some adequate form of stimulation and become conditioned to previously neutral stimuli. In other words the UCR must be the illness itself, or those physiological changes which are labelled as the illness. Speculative examples might include the induction of asthmatic attacks by exposure to bronchial irritation or the induction of colonic spasm in the presence of situational cues. In this case the physiological changes would come to be defined as illness if they were repeatedly elicited by situational cues. These examples are merely illustrative and in fact it is difficult to identify a subform of psychosomatic illness which would readily fit this model.

The precipitation of symptoms in an already existing illness offers more scope. In this case the UCR is the already established illness, and a conditioning process would involve extending the range of precipitating events to those which were previously inadequate. Patients report that the mere sight of an allergenic agent, for example cats or flowers, can precipitate attacks of asthma or sinusitis. Needless to say this type of report should not be taken as evidence for conditioning without objective observation using the controls appropriate to conditioning studies. It should be noted that this category would include conditioned emotional reactions which in turn precipitated episodes of illness. In this case we are considering autonomic conditioning rather than the interoceptive conditioning implied in the model of direct causation.

The third category would necessitate argument that conditioning processes are capable of inducing chronic stress. The concept of psychosocial stress (Levi, 1971) is interesting in that it refers to real-life forms of environmental stressors. The kinds of extreme physical stress used in animal experiments are not likely to be encountered in everyday human experience. That repeated stress is associated with hypertension has been demonstrated by Heine, Sainsbury, and Chynoweth (1969) who made the ingenious assumption that recurrent depression is itself a form of stress. If a conditioning model were to be applied to the concept of chronic stress one of the criteria of evaluation would be that inappropriate stimuli in the environment come to elicit repeated stress reactions.

In considering the possible implication of classical conditioning in psychosomatic illness it is evident that individual differences, both in conditionability and in response patterning, would need to be examined. Of the many dogs trained by Gantt only one developed apparent bronchial asthma and the same was true of the patients of Dekker *et al.* The concept of autonomic response specificity elaborated by Lacey (1967) is clearly relevant to the problem of individual response patterning. It should be noted that the role of skeletal and somatic responses and their interaction with visceral responding are not understood. The interoceptive conditioning model can involve, as described earlier, either a CS or a UCS which is exteroceptive. In an excellent review of biofeedback techniques, Miller (1978) has categorized the ways in which skeletal responses can interact with visceral responses, and has reviewed the modification of visceral responding through training. While these procedures are usually classified as instrumental learning, many of them fit equally well into the classical conditioning paradigm.

As a cautious summary it would seem that two possibilities offer the most plausible basis for implicating classical conditioning in psychosomatic illness.

The first of these is the classical conditioning of defence reactions, involving autonomic, visceral, and systemic components. Conditioning of individual components has been demonstrated in the laboratory, and it requires merely an act of imagination to suppose that this type of conditioning could occur in real-life situations. It seems almost certain that such a model would have to refer to individual differences in susceptibility to chronic impairment. One of the factors contributing an aura of plausibility to this model is that it allows for repeated exposure to environmental situations which would not of themselves be considered stressful. Similarly the process could occur below the level of conscious awareness. The second area of plausibility lies in the implications of interoceptive conditioning described in an earlier section. Again the possibility is open that visceral stimulation occurring below the level of subjective awareness leads to chronic exacerbation of visceral changes resulting in eventual organ damage.

It would be premature to offer any judgement as to the real-life operation of classical conditioning as opposed to plausible speculations. An earlier interest in conditioning in illness was based on very primitive models of conditioning and it seems reasonable to suppose that no conclusion can be drawn until contemporary conditioning procedures are used in the investigation of this field. At the same time a global model of conditioning as responsible for psychogenic illness carries little conviction in view of the known complexity of psychosomatic illnesses. The suggestion of Weiner (1976) that sub-forms of illness should be identified and examined individually must be taken seriously as the basis for future work.

Finally, whatever role is assigned to classical conditioning, it must be recognized that this is fundamentally an adaptive mechanism ensuring the survival of the individual. The circumstances under which conditioning can become maladaptive must therefore be examined. The adaptive advantages of taste aversions have been described in an earlier section. However this literature contains an interesting example of maladaptive conditioning reported by Rodgers and Rozin (1966). Thiamine-deprived rats were given a distinctively flavoured diet of adequate thiamine content. They rapidly developed the expected specific hunger for the distinctive taste of the food, particularly for their 'prepared' preference for saccharin. It was then shown that rats will continue to ingest a thiamine-free diet flavoured with saccharin in preference to an unlabelled food containing adequate thiamine until they die of thiamine deficiency. If premature death can be construed as the ultimate form of psychosomatic illness this experiment might be interpreted as a possible example of the classical conditioning of psychosomatic illness.

Acknowledgements

We gratefully acknowledge the support of the Bethlem and Maudsley Research Fund (to I.M.) and the Medical Research Council (to A.B.L.).

REFERENCES

Adam, G. (1967). *Interoception and Behaviour: an Experimental Study*. Budapest: Akademiai Kiado, Publishing House of the Hungarian Academy of Sciences.

Ader, R., and Cohen, N. (1975). Behaviorally conditioned immuno-suppression. *Psychosom. Med.*, **37**, 333–340.

Ainslee, G. W., and Engel, B. T. (1974). Alteration of classically conditioned heart rate by operant reinforcement in monkeys. *J. Comp. Physiol. Psychol.*, **87**, 373–382.

Alexander, F. (1952). *Psychosomatic Medicine*. London: Allen & Unwin.

Alexander, F., French, T., and Pollock, G. (1968). *Psychosomatic Specificity*. Chicago: University of Chicago Press.

Booth, D. A. (1977). Editorial: Satiety and appetite are conditioned reactions. *Psychosom. Med.*, **39**, 76–80.

Campbell, D., Sanderson, R. E., and Laverty, S. G. (1964). Characteristics of a conditioned response in human subjects during extinction trials following a single traumatic conditioning trial. *J. Abn. Soc. Psychol.*, **68**, 627–639.

Claridge, G. (1973). Psychosomatic relations in physical disease. In H. J. Eysenck (ed.), *Handbook of Abnormal Psychology*, ch. 19. London: Pitman Medical.

Corson, S. A., O'Leary Corson, E., and Pasamanick, B. (1963). Neuroendocrine factors in conditioned and unconditioned renal responses. *Excerpta Medica Int. Congr. Series No. 78, Proc. IInd. Int. Congr. of Nephrology, Prague*.

Corson, S. A., O'Leary Corson, E., Dykman, R. A., Peters, J. E., Reese, W. G., and Seager, L. D. (1962). The nature of conditioned antidiuretic and electrolyte retention responses. *Activ. Nerv. Sup. (Praha)*, **4**, 359–382.

Corson, S. A., O'Leary Corson, E., and Kirilcuk, V. (1970). Individual differences in respiratory responses of dogs to psychologic stress and Anokhin's formulation of the functional system as a unit of biological adaptation. *Int. J. Psychobiol.*, **1**, 1–12.

Corson, S. A., and O'Leary Corson, E. (1976). Constitutional differences in physiologic adaptation to stress and distress. In G. Serban (ed.), *Psychopathology of Human Adaptation*. New York: Plenum Press.

Dekker, E., and Groen, J. J. (1956). Reproducible psychogenic attacks of asthma. A laboratory study. *J. Psychosom. Res.*, **1**, 58–67.

Dekker, E., Pelser, H. E., and Groen, J. (1957). Conditioning as a cause of asthmatic attacks. A laboratory study. *J. Psychosom. Res.*, **2**, 97–108.

DeMaria, W. J. A., Shmavonian, B. M., Cohen, S. I., Drueger, R. P., Hawkins, D. M., Baylin, S. B., Sanders, A. P., and Baylin, G. J. (1963). Renal conditioning. *Psychosom. Med.*, **25**, 538–542.

Dunbar, F. (1943). *Psychosomatic Diagnosis*. New York: Hoeber.

Eysenck, H. J. (1967). *The Biological Basis of Personality*. Springfield, Ill.: Charles C. Thomas.

Eysenck, H. J. (1976). The learning model of neurosis—a new approach. *Behav. Res. Ther.*, **14**, 251–267.

Eysenck, H. J., and Levey, A. B. (1972). Conditioning, introversion–extraversion and the strength of the nervous system. In J. A. Gray and V. D. Nebylitsyn (eds.), *Biological Basis of Individual Behaviour*. London: Academic Press.

Furedy, J. J., and Paulos, C. X. (1976). Heart rate decelerative Pavlovian conditioning with tilt as UCS; towards behavioural control of cardiac dysfunction. *Biol. Psychol.*, **4**, 93–105.

Gantt, W. H. (1944). *Experimental Basis for Neurotic Behavior: Origin and Development of Artifically Produced Disturbances of Behaviour in Dogs*. New York: Hoeber.

Garcia, J., Hankins, W. G., and Rusiniak, K. W. (1974). Behavioral regulation of the milieu interne in man and rat. *Science*, **185**, 824–831.

Gray, J. A. (1975). *Elements of Two-process Theory of Learning*. London: Academic Press.

Heine, B. E., Sainsbury, P., and Chynoweth, R. C. (1969). Hypertension and emotional disturbance. *J. Psychiat. Res.*, **7**, 119–130.

Kamin, L. J., Brimen, C. J., and Black, A. H. (1963). Conditioned suppression as a monitor of fear of the CS in the course of avoidance training. *J. Comp. Physiol. Psychol.*, **56**, 497–501.

Kimmel, H. D., McLeod, D. C. and Burns, R. A. (1978). Trans-Switching: conditioning with tonic and phasic stimuli. *J. Exp. Psychol.*, **107**, 187–205.

Lacey, J. I. (1967). Somatic response patterning and stress: some revisions of activation theory. In M. Appley and R. Trumbull (eds.), *Psychological Stress*. New York: Appleton-Century-Crofts.

Levi, L. (1971). *Society, Stress and Disease*. Vol. I. London: Oxford University Press.

Mason, J. W. (1968). The scope of psychoendocrine research. *Psychosom. Med.*, **30**, 565–575.

Mason, J. W. (1970). Strategy in psychosomatic research. *Psychosom. Med.*, **32**, 427–439.

Miller, N. E. (1978). Biofeedback and visceral learning. *Ann. Rev. Psychol.*, **29**, 373–404.

Mischel, W. (1973). Toward a cognitive social learning reconceptualization of personality. *Psychol. Rev.*, **80**, 252–283.

Napalkov, S. V. (1963). Information process and the brain. In N., Wiener and J. Schade (eds), *Progress in Brain Research*, vol. 2, pp. 59–69. Amsterdam: Elsevier.

Obrist, P. A. (1976). The cardiovascular–behavioral interaction as it appears today. *Psychophysiology*, **13**, 95–107.

Ottenberg, P., Stein, M., Lewis, J., and Hamilton, C. (1958). Learned asthma in the guinea pig. *Psychosom. Med.*, **20**, 395–400.

Purcell, K., and Weiss, J. H. (1970). Asthma. In C. G. Costello (ed.), *Symptoms of Psychopathology: a Handbook*. New York: Wiley.

Razran, G. (1961). The observable unconscious and the inferable conscious in current Soviet psychophysiology: interoceptive conditioning, semantic conditioning and the orienting reflex. *Psychol. Rev.*, **68**, 81–147.

Rodgers, W. L., and Rozin, P. (1966). Novel food preferences in thiamine-deficient rats. *J. Comp. Physiol. Psychol.*, **61**, 1–4.

Rogers, M. P., Reich, P., Strom, T. B., and Carpenter, C. B. (1976). Behaviorally conditioned immunosuppression: replication of a recent study. *Psychosom. Med.*, **38**, 447–450.

Rotter, J. B. (1966). Generalized expectancies for internal vs external control of reinforcements. *Psychol. Monogr.* No. 80 (whole No. 609).

Seligman, M. E. P., and Hager, J. L. (eds.) (1972). *Biological Boundaries of Learning*. New York Appleton-Century-Crofts.

Selye, H. (1956). *The Stress of Life*. New York: McGraw Hill.

Spence, K. W., and Taylor, J. (1951). Anxiety and strength of UCS as determinants of amount of eyelid conditioning. *J. Exp. Psychol.*, **42**, 183–188.

Spielberger, C. D. (1972). Anxiety as an emotional state. In C. D. Spielberger (ed.), Anxiety, *Current Trends in Theory and Research*, pp. 23–49. New York: Academic Press.

Staats, A. W. (1975). *Social Behaviorism*. Homewood, Illinois: Dorsey Press.

Stunkard, A. (1975). Satiety is a conditioned reflex. *Psychosom. Med.*, **37**, 383–387.

Teplov, B. M. (1964). *Pavlov's Typology* (trans. J. A. Gray). Oxford: Pergamon Press.

Weiner, H. (1976). The heterogeneity of 'psychosomatic disease'. *Psychosom. Med.*, **38**, 371–372.

Woods, S. C., and Kulkosky, P. J. (1976). Classically conditioned changes of blood glucose level. *Psychosom. Med.*, **38**, 201–215.

Zuckerman, M. (1971). Dimensions of sensation seeking. *J. Consult. Clin. Psychol.*, **36**, 45–52.

Foundations of Psychosomatics
Edited by M. J. Christie and P. G. Mellett
© 1981 John Wiley & Sons Ltd.

13

THE PSYCHOPHYSIOLOGY OF PSYCHOPATHIC BEHAVIOUR

DAVID A.T. SIDDLE AND GORDON B. TRASLER
University of Southampton, England.

INTRODUCTION

The aim of this chapter is to review what is currently known of the psychophysiological correlates of psychopathy and psychopathic behaviour. This is a confused field of study which is complicated by the coexistence of several quite different theoretical positions and the existence of a great many more unexplicit theoretical assumptions. For this reason we have chosen to adopt, as a way of organizing the material, a framework derived from the theoretical propositions advanced by one of us (Trasler, 1973, 1978a). We hope, however, that our evaluations are substantially independent of our theoretical orientation and that readers who prefer to adopt another theoretical perspective may find here at least an annotation of the relevant work.

The most comprehensive clinical description of the psychopathic personality is contained in Cleckley's book, *The Mask of Sanity* (Cleckley, 1941, 1976). This was the source of a group of criteria for the selection of subjects which was first adopted by Lykken (1955). Hare and his colleagues have employed similar criteria in drawing samples of psychopaths for their series of studies (Hare, 1970; Hare and Cox, 1978), and have recently attempted to attain greater precision in the selection of experimental subjects by developing a 'research scale' or checklist, again based upon Cleckley's description, which appears to have relatively high interrater reliability (Hare, in press).

The nature of Cleckley's description is well conveyed by Lykken's list of criteria. This contains items of several kinds, some of which refer to the conduct of the psychopath ('he will commit theft, fraud, and other deeds for astonishingly small stakes and under much greater risks of being discovered than will the ordinary scoundrel'—p. 111), his response to attempts by others to modify his behaviour ('does not show the slightest evidence of humiliation or regret . . . no punishment will make him change his ways'—p. 111), and his responsiveness to immediate contingencies (. . . 'their excitement seeking, consequence disdaining behavior is notable in being a quite different thing than the ordinary pattern of delinquency'—p. 24). The remaining criteria have the effect of excluding people suffering from certain illnesses or defects which might explain their behavioural abnormalities ('free from irrationality and other commonly-accepted symptoms of psychosis ... average or superior intelligence ... free from any marked nervousness or other common symptoms of psychoneurosis' p. 110). A very brief account of Lykken's investigation is to be found in Lykken (1957).

Cleckley's description of the distinctive behaviour of the psychopath depicts him as dishonest, untruthful, extremely selfish, disloyal and exploitative in his dealings with others, and apparently devoid of feelings of obligation, remorse, or shame. This is a behavioural *syndrome*; none of its elements is peculiar to the psychopath, but the conjunction of all or most of these characteristics defines a person who is essentially under-socialized. It is also a description of someone who is wholly responsive to the contingencies of the moment: opportunism, impulsiveness, and unreliability—terms which are commonly used to characterize the behaviour of psychopaths—indicate the absence of those 'internalized' inhibitions which restrain other people from acting dishonestly or inconsiderately, even though there might be advantage in doing so (Trasler, 1978a).

The notion that the psychopath is under-socialized—a person who has not learned the inhibitions, the moral scruples, and awareness of social obligations which normally regulate relationships with others—implies that the condition may come about for either (or both) of two reasons. The individual may have been deprived of the opportunity to learn these things, or he may possess some defect, constitutional or acquired, which has prevented him from learning. There is general agreement that the learning process through which one acquires a conscience is usually, and certainly most effectively, accomplished through the agency of the young child's close and dependent relationship with his parents. He learns to inhibit aggressive, deceitful, or greedy behaviour because such actions attract their disapproval—a state of affairs which, because he is so dependent upon them, he experiences as distressing and alarming. It is a distinctive feature of rules or proscriptions learned in this way that they become internalized: that is to say, they continue to control the individual's behaviour when the threat to punishment or disapproval is no longer present (for a detailed discussion of this process see Aronfreed, 1968, and Hoffman, 1977). Learning of this kind will not take place in the absence of an affectional bond between the child and his parents; nor will it be effective if they are very inconsistent in giving and withholding their approval (Arieti, 1967; Bowlby, 1969).

Lykken's procedures for the selection of psychopaths for research purposes include the requirement that the family background should not be 'markedly sociopathic or deviant' (1955, p. 111a), thus ruling out some individuals whose psychopathic behaviour might be attributable to unaffectionate or grossly inconsistent parental behaviour. Several investigators regard evidence, in the case history, of marked unresponsiveness to parents' attempts to modify the individual's behaviour through persuasion or punishment as one of the grounds for suspecting him to be a psychopath; by implication, they would tend to exclude from consideration cases in which such attempts had been erratic or lacking. By omitting such cases from their samples these researchers have, of course, partially redefined the phenomenon to be explained. Lykken and Hare also exclude other categories of people (those below average in intelligence; those with symptoms of psychosis or neurosis; those known to have made genuine attempts at suicide) and in doing so, further delimit the problem. The consequence of this definitional procedure is to concentrate attention upon a sub-set of psychopathic individuals (usually called 'primary psychopaths') whose behavioural abnormalities appear to be the consequence of inability to learn through punishment—the significance of which we shall consider later. It also omits from consideration substantial numbers of people who would have been regarded as psychopathic by other investigators. Thus Lykken (1955) excluded cases in which there was evidence of 'strongly adverse or neuropathic heredity' (p. 111a), thus eliminating psychopathic individuals who have psychopathic or schizophrenic parents—who, according to Schulsinger (1977) are fairly numerous. Other investigators whose point of departure is sociological or psychiatric rather than psychophysiological have adopted different criteria for the selection of subjects for study. Bowlby (1947), for example, was especially interested in the connections between prepsychopathic behaviour in children and the absence or disruption of the affectional bond between the developing individual and his mother; his sample of 'affectionless thieves' contained many subjects who would have been ruled out of consideration if he had used those criteria which Lykken and Hare subsequently employed.

These examples serve to illustrate the important point that although research in psychopathy is always, of course, concerned with people who exhibit psychopathic behaviour, the samples used by different investigators are not necessarily, or even usually, comparable. They are sub-sets of the pool of potential subjects, defined by criteria for exclusion which in turn rest upon certain theoretical assumptions as to the nature of psychopathy. It is hardly surprising, therefore, that there have been some sharply conflicting findings about such questions as the roles of affectional deprivation and of heredity in the causation of psychopathy. It is even more important in this field than in other areas of psychophysiology to pay close attention to the means by which the author of an investigation selected his subjects, and to take this into account in interpreting the findings. Quite subtle differences in operational criteria for the selection of samples may wholly invalidate attempts to draw inferences from comparisons between several studies—a trap which even scholars expert in this field have not always managed to avoid.

The reader should be aware of another complication, also reflected in the examples we have discussed, which arises because psychopathic behaviour originates in some way (there is no agreement as to the mechanism) in the process of interaction between the developing individual and his social environment. Let us accept, for the purpose of illustration, the view outlined above— that psychopathy is the result of failure to acquire internalized controls through punishment (parental disapproval). It follows that researchers who wish to investigate the role of individual differences in the capacity to learn through punishment ought to employ samples which are defined so as to exclude people who have never been subjected to efficient parental training. If they do not do so they must be content with small or uncertain discriminations between the psychopathic subjects and their controls. Similarly, attempts to examine the role of errors in parental behaviour in the genesis of psychopathy will be greatly complicated by the possibility that some people are, for physiological reasons, less responsive to certain forms of training than others. This is one reason for studying the psychophysiology of psychopathy; until we know more about the 'input' characteristics of the individual—his capacity to respond, or not to do so, to various combinations of cues and aversive stimuli—we shall not make much progress in identifying what it is that makes some modes of parental training more efficient than others in securing internalization. Neither, of course, shall we succeed in the urgent task of devising methods of treating psychopaths. One way of summarizing what we have said about the adequacy of socialization procedures, susceptibility to aversive inhibitory conditioning, (i.e. responsiveness to punishment), and the quality of the parent–child affectional bond in securing the internalization of social rules is shown in Figure 13.1. Psychopathic behaviour may result from a deficit in one or more of these variables.

Since much of the research to be described later in this chapter has stemmed from the belief that psychopaths must be people who have particular difficulty

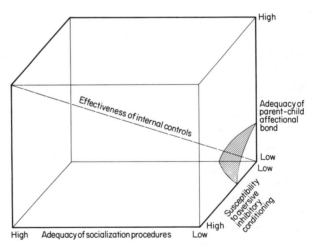

FIGURE 13.1 Diagrammatic representation of a model for the acquisition of psychopathic behaviour. Three variables, adequacy of socialization procedures, susceptibility to aversive conditioning and adequacy of parent–child affectional bond, all contribute to the effectiveness of internal controls of behaviour (dashed line). Clearly, the investigation of any one of these variables in deviant groups requires that the experimental and control samples are matched in terms of the other two. The shaded surface represents the notional 'boundary' of the acquisition of normally adequate internal control

in learning through punishment, it may make matters less confusing to the reader if we first draw attention to the essential characteristics of the kind of learning that is involved. Mowever (1950, 1960) developed a model of passive avoidance conditioning (that is, learning to inhibit behaviour which has, on previous occasions, been followed by punishment) which has been extremely influential. He suggested that the punishment elicites a state of pain or distress which becomes linked, by a process of associative conditioning, with the behaviour which immediately preceded it. When the subject again embarks upon the sequence of behaviour which previously led to punishment, his own actions function as signals (conditioned stimuli) which bring about a revival of the unpleasant state of arousal, previously elicited by punishment and now evoked as a conditioned response. This, in turn, causes the individual to break off the behavioural sequence.

Translated into language that is more appropriate for our present purpose, this means that when parental disapproval follows one of the child's actions, the distress caused by it becomes, perhaps after several repetitions of the sequence, associated with the behaviour itself. When the child is tempted to repeat the behaviour he experiences a resurgence of distress (anxiety or 'anticipatory guilt') which makes the act distasteful to him, so that he turns away and does something else. This process of 'internalization' has the effect of making the previously-punished behaviour inherently wrong, from the point of view of the individual himself (Trasler, 1978a).

This model of passive avoidance conditioning (or aversive inhibitory conditioning as it is more correctly called; the individual is not rendered passive, but diverted to an alternative activity) has a number of interesting features. It relies upon the establishment of a link, by associative conditioning, between the preliminary stages of a behavioural sequence and an unpleasant state of arousal elicited by an aversive stimulus or punisher (usually parental disapproval). It is the onset of this conditioned emotional response which subsequently brings about the inhibition of the punished behaviour. Not unnaturally, investigators have looked for evidence of some deficit in associative conditioning (that is, in the capacity to acquire or to retain a classically conditioned response) or in the ability to respond to an aversive stimulus, or conditioned stimuli associated with it, with a sufficiently vigorous increase in arousal. (There are other possible consequences of this model which will be considered in relation to the results of particular psychophysiological investigations, later in this chapter.)

In the remainder of this chapter we will examine psychophysiological investigations of psychopathy within the framework of the hypothesis that psychopathic behaviour results, in part as least, from poor aversive inhibitory conditioning which in turn leads to a failure to acquire internalized controls. Our examination will focus on physiological activity mediated by the autonomic nervous system: since some readers may not be familiar with psychophysiological methodology, we shall first provide a brief description of those measures most frequently used by investigators in this field.

AN ORIENTATION TO PSYCHOPHYSIOLOGICAL MEASURES

In general terms, psychophysiology is concerned with the relationships between psychological (or behavioural) events on the one hand and physiological activity on the other. Although it is frequently confused with physiological psychology, the differences are reasonably clear. The independent variables in physiological psychology are usually biologically based (e.g. brain lesions, drug action) and the dependent variables are usually behavioural. Psychophysiological research, on the other hand, typically investigates the effect of psychological or behavioural variables on physiological activity. Whereas physiological psychology utilizes infra-human species for research purposes, psychophysiology usually employs human subjects. For this reason, and because much early psychophysiology was concerned with emotional behaviour, many investigators, have concentrated upon physiological activity measured by surface-placed electrodes and mediated by the autonomic nervous system (ANS). More recently, however, a good deal of psychophysiological research has been concerned with the autonomic correlates of attention and information processing, and investigation of event-related cortical potentials has focused research effort on the relationship between specific cortical potentials and a variety of cognitive processes. Nevertheless, in view of the fact that many descriptions of the psychopath have emphasized abnormalities of emotional behaviour, it is perhaps not surprising that psychophysiological investigations in this area have more frequently employed autonomic rather than cortical measures. There has been particular interest in electrodermal and cardiac activity. The following sections provide an introduction to psychophysiological terminology and measurement; more detailed analyses may be found in Lykken and Venables (1971), Siddle and Turpin (1980), Siddle *et al.* (1980) and Venables and Christie (1973).

Electrodermal activity

The term 'electrodermal activity' (EDA) is a general one which covers two distinct phenomena. The first is exosomatic activity and refers to the fact that an electrical resistance is offered to the passage of a small electric current through the body from two points on the skin. The second is endosomatic activity which consists of a potential difference between two points on the body surface. The first phenomenon involves the measurements of skin resistance and its reciprocal, conductance, while the second involves the measurement of skin potential. It is the former measure which is employed more widely, particularly in relation to research on psychopathy. Although the eccrine sweat glands which seem to be of prime importance in the production of skin conductance are controlled solely by the sympathetic branch of the ANS, the transmitter substance is cholinergic (acetylcholine).

It is now usual to employ the term 'tonic' to refer to the background, ongoing skin conductance level (SCL). Short-term or phasic changes which are elicited by environmental stimulation are referred to as skin conductance responses (SCRs). Similar phasic changes also occur in the absence of external stimulation, and these are referred to as non-specific responses (NSRs). Although this is the most widely accepted terminological system, phasic changes are sometimes referred to as galvanic skin responses (GSRs) or psychogalvanic reflexes (PGRs).

A wide range of measures can be obtained from recordings of EDA. Tonic SCL is usually obtained by sampling SCL at a number of points, while frequency of NSRs is obtained simply by counting the number of phasic changes which occur in the absence of external stimulation and which exceed some amplitude criterion. A stimulus-evoked SCR is usually defined as a phasic change which occurs within 1–4 or 1–5 seconds after stimulus onset. In addition to SCR amplitude, a number of temporal measures such as latency (time from stimulus onset to response onset) and half-recovery time (time from peak response to half response amplitude) can be obtained. Finally, measures of habituation, which is defined as a response amplitude decrement as a function of stimulus repetition, can also be obtained. These may range from simple measures such as the number of stimulus presentations before an habituation criterion is reached to more complex rate measures derived from the regression of response amplitude on stimulus number.

Cardiac activity

The widespread use of cardiac activity as a dependent variable in psychophysiological research may be traced to two factors. First, recording techniques were developed from medicine and physiology and have, therefore, been available for some time. Second, cardiac activity has traditionally been associated with the concept of arousal. Cannon (1936) proposed that changes in stimulation could lead to motivational changes which were accompanied by some generalized physiological response, the purpose of which was to prepare the body's physiological state for increased behavioural drive. Since the heart was clearly involved in the regulation of metabolic requirements, it seemed reasonable to employ heart-rate as an index of physiological arousal.

More recent research, however, has indicated that this position was an oversimplification. Short-term cardiac changes have been shown to be bidirectional, with the direction of change depending upon the situation. For example, heart-rate decreases in response to sensory stimuli of moderate intensity, but increases in response to intense stimuli (Graham and Clifton, 1966) or during mental arithmetic (Blair et al., 1959). J. I. Lacey (1967) has developed a model of sensorimotor behaviour in which the direction of heart-rate change is linked to the type of situation in which stimulation occurs. He has suggested that heart-rate deceleration occurs in situations which require the intake of information from the environment, and that acceleration occurs in situations in which there is a rejection of environmental information. Moreover, Lacey (1967) and B.C. Lacey and J. I. Lacey (1974) have provided a functional explanation of the relationship between cardiac activity, cortical activity, and behaviour in that cardiac deceleration is said to be instrumental in the facilitation of sensory processing. They have argued that cardiac activity may alter cortical activity by way of a visceral afferent feedback loop mediated by the baroreceptors.

The Lacey hypothesis has generated considerable research and some of the work has emphasized the importance of the relationship between motor requirements and cardiac activity. The most elaborate hypothesis concerning somatic and cardiac activity has been proposed by Obrist and his colleagues (Obrist, 1976). Essentially, they have argued that increases in somatic activity lead to an increase in the metabolic demands of the musculature, and that this in turn results in increased heart-rate. Conversely, a decrease in somatic activity is said to lead to a decrease in heart-rate.

In addition to the theoretical positions outlined above, cardiac activity has been an important measure in research on the orienting response (OR). This is usually defined in terms of the complex of EEG, sensory, muscular, and autonomic changes which occur in response to novel stimulation. The adaptive significance of the OR is said to involve the enhancement of the information processing capacity of the nervous system (Sokolov, 1963). The defense response (DR), on the other hand, is said to be elicited by painful or aversive stimuli and to involve a decrease in sensitivity to environmental information. Whereas the OR is said to habituate rapidly with stimulus repetition, the DR is said to be highly resistant to habituation. In an influential paper in 1966, Graham and Clifton used the Lacey hypothesis and a critical review of the literature to conclude that the OR involved cardiac deceleration while the DR involved acceleration. Although some authors have suggested recently that the situation may be more complex (Turpin and Siddle, 1978), the Graham and Clifton (1966) analysis has been of considerable importance in guiding research.

PSYCHOPATHY AND AVERSIVE INHIBITORY CONDITIONING

Detailed discussions of the use of aversive inhibitory conditioning as a laboratory analogue for the acquisition of internalized controls have been presented by Trasler (1973, 1978a). Our concern at this point is to present some empirical evidence which indicates that psychopaths do in fact display deficits in such conditioning, so that there is a context within which we can review the psychophysiological data.

Lykken (1955) required psychopaths and non-psychopaths to learn a mental maze containing 20 choice-points. At each choice-point, there were four possible responses, one of which was correct. Subjects were informed as to whether a correct response had been made at each choice-point, and finding the path through the maze constituted the manifest task. One of the three incorrect responses at each choice-point was followed by an electric shock, and learning to avoid responses which were followed by shock constituted the latent task. No mention was made of the latent task during pre-experimental instructions.

Lykken's results indicated that although there was no difference between psychopaths and non-psychopaths in terms of speed of learning the manifest task, the former were inferior to the latter in terms of avoidance learning— that is, in learning to inhibit responses which were followed by shock. Similar results have been reported by Schoenherr (1964) and Schmauk (1970), although in Schmauk's study the performance of psychopaths on the latent task was inferior to that of non-psychopaths only under conditions of physical punishment (shock) and social punishment (disapproval); these differences disappeared when the punishment was loss of money. More recently Chesno and Kilmann (1975) have also reported that primary psychopaths displayed poorer passive avoidance learning than control subjects, although in this case the results were influenced by the ambient level of auditory stimulation. At high levels of background noise (95 dB), the learning differences between psychopaths and non-psychopaths disappeared.

It is clear that the statement that psychopaths are less susceptible to aversive inhibitory conditioning than non-psychopaths must be qualified. However, it is sufficient for our purposes at present to establish that this is the case under some conditions. As we have already intimated, a good deal of the psychophysiological research in the area of psychopathy has been concerned, either explicity or implicitly, with interpretations of the aversive inhibitory conditioning deficits displayed by psychopaths, and it is to those interpretations and data that we now turn.

INTERPRETATION

Classical conditioning and anticipatory autonomic activity

We have already mentioned that the Mowrer (1950, 1960) model of aversive inhibitory conditioning involves an associative conditioning link between cues associated with behaviours which are followed by punishment and an unpleasant state of arousal. It is not too surprising, therefore, that the poor aversive inhibitory conditioning of psychopaths has often been interpreted in terms of their failure to respond to signals of impending punishment; empirically, this has been investigated using classical conditioning paradigms.

The principal advocate of the hypothesis that psychopathy is a consequence of refractoriness to classical conditioning is Eysenck (1964, 1967, 1976). Eysenck relied upon a handful of studies which purported to show slower rates of acquisition of conditioned eyeblink and electrodermal responses in psychopaths than in non-psychopathic subjects. However, as he himself has pointed out (Eysenck, 1976; see also Hare, 1978a), a number of investigators have failed to find such differences. Moreover, some of the studies which seemed to show differences suffer from methodological deficiencies which preclude unambiguous interpretation (e.g. Hare, 1965a). Eysenck has also contended that experiments by Franks (1956a) and others, using eyeblink and electrodermal conditioning, have established clear differences between extraverted and non-extraverted people in respect of rates of acquisition and resistance to extinction of conditioned responses. Since, according to his theory, psychopaths are predominantly extravert in temperament, he argued that it was legitimate to infer that they were also poor conditioners (cf. Franks, 1956b).

In addition to the problem of conflicting results, which was discussed above, Eysenck's theory of psychopathy faces a number of further difficulties. First, it rests upon the assumption that individuals differ from one another in terms of a stable trait or characteristic 'conditionability', which governs their response to classical conditioning of all kinds, whether this involves appetitive or aversive unconditioned stimuli. This assumption requires, of course, that rates of acquisition and extinction from several kinds of conditioning, applied to a single group of subjects, should show a substantial measure of intercorrelation, within the limits imposed by the reliability of those conditioning techniques which can be employed with human subjects. There is, however, very little evidence to show that this is the case (Trasler, 1978b). Some recent work by Gray (1975) suggests that, on the contrary, the capacity to learn to inhibit behaviour which has previously been punished is mediated by a subsystem in the septohippocampal region of the brain which is functionally distinct, at least in part, from those systems implicated in other forms of conditioning. If this is the case, there is no reason to suppose that the readiness with which a person will develop inhibitory responses will have anything to do with his responsiveness to other kinds of conditioning, such as, for example, eyelid conditioning. It also raises the interesting possibility that some individuals may possess central nervous systems which strongly resist learning through punishment, but are normally responsive to learning by other means.

Second, the proposition that psychopaths are more extraverted than non-psychopaths is a matter of considerable controversy (Trasler, 1978a) as is, indeed, the question of whether there are reliable differences between extraverts and introverts in terms of speed of acquisition and extinction of conditioned responses (Eysenck, 1965; Franks, 1963; Lovibond, 1964).

The quasi-conditioning paradigm has involved the effects of threat of aversive stimuli on autonomic activity, and the results have generally been more consistent than those obtained from formal classical conditioning studies. Hare (1965b) measured SCL while groups of psychopaths and non-psychopaths viewed serially presented numbers in the window of a memory drum. The subjects had previously been informed that a strong electric shock would follow the number '8'. Hare reported that the psychopaths, unlike the non-psychopaths, displayed little increase in SCL prior to presentation of the number which was followed by shock. More recently, Hare (1972) has reported a large increase in SCL in non-psychopaths prior to hypodermic injection, whereas psychopaths displayed only a small increase. Similar results have also been reported by Hare, Frazelle, and Cox (1978) in relation to the threat of loud noise.

The threat of unpleasant stimuli also seems to exert consistent effects on non-specific electrodermal activity. For example, Lippert and Senter (1966) reported that threat of shock resulted in a smaller increase in the frequency of NSRs in psychopaths than in non-psychopaths, while Sutker (1970) found that the amplitude of anticipatory NSRs was smaller in psychopaths than in non-psychopaths. Similar results were reported by Hare and Craigen (1974) from a situation in which either the subject or other individuals were receiving shocks. In addition Hare et al. (1978) have reported that the threat of loud noise produces smaller increases in NSR frequency in psychopaths than in non-psychopaths. In general, then, it seems reasonable to conclude that SCL is lower and that NSRs are less frequent in psychopaths than in non-psychopaths prior to unpleasant stimulation of which the subjects have warning.

Cardiac activity, on the other hand, appears to present a different pattern. For example, Hare and Quinn (1971) reported no difference between psychopaths and non-psychopaths in terms of the classically conditioned cardiac response, and in the studies reported by Hare and Craigen (1974) and Hare et al. (1978), psychopaths displayed significantly *larger* cardiac acceleration in anticipation of an unpleasant stimulus than did non-psychopaths. Traditional arousal theory would, of course, view these data as indicating that the psychopathic groups were more aroused autonomically by the impending noxious event, whereas the electrodermal data already discussed indicate the reverse.

In order to reconcile the electrodermal and cardiac data, Hare and his colleagues (Hare, 1978a; Hare et al., 1978) have utilized the Lacey (1967) hypothesis concerning the cardiac changes which are said to facilitate sensory 'intake' and 'rejection'. Hare et al. (1978) have suggested that the anticipatory cardiac acceleration displayed by psychopaths may reflect the operation of an efficient coping mechanism which, through the hypothesized sensory rejection process, attenuates the impact of the aversive stimulus and inhibits anticipatory fear-arousal as measured by electrodermal activity.

Although this account seems to reconcile the electrodermal and cardiac data, it presents some rather severe problems. First, although the cardiac acceleration is hypothesized to attenuate the effects of the impending aversive stimulus (see Hare et al., 1978, p. 170), Hare (1980) has suggested that it may also attenuate the effects of cues which signal unpleasant stimuli, and has argued that this may help to account for the psychopath's poor aversive inhibitory conditioning. However, it is difficult to see how the effects of a stimulus which elicits a cardiac acceleration can be attenuated by some process which is thought to be controlled by that same cardiac acceleration. Moreover, even the notion that the effects of the aversive stimulus are attenuated by anticipatory cardiac acceleration faces difficulties. It will be recalled that Hare's argument rests on the fact that in situations of impending aversive stimulation, psychopaths displayed larger cardiac acceleration than non-psychopaths. However, close inspection of the data reported by Hare and Craigen (1974)—particularly those from trial 1—and of the mean data presented by Hare et al. (1978) indicates that the group differences in cardiac acceleration were due almost entirely to the changes evidenced by the psychopathic subjects. In both studies, psychopaths displayed a peak cardiac acceleration of about 4 beats per minute (bpm), while the non-psychopaths displayed changes which were within approximately plus or minus 1 bpm of the prestimulus level. On the other hand, there is some evidence from other studies which have employed either a countdown procedure or a classical conditioning paradigm and which have employed subjects who were presumably non-psychopathic (Epstein and Clarke, 1970; Headrick and Graham, 1969) that cardiac response in these situations is at least biphasic. That is, the early portion of the countdown or conditioned stimulus–unconditioned stimulus interval elicits significant cardiac acceleration which is followed by either a relative or absolute deceleration immediately prior to the aversive event. Thus, it can be argued that it is the data from the non-psychopaths in the studies of Hare and Craigen (1974) and Hare *et al.* (1978) which pose problems of interpretation and which require explanation. Moreover, interpretation of Hare *et al.*'s (1978) result is complicated by the fact that subjects had already been exposed to 30 tone presentations, including six at 120 dB, in an unsignalled condition (see Hare, 1978b). It is quite possible that these prior exposures exerted different effects on the responsiveness of psychopaths and non-psychopaths in the signalled condition.

Hyporesponsivity to aversive stimulation

It seems reasonably clear that psychopaths display less anticipatory electrodermal activity than non-psychopaths in situations of impending aversive stimulation, and it has been suggested that this may be because psychopaths are relatively unresponsive to aversive stimuli. There seems to be some evidence for this hypothesis, at least with regard to SCRs. Hare and Quinn (1971) and Hare and Craigen (1974) reported that psychopaths displayed significantly smaller SCRs to shock stimuli than non-psychopaths. However, caution is required in interpreting these data since in both studies shock was preceded by a conditioned stimulus, and there is some evidence that in this situation the conditioned stimulus may exert an inhibitory influence on response to the unconditioned stimulus (Kimmel, 1966). Thus, if the extent of this inhibitory influence differed systematically between psychopaths and non-psychopaths, the above results could not be interpreted unambiguously. Nevertheless, there is evidence from other studies which did not involve signalled aversive stimuli that psychopaths display smaller SCRs to loud tones (Hare, 1978b) and the insertion of a hypodermic needle (Hare, 1972) than non-psychopaths.

Although the electrodermal data seem consistent with regard to the effects of strong or unpleasant stimuli, there is no evidence to indicate similar group differences in terms of cardiovascular responses (Hare, 1978a, b). Thus, it is difficult to argue that psychopaths are *generally* hyporesponsive to aversive stimuli.

Arousal

One general theoretical framework adopted in relation to psychopathy concerns the notion of arousal and reactivity. In fact, several different but related views can be delineated here, and useful distinctions can be made between tonic arousal, reactivity, and habituation. Tonic arousal refers to the ongoing, background level of cortical and autonomic excitation, while reactivity refers to the magnitude of phasic arousal changes elicited by particular stimulation. Habituation is generally defined as a response decrement as a function of stimulus repetition and involves the modulation of sensory input. While some authors (e.g. Hare, 1968, 1970) have suggested that psychopaths are characterized by lower levels of tonic arousal, others (e.g. Quay, 1965, 1977) have stressed the psychopath's low reactivity and rapid habituation.

Although the two positions can be distinguished, they each have implications for the explanation of the same behaviour, namely the psychopath's apparent need for stimulation (Quay, 1977). It is argued that there is some 'optimum' level of arousal, both for information processing and learning and for pleasant affective experience, and that organisms attempt to achieve and maintain arousal at this optimal level. It is argued further that because of his hypo-reactivity, or because of rapid habituation, the psychopath will engage in impulsive, bizarre, and perhaps antisocial behaviour in an attempt to maintain arousal at an optimal level. Much of the behavioural data relevant to the arousal hypothesis have been summarized by Quay (1977), and our concern here is with the physiological aspects of the model.

Unfortunately, interpretations of psychopathic behaviour in terms of level of arousal face a number of difficulties from the psychophysiological perspective. The first concerns what is meant by 'arousal' and here the tendency in psychophysiological theorizing has been away from a view of arousal as a unitary dimension. This trend is clearly evident in the influential work of Lacey (1967) who has reviewed a considerable body of evidence which indicates that cortical, autonomic, and behavioural arousal are best viewed as 'imperfectly coupled, complexly interacting systems' (p. 15). Nevertheless, some theorists have in fact specified *cortical* under-arousal as a characteristic of psychopathy (Hare, 1970; Schalling *et al.*, 1973) and have referred to electroencephalographic (EEG) studies which purport to show a predominance of slow-wave activity in psychopaths in support of their arguments. However, even when EEG studies of arousal are considered, the inescapable conclusion seems to be that there is virtually no evidence which indicates differences between psychopaths and non-psychopaths (Gale, 1975; Syndulko, 1978).

Examination of autonomic measures such as SCL which may reflect autonomic arousal, and frequency of NSRs which may reflect cortical arousal (J.I. Lacey and B.C. Lacey, 1958), leads to much the same conclusion (Siddle, 1977). Thus, while Hare and his colleagues (Hare, 1965b, 1968) have sometimes reported lower SCL in psychopaths, this has not always been the case (Hare and Craigen, 1974; Hare *et al.*, 1978; Hare and Quinn, 1971). Non-significant differences have also been reported by other authors (Borkovec, 1970; Parker *et al.*, 1973; Schalling *et al.*, 1973, Sutker, 1970; Schmauk, 1970). A similar conflicting picture emerges from examination of NSR frequency. Although both Hare (1968) and Hare and Quinn (1971) reported fewer NSRs in psychopaths, these differences were not significant. There seems to be only one study which has shown that psychopaths display fewer NSRs than non-psychopaths under conditions of no-stimulation (Schalling *et al.*, 1973) and even here, the clear differences were observed only following a stimulation period.

Data relevant to hyporesponsivity are also contradictory. Hare (1968) found no differences in SCR amplitude to an 80 dB tone either on the first trial of an habituation series or on a trial which involved a change in stimulus intensity and pitch. In a subsequent re-analysis of these data, however, Hare (1975) has reported that when SCR amplitudes were expressed in terms of the range of responsiveness displayed by each subject, significant differences emerged; the psychopathic group displayed smaller SCRs than the non-psychopathic group both on trial 1 and on the trial involving stimulus change. Similarly, Borkovec (1970) reported that psychopaths displayed smaller SCRs than non-psychopaths, although Hare (1978b) reported differences only at high stimulus intensities.

Habituation data are meagre. Hare (1968) reported no differences between psychopaths and non-psychopaths in terms of SCR habituation, but did find that habituation of the cardiac decelerative response was faster in non-psychopaths; this finding is clearly contrary to Quay's (1965, 1977) hypothesis. On the other hand, Borkovec (1970) found no differences between psychopaths and non-psychopaths in terms of either electrodermal or cardiac habituation.

SCR recovery

Some authors have attempted to construct psychophysiological models of psychopathic behaviour by utilizing differences between psychopaths and non-psychopaths in terms of the recovery limb of the SCR. In general terms, this refers to the time from peak SCR amplitude to some specified fall in amplitude. Although a number of measures have been derived (Venables, 1974), the most frequently used is that of half-recovery time: that is, the time from maximum to 50 per cent of response amplitude.

Mednick (1974) has argued that one important factor within the aversive inhibitory conditioning paradigm is the dissipation of anticipatory fear following the inhibition of previously punished behaviour. He has argued further that if such fear dissipation serves as a reinforcer for the inhibition of behaviour, then the rate at which fear dissipates might be a critical variable; relatively rapid dissipation should result in more rapid reinforcement and thus lead to more effective avoidance learning. According to Mednick (1974), the rate at which the SCR recovers provides a measure of fear dissipation, and his position predicts that since psychopaths are characterized by poor aversive inhibitory conditioning, it might be expected that they would display slower SCR recovery than non-psychopaths.

Certainly, a number of studies have found that individuals who have committed antisocial acts display longer SCR half-recovery times than controls. Hare (1975) re-analysed his 1968 data and reported that the psychopathic group displayed longer half-recovery times than the non-psychopathic group on a trial involving stimulus change. Siddle *et al.* (1976) found that 'high antisocial' adolescents from a Borstal institution displayed significantly longer half-recovery times than a 'low antisocial' group. The groups were selected on the basis of a social history checklist which included such items as convictions for non-traffic offences, physical aggression, poor work history and pathological lying. Loeb and Mednick (1977) made use of SCR data obtained from adult subjects before any of them had been in trouble with the police. Those who were subsequently convicted of crimes on at least two occasions displayed, as a group, slower SCR recovery than those who retained clean records. All these findings were obtained with stimuli of moderate intensity and Hare (1978b) was not able to replicate the results; in this experiment, half-recovery time differences were reliable only at relatively high stimulus intensities.

The difficulty with Mednick's position concerns the assumption that SCR recovery is an appropriate measure of fear dissipation. As far as we are aware this proposition has not been tested, and one could just as easily argue, perhaps with greater face validity, that recovery of *tonic* measures reflected fear dissipation. Clearly, a good deal of basic laboratory work which involves fear-eliciting stimuli and a number of autonomic measures is necessary before we can be confident that Mednick's explanation of the SCR recovery differences between psychopaths and non-psychopaths is the correct one.

In view of the relatively long half-recovery times displayed by psychopaths, Siddle (1977) suggested that psychopaths might be characterized by an attentional deficit. Edelberg (1972) originally suggested that fast SCR recovery indicated preparation for goal-directed activity, and Venables (1974) extended this notion to suggest that SCR recovery might reflect a dimension which he termed 'openness–closedness' to the environment, with slow recovery indicating 'closedness'. It was argued, therefore, that psychopaths might represent extreme closedness to the environment, and Siddle (1977) speculated that if psychopaths were less attentive to their environment, they might become aware of relationships between stimuli more slowly; this, in turn, could explain their poor aversive inhibitory conditioning.

The major difficulty with this approach concerns the construct validity of SCR recovery measures. Although Edelberg (1972) originally related SCR recovery to extrinsic stimulus factors, more recent evidence has suggested that intrinsic factors such as prior EDA are probably more important (Bundy and Fitzgerald, 1975; Edelberg and Muller, 1977). Thus, just as in the case of Mednick's (1974) hypothesis, considerably more basic research on the mechanisms underlying SCR recovery is required before Siddle's (1977) hypothesis can be entertained.

DISCUSSION

The preceding section has indicated that, with a few exceptions, psychophysiological studies of psychopathy have generally produced contradictory data.

Obviously, procedural differences in subject selection may account for some of the discrepancies. For example, Hare and his colleagues have employed global ratings of psychopathy, while others have used the Psychopathic Deviate scale from the MMPI (e.g. Schmauk, 1970; Sutker, 1970), behaviour checklists (Borkovec, 1970), the Taylor Manifest Anxiety Scale (Schmauk, 1970) and the socialization scale from the California Psychological Inventory (Hare *et al.*, 1978), or a combination of some of these measures. In addition, we have already argued that neglect of the fact that a number of different factors may each produce psychopathic behaviour will lead to small and possibly non-replicable differences. At a theoretical level, too, the area presents a somewhat confused picture. Although a number of psychophysiological models of psychopathy have been proposed, none of them can account satisfactorily for all the data.

What empirical conclusions can we reach about the psychophysiology of psychopathy? There seems to be reasonably convincing evidence only for the fact that psychopaths display less electrodermal arousal than non-psychopaths when faced with an impending aversive event. In addition, there is some evidence that psychopaths display smaller SCRs to high-intensity stimuli and slower SCR recovery to stimuli of moderate intensity; they also display larger cardiac acceleration prior to aversive events of which they have warning. However, it is our contention that it is not possible, on the basis of the above conclusions, to construct a satisfactory psychophysiological model of psychopathic behaviour—certainly not one which could be used profitably in conjunction with other aspects of psychopathic behaviour.

On the other hand, some of the psychophysiological data, together with the theoretical orientation adopted in the Introduction, suggest, to us at least, that it may be worthwhile to examine in more detail aversive inhibitory conditioning in psychopaths. There are a number of good reasons for this. First, the available data seem to be consistent in indicating relatively poor aversive inhibitory conditioning in psychopaths. Second, the poor aversive inhibitory conditioning in psychopaths can be accommodated within a broader theory of psychopathy which might attempt to specify the role of other important variables such as the adequacy of socialization procedures and parent–child relationships. Third, as Trasler (1978a) has noted, aversive inhibitory conditioning seems to be a rather special form of learning in that it occurs in primitive organisms which are not capable of other forms of learning (Razran, 1971) and seems to be mediated by neurophysiological systems which are different from those which mediate other forms of learning (Gray, 1975).

It can also be argued that if psychophysiological investigations of psychopathy are to advance our understanding of this syndrome, they should involve situations of behavioural relevance. It is simply not sufficient, in our view, to ask *whether* psychopaths differ from non-psychopaths in terms of some aspects of physiological activity without having first formulated a clear theoretical rationale for predicting such differences. Genuine progress will only be made when there is some attempt to show that physiological changes have functional significance for some particular piece of behaviour. Thus we would like to argue that, for the reasons already discussed, physiological activity should be examined during aversive inhibitory conditioning. There appears to be only one study which has done this (Schmauk, 1970), and it has provided some interesting findings which suggest that we may reasonably expect to find robust behavioural–physiological covariation in this situation. Schmauk employed three punishment conditions—physical (shock), tangible (loss of money), and social (disapproval), and reported that the inhibitory conditioning of psychopaths was inferior under conditions of physical and social punishment, but not when the punishment was loss of money. Analysis of the electrodermal data indicated that although non-psychopaths displayed larger SCRs in anticipation of shock and social disapproval than did psychopaths, there was no difference in the loss-of-money condition. Moreover, the psychopaths displayed more anticipatory electrodermal activity under conditions of loss of money than under conditions of social disapproval.

Although Schmauk's (1970) results are sufficiently provocative to justify more work of this sort, such research should take note of several points. First, the discrepancies between cardiac and electrodermal activity noted earlier serve to underscore the shortcomings of measuring only one aspect of physiological activity, and the work of Lacey and Lacey (1974) and Obrist (1976) demonstrates quite clearly that much more may be learned from multiple physiological recording. Second, some basic research on aversive inhibitory conditioning in non-psychopaths is probably a necessary step before data from psychopaths can be interpreted unambiguously. That is, the important parameters must be established empirically with human subjects (Trasler, 1978a) in order to avoid the pitfalls of extrapolation from one species to another (Seligman, 1970). Finally, the processes underlying aversive inhibitory conditioning are themselves a matter of debate (Rachman, 1976; Seligman and Johnston, 1973) and developments in this area will need to be incorporated into explanations of psychopathic behaviour which utilize aversive inhibitory conditioning.

CONCLUSION

This chapter has attempted to review what is known about the psychophysiological correlates of psychopathy. The review indicates that, despite considerable research effort, few empirical generalizations are possible. In view of this, we contend that the formulation of models of psychopathy based solely on psychophysiological data is not an optimal strategy. Despite this rather pessimistic statement, we have also argued that a viable research strategy involves examination of the pattern of physiological activity which accompanies aversive inhibitory conditioning, and have outlined the advantages of such a strategy. It is our view that this approach may yield meaningful psychophysiological findings which could be encompassed within a genuine theory of psychopathy which would provide a theoretical account of all aspects of psychopathic behaviour.

REFERENCES

Arieti, S. (1967). *The Intrapsychic Self*. New York: Basic Books.

Aronfreed, J. (1968). *Conduct and Conscience*. New York: Academic Press.

Blair, D. A., Glover, W. E., Greenfield, A. D. M., and Roddie, I. C. (1959). Excitation of cholinergic vasodilator nerves to human skeletal muscles during emotional stress. *Journal of Physiology*, **148**, 633–647.

Borkovec, T. D. (1970). Autonomic reactivity to sensory stimulation in psychopathic, neurotic, and normal juvenile delinquents. *Journal of Consulting and Clinical Psychology*, **35**, 217–222.

Bowlby, J. (1947). *Forty-four Juvenile Thieves*. London: Baillière, Tindall & Cox.

Bowlby, J. (1969). *Attachment and Loss*, Vol. 1. London: Hogarth Press.

Bundy, R. S., and Fitzgerald, H. E. (1975). Stimulus specificity of electrodermal recovery time: an examination and reinterpretation of the evidence. *Psychophysiology*, **12**, 406–411.

Cannon, W. B. (1936). *Bodily Changes in Pain, Hunger, Fear and Rage* (2nd edn.). New York: Appleton-Century.

Chesno, F. A., and Kilmann, P. R. (1975). Effects of stimulation intensity on sociopathic avoidance learning. *Journal of Abnormal Psychology*, **84**, 144–150.

Cleckley, H. (1941, 1976). *The Mask of Sanity* (5th edn.). St Louis: Mosby.

Edelberg, R. (1972). Electrodermal recovery rate, goal-orientation, and aversion. *Psychophysiology*, **9**, 512–520.

Edelberg, R., and Muller, M. (1977). The Status of the Electrodermal Recovery Measure: A Caveat. Paper presented at the Seventeenth Annual Meeting of the Society for Psychophysiological Research, Philadelphia, October.

Epstein, S., and Clarke, S. (1970). Heart rate and skin conductance during experimentally induced anxiety: effects of anticipated intensity of noxious stimulation and experience. *Journal of Experimental Psychology*, **84**, 105–112.

Eysenck, H. J. (1964). *Crime and Personality*. London: Routledge & Kegan Paul.

Eysenck, H. J. (1965). Extraversion and the acquisition of eyeblink and GSR conditioned responses. *Psychological Bulletin*, **63**, 258–270.

Eysenck, H. J. (1967). *The Biological Basis of Personality*. Springfield, Illinois.: Thomas.

Eysenck, H. J. (1976). The biology of morality. In T. Lickona (ed.), *Moral Development and Behavior* pp. 108–123. New York: Holt, Rinehart, & Winston.

Franks, C. M. (1956a). Conditioning and personality: a study of normal and neurotic subjects. *Journal of Abnormal and Social Psychology*, **52**, 143–150.

Franks, C. M. (1956b). Recidivism, psychopathy and personality. *British Journal of Delinquency*, **6**, 192–201.

Franks, C. M. (1963). Personality and eyeblink conditioning seven years later. *Acta Psychologica*, **21**, 295–312.

Gale, A. (1975). Can EEG Studies make a Contribution to the Experimental Investigation of Psychopathy? Paper presented at the NATO Advanced Study Institute on Psychopathic Behavior. Les Arcs, September.

Graham, F. K., and Clifton, R. K. (1966). Heart-rate change as a component of the orienting response. *Psychological Bulletin*, **65**, 305–320.

Gray, J. A. (1975). *Elements of a Two-process Theory of Learning*. New York: Academic Press.

Hare, R. D. (1965a). Temporal gradient of fear arousal in psychopaths. *Journal of Abnormal Psychology*, **70**, 442–445.

Hare, R. D. (1965b). Acquisition and generalization of a conditioned fear response in psychopathic and nonpsychopathic criminals. *Journal of Psychology*, **59**, 367–370.

Hare, R. D. (1968). Psychopathy, autonomic functioning, and the orienting response. *Journal of Abnormal Psychology: Monograph Supplement*, **73**, 1–24.

Hare, R. D. (1970). *Psychopathy: Theory and Research*. New York: Wiley.

Hare, R. D. (1972). Psychopathy and sensitivity to adrenalin. *Journal of Abnormal Psychology*, **79**, 138–147.

Hare, R. D. (1975). Psychopathy. In P. H. Venables and M. J. Christie (eds.), *Research in Psychophysiology*, pp. 325–348. London: Wiley.

Hare, R. D. (1978a). Electrodermal and cardiovascular correlates of psychopathy. In R. D. Hare and D. Schalling (eds.), *Psychopathic Behaviour: Approaches to Research*. pp. 107–143. London: Wiley.

Hare, R. D. (1978b). Psychopathy and electrodermal response to non-signal stimulation. *Biological Psychology*, **6**, 237–246.

Hare, R. D. Psychopathy. In H. M. van Praag, M. H. Lader and O. J. Rafaelson (eds.), *Handbook of Biological Psychiatry*, vol. 3. pp. 249–262. New York: Marcel Dekker.

Hare, R. D. (in press) (b). A research scale for the assessment of psychopathy in criminal populations. *Personality and Individual Differences*.

Hare, R. D., and Cox, D. N. (1978). Clinical and empirical conceptions of psychopathy, and the selection of subjects for research. In R. D. Hare and D. Schalling (eds.), *Psychopathic Behaviour: Approaches to Research*, pp. 1–21. London: Wiley.

Hare, R. D., and Craigen, D. (1974). Psychopathy and physiological activity in a mixed-motive game situation. *Psychophysiology*, **11**, 197–206.

Hare, R. D., Frazelle, J., and Cox, D. N. (1978). Psychopathy and physiological responses to threat of an aversive stimulus. *Psychophysiology*, **15**, 165–172.

Hare, R. D., and Quinn, M. J. (1971). Psychopathy and autonomic conditioning. *Journal of Abnormal Psychology*, **77**, 223–235.

Headrick, M. W., and Graham, F. K. (1969). Multiple-component heart rate responses conditioned under paced respiration. *Journal of Experiemental Psychology*, **79**, 486–494.

Hoffman, M. L. (1977). Moral internalization: current theory and research. In L. Berkowitz, (ed.). *Advances in Experimental Social Psychology*, vol. 10, pp. 86–135. New York: Academic Press.

Kimmel, H. D. (1966). Inhibition of the unconditioned response in classical conditioning. *Psychological Review*, **73**, 232–240.

Lacey, B. C., and Lacey, J. I. (1974). Studies of heart rate and other bodily processes in sensorimotor behavior. In P. A. Obrist, A. H. Black, J. Brener, and L. V. DiCara (eds.), *Cardiovascular Psychophysiology: Current Issues in Response Mechanisms, Biofeedback and Methodology*, pp. 538–564. Chicago: Aldine.

Lacey, J. I. (1967). Somatic response patterning and stress: some revisions of activation theory. In M. H. Appley and R. Trumbull (eds.), *Psychological Stress: Issues in Research*, pp. 14–37. New York: Appleton-Century-Crofts.

Lacey, J. I., and Lacey, B. C. (1958). The relationship of resting autonomic activity to motor impulsivity. *Research Publications of the Association for Nervous and Mental Diseases*, **36**, 144–209.

Lippert, W. W., and Senter, R. J. (1966). Electrodermal responses in the sociopath. *Psychonomic Science*, **4**, 25–26.

Loeb, J., and Mednick, S. A. (1977). A prospective study of predictors of criminality: electrodermal response patterns. In S. A. Mednick, and K. O. Christiansen (eds.), *Biosocial Bases of Criminal Behavior*, pp. 245–254. New York: Gardner Press.

Lovibond, S. H. (1964). Personality and conditioning. In B. A. Maher (ed.), *Progress in Experimental Personality Research*, vol. 1. pp. 115–168. New York: Academic Press.

Lykken, D. T. (1955). A study of anxiety in the sociopathic personality. Unpublished doctoral dissertation, University of Minnesota. Ann Arbor: University Microfilms, No. 15, 944.

Lykken, D. T. (1957). A study of anxiety in the sociopathic personality. *Journal of Abnormal and Social Psychology*, **55**, 6–10.

Lykken, D. T., and Venables, P. H. (1971). Direct measurement of skin conductance: a proposal for standardization. *Psychophysiology*, **8**, 656–672.

Mednick, S. A. (1974). Electrodermal recovery and psychopathology. In S. A. Mednick, F. Schulsinger, J. Higgins, and B. Bell (eds.), *Genetics, Environment and Psychopathology*, pp. 135–146. Oxford: North-Holland.

Mowrer, O. H. (1950). *Learning Theory and Personality Dynamics*. New York: Ronald.

Mowrer, O. H. (1960). *Learning Theory and Behavior*. New York: Wiley.

Obrist, P. A. (1976). The cardiovascular–behavioral interaction—as it appears today. *Psychophysiology*, **13**, 95–107.

Parker, D. A., Syndulko, K., Maltzman, I., Jens, R. and Ziskind, E. (1973). Orienting and Habituation in Sociopahic and Normal Subjects. Paper presented at the Thirteenth Annual Meeting of the Society for Psychophysiological Research, Galveston, October.

Quay, H. C. (1965). Psychopathic personality as pathological stimulation seeking. *American Journal of Psychiatry*, **122**, 180–183.

Quay, H. C. (1977). Psychopahic behavior: Reflections on its nature,origins, and treatment. In F. Weizmann and I. Uzgiris (eds.), *The Structuring of Experience*. New York: Plenum.

Rachman, S. (1976). The passing of the two-stage theory of fear and avoidance: fresh possibilities. *Behaviour Research and Therapy*, **14**, 125–131.

Razran, G. (1971). *Mind in Evolution*. Boston: Houghton Mifflin.

Schalling D., Lidberg, L., Levander, S. E., and Dahlin, Y. (1973). Spontaneous autonomic activity as related to psychopathy. *Biological Psychology*, **1**, 83–97.

Schmauk, F. J. (1970). Punishment, arousal, and avoidance learning in sociopaths. *Journal of Abnormal Psychology*, **76**, 325–335.

Schoenherr, J. C. (1964). Avoidance of noxious stimulation in psychopathic personality. Unpublished doctoral dissertation, University of California at Los Angeles, 1964. Ann Arbor: University Microfilms No. 8334.

Schulsinger, F. (1977). Psychopathy: heredity and environment. In S. A. Mednick and K. O. Christiansen (eds.), *Biosocial Bases of Criminal Behavior*, pp. 109–126. New York: Gardner Press.

Seligman, M. E. P. (1970). On the generality of the laws of learning. *Psychological Review*, **77**, 406–418.

Seligman, M. E. P., and Johnston, J. C. (1973). A cognitive theory of avoidance learning. In F. J. McGuigan and D. B. Lumsden (eds.), *Contemporary Approaches to Conditioning and Learning*, pp. 69–110. Washington, D.C: Winston & Sons.

Siddle, D. A. T. (1977). Electrodermal activity and psychopathy. In S. A. Mednick and K. O. Christiansen (eds.), *Biosocial Bases of Criminal Behavior*, pp. 199–211. New York: Gardner Press.

Siddle, D. A. T., Mednick, S. A., Nicol, A. R., and Foggitt, R. H. (1976). Skin conductance recovery in antisocial adolescents. *British Journal of Social and Clinical Psychology*, **15**, 425–428.

Siddle, D. A. T., and Turpin, G. (eds.) (1980). The measurement, quantification and analysis of cardiac activity. In I. Martin, and P. H. Venables, (eds.), *Techniques in Psychophysiology*, pp. 139–246. London: Wiley.

Siddle, D. A. T., Turpin, G., Spinks, J. A., and Stephenson, D. (1980). Peripheral measures. In H. M. van Praag, M. H. Lader and O. J. Rafaelson (eds.), *Handbook of Biological Psychiatry*, vol. 3. pp 45–78. New York: Marcel Dekker.

Sokolov, E. N. (1963). *Perception and the Conditioned Reflex*. Oxford: Pergamon.

Sutker, P. B. (1970). Vicarious conditioning and sociopathy. *Journal of Abnormal Psychology*, **76**, 380–386.

Syndulko, K. (1978). Electrocortical investigations of sociopathy. In R. D. Hare and D. Schalling (eds.), *Psychopathic Behaviour: Approaches to Research*, pp. 145–156. London: Wiley.

Trasler, G. B. (1973).Criminal behaviour. In H. J. Eysenck (ed.), *Handbook of Abnormal Psychology (2nd. ed.)*, pp. 67–96. London: Pitman.

Trasler, G. B. (1978a). Relations between psychopathy and persistent criminality—methodological and theoretical issues. In R. D. Hare and D. Schalling (eds.), *Psychopathic Behaviour: Approaches to Research*, pp. 273–298. London: Wiley.

Trasler, G. B. (1978b). Review of the third edition of H. J. Eysenck's *Crime and Personality*. *British Journal of Criminology*, **18**, 190–193.

Turpin, G., and Siddle, D. A. T. (1978). Cardiac and forearm plethysmographic responses to high intensity auditory stimulation. *Biological Psychology*, **6**, 267–281.

Venables, P. H. (1974). The recovery limb of the skin conductance response. In S. A. Mednick, F. Schulsinger, J., Higgins, and B. Bell (eds.), *Genetics, Environment and Psychopathology*, pp. 117–133. Oxford: North-Holland.

Venables, P. H., and Christie, M. J. (1973). Mechanisms, instrumentation, recording, and quantification. In W. F., Prokasy and D. C. Raskin (eds.), *Electrodermal Activity in Psychological Research*, pp. 1–124. New York: Academic Press.

Foundations of Psychosomatics
Edited by M. J. Christie and P. G. Mellett
© 1981 John Wiley & Sons Ltd.

14

PAIN AND PERSONALITY

MICHAEL R. BOND
Professor of Psychological Medicine,
University of Glasgow, Scotland.

INTRODUCTION

Personality is a blend of emotional, cognitive, and motivational qualities reflected in the behaviour of each individual. Although unique in its exact composition, personality has general qualities, for example emotional traits and intelligence levels, which may be assessed psychometrically or in terms of responses to certain psychological stimuli. General intelligence, except at its lowest levels, plays a relatively small part in influencing the experience of pain and behaviour associated with it, whereas emotion, perceptual, and motivational factors, play an important part and consequently form the basis of most psychological and psychiatric studies of pain. Individuality in pain experiences is chiefly described by relating it to personality factors and to the effects of culture upon learning and behaviour. The former may be based upon a descriptive typology of the kind used in psychiatric practice, or upon psychometric techniques for assessment of different dimensions of personality. Furthermore, the latter is used as a basis for the elaboration of descriptive systems which incorporate patients' patterns of behaviour described in detail by Sternbach (1974a). Integration of this aspect of pain into a more general account of its nature, clinical analysis and treatment is to be found in Bond, 1979.

PAIN, COMPLAINT BEHAVIOUR, AND MEASURES OF PERSONALITY CHARACTERISTICS

Several personality traits play a significant part in influencing the severity of pain and associated behaviour. They include proneness to anxiety and depression, hysterical, and hypochondriacal traits. These attributes also predominate in neurotic disorders associated with pain and all have been subjected to measurement in acute and chronic painful illnesses.

Most people become anxious when they first become ill and, if pain is experienced, levels of anxiety tend to be greater and may occasionally require medical treatment in acutely painful disorders. Moreover, in addition to the fact that those who are most prone to anxiety have the greatest sensitivity to pain (Schalling and Levander, 1964), rising levels of anxiety are associated *pari passu* with increases in the severity of pain. Clearly it is important for a clinician to be aware of each individual's proneness to anxiety if severity of pain is to be kept to a minimum. Anxiety is often present in chronic illnesses in which, however, depression of mood tends to predominate. Sternbach (1974a) states that anxiety in acutely painful illnesses is of a generalized kind, whereas in chronic disorders it becomes more specifically attached to certain symptoms appearing as hypochondriasis.

Using the Eysenck Personality Inventory several workers have demonstrated that complaints of pain severity are directly related to neuroticism scores (S. G. B. Eysenck, 1961; Lynn and Eysenck; 1961, Pilling, Brannick, and Swenson, 1967; Bond and Pearson, 1969; Bond, 1971, 1973), and Bond (1978) correlated the latter, which measure proneness to anxiety, with overt anxiety using the Taylor Manifest Anxiety Scale. Increased levels of neuroticism in chronic painful illnesses have been reported by Woodforde and Merskey (1972), Bond (1973) and Sternbach and Timmermans (1975). Furthermore, Sternbach (1974a) analysed the elements of increased neuroticism levels in acute and chronic back-pain patients using the Minnesota Multiphasic Personality Inventory. He reported that those in acute pain show high scores for hypochondriasis and hysteria, whereas those with chronic pain not only score higher than pain-free individuals on these scales but also on the depression scale. These findings indicate that both acute and chronic pain cause preoccupation with bodily functions, but whereas those with acute pain express agitation, reflected in increased scores on the mania scale, those with chronic pain tend to be depressed.

It is known that pain relief is associated with a fall in levels of neuroticism (Kissen, 1964; Sternbach and Timmermans, 1975), and it is assumed by most, and this view was put forward vigorously by Sternbach (1974a), that raised levels of neuroticism are the consequence of illness and pain. Sainsbury (1960), in a discussion of psychosomatic disorders, suggested that raised levels of neuroticism may predispose towards certain illnesses, and this seems appropriate for certain chronic painful illnesses, for example rheumatoid arthritis. Opinions about the relationship between neuroticism, illness, and pain were subjected to further scrutiny by Bond (1973) who proposed that each individual has a given personality 'setting' in which changes occur at the time of ill health. In his view, which takes account of the comments of Sainsbury, Sternbach and others, he suggests that neuroticism levels may increase or decrease at times of illness or stress, depending upon their levels in normal health. His hypothesis is based upon results of studies of patients with cancer, some of whom had very low neuroticism scores until their pain was relieved by cordotomy, after which, in a proportion of low neuroticism patients, scores rose towards the mean value for the test. In others, who had raised levels of neuroticism, scores fell. In another study, Bond and Pearson (1969) noticed that amongst women with advanced cancer of the cervix, those who were pain-free had very low levels of neuroticism. This observation complements those of Kissen and Eysenck (1962), who studied lung cancer patients, and of Huggen (1968). However, whereas Kissen and Eysenck saw low neuroticism scores in cancer patients representing a very reduced level of emotionality or denial of anxiety about illness, Huggen saw them as artifacts in the test scores. However, Sternbach (1968) supports Kissen and Eysenck (1962) and Bond and Pearson (1969), by emphasizing that very low levels of neuroticism or denial occur in certain individuals as part of their reaction to the stress of illness and pain.

One very definite practical issue has emerged from the observations linking anxiety and pain. First, it is generally agreed that the most effective way to treat pain is by preventing it from building up to high levels. Build-up of pain tends to occur in 'on-demand' treatment regimes relying on patients to ask for drugs, because even today British patients believe that they 'should bear pain as long as possible' (Bond, 1978), although this attitude brings with it rising levels of anxiety about eventually gaining relief. Second, it is well established that postoperative pain is substantially less if patients are prepared beforehand by relaxation and counselling (Egbert et al., 1964), or by the use of counselling and anxiolytic drugs.

The assessment of levels of pain is an essential part of providing adequate relief and the relationship of personality to 'complaint behaviour' must be taken into account. Furthermore, cultural attitudes to pain tend to exert a strong effect upon each individual's behaviour when he or she is in pain, apparently to the disadvantage of some and to the advantage of others, as will become clear later.

The extraversion–introversion dimension of personality appears to be closely related to complaint behaviour. Bond and Pearson (1969) reported that amongst a group of women with advanced cancer of the cervix, all of whom had raised levels of neuroticism, extraverts were more likely to complain of pain than introverts despite the fact that the latter had slightly higher levels of pain measured using an analogue scale. This finding would not be expected from a consideration of laboratory studies of introverts and extraverts which reveal that the latter have higher levels of pain tolerance than the former; a matter which has been the subject of several papers and which was thoroughly reviewed and confirmed by Barnes (1975). The clinical paradox was explained by S. G. B. Eysenck (1961). She reported that extraverts communicate their distress more readily than introverts, and related laboratory findings to work by Petrie (1967). Petrie isolated a personality variable which she named 'perceptual reactance' using it to identify three types of individual: the reducer, the moderate, and the augmenter. The reducer tends subjectively to decrease what is perceived, and the augmenter to increase a similar perception. Petrie has demonstrated that the reducer is more than usually tolerant of pain when induced experimentally, and the augmenter less than usually tolerant. In Eysenck's view reducers exhibit the same response as extraverts to noxious stimuli and augmenters resemble introverts in the laboratory, but, when ill, extraverts communicate or complain of their experience much more freely. It is worth noting that the freedom with which patients complain is not an accurate guide to the origin of their pains in terms of the contribution of organic and psychogenic factors to it, because they are equally likely to occur (Baker and Merskey, 1966; Woodforde and Merskey,

1972). Nevertheless, there are several clinical studies in which examination of the neuroticism–stability and extraversion–introversion dimensions of personality have revealed helpful information about the contributions of these personality factors to our understanding of the pain intensity and complaint behaviour of individuals with painful disorders.

Lovell and Verghese (1967) found that amongst men who had had a myocardial infarct the highest neuroticism scores were obtained from those who experienced angina and left chest pain, not thought to have an organic basis. Second-highest scores were obtained from men with angina alone, and lowest scores from men who were symptom-free. Interestingly the angina/left chest pain group were mostly of an asthenic build, leading the authors to conclude that there is a relationship between body-build and the outcome of the illness which might be a useful indicator when assessing the likelihood of patients' ability to cope with their symptoms. Their findings complement earlier studies of Ostfeld et al. (1964) who carried out a prospective study on men with coronary artery disease and found that angina occurs most often amongst those with high levels of emotional lability and suggestibility.

Considering sufferers of headache, Philips (1976) wrote, 'there is widespread agreement on the general personality characteristics of headache sufferers . . . as being tense, driving, obsessionally perfectionist people with unexpressed and unresolved resentments and hostilities'. However, she obviously felt the need to make a more accurate appraisal of this matter because she also reported that those who have studied migraine (Selinsky, 1939) and tension headache (Martin, Rome, and Swenson, 1967) in detail have not found major personality differences between the groups. And furthermore, Walters and O'Connor (1971) and Howorth (1965) were unable to distinguish the personality characteristics of sufferers from migraine or tension headache from members of the general population not subject to these forms of headache. Using measures of neuroticism, introversion–extraversion, and psychoticism, and a lie scale (Eysenck and Eysenck, 1976), Philips was also unable to distinguish between migraine, muscle tension and mixed headache sufferers, and headache-free individuals. However, she did discover that headaches were more severe in women with high neuroticism scores and that high levels of medication were required by extraverted tension headache sufferers with high levels of neuroticism. In attempting to explain the variations in the studies of headache mentioned she concluded that doctors at special clinics for headache sufferers are more likely to see patients who are neurotic extraverts than others, and that their studies are biased accordingly.

Levels of preoperative anxiety bear a significant relation to postoperative levels of pain. Parbrook, Steel and Dalrymple (1973) reported that persistently high levels of neuroticism assessed with the Eysenck Personality Inventory are associated with the highest levels of pain and pulmonary complications after surgery as a result of involuntary restriction of movements of the chest wall due to the pain these movements produced. The predisposition of anxious patients to higher levels of postoperative pain than their more stable fellows bears an interesting relationship to the use of standard doses of analgesics in the post-operative period. Generally, analgesics are given in similar doses to all patients and usually little account is taken of individual personality differences as factors which influence the severity of pain. However, this issue is now attracting the attention of research workers, for example Bond, Glynn, and Thomas, (1976) examined postoperative levels of pain and their relation to personality character-istics. The study was conducted on 25 men, each of whom received pentazocine (Fortral) in a dose calculated upon body-weight at 4-hourly intervals on the first day after surgery for a prolapsed intervertebral disc. None of the men had any other physical disorder or history of mental illness. Measurements of pain revealed that, despite comparable blood levels of the analgesic, highest levels were experienced by neurotic extraverts. It was also found that the differences in pain between them and patients with other personality characteristics in-creased from the first hour after injection of the drug; that is, when blood levels of the analgesic were falling.

In addition to taking account of personality differences when considering analgesic drug treatment clinicians should also be aware of the fact that pain levels vary during the day. Folkard, Glynn, and Lloyd, (1976) have shown that pain levels exhibit a diurnal variation in patients with intractable pain. The lowest levels of pain are experienced in the morning and the highest levels towards the end of the day, but this pattern does not fit variations in levels of alertness or body temperature. Examination of personality scores on the Eysenck Personality Inventory reveals that introverts seem to feel more pain than extraverts before noon and less after this time. Folkard and his co-workers also found that pain levels of patients with high neuroticism scores tend to rise later in the day than those with low scores. The increase of pain over the day was significantly greater for women than for men and, amongst the women, for those at home when compared with those out at work, suggesting that the distracting effect of work and social interactions reduce pain.

Depression and pain are linked in two ways: first a painful illness, especially if chronic, tends to produce depression of mood and this is the result of combin-ed physical and psychological stresses. The presence of depression is associated with lower levels of tolerance for pain which will rise if the depression is treated. Treatment is most successful amongst patients with previously good personality characteristics, and Sternbach (1974a) has pointed out that depression will be relieved by drug treatment if the patient has a reactive depressive profile on the Minnesota Multiphasic Personality Inventory. Secondly, pain is common in depressive illness. Merskey and Spear (1967) reported that pain is present in just over 50 per cent of psychiatric inpatients and Baker and Merskey (1966) found that 59 per cent of patients in general practice with emotional disorders had pain. Pilling, Brannick, and Swenson, (1977) reported that the number of men and women psychiatric patients with depression and pain is similar, with 63 per cent and 65 per cent in each group. At times physical and mental pain (i.e. depression) coexist, but a small number of patients may present with pain only, which masks underlying depression. This has been reported in patients with atypical facial pain by Lascelles (1966) who observed that the sufferers complain of pain, lethargy, fatigue, tension, and disordered sleep. He also noted that they have marked obsessional personality characteristics and that if the symptoms have been present for 6 months or less response to treatment with antidepressant drugs is good.

Apart from the influence of levels of neuroticism, extraversion–introversion, and depression, pain experience and associated behaviour are also influenced by attitudes towards pain and its significance to the sufferer. This matter has been examined by investigations of hypochondriacal, and conversion disorders in which pain predominates, and of those individuals who maintain abnormal tenure of the sick role state when in pain.

Hypochondriacal personality traits are taken to represent a particular attitude towards health which has been defined as, 'fascinated absorption by the experience of a physical or mental impairment' (Ladee, 1966). Kenyon (1976) proposed that 'hypochondriacal traits, symptoms, ideas, and fears, should carry with them the implication that there is morbid preoccupation with mental and bodily functions or state of health'. Pilowsky (1967), in a factor analysis of data from psychiatric patients, identified three elements of hypochondriasis; namely, preoccupation with body functions, fear of disease which patients seek to deny, and a conviction of the presence of bodily disease which is held with delusional intensity. According to Kenyon 70 per cent of hypochondriacal patients in his study had pain, with headaches in 55 per cent, chest pain in 20 per cent, and abdominal pain in 16 per cent. He also observed that complaints of diffuse and vague pains, especially in muscles, are common, and that others have reported the following types of pain in hypochondriacal disorders: atypical facial pain (Webb and Lascelles, 1962), right iliac fossa pain in women (Merskey and Spear, 1967), abdominal pain in children (Apley, 1975). Patients presenting with hypochondriasis and pain are likely to have a long history of illness, fewer affective symptoms than other patients, and a poorer chance of recovery by the time of discharge. Kreitman et al. (1965) reported that hypochondriacal patients are more likely to have had a psychosomatic disorder in childhood when compared with depressed patients without physical symptoms. They concluded that the development of somatic symptoms is a defence against severe psychic stress and that this reaction is learned in childhood, chiefly from a mother who responds emotionally to her child only when it is ill.

Hysterical personality traits, and in particular the tendency to exaggerate personal experiences, to be demanding, and to be manipulative, influences the presentation of a painful illness and the interpretation of symptoms by doctors. Thus at times the 'pain behaviour' of an hysteric may be so exaggerated that even very experienced doctors are unable to determine the meaning of physical symptoms and reject a diagnosis of organic disease (Bond, 1978).

Conversion disorders in which the primary gain to the patient is relief from intolerable levels of emotional tension, for example generated by hostility and guilt, may be manifest as painful disorders. The pain tends to have characteristics which enable doctors to differentiate it from pain which is due chiefly to a physical cause, the word chiefly being used because in conversion disorders there is a physical abnormality at times. Pain is usually described as constant and severe although it seldom wakens the patient from sleep. It is most often experienced in the face and may also occur at the site of a previous injury or surgical operation, giving rise to difficulties in diagnosis. The pain may be inconstant in position, crossing dermatome boundaries and areas for referred pain. The term psychogenic pain is often used to describe this form of pain and in an extensive review Sternbach (1974a) cautions against the misuse of the term, concluding that psychogenic pain is best described as 'pain which is better understood in psychological and physical language although the quality of the experience does not differ appreciably amongst those who suffer it compared with individuals with pain due to physical causes'. He chooses this description to avoid the artificiality of having to propose either a psychological or physical cause for the pain, because this is so often impossible. The appearance of a conversion syndrome is not dependent upon any specific premorbid personality characteristic and this has been confirmed by those who have compared the personality profiles of sufferers of pain which is either primarily psychogenic, or somatogenic (Pilling *et al.*, 1967, Woodforde and Merskey, 1972). Sternbach (1974a) reports that amongst patients with psychogenic pain levels of hypochondriasis are greater than those of depression and that when pain is part of a conversion disorder overt neurotic symptoms are less in evidence than in pain-free psychiatric patients.

The appearance of physical pain as a conversion symptom may be related to a low level of self-esteem. This is restored by suffering pain which has the effect of making the individual believe that he or she would function well in all areas of life if it were not for pain. Elton, Stanely, and Burrows (1978), gave support to this idea by measuring levels of self-esteem before and after treatment in pain-prone patients and patients with chronic pain due to a definite physical cause. The pain-prone patients had significantly lower levels of self-esteem than others initially but, after psychological treatments lasting 3 months, their pain levels were lower and their self-esteem had increased significantly.

Psychodynamic studies of psychogenic pain owe much to two germinal papers by Szarsz (1957) and Engel (1959) who described the personality characteristics of the sufferers of this symptom. Engel described the pain-prone person as constitutionally gloomy, pessimistic, guilt-ridden, depressive, and self-punitive. He claimed that the last-named trait stemmed from early childhood abuses and maltreatment by parents. In those early years punishment for badness becomes a signal for the development of guilt and also for the later experience of forgiveness and reunion with loved ones: thus the meaning of pain becomes ambiguous. In adult life the pain-prone person seems to develop his or her pain just when success or achievement of an important goal is within reach. Thomas Szarsz described 'L'homme douloureux', as an individual for whom being in pain is a way of life, and a means for creating and controlling the environment. Inevitably these characteristics lead to frequent encounters with doctors, and challenges to their skills, leading to the performance of increasingly obscure or dangerous investigations which almost always prove to be inconclusive but which may cause damage and certainly reinforce the patient's abnormal behaviour.

Mechanic (1977) states that 'motivational needs and coping are important aspects of illness response', and continues by describing illness behaviour as 'the varying perceptions, thoughts, feelings and acts affecting the personal and social meaning of symptoms, illness, disabilities and their consequences'. Pilowsky and Spence (1976) defined the sick role as 'the ways in which symptoms may be differentially perceived, evaluated and acted (or not acted) upon by different kinds of persons', and have extensively studied abnormal tenure of it. Their studies show how illness behaviour may serve to control relationships and satisfy personal needs, and that pain in particular often plays an important part in personal interactions. As Szarsz pointed out, pain may serve as a means of communicating distress of an emotional kind, as a means of manipulating others, as a means of expressing hostility, or as a means of relieving guilt. Pilowsky and Spence have extended these observations by quantitative assessments of illness behaviour and their work is based upon the use of an Illness Behaviour Questionnaire (Pilowsky and Spence, 1975), which was designed to eliminate the confusion which often arises when the traditional psychiatric terms hypochondriacal, hysterical, psychogenic, and functional are used. They showed that, when compared with pain-free psychiatric patients, individuals with chronic pain who attended a pain clinic had a greater conviction of disease and level of somatic preoccupation, and that they also had a tendency to deny current life difficulties. They made the point that the patient with chronic pain has a tendency to feel depressed though not suffering from a frank depressive illness.

In a factor analysis of data obtained using an Illness Behaviour Questionnaire Pilowsky and Spence (1975) identified a specific factor which they labelled 'affective inhibition' and stated that those exhibiting this characteristic 'may fail to assert themselves adequately in other areas of social functioning and so chronically experience frustration and the physiological arousal that invariably accompanies it'. They found that of 100 patients attending a pain clinic or psychiatric department 27 did not express personal and angry feelings easily, and suggested that this may be an important mechanism amongst those who develop musculoskeletal pain. Patients who do not reveal their feelings easily may have a self-punitive attitude and experience significant affective disturbances more often than those who express irritability and anger freely. Thus there is support for the descriptive approach favoured by Engel (1959), and Freud's hypothesis that in depressive illnesses anger is inhibited—a view which is still held but only for a proportion of those who have a depressive illness.

The work of Pilowsky and Spence emphasized the views of earlier workers that it is important to study behaviour patterns in chronic-pain patients and to relate these to the meanings of pain for different patients. This subject has been advanced in another direction by Sternbach et al., (1973); and Sternbach (1974b), who have written at length about the significance of pain to patients, and in particular its role in their interaction with family, friends, medical professionals, and others. They have reported the interactions as 'games' of which there are several types. For example, a patient may be a 'home tyrant' because he or she manipulates the home environment to escape the responsibilities of family life and to attract attention and sympathy by evoking guilt in others. The person may become a 'pain professional'; one who plays a game for financial rewards through chronic sickness, or an addict who plays for drugs of addiction though expressing a dislike for need of them. The 'somatizer' has perfect health—except for pain which serves as an expression of unresolved emotional conflicts. Finally, a patient may be a 'confounder' because he or she seems concerned only to defeat the efforts of doctors to make a diagnosis and treat their symptom. This is an exercise which, paradoxically, appears to fulfil unmet needs for emotional support and, at times, for punishment, although doctors are usually unaware of their true role in the patient's emotional life.

PERSONALITY AND PAIN THRESHOLDS

There are two thresholds for noxious stimuli. The first is the point at which the initial quality of the stimulus—for example, warmth, coldness or pressure changes, and pain is experienced, and the second is that at which pain becomes unbearable. The upper limit is regarded by some as a measure of pain tolerance and the interval between the thresholds as sensitivity to pain. Others regard the threshold interval as a measure of tolerance. Both thresholds are based upon physiological mechanisms, but whereas the lower one is relatively constant within and between different individuals the upper one is influenced to a considerable extent by psychological factors, including personality, attitudes to pain, the meaning of pain, and the setting in which it is experienced (Bond, 1979). It also varies with age, sex, and occupational status (Merskey and Spear, 1967). Tolerance of pain is lower in individuals who are anxious, especially when their anxiety is acute, and it is probably because of the effects of anxiety that a fall in pain thresholds during illness is reported by most workers; especially in levels of tolerance (Bond and Pearson 1969; Parbrook, Steel, and Dalrymple, 1973). However, it seems that a fall in thresholds in illness is not inevitable because Keele (1968) reported that amongst patients who had had a myocardial infarct some had elevated pain thresholds, less pain from the illness and required less analgesic medication than others. Dalrymple, Parbrook, and Steel (1973) found that lung vital capacity after upper abdominal surgery was higher amongst patients with the highest postoperative pain thresholds, that is amongst the least neurotic patients, although for the whole population studied threshold levels fell. Therefore it seems that the extent to which pain thresholds fall, and the point from which they fall, varies from person to person and that both the initial setting of the threshold for tolerance and the degree to which it changes is closely related to personality characteristics.

Sternbach et al. (1974) utilized the interval between thresholds to compute a 'tourniquet pain ratio'—a method for comparing patients' reports of pain arising from disease processes with artificially induced pain due to forearm ischaemia. The technique was devised to eliminate the heavy psychological bias that is thought to distort subjective estimates of pain due to a physical cause. In patients with chronic pain subjective estimates of pain are usually higher than the value computed from the tourniquet pain ratio and much higher where there are major psychological factors influencing patients' spontaneous reports of pain. Surprisingly, Sternbach and his colleagues were unable to find a correlation between subjective estimates of pain and personality variables measured with the Minnesota Multiphasic Personality Inventory.

In work reminiscent of Petrie's studies of perceptual reactance, Adler and Lomazzi (1973) investigated the relation between perceptual style as an aspect of personality, and pain tolerance levels. The construct they used to assess perception was developed by Witkin, Dyk, and Faterson (1962) known as field-dependence, field-independence. The field-independent person is alleged to have a more developed body image, a more accentuated self-identity and more developed psychological defence mechanisms than the field-dependent person. As a consequence the former experience greater vividness of perception of afferent sensory input and should have lower thresholds for pain. Sweeney and Fine (1965) confirmed this when they reported that field-independent subjects have a lower tolerance for a cold pressor stimulus. However the work of others in this area seems contradictory and Adler and Lomazzi were not able to confirm their hypothesis that there is a significant relationship between field orientation and pain tolerance. They attributed this to the interference effect of anxiety in their subjects. In a second experiment Adler, Gervasi and Holzer (1973) used an anxiolytic agent and on this occasion found that the correlations they sought were present in the least anxious subjects who were also those who used fewest manoeuvres to distract themselves from pain. They concluded, 'an individual's perceptual style and pain tolerance are correlated only when psychological factors like anxiety, etc., are relatively in abeyance'.

THE INFLUENCE OF LEARNING AND SOCIOCULTURAL FACTORS UPON PAIN SEVERITY AND THE DEVELOPMENT OF ASSOCIATED BEHAVIOUR PATTERNS

It is believed that the withdrawal response to noxious stimuli is innate and one upon which, in normal development, each person gradually builds his or her repertoire of 'pain behaviour'. This is shaped by personal experiences and those of others around us, by attitudes towards pain in the family, and by wider cultural influences. Within the first year or two of life a child learns to avoid situations leading to pain and, with increasing sophistication, puts the experience of pain into words. The influence of birth order and family size upon behaviour associated with pain has been of interest to various workers but their conclusions do not give a uniform picture. It has been shown that firstborn and only children, together with those from very small families, tend to be brought up to be more protected and dependent than those from large families, and

Collins (1965) found that the former group had higher levels of pain tolerance. However, Schachter (1959) reported lower levels of pain tolerance in firstborn children, and Ryan and Kovacic (1975) and Nisbett (1968) inferred this from studies in which they found lower pain thresholds in non-athletes and the fact that fewer firstborn children took part in contact sport athletics. In contrast, Gonda (1962) had shown previously that in adult life those who were younger children in large families complain more about pain. Merskey and Spear (1967) comment that this may reflect a younger child's use of pain as a means of attracting attention and affection from the mother.

Schultz (1975) states that a child's perception of pain follows a characteristic pattern of development during childhood and, in addition, that apart from learning the obvious meaning of pain, namely that it commonly indicates injury to the body, he or she also develops patterns of behaviour in which pain takes on meanings, for example in gaining attention and affection, or as a means of manipulating others. This is a reiteration of Engel's earlier views about childhood development and pain, in which he also holds that pain and aggression become linked in childhood when the child learns that pain can become an expression of aggression and power. Moreover at that time the child also learns the effects of inflicting pain on others and the self, and that the latter can become a means of controlling one's own aggression. Engel stated that at this time of life pain may be experienced in association with loss of a loved one, and that physical pain may occur in the same circumstances in adult life. Thus during childhood the patterns of later adult illness behaviour, including the use of pain, are laid down; obviously modelling is an important aspect of the learning process and is relevant to the development of pain complaint behaviour. For example, it has been shown that complaints of chronic pain are more common amongst those raised in an atmosphere of strife, frequent physical punishments for misdeeds, and homes where pain was a part of another's neurotic behaviour.

Sex differences emerge during childhood as boys learn the general attitude of their society towards pain; for example the British view that they should bear pain quietly, though anxious or afraid. By contrast the girls are allowed greater freedom of complaint though they too learn that excessive expressions of emotion are not readily tolerated and these modes of behaviour are central to an understanding of ethnic and cultural attitudes to sickness and pain; an issue which is of increasing importance in Britain where the ethnic structure has changed appreciably in the past 25 years and continues to alter. The British attitude to bearing pain typified by the phrase 'stiff upper lip' is not that of other ethnic groups and doctors, above all others, must recognize this fact. Northern and Western Europeans tend to exhibit less emotion and complain less when in pain than Southern Europeans or those of the Latin races. In the often-quoted study in the United States by Zborowski (1952) the complaint behaviour of three different ethnic groups was found to differ substantially. Thus, he reported that individuals of Old American stock, who are closest in their origins and attitudes to native-born British people, and American-Irish, are phlegmatic and matter-of-fact about pain. By contrast Italian-Americans complain more freely and expect treatment sooner. Jewish-Americans behave similarly, openly seeking support and sympathy from relatives and friends, which is freely given, and there is good reason to believe that this form of behaviour, in which a catharsis takes place, lowers tensions and reduces pain and suffering. The factor governing behaviour for all groups seems to be the level of approval given by society for the public expression of pain and emotion. Sternbach and Tursky (1965), and Tursky and Sternbach (1967)—in studies of Americans of Irish, Italian, and Jewish origins—confirmed the cultural differences Zborowski described and also observed that these are related to levels of pain tolerance and physiological responses to noxious stimuli. British attitudes to pain are reflected in recent work by Bond (1978) on two groups of patients in Scottish hospitals. He found that irrespective of whether their pain was acute or chronic all patients felt they should bear pain as long as possible. The study also revealed that nurses trained to deal with pain problems give patients their analgesics more promptly and give greater emotional support than those who have not had this advantage. Clearly the effect of cultural attitudes to pain, reviewed extensively by Wolff and Langley (1975), and an individual's personality interact to give a wide range of behaviour patterns some of which have been described in this chapter.

Attempts have been made by Lynn (1971) and Lynn and Hampson (1975) to study personality characteristics of different ethnic groups as they present in their own countries. They carried out an exercise to determine differences in levels of anxiety amongst national groups. Lynn claims that a general factor, namely a population anxiety level, may be determined by examining the inter-correlation of the prevalence rates and consumption figures of a number of national demographic and epidemiological phenomena. From the results of a study in which twelve variables were used (national prevalence rates for suicide, crime, murder, illegitimacy, divorce, alcoholism, chronic psychosis, coronary heart disease, accidents, and the consumption per head of population of calories, caffeine, and cigarettes), Lynn and Hampson computed national differences in extraversion and neuroticism. They concluded that the Japanese tend to be the most introverted and Americans the most extraverted peoples. Austrians had the highest neuroticism scores, and the Irish—closely followed by the British—the lowest scores. The relevance of these findings to our understanding of individuals in pain seems very tenuous at present and requires further clarification.

We know that interaction between the individual and his or her environment, and in particular with those with whom he or she is in daily contact, has had important consequences for the development of methods of treatment of chronic pain states. More specifically it has led to the development of social modelling techniques. Craig and Coren (1975) have found that experiences of pain and physical distress can be altered appreciably by social communications operating independently from the effects of drugs and surgery. Whether or not changes of this kind really reflect alterations in levels of personal distress or in complaint behaviour is uncertain and Craig and Neidermayer (1974) and Craig, Best, and

Ward (1975) have examined the problem in laboratory experiments in order to clarify the situation. They have shown that, amongst volunteers, tolerance for electric shocks, reflected in changes in pain thresholds, is influenced significantly by the behaviour of 'models' to whom the subjects of the experiments are exposed. Thus the presence of an intolerant model lowers tolerance in the subject but a tolerant model does not appear to alter sensitivity. However, the latter situation does result in less willingness to report physical distress. Therefore it appears that both the experience of pain and complaint behaviour vary in response to social influences and, as Craig and Coren (1975) state:

> if you tell a patient that the ongoing stimulation is painful, via the presence of an intolerant model, you may actually be increasing his vulnerability to the sensory experience of pain. If you tell him that the ongoing stimulus is not painful, via a tolerant model, you do not affect the actual internal sensory experience but rather reduce his willingness to report his distress.

It is interesting to speculate whether the influence of the model presented by a stoical and uncomplaining Britisher in a hospital ward merely silences an individual from a different ethnic background leaving him with the same degree of pain or, more probably, with greater pain as a result of raising his level of emotional tension by suppressing his normal patterns of behaviour!

In conclusion, pain is a subjective experience the appearance and severity of which is dependent upon physiological, psychological, and social factors. The interplay between these factors varies from person to person, and from time to time for any given individual, accounting for the great variations in levels of pain and patterns of complaint behaviour seen amongst ill people. The fact that pain may be a reflection of emotional problems or a means of manipulating illness is often forgotten or not appreciated, and it is only by understanding the way in which our behaviour is moulded by life experiences that we can make accurate assessments of people in pain and develop appropriate methods of management.

REFERENCES

Adler, R., and Lomazzi, F. (1973). Perceptual style and pain tolerance—I. The influence of certain psychological factors. *J. Psychosom. Res.*, **17**, 369–379.

Adler, R., Gervasi, A., and Holzer, B. (1973). Perceptual style and pain tolerance—II. The influence of an anxiolytic agent. *J. Psychosom. Res.*, **17**, 381–387.

Apley, J. (1975). *The Child with Abdominal Pains*, 2nd Edn. Oxford: Blackwell Scientific Publications.

Baker, J. W., and Merskey, H. (1966). Pain in general practice. *J. Psychosom. Res.*, **10**, 383–387.

Barnes, G. E. (1975). Extraversion and pain. *Br. J. Soc. Clin. Psychol.*, **14**, 303–308.

Bond, M. R. (1971). The relation of pain to the Eysenck Personality Inventory, Cornell Medical Index and Whitely Index of Hypochondriasis. *Br. J. Psychiat.*, **119**, 671–678.

Bond, M. R. (1973). Personality studies in patients with pain secondary to organic disease. *J. Psychosom.*, **17**, 257–263.

Bond, M. R. (1980). Personality and pain. In S. Lipton (ed.), *Persistent Pain, Modern Methods of Treatment*, vol. II. London: Academic Press.

Bond, M. R. (1979). *Pain, its Nature, Analysis and Treatment.* London, Edinburgh, and New York: Churchill Livingstone.

Bond, M. R., Glynn, J. P., and Thomas, D. G. (1976). The relation between pain and personality in patients receiving pentazocine (Fortral) after surgery. *J. Psychosom. Res.*, **30**, 369–381.

Bond, M. R., and Pearson, I. B. (1969). Psychological aspects of pain in women with advanced carcinoma of the cervix. *J. Psychosom. Res.*, **13**, 13–19.

Collins, L. G. (1965). Pain sensitivity and ratings of childhood experience. *Percep. Mot. Skills*, **21**, 349–350.

Craig, K. D., Best, H., and Ward, L. M. (1975). Social modelling influences on psychophysical judgements of electrical stimulation. *J. Abn. Psychol.*, **84**, 366–373.

Craig, K. D., and Coren, S. (1975). Signal detection analysis of social modelling influences on pain expressions. *J. Psychosom. Res.*, **19**, 105–112.

Craig, K. D., and Niedermayer, H. (1974). Autonomic correlates of pain thresholds influenced by social modelling. *J. Person. Soc. Psychol.*, **29**, 246–252.

Dalrymple, D. G. Parbrook, G. D., and Steel, D. F. (1973). Factors predisposing the post-operative pain and pulmonary complications. *Brit. J. Anaesth.*, **45**, 589–597.

Egbert, L. D., Battit, G. E., Welch, C. E., and Bartlett, M. K. (1964). Reduction of post-operative pain by encouragement and instruction of patients. *New Eng. Med. J.*, **270**, 825–827.

Elton, D., Stanely, G. V., and Burrows, G. D. (1978). Self-esteem and chronic pain. *J. Psychosom. Res.*, **22**, 22–30.

Engel, G. L. (1959). 'Psychogenic' pain and the pain prone patient. *Am. J. Med.*, **26**, 899–918.

Eysenck, H. J., and Eysenck, S. G. B. (1976). *Manual of the Eysenck Personality Questionnaire.* London: Hodder & Stoughton.

Eysenck, S. G. B. (1961). Personality and pain assessment in childbirth of married and unmarried mothers. *J. Ment. Sci.*, **107**, 225–239.

Folkard, S., Glynn, C. J., and Lloyd, J. W. (1976). Diurnal variation and individual differences in the perception of intractable pain. *J. Psychosom. Res.*, **20**, 289–301.

Gonda, T. A. (1962). The relationship between complaints of persistent pain and family size. *J. Neurol., Neurosurg. Psychiat.*, **25**, 277–281.

Howorth, E. (1965). Headache, personality and stress. *Brit. J. Psychiat.*, **111**, 1193–1197.

Huggen, R. E. (1968). Neuroticism, distortion and objective manifestations of anxiety in males with malignant disease. *Brit. J. Soc. Clin. Psychol.*, **7**, 280–285.

Keele, K. D. (1968). Pain complaint threshold in relation to pain of cardiac infarction. *Brit. Med. J.*, **1**, 670–673.

Kenyon, F. E. (1976). Hypochondriacal states. *Brit. J. Psychiat.*, **129**, 55–60.

Kissen, D. M. (1964). The influence of some environmental factors on personality inventory scores in psychosomatic research. *J. Psychosom. Res.*, **8**, 145–149.

Kissen, D. M., and Eysenck, H. J. (1962). Personality in male lung cancer patients. *J. Psychosom. Res.*, **6**, 123–127.

Kreitman, N., Sainsbury, P., Pearce, K., and Costain, W. R. (1965). Hypochondriasis and depression in outpatients at a general hospital. *Brit. J. Psychiat.*, **111**, 607–615.

Ladee, G. A. (1966). *Hypochondriacal Syndromes.* Amsterdam: Elsevier.

Lascelles, R. G. (1966). Atypical facial pain and depression. *Brit. J. Psychiat.*, **112**, 651–659.

Lovell, R. R. H., and Verghese, A. (1967). Personality traits associated with different chest pains after myocardial infarction. *Brit. Med. J.*, **2**, 327–330.

Lynn, R. (1971). *Personality and National Character.* Oxford: Pergamon Press.

Lynn, R., and Eysenck, H. J. (1961). Tolerance for pain, extraversion and neuroticism. *Percept. Mot. Skills*, **12**, 161–162.

Lynn, R., and Hampson, S. L. (1975). National differences in extraversion and neuroticism. *Br. J. Soc. Clin. Psychol.*, **14**, 223–240.

Martin, M. J., Rome, H. P., and Swenson, W. M. (1967). Muscular contraction: a psychiatric review. In A. P. Friedman *et al.* (eds.), *Research and Clinical Studies on Headache*. Basel, New York: Karger.

Mechanic, D. (1977). Illness behaviour social adaptation and the management of illness. *J. Nerv. Ment. Dis.*, **165**, 79–87.

Merskey, H., and Spear, F. G. (1967). *Pain: Physiological and Psychiatric Aspects*. London: Baillière, Tindall, & Cassell.

Nisbett, R. E. (1968). Birth order and participations in dangerous sports. *J. Person. and Soc. Psychol.*, **8**, 351–353.

Ostfeld, A. M., Lebovits, B. Z., Shekelle, R. B., and Paul, O. (1964). A prospective study of the relationship between personality and chronic heart disease. *J. Chron. Dis.*, **17**, 265–276.

Parbrook, G. D., Steel, G. F., and Dalrymple, F. G. (1973). Factors predisposing to postoperative pain and pulmonary complications. *Brit. J. Anaesth.*, **45**, 21–32.

Petrie, A. (1967). *Individuality in Pain and Suffering*. Chicago: University of Chicago Press.

Philips, C. (1976). Headache and personality. *J. Psychosom. Res.*, **20**, 535–542.

Pilling, L. F., Brannick, T. L., and Swenson, W. M. (1967). Psychologic characteristics of psychiatric patients having pain as a presenting symptom. *Canad. Med. Ass. J.*, **97**, 387–394.

Pilowsky, I. (1967). Dimensions of hypochondriasis. *Brit. J. Psychiat.*, **113**, 89–93.

Pilowsky, I., and Spence, N. D. (1975). Patterns of illness behaviour in patients with intractable pain. *J. Psychosom. Res.*, **19**, 279–288.

Pilowsky, I., and Spence, N. D. (1976). Pain, anger and illness behaviour. *J. Psychosom. Res.*, **20**, 411–416.

Ryan, E. D., and Kovacic, C. R. (1975). 'Pain tolerance and athletic participation'. In M. Weisenberg (ed.), *Pain, Clinical and Experimental Perspectives*, pp.127–132. St Louis: C. V. Mosby Co.

Sainsbury, P. (1960). Psychosomatic disorders and neurosis in outpatients attending a general hospital. *J. Psychosom. Res.*, **4**, 261–273.

Schachter, S. (1959). *The Psychology of Affiliation*. Stanford: Stanford University Press.

Schalling, D., and Levander, S. (1964). Ratings of anxiety proneness and responses to electrical pain stimulation. *Scand. J. Psychol.*, **5**, 1–9.

Shultz, N. V. (1975). How children perceive pain. In M. Weisenberg, (ed.), *Pain, Clinical and Experimental Perspectives*, pp. 105–110. St Louis: C. V. Mosby Co.

Selinsky, H. (1939). Psychological study of the migraine syndrome. *Bull. N.Y. Med.*, **15**, 757–763.

Sternbach, R. A. (1968). *Pain: A Psychophysiological Analysis*. New York and London: Academic Press.

Sternbach, R. A. (1974a). *Pain Patients, Traits and Treatments*. New York and London: Academic Press.

Sternbach, R. A. (1974b). Varieties of pain games. In J. J. Bonica (ed.), *Advances in Neurology*, vol. 4, pp. 423–429. New York: Raven Press.

Sternbach, R. A., Murphy, R. W., Timmermans, G., Greenhoot, J. H., and Akeson, W. H. (1974).Measuring the severity of clinical pain. In J. J. Bonica (ed.), *Advances in Neurology, Vol. 4*, pp. 281–288. New York: Raven Press.

Sternbach, R. A., and Timmermans, G. (1975). Personality changes associated with reduction of pain. *Pain*, **1**, 177–181.

Sternbach, R. A., and Tursky, B. (1965). Ethnic differences among housewives in psychophysical and skin potential responses to electric shock. *Psychophysiol.*, **1**, 241–246.

Sternbach, R. A., Wolff, S. R., Murphy, R. W., and Akeson, W. H. (1973). Traits of pain patients: the low-back 'loser'. *Psychosomatics*, **14**, 226–239.

Sweeney, D. R., and Fine, B. H. (1965). Pain reactivity and field-dependence. *Percept. Mot. Skills*, **21**, 757–758.

Szarsz, T. S. (1957). *Pain and Pleasure: A Study of Bodily Feelings*. New York: Basic Books.

Tursky, B., and Sternbach, R. A. (1967). Further physiological correlates of ethnic differences in responses to shock. *Psychophysiol.*, **4**, 67–74.

Walters, W. E., and O'Connor, P. J. (1971). Epidemiology of headache and migraine in women. *J. Neurol. Neurosurg. Psychiat.*, **34**, 148–153.

Webb, H. E., and Lascelles, R. G. (1962). Treatment of facial and head pain associated with depression. *Lancet*, **1**, 355–356.

Witkin, H. A., Dyk, R. B., and Faterson, H. F. (1962). *Psychologic Differentiation Studies of Development*. New York: Wiley.

Wolff, B. B., and Langley, S. (1975). Cultural factors and the response to pain. In M. Weisenberg, (ed.), *Pain, Clinical and Experimental Perspectives*, pp. 144–151. St Louis: C. V. Mosby Co.

Woodforde, J. M., and Merskey, H. (1972). Personality traits of patients with chronic pain. *J. Psychosom. Res.*, **16**, 167–172.

Zborowski, M. (1952). Cultural components in responses to pain. *J. Soc. Issues*, **8**, 16–30.

SECTION 5

Environment

Foundations of Psychosomatics
Edited by M. J. Christie and P. G. Mellett
© 1981 John Wiley & Sons Ltd.

15

CULTURE AND ILLNESS: EPIDEMIOLOGICAL EVIDENCE

MICHAEL MARMOT
*Department of Medical Statistics and Epidemiology,
London School of Hygiene and Tropical Medicine.*

INTRODUCTION

The culture in which people live affects their beliefs, their attitudes, their behaviour, and their social groupings. This may influence their disease patterns in a variety of ways. In this chapter major attention will be paid to the evidence from population studies that cultural forces, acting through psychosomatic pathways, may play a role in the aetiology of disease. To put this in context, the various ways culture may influence disease will first be considered.

Behaviour affects exposure of individuals to 'noxious' agents

Cultural and social influences clearly affect a wide variety of behaviours relevant to disease. Dietary habits, physical activity patterns, religious practices, smoking, alcohol and other drug-taking are all intimately bound up with cultural traditions, and may all influence risk of disease. In medical epidemiological studies, the risks associated with factors such as smoking, intake of certain foods, or obesity, are studied. Often scant attention is paid to the influences shaping dietary patterns, obesity, or smoking. The behavioural sciences can provide invaluable aid from their study of these influences (Jenkins, 1972). In particular, the way people from different cultures react to proposed health innovations had been intensely studied by anthropologists and health educators (Paul, 1955).

Behaviour may affect risk of disease via psychosomatic pathways

Culture may influence risk-related behaviour as described above. It may also have a more direct influence because social encounters have a symbolic meaning, influenced by the culture (Brown, 1976). The psychosomatic pathways by which such symbolic influences may exert their effect are the subject of other chapters of this book. The main emphasis of this chapter will be epidemiological studies that relate social and cultural factors of population groups to risk of disease. As will be seen, a central problem in these studies is to disentangle 'physical' effects on the body from 'psychosomatic' effects.

Culture affects illness behaviour

Cultural traditions affect what people recognize as disease and what they do about it once they define themselves as sick (Mechanic, 1972). This has been a principal focus of medical anthropology (Fabrega, 1974) and will not be dealt with further here.

Ecological relationships

The size, complexity, and level of development of a society affects its disease patterns. Fenner (1971) has summarized the interaction between group size, agricultural and living arrangements, and exposure to micro-organisms, in societies of differing levels of complexity. Thus, hunter–gatherers who live in isolated bands of 30 or so individuals are not subject to infectious diseases such as measles that require a human reservoir and a pool of susceptibles for their transmission. The group size is too small to sustain transmission of the virus. On the other hand, such small groups will be subject to diseases transmitted from animals to man by a vector such as the mosquito. Dunn has shown that, hunter–gatherers, who disturb the ecosystem very little, are subject to a wider variety of parasites than agriculturalists who make a greater impact on the ecosystem (Dunn, 1968, 1972).

Agriculturalists living in larger population groups are subject to the major epidemic diseases requiring direct person-to-person transmission. Contact with rivers and stagnant water are liable to allow the cycle of transmission of diseases such as schistosomiasis and malaria to be set up (Wiesenfeld, 1967).

Living in large urban areas brings its own problems of pollution of air and water, crowded living conditions, and later, the disorders associated with modern urban life, such as cancer and heart disease (Furnass, 1970).

EVIDENCE FOR PSYCHOSOMATIC PATHWAYS IN DISEASE AETIOLOGY

Three main types of enquiry are important in demonstrating that social and psychological factors may have direct influence on physiology and pathology— i.e. via neuroendocrine pathways.

Animal studies

There is a vast literature demonstrating that, in experimental animals, social and psychological factors will accelerate the rate of occurrence of a variety of diseases (e.g. see Henry and Stephens, 1977; Calhoun, 1962). These studies establish the plausibility of the proposition that psychosocial factors are important in disease aetiology. They also demonstrate the mechanisms by which such factors might operate. Thus, for example, it has been shown that when mice, raised in isolation to be socially incompetent, are exposed to a mouse colony, they develop high blood pressure, and other vascular and renal disease, with increased frequency (Henry, Meehan, and Stephens, 1967, Henry, Ely, and Stephens, 1971). This demonstrates very neatly the possible influence of psychosocial stimuli on the adrenocortical and sympathomedullary systems of the mouse, and on the development of disease. The applicability of these studies to humans must of course be questioned. In particular the nature of the deleterious psychosocial stimuli can only be defined by studying humans.

Laboratory/clinical studies on humans

Other chapters in this book provide ample evidence for the effect of psychosocial factors on physiological and biological function. Such laboratory studies on individuals are crucial in the investigation of possible disease pathways. For obvious ethical reasons, however, such studies cannot demonstrate that the risk of actual disease in humans is increased by psychosocial stimuli. For example, it may be shown that certain stressful circumstances may lead to changes in blood pressure and hormonal secretions (Kiritz and Moos, 1974). The next step is to show that such transient changes in function may result in pathological changes, clinical disease, and death. The evidence for this step is more circumstantial, and has come from epidemiological studies.

Epidemiological studies

Epidemiology has departed from its origins in the study of infectious disease and is now more generally concerned with the study of the distribution of disease in populations. By studying the rates of disease of people living in different cultures or in different social groups, the influence of cultural and social factors may be determined. A crucial task in such studies is to distinguish between factors that influence neuroendocrine pathways and factors that exert their effect by influencing health-related behaviours such as diet or smoking. For example, in the United Kingdom working-class people have a higher mortality from almost every cause of death (OPCS, 1978). It is known that there are social class differences in smoking, in food habits, in other patterns of consumption, in family structure, in housing, and many other environmental factors. Merely showing that patterns of disease differ in different social or cultural groups is not per se an argument that these differences are psychosomatic in nature. Nevertheless, as will be shown, it may be possible by epidemiological enquiry to distinguish psychosomatic from other social or cultural factors.

CONCEPTUAL FRAMEWORK

Multifactorial aetiology

All diseases are multifactorial in origin. As Dubos (1965) has pointed out, exposure to an infecting organism is usually insufficient to account for the occurrence of clinical disease. Host resistance or environmental stimuli may also play a part in determining the outcome of an infection. The crucial question here is whether, in an individual who is otherwise liable to a particular disease, psychosocial factors may change the risk of disease. It is suggested that they may do this by affecting the individual's general level of resistance to disease or by acting as a precipitant in an otherwise predisposed individual. Thus it is not claimed that psychosocial factors can, in the absence of other causal agents, lead to physical disease. It is possible that this may be true for 'disturbances of mood, thought and behaviour' (Hinkle and Wolff, 1958) but unlikely for other diseases.

Specificity

This has important implications. As Cassel has argued, it is not very useful to think of psychosocial factors as aetiological agents with the same specificity as micro-organisms. Nor should one expect to find a dose–response relationship between a presumed psychosocial causal factor and disease (Cassel, 1976). If the effect of psychosocial factors is to change susceptibility, the disease process that results will to some extent be determined by the presence of other causal agents. For example, a relationship has been shown between the onset of tuberculosis and the occurrence of stressful life events (Holmes, 1956). Clearly without the presence of the infecting organism the stressful life event could not increase the risk of clinical tuberculosis. In the presence of different predisposing factors stressful life events have been shown to be related to other respiratory illness (Jacobs et al., 1970), to clinical depression (Brown and Harris, 1978) and possibly to coronary heart disease (de Faire and Theorell, 1977).

While one cannot expect specific psychosocial factors to have specific diseases associated with them, there may be some degree of specificity. Certain factors may be more related to adrenal medullary catecholamine response and high blood pressure; others more related to the pituitary–adrenocortical axis (Henry and Stephens, 1977). Nevertheless it seems a reasonable working hypothesis that 'any disease process, and in fact any process within the living organism, might be influenced by the reaction of the individual to his social environment or to other people' (Hinkle, 1973).

Nature of the psychosocial factors considered

The general proposition being considered is that cultural factors may play a role in the aetiology of disease by the way they influence psychosocial factors, which is turn influence neuroendocrine pathways and pathology. These psycho-social factors may act in a positive or negative way i.e. they may be 'stressful' or protective. A central problem that has bedevilled this field has been the decision as to what constitutes a stressful factor. What is highly negative to one person may be neutral or even positive to another. For example, it was stated above that people of working class are at higher risk of disease than those of middle or upper class. It is possible that to be working class is to be subject to more 'stress', but the reverse may also be true. The point is that 'social class' by itself has no meaning. By itself it does not help us to decide whether 'stress' is related to disease. Thus in any particular instance it may be difficult to decide whether a particular feature of the social environment is stressful, because we do not know the *meaning* of that feature to the individual who is experiencing it. Yet, as Hinkle (1961) argues, an individual's response to the social environ-ment is not entirely idiosyncratic and un-knowable 'as precise knowledge of a man's cultural background allows one to make a large number of work-ing assumptions about him with a probability that these will be correct'. To take an example, it is probably reasonable to assume that bereavement is a stressful event for most people. On the other hand, an event such as a change of job may be stressful for some and not for others. More detailed knowledge of an individual's background is required before an inference can be made with any degree of confidence.

As can be seen, many studies in this area (and most of those described in the succeeding sections) have a gap in the chain of evidence. A particular social or cultural feature is measured and related to risk of disease. The gap is the evidence that the social or cultural feature was indeed stressful or supportive to the individual who experienced it. Because of this gap it is often necessary to creep up on the evidence in a circumstantial way. The particular lines of study that will be illustrated are:

(a) patterns of illness related to specific cultures;
(b) illness associated with cultural change;
(c) illness associated with stressful life-events.

ILLNESS RELATED TO SPECIFIC CULTURES

Blood pressure

There has been much interest, most of it somewhat vague and ill-focused, in the diseases that accompany urbanization or modernization. Nevertheless it is clear that there are consistent patterns, apart from the obvious ones related to infectious disease referred to in the first section. It has now been a common observation that there are societies round the world where the average blood pressure is low and shows little rise with age (Henry and Cassel, 1969). These societies are all characterized as being small-scale, rural, with the members of the society living a traditional or unacculturated way of life. By contrast urban societies show a much greater average blood pressure, which rises steeply with age, and the prevalence of clinically defined hypertension is high.

There are numerous dietary, genetic, and other differences which might account for these blood pressure differences. In an effort to narrow down the range of possibilities, there has been a second generation of studies that have compared people of similar ethnicity living under different conditions. One of the earlier ones was from South Africa. Scotch and his co-workers compared the blood pressure distributions in two Zulu communities (Scotch, 1960, 1963). One was in a rural area; the other was urban. The people living in the two areas were similar ethnically, but the blood pressures were higher in the urban area and showed a greater rise of pressure with age. This study did not examine dietary or other possible biological explanations for the change, but it makes a genetic explanation most unlikely.

A study from East Africa of Kenyan men showed similar findings. Shaper compared the blood pressures of nomadic Kenyan warriors who had entered the Kenyan army, with those who did not enter (Shaper, 1972). After 6 months in the army the blood pressures of the army recruits were higher than the controls. This difference was still in evidence after 6 years. Again, it is unlikely that genetic differences could account for the change in blood pressure. This study further showed that although blood pressure is strongly related to body-weight, changes in body-weight did not appear to be the explanation of the changes in blood pressure.

Studies of Polynesian Islanders show similar changes in blood pressure, but in addition these studies have started to focus more closely on psychosocial factors. Prior and his colleagues noted that Polynesians living in New Zealand show the typical high blood pressures, and rise with age, of whites in New Zealand (Prior, 1974). By contrast Polynesians living on Pacific island atolls such as the Tokelau Islands show low blood pressures and little rise with age (Prior et al., 1974). In order to study the modernization process in an intermediate stage, they had previously studied two groups of Polynesians living on the Cook Islands (Prior et al., 1968). The unacculturated group lived under a subsistence-level economy on the isolated coral atoll of Puka-Puka. The more modernized group had lived under town conditions and a cash-economy for at least 10 years. The blood pressure distributions of the two groups are shown in Figure 15.1. It is clear that the Pukapukans show the unacculturated pattern of blood pressure described and the Raratongans, in town conditions, show more evidence of the increase with age. Apart from the social and economic differences between the two places, there were dietary ones also. In particular, salt consumption was higher on Raratonga than on the less modern Puka-Puka. Although the amount of salt consumed by individuals in the study was unrelated to the blood pressures of individuals, it nevertheless seems likely that the higher blood pressures on Raratonga are, to some extent, related to the higher level of salt consumption.

This study illustrates the difficulty of disentangling psychosocial factors from other cultural factors. What is needed is a more precise measure of the

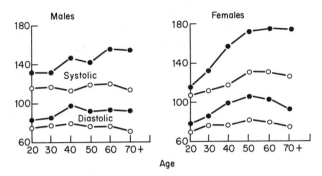

FIGURE 15.1. Mean blood pressures of similar people living under different degrees of culture contact: ●—● Raratonga; ○—○ Puka-Puka (from Prior *et al.*, 1968)

psychosocial factors involved. This was supplied in a later study of Tokelauan migrants in New Zealand (Beaglehole *et al.*, 1977). It was reasoned that if the higher blood pressures of Polynesians in New Zealand were related to living in a modern urban society, then the more that the migrants were part of that society, the higher should be their blood pressures. To test this they developed a measure of 'social interaction' which reflected the degree to which the Tokelauans were part of New Zealand society. A significant correlation was observed between the degree of social interaction with New Zealand society and level of blood pressure. It is possible that those Tokelauans who were more 'westernized' had different diets or were different in other respects from those who were more traditionally Tokelauan. Nevertheless this study is certainly consistent with the possibility that psychosocial factors play an important part in the cultural influence on disease patterns.

Coronary heart disease

Coronary heart disease (CHD) also shows wide variations in occurrence around the world. In general it is more common in countries that are modernized, industrialized, and urbanized. As with studies of blood pressure, one approach the exploring the reasons for these differences has centred on the study of migrants. The rate of CHD experienced by migrants is influenced both by the rate of disease prevailing in the old country and the rate prevailing in the new (Reid, 1971). This has been shown to be true for migrants to Israel (Medalie, Kahn, and Neufeld, 1973a), to the United States (Kreueger and Moriyama, 1967) and to Australia (Stenhouse and McCall, 1970).

In Israel it has been shown that immigrants from the Yemen, where CHD rates are low, initially have low CHD rates after arrival in Israel. The disease rates increase with increasing length of stay in Israel (Brunner *et al.*, 1971), and is higher among the offspring of the Yemeni migrants who are born in Israel (Medalie *et al.*, 1973b). This higher rate of heart disease among the long-term Yemenite migrants is accompanied by a rise in serum cholesterol concentration

(Toor, Katchalsky, and Agmon, 1957). The role of changing dietary patterns in this change in serum cholesterol and heart disease risk has been questioned (Cohen, Bavly, and Poznanski, 1961), but it seems likely that diet does play some role (Groen, Dreyfuss, and Guttman, 1968). It has been suggested that psychosocial factors may also play a role in this changing pattern of heart disease. Indeed separate studies in Israel have shown an association between work and social problems and CHD prevalence (Groen et al., 1968). What is lacking is the clear demonstration that the increased CHD risk experienced by Yemenite Jews in Israel is related to the problems they encounter in Israeli society, or to other psychosocial factors.

It has proved possible to approach the issue of psychosocial factors more directly in a study of Japanese migrants to the USA. The USA is typical of industrialized countries in having a high rate of CHD. By contrast Japan although affluent and highly industrialized, has a very low rate of CHD—about one-sixth that of the USA. It has been reported that Japanese men who migrated to the USA have a mortality from CHD that is intermediate between the low rate in Japan and the high rate in the USA (Gordon, 1957, 1967). Further, men who migrated to California have a higher heart disease mortality than those who migrated only as far as Hawaii. The Hawaii population is made up of a wide variety of ethnic groups and is not typical of the rest of the USA—having marked oriental and Pacific cultural influences. It was thus tempting to suggest that the more American the Japanese become the more their heart disease rates become Americanized. As with the other studies reported above, the task was to investigate which features of Americanization might be responsible for the change in heart disease rates: changes in diet, physical activity, smoking, social grouping, others? A later study of Japanese men living in Japan, Hawaii, and California confirmed the Japan–Hawaii–California gradient of heart disease (Syme et al., 1975), but showed that the change in disease rates was unlikely to be due only to changes in smoking, serum cholesterol, or blood pressure (Marmot et al., 1975).

It had been proposed that the Japanese are protected from heart disease because their culture contains devices that act as buffers against stress (Matsumoto, 1970). Matsumoto suggested that the strong, tightly knit, social group in Japan acts as a means of social support. Competitiveness in Japan tends to be between groups rather than individuals, so the individual person is less vulnerable to social stress. To test this hypothesis a study was conducted among Japanese men living in California (Marmot and Syme, 1976). From the answers to a questionnaire, a scale was constructed that reflected the culture of upbringing of each individual, whether traditional Japanese or more 'acculturated' and non-traditional. On the basis of his answers to the questionnaire, each individual could then be assigned an acculturation score. The relationship between culture of upbringing and prevalence of coronary heart disease is shown in Figure 15.2. As can be seen, the more traditional men had a lower CHD prevalence than the non-traditional men. Because of the possibility that being brought up to be traditionally Japanese may have been associated with

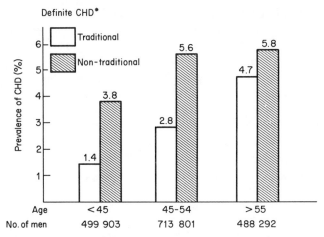

FIGURE 15.2. Prevalence of CHD by culture of upbringing
(from Marmot *et al.*, 1976)

eating a more Japanese diet, the population was further classified according
to dietary preference. This made little difference to the association between
culture of upbringing and CHD. Similarly the lower rate amongst the traditional
men was shown not to be due to differences in smoking, in obesity, in plasma
cholesterol, or in blood pressure. As a more specific test of Matsumoto's hypothesis the population was further classified according to the degree to which they
sought personal contact and social support, at work and socially, amongst
Japanese rather than non-Japanese people. With this further analysis, the
apparent protection of the more traditional Japanese men was even more
striking (Marmot and Syme, 1976). Thus this study did not directly measure
'stress' either, but it did show an association between CHD and particular
cultural traits that was independent of the known biological risk factors for
heart disease.

In this study of Japanese it was assumed that Japanese culture has protective
features. Alternatively, it is logically possible that American culture may have
harmful features. In particular a coronary-prone behaviour pattern has been
described in America—so-called type-A behaviour (Friedman and Rosenman,
1959). This behaviour pattern includes time-urgency, striving, ambition and
competitiveness, aggressiveness, and preoccupation with vocational deadlines.
In a large prospective study, men were classified as type-A or its converse
type-B, and their risk of developing heart disease was followed. After $8\frac{1}{2}$ years
of follow-up, the men who displayed behaviour pattern A had twice the CHD
incidence of men who had been classified as type B. This increase in risk was
independent of other known coronary risk factors (Rosenman *et al.*, 1975).

It is not completely clear what one should understand by 'type-A behaviour
pattern'—how much is a deeply rooted psychological trait, and how much is a
reaction to a particular social or cultural environment. That this behaviour

pattern may be a Western phenomenon is suggested by Cohen's study of Hawaiian Japanese—a group whose CHD rate is less than half that of white Americans (Cohen, 1974). She used the Jenkins Activity Survey, designed to test for the coronary-prone pattern, and found type-A behaviour to be very much less common than in white Americans. Thus although it would be desirable to understand more of the origins of the type-A behaviour pattern and its appearance in different population groups (Jenkins, 1971) it seems possible that it is a culturally determined reaction of particular personality types to stressful demands made by the environment.

ILLNESS ASSOCIATED WITH CULTURAL CHANGE

In the previous section consideration was given to the proposition that cultures may have specific characteristic that may be stressful or protective and thus related to disease. If this is so, members of a particular culture will be expected to manifest the disease pattern characteristic of that culture. Cassel, Patrick, and Jenkins (1960) have suggested that, in addition, the process of social or cultural change in itself may be stressful and that such stress may increase an individual's predisposition to disease. They argued that the stress arises when an individual is confronted with a situation for which his background and previous experience have left him unprepared. Therefore an individual who has undergone recent change from one culture to another will have new and possibly conflicting demands made upon him that he cannot adequately deal with. The resultant stress may be potentially pathogenic. With this hypothesis in mind they instituted a study of rural mountaineers in Appalachia who had come to work in a factory (Cassel and Tyroler, 1961). They divided their population into two groups:

(a) those who had themselves been mountaineers and came to work in a factory, i.e. were first generation of the family to pursue factory work; and
(b) those factory workers whose fathers had moved from mountaineering to factory work, i.e. the individuals studied were second-generation factory workers.

They found that the first-generation factory workers showed a higher rate of illness as measured by responses to the Cornell Medical Index and by sickness absenteeism, than the more 'experienced' second-generation factory workers. This was as predicted by the hypothesis, namely that those subject to recent change would experience greater health consequences.

That this process of social and cultural change may be endemic in the modern American way of life was suggested in a separate series of studies (Syme et al., 1964, 1965, 1966). In both a rural and an urban community in the USA, it was found that men who had experienced occupational or geographical mobility had higher rates of CHD than men who were stable. The implication was that a discontinuity or incongruity between past and present circumstances would provide a potentially stressful situation.

The blood pressure findings of the study of Zulu in South Africa (see the section on Illness related to specific cultures) have been similarly interpreted (Scotch, 1963). The Zulu who were urban dwellers had higher blood pressures than rural residents. Contrary to original expectations, however, it was the most recent migrants to the city who showed the highest blood pressures, rather than the long-term residents (Gampel *et al.*, 1962). Scotch (1963) interpreted these and other data to mean that the individual at highest risk of high blood pressure was he whose way of life and beliefs were not adapted to the environment in which he found himself.

It will be appreciated that we have the potential for considerable confusion. The hypothesis elaborated in the earlier section was that certain cultures have particular disease patterns associated with them. From this one would predict that the longer a migrant had lived under a new culture, the more likely would he be to experience the disease pattern of that culture. As migration usually takes place from a lower CHD to a higher CHD culture, this usually means an increased risk of CHD. In direct contrast to this, the hypothesis elaborated in this section would predict that it is the new arrivals to a culture that would experience the most stress and therefore be at greater risk of CHD. Despite the apparent conflict, there may be elements of truth in both arguments; i.e. there may be a risk of disease associated with cultural change *and* certain cultures may have distinctive disease patterns associated with them. Mere argument or mental gymnastics will not settle the issue. We need (i) a clearer formulation of the hypothesis relating psychosocial factors to disease, and (ii) more precise measurement of what is actually happening in the individual; i.e. whether or not the individual experiences a situation as stressful. An example of this approach is given in the next section.

LINKING CULTURE AND PSYCHOSOCIAL FACTORS TO DISEASE

Groen has developed a general hypothesis that links both biological risk factors for CHD and psychosocial factors to Western culture. To Groen:

> it appears that most of the risk factors which have been shown to play a role in the multi-factorial causation of CHD are related to both the social structure and ways of life of 'western' society in general and to certain personality and situational characteristics which make these 'western' psycho-social behaviour patterns more risky for some individuals than for others (Groen, 1976).

In particular he formulates the hypothesis that the risk of coronary heart disease is increased as a result of three factors:

(1) a certain personality which predisposes some individuals more than others— this personality is shaped by the culture, by heredity and by previous experiences;

(2) the presence of interhuman conflict which acts as a more immediate precipitant—this includes both stressful events and lack of support from family and social group;
(3) a certain behaviour by which the individual, because of his personality, responds to this conflict.

Groen is then able to fit into this framework much of the research linking psychosocial factors to CHD. The test of a good hypothesis, however, is not how well it ties together observed data—any hypothesis can be twisted to do that—but how well it predicts new observations. This is especially true given the crucial problem of judging whether a particular situation is 'stressful' to the individual experiencing it. Using this framework, Groen and co-workers conducted a prospective study of CHD among Israeli civil servants. They classified the men in the study as to the severity of problems with family, with co-workers, with superiors, with finances, and with work. There was a clear association between severity of problems reported and incidence of angina pectoris (Medalie *et al.*, 1973). There was also an association between the number of countries an individual had lived in, and the risk of angina. Men who were judged to have anxiety—on the basis of reported tenseness, anxiety, and sleep problems—had twice the incidence rate of angina as men judged to be free from anxiety. In a later analysis it was shown that among men who were judged to have anxiety, those who reported that they had the love and support of their wife had a lower incidence of angina than those anxious men who lacked their wife's love and support (Medalie and Goldbourt, 1976). The prediction of angina pectoris was independent of dietary intake of fat, and of other predictors of coronary disease. Thus this study supported the hypothesis of an increase in risk of angina pectoris associated with social problems and conflicts, and a decreased risk associated with emotional support. One cautious note is appropriate as, by and large, the association was limited to angina pectoris. There was little association between these factors and the incidence of myocardial infarction. Such a finding is not unique as angina pectoris and myocardial infarction, although both manifestations of underlying CHD do not share precisely the same aetiological factors. On the other hand, it is possible that the psychosocial factors considered were more related to the experience of recurrent pain than to disease of the coronary arteries, i.e. people who were anxious or experienced problems might be more likely to report pain. This is possible, but it seems unlikely that this alone could account for the increased emergence of the well-defined syndrome of angina pectoris.

An important point to be emphasized about this study is that it made a minimum number of assumptions about what an individual perceived as stress. Although it proceeded from the general hypothesis that features of the 'western' Israeli culture may be stressful, each individual in the study was assessed as to the presence or absence of problems and support. It was not necessary to make a general assumption about the stressfulness of the culture in which they lived.

This study confirmed that migrants to Israel from Europe had a higher

CHD rate than migrants from other parts of the Middle East. To strengthen the argument that this difference in rates was related to cultural differences in psychosocial factors, one would like to have seen an analysis of the frequency of interpersonal problems and emotional support among the different ethnic groups in the study. It would be important to know if the higher CHD rates amongst the Jews of European origin was the result of a greater frequency of psychosocial problems.

Non-vascular disease

Most of this literature has been concerned with vascular disease. This is under-standable as much of the literature concerning culture and health has concentrated on Westernization, and vascular diseases are the major causes of death in Western society. As stated at the beginning of this chapter, there is no *a priori* reason why other diseases should not similarly be associated with these psychosocial factors. This can be illustrated with two examples.

Nuckolls, Cassel and Kaplan (1972) interviewed 170 primiparous women during the early stages of their pregnancy. A standard questionnaire was administered that assessed recent major life-changes that require adaptation (Holmes and Rahe, 1967). In addition each subject was assessed according to the psychological and social support she could receive during the pregnancy— this was termed her 'psychosocial assets'. The outcome of pregnancy was judged as to whether there were one or more complications. If a woman had a low life-change score before pregnancy, the presence of psychosocial assets made little difference to the outcome of the pregnancy. The relationship between

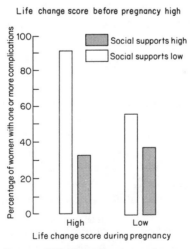

FIGURE 15.3. Complications of pregnancy by life change score and level of social support (from Nuckolls *et al.*, 1972)

psychosocial factors and outcome of pregnancy for women with a high life-change score prior to pregnancy is shown in Figure 15.3. If a woman reported few life-changes during pregnancy, the pressure of social support made little difference to the pregnancy complication rate. By contrast, for women who had a high life-change score during pregnancy, those who could count on social support had a lower complication rate than those who could not.

The Holmes and Rahe scale to measure life events and other measures of stressful life events have been extensively used in epidemiological studies (see Dohrenwend and Dohrenwend, 1974). These measures question individuals about what events from a standard list have happened in their lives during the recent past. One criticism that has been made of such measures is that they do not tell us whether a particular individual experiences a particular event as stressful (Brown, Brohlchain, and Harris 1976). The measures tell us that the event occurred but not the effect on the individual. These authors went to some length to avoid this problem in a study of depressive illness in women (Brown *et al.*, 1976). Women who were depressed, and a control sample of non-depressed women, were interviewed. At the interview an assessment was made by the trained interviewer of whether a significant event had occurred in the subject's life and whether it had been stressful. It was found that women who were depressed had a higher frequency of prior stressful life events than the control sample. Women were then classified as to their 'vulnerability' by such factors as not having an intimate relationship with anyone, or having three or more young children to look after. Women who were thereby classed as vulnerable appeared more liable to depression in the face of a stressful event than women who were not.

These two studies—one of outcome of pregnancy, the other of clinical depression—support the contention that psychosocial factors may be both stressful and protective against the onset of physical and mental illness.

CONCLUSION

The studies to which reference has been made are a small fraction of the vast literature implicating cultural and psychosocial factors in disease aetiology. They were chosen to illustrate the plausibility of the general proposition linking culture to illness, and the difficulties of studying it. As long as broad general concepts such as 'culture', 'cultural change', 'stress', and 'illness' are used it remains difficult to establish any sort of precise causal link, let alone under-stand the neuroendocrine pathways involved. To understand the link better, two strategies of research are needed. First, the development of measures of stressful factors that have some meaning in themselves. All too often, a vague indicator of stress appears to be related to some disease, and the interpretation of its meaning is very much *post hoc*. With the development of measures that relate to what is actually going on, hypotheses can be tested, and rejected if found wanting. In general, in the studies reviewed, the more specific the psychosocial measure the more compelling was the evidence relating it to disease.

Second, having shown a close association between a specific psychosocial measure and disease, it is necessary to show that this apparent association is not due to some third factor. Obviously if a recent migrant to the city is found to have a rise in blood pressure, it is important to know if this is related to his loss of social support from the extended family or whether it is really due to his increased consumption of salt and of calories.

As shown above, these are not impossible tasks and we have an increasing understanding of the nature of stressful life events and of the social supports that can protect against them. One issue that has been left unresolved is the nature of the diseases that may be associated with psychosocial factors. It seems fairly clear that at least some psychiatric disturbances are related to psychosocial factors. The position is less clear when it comes to physical disease. The distinction between so-called psychosomatic disease and physical diseases is becoming blurred. On the one hand there is the position of Cassel (1976) and Syme (1967) that the risk of all diseases may be affected by psychosocial factors. On the other hand, there is the view that different classes of disease are related to different types of psychosocial factors (Henry and Stephens, 1977). Much more precise work is needed before this issue can be settled.

It is proper to question the relevance of this general line of research. It may be argued that it is not very useful to show that an anxious person has a higher risk of disease. What is required is an understanding of why the person was anxious in the first place. The demands of research aimed at demonstrating that an association exists are different from the demands of understanding the social causes of illness from the public health or preventive medicine viewpoint. As has been argued, the former requires close attention to detail of individual responses to the environment. The public health viewpoint requires the link to be made with the social or cultural environment, with the ultimate aim of seeking factors that can be changed. The studies of migrants indicate that marked changes in disease occur when the cultural environment is changed. Perhaps it is not too Utopian to believe that a better understanding of the relationships involved will allow the harmful effects of the cultural and social environment to be modified or reversed.

REFERENCES

Beaglehole, R., Salmond, C. E., Hooper, A., Huntsman, J., Stanhope, J. M., Cassel, J. C., and Prior, I. A. M. (1977). Blood pressure and social interaction in Tokelauan Migrants in New Zealand. *Journal of Chronic Diseases*, **30**, 803–812.

Brown, G. W. (1976). Social Causes of Disease. In D. Tuckett (ed) *An Introduction to Medical Sociology*, pp. 291–333. London: Tavistock.

Brown, G. W., Bhrolchain, M., and Harris, T. O. (1976). Social class and psychiatric disturbance among women in an urban population. In R. M., Acheson, and L. Aird, (eds.), *Seminars in Community Medicine*, vol. 1, *Sociology*, pp. 51–82. London: Oxford University Press.

Brown, G. W., and Harris, T. (1978). *The Social Origins of Depression*. London: Tavistock.

Brunner, D., Meshulam N., Altman S., Bearman, J., Loebl, K., and Wendhos, M. E. (1971). Physiologic and anthropometric parameters related to coronary risk factors in Yemenite Jews living different time spans in Israel. *Journal of Chronic Diseases*, **24**, 383–392.

Calhoun, J. B. (1962). A 'behavioral sink'. In E. L. Bliss, (ed.), *Roots of Behaviour: Genetics, Instinct, and Socialization in Animal Behaviour*, pp. 295–315. New York: Harper.

Cassel, J. C. (1976). The contribution of the social environment to host resistance. *American Journal of Epidemiology*, **104**, 107–123.

Cassel, J. C., Patrick, R., and Jenkins, C. D. (1960). Epidemiological analysis of the health implications of culture change: a conceptual model. *Annals of the New York Academy of Sciences*, **84**, 938–949.

Cassel, J., and Tyroler, H. A. (1961). Epidemiological studies of culture change. I. Health status and recency of industrialization. *Archives of Environmental Health*, **3**, 31–39.

Cohen A. M., Bavly, S., and Poznanski, R. (1961). Change of diet of Yemenite Jews in relation to diabetes and ischaemic heart disease. *Lancet*, **2**, 1399–1401.

Cohen, J. B. (1974). Sociocultural change and behaviour patterns in disease etiology: an epidemiological study of coronary disease among Japanese Americans. *Unpublished Ph.D. dissertation*, University of California, Berkeley.

Dohrenwend B. S., and Dohrenwend, B. P. (eds.) (1974). *Stressful Life Events: Their Nature and Effects*. New York: Wiley.

Dubos, R. (1965). *Man Adapting*. New Haven: Yale University Press.

Dunn, F. L. (1968). Epidemiological factors: health and disease in hunter–gatherers. In Lee, R. B., and Devore, I. (eds.), *Man the Hunter*, pp. 221–228. Chicago: Aldine.

Dunn, F. L. (1972). Intestinal parasitism in Malayan aborigines (Orang Asli) *Bull. Wld. Hlth. Org.*, **46**, 99–113.

Fabrega, H. (1974). *Disease and Social Behaviour*. Cambridge, Mass.: MIT Press.

de Faire U., and Theorell, T. (1977). Life changes and myocardial infarction. Epidemiological and clinical considerations. *Preventive Medicine*, **6**, 302–311.

Fenner, F. (1971). Infectious disease and social change. *Medical Journal of Australia*, **1**, 1043–1050.

Friedman, M., and Rosenman, R. H. (1959). Association of a specific overt behaviour pattern with blood and cardiovascular findings. *Journal of the American Medical Association*, **169**, 1285–1292.

Furnass, S. B. (1970). Changes in non-infectious diseases associated with the processes of civilisation. In S. V. Boyden, (ed.), *The Impact of Civilization on the Biology of Man*, pp. 77–101. Sydney: University of Toronto.

Gampel, B., Slome, C., Scotch, N., and Abramson J. H. (1962). Urbanization and hypertension among Zulu adults. *Journal of Chronic Diseases*, **15**, 67–70.

Gordon, T. (1957). Mortality experience among the Japanese in the United States, Hawaii and Japan. *Public Health Reports*, **72**, 543–553.

Gordon, T. (1967). Further mortality experience among Japanese Americans. *Public Health Reports*, **82**, 973–984.

Groen, J. J. (1976). Psychosomatic aspects of Ischaemic (coronary) heart disease. In O. Hill (ed.), *Modern Trends in Psychosomatic Medicine*, vol. III, pp. 288–329. London: Butterworths.

Groen, J. J., Dreyfuss, F. and Guttman L. (1968). Epidemiological, Nutritional and Sociological Studies of Atherosclerotic (Coronary) Heart Disease among different ethnic groups in Israel. *Progress in Biochemical Pharmacology*, **4**, 20–25.

Henry, J. P., and Cassel, J. C. (1969). Psychosocial factors in essential hypertension. *American Journal of Epidemiology*, **90**, 171–200.

Henry, J. P., Ely, D. L., Stephens, P. M., Ratcliffe, H. G., Santisteban, G. A., and Shapiro, A. P. (1971). The role of psychosocial factors in the development of arteriosclerosis in CBA mice: observations on the heart, kidney, and aorta. *Atherosclerosis*, **14**, 203–218.

Henry, J. P., Meehan, J. P., and Stephens, P. M. (1967). The use of psychosocial stimuli to induce prolonged systolic hypertension in mice. *Psychosomatic Medicine*, **29**, 408–432.

Henry, J. P., and Stephens P. M. (1977). *Stress, Health, and the Social Environment.* New York: Springer-Verlag.

Hinkle, L. E. (1961). Ecological observations on the relation of physical illness, mental illness, and the social environment. *Psychosomatic Medicine*, **23**, 289–296.

Hinkle L. E. (1973). The concept of 'stress' in the biological and social sciences. *Science, Medicine and Man*, **1**, 31–48.

Hinkle, L. E., and Wolff H. G. (1958). Ecologic investigations of the relationship between illness, life experiences and the social environment. *Annols of Internal Medicine*, **49**, 1373.

Holmes, T. (1956). Multidiscipline studies of tuberculosis. In P. J. Sparer, (ed.), *Personality Stress and Tuberculosis*. International Universities Press cited by Cassel, (1976).

Holmes, T. H., and Rahe, R. H. (1967). The social readjustment rating scale. *Journal of Psychosomatic Research*, **11**, 213–218.

Jacobs, M. A., Spilken, A. Z., Norman, M. M., and Anderson, L. S. (1970). Life stress and respiratory illness. *Psychosomatic Medicine*, **32**, 233–243.

Jenkins, C. D. (1971). Psychologic and social precursors of coronary disease. *New England Journal of Medicine*, **284**, 244–255, 307–317.

Jenkins, C. D. (1972). Social and epidemiologic factors in psychosomatic disease. *Psychiatric Annals*, **2**, 8–21.

Kiritz, S. and Moos, R. H. (1974). Physiological effects of the social environment. *Psychosomatic Medicine*, **36**, 96–114.

Krueger, D. E., and Moriyama I. M. (1967). Mortality of the foreign born. *American Journal of Public Health*, **57**, 496–503.

Marmot, M. G., Syme, S. L., Kagan, A., Kato, H., Cohen, J. B., and Belsky, J. (1975). Epidemiologic studies of coronary heart disease and stroke in Japanese men living in Japan, Hawaii and California: prevalence of coronary and hypertensive heart disease and associated risk factors. *American Journal of Epidemiology*, **102**, 514–525.

Marmot, M. G., and Syme S. L. (1976). Acculturation and coronary heart disease in Japanese-Americans. *American Journal of Epidemiology*, **104**, 225–247.

Matsumoto, Y. S. (1970). Social stress and coronary heart disease in Japan: a hypothesis. *The Milbank Memorial Fund Quarterly*, **48**, 9–36.

Mechanic, D. (1972). Social psychologic factors affecting the presentation of bodily complaints. *New England Journal of Medicine*, **286**, 1132–1139.

Medalie, J. H., and Goldbourt, U. (1976). Angina pectoris among 10,000 men. II. Psychosocial and other risk factors as evidenced by a multivariate analysis of a five year incidence study. *American Journal of Medicine*, **60**, 910–921.

Medalie, J. H., Kahn, H. A., Neufeld, H. N., Riss, E., Goldbourt, U., Perlstein, T., and Oron, D. (1973a). Myocardial infarction over a five-year period. I. Prevalence, incidence and mortality experience. *Journal of Chronic Diseases*, **26**, 63–84.

Medalie, J. H., Snyder, M., Groen J. J., Neufeld, Ris. E. and Goldbourt, U. (1973b). Angina Pectoris among 10,000 men. 5 year incidence and univariate analysis. *American Journal of Medicine*, **55**, 583–594.

Nuckolls, C. B., Cassel, J., and Kaplan B. H. (1972). Psychosocial assets, life crises and the prognosis of pregnancy. *American Journal of Epidemiology*, **95**, 531–541.

Office of Population Censuses and Surveys (1978). Occupational mortality. *The Registrar General's Decennial Supplement for England and Wales 1970–1972, Series DS, No. 1.* London: HMSO.

Paul, B. D. (ed.) (1955). *Health, Culture and Community*. New York: Russel Sage Foundation.

Prior, I. A. M. (1974). Cardiovascular epidemiology in New Zealand and the Pacific. *New Zealand Medical Journal*, **80**, 245–252.

Prior, I. A. M., Evans, J. G., Harvey, H. P. B., Davidson, F., and Lindsey, M. (1968). Sodium intake and blood pressure in two Polynesian populations. *New England Journal of Medicine*, **279**, 515–520.

Prior, I. A. M., Stanhope, J. M., Evans, J. G., and Salmond, C. E. (1974). The Tokelau Island migrant study. *International Journal of Epidemiology*, **3**, 225–232.

Reid, D. D. (1971). The future of migrant studies. *Israel Journal of Medical Science*, **7**, 1592–1596.

Rosenman, R. H., Brand, R. J., Jenkins, C. D., Friedman, M., Straus, R., and Wurm, M. (1975). Coronary heart disease in the Western Collaborative Group Study. Final follow-up experience of $8\frac{1}{2}$ years. *Journal of the American Medical Association*, **233**, 872–877.

Scotch, N. (1960). A preliminary report on the relation of sociocultural factors to hypertension among the Zulu. *Annals of the New York Academy of Science*, **84**, 1000–1009.

Scotch, N. (1963). Sociocultural factors in the epidemiology of Zulu hypertension. *American Journal of Public Health*, **53**, 1205–1213.

Shaper, A. G. (1972). Cardiovascular disease in the tropics. III: Blood pressure and hypertension. *British Medical Journal*, **3**, 805.

Stenhouse, N. S., and McCall, M. G. (1970). Differential mortality from cardiovascular disease in migrants from England and Wales, Scotland and Italy, and native-born Australians. *Journal of Chronic Diseases*, **23**, 423–432.

Syme, S. L. (1967). Implications and future prospects. In S. L., Syme and L. Reeder, (eds.), Social stress and cardiovascular disease. *Milbank Memorial Fund Quarterly*, **45** (2), 175–180.

Syme, S. L., Hyman, M. M. and Enterline P. E. (1964). Some social and cultural factors associated with the occurrence of coronary heart disease. *Journal of Chronic Diseases*, **17**, 277–289.

Syme, S. L., Hyman, M. M., and Enterline, P. E. (1965). Cultural mobility and the occurrence of coronary heart disease. *Health and Human Behavior*, **6**, 178–189.

Syme, S. L., Borhani, N. O., and Buechley, R. W. (1966). Cultural mobility and coronary heart disease in an urban area. *American Journal of Epidemiology*, **82**, 334–346.

Syme, S. L., Marmot, M. G., Kagan, A., Kato, H., and Rhoads, G. (1975). Epidemiologic studies of coronary heart disease and stroke in Japanese men living in Japan, Hawaii and California. Introduction. *American Journal of Epidemiology*, **102**, 477–480.

Toor, M., Katchalsky, A., Agmon, J. and Alallow, D. (1957). Serum lipids and atherosclerosis among Yemenite immigrants in Israel. *Lancet*, **1**, 1270.

Wiesenfeld, S. L. (1967). Sickle-cell trait in human biological and cultural evolution. *Science*, **157**, 1134–1140.

Foundations of Psychosomatics
Edited by M. J. Christie and P. G. Mellett
© 1981 John Wiley & Sons Ltd.

16

HOW SOCIETY DEFINES SICKNESS: ILLNESS BEHAVIOUR AND CONSULTATION

MICHAEL WADSWORTH
Department of Community Health, University of Bristol, England

and

JACK INGHAM
University Department of Psychiatry, Royal Edinburgh Hospital, Scotland.

Modern medical practice in the Western world presents a confusing paradox. Although knowledge in curative medicine and surgery has grown enormously over the last 30 or 40 years, demands on the health services have actually grown rather than lessened as expected by Beveridge at its inception (Wadsworth, Butterfield, and Blaney, 1971). Some of the increase in demand may be because effective help is now available for previously untreatable conditions, and because there is now more illness of a kind that takes longer to treat. There is, however, another very important factor that has more to do with changing social attitudes to illness than with medical knowledge or patterns of illness. Attitudes to many kinds of distress and deviance have moved towards their acceptance as illnesses, and the ready availability of medical assistance from a free health service has, in itself, helped to produce such changes. So the paradoxically increased demand on the health services could be due in part to a more inclusive use of the term 'illness'. People are now prepared to regard things that would previously have been ignored, or dealt with in some other way, as legitimate reasons for seeking medical advice. In this chapter we shall see what light the behavioural sciences can throw upon the influence of social attitudes and concepts of illness upon people's behaviour when they are ill or consider themselves to be ill. We shall be particularly concerned with such questions as whether, and at what point, an individual decides to consult his doctor, declaring himself to be ill.

One of the factors underlying the change in social attitudes about illness is a gradual but fundamental shift in the prevailing pattern of disease. Infectious disease has gradually given way to conditions which are generally less striking in onset, longer in duration, and often less certain in their cure. The older kind of disease pattern may be characterized by conditions such as lobar pneumonia or mastoiditis, and the newer by diabetes or arthritis. These changes in the contemporary pattern of disease have brought the need for a change in ideas about causation for the layman and doctor alike. Germ theories considered the relation between host and environment, that is personal predisposition to illness, and environmental factors, such as air pollution. More complex notions of multifactorial causality now consider the influence of personal behaviour, as well as the relations between host and environment. Some theories have looked for environmental and psychological features which are more common amongst sufferers than non-sufferers (Dohrenwend and Dohrenwend, 1969); others have looked more widely and considered the whole question of adaptive response (Raab, 1971), preferring to see man not simply as a psychophysiological system *reacting* to external factors but rather as part of the process itself. Sheldon (1970) explained that:

> One must assume that there is a train of events such that each insult, possibly trivial in itself, increases the tendency for other insults to develop until death supervenes. A similar process was found in the midtown Manhattan study (Langner and Michael, 1963), where it was found that if defined stresses acted in an additive fashion to increase the risk of mental illness, this would produce a similar picture. Therefore, one might hypothesize an alternative explanation to somatic mutation: continually added insults may sequentially modify the capacity of feedback mechanisms to maintain a steady state, especially under stress.

Such concern for cause has, naturally, been closely bound up with diagnosis and with the study of the natural history of disease. It has been complicated by the characteristically insidious onset of some chronic conditions, an onset which takes place over a long time-scale, so that the question of when normality or good health stops and illness begins cannot usually be definitively answered. This is particularly difficult in conditions where diagnosis depends, at least in part, on an interpretation of measurements that are continuously distributed in the whole population, measurements for example of blood sugar or blood pressure. Thus, the question of when a blood pressure reading is 'normal' and when it indicates pathology is often a matter of individual judgement rather than certain knowledge. The so-called Platt—Pickering controversy is about the interpretation of blood pressure readings (G.W. Pickering, 1963) since it is by no means universally agreed which individuals should be placed in the categories sick, ill, or diseased on this basis. A woman with advanced cancer of the cervix and many secondaries may look ill and feel ill, and no one would have any doubt about placing her in the sick group. Suppose, however, that the condition had been detected at a much earlier stage by cervical screening tests when she was symptom-free, could she then be said really to be ill? What about an even earlier stage when the pathological processes may already have begun, though as yet remaining undetectable? Even with conditions like cancer, which everybody would accept without hesitation as an illness, it is difficult to define the point at which the illness begins. With other conditions there are problems about whether the state concerned can ever be regarded as an illness at all. Homosexuality, for example, can cause great misery and suffering and is regarded by some as an illness. There are many other sources of distress, however, that could not by any stretch of the imagination be called illnesses and a state that causes distress to one person may be neutral or even enjoyable to another.

Concepts which are blurred at the edges are very common in ordinary language, and in everyday life words like sick, ill, and diseased are used frequently without any misunderstandings or difficulties arising. However, there are many instances where greater precision is required. To classify a person as sick carries certain implications—medical, scientific, administrative, or legal in nature—which determine how people interact with him. A lack of precision may adversely affect the individual, or society at large.

Doctors are sometimes asked by the judiciary to decide whether prople are mentally ill and thus free from the burden of criminal responsibility. Kendell (1975) suggested this as one reason why psychiatrists, as the doctors specializing in mental disorders, have been more preoccupied with the problem of defining illness than have other medical specialists. The 'medical model' of mental illness, which is the basis of such decisions, has been attacked from several sources and is said to confuse illness with distress that is more social than medical in nature (Ryan, 1976; Szasz, 1960). Psychiatrists, therefore, have been forced to consider very carefully what they mean by illness so that they can be clear what territory they are defending.

In this chapter we shall give examples of social science contributions and concern in medicine, paying particular attention to studies of individuals rather than those of wider issues. Our first concern, however, must be with the definition of disease, not as an academic or theoretical exercise but because the definition conditions how the individual comes to be classified as sick.

MEDICINE IN SOCIETY

Definition of disease

The World Health Organization defines health as 'a state of complete physical, mental and social well-being', but the key question is whose definition of a state of disease is to be seen as legitimate? It is helpful to follow Kendell's (1975) explanation of types of definition and their inadequacies. From the most objective view disease might be defined simply as a lesion, or structural damage, or biochemical abnormality; but physical characteristics usually vary from individual to individual so that it is not necessarily clear whether a given departure from the norm can be attributed to normal variation or pathology, and there exist many syndromes that all would accept as illness, of which the physical basis has not yet been demonstrated. Kendell quotes trigeminal neuralgia, senile pruritus, proctalgia fugax, dystonia musculorum, and migraine as examples.

Disease might also be defined as that which doctors treat. Kraupl Taylor (1971) has suggested that people could be regarded as ill if they or others were convinced that they needed medical attention. However, the individual as sole arbiter of whether he is ill or not is unsatisfactory because some people who should be complaining do not do so and others do complain, apparently without having adequate reasons. If the decision were left to other people, doctors, or society at large, then no one could be ill until he was recognized as such, with the danger that all deviants could be defined as ill, opening the door to the many inconsistencies and abuses that Szasz (1960) has warned of. Clearly society should not be able to rid itself of awkward individuals simply by labelling them as mentally ill.

Disease might be defined simply as suffering, but many sick people do not complain or suffer, either because they are symptomless or because they stoically ignore what others would complain about. A man with cancer of the lung, yet no symptoms, would be regarded by everyone as ill and urgently in need of treatment, as would a schizophrenic patient convinced that the voices he keeps hearing are real. Other people complain excessively both to doctors and relatives without anyone being convinced even after intensive investigation that they are genuinely ill.

Disease could also be regarded as adaptation to stress. Meyer (1907) insisted that all diseases were reactions of the whole organism to its total environment rather than the effects of external noxious agents or internal structural lesions. He also stressed the uniqueness of every individual's environment, and thus argued that the reaction constituting his disease must also be unique. This of course makes it difficult to classify diseases and to provide a criterion for distinguishing between health and illness.

If disease is seen as imperfection, then any departure from an ideal state of perfect health is an illness. According to Kendell the most influential philosophy of this kind is the psychoanalytic theory of psychological illness. As perfect health can never be achieved in practice, sickness becomes man's universal lot. But we need to be able to think of degrees of ill health in order to decide, for example, which individuals most need the limited resources of a health service. This inevitably leads us to consider a statistical concept of disease. Many biological characteristics are graded, depending on polygenic inheritance, where the abnormal and normal shade into one another without any marked discontinuity. It has become apparent that many illnesses are of this kind as well; for example, essential hypertension (Oldham et al., 1960). To distinguish such diseases from other departures from normality which may be neutral or even advantageous, Scadding (1967) stipulated that to qualify as a disease the abnormal phenomenon must place the affected individual at a biological disadvantage, reducing his chances of survival and/or his chances of procreation. Scadding's definition of disease is 'The sum of the abnormal phenomena displayed by a group of living organisms in association with a specified common characteristic or set of characteristics by which they differ from the norm for their species in such a way as to place them at a biological disadvantage.' This definition also has its disadvantages: for example a characteristic which is a biological disadvantage in one environment may be beneficial in another. Sickle-cell anaemia is a disadvantageous trait in most environments, but where malaria is endemic it is positively beneficial.

It is as well to remember that the definition useful to one group of individuals is not necessarily useful to another. If a distressed patient visits a psychiatrist to seek help it may not matter to the doctor whether the patient is really ill or whether he is suffering from normal psychosocial stresses. He will give what help he can in either case. However, to a judge faced with the decision of sending an accused individual to prison or for medical advice, the question is crucial. So it may be for the general practitioner who is deciding whether a case of minor illness is one that justifies a certified time off work.

It is evident that any satisfactory definition of illness or disease must make clear the distinction between disease and distress. It is interesting that the words stress, distress, and disease originally meant the same thing. Another psychiatrist, Rees (1976), has recently pointed this out. 'Stress' was first used in the fifteenth century and is a shortened form of 'distress'. Disease originally meant dis-ease or discomfort or lack of well-being. Historically the words are very closely linked and it is only in comparatively recent times that the distinction has been made. The meanings still tend to change in ordinary language and may well continue to do so. Many recent discussions of the nature of health and illness also fail to make the distinction between distress and disease, as does the World Health Organization's definition (see p. 343). On this definition any departure from 'well-being' in any sense of the word must be regarded as ill health, disease, or sickness. Rees (1976) defines disease as 'disability arising from bodily or mental malfunction which imposes difficulty in coping with everyday work and responsibilities, interferes with wellbeing and produces distress'. He accepts that he has introduced this definition 'purely for pragmatic purposes' and it clearly suffers from some of the difficulties already mentioned, particularly in that it leaves undefined the term '*malfunction*'. The word '*illness*' used in the context of psychological symptoms gives rise to a special problem of definition that does not apply to illnesses that can be defined in terms of directly observable physical changes. External stress, for example, does produce distress and under certain circumstances 'can lead to a disorganization of behaviour or maladaptation or a dysfunction which may lead to disease' (Rees, 1976). In the case of psychological illness the criterion for defining the condition will involve symptoms that are largely psychological in nature, being detectable only by what the patient says about his or her own feelings. The special problem is that the feelings concerned are those which can arise directly as the distress associated with stress. That is to say that the same symptoms in different degrees and in different configurations may be 'normal' psychophysiological responses to stress or symptoms of illness. A recent attempt to overcome this difficulty is the introduction of a concept of '*personal illness*' by Foulds (1976). It is difficult to define this concept concisely but

> when we become at least partially impaired in those functions which constitute us persons and when this impairment is sufficiently distressful to us, or to others acting on our behalf, that means are sought to restore our personhood, we may be said to be personally ill (Foulds, 1976).

The essential nature of a personal illness is a breakdown of existing relationships between the individual and his environment, chiefly his social environment. When this happens he may be said to suffer from personal illness and this means that the modes of adjustment and coping, that have previously served to keep him functioning within the behavioural boundaries set by the relationships he has held in his social system, no longer work. He either succumbs and virtually ceases to function, or the changes that are called symptoms, abnormal behaviour, etc., take place and these keep him functioning to some degree. It is possible that a definition along these lines may help to overcome some of the problems associated with other uses, but further development of the concept is needed and it remains to be seen how useful it will become.

The truth is that we still know too little about the normal and abnormal in psychophysiological functioning to be able to make an entirely satisfactory distinction between them. However, individuals and social agencies are frequently forced to make such a distinction, to decide whether a person is ill or not. So we can ask what is in many ways a more sensible question and one that can be answered if we seek the right information. What is society's operational definition? What are the factors that determine the labelling of an individual as a 'legitimate' patient with an illness?

Control of disease

Each of the definitions of disease offered here carries implications for its prevention, control, and management. These medical difficulties in drawing lines or thresholds where fitness stops and sickness starts are paralleled in problems of knowing how to delineate a 'legitimate' medical interest in the lives of individuals. The wide-ranging searches for causes, and the increasing ability to detect illness early in its natural history—even before the potential sufferer is aware of symptoms—have implicated the need for care and concern about the food and drink we consume, how we spend our leisure, the exercise we take, and the drugs we are prescribed. So the possibility of medical concern for the things other than frank illness becomes an important topic. There is therefore debate about the interface between medicine and society, and this takes place at two levels: first as debate about direct control, and also as concern with less obvious forms of persuasion.

Direct medical control of some aspects of life is no new thing, and arguments for it are usually concerned with the management of a medical problem which is also seen as a social problem. There are laws, for example, about the incarceration of tuberculosis sufferers, and regulations about cigarette advertising, and the treatment of drug addicts involves considerable control over people (who usually do not consider themselves to be sick) by way of regulation of amounts of drugs made available and restrictions of the time and place at which they may be obtained. More at a persuasive than a coercive level are the effects of medical advice about such things as diet. Myers (1963) compiled an 'ideal man' from what was then medical advice about life style and discovered that he would be

> an effeminate municipal worker or embalmer completely lacking in physical or mental alertness and without drive, ambition, or competitive spirit; who has never attempted to meet a deadline of any kind; a man with poor appetite, subsisting on fruits and vegetables laced with corn and whale oil, detesting tobacco, spurning ownership of radio, television, or motor car; with full head of hair but scrawny and of unathletic appearance, yet constantly straining his puny muscles by exercise. Low in income, blood pressure, blood sugar, uric acid and cholesterol, he has been taking nicotinic acid, pyridoxine, and long term anti-coagulant therapy ever since his prophylactic castration.

Persuasive medical advice may assume a subtle form of social pressure because of arguments about the cost to society of cigarette smoking, or choosing not to wear car seat-belts. There are also occasions when the doctor may feel, and even indicate, that the condition in question is 'self-inflicted', and there is a tendency to use such terms not only in illness such as venereal disease but in some stress conditions too. It is, however, certainly open to question how far in our kind of society an individual may be held responsible for his physical reaction to stress, any more than nineteenth-century paupers could reasonably be said to be 'responsible' for their suffering of the illnesses associated with poverty.

At a more general level Parsons (1951) has argued that there are social pressures to remain healthy, and observed that society sees the role of a patient as undesirable; necessarily so because patients are exempt from many everyday responsibilities required for the smooth running of society. More recently a very vigorous argument about medical control has been set off by the work of Illich (1976):

> In a medicalised society the influence of physicians extends not only to the purse and the medicine chest but also to the categories to which people are assigned. Medical bureaucrats subdivide people into those who may drive a car, those who may stay away from work, those who must be locked up, those who may become soldiers, those who may

cross borders, cook or practice prostitution, those who may not run for the vice-presidency of the United States, those who are dead, those who are competent to commit a crime and those who are liable to commit one.

Whatever definition of disease is considered, and whatever forms of control are postulated, it is in almost every case the sufferer himself who must first decide that he is ill and that he should seek help. Therefore as well as being involved in the debate about medicine and society, social scientists are also very concerned with the effects on individuals of changes in the prevailing pattern of disease, in medical searches for causes, and in social pressures on individuals in their use of medical care. Two problems are of particular interest. First is the failure of people to use medical care services when they evidently need them and when the care is free, and the not-uncommon failure of people to follow the doctor's advice when they request it. Second is the tendency of people to use the services when they are not needed or when some other service would be more appropriate.

MEDICINE AND THE INDIVIDUAL

Going to the doctor

Quite a lot is known about the kinds of people who tend to make greatest use of front-line medical-care services. The concept of consultation-prone people and families is well known to all general practitioners, who see a relatively small percentage of their patients taking up a disproportionately high percentage of their time. Studies of this phenomenon have tried to identify characteristics of consultation-prone individuals to seek clues as to how to control it.

Statistical studies have already provided some information about factors associated with contact rates of patients registered on general practice lists. Women have more contacts with their GPs than men during the years of the childbearing period, the greatest difference occurring in the 20–30 year age-group. For both sexes there is a peak in contact rate during early childhood, and for men a steady increase from early teens to old age with a peak around 60 (Banks *et al.*, 1975; Kasl and Cobb, 1966; McKinlay, 1972; Ashford, 1972). Marital status, education, occupation, and social class are also differentially associated with the demand for medical care. Of course, contacts are not randomly distributed in time but are grouped around episodes of illness.

Statisticians have derived theoretical frequency distributions of contact rates from different theoretical models and, for surgery attendances, have found that it is possible to obtain a better fit with the observed distributions by taking into account this episodic nature of illness. Ashford and his colleagues (Ashford, 1972) obtained the best fit by a distribution which included two measures; one described various degrees of 'proneness' or predisposition to illness, and the other variations in the number of contacts arising from each episode.

Sociologists, social psychologists, and psychiatrists have looked at the social and emotional circumstances, as well as the personalities of consultation-prone individuals. Kessel (1960) showed that excessive attendances were associated with neuroses, social problems, emotional disturbance, and conflicts within the family, and a number of other authors have shown the associations in individuals (Watts, 1962; Brown and Fry, 1962; Ryle and Hamilton, 1962; Grad and Sainsbury, 1963; Balint, 1968). Jacob (1969) showed that personality is also important; in his study, patients who made frequent demands for medical care tended to have high neuroticism scores on the Maudsley Personality Inventory and also tended to be more introverted than patients making lower demands. The personality of an individual may also influence the number of consultations made by other members of his family. Polliak (1971) used the Cornell Medical Index (CMI), a symptom inventory which also reflects emotional and personality variables (Brodman, Erdmann, and Wolff, 1956) and found that consultation rates were significantly associated with CMI scores of the individual patient. It was particularly interesting that there was also a correlation between consultation rates of young children and the CMI scores of each of their parents. McArdle, Alexander, and Murray Boyle, (1974) studied a group of patients who had made an average of more than 20 contacts each in one year; unemployment and loneliness occurred frequently in this group. Beresford *et al.*, (1977) found in their female population that women with poor housing amenities consulted their doctors more often than others. Those who had lived longest in the area, were attached to the neighbourhood, and were used to the stresses of city life consulted less often.

The possibility that attendance rates are more closely linked to illness frequency and severity than to anything else is, surprisingly, one that has often been overlooked. Most results discussed so far could easily be accounted for in this way. The age and sex groups known to have higher consultation rates are clearly those at higher risk of becoming ill, like the very young and the very old. Investigations of the non-illness variables discussed earlier have failed to take account of illness severity. We need investigations that measure the severity of illness and take it into account in assessments of the influences of the other factors. Certain aspects of illness may be more important than others in this respect. An illness that has seriously disrupting effects on a person's life may be more likely to lead to a consultation than another, perhaps more severe, which is less incapacitating. Mechanic and Greenley (1974) found that 45 per cent of a random sample of students had abnormally high scores on a scale of psychological distress compared with 75 per cent amongst those who sought treatment. However, only 10 per cent of the random sample reported that their problems often prevented activities, whereas half of the treatment-seeking sample did so. Mayo (1969) compared neurotic patients with a group of 'normals with symptoms', that is people who had neurotic symptoms but had not sought medical assistance for them. Using Foulds' Hostility and Direction of Hostility Questionnaire (HDHQ) it was found that both neurotics and normals with symptoms had significantly higher total hostility scores than normals. People with neurotic symptoms who sought treatment were more likely to be intropunitive, that is to blame themselves for their problems, than people with the same symptoms who did not seek treatment, but tended to blame the outside world. There is also some support for a notion that the extrapunitiveness of normals with symptoms who did not seek treatment would be reflected in their interpersonal relationships. They did in fact show poorer home adjustment on Bell's Adjustment Inventory. These findings have been largely confirmed recently by Foulds and Bedford (1977).

Other studies have also shown that the demand for primary care does not precisely reflect the presence of morbidity. Dunnell and Cartwright (1972) found that, on average, adults experienced symptoms of illness on about one day in four, but that only a small proportion of these symptoms led to a demand for medical care. Even more frequent symptoms have been found in women aged 20–44, a group known to have high GP contact rates (Banks et al., 1975). In this study women were asked to complete a health diary daily over a period of 4 weeks, and symptoms were reported on an average of 10 days out of the 28. Symptoms tended to be grouped in episodes of more than one day, and taking this into account it was found that, on average, there was one patient-initiated consultation for 37 symptom episodes. Symptoms most frequently reported—for example, headaches—were not those that were most frequently presented to the general practitioner, such as coughs, sore throats, and abdominal pain. The anxiety level, assessed using Cattell's Anxiety Scale, was positively associated with consultation rate independent of symptom severity.

The nature of the complaint may also be an important factor in determining when medical care is consulted. During the time of insidious onset of a condition the sufferer will experience bouts of minor complaints such as boils, dizziness, low back pain, or indigestion. These are usually self-limiting and because they appear amenable to self-treatment the sufferer may be lulled into accepting them, and therefore to the acceptance of a gradual but increasing deviation from health. During this onset he is likely to accommodate his behaviour to suit the symptoms in a homeostatic manner, thus increasing the chance of a later, rather than an earlier, first medical consultation in the course of the illness (Wadsworth, 1974).

Another factor that is often thought to increase the likelihood of a consultation is stress. Miller, Ingham, and Davidson (1976) compared a group of patients recently self-referred to general practice, with other individuals of the same age and sex who had not recently consulted. Information about recent life events was collected using an adaptation of methods devised by Brown et al. (1973, 1975). This index of stress discriminated significantly between consulters and non-consulters, but it was also strongly associated with severity of psychological symptoms, though hardly at all with physical symptoms. The difficulty of distinguishing between stress, distress, and disease has already been mentioned. The psychological symptoms assessed in this investigation may in fact be made up of the natural distress resulting from the stresses concerned.

Counting symptoms is only a partial resolution of the problem of allowing for illness severity in assessing the effect of non-illness factors. The people who do not consult may have symptoms as frequently, but they do not necessarily have them as severely, as those who do seek treatment from their doctors. Mechanic and Greenley (1974) took into account the amount and seriousness of symptomatology and showed that a number of sociocultural characteristics remain as determinants of help-seeking even when symptom seriousness is controlled. They also showed that the non-symptomatic determinants of help-seeking seem to be more influential with symptoms of a moderate or mild character than with severe symptoms. Wing (1976) and Ingham and Miller (1976) have drawn attention to the fact that, whilst the psychological symptoms of those who do not consult their doctors include many that are as severe as those reported by patients, they are still in the zone that would be regarded as borderline for the purpose of determining the presence of clearly defined pathology. A true comparison group for looking at factors other than illness determining self-referral consists of those who are in this overlapping zone of severity.

Studies like those of Miller, Ingham, and Davidson previously cited, confound individual proneness to consultation with temporary factors associated with episodes of consultation. The people who consulted and who were found to have experienced threatening life events may be people with a tendency to consult frequently who also, perhaps for the same reasons, tend to experience over a long period of time a higher number of threatening life events than do other people. It is necessary to distinguish these two sets of associated variables, and Roghman and Haggerty (1972) have attempted to do so. They asked a random sample of 512 mothers to keep a health calendar over a period of 28 days and also to record any upsetting events at work, in the house, with the children, with the husband, and so on. Each mother was also asked to record illness and any use of health services for all members of the family. It was found that illness episodes accompanied by stress has a lower chance of medical contact than illness episodes without stress. 'The mother seems to realise stress as the cause of these short illnesses and does not expect any help from the physician.' For illnesses lasting 5 or more days stress seemed to be less important, though the numbers were small.

Relatively fewer studies have tried to define medical and social characteristics of non-attenders. Failure to use services is sometimes a matter of social pressure on the individual, perhaps taking the form of not feeling able to take time off work or the neglect of parental duties, which may be necessary in an official declaration of illness (see e.g. Robinson, 1971). Zola (1973) suggests that some social events, such as trouble at work or home, may act as a 'final straw' or trigger that ultimately makes someone, who has seriously delayed getting advice, consult a doctor about his complaint. Strauss (1970) has argued that previous experience of medical care may act as a deterrent, both because of the procedures and treatments undergone and because of the perceived lack of friendliness and helpfulness in the doctors (see also Stimson and Webb,

1975). But as well as weighing the pros and cons of going to the doctor, an individual may not even see his complaint as something which is appropriate for medical treatment, as Cartwright, Hockey, and Anderson (1973) found, and as McKinlay (1973) noted in his investigation of the relative under-use of antenatal clinics by women from the lower social class. Some will seek advice from friends or relatives or non-medical healers, and this is known as lay referral (Wadsworth, Butterfield, and Blaney, 1971; McKinlay, 1973; Dunnell and Cartwright, 1972). Some will see their complaints as so socially unacceptable that they will delay help-seeking (e.g. in venereal disease), whilst others will see theirs as so common in their society that there is little point in treatment or in certain forms of treatment (Wadsworth, Butterfield, and Blaney 1971).

Kessel and Shepherd (1965) took a group who did not visit the doctor at all during the first 10 years of the National Health Service, and found them more likely to see themselves as being healthy and to worry less about their health. This was true even though they had the same number of recent trivial ailments than more frequent attenders, but they managed them in most instances without going to the doctor. There was an indication that the non-attenders had perhaps had less experience of serious illness in the past. The authors drew the reassuring conclusion that 'broadly speaking, those who seldom or never consult their practitioners appear to be healthy'. This may seem rather obvious, but to the epidemiologist it is an important observation because it is often suggested that prevalence rates of serious illness may be greatly underestimated by taking numbers of patients coming to the general practitioner as an index.

Individual coping with disease

Recently more detailed studies of people as patients, both in clinics and in their homes, have been concerned with the social meaning of illness for the individual; how he reacts to, contends with, and perceives his illness and its treatment. This led the sociologist David Mechanic to introduce the concept of 'illness behaviour', defined as 'the ways in which given symptoms may be differentially perceived, evaluated and acted (or not acted) upon by different kinds of persons' (Mechanic, 1962). If a person is motivated to become a patient and is successful in convincing his family, friends, and society at large that he is ill, he may be said to have adopted the 'sick role' (Parsons, 1951).

It is easy to account for any feeling of distress by attributing it to illness and, particularly in the absence of other ways of coping with the true sources of the distress, the sufferer may adopt the sick role in an attempt to seek relief. This form of illness behaviour is not necessarily recognized as such by the sufferer, nor is it necessarily successful. Whether he attempts it, however, and whether he is successful in getting other people to accept him in his self-allotted role are clearly important issues in society's operational definition of illness. Now that we have seen this form of illness behaviour as a way of coping with stress, we must consider what is known of the psychology of coping in general.

Threat produces distress and there is strong evidence that it can also produce illness. However, it is clear that this does not always happen; some individuals, under some circumstances, can undergo severe stress of a kind that would produce illness in others without any ill effects. It is easy to put this down to individual variations in susceptibility. Some people are more prone to illness than others, and there are also qualitative variations in probable symptom patterns (Lacey and Van Lehn, 1952), but this does not get us very far. We need to enquire into the circumstances and conditions that determine the individual variations, and here we are in an area of great complexity. Modifiers of susceptibility to stress-induced illness may be positive or negative and include the four general categories:

(1) external physical agents such as infectious agents, toxic substances, and nutrition;
(2) internal physical factors, e.g. genetic constitution, physical fitness, and immunity;
(3) psychological factors; the individual's personal resources and capacity for coping with threat—this interacts very closely with;
(4) external socioeconomic factors. Social resources include support from close confidants (see Brown, 1976) which probably affords some protection against the adverse effects of threat.

Coping has been studied by Lazarus and other psychologists (Lazarus, Averill, and Opton, 1974; Lazarus, 1966; Janis, 1962). Mature and effective 'adaptive' coping occurs most readily when the threat is moderate, that is in 'low stakes situations', whereas maladaptive 'primitive and unrealistic' coping takes over when threat is intense and involves 'high stakes'. It is under these conditions of high threat that we find what Janis has called 'regressive' solutions such as are observed in psychopathological states. It is tempting to equate some of the manifestations of illness that have been attributed to threat with primitive coping responses. Indeed illness as coping is not necessarily 'primitive'. The illnesses of Florence Nightingale or Charles Darwin for instance (G. Pickering, 1974), may have been highly adaptive strategies though not necessarily consciously formulated as such, enabling the patients not only to cope with the frustrations that brought them on, but to achieve their goals with quite remarkable success. It may sometimes be an arbitrary decision whether to regard the adoption of the sick role as in the cases of Charles Darwin and Florence Nightingale as illness or illness behaviour. 'It has been noted that not all organically "sick" people necessarily define themselves as ill, nor are all self-defined "sick" people likely to be recognized as such by legitimate medical authorities' (Shuval, 1972). In discussing some social aspects of adaptation and coping Mechanic (1974) has stressed the importance of institutionalized solutions to environmental problems, and these change as the problems change. 'With rapid technological and social change', he writes, 'institutionalized solutions to new problems are likely to lag behind, and the probability increases that a larger proportion of the population will have difficulties in accommodating to life's problems'. Adopting the sick role is a modern institutionalized solution to many present-day problems. For example, a patient consulting the doctor with typical early symptoms of depression such as tiredness, insomnia, anxiety, headaches, inability to concentrate, lack of interest, feelings of being unable to cope with work, may well have experienced a number of live events of quite a threatening nature in the recent past. Is this an example of threat-induced illness; of illness as a maladaptive coping response; or of institutionalized illness behaviour that solves, or partially solves, the environmental problem? It may be possible to ask the same question of many groups of physical symptoms as well. It may be that elements of all three must be introduced if we are to develop a theory that is of value, both scientifically and to the individual. Perhaps all are describing the same events in different words, but it does seem that the central problem facing us is to develop a methodology that will deal adequately with the interaction between life circumstances and personality (Lazarus *et al.*, 1974). Given a series of events occurring to a known individual in known circumstances, what is his response likely to be? Will he manifest symptoms? Will he cope adaptively? Will he seek help and from whom? No existing formulation comes anywhere near supplying the answers to these questions in individual cases. The most important question of all, perhaps, is how can he best be helped?

Such considerations have led social scientists to take a particular interest in the illness itself, since the individual's lifestyles and chances are now recognized as being not only closely tied to how he copes with sickness, but also as enmeshed with its causes. This kind of work is to be seen in the study of coronary heart disease where the importance of how the individual reacts to societal and family pressures is well recognized for its effect on interactions with the biochemical and physiological systems (Raab, 1971). This, of course, raises many important questions about the quality of reactions, the nature of stress and distress, how far reactions are determined by the type of event experienced, how far by traits shown in answers to personality inventories, and how far by previous experience which, as the midtown Manhattan studies suggest, may have a cumulative effect (Langner and Michael, 1963). Brown (1976) has contributed to the unravelling of causal and predisposing social factors in psychiatric disturbance in women, and observes that the 'potential influences are so many that it is easy to become lost without the guidance of ideas that firmly link the disease with the immediate social context, past and present'.

Progress with unravelling the very long-term effects of experiences will come from prospective studies; that is those in which we have regular follow-up of a population, so that we may compare later illness and behaviour in those who had certain experiences which we hypothesize to be of importance, with the illness and behaviour of those who did not. This method, of course, avoids problems associated with the recollection of earlier events. In the National Survey of Health and Development, for example, it has been possible to examine the relation between the experience of certain emotionally disturbing events occurring before age 5 years with later behaviour, in males. Discriminant analysis of these data correctly selects a very high proportion of those who later commit sexual and violent crimes. Those who are wrongly selected by this method, i.e. who have the experience, but who do not become criminals, have a prevalence of admissions to psychiatric hospitals and of dueodenal ulcers and colitis which is considerably higher than in others who have not had this experience (Wadsworth, 1979).

The medical care of the patient

Just as the role of the individual and his personal and social behaviour are increasingly seen as having importance in the genesis of illness and in the decision about when to consult medical care, so it is equally important in the process of recovery from, or accommodation to, illness. As Ford et al. (1967) observed, the doctor can work effectively with a patient who is 'responsive to treatment'. Communication is, naturally enough, used by the doctor in the treatment of disease, and so good rapport and understanding between doctor and patient are of the greatest importance. In his study of children with poliomyelitis Davis (1960) found that

> uncertainty, a *real* factor in early diagnosis and treatment of the paralysed child, came more and more to serve the purely managerial ends of the treatment personnel in their interaction with parents. Long after the doctor himself was in no doubt about the outcome, the perpetuation of uncertainty in doctor to family communication, although perhaps neither premeditated nor intended, can none the less be understood in terms of its function in the treatment system.

Poor rapport may be difficult for the doctor to detect since what Webb and Stimson (1976) call 'a facade of compliance and acquiescence' will often mask any conflict that the patient may feel. This is particularly important since recent studies are beginning to confirm that poor rapport as perceived by the patient—and relatively few studies have considered the patient's views of the doctor/patient relationship—is associated with a lack of compliance with the prescribed treatment regime. In their notable series of studies of child patients Korsch and Negrete (1972) found that 'when the doctor does express negative feelings, the mother is likely to be dissatisfied with the visit and fail to comply with his advice. Conversely a substantial showing of positive affect by the doctor to the mother enhances her satisfaction and compliance.'

If improvement of the affective quality of the doctor/patient relationship enhances communication, it also seems to work the other way round. An improvement in communication enhances the relationship. Ley (1976), in a recent review of studies, concluded that much of the lack of compliance and satisfaction with communications could be accounted for by failure in understanding and memory, complicated by diffidence on the part of the patients in requesting enlightenment. He and his colleagues showed that worthwhile improvements could be obtained by efforts to increase comprehensibility, and that increases in understanding led to significantly greater satisfaction with communications.

More recent studies of doctor/patient communications have taken account of time passing, by seeing the consultation in its social context rather than as an isolated incident, so that it is becoming possible to see how the individual's views of his condition and its treatment change in response to his perceptions of the treatment and of its effects on his life. Thus rather than investigate communications between doctors and patients simply by studying what patients know about particular conditions or how many of the prescribed pills they have taken, this method takes as wide a view as possible in both time and subject-matter in order to see the social context of events and have patients' views of these contexts. Assumptions about social context are not made from structural information on social class or education or income.

West's (1976) work makes a particularly important contribution to this field. He observed a small series of consultations about epilepsy in children, beginning with the first visit to the hospital physician, and continuing with the subsequent consultations. West describes this visit as 'a crucial definitional encounter for the parent... characterized by a rigid structure where parents have only a limited opportunity to initiate anything other than complementary definitions. *They appear* remarkably passive in this interview.' At subsequent consultations parents began to negotiate with the doctor for better definitions or for changes in the treatment, and some challenged the doctor on the diagnosis and the management of the illness, suggesting, for example, that from their observations of the child it might be best to change or reduce the dosage of a drug. From the home interviews it became clear that some parents were dissatisfied with, or worried about, their child's treatment but they still felt it necessary to maintain good relationships. As West says 'rather than effecting a change in their future presentations to the doctor, they may sustain a definition of the situation corresponding to that held by the doctor while "believing" in another and acting according to their "privately" held definition'. He even reports a case in which the mother's previous experience with another epileptic child led her to ignore the doctor's instructions for medication for 5 years '*but*, in order to maintain the appearance of the "good" mother, she regularly went to her G.P. to obtain repeat prescriptions'. By using this observational method over time West has shown that patients do not necessarily opt for *either* professional *or* lay treatment, and that they do not simply take the doctor's definition and advice for granted.

There is therefore much to be gained by social science studies of behaviour in illness of those who are already patients. Such investigations should provide clues about assessing various kinds of treatment programmes, and sharpen clinicians' perceptions of a need for continuing awareness of individual differences and their importance, even after the diagnosis has been made and the plan for treatment worked out.

CONCLUSION

We have seen how difficult it is to define illness precisely. In any population there are people suffering distresses that give rise to wide disagreements concerning whether they are illnesses or not. There is no single definition of illness that does not produce its own anomalies and ambiguities.

This in itself leads to some of the difficulties discussed under Control of Disease (see p. 346). Some individual freedom is often relinquished voluntarily, sometimes even compulsorily, in return for medical help in dealing with illness. In cases of dangerous infection, for example, people may be isolated, or prevented from handling food. Courts may require people to be given treatment for serious mental illness or compulsorily detained in hospital, particularly if there is a risk of personal injury to the patient or others. On the other hand, people can also be relieved of some of their responsibilities on grounds of illness, including the responsibility to work in order to maintain themselves and their families. It is obviously desirable that illness is defined in such a way that it can be clearly recognized, but in practice this not always possible. Society is often forced to use criteria that have little to do with illness as such. It is usually a matter of individual decision about when an illness is sufficiently disruptive as to require medical advice. Naturally enough, studies of decision-making about getting medical advice have investigated social pressures, individual characteristics and the signs and symptoms themselves, in attempts to find explanations for differences in consultation behaviour. Social pressures studied and hypothesized to be of relevance are wide-ranging and include personal relationships, work, others' views of such illness, perceived class differences between doctors and patients, and relative social isolation of the sick, with an implicit pressure for them to do all they can to regain a state of good health. However, we are not only concerned with the social pressures on people who are undeniably sick. We have pointed out how easily the distresses of life that have nothing to do with illness can be confused with illness, particularly psychological illness, and if people suffering such distresses cope by adopting the sick role it may be against the interest both of the individual and of society.

Some progress has been made, albeit limited, in exploring the coping mechanisms that people use in dealing with the trials and tribulations of their lives. The borderline between 'normal' distress and the distress resulting from illness is very blurred and the relationship between them is not clearly understood. It is evident that there is an association between stress, distress, illness, and illness behaviour, but the network of causation in this area is very complex. Stress and distress can cause illness; illness can cause distress; distress can be confused with illness. We clearly need a much more systematic and comprehensive theory of the transition from states of normal distress to illness and the adoption of the sick role. Hypotheses derived from such theory can be tested by prospective studies of small samples, once we are able to detect subjects who are at high risk of developing psychological or stress-produced illness or are becoming a serious burden to the health service.

At the same time continuing evaluative work on the delivery of health-care services and their acceptance will help to direct service planning, aided by investigations of self-help, which will in turn offer much needed advice about the individual's concepts of illness and how to cope with it. It should eventually be possible to extend evaluation studies to include experimental work to compare the effectiveness of different kinds of services, and preventive and health education campaigns.

Research in this area can be difficult and costly but the potential gain is great. When we understand more about the early stages of illness, and about health and illness behaviour related to stress, it will be feasible to use this knowledge in preventive measures, including health education as well as medical and nursing care. For example, it should be possible to advise practitioners about the importance of various kinds of life events and the ways in which they are handled at different ages and states of life. Of course, the difficulty lies, as ever, in the translation of research findings, such as those reported and discussed in this chapter, into practice. As a recent report on child health says in discussing preventive paediatrics:

> even if there were an agreed body of knowledge about parenting to be transmitted (and there is not) and one could work on the assumption that knowledge always changes behaviour (which one cannot) it would still be necessary to bear in mind how much the interpersonal relationships and integrity of the parents affect their ability to be successful. So many previous well-meaning programmes aimed at changing behaviour for the benefit of health have fallen short of their objective... (Fit for the Future, 1976).

Social and psychological studies of illness behaviour can help health educators and practitioners towards overcoming these problems. The results should be a reduction of health care costs to the community and a gain to individuals in terms of human happiness and fulfilment.

REFERENCES

Ashford, J. R. (1972). Patient contacts in general practice in the National Health Service. *The Statistician*, **21**, 265–289.

Balint, M. (1968). *The Doctor, his Patient and the Illness*, 2nd edn. London: Pitman Medical.

Banks, M. H., Beresford, S. A. A., Morrell, D. C. Waller, J. J., and Watkins, C. J. (1975). Factors influencing demand for primary medical care in women aged 20–44 years: a preliminary report. *International Journal of Epidemiology*, **4**, 189–195.

Beresford, S. A. A., Waller, J. J., Banks, M. H., and Wale, C. J. (1977). Why do women consult doctors? Social factors and the use of the general practitioner. *British Journal of Preventive and Social Medicine*, **31**, 220–226.

Brodman, K., Erdmann, A. J., and Wolff, H. G. (1956). *Cornell Medical Index Health Questionnaire*. New York: Cornell University Medical College.

Brown, A. C., and Fry, J. (1962). The Cornell Medical Index Health Questionnaire in the identification of neurotic patients in general practice. *Journal of Psychosomatic Research*, **6**, 185–190.

Brown, G. W. (1976). Social causes of disease. In Tuckett, D. (ed.), *An Introduction to Medical Sociology*, pp. 291–333. London: Tavistock.

Brown, G. W., Sklair, F., Harris, T. O., and Birley, J. L. T. (1973). Life-events and psychiatric disorders. Part 1: some methodological issues. *Psychological Medicine*, **3**, 74–87.

Brown, G. W., Bhrolchain, M. N., and Harris, T. O. (1975). Social class and psychiatric disturbance among women in an urban population. *Sociology*, **9**, 225–254.

Cartwright, A., Hockey, L., and Anderson, J. L. (1973). *Life before Death*. London: Routledge & Kegan Paul.

Coelho, G. V., Hamburg, D. A., and Adams, J. E. (1974). *Coping and Adaptation*. New York: Basic Books.

Davis, F. (1960). Uncertainty in medical prognosis: clinical and functional. *American Journal of Sociology*, **66**, 41–47.

Dohrenwend, B. S., and Dohrenwend, B. P. (1969). *Social Status and Psychological Disorder: a Casual Inquiry*. New York: Wiley.

Dunnell, K., and Cartwright, A. (1972). *Medicine Takers, Prescribers and Hoarders*. London: Routledge & Kegan Paul.

Fit for the Future (1976). The Report of the Committee on Child Health Services, p. 154. London: HMSO.

Ford, A. B., Liske, R. E., Ort, R. S., and Dewton, J. C. (1967). *The Doctor's Perspective*. Cleveland. Western Reserve University Press.

Foulds, G. A. (1976). *The Hierarchical Nature of Personal Illness*. London: Academic Press.

Foulds, G. A., and Bedford, A. (1977). Personality and coping with psychiatric symptoms. *British Journal of Psychiatry*, **130**, 29–31.

Grad, J. & Sainsbury, P. (1963). Mental illness and the family. *Lancet*, **1**, 544–547.

Illich, I. (1976). *Limits to Medicine*, pp. 76–77. London: Marion Boyars.

Ingham, J. G., and Miller, P. McC. (1976). The concept of prevalence applied to psychiatric disorders and symptoms. *Psychological Medicine*, **6**, 217–225.

Jacob, A. (1969) The personality of patients in the 'artificial' practice. *Journal of the Royal College of General Practitioners*, **17**, 299–303.

Janis, I. L. (1962). Psychological effects of warnings. In G. W. Baker, and D. W. Chapman (eds.), *Man and Society in Disaster*, pp. 55–92. New York: Basic Books.

Kasl, S. V., and Cobb, S. (1966). Health behaviour, illness behaviour and sick role behaviour. *Archives of Environmental Health*, **12**, 246–266.

Kendell, R. E. (1975). *The Role of Diagnosis in Psychiatry*. Edinburgh: Blackwell Scientific Publications.

Kessel, N., and Shepherd, M. (1965). The health and attitudes of people who seldom consult a doctor. *Medical Care*, **3**, 6–10.

Kessel, W. I. N. (1960). Psychiatric morbidity in a London general practice. *British Journal of Preventive and Social Medicine*, **14**, 16–22.

Korsch, B., and Negrete, V. F. (1972). Doctor–patient communication. *Scientific American*, **227** (August), 66–74.

Kraupl Taylor, F. (1971). A logical analysis of the medico-psychological concept of disease. *Psychological Medicine*, **1**, 356–364; **2**, 7–16.

Lacey, J. I., and Van Lehn, R. (1952). Differential emphasis in somatic response to stress: an experimental study. *Psychosomatic Medicine*, **14**, 71–81.

Langner, T. S., and Michael, S. T. (1963). *Life Stress and Mental Health*. New York: Free Press.

Lazarus, R. (1966). *Psychological Stress and the Coping Process*. New York: McGraw-Hill.

Lazarus, R. L., Averill, J. R., and Opton, E. M. (1974). The psychology of coping: Issues of research and assessment. In D. A. Hamburg, and J. E. Adams, (eds.), G. V. Coelho, *Coping and Adaptations*, ch. 10. New York: Basic Books.

Ley, P. (1976). Towards better doctor–patient communication. In A. E. Bennett (ed.), *Communication between Doctors and Patients*. Oxford: Oxford University Press.

Mayo, P. R. (1969). Women with neurotic symptoms who do not seek treatment. *British Journal of Medical Psychology*, **42**, 165–169.

McArdle, C., Alexander, W. D., and Murray Boyle, C. (1974). Frequent attenders at a health centre. *The Practitioner*. (November), 696–702.

McKinlay, J. B. (1972). Some approaches and problems in the study of the use of services — an overview. *Journal of Health and Social Behaviour*, **13**, 115–152.

McKinlay, J. B. (1973). Social networks, lay consultation and help-seeking behaviour. *Social Forces*, **51**, 255–292.

Mechanic, D. (1962). The concept of illness behaviour. *Journal of Chronic Diseases*, **15**, 189–194.

Mechanic, D. (1974). Social structure and personal adaptation. In G. V. Coelho, D. A. Hamburg, and J. E. Adams, (eds.), *Coping and Adaptation*, Ch. 3. New York: Basic Books.

Mechanic, D., and Greenley, J. R. (1974). The prevalence of psychological distress and help-seeking in a college student population. *Social Psychiatry*, **11**, 1–14.

Meyer, A. (1907). Fundamental conceptions of dementia praecox. *Journal of Nervous and Mental Disease*, **34**, 331–336.

Miller, P.McC, Ingham, J. G., and Davidson, S. (1976). Life events, symptoms and social support. *Journal of Psychosomatic Research*, **20**, 515–522.

Myers, G. S., quoted in Lasagna, L. (1963). *Life, Death and the Doctor*, pp. 215–216. New York: Alfred Knopf.

Oldham, P. D., Pickering, G., Fraser Roberts, J. A., and Sowry, G. S. C. (1960). The nature of essential hypertension. *Lancet*, **1**, 1085–1093.

Parsons, T. (1951). *The Social System*, Ch. X. Glencoe: The Free Press.

Pickering, G. (1974). *Creative Malady*. London: George Allen & Unwin.

Pickering, G. W. (1963). The interitance of arterial pressure. In Pemberton J. (ed.), *Epidemiology—Reports on Research and Teaching*. London: Oxford University Press.

Polliack, M. R. (1971). The relationship between Cornell Medical Index scores and attendance rates. *Journal of the Royal College of General Practitioners*, **21**, 453–459.

Raab, W. C. (1971). Cardiotoxic Biochemical effects of emotional–environmental stresses. Fundamentals of Psychocardiology. In L. Levi (ed.), *Society, Stress and Disease*, pp. 331–337. London: Oxford University Press.

Rees, W. L. (1976). Stress, distress and disease. *British Journal of Psychiatry*, **128**, 3–18.

Robinson, D. (1971). *The Process of Becoming Ill*. London: Routledge & Kegan Paul.

Roghman, K. J., and Haggerty, J. (1972). Family stress and the use of health services. *International Journal of Epidemiology*, **1**, 279–286.

Ryan, J. (1976). The production and management of stupidity: the involvement of medicine and psychology. In M. E. J. Wadsworth, and D. Robinson (eds.), *Studies in Everyday Medical Life*. London: Martin Robertson.

Ryle, A., and Hamilton, M. (1962). Neurosis in fifty married couples. *Journal of Mental Science*, **108**, 265–273.

Scadding, J. (1967). Diagnosis: the clinician and the computer. *Lancet*, **2**, 877–882.

Sheldon, A. (1970). Toward a general theory of disease and medical care. In A. Sheldon, F. Baker, and C. P. McLaughlin (eds.), *Systems and Medical Care*, p. 94. Cambridge, Mass.: MIT Press.

Shuval, J. T. (1972). The sick role in a setting of comprehensive medical care. *Medical Care*, **11**, 50–59.

Stimson, G., and Webb, B. (1975). *Going to See the Doctor: The Consultation Process in General Practice*. London: Routledge & Kegan Paul.

Strauss, A. (1970). Medical ghettoes. In A. Strauss (ed.), *Where Medicine Fails*. Chicago: Aldine.

Szasz, T. S. (1960). The myth of mental illness. *American Psychologist*, **15**, 113–118.

Wadsworth, M. E. J. (1974). Health and sickness. *Journal of Psychosomatic Research*, **18**, 271–276.

Wadsworth, M. E. J. (1979). *Roots of Delinquency*. Oxford: Martin Robertson.

Wadsworth, M. E. J., Butterfield, W. J. H., and Blaney, R. (1971). *Health and Sickness: The Choice of Treatment*, pp. 1–4. London: Tavistock Publications.

Watts, C. A. H. (1962). Psychiatric disorders. In *Morbidity Statistics from General Practice*, vol. III: *Disease in General Practice*. The Res. Comm. of the Council of the Coll. of Gen. Prac. Studies on Medical and Population Subjects, No. 14, London: HMSO.

Webb, B. and Stimson, G. V. (1976). People's accounts of medical encounters. In M. E. J. Wadsworth, and D. Robinson (eds.), *Studies in Everyday Medical Life*. London: Martin Robertson.

West, P. (1976). The physician and the management of childhood epilepsy. In M. E. J. Wadsworth, and D. Robinson (eds.), *Studies in Everyday Medical Life*. London: Martin Robertson.

Wing, J. K. (1976). A technique for studying psychiatric morbidity in in-patient and out-patient series and in general population samples. *Psychological Medicine*, **6**, 665–671.

Zola, I. K. (1973). Pathways to the doctor: from person to patient. *Social Science and Medicine*, **7**, 677–689.

Foundations of Psychosomatics
Edited by M. J. Christie and P. G. Mellett
© 1981 John Wiley & Sons Ltd.

17

IN VIVO OR *IN VITRO?* SOME EFFECTS OF LABORATORY ENVIRONMENTS, WITH PARTICULAR REFERENCE TO THE PSYCHOPHYSIOLOGY EXPERIMENT

ANTHONY GALE

Department of Psychology, University of Southampton, England

and

SUE BAKER

Department of Applied Psychology, University of Wales.

INTRODUCTION: WHAT'S THE PROBLEM?

If you are reading this book then you may perhaps be a member of the medical profession who wants to know what the psychological sciences can offer in understanding psychosomatic disease. You will already know that psychologists have dozens of theories and many hundreds of experiments. You will also have discovered that psychological theories are like delicate plants which flourish only in certain environments. Tweedledum's subjects in Tweedledum's laboratory produce results consistent with Tweedledum's theory. But what happens when Tweedledee tries to replicate Tweedledum's experiments? It seems that Tweedledum's power to obtain 'correct' findings depends more on processes analogous to placebo-type effects than to the laws of physics.

The primary source of doubt about the psychology of the psychology experiment is Rosenthal, who in his early studies showed that the experimenter's expectations were a powerful influence on the outcome of experiments. In the classic Rosenthal study, students were presented with 'maze-bright' and 'maze-dull' rats, especially bred for the purpose. The students went off to run their rats in their mazes, and returned with the expected outcome. Dull rats were bad at maze-running, bright rats were good. In fact, the rats had been selected at random, and there was no inherent difference between them. Somehow the students, in their handling of the rats, in their observations, and in their data tabulation, had unwittingly ensured that their instructor heard what they expected him to hear. Somehow, they had made their rats behave in different ways. Recently Rosenthal and Rubin (1978) have reviewed 345 studies and conclude that these and similar effects are still robust and have withstood the tests of time and criticism. It is a paradox, then, that an effect which undermines our confidence in experiments has itself been demonstrated in so many experiments!

We, the authors, are psychophysiologists and virtually all our work is laboratory work, so we have a proper concern with this issue. As you will see, we have carried out experiments which demonstrate physiological effects in laboratory environments, which can appear quite powerfully even though they are not part of the explicit procedure. Psychophysiological research is particularly relevant to psychosomatics, because it is concerned with the integration of physiological, experiential, and behavioural data. In psychosomatics we see the implication of psychological factors in physiological disease. Indeed the five key questions of psychosomatic disorders, all call for a psychophysiological approach. What are the basic mechanisms involved in the formation of a psychosomatic disease? Why do other symptoms not develop, symptoms which are also seen in stress, namely depression, anxiety, or psychosis? What marks out the individual who suffers from psychosomatic disorders? Why do some people develop ulcers and others asthma? And finally, what treatments are appropriate? Because the answer to all these questions must involve the interrelationship between mind and emotion—the integration of the psychological and the physiological—psychosomatic disorders have been an appropriate focus for psychophysiological research and theory.

The question then arises, what is the appropriate method to study such problems? By far the majority of psychological research studies have been carried out in the laboratory rather than the field. The laboratory researcher argues that only in the laboratory can he gain control of the experiment. He is concerned with the testing of very specific hypotheses and this involves the systematic manipulation of experimental variables, free from extraneous interference or confounding. Moreover, the experiment is essentially simple in conception, and relatively few variables are handled simultaneously for psychological theory is not yet capable of handling very complex results or multiple interactions. The laboratory researcher denies, as a matter of conscious strategy, the complexity of Nature. Laboratory studies enable him not only to simplify but also to build up a series of studies, each one related logically to the ones which went before it, gradually developing a coherent database for his theory. Work in the *field* removes virtually all this control. Life in the real world is too complex, for too much happens, much too quickly, even for the human observer to record the salient events. Nor are natural events repeated in a way which allows for estimates of variance and error. Thus the essential features of the logic of laboratory experimentation are abused; the experimenter cannot identify this or that variable as crucial, he cannot eliminate systematically this or that source of error, he cannot build up a coherent database.

The problem is, of course, that psychophysiological disorders develop over time. They also develop in the real world of the individual, in the context of his home and working environment. The stress which he may experience is mediated by well-established habits of coping or failing to cope with problems. Such problems arise in his interactions with other people, in handling his emotions, in making decisions. If this is the arena in which life's battles are fought, how do we capture a slice of life and re-create in the laboratory the stimuli which trigger off his emotional responses? Can we somehow simulate the real world in such a way as to sample his responses to the real world? Can we recover the complexity and yet still retain the power of the experimental approach? The answer to these questions calls for considerable ingenuity in the art of experimentation.

However, there is yet a further difficulty. The experiment itself is a very special event, since it subjects the individual to novel experiences and novel demands. The role which is required of him as an experimental subject is very unlike his role as a student, a friend, a family member, or any other role he serves in life. Being a subject is hardly like opening a newspaper, or getting on a bus, or studying, or sitting for an examination which will determine your future. In recent years several psychologists have argued that the experience of being an experimental subject is so unusual that the data which emerge from psychological experiments are not to be trusted. They claim that laboratory experiments do not sample life and the results therefore cannot be generalized to life. The most extreme proponents of this view hold that very radical changes are required both in psychological methods and psychological theorizing before we shall ever develop a veridical psychology. If psychology is to be applied to the real world then it must sample the real world. This is not a novel idea, for many developments in psychological research can be seen in terms of an improvement in the ecological validity of experimentation.

This controversy must clearly affect those who look to the psychologist for guidance. Many professional workers are faced with problems which seem to have a psychological component. Therefore they seek for an understanding of the psychological input to the problem and wish to know whether there can be a psychological input to its solution. The problems they have to deal with are real-life problems, not laboratory problems. They will therefore wish to know whether they can trust psychological theories and advice which emerge from the laboratory, or whether they should treat them with caution.

The aim of this chapter, then, is to review some of the studies which reveal effects of the laboratory environment. By 'environment' we do not simply mean the bricks and mortar, but the people, the artifacts and the activities to be found in the laboratory.

We look first at the changing role of the experimental subject over time. When experimental psychology first began, the subject was a bit of an expert; now he seems to be treated as a naïve simpleton. What implications does this have for the data he produces? Does this brand of treatment raise ethical issues? Are subjects selected according to proper sampling procedures, and if not might there be a systematic bias in results? We then consider what we view as defects of some psychophysiological strategies in research and point to the dangers of misinterpretation when the experimenter fails to ask himself 'What does it feel like to be a subject in my laboratory?' We briefly review data on experimenter and subject effects, particularly those attributable to sex differences. If the psychology experiment is a special sort of social psychological event, then what theories from social psychology are applicable to the experiment? Can social psychological theory itself help us to be better experimenters? Finally, we present a model of sources of 'arousal' in the psychology experiment, a model which has helped us to improve our own experimentation and make sense of our results. This is particularly pertinent, when one is concerned with the measurement of *emotional* responses. We conclude with some guidelines which we hope will help the reader to carry out sensitive experiments and will help him to look critically at studies in the literature.

We must not mislead the reader. The laboratory environment, in spite of the problems it raises, will be the home of the bulk of psychological research for a long time to come. It is the only place where proper control is possible. This does not mean that the psychologist should eschew field studies, for it is in the real world that he derives the very ideas he tests in the laboratory. The good psychological scientists moves back and forth between the backroom bench and the factory floor. The identification of sources of error represents an advance in method. Problems with laboratory research should be recognized and then handled. They are a challenge to ingenuity and creativity rather than a cause for despair.

Who has the courage to predict what psychological research will look like a hundred years from now? We can raise a chuckle over the antics of ancient Egyptian astrologers, feel amused by the sorcerer's apprentice, or feel patronizing about the confusion of epilepsy with divine inspiration. But this was the science of the time. Even nowadays there are Nobel prizewinners who ploughed a lonely furrow, rejected by established authority.

Let us allow ourselves some literary indulgence and look forward to future history, tempered by a humility engendered by our awareness of how past events appear from our vantage point in the present. What will a future historian of contemporary psychology think of our science? Perhaps he might see us as a community of unwitting religious fanatics, members of a pan-national conspiracy, replete with ritual, initiation procedures, and masonic rule-books; some sort of institutional psychosis; a *folie à N*. The laboratory we love might be seen as a temple wherein the psychologist professes his faith and gives vent to his delusions. Young graduate psychologists are novitiates or acolytes, some of whom might be lucky enough, in their time, to become high priests. Does the teacher of contemporary psychology indoctrinate his students to become as misguided as he is, or rather, does he educate them to become good scientists? Silverman (1977) suggests that there are subtle processes of socialization, part and parcel of undergraduate and postgraduate education, which induce conformity and stifle natural curiosity in the psychology student, directing his attention away from the very original questions which led him into being a student of mental life in the first place. Thus belief in the rigours of experimental design and statistical manipulation is really part of dogma which sets up a self- contained set of rules which inhibit freedom of thought.

When one looks back at the controversies which have raged across psychology in even its own brief history, then speculations such as these seem less far-fetched.

Let us return to the present.

THE CHANGING ROLE OF THE SUBJECT IN THE PSYCHOLOGICAL LABORATORY

We owe a great deal in this discussion to a seminal paper by Schultz (1969) and a recent monograph by Silverman (1977) which extends and elaborates upon Schultz's arguments. Schultz identifies several problem areas in the evolution, throughout the history of psychology, of the role of the subject. Firstly, what is a 'good' subject? For the original introspectionist school, the subject was an expert observer, attending to his psychological processes with a trained eye. Subjects whose observations were unreliable, because their reports fluctuated from occasion to occasion, were excluded. A long apprenticeship in techniques of introspection was essential. We might well question whether the objectives of the original workers were indeed attainable; however, the important point is that subjects were *trained* observers. The interest of the functionalists in individual differences led them to be interested in those differences of response which Titchener wanted to discard. Thus the notion of the naïve and untrained observer became possible. With the growth of methodological behaviourism, however, the cycle became complete. The subject now *behaved* and the experimenter was the observer; the subject became the object of the experimenter's observations. Subjective comment, or report of personal experience on the part of the subject, were again considered unreliable and untrustworthy. Thus the subject lost status and importance within the laboratory set-up. More recently the emphasis has shifted again, with the development of humanistic psychology, where experimenter and subject are seen as sharing a common voyage of exploration; but the humanist tradition has not yet reached many psychological laboratories and the subject-as-object role is the predominant one. Schultz argues that the shift from subject to object apparent in views of the subject's role has serious consequences for the way he is treated, and implications for the interpretation of his behaviour. He states:

> This image of the subject as object is reinforced by the mechanomorphic tendencies of behaviourism whose model of man is that of an organic machine—an inanimate, determined, reacting, empty organism. The tendency to view subjects as mechanical objects to be poked, prodded, manipulated and measured, causes the experimenter–subject dyad to be of the order of Buber's I–It relationship. The relationship is not that of person-to-person, but rather that of person-to-thing, with its attendant tendencies of domination, manipulation and control.

He goes on to argue that such a view of the subject as object leads us to forget that the subject has thoughts and feelings of his own and that these thoughts and feelings might play an important part in the way he reacts to the experimental situation, the manner in which he responds and the data he produces.

He next considers biases in the sampling of subjects. Studies by Smart (1966) and Schultz (1969) and indeed a later study by Jung (1969) indicate, both by an analysis of subject populations in studies reported in prestigious journals and on the basis of questionnaire responses by researchers, that subject populations are biased in the following ways. Between 32 and 80 per cent of experimental subjects were first-year introductory psychology students. Between 70 and 90 per cent of subjects were one sort of student or another. The ratio of males/females is approximately three to one. It is common criticism of Freud that his 'experimental subjects' were middle-class, middle-aged, Victorian, Viennese, sexually frustrated/inhibited, rich, Jewish women. According to Schultz's data the majority of contemporary experimental psychology is conducted upon middle-class, late adolescent, highly intelligent, American, male, Caucasian, first-year undergraduates, many of whom are required to participate as part of a course and even obtain credits for participation. It should be remembered that the standard textbook criticism of Freud's brand of methodology is presented by the exponents of contemporary experimental psychology. The problem is that, just like Freud's patients, the subjects yielded by such sampling are likely to convey with them to the laboratory a common set of attitudes, expectations, and interpretations. Thus much experimental psychology can be said to be subject to systematic bias rather than random error. Generalization from such biased populations is hardly likely to be trustworthy. Such groups are not only highly selected but may attend for common reasons; Jung's findings lead us to believe that 90 per cent of college students who participate are in some sense coerced into participation.

We then have to ask, what may be the motives and intentions of such press-ganged subjects? Are their actions, as recorded by the experimenter, *prima facie* responses to the explicit instructions and stimuli which the experimenter presents? What are the consequences of being forced to act as if one is not forced, to have to please when one does not necessarily wish to please?

It is not fair to characterize the experimenter as the tyrant and the subject as the victim. Schultz and Silverman claim both are victims of a *zeitgeist*. They suggest that both experimenter and subject act in collusion to produce data. This, they claim, is an abuse of the term. The origin of the term 'data' is the Latin word *datum* which means *given*; thus Nature gives and the psychologist experimenter receives. Not so, they say, for the experimenter and subject are playing a part, acting out roles prescribed by tacit conventions which reflect the contemporary culture of psychology. Does the subject merely do what the experimenter tells him to do, by covert and unwitting mutual agreement, or what he, the subject, believes the experimenter wants him to do? The argument is that when the subject is treated as an object and not encouraged to say how he feels about the experiment, the experimenter is less likely to realize what he has done wrong. Better not to hear bad news.

Of course there is nothing special about this problem. In the medical environment one is required to interview patients, to talk to them about their life circumstances, to explain to them what one considers to be the sources of their discomfort. All too often, studies of doctor–patient interaction have shown that doctor and patient have widely differing conceptions of what occurred and what was said. The patient who is encouraged to speak for himself is more likely to reveal his understanding of the situation.

Just as the way in which the doctor talks to his patient has implications for diagnosis and treatment, so also the way the psychologist deals with his subject has implications for the model of man which the psychologist constructs. Shotter (1975) suggests that psychologists, by virtue of the nature of their activities, help to create a particular image of Man within society. If psychological theories treat the person wholly as a mechanism or wholly as an organism, rather than a conscious, willing, and responsible source of action, then society's view or image of man will reflect this limited view.

Consider psychosomatic disorders. If one thinks wholly in terms of autonomic nervous system imbalance or biochemical disturbance, then one tends to forget the psychological world of the patient. Yet the expression of emotion is filtered through layers of experience and learning, through the individual's past experience and expectations of future experience. The thinking, perceiving, and decision-making model of the person cannot be separated from his physiology.

It is worth mentioning that Schultz and Silverman do not limit their arguments to mere expediency, to the contamination of experimental data by inappropriate research strategies. They also claim that the treatment of the subject has moral or ethical implications, leading to a diminution of the subject as a human being and invading his rights of personal dignity and privacy. Even if we do not agree with this value-judgement it would be difficult to deny that if the *subject* resents what he sees as an invasion of his privacy, then he is unlikely to provide a direct and frank response. We shall return to these points later when we offer advice on experimental technique.

What we hope we have made clear so far is that the particular view which the experimenter holds of the subject will affect: recruitment, population sampling, subject response to the experimenter, subject expectations, subject willingness to participate, the quality of experimenter–subject interaction, the design of the laboratory as a place in which to conduct research, the nature of the tasks employed, the duration of sampling of responses, the provision of feedback to the subject, the instructions given, the classes of data gathered, the manner in which they are gathered, and the ways in which they are interpreted.

SOME STRENGTHS AND WEAKNESSES IN CONTEMPORARY PSYCHOPHYSIOLOGY

In this brief section we apply some of the points we have made so far to a context with which we are familiar: the use of the laboratory in psychophysiological research, and the characteristics of certain forms of psychophysiological research which, we believe, adopt too narrow a view of the person.

In a later section we shall see how useful psychophysiological methods may be in the very appraisal of the psychological experiment itself. Chapman's studies (see p. 376 below) indicate how simple measures of bodily activity reflect subtle changes in procedure, and the differing views of the experimenter held by the subject. These techniques enable us to obtain an unique and non-intrusive running record of the subject's emotional response to the experimental situation. This helps us to pinpoint those aspects of the situation which might or might not be of importance in terms of the total variance observed. However, psychophysiology is more than a technique, or mere handmaiden for improving other methodologies. Psychophysiology is said to be of value for its own sake, acting as a potential bridgebuilder and integrating different approaches within psychology. Although anchored to a biological approach, its concern with human subjects, rather than the infra-human species studied by physiological psychology, enables psychophysiology to sample also the experiential and behavioural domains. At the same time, there is a long-standing concern not only with general laws of behaviour but with individual variations. Psycho-physiological measures provide a rich database for both ipsative and normative scoring; it enables us to adopt both an ideographic and a nomothetic approach. Nor is psychophysiology locked within the individual; there is a recognition of the social origins of behaviour and the importance of other persons as psychological stimuli. In the context of psychopathology in particular, the psychophysiologist has been obliged to recognize that patient groups exhibit behavioural and experiential anomalies as well as disruption of the patterning of physiological response. Thus the potential for a synthesis of a variety of approaches to the person is considerable. In the early days of psychophysiology the pioneers addressed several major problems. More recently, however, there has been considerable preoccupation with electronic hardware and problems of quantification. Recent developments in electronics and computing have put many of these problems behind us, however, and psychophysiology is ready for a great leap forward. We are rather concerned that researchers in the field are too preoccupied with the physiological to remember the other aspects of the person. All too frequently, physiological indices of response are the only dependent variables. Subtle measures of performance are rare, and very few subjects are asked to indicate changes of emotion *experienced* during the experiment. We have a suspicion that many of our colleagues do think of subjects as a stimulus–response lump. To the reader this may seem like a private and somewhat academic battle, but as we have already suggested the sampling of both the physiological and the experiential is essential to the development of models of psychosomatic disorders. There is a more lengthy discussion of this problem in Gale (1973) and Gale (1980).

Psychophysiological laboratories, in their very construction, reflect a lack of sensitivity to the feelings of the subject. There is often no attempt even in pur-pose-built constructions to conceal from the subject's view the electronic gadgetry, flashing lights, meters and other gear which may make the laboratory reminiscent of a Frankensteinian cellar. We would argue that it should look like a drawing room! But taking inspiration from the Pavlovian experimental chamber, the psychophysiologist sometimes encases his subjects alone in a soundproofed cubicle which resembles an enormous meat safe, and locks him in, with a thump of chromium handles and bolts. More often than not, the subject sits or lies supine on a dentist-type chair, passive and physically inactive, and trussed up with wires and transducers. Imagine introducing to a situation like this a patient suffering from anxiety, in the hope that you may measure his spontaneous responses to some mild form of stimulation! Generally, before the experiment begins there is a 'rest' period, during which the subject is said to subside, physiologically, to some sort of baseline. This notion seems to us to be based on the principle that the longer you wait for the unexpected, the more relaxed will you feel. In many cases, the experimenter cannot tell the whole story before the procedure begins, so that the waiting period before the first critical experimental event occurs could be as long as half an hour; even an experienced operator takes time to instal his electrodes and check that his records are artifact-free.

Gale and Smith (1980), while preparing a brief for the construction of laboratories, conducted a survey of a large sample of psychophysiologists. One of the topic headings on their questionnaire was 'the psychosocial environment'. Many respondents simply ignored this aspect, preferring to consider problems of computer installation, soundproofing, air-conditioning and electrical interference. Only two respondents wrote in any detail about the problems of dealing with subjects as people, and with training assistants to adopt the sort of attitudes towards *rapport* which are common currency in psychometric testing. We suspect that the predominant emotion felt in a psychophysiological experiment is anxiety which undoubtedly, in the case of clinical groups, is likely to be accentuated. This problem can of course be overcome. One can spend time with subjects, conceal the more frightening parts of the apparatus, explain what the experiment is about, and delay the taking of measurements proper for a second visit. So many studies are based upon data derived from the person's very first visit to the laboratory. One of the best ways to keep the subject's mind away from extraneous aspects of the experimental environment is to give him a challenging and interesting task to perform.

To complete this section, we insert an extract from an earlier review by Gale (1973) of studies of extraversion and the EEG.

> Let us consider what happens to the subject when he enters the psycho-physiological laboratory, and in addition what he may feel or think before, during and after the visit. Firstly, how exactly did he come to be there? He may be responding to an advertisement in the student newspaper, he may have received a letter telling him that he was selected at random from the university list, he may have been asked to come during a tutorial meeting, he may have been accosted on the campus by a complete stranger, he may have been asked to volunteer

in a lecture. How then does the subject perceive the experimenter? Is this a research assistant doing a job, or a postgraduate student doing this for a higher degree, or a lecturer who is in the position to evaluate me? Such factors, I suggest, must affect the way in which the subject perceives and interprets the demand characteristics of the task and also the extent of his cooperation. Again, if he has heard that psychologists on the campus are conducting experiments which involve deception, he may be suspicious of the nature of the experiment and may even have decided from the outset to pretend to cooperate while inwardly scowling with amusement. He sees, as he comes in, a number of electronic gadgets equipped with moving parts and flashing lights. He is informed that he is to be attached to this machinery. He is informed that no harm will come to him. Strange or unusually smelling substances are rubbed into his skin. He may have been asked to remove some part of his clothing. Electrodes are placed on to him and wires clipped on to them. In all probability, he has been placed in a room which is devoid of stimulation; possibly, the lights are turned out and he is shut in and alone. If the cubicle is not perfectly sound-proofed, he may hear persons commenting on *his* brainwaves, or *his* heartbeat, they may talk of getting 'rid of the hum' or 'switching up the gain' and so on. May we now speculate about what this person is thinking? The situation bears fair resemblance to a projective test. He may, in fact, be asking of himself the sorts of things the subject is asked to ask of a TAT picture. 'Who are these people? What do they want? What is going to happen? Why are they here?' A number of possible thoughts, questions, statements and answers may be running through his head. 'This is horrible. This isn't as bad as I thought. This is a waste of time. When is it going to end? What is going to happen? Are my brain waves normal? Can they see anything wrong with them? What will he think of me if I don't do things correctly? She's very attractive, I wonder if I could ask her for a date? It was rather nice when she rubbed the jelly in. I said I understood when he told me the instructions, but now I'm here, I'm not sure that I do understand. What exactly is this experiment trying to measure? I hate it in this dark room. How nice it is to lie back and relax. Now what was that problem I was working on before I came in? Did I put jam on the shopping list? Ouch, what a horrible noise. Oh, that one wasn't too bad. What a bore, I hope it will finish soon. I just can't keep my mind free, I hope it doesn't matter. I'm tempted to count the tones. I can't stand this any longer. This is all pointless. What a ridiculous way to spend a morning. Is that a fan I hear. It's getting close in here; I hope my deodorant works. Am I really supposed to do nothing? Oh dear, I nodded off; I wonder if they can tell. Shall I say anything afterwards?'

We may well ask upon reading this, are there really such things as 'resting' levels? Looked at from the phenomenological point of view, the subject is not only not at rest but is free to undergo a broad range of experiential events. He is certainly not under stimulus control. He is no less 'mentally active' than he would be during a nightmare.

EXPERIMENTER EFFECTS

Rosenthal has distinguished between two types of experimenter effect; experimenter bias induced by knowledge of the hypothesis he is testing (as in the 'maze-bright' rat study), and experimenter attributes. We do not have room here to redocument Rosenthal's well-known studies of experimenter expectancy. These have been dealt with extensively, and an excellent summary, so far as psychophysiology is concerned, is to be found in Christie and Todd (1975). We are concerned here with the attributes of the experimenter, and in particular, sex of experimenter, as an important aspect of the laboratory situation. As we shall show below, sex effects have been identified as a source of error, by a number of workers, and recent psychophysiological data provide a moderately consistent picture. As we have already pointed out, the psychological experiment may be regarded as a social situation in which the interaction between subject and experimenter has implications for experimental outcome. However, as Silverman has pointed out (1974) experimenter sex effects are still ignored by most researchers. In psychophysiological studies, experimenter–subject interactions are particularly important since the procedures may involve bodily contact, partial removal of clothing, skin abrasion, touching, and application and removal of electrodes. In such a situation the subject's personal space is invaded in a manner which would only be tolerated from an intimate, or in the constrained environment of the medical practitioner's consulting room. If such an intrusion is mishandled it could contribute to the depersonalizing of the subject both in his own mind and in the mind of the experimenter. The subject may feel 'my body is being treated as an object' while the experimenter may adopt the view that this other person's body is merely a surface for electrodes. The subject might infer that indeed he is to behave like a machine; one way in which he is able to produce the data which theory demands of him.

Of course, the situation is not straightforward, because it has unique properties. Could the subject (or the experimenter) feel 'natural' in such a situation? Invasion of personal space by a stranger of either sex is likely to raise all sorts of confusion and anxiety in the subject. The experimenter is likely to develop a stereotypic pattern of behaviour, including an allegedly reassuring, but probably anxiety-inducing patter, following a script which becomes progressively less convincing as more and more subjects pass through the laboratory. Needless to say, although psychophysiology is a special case, it is not so special that similar effects will not be found under other laboratory conditions.

The data from earlier studies concerning the effects of experimenter sex are equivocal. Cieutat (1965) has shown, for example, that a female experimenter elicited better intellectual performance from subjects than did a male experimenter, while Rikli (1976) found that male experimenters tended to receive better overall performance from subjects. However, both the type of task and the age of subjects differed. Rikli used sporting tasks, with an older population. Such studies raised three difficulties. Firstly, reviewers of the literature agree (Rumenik, Capasso, and Hendrick, 1977) that sex effects are most frequently seen with younger subjects. Secondly, many such experiments confound sex of experimenter with possible attributes of *particular* experimenters, since only one experimenter of each sex is employed. Of 63 studies reviewed by Rumenik *et al.*, only 39 employed at least two experimenters of each sex. They recommend that any statistical analysis should be conducted taking individual experimenters as separate levels within a factor, rather than collapsing data across sex. As Rumenik *et al.* conclude: 'If sex differences affect role relations outside of the laboratory, it is unrealistic to expect such influences suddenly to cease to exist within an experiment.'

However an equally crucial variable is the type of task employed. Some experimental tasks are difficult and challenging, while the majority are simpleminded and boring. As we shall see, Zajonc's (1965) social facilitation theory predicts differential performance effects for difficult and simple tasks, as a function of physiological arousal level within the subject. The fluctuations in arousal in this context will be induced by the presence of another person (the experimenter, or other subjects). Moreover, proximity and degree of eye contact have also been shown to affect the level of arousal of the subject (Gale *et al.*, 1975).

AND SUBJECT SEX EFFECTS

A number of more recent and unpublished psychophysiological studies indicate quite consistently that male subjects are more aroused than females. Baker (1978) tested subjects alone or in pairs, with friends or strangers, and under competitive and non-competitive instructions. Female pairs, although aroused by competition, were typically less aroused than males, particularly when paired with a friend. In a smaller-scale study, using only one male and one female experimenter, the male experimenter was shown to be more arousing than the female. Gale, Kingsley, and Smith (1978) obtained both sex-of-experimenter and sex-of-subject effects in two studies. One employed two experimenters of each sex, and the other employed the subjects as their partner's confederate, measuring physiological responses in both partners. Again female subjects were less aroused, and female experimenters or confederates induced less arousal. These physiological data were confirmed by ratings derived from the Thayer High Activation Scale. Hevey (1981) has obtained similar results. Her most arousing condition involved a combination of male experimenter with male subject. However, whereas Baker, and Gale *et al.*, employed only the EEG as their indicator of arousal, Hevey used a number of physiological measures, not all of which yielded identical results. The next stage in such studies (given their consistency) is to examine the situation in more detail, to determine what characteristics of subject and experimenter bring about the effects. Are there differences either in the behaviour of experimenters of different sex, or in the evaluation of the situation by subjects of different sex, which leads females to be less aroused? Rosenthal (1967) suggests that male experimenters are more friendly and that they are more protective in their treatment of female subjects in particular. According to Singer and Llewellyn (1973) there is a tendency for subjects to be more affected by experimenters of the opposite sex, and this is particularly true for female subjects (Gall and Mendelsohn, 1966). One of the studies which contradicts recent psychophysiological work is that by Fisher and Kotses (1974), who showed female experimenters to be *more* arousing. They account for this result in terms of the novelty effect of encountering a female experimenter in a male-dominated laboratory environment. In our own work, experimenter and subject sex effects are considerable when compared with other experimental manipulations. We would therefore wish to agree with Rumenik *et al.*'s conclusion that experimental designs should include control for both sex-of-experimenter and sex-of-subject effects, even if this involves considerable expense. Those who fund research need to be convinced, however, that such precautions are essential. Until these effects have been studied extensively, we cannot tell how influential they might be across the range of psychological enquiry.

THEORETICAL VIEWPOINTS RELEVANT TO THE LABORATORY SITUATION

In this section we turn psychology in upon itself to investigate the experimental situation. Theoretical constructs like social facilitation, evaluation apprehension, and attribution are clearly relevant, since experimental studies always involve the presence of others, the measurement of the behaviour of one person by another, and the interpretation of the meaning of interaction by the subject.

For a great deal of our lives our time is spent with others and it could be argued that many of the adaptive responses of our nervous system are designed to facilitate interaction. We are all aware that our behaviour varies from context to context. The public face we adopt in communicating with colleagues differs from the private face reserved for close friends, family members, and intimates. Zajonc's theory of 1965 was an essentially biological theory to explain why the individual's behaviour when he is alone is different from his behaviour in company. Certain responses are facilitated in the presence of others. The concept of arousal is central to the theory, for other persons—by their mere presence—are said to arouse us, physiologically. Potential responses to situations are said to be organized in hierarchies, and increased arousal leads to the emission of the most probable response. In complex or novel situations such responses, developed for more familiar contexts, may well be quite inappropriate. High levels of arousal, in novel or complex situations, will then disrupt performance. This socially induced arousal will of course be of benefit in familiar situations and in the performance of simple tasks.

The laboratory presents a novel, confusing, and puzzling situation to the subject. He is required by the other person present to perform tasks with which he is unfamiliar. Under such conditions, therefore, he is likely to produce inappropriate responses, which are not the responses he would produce were he unaffected by the extraneous factors. The sample of the behaviour taken by the experimenter is a sample of high-probability responses which are not necessarily those which the subject might give to the task in question under less threatening circumstances. For such an explanation of the subject's behaviour, one requires more than Zajonc's notion of the mere presence of others. The function of the encounter, the evaluation of the subject by the experimenter, and the subject's interpretation of the purpose of the experiment need to be taken into account. Rosenberg (1969) used the term 'evaluation apprehension' to describe the person's anxiety about what others think of him. This will apply to the subject whether his performance is evaluated explicitly (as in an intelligence test) or not. The notion of evaluation anxiety is seen to apply to the whole person rather than to some minor aspect of his behaviour. Chapman (1973) demonstrated that muscle tension and reported feelings of being evaluated were increased when the subject listened to humorous material via a publicly audible loudspeaker, rather than through personal headphones. In neither situation was there any explicit indication that his response to the material was to be judged in any way. The mere fact that under the loudspeaker condition both the humorous material and the subject's responses to it were publicly available, induced arousal and evaluation anxiety. The notion of evaluation anxiety can be used to explain differences in our behaviour with different groups of people. Friendship, prior acquaintance, status, working relationships, and so on, imply different levels of potential evaluation and facilitate or constrain our behaviour accordingly. We would argue that the testing situation is an extreme example. The presence of others and the notion of evaluation anxiety are difficult to overcome in the laboratory. It does not matter whether the experimenter is actually present in the room or not, there will always be a lesser or greater residue of anxiety. However, speculation about physiological arousal and evaluation anxiety does not tell the full story; we have not yet considered the subject's cognitive responses to the testing situation. Generally speaking, the experimenter alone knows the true purpose of the experiment and it is left to the subject to deduce its real nature. Sometimes, of course, he has to be deliberately deceived. Social psychologists have employed the notion of attribution to describe the way in which we interpret the causes of events. Orne (1962) contends that subjects are strongly motivated to discover the experimenter's intention in bringing them to the laboratory. The subject seeks for cues from the experimental situation and the experimenter's behaviour in order to explain his reason for being there. This is just a special case of the general perceptual principle outlined by Bartlett (1932) whereby we seek to make situations meaningful. The very ambiguity and novelty of the experimental situation increases 'effort after meaning'. Orne (1962) claims that there are three stages in the subject's encounter with the laboratory: determining the 'demand characteristics', setting up a hypothesis, and then validating it. This hypothesis may of course have nothing to do with the *real* intention of the experiment, but it determines the pattern of the subject's responses.

In testing Sokolovian and related models of the orientation reaction, many psychophysiologists have placed their subjects in just this type of ambiguous situation. Subjects are told to relax, but not go to sleep, that they will hear noises to which they do not need to attend, and that they must keep their minds 'clear of thoughts'. Having prepared the subject for physiological recording, the experimenter then exposes him to short bursts of sound at widely spaced and irregular intervals. We have calculated that in the typical habituation of the orientation reaction experiment, the subject is exposed to explicit stimulation for only 3 per cent of the total experimental time. There is a current controversy in the psychophysiological literature as to whether one needs to resort to cognitive interpretations to explain the experimental data! We have argued that the best psychophysiological experiments involve those situations in which the subject is actively involved in an interesting and challenging (but not threatening) task. Baker's data (1978) indicate that the presence of another person to share the experience goes some way to reducing the subject's arousal. It is our impression that situations which are easily understood and enjoyed by the subject lead to fewer problems of measurement; the muscle artifacts which seem to worry so many psychophysiological researchers do not worry us.

We argue, therefore, that one needs to have a psychological model of the psychology experiment, and to apply to it relevant aspects of social psychological theory, if one is to appreciate fully what goes on in the laboratory environment and to construct meaningful experiments. In psychophysiology, and in psychophysiological studies of psychosomatics in particular, one is concerned with measuring responses to stimuli which have emotional meaning. It is therefore essential that one is able to partial out emotions that the subject brings with him from those which arise merely from attending the laboratory and acting as a subject from those which are truly triggered by the experimental stimuli.

To aid us in our own research we have developed a model which incorporates the different types of emotional arousal which we believe are present and operate upon the data which emerge from our polygraph. We deal with this model briefly in the following section. A more extensive account is given by Gale (1977), when an attempt is made to weave a body of data within the model, and by Spratt and Gale (1979) in relation to data derived from schizophrenic patients.

AN AROUSAL MODEL FOR THE LABORATORY ENVIRONMENT

Many psychophysiological data have been confounded by a failure to recognize that not only is the laboratory a strange and possibly hostile environment, but that dynamic changes occur within the subject as a function of being in the laboratory and as a function of becoming used or adapted to the laboratory. We have already considered above the accepted distinction of 'rest' and 'task' periods. There we argued that this distinction was probably invalid. While waiting for the task to commence, the subject is probably in a state of curious (if not anxious) anticipation. The quality of this anticipation will be determined by the subject's perception of the laboratory and the demand characteristics. It is hardly a period of 'rest', nor is it free from contamination with perceived characteristics of the task. Nor is this just a matter of terminology since such 'rest' periods are typically taken as baseline periods against which to estimate the degree of response to the explicit stimuli which the experimenter later presents. We believe, even so, that the distinction between 'task' and 'rest' falls far short of the number of categories of experimental phases which are required. Our model is a simple serial cumulative model, with nine separate stages, first described by Gale (1977). The components of the model are element-ary and perhaps rather obvious, and they are based not only on our own research but upon a long history of data and theory. As yet our model has been used *post hoc* to explain data, and has not yet been subjected to rigorous test; how-ever we think it makes sense. Although the model was devised to handle data from psychophysiological experiments we see no reason why it should not apply equally well to psychological experiments in general.

The nine components of the model are labelled as follows. First, there is the arousal that comes from the stable and relatively permanent characteristics of the subject; that is, arousal differences associated with sex, first-order personality differences (e.g. extraversion–introversion), and some forms of chronic patho-logy or levels which may be induced by prolonged periods of institutional life (e.g. in chronic schizophrenia). The subject brings this type of arousal to the laboratory with him. Quite often such traits may be those which the experi-menter wishes to explore. Our argument is that if he ignores *other* sources of arousal (which we come to below) then these stable sources may become washed out in the data. At the same time these permanent characteristics, even if they are not the concern of the experimenter, can inflate the error term if they are ignored. Eysenck has argued on several occasions that studies which do not account for individual differences throw out the baby with the bathwater of the error term. If it is claimed that permanent traits like extraversion—introversion account for a significant proportion of the variance of everyday behaviour, then it is likely that they will account for a detectable proportion of the variance in the laboratory. Thus our first sort of arousal, coming from permanent characteristics, can either be a key factor which is influenced by other sources of arousal, or be a source of confounding itself.

Secondly, there is arousal which varies with naturally recurring rhythms, such as the menstrual cycle and circadian changes. For example there are several demonstrations of the effect of time of day upon arousal and the efficiency of human performance. It has even been suggested that women volunteer to participate in experiments at particular times of the menstrual cycle! In the case of clinical groups, fluctuations in arousal may occur as a function of pattern and type of medication; thus long-acting treatment with major tranquillizers will lead to fluctuations in state both prior to and following medication. Such fluctuations are not, of course, 'natural' but they are often beyond the experimenter's control. Again, this second source of arousal is brought, by the subject, to the laboratory with him. The skilful experimenter will consider in advance whether such sources of variation are likely to affect his experiment. He can ignore them, examine them for their own intrinsic interest, or adopt designs which allow for their effects.

Thirdly, there is the manner in which subjects are recruited and the effect this has upon their expectations when they arrive. The experimenter should prepare his recruitment campaign very carefully, deciding what exactly is to be revealed, how long subjects might be expected to spend in the laboratory, and so on. If the method of recruiting is too anxiety-inducing then it will, of course, serve to eliminate certain subjects at the outset. Spratt (1975), following the pertinent comments of Venables (1967), spent several weeks working with psychiatric patients in an occupational therapy unit before he invited them to visit his laboratory. Thus his intention was to become known as a reasonable and non-threatening person, before he raised the matter of participation in his experiments.

Then fourthly is the arousal which comes from the subject's initial encounter with the laboratory. Sensitivity to this source of arousal is crucial in the design of studies with patients and other special-criterion groups. We have referred earlier to some of the way in which the individual might respond upon initial encounter with a psychophysiological laboratory. Spratt, following the suggestions in Venables (1967), studied the effect of repeated visits to the laboratory in his carefully selected group of schizophrenic patients, whom he had already come to know quite well. Nevertheless, they were very highly aroused on their first visit, performed at tasks very poorly, and showed little systematic physiological response to the experimental stimuli. This was not the case for a control group of non-hospitalized subjects of similar age and socioeconomic status. On the second visit, however, the patients were significantly less aroused than on the first occasion, were able to perform the tasks set to them, and showed physiological responses to stimuli in a manner which did not differentiate them from other groups. Spratt argued that theories about high levels of arousal in chronic schizophrenics and about the effects of high levels of arousal upon selective attention should have led exactly to these results. In other words one would expect any first visit by patients to a novel environment to be quite disruptive of attentional processes. His patients knew him well, had expressed willingness to participate, and had come only a short distance to his laboratory. One wonders how many 'facts' about performance and physiological response in schizophrenics are based upon a sudden, possibly unwarned, and single visit? Yet theories about schizophrenia, based upon such data, refer to the patient's life as a whole, not just to his response to frightening experiences. A characteristic of Spratt's work is his commitment to treating schizophrenic patients as persons rather than patients.

The fifth component in the model is the arousal which is associated with processes of task-acquisition, and grasping what the psychometrician calls the conventions of the test. A standard intelligence test which you may have performed is the AH5; this has a practice session which can take almost half the time to complete and score as the test itself. Mental testers seem to be much more aware than are experimental psychologists of the need to establish rapport and ensure that the subject really knows what he has to do and what is expected of him. Mental testers also have a concept of 'face validity' which is a measure of the apparent authenticity of the test, for they recognize that subjects will be unwilling to co-operate when the test looks silly or irrelevant to its professed purpose. Our own experience is that the life of the psycho-physiologist is more complicated than that of the tester, since he also has his apparatus to worry about; therefore it is tempting to want to get on with things and rush the subject through the procedure, before there is any risk of equipment faults developing!

The sixth sort of arousal comes with task mastery. As people become accustomed to the task their level of arousal alters. Again, sampling could occur at the wrong point in time for a particular function, for a particular subject. Inspection of most time-in-task data reveals a shift in arousal level or performance level as a function of time (e.g. Gale, Davies, and Smallbone, 1977). Thus a testing schedule which involves strict standardization of procedure for all subjects might capture some at the task mastery stage, while others are still acquiring the task.

The seventh source of arousal within our sequential model is the one to which researchers typically pay exclusive attention (ignoring the previous six!), and we call it task-specific arousal. Some tasks increase activation with time, others induce a decrease, while yet others are said to maintain a stable level. Thus vigilance tasks typically show a decline in performance over time which is said to be associated with decreased levels of arousal. In short-term memory tasks, performance can improve during the session.

The eighth component we call situational arousal. This is a bit of a mixed bag and includes extraneous sources as well as explicit aspects of the procedure. Thus it necessitates consideration of whether the subject performs alone or close to another person, the sex of the experimenter, the atmosphere of the laboratory, provision of incentives or punishments, the general ambiance, and so on. We have described how some of our own studies have focused on this aspect. Presence of others, sharing the situation, appears to have relaxing effects upon subjects so long as explicit competition is absent. The availability of other stimulation might well affect subjects, particularly when the task employed takes up only a small part of their field of attention. For example, in his review of studies of the relationship between extraversion–introversion and the EEG, Gale (1973) points out that the discrepant results in the literature can be accounted for in terms of the amount of stimulation available, particularly since extraverts are said to be 'stimulus-hungry'. In most of these experiments subjects are merely required to lie still with their eyes closed and 'do nothing'. Gale argues that extraverts, being already low-aroused, are obliged to cogitate if they are to keep awake; introverts, already high-aroused, are glad of the relief from stimulation which such boring experimental conditions allow. Thus, contrary to prediction, many studies have shown extraverts to be high-aroused and introverts to be low-aroused. The experimenters were measuring our eighth component rather than the first!

Finally we have arousal which comes from feedback, either explicit from the procedure or the task, or given to the subject by himself. The feedback need not be an overt characteristic of the task but may be conveyed inadvertently by the experimenter or interpreted on the basis of his performance, by the subject. This notion of feedback includes self-evaluation, evaluation anxiety and aspects of self-esteem. We assume that physiological arousal does alter in association with our feelings of pride, disappointment, or even persistence in the light of apparent failure. This ninth component completes our model of the sources of arousal that operate during an experimental session. To summarize the different sources, they are: stable characteristics, rhythmic variation, manner of recruitment, laboratory encounter, task acquisition, task mastery, task specific, situational, and feedback.

Let us assume that each of these types of arousal is associated with a physiological *response* to a specific stimulus. Such a response will be characterized by differential threshold, rise time, peak amplitude, dwell time, recovery period, and perhaps homeostatic overshoot. It may also be followed by a period of refractoriness. It is then difficult to think of our model as merely sequential; it also has cumulative properties. Even putting aside the thorny problem of the distinction between arousal and arousability, we can see that each earlier stage has a potential to influence later stages. Unless each type of arousal is allowed to decay below threshold, then we have a complex and interactive situation since later sources of arousal in the sequence are influenced by antecedent states. If Spratt had stopped his research after his subjects' first visit, then he might have concluded that schizophrenic patients are so chronically over-aroused that they can do virtually nothing which involved attention. Laboratory encounter arousal could have been confounded with trait arousal. Of course this does not apply merely to psychiatric groups; even undergraduates can feel anxious.

One can see that the full demonstration of our model calls for an extensive laboratory study. However we wish to suggest that the model is plausible, that teasing out the various components of arousal might be a worthwhile enterprise, and that in psychosomatic research in particular, the model needs careful attention. The key question to ask is: 'If I have demonstrated increased or decreased arousal in this or that experimental group, what is the arousal *in response to*?'

SOME ADVICE ON RESEARCH TACTICS

If the reader has followed our arguments and thinks them sound, then the next section will not be surprising. In the space available we shall limit ourselves to a brief list. This will not represent the full picture but will act as a schematic guide.

(1) When you design your experiment, think exactly what it is you wish to measure and what it is you wish to exclude. If you wish to do a laboratory study, consider the ecological validity of your procedure. For example, do you use standard stimuli or tailor them carefully for each subject; in the case of phobias, say, will you choose 'general phobic stimuli' like spiders or homicide slides, or ask the subjects themselves to provide the stimuli which are fear-provoking for them.

(2) In selecting subjects, ask whether it matters to your hypothesis whether you sample the general population, or limit yourself to a highly specific group? You may consider whether large numbers are essential or whether re-repeated visits from a few individuals might generate data more relevant to your hypothesis. They will certainly provide more stable data.

(3) Always try out your procedure first; never rush headlong into testing. Act as your own subject, asking a friend to be experimenter. Ask yourself and colleagues who act as guinea pigs: 'What is my response to this situation, what would my response be if I were a complete stranger to my laboratory?'

(4) Spend a great deal of time preparing your laboratory, so that it looks a pleasant place to be in. Draft several recruitment letters or posters, try several versions of your experimental instructions, and practise again and again the routine to be followed when subjects arrive.

(5) There is now a great deal of evidence to show that single experimenters might have a profound influence on outcome. Consider the costs and benefits of training and even paying different experimenters; your decision will depend very much upon the nature of the investigation. We suspect that, in the case of clinical groups, the individual experimenter can be a crucial source of variance.

(6) Treat subjects as visitors to your home, rather than objects to be used and discarded. Try not to be defensive when asked questions and give your subject time and opportunity to express his doubts and worries. When the experiment is over, provide an opportunity for him to record his personal response; and take note of it.

(7) Do not limit yourself merely to physiological measurement. This will provide you with a very limited database which will be difficult to interpret.

(8) Pace your experiment very much to the population you are testing. You may be used to testing student subjects at a rapid rate. Psychiatric patients might well need a morning or afternoon each.

(9) Try to use an interesting and absorbing task; this not only gives a straight-forward and unambiguous meaning to the experiment for the subject, but provides a means of eliminating distraction either arising from his own anxieties or from the experimental environment.

(10) Finally, without being too masochistic, engage in regular sessions of

self-questioning about your procedures. It is very easy to deceive oneself that nothing is wrong. However, the more experience one has of research the more one realizes that its purpose seems to be to teach you to do research better next time!

If you follow these guidelines we believe you will be able to overcome some of the problems which arise in laboratory environments. We must emphasize that demonstrations of artifact do not invalidate procedures. Even a statistically significant experimenter effect may not account for very much for the total variance observed. The art is to locate these sources of error and control for them. Many of the artifacts identified in the laboratory will have their counterparts in field studies. The choice of a context for your experimentation depends very much on a complex decision-making process. In the case of psychological disorders the laboratory has probably produced some very misleading data; however, we do not consider this to be a *necessary* consequence of using a laboratory.

Experimentation is an art as well as a science; the artist takes many years to develop his skill.

REFERENCES

Baker, S. M. (1978). Social facilitation, coaction and performance. Unpublished Ph.D. thesis, University of Wales.

Bartlett, F. C. (1932). *Remembering: A Study in Experimental and Social Psychology*. Cambridge: Cambridge University Press.

Chapman, A. J. (1973). An electromyographic study of apprehension about evaluation. *Psychological Reports*, **33**, 811–814.

Christie, M. J., and Todd, J. L. (1975). Experimenter–subject–situational interactions. In P. H. Venables, and M. J. Christie (eds.) *Research in Psychophysiology*, pp. 50–68. London: Wiley.

Cieutat, V. J. (1965). Examiner differences with the Stanford–Binet I. Q. *Perceptual and Motor Skills*, **20**, 317–318.

Fisher, L. E., and Kotses, H. (1974). Experimenter and subject sex effects in the skin conductance response. *Psychophysiology*, **11**, 191–196.

Gale, A. (1973). The psychophysiology of individual differences: studies of extraversion and the EEG. In P. Kline, (ed.), *New Approaches in Psychological Measurement*. London: Wiley. pp. 211–256.

Gale, A. (1977). Some EEG correlates of sustained attention. In R. R. Mackie, (ed.), *Vigilance: Theory, Operational Performance and Physiological Correlates*, New York: Plenum Press, pp. 263–283.

Gale, A. (1980). Psychophysiology: a bridge between disciplines. (Inaugural Lecture). University of Southampton.

Gale, A., Davies, R., and Smallbone, A. (1977). EEG correlates of signal rate, time in task and individual differences in reaction time during a five-stage sustained attention task. *Ergonomics*, **20**, 363–376.

Gale, A., Kingsley, E., and Smith, D. G. (1978). Effects of experimenter and subject sex upon the EEG. Paper presented at the Annual Conference of the Social Psychology Section of the British Psychological Society.

Gale, A., and Smith, D. G. (1980). On setting up a psychophysiological laboratory. In

I. Martin and P. H. Venables (eds.), *Techniques in Psychophysiology*. London: Wiley. pp. 565–582.

Gale, A., Spratt, G. S., Chapman, A., and Smallbone, A. (1975). EEG correlates of eye contact and interpersonal distance. *Biological Psychology*, 3, 237–245.

Gall, M., and Mendelsohn, G. A. (1966). Effects of facilitating techniques and subject–experimenter interaction on creative problem solving. Unpublished manuscript, University of California, Berkeley.

Hevey, D. (1981). Social interactional aspects of psychophysiological experiments. Unpublished Ph.D. thesis, University of Southampton.

Jung, J. (1969). Current practices and problems in the use of college students for psychological research. *Canadian Psychologist*, 10, 280–290.

Orne, M. T. (1962). On the social psychology of the psychology experiment: with particular reference to demand characteristics and their implications. *American Psychologist*, 17, 776–783.

Rikli, R. (1976). Physical performance scores as a function of experimenter sex and experimenter bias. *Research Quarterly*, 47, 776–783.

Rosenberg, M. J. (1969). The conditions and consequences of evaluation apprehension. In R. Rosenthal and R. Rosnow (eds.), *Artifact in Behavioral Research*, New York: Academic Press, pp. 280–349.

Rosenthal, R. (1967). Covert communication in the psychological experiment. *Psychological Bulletin*, 67, 357–367.

Rosenthal, R., and Rubin, D. B. (1978). Interpersonal expectancy effects: the first 345 studies. *Behavioral and Brain Sciences*, 3, 377–415.

Rumenik, D. K., Capasso, D. R., and Hendrick, C. (1977). Experimenter sex effects in behavioral research. *Psychological Bulletin*, 84, 852–877.

Schultz, D. P. (1969). The human subject in psychological research. *Psychological Bulletin*, 72, 214–228.

Shotter, J. (1975). *Images of Man in Psychological Research*. London: Methuen.

Silverman, I. (1974). The experimenter: a (still) neglected stimulus object. *Canadian Psychologist*, 15, 258–270.

Silverman, I. (1977). *The Human Subject in the Psychological Laboratory*. New York: Pergamon Press.

Singer, R. N., and Llewellyn, J. H. (1973). Effects of experimenter's gender on subjects' performance. *Research Quarterly*, 44, 185–191.

Smart, R. (1966). Subject selection bias in psychological research. *Canadian Psychologist*, 7a, 115–121.

Spratt, G. S. (1975). EEG Correlates of attention in schizophrenic persons. Unpublished Ph.D. thesis, University of Wales.

Spratt, G. S., and Gale, A. (1979). An EEG study of visual attention in schizophrenic patients and normal controls. *Biological Psychology*, 9, 244–269.

Venables, P. H. (1967). Partial failure of cortical–subcortical integration as a factor underlying schizophrenic behaviour. In Romano, J. (ed.), *The Origins of Schizophrenia*. Amsterdam: Excerpta Medica Foundation.

Zajonc, R. B. (1965). Social facilitation. *Science*, 149, 269–274.

Foundations of Psychosomatics
Edited by M. J. Christie and P. G. Mellett
© 1981 John Wiley & Sons Ltd.

18

THE TREATMENT ENVIRONMENT

ALISTAIR M. GORDON
The Retreat, York, England

INTRODUCTION

Environmental psychology is a relatively recent field of scientific study (Insel and Moos, 1974), but its origins can be traced to the expanding concern with human ecology in this century. Social ecology focuses particularly on the interaction between man and his environment, and many of its percepts are readily evidenced in our daily lives. We are all aware that environmental settings influence our behaviour. The physical attributes and social expectations of differing environments demand a range of behaviours specifically appropriate to their unique challenges. The work and the home environment evoke identifiably different behavioural responses; the public social setting inhibits behaviour appropriately displayed in a private social environment. Social ecology attempts to study this interaction of man with his social and physical environment, and to observe and measure the effect of such variables as the physical constraints of the environment, its organizational structure, the personal characteristics of its inhabitants, its emotional climate, and its functional objectives. The observations of social ecology have helped in identifying maladaptive behavioural patterns and their potential for response to modifications in the environment (Moos, 1974).

Hospitals as stressful environments have received less public attention than high-rise flats, council estates, traffic congestion, pollution, and the effects of natural or man-made disaster. Hospitals invoke two contrasting attitudinal reactions. In health they may provide a sense of reassurance against the threat of illness, but in sickness they present a more frightening aspect, symbolizing the apprehension of disease and death. Hospital staff may initially share these perceptions, but their occupational familiarity with the hospital environments, its sights, sounds, experiences, and techniques, allows them the time and opportunity to accustom themselves to the setting and develop the defences necessary to cope with its unique stresses. This psychological adjustment is necessary if they are to work with equanimity in the hospital environment but it may also handicap their ready perception of the impact of the hospital experience on their patients. Environments are instrumental in shaping adaptive behaviour, and while the hospital environment can facilitate coping behaviour in staff members, it may inhibit coping behaviour in patients who approach the environment with a different percept and in a different functional role.

In the past 20 years the expanding study of psychosomatic medicine has shown developing interest in the treatment environment as an influence in disease and its management (Lipowski, 1974). Sociologists have contributed to hospital design and planning (Brown, 1961). Psychophysiology has demonstrated that environment can effect physiological processes and psychologists have increased awareness that individual psychological differences are incompletely defined without attention to their environmental setting. Psychiatrists and physicians have described mental disturbances related to treatment experience (Kornfeld, 1972). The technological advances and increased use of apparative techniques have accentuated awareness of the stress in the hospital both for patients and staff, and revealed more clearly in the clinical setting that reactions to hospital environments do occur (Gordon, 1976). Aspects of the treatment environment which provide little challenge to the healthy person may develop a different significance in illness when the mental capacity for adaptation is impaired and the physical possibilities for modifying the environment are restricted. The scope of psychosocial investigation of the hospital environment has expanded rapidly. Earlier studies focused on objective physical features such as ward design (Thompson, 1955; Trites et al., 1969). The enormous complexity of environmental factors is now increasingly recognized, and a web of interacting events—the daily routine, the diagnostic tests, the nature of illness and treatment, the staff attitudes, the patient's experience and personality, the access to visitors, the decor, and facilities—all contribute to a subjective perception which determines emotional response to the hospital experience. Although objective physical features may be more readily defined, it is important to realize that a patient may not only be affected by the environment as it exists, but also by his subjective perception of the environment as it appears to be. Attention to the subjective experience of the treatment environment is not only valuable as a humane intervention. The mental and psychophysiological disturbances which are an accompaniment of emotional distress may influence the course of disease. Clinical states such as anxiety and depression affect electrolyte and endocrine balance with measurable physiological effects, particularly in neurological and cardiovascular functions. Studies of the treatment environment increase our understanding of the role of the hospital setting in re-establishing physical and mental well-being, and enhance patient care by defining the physical and social environment in which advancing technical skills may achieve their optimal efficacy.

THE METHODOLOGY OF TREATMENT ENVIRONMENT STUDIES

Treatment environments are difficult objects for investigation. Their extreme multifaceted complexity, and the intrinsic contribution of subjective perception to environmental responses, are factors which do not adapt readily to the systematic approaches of validated scientific method. The natural pattern of development of treatment environment studies is itself a handicap in research design. Treatment environments are not controlled research laboratory settings but living therapeutic environments where the claims of research validation dwindle in the face of urgent treatment needs. Studies are commonly inaugurated by a clinical observation of an extreme emotional reaction in a specific setting. Appraisal of the situation may suggest that environmental factors are contributory, and a more detailed observation of other patients in the environment follows. Such observations are often made by a liaison psychiatrist who has not been involved in primary care and whose perceptual sensitivity to the environment is less blunted because of his initial detachment from the team and their aims. The relevance of these observations may be readily apparent to the therapeutic team, although previously overlooked because of the different claims on their attention. Once recognized, environmental modifications can be instituted with therapeutic benefit. This beneficial flexibility produces problems for the researcher who finds that environmental variables change as the study progresses and the stability of variables, essential to systematic research, is nullified. As a result, most studies of treatment environments emerge as largely descriptive and heavily loaded with unverifiable subjective observations. Therapists who have had practical experience in treatment environments will not denigrate the importance of such subjective perceptions, but attempts have been made to achieve a more scientific approach to investigation. The unwieldy sprawl of 'treatment environments' may be partially contained by focusing on single facets of the environment or concentrating on specific environmental units which allow some containment of observation in time and space dimensions. The main methodological approaches include:

(1) Clinical studies of psychological reactions. The commonest approach remains the descriptive account of the incidence, behavioural manifestations, and psychopathology of psychiatric disturbance in particular environments. Psychometric measurements of mood states such as anxiety or depression, using self rating or observer rating, and occasionally psychophysiological measures such as heart-rate, blood pressure, or catecholamine levels, have provided some validation of the clinical observations and their implications in physical health.
(2) Comparative studies. Treatment environments rarely lend themselves to valid controlled studies, even where comparative patient groups share a common diagnosis. The selection criteria for special treatment procedures inevitably differentiate treatment environment patients from controls. Attempts at comparative studies include 'before and after' studies of changing environments, e.g. transfer of patients to new ward settings, and comparison of patients in two distinct environments, e.g. myocardial infarction patients in intensive-care units and in general wards. The problem of controlling all variables in comparative studies remains unresolved in functioning clinical units.
(3) Studies of environmental climate. The development of climate scales which attempt to measure and characterize the psychosocial qualities

of environment have been devised. Common dimensions which emerge from these studies include: relationship dimensions, measuring the nature and quality of personal relationships, and support systems; personal development dimensions, measuring the potential for growth and development of self-esteem; system maintenance dimensions, measuring order, control, and flexibility in the environment. Their application in clinical medicine has rarely extended beyond the psychiatric or rehabilitation settings (Insel and Moos, 1974).

(4) Studies of individual differences. Studies which attempt to define the individual qualities which enhance vulnerability to environmental stress have employed a range of measures derived from the psychological study of individual differences. Personality questionnaires, intelligence tests, symptom-sign inventories and attitudinal scales have introduced some qualitative assessment in predictive studies of treatment response.

Few of the studies discussed can withstand criticism on the grounds of scientific verification. It must be understood that they have rarely developed from the pursuit of scientific respectability but arise from a growing awareness of factors in health care which should not be neglected simply because of their elusiveness to scientific measurement.

SPECIFIC TREATMENT ENVIRONMENTS

Social therapy and the psychiatric unit

The development of the social sciences in relation to medicine, particularly the concern with environment as an integral aspect of medical treatment, has been a major influence in twentieth century medicine. The application of social therapy is most apparent in psychiatry, where it has transformed the secluded custodial asylum of the nineteenth century and led towards the district general hospital psychiatric unit of today (Clark, 1977). The concepts of the 'therapeutic milieu' and the 'therapeutic community', inaugurated in practice by Maxwell Jones in the 1950s, are now widely applied throughout psychiatric units in Britain and are influential in the function of community health centres, residential institutions, rehabilitation units, occupational units, and day centres where the aim of change employs social influence as a tool.

The therapeutic milieu has been developed, diluted, and adapted in such a variety of settings that it no longer maintains any precise definition as an applied technique. Certain concepts, however, remain characteristic. All residents, both staff and patients, are regarded as active contributors to the therapeutic process. The conventional separation of function between hospital staff and their patients is diffused by a democratization which includes shared involvement in group decisions and activities, a loss of symbolic differentiators such as uniform dress, and a merger of the accepted skills of differently trained staff which modifies their conventional roles. The total community undertakes some accountability for its responsible socialized function and the authoritarian structure of the conventional hospital unit is altered in the direction of permissiveness and tolerance. The function of individuals within the community is reviewed communally and the aim of behavioural alteration achieved through social analysis in a setting of group interaction. Not all psychiatric disorders or all psychiatric settings are appropriate for a total therapeutic milieu approach but few units are without some facets which reveal its impact.

Social therapy has certainly increased the social acceptance of psychiatric disorder and strengthened the links between physical medicine and psychiatry, but its efficacy as a treatment technique, though generally accepted, is not easily assessed by objective scientific methods. The numerous observational and descriptive studies of therapeutic communities and social therapy settings convey a subjective impression of positive gain, but quantitative studies of psychiatric hospital atmosphere and their physical environments are few. Gurel's study (1974) of 41 psychiatric hospitals aims to relate indices of hospital atmosphere to measures of effectiveness. Employing factor analysis, he identified two factors where social therapy concepts of global activity and less authoritarian atmosphere were present. These two factors were most apparent in two types of hospital setting, differentiated by their orientation—either sociotherapeutic with a basic community orientation, or medicotherapeutic with a basic teaching/research orientation—though both shared a non-traditional approach to therapy. Such units tended to be smaller hospitals, not exclusively psychiatric, with smaller proportions of chronic patients, higher staff ratios, active teaching programmes, and volunteer services. They tended to be more urban in location, more psychotherapeutic in orientation, more involved in community care programmes, and more costly in operation. His findings support current thought about the value of social therapy in mental hospitals and its positive effect on patient care, but the specific features of social therapy or the constructive grouping of such features remain unidentified and unquantitated.

Two studies of changing physical ward environment provide observations on the impact of altered environment on behaviour in psychiatric patients. Holahan and Saegert (1973) described a controlled study of in-patients, allocated randomly to an old admission ward and a remodelled ward, designed to encourage social interaction. Decreased passivity, increased socialization, and augmented positive attitude were measurable in the redesigned ward, indicating that desirable behaviour can be obtained by environmental manipulation. Their observation that poor and inappropriate ward design can foster the very behaviour for which patients are admitted echoes the observations from the wards of Britain's nineteenth-century asylums. De Vries (1968) noted the effect of changing both physical and social environment in a study of patients moving to a newly designed unit. Patients were able to choose both their rooms and their room-mate in a comparative three-way study. The physical environmental change certainly effected a lasting shift to more appropriate behaviour but the participation in social environmental change did not significantly enhance the effects of the physical change.

The concepts of social therapy have made less extensive impact in general medical hospitals where changes have been largely confined to the physical environment, improving appearance, facilities, and physical comfort. It is in the special units of general hospitals where the effect of environment has been most extensively studied and where awareness of the psychosocial influence of environment has contributed to changes in management.

Reception area

On entering a hospital for examination or treatment, a patient is rarely greeted by an eager physician at the door but is directed to a reception area or waiting room. Few physicians in their private practice can ignore the importance of the interactions between reception staff and patients, and seek a receptionist who can cope with the diverse demands of patient contact with control and courtesy, calmness and concern. In hospitals where the staff and patient numbers inevitably affect the quality of personal interactions, waiting rooms can become distancing, impersonal spaces, where isolated individuals sit silent behind magazines after a perfunctory registration, awaiting a call to an unsighted doctor concealed behind the doors of the examination room. The design of less cheerlessly clinical reception areas, the provision of canteen facilities, children's toys, the employment of lay personnel as ward clerks, all reflect the developing awareness that the anxiety of waiting time in reception areas merits attention. But waiting time can also be incorporated into the therapeutic process, as Hoffman and Futterman (1971) described in their study of a waiting room in a paediatric oncology clinic. Impressed by the passive, uncommunicative interaction between families attending a clinic for leukaemic children, they introduced a psychotherapist and occupational therapist into the waiting area itself. By inaugurating a play group for the sick children, parent group interaction actively developed, and with therapist support, anxieties of separation, mutilation, and death were confronted, changing the silent, tense inactive environment to a lively area of interaction which was constructively channelled in a therapeutic manner. The waiting room became an extension of the therapeutic setting which obviated the need to eliminate or reduce waiting time.

The operating suite

The surgical theatre and recovery rooms are hospital areas where consciousness is generally reduced by anaesthesia, and it has often been thought unnecessary to consider the impact of this environment on patients because of their diminished levels of conscious awareness. The environment of the surgical patient typically involves three areas: a preoperative waiting area where anaesthetic induction occurs, the theatre itself, and a postoperative recovery room. Observations in these three areas have challenged the assumption that they are essentially free from environmental stress. Egbert *et al.* (1963) stress the value of a pre-operative visit by the anaesthetist in diminishing lay fears of a routine procedure. He recommends that patients are transferred to a preoperative preparation room where anaesthetic premedication is given and patients are prepared for their postoperative experience in the recovery room.

In the theatre itself, patients who receive procedures under local or spinal anaesthesia will require special attention to their conscious awareness of a frighteningly strange environment with its disquieting sounds, clinical comments, and sometimes a view of their operation reflected in the theatre light. The assumption that patients under general anaesthesia are always oblivious to theatre activities has been challenged by Levinson (1965) who describes how patients may recall comments made during apparent total anaesthesia. The use of muscle-relaxants can often conceal the true depth of anaesthesia. Postoperative depression or anxiety may relate to remarks, especially comments on unfavourable findings, made during surgery and Cheek (1959) has demonstrated the recall of such comments under hypnosis.

Winkelstein, Blacher, and Meyer (1965), in a study of recovery-room patients, demonstrated that patients could not only respond lucidly to an interview shortly after leaving theatre but could recall much of the interview content 24 hours later. They stress that recovery-room patients are not oblivious of their surroundings and the sight of other distressed patients or of postoperative complications, the presence of unexpected mechanical apparatus (such as intravenous drips, catheters, airways, and nasogastric tubes), inadequate analgesia and the absence of familiar orientating stimuli may evoke emotional distress. The authors suggest the use of individual cubicles, stress the need for human contact to balance the mechanical interventions, and advise a quick return to the general ward. Although severe psychological reactions may be rare in the operating suite itself, studies of intensive-care unit (ICU) situations indicate that psychological responses, minimized or contained in the ICU, may emerge on transfer and become manifest after the patient leaves a stressful environment. The brief duration and limited conscious exposure in the surgical suite should not be accepted as obviating environmental stress.

Isolation units and sensory deprivation

Man depends on a rich array of sensory stimuli to maintain his cortical alertness and to orientate him within his environment. Restriction of sensory input, or an alteration in the quality of experienced sensation imposed by a fixed structure or reduced patterning of sensory stimuli, can produce changes in cerebral function. The integrity of the psychological state is dependent on adequate perceptual contact with the external environment (Solomon, Leiderman, Mendelson, and Lindeman, 1957). In 1956, Lilly described the effects of a reduction in the ordinary levels of sensory input on healthy people. In his laboratory experiment volunteers were exposed to the sensory monotony of a prolonged immersion. This experimental environment produced a reduction in visual, auditory, and tactile stimuli associated with limited mobility, and Lilly observed the rapid development of a confusional state with disorientation and hallucinations. Subjects manifested impairment of organized thinking, increased suggestibility and an intense desire for extrinsic sensory stimuli. Mendelsohn, Solomon, and Lindeman, (1958) described a similar mental state in poliomyelitis patients, treated in a tank respirator (iron lung). Some patients developed an acute psycho-organic reaction with confusion, disorientation, delusions, and hallucinations. Their hallucinations could be in any of the sensory modalities. Mendelsohn et al., (1958) found no evidence of toxic or metabolic disturbance in these patients and ascribed their psychotic state to the effects of sensory deprivation. Positive pressure respirators have rendered the tank respirator obsolete but the psychological effects of acute sensory deprivation are now acknowledged and are evidenced in treatment situations where sensory restriction and isolation are imposed on patients.

The bilateral eye bandaging formerly common following cataract extraction produced just such a situation of acute sensory deprivation. Psychotic reactions were not infrequent after cataract surgery and the appearance of delusions, disorientation, hallucinations, anxiety, somatic complaints, and psychomotor restlessness complicated post-operative management. Linn et al. (1953) studied the effect of bilateral eye masking in 21 cataract patients, both pre- and postoperatively. A brief period of preoperative masking was associated with anxiety but no psychotic phenomena. Postoperative patients were bilaterally bandaged for 3 days and almost all showed some altered behaviour. Delusional symptoms developed in 60 per cent of patients. Psychological symptoms usually resolved within 48 hours when the bandaging was removed, but occasionally persisted or actually appeared after unmasking. Increasing age, and the presence of organic brain disease, increased the incidence of this postoperative psychosis. Current surgical practice has incorporated these findings in postoperative management, and bilateral bandaging is either brief or avoided altogether.

Isolation systems which provide a protected sterile environment have been developed to reduce the incidence of exogenous infection in various medical situations: organ transplant, thoracic surgery, burns, immune disease, radiation injury, and cytotoxic therapy. The two basic designs in use are the plastic tent isolator and the cubicle isolator with laminar airflow (Trexler, 1973). In these isolators, which separate patients from any direct physical contact, patients must maintain the sterility of their environment in a strict routine, may require irradiated food which is tasteless, are restricted in mobility, must adjust to the distorting 'space-suit' uniforms of the staff, cope with reduced social contact, and view a restricted visual environment. The psychological effects of gnotobiotic isolation have been studied in patients with leukaemia where the threat of fatal illness compounds any environmental stress. A diagnosis of fatal illness combined with a treatment regime in such a restrictive environment imposes considerable stress on individual adaptation. There are, however, no reports of psychotic reactions during isolator therapy. Holland, Harris, and Plumb (1970) noted the distress caused by the deprivation of human touch. Gordon (1975) comments on the anxiety apparent before entry to the isolator and its reemergence at times of physical deterioration and on discharge. Kohle, Simons, and Weidlich (1971) describe the ambivalence and conflicts which arise in relation to the dependency produced by isolation, often manifested in paranoid or aggressive interactions with staff members. The lack of acute psychiatric disturbance in the isolator reflects an awareness of the potential stress of this environment and the units studied have paid particular attention to maintaining mobility, fostering socialization, preserving orientation, and counteracting monotony with diversionary occupational therapy as well as incorporating psychological counselling and support in the treatment programme.

Gnotobiotic isolation has also been used for children with immune deficiency disorders and here the length of therapy is considerably more prolonged. Teller (1973) describes the rearing of hypogammaglobulinaemic twins from birth to $2\frac{1}{2}$ years, in a complex of isolators. He found that levels of sensory and social stimulation could be maintained, but the limited possibilities for experience, imitation, physical interaction, and motor behaviour created a learning deficit which was not compensated for by the use of play therapy. A lack of spontaneous activity, stereotyped behaviour, and prolonged dependency were developmental abnormalities associated with the environment. In this situation even the greatest possible attention to the problems of the isolator environment had proved insufficient to rectify its deficiencies.

The commonest disorders requiring isolation in hospitals are the infectious diseases. The physical features of isolation in this situation are generally less intense. A single room with barrier nursing practices may be less intimidating than isolation in a plastic tent, but a severely ill patient may still find that the social separation, the strange masked and gowned staff, and the limited visual and occupational stimulation intensifies anxiety, occasionally contributing to an acute psychotic reaction. Even in this less extreme setting of isolation, attempts to maintain socialization, orientation, and occupation combined with a reduction of sensory monotony will assist smooth recovery.

Cardiac surgery

The development of cardiac surgery in the 1950s was associated with reports of an increased incidence of postoperative psychiatric disturbance (Abram, 1971). The psychiatric complications of closed-heart surgery were initially attributed to the scale of the surgical procedure and the psychological significance of the heart as an ailing organ. In the 1960s, with the development of cardiopulmonary bypass technology, open cardiac surgery expanded and reports of an even greater incidence of postoperative confusional states appeared (Blachly and Starr, 1964; Egerton and Kay; 1964, Kornfeld, Zimberg, and Malm, 1965). The typical postcardiotomy delirium followed a lucid postoperative period of 3–4 days. Disorientation, impaired cognitive function, illusions, hallucinations, and paranoid delusions were common features. Although the physiological disturbances of bypass surgery were acknowledged as major aetiological factors in precipitating delirium, the treatment environment also contributed. The presence of intravenous tubing and electrocardiogram (ECG) leads, the regular flashing of the cardiac monitor, the persistent hiss of the enveloping oxygen tent, the frequent disturbances of nursing and medical observations, the constant illumination, pain, and limited mobility all combined to produce an environment which fostered sleep-deprivation in a setting of sensory monotony. The aetiological role of this environment was further substantiated when it was observed that transfer to a standard hospital ward often resolved the delirium in 1–2 days.

The observations have been a major influence in altering recovery-room design and procedure. The prevention of sleep-deprivation by modifications in nursing procedure and the maintenance of normal biological sleep rhythm; the use of private cubicles to limit disturbance from other ill patients; the distancing, restricted use, or early removal of monitoring equipment; the provision of more rewarding and reorientating visual stimuli than blank, white walls; are suggestions which have been incorporated in current intensive-care technique. Lazarus and Hagens (1968) describe how modifications in environment alone reduced the incidence of postcardiotomy delirium.

Heller, Frank, and Malm (1970) re-examined the pattern of psychiatric complications to cardiac surgery in the late 1960s. They confirmed the reduced incidence of postcardiotomy delirium, but noted the appearance of an early postoperative organic brain syndrome which presented as disorientation without frank psychotic features or a preceding lucid interval. The development of postcardiotomy delirium was associated with advancing age, the severity of the preoperative cardiac condition, and the length of time on cardiopulmonary bypass, while the development of the early brain syndrome related to preoperative organic brain damage, the length of cardiac surgery, and the degree of hypothermia during surgery. The authors recognized the contribution of improved surgical technique to the decline in postoperative delirium, but acknowledged that modifications in recovery-room procedure, reduced staff anxiety, wider public knowledge, and psychological counselling have also assisted postoperative recovery. A complexity of functional and organic elements combine to predispose patients to postcardiotomy psychosis. These observations from cardiac surgery patients appear equally relevant in other postoperative psychoses.

More recent studies have focused on the individual differences in patients which contribute to psychiatric disturbance following cardiac surgery. Henricks and Waters (1972) classified preoperative cardiac patients, using their scores on the Minnesota Multiphasic Personality Inventory. Male patients rated more highly on depression, and females more highly on anxiety. Different patterns of preoperative psychiatric symptomatology were associated with different types of response to surgery. After surgery psychiatric complications in women, for example, were more frequent where high ratings for denial of anxiety or significant psychological disturbance had been measured pre-operatively. Individual differences can also affect long-term outcome. In a 15-month follow-up study of cardiac surgery patients, Kimball (1969) found the best functional recovery in patients whose preoperative function was characterized by realistic limits without denial of morbidity. Postoperative psychoses were commonest in patients who denied anxiety and voiced vague optimism without clear objectives, while postoperative mortality was highest in patients identified preoperatively as depressed.

Heller, Frank, and Malm (1974) found that poor postoperative adjustment at 1-year follow-up related more strongly to poor preoperative psychological adjustment than to actual physical outcome. Patients with paranoid or depressed traits preoperatively were particularly at risk. Psychological counselling and preparation for surgery might beneficially include intervention which takes these differing types of response into account. Increased passivity with greater dependence was generally common at follow-up, but anxiety, depression, somatic preoccupation, social withdrawal, and paranoid feelings characterized the patients with the poorest adjustment. The authors noted that patients with aggressive or confronting coping mechanisms did less well during convalescence, asserting themselves in hedonistic, unreflective action which was often inappropriate.

Intensive-care units

Following the observations on the relation between hospital environment and postcardiotomy delirium, attention shifted to the environmental effects of intensive-care units (ICUs) which has expanded rapidly since the 1950s. The high incidence of psychiatric disturbance after cardiac surgery has not been replicated in studies of ICU patients and the role of environmental stress in any observed disturbance in the ICU has been questioned. Few patients in the ICU have undergone a physiological assault equivalent to the dual challenge of major cardiac surgery and artificial perfusion, but organic vulnerability may be only one relevant factor in this reduced incidence of psychiatric disturbance. ICU design has benefited from a growing awareness of environmental stress and has generally incorporated structural, procedural, and attitudinal features which minimize the more negative aspects of treatment environments. When Sgroi, Holland, and Marwitt (1968) compared ICU patients with a group of comparably ill patients treated in a general hospital ward, no difference in ratings for anxiety or depression emerged between the groups. Delirium occurred more frequently in the ICU patients but environmental factors were not considered instrumental in its development. Hewitt (1970) asked 100 patients to complete a questionnaire on their subjective experience in a six-bedded surgical ICU. The commonest difficulties reported were inadequate sleep and rest. Nasopharyngeal suction emerged as the most distressing mechanical treatment. Few patients could recall much of their time during mechanical ventilation. Despite the low levels of reported psychological disturbance, Hewitt advised a minimum of clinical recordings, indirect lighting, individual cubicles, and adjustable beds to reduce environmental stress. In this unit, explanation of procedure before entry, continuity of staff care, open visiting arrangements, and brevity of stay (86 per cent remained only 1–4 days) all contributed to patient tolerance. Hewitt acknowledges that the existence and experience of his study implies the presence of a sensitized and aware team which must influence patient response. The application of intensive care procedures remains various in different settings with different techniques, staff, and patients, and psychological reactions to the ICU environment are still observed.

The intensive-care situation which has attracted most interest is the coronary care unit (CCU). These vary widely in design, ranging from the side room in a general ward to a purpose-built unit with individual cubicles and a central nursing station. They share in common a concentration of technical equipment, such as electronic monitors and continuous ECG machines, and a high staffing level with specialized nursing and medical personnel. The patients share a single common acute disorder, myocardial infarction. Many of the patients are not in great physical distress after the acute stages of their heart attack, but their medical situation remains critical and the physiological effects of psychological disturbance can effect both morbidity and mortality.

The incidence of psychological disorder in the CCU varies widely in different studies. Parker and Hodge (1967) observed an acute psychorganic reaction similar to postcardiotomy delirium, in a twelve-bed open ward unit. Sensory monotony and sleep deprivation emerged as major contributors in its development. This confusional state responded best to removal to a general ward. Hackett, Cassem, and Wishnie (1968), studying a four-bed CCU, found a low incidence of delirium and little evidence or psychological disturbance related to environmental factors. Anxiety was evident in 80 per cent of their patients, and depression in 60 per cent, but the degree of disturbance appeared appropriate to the stress of physical illness. In the study of Cay et al. (1970) investigating 203 male patients in a CCU of single-room design, 88 per cent were reassured by their stay and only 5 per cent were distressed by the unit. Major psychiatric disturbance was rare. The authors relate this high level of patient confidence to staff efficiency, individual attention, clear explanation of the mechanical equipment, continuity of nursing staff for each patient, as well as advanced medical care. Patients who were not reassured by the unit showed higher anxiety levels on psychometric testing. Dominian and Dobson's (1969) psychometric observations in a three-bedded CCU revealed little anxiety related to the unit. Such contrasting reports may reflect the differing effects of units which vary in structure and technique, but no comparative study of psychological responses to different types of CCU is available. It would be incautious to assume that CCUs are without any potential environmental stress.

The impact of the CCU environment may invoke varied response in patients. Some patients may perceive the concentration of staff and equipment as reassuring at a time when they feel their lives are threatened. Other patients may construe the facilities as a continual indication of the critical nature of their condition and view the experience with intensified apprehension. Patients may meet with this challenge by effective use of denial, reducing conscious awareness of their situation, and repressing anxiety. Hackett has observed that overt anxiety appears to be associated with increased mortality following infarction and suggests that denial may favour survival in the immediate post-infarct period. He advises the routine use of minor tranquillizers to contain anxiety, rather than a full exploration of specific fears at this stage. Experienced staff will be familiar with commoner sources of concern and attempt to minimize their patients' exposure to the more distressing aspects of coronary care techniques.

One potential stress in the CCU is the witnessed death of a fellow-patient, particularly when it follows an unsuccessful attempt at resuscitation. Bruhn et al. (1970) observed increases in blood pressure and heart-rate in patients who had witnessed the death of a fellow-patient. Although other authors (Hackett, Cassem, and Wishnie, 1968; Grace, 1969) noted little expressed anxiety or fatal complications following the witnessing of a cardiac arrest, most patients expressed a preference for a single room which would protect them from such exposure. Although Bruhn et al. (1970) observed no difference in the incidence of arrhythmias when patients were transferred from an open ward to individual cubicles, a relationship between cardiac arrhythmias and catecholamine levels is established (Jewitt et al., 1969). The significant therapeutic achievements of the CCU should not prevent a continued awareness of the importance of reducing anxiety through attention to the potential hazards of the environment.

Patients must adapt to the experience of coronary care not only on entry but also on leaving the unit. Klein et al. (1968) noted an increase in catecholamine excretion and in cardiovascular complications on transfer from the CCU. They attributed these complications to the anxiety of abrupt removal from the security of a specialized protective setting which obviated any feeling of relief at the physical improvement implied by transfer. Changes in transfer procedure, including an early explanation of the possibility of abrupt transfer and some continuity of medical and nursing staff on transfer, were accompanied by a decline in cardiovascular complications and a lower incidence of raised catecholamine excretion. Cay et al. (1970) described anxiety or depression in 62 per cent of their male patients on transfer but noted that their dependence on their monitors subsided quickly. Although patients with a history of previous psychiatric disturbance were more likely to be distressed by the unit, transfer reactions were not related to the extent of psychological distress manifested during their stay on the unit. These observations on transfer anxiety contrast with Hewitt's report (1970) from a surgical ICU, where 76 per cent of patients expressed pleasure at their return to a general ward and only 4 per cent were disquieted by the move.

Although the CCU generally emerges as a less challenging environment than the ICU, producing fewer adverse effects, many patients develop a state of invalidism on discharge with restriction of function. Wynn (1967) reports unwarranted emotional distress after discharge in 50 per cent of 400 patients with ischaemic heart disease, often producing a psychological disability more handicapping than their actual physical limitations. Investigation of the sources of their distress suggested that fear had been induced in 22 per cent by their medical staff and in 15 per cent by the effects of their hospital treatment. It is difficult to separate the effects of cardiac illness itself from the effects of treatment, but the denial of anxiety, common in the early stages of treatment, may prove less effective on discharge.

While the CCU may provide a sense of reassurance in the acute phase of illness, the intensity of this therapeutic experience may contribute to a sense of continued apprehension after discharge, by signifying to patients the potential severity of their illness. Dominian and Dobson (1969) note the need for re-assurance in the rehabilitation phase. Patients discharged without arranged follow-up were re-referred more frequently than patients who held a follow-up appointment. Anxieties provoked by the treatment environment are one area that might be helpfully explored with the patient prior to discharge.

The burns unit

As a physical therapeutic environment, the burns unit incorporates many of the features of intensive care, including isolation to diminish the incidence of infection. A patient injured by burning has sustained one of the most acute and terrifying threats to survival and has to contend with severe pain, the visible distortion of their familiar body image, repeated surgical procedures, anaesthesia and a protracted convalescence. Psychological studies of burn patients have largely focused on the considerable emotional problems experienced by patients and examined the interactions between their disturbance and their hospital environment. Emotional instability is a frequent observation in the early stages following admission, often reflected in demanding, unco-operative or depressed behaviour. Psycho-organic reactions with confusion may further handicap environmental adaptation. As physical recovery proceeds the patient encounters an array of psychological challenges: feeling of guilt or anger at the cause of their injuries; compulsive ruminations on the traumatic event and vivid, terrifying recall of the incident; prolonged separation from their usual social environment; anxiety about future possibilities for occupation and leisure activities; fears of dependency and personal rejection; the confrontation with disfigurement; and altered sexual attractiveness. Hamburg, Artz, and Reiss (1953), in a study of extensive full skin thickness burn patients, noted their use of familiar adaptive mechanisms such as suppression, repression, and denial, their constriction of emotion, their heightened sensitivity to rejection, and their overt hostility, often directed towards the staff. They conceive management of these emotional problems as an integral part of therapy and propose features of the physical and emotional environment of the burns unit which could facilitate adaptation. The fostering of confidence and restriction of feelings of rejection are encouraged when one primary doctor is involved with each patient. Socialization must be maintained to limit rejection, and the avoidance of isolation or use of an atmospheric isolation which still allows social contact is important. Ready contact with relatives and with recovering patients can foster the aptitude for recovery. Occupational therapy programmes, both diversionary and constructive, encourage both socialization and self-assistance.

The accent is on the development of a positive emotional climate for recovery but the physical environment remains an integral part of such development. The adjustment of patients is also dependent on integral aspects of their own personality. Andreasen, Noyes, and Hartford (1972) used a standard psychiatric history-taking procedure to assess premorbid psychopathology and its significance in the recovery of burns patients. Psychological complications in the recovery phase related more to premorbid psychological adjustment and to poor adjustment to previous physical problems than to the extent or severity of burn injuries. Patients exposed to more frequent changes in life, and greater life stresses before injury, adapted less well. Psychiatric evaluation may assist in identifying patients in whom environmental considerations merit particular attention.

Haemodialysis

Psychological reactions to haemodialysis are less dramatic than with open-heart surgery, but the need for patient selection, where demand for treatment exceeds availability, has focused attention on psychological adaptation to haemodialysis. No accurate predictors of psychological adjustment to dialysis have emerged but the numerous studies have increased awareness of the psychological problems created by a treatment in which continued survival is dependent on a machine. The patterns of adaptation required for successful adjustment to a personal environment which involves an extension of the concept of bodily function to include a large mechanical aid have been examined, and psychological traits which favour good adjustment to this new environment have been sought. Although most studies have focused on psychiatric evaluation of patients and reflect psychological difficulties familiar to many chronic disorders, the therapeutic environment and treatment regime emerge as distinctive stressors and create a focal area where mental problems may be demonstrated in behavioural responses to treatment procedure.

Reichsman and Levy (1972) describe three stages in psychological adaptation to haemodialysis. The familiar depression of chronic renal disease generally resolves in the first 1–6 months of dialysis as physical health improves and optimism emerges. A period of disenchantment and discouragement often follows the stress of resuming a more active role at home or at work. Physical complications, such as arteriovenous shunt clotting, may develop and a mood of hopelessness and depression re-emerges. In the final stage of long-term adaptation, fluctuations occur in physical health and emotional stability. Denial may recur as a predominant defence mechanism, and increased dependence on staff and equipment may lead to expressed ambivalence with periods of projected hostility.

These clinical observations are generally supported by Gentry and Davis (1972) who employed a battery of psychological tests (including measures of IQ, anxiety, depression, and social desirability) to quantify changes in adaptation during dialysis. As the number of dialysis treatments increased, ratings for anxiety and depression declined and social desirability ratings increased. Gentry and Davis propose that these observations support a hypothesis of an increase in denial as treatment progresses, which provides protection against overt emotional decompensation. Social desirability, a measure of staff acceptance and toleration, may reflect acceptance of dependent feelings with repression of aggression. The authors note that this correlation of their test results with the number and frequency of treatments may really reflect the severity of illness and the greater need for defence of denial in sicker patients.

Greenberg, Davis, and Massey (1973) comment on the organic impairment of intellectual function in chronic renal disease and its effects on the capacity for learning to comply with a dialysis programme. Although no psychotic behaviour or gross emotional maladjustment emerged in patients in their 3-year study, reduced affective responsivity developed. Successful adaptation was related to a higher IQ, less defensiveness about anxiety, more familial support, and fewer psychosomatic complaints.

Crammond, Knight, and Lawrence (1967) noted the inclusion of the therapeutic procedure in psychological adaptation. The concern of patients with their illness and progress often focused on a preoccupation with their arteriovenous shunts, and the strict dietary regime was frequently the object of displaced hostility. Anxiety re-emerged at times of staff changes, reflecting the dependency of patient/staff relationships.

Dialysis patients are rarely treated in isolation and Wright, Sand, and Livingstone (1966) note the supportive aspects of group treatment in the dialysis unit. While group identification can lessen both anxiety and the need for denial, the patient group can have negative aspects for the depressed patient who has difficulty in establishing group contact or for the patient who for a prolonged period has a poor response to treatment. The group can make a joint contribution to their programme by creating a conscious ethos of competition in the maintenance of dietary regimes.

Constructive suggestions to improve the treatment environment have followed from such studies. Therapeutic support and education of the family increases their capacity for involvement; a possible outlet for the tensions and hostility which develop during such a strict treatment regime may possibly be provided by the inclusion of a physiotherapist in the team; staff changes should be graduated with an overlap of replacement staff; staff should strive for a supportive role which neither encourages total dependency nor demands independence, while recognizing the fluctuating and ambivalent feelings of patients concerning independence; the positive fostering of a supportive patient group milieu. Such studies have certainly assisted in educating staff to the changing needs and changing responses of their patients and increased their capacity to accept and assist their patients during their less co-operative phases. Although it has been proposed that the real stresses for patients in chronic dialysis relate to social factors in their outside environment—job losses, marital stress, restricted sociability—rather than their treatment experience, the manifestations of such stress commonly present in the treatment environment. Attention to the treatment milieu can assist in diminishing the impact of external social change.

The internal environment—organ transplant and cardiac pacemakers

The environment of treatment encompasses not only the external events which confront patients but also adaptation to therapeutic alterations in their internal environment and their body image. Most illness involves some perception of bodily change but the effect of therapy on the internal environment has been dramatically accentuated by the development of organ transplantation. Transplanted organs feel no different in somatic sensation but the psychological concomitants of transplantation are considerable and form one of the most emotive topics in modern medicine. The impact of a transplantation programme can alter the environmental climate of a hospital unit. Kraft and Vick (1971) describe the gradual development of a 'transplantation milieu' in one of the first cardiac transplant units. The problems of administration and publicity, the unrealistic prognostic aspirations of the patients, the competition for organs, and the shift from an acute unit to a chronic unit of invalid 'waiters' always anticipating the sudden announcement of transplant surgery demanded a total reorientation of the unit. The initial planning had dealt only with technical skills and biological techniques, lacking appreciation of the complex requirements of transplant patients. These necessitated the development of new procedures which carefully interrelated medical and psychosocial skills. The needs of the donor's family as well as the recipient must be considered.

The pressure for transplanted organs, and the inevitable selection involved, has slanted interest in the psychosocial aspect away from the stresses encountered and towards the individual psychological differences which favour good adaptation. Christopherson and Lunde (1971) stress the importance of pre-transplant screening in both the prediction and influence of psychosocial adjustment in survivors. Factors which related to a good post-transplant adjustment were supportive family communications, an awareness of possible death, and positive time-limited reasons for transplantation—a compilation of events and attitudes which imply a reality-based perception of the treatment environment. In contrast, denial emerged frequently in patients with poor outcome, especially during experience of a 'rejection' of their transplant.

The more extensive experience with renal transplant has provided some observations on patients' adaptation to the change in internal environment.

Crammond (1971) comments on the preference of transplant recipients for cadaver kidneys which can be psychologically assimilated with less sense of obligation. Aesthetic objections were rarely voiced by recipients and the disturbances in body image, though present, were usually minimal. He comments on the importance of recognizing and alleviating the stress imposed on families, particularly as the best outcome is seen in assertive, energetic patients who had the advantage of a close familial support. Penn *et al.* (1971) stress the importance of establishing a ward environment which operates as a psychotherapeutically supportive group milieu. In their experience with renal and hepatic transplant patients, they advise reducing isolation, open visiting, fostering patient interaction, and introducing psychotherapy, and social and occupational rehabilitation, to create such an environment. The authors note the frequent development of pre- and post-operative anxiety and depression in transplant patients, but advise against transplantation where a history of functional psychosis or severe personality disturbance is present.

The implantation of an electrial cardiac pacemaker is another therapeutic situation in which perception of the internal environment may affect treatment response. Blacker and Basch (1970) found preoperative anxiety was common and some preoccupation with pacemaker function persisted on discharge, but the predicated conflicts over control and mastery in response to the presence of an 'artificial organ' were not apparent. Postoperative psychoses were rare, and eventual adaptation was largely dependent on personality characteristics. Stonehill and Crisp (1969) had the opportunity to study a series of 120 patients which included both externally and internally sited pacemakers. Depressive symptom scores were raised in both groups but patients with external pacemakers scored significantly higher for depression. Measures of anxiety were abnormally raised though patients tended to deny anxiety. The external pacemaker siting, with its constant visible presence and exposure to accidental damage, appeared to demand a greater reorganization of body image. In the few patients who had required resiting of their pacemaker, the change to an external siting was associated with an elevated symptom score for anxiety and depression.

THE STAFF

The hospital population includes staff as well as patients and, although their perception of their environment may be very different, staff members are not immune from environmental stress despite their familiarity with their occupational setting. Special units require a particular adaptation from staff members and pose problems for them which are peculiar to the specific challenges, yet distinct from the stresses experienced by patients. No objective studies of staff reactions to special units have emerged but liaison psychiatrists have frequently provided descriptive observations on staff behaviour, and attempted to analyse the stressful aspects of these environments for staff members. Many of the special units present similar challenges, particularly for the nurses

(Kornfeld, 1969). They are dealing constantly with seriously ill patients, work under pressure with little opportunity for relaxed and convivial patient contact, experience a close and frequent exposure to death, and receive few rewarding expressions of gratitude from patients who have been transferred to general wards on recovery. They need to master a range of technical equipment yet much of their busy routine involves repetitive duties like monitoring and charting. They may be required to take rapid decisions in management which are not within the conventional areas of nurse responsibility, are vulnerable to hypercriticism from stressed physicians, and face repeatedly the experience of therapeutic failure because of the severity of their patients' conditions. It is hardly surprising that special units often have a rapid turnover in staffing and the quick change in staff and patient populations limits the development of cohesive relationships which could enhance morale.

Several studies comment on the high anxiety levels engendered by special-unit nursing and the protective behavioural responses adopted as a defence against anxiety. Vreeland and Ellis (1969) recognize that intensive-care nursing offers the rewards of prestige and a high level of nursing achievement, but many of the valued skills lie in the areas of mechanical and technical competence. Intensive-care nursing often attracts nurses who are partially protected by a limited awareness of emotional stress and have little facility for empathy. Hay and Oken (1972) indicated that a positive group cohesion can develop, but its perceptions may be restricted by an orientation more towards efficiency and practicality than to the expression or reception of emotion. The anxiety of the empathic nurse may be contained by a defence of detachment which distances her from stressful events, or by a physical withdrawal in which involvement primarily focuses on the equipment or the routine. In this setting the anxieties of relatives are often inadequately handled as they impose an extra intrusion which cannot be dealt with by mechanical means.

These problems created for staff by the environment have been minimized or resolved in some units. The use of ward assistants to relieve nurses of routine clerical duties; the introduction of staff group meetings where problems can be shared and affect discharged; an induction period for new staff to familiarize them with the demands on knowledge and expertise; high staffing levels; a full-time medical officer and ready access to immediate medical assistance; clear delineation of the areas of nursing responsibility, have all contributed to the elevation of morale and decreased the emotional burden of intensive-care nursing.

There have been no studies on the impact of special units on doctors. Medical staff generally have the opportunity to move out from the constant pressures of special care, unlike the nurse who experiences little chance of escape from the ward environment. Doctors are not immune from emotional stress in general, nor from occupational stress in particular.

Vaillant and McArthur, (1972) found that emotional instability was more common in physicians than in their socioeconomic peers, and related strongly to qualities of childhood experience. They note that medical practice can be particularly stressful for the unstable doctor when he is exposed to emotional demands or to a failed expectation of reward from patient involvement. The special units combine a high level of service demand with the frequent experience of therapeutic failure, and may create an environment where the vulnerabilities of the less stable physician are exposed.

CONCLUSION

The expanding fields of social and psychosomatic medicine have contributed to an awareness that the environment of the treatment situation has implications in illness behaviour, treatment response, and recovery. Studies of the treatment environment remain largely subjective but have influenced hospital design and treatment procedure. There can be little doubt that this area of psychosomatic medicine has exerted a humanitarian influence on patient care, but an awareness of the effects of environment on both physical and emotional health has established the importance of environmental considerations in total patient care. The observations from the studies of specific treatment environments have already modified management in these settings, and the findings have also exerted a generalized influence on the approach to treatment in less specialized situations. Medical advances continue to create new environmental challenges. A constant alertness to the treatment environment must be maintained if the advances of the future are to fulfil their therapeutic potential.

REFERENCES

Abram, H. S. (1971). Psychotic reactions after cardiac surgery—a critical review. *Semin. Psych.*, **3**, 70–78.

Andreasen, N. J. C., Noyes, R., and Hartford, C. E. (1972). Factors influencing adjustment of burns patients during hospitalisation. *Psychosom. Med.*, **34**, 517–525.

Blachly, P. H., and Starr, A. (1964). Post cardiotomy delirium. *Amer. J. Psychiat.*, **121**, 371–375.

Blacker, R. S., and Basch, S. H. (1970). Psychological aspects of pacemaker implantation. *Arch. Gen. Psych.*, **22**, 319–323.

Brown, E. L. (1961). *The Use of the Physical and Social Environment of the General Hospital for Therapeutic Purposes.* New York: Russell Sage Foundation.

Bruhn, J. G., Thurman, E., Jr., Chandler, B. C., and Bruce, T. A. (1970). Patients' reactions to death in a coronary care unit. *J. Psychosom. Res.*, **14**, 65–70.

Cay, E. L., Vetter, N. J., Philip, A. E., and Dugard, P. (1970). Psychological reactions to a coronary care unit. *Scand. J. Rehab. Med.*, **2–3**, 78–84.

Cheek, D. S. (1959). Unconscious perception of meaningful sounds during surgical anaesthesia as revealed under hypnosis. *Amer. J. Clin. Hypnosis*, **1**, 101.

Christopherson, L. K., and Lunde, D. T. (1971). Selection of cardiac transplant recipients and their subsequent psychosocial adjustment. *Semin. Psych.*, **3**(1), 36–45.

Clark, D. H. (1977). The therapeutic community. *Br. J. Psychiat.*, **131**, 553–564.

Crammond, W. A. (1971). Renal transplantations—experiences with recipients and donors. *Semin. Psych*, **3**(1), 116–132.

Crammond, W. A., Knight, P. R., and Lawrence, J. R. (1967). The psychiatric contribution to a renal unit undertaking chronic haemodialysis and renal homotransplantation. *B. J. Psychiat.*, **113**, 1201–1212.

De Vries, D. L. (1968). Effects of environmental change and of participation on the behaviour of mental patients. *J. Consult. Clin. Psychol.* **32**, 532–536.

Dominian, J., and Dobson, M. (1969). Study of patients' psychological attitudes to a coronary care unit. *Br. Med. J.*, **4**, 795.

Egbert, L. D., Battit, G. E., Turndorf, H., and Beecher, H. K. (1963). The value of the preoperative visit by an anesthetist. *J. Amer. Med. Assoc.*, **185**, 553.

Egerton, N., and Kay, J. H. (1964). Psychological disturbances associated with open heart surgery. *Br. J. Psychiat.*, **110**, 444–449.

Gentry, W. D., and Davis, G. C. (1972). Cross sectional analysis of psychological adaptation to chronic haemodialysis. *J. Chron. Dis.*, **25**, 545–550.

Gordon, A. M. (1975). Psychological aspects of isolator therapy in acute leukaemia. *Br. J. Psychiat.*, **127**, 588–590.

Gordon, A. M. (1976). The effects of treatment environments. *J. Psychosom. Res.* **20**, 363–366.

Grace, W. J. (1969). Terror in the coronary care unit. *Amer. J. Cardiol.*, **30**, 746.

Greenberg, R. P., Davis, G., and Massey, R. (1973). The psychological evaluation of patients for a kidney transplant and haemodialysis programme. *Amer. J. Psychiat.*, **130**, 274–277.

Gurel, L. (1974). Dimensions of the therapeutic milieu. *Amer. J. Psychiat.*, **131**, 409–414.

Hackett, T. P., Cassem, N. H., and Wishnie, H. A. (1968). The coronary care unit: an appraisal of its psychological hazards. *New Engl. J. Med.*, **279**, 1365–1370.

Hamburg, D. A., Artz, C. P., and Reiss, E. (1953). Clinical importance of emotional problems in the care of patients with burns. *New Engl. J. Med.*, **248**, 355–359.

Hay, D., and Oken, D. (1972). The psychological stress of I. C. U. nursing. *Psychosom. Med.*, **34**, 109–118.

Heller, S., Frank, K. A. and Malm, J. (1970). Psychiatric complications of open heart surgery. A re-examination. *New Engl. J. Med.*, **283**, 1015–1019.

Heller, S., Frank, K. A., and Malm, J. (1974). Psychological outcome following open heart surgery. *Arch. Intern. Med.*, **134**, 908–914.

Henricks, T. F., and Waters, W. F. (1972). Psychological adjustment and response to open heart surgery. *Br. J. Psychiat.*, **120**, 491–496.

Hewitt, P. B. (1970). Subjective follow-up of patients from a surgical intensive therapy ward. *Br. Med. J.*, **4**, 669–673.

Hoffman, I. and Futterman, E. H. (1971). Coping with waiting. *Comp. Psychiat.*, **12**, 67–81.

Holahan, C. J. and Saegert, S. (1973). Behavioural and attitudinal effects of large scale variation in the physical environment of psychiatric wards. *J. Abnorm. Psychol.*, **82**, 454–462.

Holland, Harris, S. and Plumb, M. J. (1970). *Psychological Aspects of Physical Barrier Isolation.* Proceedings of the XIII International Congress of Haematology, Munich.

Insel, P., and Moos, R. (1974). Psychological environments. *Amer. Psychol.*, **29**, 179–188.

Jewitt, D. E., Mercer, C. J., Reid, D., Valori, C., Thomas, M., and Shillingford, J. (1969). Free noradrenaline and adrenaline excretion in patients with acute myocardial infarction. *Lancet*, **1**, 635.

Kimball, C. P. (1969). A predictive study of adjustment to cardiac surgery. *J. Thorac. Cardiovasc. Surg.*, **58**, 891–896.

Klein, R. F., Kliner, V. S., Zipes, D. P., Troyer, W. G., and Wallace, A. G. (1968). Transfer from a coronary care Unit. *Arch. Intern. Med.*, **122**, 104–108.

Kohle, K., Simons, C., and Weidlich, S. (1971). Psychological aspects in the treatment of leukemia in the isolated bed system 'Life Island'. *Psychother. Psychosom.*, **19**, 85.

Kornfeld, D. S. (1969). Psychiatric view of the I. C. U. *Br. Med. J.*, **1**, 108–110.

Kornfeld, D. S., (1972). The hospital environment: its impact on patients. *Adv. Psychosom. Med.*, **8**, 252–270.

Kornfeld, D. S., Zimberg, S., and Malm, J. R. (1965). Psychiatric complications of open heart surgery. *New Engl. J. Med.*, **273**, 287–292.

Kraft, I. A., and Vick, J. (1971). The transplantation milieu, St Luke's Episcopal Hospital, 1968–69. *Semin. Psychol.*, **3**, 17–25.

Lazarus, H. R., and Hagens, J. H. (1968). Prevention of psychosis following open heart surgery. *Amer. J. Psychiat.*, **124**, 1190–1194.

Levinson, B. W. (1965). States of awareness during general anaesthesia. *Br. J. Anaesth.*, **37**, 544.

Lilly, J. C. (1956). Mental effects of reduction of ordinary levels of physical stimuli on intact, healthy persons. *Amer. Psych. Assoc. Psychiat. Res. Rep.*, No. 5.

Linn, L., Kahn, R. L., Coles, R., Cohen, J., Marshall, D., and Weinstein, E. A. (1953). Patterns of behaviour disturbance following cataract extraction. *Amer. J. Psychiat.*, **110**, 281–289.

Lipowski, Z. J. (1974). Consultation-liaison psychiatry: an overview. *Amer. J. Psychiat.*, **131**, 623–630.

Mendelsohn, J., Solomon, P., and Lindeman, E. (1958). Hallucinations of poliomyelitis patients during treatment in a respirator. *J. Nerv. Ment. Dis.*, **126**, 421–428.

Moos, R. (1974). *Evaluating Treatment Environments*. New York: Wiley.

Parker, D. L. and Hodge, J. R. (1967). Delirium in a coronary care unit. *J. Amer. Med. Assoc.*, **201**, 702.

Penn, J., Bunch, D., Olenik, A. and Abowna, G. (1971). Psychiatric experience with patients receiving renal and hepatic transplants. *Semin. Psychol.*, **3**, 134–144.

Reichsman, F., and Levy, N. B. (1972). Problems in adaptation to maintenance haemodialysis. *Ann. Intern. Med.*, **130**, 859–865.

Sgroi, S, Holland, R., and Marwitt, S. (1968). Psychological reactions to catastrophic illness. *Psychosom. Med.*, **30**, 551–552.

Solomon, P., Leiderman, P. H., Mendelson, J., and Wexler, D. (1957). Sensory deprivation —a review. *Amer. J. Psychiat.*, **114**, 357–363.

Stonehill, E., and Crisp, A. H. (1969). Aspects of the psychological status of patients treated with cardiac pacemakers. *Postgrad. Med. J.*, **45**, 423–427.

Teller, W. M. (1973). Rearing of non-identical twins with lymphopenic hypogamma globulinaemia under gnotobiotic conditions. *Acta Paediat. Scand. (Suppl.)*, **240** (1) 45.

Thompson, J. D. (1955). Patients like these four-bed wards. *Mod. Hosp.*, **85**, 84–86.

Trexler, P. C. (1973). An isolator system for the maintenance of aseptic environment. *Lancet*, **1**, 91.

Trites, D. K., Galbraith, F. D., Leckwart, J. S., and Sturdavant, M., (1969). Radical nursing units prove best in controlled study. *Mod. Hosp.*

Vaillant, G. E. and McArthur, C. (1972). Some psychological vulnerabilities of physicians. *New Engl. J. Med.*, **287**, 372–5.

Vreeland, R. and Ellis, G. (1969). Stresses on the nurse in the I. C. U. *J. Amer. Med. Assoc.*, **208**, 332–334.

Winkelstein, C., Blacher, R. and Meyer B. (1965). Psychiatric observations on surgical patients in recovery rooms. *N. Y. St. J. Med.*, **65**, 865–870.

Wright, R. G., Sand, P., and Livingstone, G. (1966). Psychological stress during haemodialysis for chronic failure. *Ann. Intern. Med.*, **64**, 611–621.

Wynn, A. (1967). Unwarranted emotional distress in men with ischaemic heart disease. *Med. J. Aust.*, **2**, 847–851.

Foundations of Psychosomatics
Edited by M. J. Christie and P. G. Mellett
© 1981 John Wiley & Sons Ltd.

19

THE HOME ENVIRONMENTS OF SCHIZOPHRENIC PATIENTS, AND THEIR RESPONSE TO TREATMENT

JULIAN LEFF
Social Psychiatry Unit,
Institute of Psychiatry, London
and
NICHOLAS TARRIER
Clinical Department of Pharmacology
Institute of Psychiatry, London.

INTRODUCTION

Schizophrenia was first formulated by Kraepelin as a degenerative disease of the brain, distinguished from senile dementia by its early onset. This conceptualization of the disease dominated thinking in the early part of the century and led to successful attempts to establish a genetic basis for schizophrenia. However, the earlier genetic studies, which indicated a very substantial inherited component, have been undermined by subsequent work of greater methodological rigour. Recent findings suggest that inheritance cannot account for more than 70 per cent of schizophrenia at the most generous estimate (Shields, 1967). This leaves plenty of room for environmental influences to operate. With the development of psychoanalytic schools of thought, and their unprecedented domination of American psychiatry, a number of influential theories about the environmental origin of schizophrenia were formulated in the United States. These include the 'double-bind' theory of Bateson (Bateson *et al.*, 1956), Lidz's (1967) 'marital schism and marital skew', and Wynne's (Wynne *et al.*, 1958) concept of 'pseudomutuality'. These theories were put forward as complete explanations for the appearance of schizophrenia, without even a nod in the direction of the genetic evidence. Hence, a gulf appeared between the geneticists and the environmentalists, which was rendered more damaging by the fact that the environmental theories rested on very shaky evidence (Hirsch and Leff, 1975). That gulf still exists, though a few bridges have been thrown across it. The psychosomatic approach is one of these bridges, but has been difficult to apply in this area for a number of reasons. One persistent problem has been the difficulty of finding a conceptual link between organic and environmental theories of schizophrenia. Each of these areas has developed its own language, with environmental neologisms such as 'double-bind' and 'pseudomutuality' on one hand, and technical terms such as transmethylation and balanced polymorphism on the other. A common language needs to be developed before communication can occur between workers in these different fields. This will probably entail the coining of further neologisms that will stand for bridging concepts.

Another problem entails the accuracy of measurement. A central issue has been the definition of schizophrenia and the standardization of clinical assessment. This has now been achieved by the development of semistructured clinical interviews and computer programs that process the clinical data and lead to a diagnosis, e.g. Present State Examination and Catego Program in the UK (Wing, Cooper, and Sartorius, 1974) and Psychiatric Status Schedule and Diagno Program in the USA (Spitzer and Endicott, 1968). In the past, there has been a gross disparity between the accuracy of biochemical and physiological measures and the inaccuracy of clinical measurement. Use of the tools referred to above should amend this situation, but problems remain in the area of measuring features of the social environment. For example, it has so far proved impossible to get agreement, even between experts, on what constitutes a 'double-bind' statement (Ringuette and Kennedy, 1966), but certain features of the social environment can now be measured reliably and are shown to have an important effect on the patient suffering from schizophrenia. It is with these features that the bulk of this chapter will be concerned.

Life events

Firstly we need to consider the concept of life events. These are sudden, unusual occurrences in a person's life which require a greater or lesser degree of psychological adjustment. They can be viewed as particular kinds of stress, and indeed represent one method of operationalizing that unwieldy concept. A number of attempts have been made to implicate life events in the aetiology of both psychiatric and physical illnesses (Rahe, 1968; Connolly, 1972; Paykel, 1974). Although these efforts have almost always appeared to be successful, there are two main pitfalls in this area of research, into one or other of which most workers have plunged headlong. The first involves confusing illness behaviour with life events, and is bound up with the accurate determination of the onset of the episode of illness under consideration. It is usually simple to determine the date of onset of a myocardial infarction as long as it produces symptoms, but this is not always the case with an episode of schizophrenia. The appearance of delusions or hallucinations may be sudden and dramatic, but this may be preceded by a period of weeks, months, or even years during which the patient's behaviour is insidiously altered by a progressive disease process. It is not uncommon for a person's concentration, clarity of thought, and drive to be adversely affected some time before a schizophrenic illness declares itself with more florid psychotic symptoms. It is evident that this prodromal decline in function might well lead to dismissal from a job, or break-up of an important emotional relationship. If the experimenter were unaware of this possibility he would identify the loss of job, or break-up of the relationship, as life events preceding the episode of schizophrenia and would impute to them an aetiological role, an interpretation which would be the exact reverse of the truth. To guard against this kind of error, Brown and Birley (1968) categorized life events as being independent, that is completely outside the patient's control, or possibly dependent, that is to some degree within the patient's control but most unlikely to be the result of behaviour consequent upon the illness. Happenings which were probably caused by such behaviour, as in the loss of a job through inefficiency, were excluded. In addition to employing this categorization, it is necessary to determine the onset of an episode as accurately as possible, and conservatively, that is with a bias towards placing it as far back in time as is consistent with the evidence.

The second problem is the assessment of the significance of particular events for the individual patient. It is evident that an event like the death of a mother-in-law could occasion profound grief in one person, but a great sense of relief in another. The difficulty in assessing the impact of events in an individual stems from the retrospective nature of the enquiry. Virtually every study conducted to date has been retrospective, starting with the patient who has developed an illness and enquiring backwards in time. Illness, particularly of a psychiatric nature, often changes a person's perception of the world. Thus a depressed patient tends to exaggerate the importance of minor reverses, while a paranoid patient may see a special personal significance in trivial occurrences. These considerations invalidate attempts to use the patient's judgement to assess the significance of events *retrospectively*. The problem could be largely resolved by prospective studies, but these are so far rare.

Another approach, used by Rahe *et al.* (1971), is to rely on the 'man in the street' to give a common-sense view of the relative significance of particular events. These workers asked a panel of judges, drawn from representative strata of society, to rate a long list of events on a numerical scale according to their expected impact. The consensus view of the panel was then used in studies on patients. This is an interesting strategy, but is likely to be influenced by cultural factors, so that an American scaling of life events might not be applicable to an English population. An even greater disparity might be anticipated between rural and urban populations.

Brown and Birley (1968) side-stepped this problem by drawing up a list of life events on the basis of their infrequency of occurrence and deliberately ignoring possible variations in their significance for individual patients. They used this technique to compare a group of normal people, drawn from local factories, with a group of schizophrenic patients recently admitted to hospital. The normal controls exhibited a steady rate of life events, 14 per cent of the group reporting a life event for each 3-week period over the course of 3 months covered by the retrospective enquiry. The same proportion of schizophrenics reported life events for each of the 3-week periods except the most recent. During the 3 weeks immediately preceding the onset of florid symptoms, 46 per cent of patients reported a life event. This represents a significant difference from the control group and indicates a link between life events and the onset of schizophrenia. The data further suggested that schizophrenics who relapsed following the discontinuation of their medication had not experienced an excess of life events. This finding was difficult to interpret because of the possible self-selection of patients who discontinue medication. However, it suggested an interesting interaction between life events and maintenance therapy which was deserving of further study.

This issue was taken up in two trials of maintenance therapy in schizophrenia in which patients were randomly assigned to treatment with an active drug, or a placebo, thus eliminating the complexities introduced by self-selection. One of the trials was of oral medication (chlorpromazine and trifluoperazine) in acute schizophrenia (Leff and Wing, 1971), while the other was of long-acting injections (fluphenazine) in chronic schizophrenia (Hirsch et al., 1973). The same techniques of assessment were used in both trials, including Brown and Birley's life events questionnaire. It was therefore considered justifiable to pool the data, producing large enough groups of patients for statistical analysis. Four groups of patients were compared in terms of life events; patients on placebo who relapsed or remained well, and those on active drug who relapsed or remained well. Three of these groups included a low percentage of patients experiencing a recent life event. Only the patients who relapsed while on active drug had a significant excess of life events. In fact, of the nine patients in this group, eight had experienced a life event in the 5 weeks before relapse of their schizophrenia. Leff et al. (1973) interpret this finding as indicating that schizophrenic patients in the community, who are not on maintenance phenothiazines, will relapse in response to the stress implicit in everyday life. Schizophrenics on phenothiazines are protected against this relatively low level of stress, but life events can break through this drug protection and precipitate relapse.

This cannot stand as a complete explanation, however, because it fails to account for the trial patients who remained well on phenothiazines. These patients' lives were not completely devoid of events; rather, they experienced the same rate of events as the normal subjects in Brown and Birley's study. It was considered possible that these events might be less stressful than those occurring to the patients who relapsed while on drugs, but a comparison showed no difference in the kinds of events occurring in the two groups. As the patients who remained well and who relapsed on drugs were not distinguished by any clinical or historical features, there must be some other environmental factor that explains the relapsed patients' vulnerability to life events. Such a factor has been identified, but not in the same drug trials, which already had a complex enough design.

RELATIVES' EXPRESSED EMOTION

The environmental feature in question is the emotional atmosphere generated by the relatives with whom the patient lives. The importance of this was suggested by a follow-up study of 156 long-stay male schizophrenic patients who were discharged from hospital (Brown, 1959; Brown, Carstairs, and Topping, 1958). It was found that the risk of readmission was related to the type of living group to which the patient returned on discharge, being greater in patients living with relatives than in those living on their own. This was confirmed in a subsequent follow-up study of 300 schizophrenic patients who were interviewed 5 years after their key admission (Brown et al., 1966). The findings from these two studies were suggestive of a link between relapse of a schizophrenic illness and some feature of home life with a relative.

Brown and his colleagues assumed that it was the emotional atmosphere that was important and went about developing an appropriate set of measures (Brown and Rutter, 1966; Rutter and Brown, 1966). It was not considered practical to sample emotional behaviour in the home directly. Instead, the measures were made from an interview with the relative at the time the patient was admitted to hospital. Emotions tend to run high at such times of crisis, and it was assumed that emotions expressed by the relative in the course of the research interview were in some way representative of an enduring atmosphere in the home. Ratings were made on four scales; critical comments, hostility, warmth, and emotional over-involvement. A high inter-rater reliability was achieved on these measures both in live interviews and from tape recordings.

Brown, Birley, and Wing (1972) used these measures in a follow-up study of 101 schizophrenic patients, all of whom were living with relatives. The patients were followed for 9 months after their discharge from hospital, to determine the proportion relapsing with a recurrence of schizophrenic symptoms. Relapse was significantly associated with three of the measures assessed from the interview with the relative at the time the patient was admitted to hospital: critical comments, hostility, and emotional over-involvement. On the basis of the scores on these measures, families were assigned to high or low Expressed Emotion (EE) groups. The relapse rate of patients from high EE homes was 58 per cent, compared with 16 per cent from low EE homes ($p < 0.001$). There was no difference in the pattern of these results between patients living with parents and those living with spouses. Hence, the EE of the relative has a powerful effect in determining the course of a schizophrenic illness.

These impressive results can be viewed from a different standpoint: nearly half the patients living in high EE homes managed to remain well despite the difficult atmosphere. It is possible to attribute their survival to two protective factors: maintenance phenothiazines and reduced social contact with their relative. Two-thirds of the patients took the one of the major tranquillizers for most of the follow-up period. For patients living in low EE homes there was very little difference in relapse rates whether they took these drugs or not.

Patients living in high EE homes stood a better chance of remaining well if they took phenothiazines, although the effect did not quite reach statistical significance.

Social contact with the relative was assessed by constructing a time budget of a typical week and determining how many hours patient and relative actually spent in the same room together. An arbitrary cut-off point of 35 hours per week was used, more than this being counted as high social contact, and less as low social contact. It was found that the amount of contact made no difference for patients living with low EE families. However for those in high EE homes, patients in low social contact with their relative had a significantly lower relapse rate than those in high contact.

These findings of a link between relative's EE and schizophrenic relapse, and the protective nature of phenothiazine medication and of reduced social contact, seemed of such theoretical and practical importance that it was considered desirable to attempt to replicate them. Vaughn and Leff (1976a) have now done this using the methods and design of the earlier study but applying them to a completely different group of schizophrenic patients. These workers introduced one modification, which was to shorten the family interview of Brown and Rutter from its original 4 or 5 hours to no more than $1\frac{1}{2}$ hours. Vaughn and Leff (1976b) found that this could be done without losing any of the predictive power of the EE measures. The results of Vaughn and Leff's study repeated almost figure for figure those of the earlier work. Once again a significance association was found between EE and schizophrenic relapse, 50 per cent of patients from high EE homes relapsing compared with 12 per cent from low EE homes. Both maintenance phenothiazines and reduced social contact with the relative were found to exert a significant protective effect in high EE homes, but to make no difference to the relapse rates of patients from low EE homes.

It is gratifying that such close correspondence was found between the results of two studies conducted 10 years apart by different researchers on different groups of patients. It allowed the pooling of data from both studies, which produced a total group of 128 schizophrenic patients. A sample of this size can be broken down into a number of subgroups, hence providing the answer to an important question; are the protective effects of maintenance phenothiazines and reduced social contact additive? An analysis of the outcome of various subgroups is presented in Figure 19.1.

It can be seen from this analysis that the two protective factors do have an additive effect, as the relapse rate of patients with both factors present (subgroup 3) is considerably lower than the relapse rates of patients with either one or other of the factors present (subgroups 4 and 5). Furthermore, since the relapse rate of patients in subgroup 3 is virtually identical with the rates in subgroups 1 and 2, we can conclude that the combination of maintenance phenothiazines and reduced social contact gives virtually complete protection against the deleterious influence of a high EE home. It is noteworthy that patients in subgroup 5, who are on regular phenothiazine treatment,

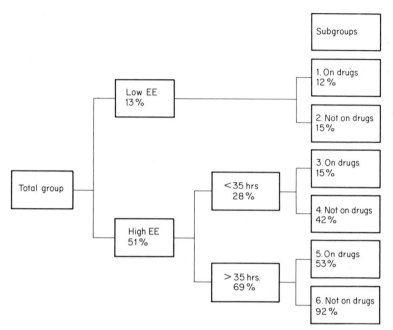

FIGURE 19.1. Nine-month relapse rates of total group of 128 schizophrenic patients: low EE = 71 patients; high EE = 57 patients

have a relatively high relapse rate (53 per cent), indicating that the protective effect of drugs can be overwhelmed by a high EE atmosphere, and that they need to be combined with some form of social intervention. It is also evident from the relapse rates in subgroups 1 and 2 that phenothiazines exert no prophylactic effect on schizophrenics living in low EE homes, over a 9-month period.

A PSYCHOSOMATIC SYNTHESIS?

We are now in possession of some key facts linking the responsiveness of schizophrenic patients to their social environment with the prophylactic effectiveness of maintenance phenothiazines. To recapitulate:

(1) the onset and relapse of schizophrenia are associated temporally with the occurrence of life events;
(2) maintenance phenothiazines protect schizophrenics against everyday happenings, but are often ineffective in cushioning them against the impact of life events;
(3) the emotional atmosphere in the home plays a crucial role in the aetiology of schizophrenic relapse;
(4) maintenance phenothiazines provide partial, but not complete, protection against the deleterious influence of the emotional atmosphere;

(5) complete protection is given only when drug treatment is combined with a particular kind of social behaviour, namely reduced contact with the critical or over-involved relative;

(6) maintenance phenothiazines do not seem to exert any protective effect in a low-keyed emotional atmosphere.

We can formulate a general principal that accommodates these findings. *Schizophrenia develops in response to 'stress', either acute (life events) or chronic (emotional atmosphere). Maintenance phenothiazines partially modify the schizophrenic response to 'stress', but are only fully effective when combined with social measures. The prophylactic effect of drugs is not demonstrable in the absence of 'stress'.* The effect of the social influences measured must be mediated through psychological mechanisms, since neither life events nor relatives' EE have a direct physical impact on the schizophrenic patient. On the other hand the phenothiazines must be operating on the physical substrate of schizophrenia, which probably results from a genetic defect. The demonstration of a complex interrelationship between the sensitivity of schizophrenia to social influences and the prophylactic effectiveness of drugs requires an explanation in terms of a synthesis between psychological and somatic phenomena. This brings us back to the problem, raised in the Introduction, of finding a conceptual framework that can act as a link between these separate 'universes of discourse'. If we approach the problem from the somatic end, it is clear that biochemical theories of schizophrenia are of little help. A number of competing theories flourish, based on rather insubstantial evidence, and taking little account of social phenomena. The field of psychophysiology looks much more promising.

From the first beginnings of the subject psychophysiologists have grappled with the concept of environmental stress and have attempted to measure its impact on the individual in physiological terms. One of the greatest problems has been the relationship between peripheral indices of autonomic response, such as electrodermal activity or pulse-rate, and activity in the central nervous system. The peripheral autonomic measures are relatively simple to obtain, whereas the central nervous system is virtually inaccesible to the physiologist. Sophisticated methods of analysing the electroencephalogram have been developed, but have failed so far to identify sufficiently specific patterns of activity. In the absence of such specificity, a global concept of central arousal has flourished, almost entirely based on inference from peripheral autonomic measures. Despite its speculative nature this concept has proved very popular as a way of linking psychological phenomena with physiological events. In fact, it was utilized to explain certain kinds of social behaviour in chronic schizophrenics over 15 years ago (Venables and Wing, 1962).

PSYCHOPHYSIOLOGY OF SCHIZOPHRENIA

There is a large body of work on measures of arousal in schizophrenics, but the findings are often contradictory. The most consistent results are that

THE HOME ENVIRONMENTS OF SCHIZOPHRENIC PATIENTS

schizophrenic patients show a faster heart-rate than normals, and exhibit more spontaneous fluctuations of skin conductance responses and slower habituation. The contradictory nature of results from different studies is partly attributable to the lack of standardized clinical measures leading to non-comparability of samples of 'schizophrenic' patients. It seems likely that the variation in results may also be partly due to a fallacy concerning the nature of the laboratory. The assumption is that the laboratory is a neutral environment. However, it is conceivable that some schizophrenics could find it very threatening if, for example, it fitted in with their delusions of being controlled by electrical forces, or of being experimented on. For this reason it seems preferable to conduct psychophysiological studies of schizophrenia in a setting in which some measures can be made of the social environment. We chose to do so in the patient's own homes, where the level of social stimulation had already been assessed in terms of the relatives' EE.

Consequently, 21 schizophrenic patients in the community, who had taken part in Vaughn and Leff's (1976a) study, were visited in their homes in order to conduct a psychophysiological investigation (Tarrier et al., 1979). The patients were asked to take part in these tests in their homes over a 9-month period, with a minimum of 3 months between each test. Twenty-one physically healthy age- and sex-matched normal subjects with no history of psychiatric illness were recruited as a control group and underwent identical tests to those of the patients in their own homes. Recordings were made with a portable polygraph which measured heart-rate and skin resistance. In view of the earlier findings of the importance of social contact with the relative, it was considered necessary to record both in the presence and the absence of the key relative. Consequently, for the first 20 minutes skin resistance and heart-rate were recorded with only the subject and the experimenter in the room. The subject's key relative was then asked to enter the room and a further 20 minutes of record were taken. During the testing period patients and relatives were encouraged to talk about the illness, experiences in hospital, and psychiatry in general. With the control subjects and their relatives the topic of conversation was psychiatry in general. Although the experimenter was aware which were the control subjects, he was unaware whether the patients belonged to high or low EE groups. After the test, both patient and relative completed a questionnaire enquiring whether the patient had experienced a life event within the 3 weeks prior to the test.

Recordings for 15 minutes before and after the relative's entry were analysed. The number of spontaneous fluctuations of skin conductance per minute was calculated for the 30-minute period, and is presented in Figure 19.2 for the first occasion of testing. At the beginning of the recording session all three groups show high levels of arousal, but particularly the two patient groups. Over the 30 minutes the control subjects show a progressive and steady decline in arousal, with a brief interruption on the entry of the relative. By contrast, both patient groups remain highly and equally aroused for the first 15 minutes until the relative enters. Thereafter, the low EE patients show a rapid decline in the level of arousal, which reaches that of the control subjects.

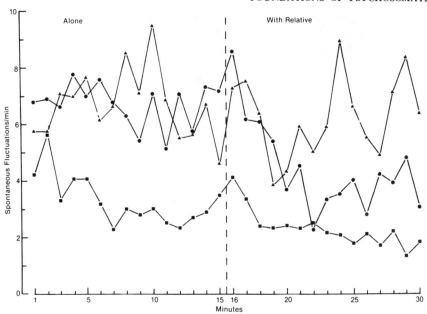

FIGURE 19.2. Mean number of spontaneous fluctuations per minute during the test period. High EE patients (triangles, $N. = 11$); low EE patients (circles, $N. = 10$); and controls (squares, $N. = 21$). (Reproduced by permission of American Medical Association Publications from *Archives of General Psychiatry* (1979), **36**, 311–15. Copyright 1979, American Medical Association)

The high EE patients, however, show a significantly higher immediate response to the relative's entry, and then show no major change in their level of arousal. As a consequence they are as highly aroused 30 minutes after the beginning of the experiment as they were initially.

These results for the high EE patients confirm earlier findings that schizophrenics are more highly aroused than normal people, and that they fail to habituate to novel stimuli. The results for the low EE patients, however, require this view of schizophrenics as a whole to be modified. These patients are able to adapt to new stimuli *in the presence* of their low EE relative. The low EE relatives are not merely neutral, as we had supposed, but are providing a positively supportive atmosphere for the schizophrenic patients.

This marked difference between the two groups of patients in their response to the relative only became evident on the first occasion of testing. On the second occasion the two patient groups were indistinguishable, both starting off at lower levels of spontaneous fluctuations than on the first test and steadily declining over the whole 30 minutes. By the third occasion the patients' initial levels of arousal and subsequent adaptation closely resemble those of the control group on their first occasion of testing.

The different responses of the patient groups on the three occasions of testing are illuminated by the data on the occurrence of life events in the 3

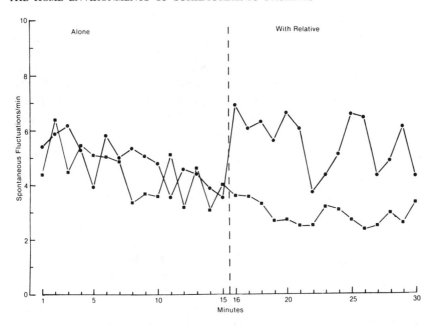

FIGURE 19.3. Mean number of spontaneous fluctuations per minute during test period for patients on occasions preceded by life event (circles, $N. = 7$) and same patients on occasions when no life event had been experienced (squares, $N. = 7$). If a patient had two occasions succeeding a life event (or not), mean of both was calculated. Patients who experienced (or did not experience) a life event on all three occasions were excluded from the graph. (Reproduced by permission of American Medical Association Publications from *Archives of General Psychiatry* (1979), **36**, 311–15. Copiright 1979, American Medical Association)

weeks before each test. Patients who had experienced a life event in the period before one testing occasion, but not on the other testing occasions were selected from both high and low EE families. The responses of these patients when they had experienced an event were compared with their responses on occasions when no life event preceded testing. Hence, the patients were acting as their own controls. This comparison is presented in Figure 19.3. Before the entry of the relative the graphs of patients on occasions with and without life events are indistinguishable. Following the entry of the relative, a striking increase in spontaneous fluctuations occurs on occasions with life events. Thereafter, the patients remain highly aroused and show no signs of a decline in arousal. By contrast, on no-life-events occasions the patients show a steady reduction in spontaneous fluctuations which is not affected by the relative's entry. The patients experiencing a life event were unfortunately too few to separate meaningfully into high and low EE groups, so that interactions between life events and relatives' EE could not be analysed statistically. Nevertheless, it is evident that on life-event occasions the relative greatly increases the patient's level of arousal compared to the no-event times. Thus, there is an interaction between the arousing effects of a recent life event and of the relative's presence, so that in conjunction they increase the spontaneous fluctuations shown by the patient. Each on its own, however, is insufficient to do this. This inter-actional effect illuminates the differences between the records obtained on the first and on subsequent occasions of testing. Only on the first occasion did the novelty of the testing procedure act analogously to a life event, both consti-tuting novel stimuli requiring adaptation. Under these circumstances signi-ficant differences were revealed between high and low EE patients in their responses to their relatives. By the second time the investigator visited their home, the procedure had lost its novelty and was no longer sufficiently arous-ing to produce differential responses to the relatives in the two patient groups.

Whether or not this interpretation is supported by further work, the data show that spontaneous fluctuations of skin conductance in the patient are sensitive both to the level of expressed emotion in the relative and the occur-rence of life events. Since these environmental factors must be impinging on the patient through psychological mechanisms, this is compelling evidence that a central response to 'stress' is being detected peripherally. We saw earlier that maintenance phenothiazines partially modify the schizophrenic patient's response to life events and to EE. It is of great interest, therefore, to determine whether this effect is detectable by the psychophysiological measures employed in this study.

The patients from low and high EE homes were divided into those currently taking regular maintenance phenothiazines and those not. Spontaneous fluctuations in patients on regular medication were found to decrease in response to the relative, but to increase in those not taking drugs, the difference between the groups reaching significance. Thus, regardless of the level of EE, regular maintenance with phenothiazines reduces the patient's peripheral autonomic response to the presence of the relative.

The number of patients not on regular phenothiazine medication was too small to analyse high and low EE groups separately, but this analysis could be performed for patients on regular medication. It was found for patients on maintenance drugs that those in high EE homes had a mean pulse rate of 75.9 beats per minute, compared with 82.0 beats per minute for those in low EE homes, a significant difference. Phenothiazines are known to raise the heart-rate by a peripheral effect on the autonomic nervous system. It is possible that the higher pulse-rate in low EE patients reflects a predominantly peri-pheral autonomic effect of phenothiazines, whereas the lower pulse-rate in the high EE patients suggests that central tranquillizing effects of phenothiaz-ines are predominant in this group.

Unfortunately, interpretation of the effect of phenothiazines on the psycho-physiology of the different groups of patients has to be speculative, as the numbers of patients were restrictively small. We initially employed psycho-physiological measures in the hope that they would bridge the gap between social and pharmacological influences on schizophrenia. We have met with only partial success. We have been able to distinguish between different social environments—eventful and event-free, high and low EE—by the peripheral autonomic responses of the patients. By itself this is an encouraging achievement which endorses the use of skin conductance as an index of *psychological* responsiveness. However, we have been unable to analyse satisfactorily the effect of maintenance phenothiazines on patients from different social environments in terms of their psychophysiology. This may be possible with larger groups of drug-free patients and further study of this area is clearly indicated. However, we have some evidence from the pulse-rates that phenothiazines have different modes of action in schizophrenic patients from high and low EE homes. On this somewhat flimsy basis we can construct a hypothesis that suggests further experiments.

Schizophrenics living in low EE, event-free environments are in a state of low arousal. Maintenance phenothiazines in these patients have no significant effect on the central nervous system, but rather a predominant peripheral effect which is useless for the prevention of schizophrenic relapse. Patients who experience life events or who live in high EE homes are in a state of high arousal. Maintenance phenothiazines have a predominant central effect in these patients, reducing arousal to a level where a schizophrenic relapse becomes less likely. However the combination of a life event and a high EE relative increases arousal to a dangerous level, which maintenance phenothiazines are incapable of reducing sufficiently, so that a schizophrenic relapse is very likely to ensue. Patients can reduce arousal by increasing their social distance from the high EE relative and hence can potentiate the protective effect of maintenance phenothiazines.

We still have considerable reservations about the term 'arousal'. We do not know what the psychological phenomena are that are reflected in the peripheral autonomic responses. Furthermore we have no conception of the way in which a high state of central arousal is converted into a schizophrenic episode. Some measures of psychological phenomena need to be included in studies which also encompass pharmacological, physiological, and social indices. In our view only a multidisciplinary approach of this kind is likely to yield an understanding of schizophrenia.

REFERENCES

Bateson, G., Jackson, D. D., Haley, J., and Weakland, J. H. (1956). Toward a theory of schizophrenia. *Behavioural Science*, **1**, 251–264.

Brown, G. W. (1959). Experiences of discharged chronic schizophrenic mental hospital patients in various types of living group. *Millbank Memorial Fund Quarterly*, **37**, 101–131.

Brown, G. W., and Birley, J. L. T. (1968). Crises and life changes and the onset of schizophrenia. *Journal of Health and Social Behaviour*, **9**, 203–214.

Brown, G. W., Birley, J. L. T., and Wing, J. K. (1972). Influence of family life on the course of schizophrenic disorders: a replication. *British Journal of Psychiatry*, **121**, 241–258.

Brown, G. W., Bone, M., Dalison, B., and Wing, J. K. (1966). *Schizophrenia and Social Care*. Maudsley Monograph No. 17. London: Oxford University Press.

Brown, G. W., Carstairs, G. M., and Topping, G. G. (1958). Post hospital adjustment of chronic mental patients. *Lancet*, **2**, 685–689.

Brown, G. W. and Rutter, M. (1966). The measurement of family activities and relationships: A methodological study. *Human Relations*, **19**, 241–263.

Connolly, J. (1972). Life Events Before Myocardial Infarction. M. Phil. Thesis, University of London.

Hirsch, S. R., Gaind, R., Rohde, P. D., Stevens, B. C., and Wing, J. K. (1973). Out-patient maintenance of chronic schizophrenic patients with long-acting fluphenazine: a double-bind placebo trial. *British Medical Journal*, **1**, 633–637.

Hirsch, S. R., and Leff, J. P. (1975). *Abnormalities in Parents of Schizophrenics*. Maudsley Monograph No. 22. London: Oxford University Press.

Leff, J. P., Hirsch, S. R., Gaind, R., Rohde, P. D., and Stevens, B. C. (1973). Life events and maintenance therapy in schizophrenic relapse. *British Journal of Psychiatry*, **123**, 659–60.

Leff, J. P., and Wing, J. K. (1971). Trial of maintenance therapy in schizophrenia. *British Medical Journal*, **3**, 599–604.

Lidz, T. (1967). The family, personality development, and schizophrenia, In *The Origins of Schizophrenia*. Excerpta Medica International Congress Series, No. 151.

Paykel, E. S. (1974). Recent life events and clinical depression. In E. K. Gunderson, and R. H. Rahe (eds.), *Life Stress and Illness*, pp. 134–163. Springfield: Thomas.

Rahe, R. H. (1968). Life-change measurement as a predictor of illness. *Proceedings of the Royal Society of Medicine*, **61**, 1124–1128.

Rahe, R. H., Lundberg, V., Bennett, L., and Theorell, T. (1971). The Social Adjustment Scale: a comparative study of Swedes and Americans. *Journal of Psychosomatic Research*, **15**, 241–249.

Ringuette, E., and Kennedy, T. (1966). An experimental study of the double-bind hypothesis. *Journal of Abnormal Psychology*, **71**, 136–141.

Rutter, M., and Brown, G. W. (1966). The reliability and validity of measures of family life and relationships in families containing a psychiatric patient. *Social Psychiatry*, **1**, 38–53.

Shields, J. (1967). The genetics of schizophrenia in historical context. In A. Coppen, and A. Walk (eds.), *Recent Developments in Schizophrenia*. pp. 22–41. Ashford: Headley Poros.

Spitzer, R. C., and Endicott, J. (1968). Diagno: a computer program for psychiatric diagnosis utilising the Differential Diagnostic Procedure. *Archives of General Psychiatry*, **18**, 746–756.

Tarrier, N. Vaughn, C., Lader, M. H., and Leff, J. P. (1979). Bodily reactions to people and events in schizophrenia. *Archives of General Psychiatry*, **36**, 311–315.

Vaughn, C., and Leff, J. P. (1976a). The influence of family and social factors on the course of psychiatric illness: a comparison of schizophrenic and depressed neurotic patients. *British Journal of Psychiatry*, **129**, 125–137.

Vaughn, C., and Leff, J. P. (1976b). The measurement of expressed emotion in the families of psychiatric patients. *British Journal of Social and Clinical Psychology*, **15**, 157–165.

Venables, P. H., and Wing, J. K. (1962). Level of arousal and the subclassification of schizophrenia. *Archives of General Psychiatry*, **7**, 114–119.

Wing, J. K., Cooper, J. E., and Sartorius, N. (1974). *The Measurement and Classification of Psychiatric Symptoms*. London: Cambridge University Press.

Wynne, L. C., Ryckoff, I., Day, J., and Hirsch, S. (1958). Pseudo-Mutuality in the family relations of schizophrenics. *Psychiatry*, **21**, 205–220.

INDEX